MW00476354

DRUGS AND THUGS

Also by Russell Crandall

The Salvador Option: The United States in El Salvador, 1977–1992

America's Dirty Wars: Irregular Warfare from 1776 to the War on Terror

The United States and Latin America After the Cold War

Gunboat Democracy: U.S. Interventions in the Dominican Republic, Grenada, and Panama

Driven by Drugs: U.S. Policy Toward Colombia

The Andes in Focus (co-editor with Guadalupe Paz and Riordan Roett)

Mexico's Democracy at Work (co-editor with Guadalupe Paz and Riordan Roett)

DRUGS AND THUGS

◆ ◆ ◆

THE HISTORY AND FUTURE OF
AMERICA'S WAR ON DRUGS

Russell Crandall

Yale UNIVERSITY PRESS   NEW HAVEN AND LONDON

Published with assistance from the Louis Stern
Memorial Fund.

Copyright © 2020 by Russell Crandall.
All rights reserved.
This book may not be reproduced, in whole or in part,
including illustrations, in any form (beyond that copying
permitted by Sections 107 and 108 of the U.S. Copyright
Law and except by reviewers for the public press), without
written permission from the publishers.

Yale University Press books may be purchased in quantity
for educational, business, or promotional use. For
information, please e-mail sales.press@yale.edu (U.S. office)
or sales@yaleup.co.uk (U.K. office).

Set in Scala type by IDS Infotech Ltd.
Printed in the United States of America.

ISBN 978-0-300-24034-4 (paperback : alk. paper)
Library of Congress Control Number: 2020931397
A catalogue record for this book is available from the British
Library.

This paper meets the requirements of ANSI/NISO
Z39.48-1992 (Permanence of Paper).

10 9 8 7 6 5 4 3 2 1

In memory of PBA
traveler, teacher, friend

Primum non nocere

CONTENTS

PART 2 | SUPPLY-SIDE CRUSADE

PART 3 | THE HOME FRONT

Introduction

I think if you were Satan and you were settin around tryin to think up
somethin that would just bring the human race to its knees what you
would probably come up with is narcotics.

—A character in Cormac McCarthy's novel No *Country*
for Old Men (2005)

Mea Culpa

Images of America's drug problem and the war against it are as disturbing
as they are indelible. In Mexican deserts, hazmat-suited police heft bodies
from mass graves. On a rooftop in Medellín, Colombian soldiers pose over the
corpse of Pablo Escobar, the cocaine kingpin once dubbed "the world's greatest outlaw." Honduran gangs murder civilians by the busload. Privatized
American prisons overflow with convicted drug offenders. Hueys hover over
coca fields in faraway Colombia, clouds of the herbicide glyphosate trailing
behind them. Taliban guerrillas joust for control of poppy plantations. In Chicago and other American cities, children lie sprawled on sidewalks, casualties
of drive-by shootings, while heroin addicts overdose on fentanyl a few blocks
away. Sons, mothers, daughters, and fathers in suburbs and rural hamlets
succumb to OxyContin and methamphetamine in small-town shopping malls
and parking lots. One sees in the media the statistic that during the quarter
century before this book was published, more than seven hundred thousand
Americans died from drug overdoses; the past four years have witnessed more
citizens dying from overdoses than were killed in the Iraq and Vietnam wars

combined. The death rate was so staggering that the nation's life expectancy actually dropped in three of these years, a remarkable outcome for a country not at war.[1]

For many Americans, such images comprise the sum of understanding of the conflict: a torrent of violence and indignity, with little connection between one episode and the next and little sense, if any, of a coherent strategy to bring this tragedy to an end. Indeed, the roots, scope, and impact of the war on drugs are largely unknown, in part because there has been no objective synthesis of the conflict that captures both the macro and micro, the broad historical patterns that describe the conflict's contours and the human stories through which those lines have been drawn. This book charts both, and in doing so, it attempts to present an unvarnished and comprehensive reckoning of one of America's longest-standing, most controversial, and least successful efforts in foreign and domestic policy.

This book is a confession of sorts. Having left my last stint in government service at the Pentagon and the White House in 2011, I realized that I did not have a clear sense of the history or impact of America's war on drugs. "He that lieth down with dogs shall rise up with fleas," as Benjamin Franklin's Poor Richard once put it. And in this case, considering the years I spent with the flea-ridden dog that is the drug war, I now view my professional experiences with a sense of doubt and trepidation.

Primum non nocere. I cannot swear to not having harmed. But there were also times inside government when I was able to help make a positive impact on, say, a bilateral U.S.-Colombian security strategy. As a scholar of Latin America's politics and history for the past two decades, I have conducted much of my scholarly research in that enchanting region and have come to know the people and the cultures relatively well. I am especially aware of the harms that drug-related violence has inflicted on these vulnerable countries. My own attempt at redemption is to write this sweeping tale of the history and logic behind a war that continues to perplex us.

I offer neither a wholesale condemnation nor an outright defense of this long drug war. Instead, I offer insight by being willing to consider the entirety of the evidence amid a deeply polarized and highly selective discourse of the policies, controversies, failures, and successes of the past 30 or 50 or 125 years—even the start date of the conflict is a matter of dispute. To preserve the clarity of analysis, I reserve my policy recommendations for the conclusion, only after readers have had the opportunity to digest the story in full.

Changing Perceptions

Since the early 1970s, the drug war has cost more than a trillion taxpayer dollars, or roughly ten times the price tag of the Gulf War (inflation-adjusted U.S.$102 billion) or three times that of World War I (inflation-adjusted U.S.$334 billion). Despite decades of effort to eradicate them, illicit drugs produced domestically and abroad continue to proliferate. As I wrote this introduction in the autumn of 2019, the heroin market was capitalized around $55 billion. In 2013, upward of 450 tons of heroin were manufactured and trafficked worldwide. Yet in a sign of the eternal ebb and flow of drug use, cocaine consumption plunged by 50 percent (from 300 to 150 metric tons) from 2006 to 2010. One Brookings Institution report identified a dozen interpretations of what caused this precipitous drop: more aggressive "supply side" drug-lab busts in Colombia, longtime cocaine users "aging out" of the drug, greater demand for coke in countries other than the United States. But jump forward to 2017, and we find the U.S. Department of State warning of "troubling early signs that cocaine use and availability is on the rise in the United States for the first time in nearly a decade."[2]

In recent years, the costs of drug addiction and the drug war itself have become personal for a larger share of Americans than ever before. In 2016, four in ten Americans said they knew someone who was currently or had once been addicted to prescription painkillers. With usage rising by 300 percent over the past decade, Vicodin, Percocet, OxyContin, and other drugs containing the narcotic hydrocodone became the most commonly prescribed medications in America. In 2015, opioid overdoses killed 52,000 people and overtook guns as a cause of death in the United States; two years later, the number had surged to 72,000, roughly half of these involving the ultra-potent synthetic opioid called fentanyl. Between 1999 and 2017, four hundred thousand Americans, a veritable "war's worth of dead," suffered fatal overdoses of prescription or illegal opioids alone. For each of those deaths, another thirty Americans wound up in emergency rooms with opioid complications. The ensuing crackdown on the prescription painkiller epidemic came with unintended harmful consequences—what policy analysts refer to as "blowback"—as users sought a "cheaper more accessible high": heroin. In parts of North Carolina in 2017, heroin was cheaper and easier to score than alcohol. Just two years later up in Baltimore, cheaper and far more potent fentanyl was making even heroin scarce—an absence local addicts had not reckoned with in decades. In a 2017 report, the opioid epidemic was reckoned to cost the nation over $500 billion each annually.[3]

The opioid epidemic even reached the 2016 presidential campaign trail. According to one press account, the opioid scourge "skyrocketed to the top of voters' lists of political priorities in the same bands of America—rural states, the suburbs, and notably the early voting state of New Hampshire." GOP candidates lined up with Democrats to label the heroin epidemic a "health crisis" rather than a crime.[4]

According to some analysts, this reflected a surprising new tenor in Republican rhetoric on drug policy, which for so long had been staunchly prohibitionist. Some GOP politicians began to advocate for dealing with low-level drug users with more treatment and less incarceration—a plank long advocated by Democrats. In 2015, Republican Chris Christie, the governor of New Jersey, routinely compared the moral need to treat drug addicts with therapy to the need to treat smokers who had become cancer patients (like his own mother) with chemo. He told a small gathering of voters in New Hampshire, "No one came to me and said, 'Don't treat her; she got what she deserved.' We need to start treating people in this country, not jailing them."[5]

This was not the only dimension in which perceptions of drug use and drug policy were beginning to show signs of change. By 2019, ten states and the District of Columbia had legalized recreational marijuana and thirty-three had legalized medicinal cannabis, leading to what one cheeky news article called the increased sense of the nation becoming the "land of the red, white, and green."[6] In Colorado, where the legal weed industry was most active, sales jumped from an estimated $1.5 billion in 2013 to $2.7 billion a year later, according to cannabis industry estimates. Perhaps the surest sign of the times came when a prominent *Wall Street Journal* writer penned a tongue-in-cheek column about his legal cannabis-altered experience attending a Las Vegas mega-prizefight. Taken together, the Republican change in tone and the creeping liberalization of pot suggested that the United States during the 2010s had reached an inflection point in its two-century-long relationship with banned substances.[7]

Party Like It's 1987

At least, that's one version of the story. Another is that, even as half of American citizens lived in states in which marijuana was legalized to one degree or another, in other parts of the massive drug war very little had changed over the past three decades. Those who observe the present and see a "new era" for drug policy marked by widespread liberalization might want to think twice before committing to such a conclusion. The inertia of the Beltway policymaking machine ensured that the global supply-side drug war was rolling along in much the same way it had in, say, 1987.

A few years ago, I met a new neighbor in the small college town of Davidson, North Carolina, where I live. This neighbor had been a Navy submarine officer in the 1990s. One of his missions, he told me, involved "parking" the high-tech stealth sub just outside Colombia's maritime boundary so that the ship's surveillance technology could track the cell phone calls of Colombian drug kingpins. Of course, deploying this sort of high-end military hardware is certainly not unique to the drug war. The Pentagon does very much the same across the globe in unconventional counterinsurgency and counterterrorism operations that might or might not have a drug component. It would be easy to assume that the Colombian coastline sub operation was how we *used* to run the international side of the drug war. Surely that would have expired with the bust-up of the Medellín and Cali cartels in the 1990s, and certainly by the time Colombia's Revolutionary Armed Forces (FARC) handed in their arms in 2017. But the reality is that the United States and counterpart countries continue to employ this exact strategy today. In fact, most current supply-side operations use tactics that emerged in the 1980s and 1990s—only now with a far bigger budget.[8]

In November 2017, American B-52s, F-16s, A-29s, and F-22s launched a ferocious airstrike on ten Taliban poppy-processing plants. It was a move taken right out of the 1990s and 2000s playbook that was used on Colombia. The strike also happened to follow years of alternative approaches to curbing the production of opium poppy, including the use of aerial herbicides, the burning of poppy fields, and a "crop substitution campaign that encouraged and paid farmers to grow almonds, apricots, green vegetables and saffron instead of poppy." Even still, as the Army commander in Afghanistan, General John W. Nicholson Jr., noted, the expenditure of ammunition was unlikely to have much of an impact on the heroin and opiate supplies entering the United States, of which drugs from Afghanistan accounted for only about 4 percent. In 2018, the federal government was still executing the same policies, in the same ways, and in pursuit of the same outcomes as the previous two generations of policymakers.[9]

Drug War as Cultural War

On August 8, 2017, after the nation's opioid death toll that year reached a record 59,000 (it would top out at 72,000), President Donald Trump briefed the press on an upcoming meeting with his task force on this public health scourge. Echoing Nancy Reagan's abstinence crusade three decades ago, he affirmed, "The best way to prevent drug addiction and overdose is to prevent people from abusing drugs in the first place. If they don't start, they won't have a problem. If they do start, it's awfully tough to get off. So if we can keep them from going on and maybe by talking to youth and telling them: No good, really bad for you in every way. But if they don't start, it won't be a problem." Legions of drug war critics jumped on the president's comments. The *Guardian*'s Chris McGreal, for one, complained, "The president's exhortation to follow Nancy Reagan's miserably inadequate advice and Just Say No to drugs is far from useful. The then first lady made not a jot of difference to the crack epidemic in the 1980s." The purpose of this vignette is to broach a point that this book will spend considerable time elaborating: the war on drugs is rife with inconsistencies and contradictions and paradoxes. For any claim you can make with certainty about the war on drugs, its opposite is likely also true. This inherent tension is a large part of what makes the war so difficult to understand in full.[10]

Further complicating this tension is the fact that much of the political debate and analysis concerning the drug war has for so long been poisoned by partisanship, ideology, and acrimony. This has made it almost impossible for the public to get an accurate view of the war's many sides. Time and again, as we will see in this book, what appears to be the "war on drugs" is in fact a "war *over* the war on drugs." Much of what we think we know about drugs, their effects, their regulation, and the crises they have caused has been portrayed through one of two competing prescriptive lenses—the "Legalize it!" view and the "Lock 'em up!" view.

The "Legalize it!" camp presents the drug war as a series of failed policies imposed in the name of a puritanical war on private citizens, especially minorities and the poor. Drug prohibition, in this narrative, serves industries that profit from the war's spoils: privatized prisons, drug-testing industries, and military contractors, to name some of the most prominent. These vocal and well-organized proponents contend that decriminalization of narcotics would save billions in futile interdiction efforts and untold sums in the criminal justice system. Moreover, savings from demilitarization would free up funding for prevention education and treatment, which should be the aim of sensible drug policy anyway. They point to statistics like the one-fifth of the incarcerated population that is serving time related to a drug charges or convictions.

The "Lock 'em up!" camp represents the belief that Americans indulge because drugs are either readily accessible or socially tolerated. In this thinking, drug use is a moral ill, and to tolerate it is to invite a return to the crime-ridden

horrors of New York City circa 1975. The conservative camp believes that social stigmatization and punishment are effective deterrents and that the key to
solving the drug scourge lies in discouraging people from using drugs and
preventing the substances from crossing American borders or from being
produced inside them.

Although both narratives have obvious weaknesses, it is not my intention
to split the difference between these two polarized interpretations. This book
dissects the truisms on either side, such as the view that eradicating coca crops
and restricting the purchase of precursor chemicals is the "magic bullet" that
would fix the drug scourge; or the equally erroneous view that the current
drug war is analogous to 1930s-era Prohibition and that the legalization that
ended the latter would magically solve the former.

As we shall see, a broad view of the war against illegal drugs requires proper
assessments of several related phenomena: the physiological effects of available drugs; the extent of their consumption; prevailing social attitudes about
specific substances; and the prevailing state of evidence on the physical and
social harms that attend the use of a drug when the substances are consumed
by large segments of the population.

The Snake That Eats Its Own Tail

To be sure, the war on drugs is a beast. Its strategic, financial, and moral costs
are comparable to those of the conflicts in Vietnam and Iraq. Yet dismissing the
war on drugs as a monumental failure is also inaccurate and counterproductive.
The aim here is not to condemn or defend the drug war to date but to explain it
and propose an alternative way forward. Only after we've looked at America's
drug habit and the associated war against it with a measure of objectivity can we
begin to judge it. This book proceeds by interrogating the interconnectedness
and disconnectedness of domestic drug policy, the military-narcotic-industrial
complex, and human lives on the ground. It covers the panoply of players—the
web of users, cultivators, processors, traffickers, combatants, and regulators
who are engaged in the war on drugs. The history begins with the premise that,
although the war on drugs is most often associated with the hawkish approaches
of the Nixon and Reagan administrations, the American drug war in fact began
in the early 1900s with crackdowns on opium, cocaine, marijuana, and, most
dramatically, alcohol. Through the years, the drug war has accumulated new
fronts, new tactics, new dimensions. And it continues to evolve, even if "evolution" often looks far more like repetition than progress.

As the narrative progresses, several themes become apparent. First, for most of its duration, the U.S.-led drug war has operated with no real rearview mirror, no mechanism to enable policymakers to use the past as a guide. Each new decision—whether spraying coca fields in Colombia or enacting legislation to reduce prescription drug abuse—carries its own motivation and logic. This frustrating and counterproductive status quo is often the result of bureaucratic and political inertia, rather than malicious intent.

Second, drug policies often produce a common result, the "balloon effect." When you squeeze a balloon, the air moves but never disappears, and similarly, when the United States applies pressure to one area of the drug trade, similar (or worse) conditions often emerge elsewhere. Events in Colombia are illustrative: just months after the U.S.-backed takedown of Escobar's cartel in the 1990s, the Cali cartel filled the void—and then some. When Washington and Bogotá decapitated the Cali mob, control of cocaine trafficking atomized to smaller and far less visible "mom-and-pop" cartels that continue to control the illicit market in Colombia to this day. The now familiar term is often associated with the early days of the supply-side war in the late 1980s, but the balloon effect is alive and well today. When the federal government outlawed precursor chemicals used to make methamphetamines in 2005, production shifted south, and meth became the flagship product for Mexican narco gangs like the Sinaloa cartel. Similarly, the legalization of marijuana in U.S. states has pushed Mexican traffickers that had been banking on pot to shift to heroin and fentanyl.[11]

Finally, like the ouroboros, the snake that eats its own tail, the war on drugs is a saga far more circular than linear in form. The searing images that opened this introduction have beset America's drug story for decades. Any of those images could have described a scene in 1982, 1992, 2002, or 2012, and it's highly likely that they will typify 2022 and 2032 as well. For a host of reasons that this book details, there is little evidence to suggest that the U.S. drug war will reach a happy ending—or any ending at all. Despite this bleak outlook, it is a worthy consideration to look at the drug war in all its complexity, so that even if it never ends, its lessons can help us limit the damage done to future generations.

PART 1:
DRUGS AND THE DRUG WAR
IN CONTEXT

1 • Drugs 101

A bit of history is in order. For at least four thousand years, humans have used drugs for all kinds of reasons, including achieving alternative states of consciousness. Excavations have uncovered colored stains on human teeth that date back to sometime between 2400 and 2000 B.C.E. In the thin air of the Andes Mountains in 2000 B.C.E., indigenous Peruvians were making pipes for smoking hallucinogenic herbs. By A.D. 700 the Chinese were cultivating opium. In A.D. 900 an Abyssinian herder noticed that his animals would become nervous after eating the shiny red fruit of a tree that would one day be called coffee. A farmer in Yemen discovered the stimulant *khat,* similar to amphetamine, by watching goats get excited after chewing the leaves. In the seventeenth century, European explorers returned home from the New World with the mild psychoactives coffee, tobacco, and chocolate, which constitute the core of modern stimulation. Forensic tests on clay tobacco pipes dug up in William Shakespeare's yard in Stratford-upon-Avon have led some to conclude that that the Bard "might have written some of his famous works while high."[1]

Physician Andrew Weil contends that, because of its striking ubiquity, drug use may well "represent a basic human appetite." Some scientists have even suggested that the desire to alter our consciousness is the "fourth drive" in every human mind—after the desires to drink, eat, and have sex—making it "biologically inevitable." Our own brains naturally produce chemicals that induce state-changes like those of coca, poppy, and cannabis. Endorphins, for instance, are morphine-like compounds that make us feel good and sometimes euphoric. In the estimation of UCLA psychopharmacologist Ronald K. Siegel, "The experience you have in orgasms is partially chemical—it's a drug. So people deny they want this? Come on! . . . It's fun. It's enjoyable. And it's chemical. That's intoxication." Siegel's sense, as he told journalist Johann Hari, is that this fact alone should give us pause about being so reflexively anti-drug.[2]

There are those who argue that the majority of our daily activities are actually directed at altering consciousness. We cultivate friendships in order to feel love and lessen loneliness; we eat certain foods to enjoy their transient impact on our tongues; we read books for the pleasure of seeing the world through the author's prism. For philosopher and neuroscientist Sam Harris, "Every waking moment—and even in our dreams—we struggle to direct the flow of sensation, emotion, and cognition toward states of consciousness that we value." Drugs—legal or illegal, accepted or vilified, innocuous or dangerous—are a means toward this goal.[3]

That said, a significant proportion of drug use does carry risks, harms, and costs. In the United States and most other countries, alcohol and tobacco, because they are far more prevalent and socially accepted and available to users at low cost, carry by far the highest burdens in the form of healthcare costs, addiction treatment, and criminal behavior resulting from intoxication. Opiates such as heroin and pharmaceutical codeine have relatively high rates of addiction, and for many of those dependent on such drugs, the need to satisfy the associated cravings becomes all-consuming. Even cannabis consumption carries some public health consequences. A higher frequency of accident and injury is the most significant, but there are also increased risks for certain cancers and mental disorders, including psychosis and schizophrenia, for a small subset of the population already predisposed to these illnesses.[4]

Many readers will balk at some part of the preceding analysis. It aims for objectivity, but there are claims in these opening paragraphs that will provoke visceral or even indignant opposition in some. Unfortunately, much of the contemporary public debate about drugs tends to deal in absolutes: drugs are either wholly evil or wholly harmless. In fact, the values and disvalues we assign to these substances are highly contingent on the prevailing social and political winds at the time when they are being considered. One of the main contentions of this book is that we can only make progress toward a more sensible drug policy if we clearly understand these substances and their use and governance in historical context.

To achieve that kind of clarity, it's important to define a few terms and concepts at the outset. The term *drug* describes a chemical that affects our biological function in ways other than providing hydration or nutrition. Some drugs are synthetic; others are natural. In either case, they can be harmful or benign or both. To illustrate, alcohol is a drug that changes a drinker's cognitive and motor abilities. It also ranks high in dimensions of risk, generating more physical and societal harms than any other substance.

A psychoactive drug becomes *abusable* when users seek it out not to ameliorate any physical affliction but because they enjoy its effects on consciousness. By this definition, aspirin is a drug, but not a psychoactive one. An *abusable* psychoactive drug is one whose effects are "sufficiently pleasant" that users take it for reasons other than to treat an ailment.[5]

The term *narcotic* often comes up in discussions of the war on drugs. Derived from the Greek word *narko*, to make numb, the term was first associated with psychoactive compounds with soporific or anesthetic properties, such as mandrake root and poppy juice (opium). In the American medical community, the term is a value-neutral descriptor for a substance that binds at opioid receptors, and it is most often associated with opiates such as morphine and heroin. In the American legal realm, though, the term is more haphazardly applied—often with a negative connotation—as a catch-all for any illegal drug. Cocaine is often labeled a narcotic even though, in a physiological sense, it functions as a stimulant.[6]

All told, the moniker *drug* is a controversial and complicated one. As the scholar David Courtwright has pointed out, it has the advantage of being brief. For this book's purposes, I use *drugs* as a handy and neutral term of reference for a variety of legal and illegal psychoactive substances, mild or powerful, used for medical and nonmedical reasons. This roster includes alcohol, caffeine, tobacco, cocaine, opium, heroin, methamphetamine, psilocybin (the active compound in "magic mushrooms"), MDMA (ecstasy), and lysergic acid diethylamide (LSD), among many others.[7]

This book is principally concerned with America's war on *illegal* drugs. However, assignations such as "legal," "illegal," "controlled," and "regulated" further complicate the picture, because the lists of licit and illicit substances in America—not to mention the attitudes of permissiveness or stigma that attend those labels—have changed so much over the past century. In the United States of 1925, alcohol was an illicit drug, and amphetamine was available over the counter. Psychoactive cannabis, which grew wild across the rural United States, was widely considered an "attractive alternative" to booze. LSD, of course, had not yet been synthesized.[8] This is all to suggest that—at least as far as psychoactive substances are concerned—the legal categories that happen to obtain at a given moment in history are contingent, and they tend to track influential and persuasive voices more than any sort of objective truth.

And You Know It's Harming You, But You Still Do It

Not all drugs carry the same risks. Some drugs of incredible power and utility, such as psilocybin and LSD, pose no demonstrated risk of physical addiction and tend to be physically well tolerated. Yet drug policies in most countries treat users of these drugs the same as users of far more physically and socially burdensome substances, such as methamphetamine and heroin. At the same time, people in almost every society in the world enjoy drugs such as alcohol and tobacco *ad libitum* even though they have devastated people's lives for centuries. At any one time, the United States has twice as many alcohol abusers than abusers of all other illicit drugs together.[9]

In the United States, cocaine boomed in the early to mid-1980s, with an estimated eight million regular users (5 to 8 percent of whom developed a severe addiction). That number has since declined by two million. Pot use has followed a different trend. "Regular use" among teens in 1976, for example, was 37 percent; in 1991, it was 12 percent; in 2013, 23 percent. At the time of this writing, half of American teens will use an illicit drug by the time they are seniors in high school. Any slice of drug use almost invariably reveals these types of ebbs and flows, but *drug use itself* is a constant, despite the illegality, scarcity, and expense of many of these substances.[10]

For politically progressive or libertarian observers, most drug use is socially harmless and personally beneficial, if "pleasure and relaxation" can be considered benefits. Johann Hari, himself a former addict, writes:

> Some drug use causes horrible harm, as I know very well, but the overwhelming majority of people who use prohibited drugs do it because they get something good out of it—a fun night out dancing, the ability to meet a deadline, the chance of a good night's sleep, or insights into parts of their brain they couldn't get to on their own. For them, it's a positive experience, one that makes their lives better. That's why so many of them choose it. They are not suffering from false consciousness, or hubris. They don't need to be stopped from harming themselves, because they are not harming themselves.[11]

Yet there's no denying that drug abuse is real. Author Bruce Barcott once heard J. Michael Bostwick, a physician at the Mayo Clinic in Minnesota, define abuse in these crisp terms: "When I see a patient, I don't weigh their personality type and brain chemistry. I ask, 'Is your life screwed up? How are your relationships doing? How are you doing in school? How are you doing at work?' "

If drug use was exacerbating problems in these aspects of their lives, then his patients were substance abusers. A Texan pot farmer put it to Barcott in a similar vein: "If you're using cannabis to engage with the world, that's good. If you're using it to disengage from the world, that's not so good." In this more permissive interpretation, for most who succumb to its powers, drug abuse is actually relatively ephemeral. An overlapping and even smaller group, however, loses control over drug-taking itself. Among those who start using injected heroin, about a quarter will develop addictions. Cocaine has an addiction tendency of 15–16 percent. For booze, it's 12–13 percent. Pot is roughly 8 percent. However, as Barcott reminds us, America's most addictive drug is not any of these substances. The undisputed winner is tobacco: a third of users who experiment with cigarettes wind up addicted.[12]

Drug addicts form a minority of drug users, yet they account for the vast majority of the physical and social problems associated with drug use. For this reason, it's worth trying to understand what addiction means. Dr. Howard Markel reminds us in his splendid book *An Anatomy of Addiction* that the word comes from the Latin *addico,* to devote. Markel expanded in a press interview:

> In antiquity, it was an edict of Roman law. So that if I owed you a great deal of money . . . and I couldn't pay you back, you would take me before a judge. And he would make me your addict, your slave, until—I'd have to work for you until I could pay you off.

Addiction signifies a structural and chemical change in the brain. As Markel put it, "Once you change a cucumber into a pickle, you can't change that pickle back into a cucumber. So you have to come up with other means, very clever means of medical and psychological treatment to try to help people get off their drugs of choice."[13]

Addicted drug abusers have a "chronic, relapsing" psychic compulsion to maintain use of their drugs. However, "compulsive" is not the same as "involuntary": addicts can usually control their behavior to some extent. It is a falsehood that addicts will always buy a drug, whatever the asking price. "Like other consumers, they are sensible of cost. If it rises high enough they will seek substitutes, make do with less, or quit altogether." Contrary to what is often assumed, addicts tend to decrease use when price increases or availability decreases. They also abstain or cut back if punishments or rewards are significant and predictable. Make no mistake, though: addicted users often go to great and destructive lengths to keep using—far more than they do for goods they don't have a psychic compulsion to consume. As one would imagine, this is especially true in the short term, when addicts are experiencing the effects of withdrawal.[14]

Dr. Gabor Maté, a physician with more than two decades of palliative care experience, worked for ten years in Vancouver's Downtown Eastside—one of North America's most drug-ridden urban settings—treating hard-core drug addiction, mental illness, and HIV/AIDS. To get a clear view of what drug addiction looks like in all its devastation, it's worth looking at a passage from *In the Realm of Hungry Ghosts,* Maté's memoir of the wrenching, nurturing work of caring for addicts in Vancouver.

> In the Downtown Eastside the angel of death slays with shocking alacrity. Marcia, a thirty-five-year-old heroin addict, had moved out of her [housing service] residence and was living in a tenement half a block away. One morning, I received a frantic phone call about a suspected overdose. I found Marcia in bed, her eyes wide open, lying on her back and already in rigor mortis. Her arms were extended, palms outward in a gesture of alarmed protest as if to say: "No, you've come to take me too soon, much too soon!" Plastic syringes cracked under my shoes as I approached her body. Marcia's dilated pupils and some other physical cues told the story—she died not of overdose but of heroin withdrawal. I stood for a few moments by her bedside, trying to see in her body the charming, if always absent-minded, human being I had known. As I turned to leave, wailing sirens signaled the arrival of emergency vehicles outside.
>
> Marcia had been in my office just the week before, in good cheer, asking for help with some medical forms she needed to fill out to get back on welfare. It was the first time I'd seen her in six months. During that period, as she explained with nonchalant resignation, she had helped her boyfriend, Kyle, blow through a $130,000 inheritance—a process selflessly aided by many other user friends and hangers-on. For all that popularity, she was alone when death caught her.[15]

The extent to which addiction is a consequence of substances or of outside risk factors, such as poverty and social isolation, is a subject of ongoing dispute. Some experts view drugs as "germ-like pathogens" able to artificially stoke insatiable desires. One such proponent was Nils Bejerot: "No disturbed personality and no underlying social problems are required for an individual with a drug dependence." Rather, "exposure" is the crucial factor. Simple access, the argument goes, explains why doctors in Western countries have long

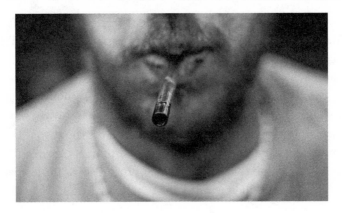

A man holds a used crack pipe in his mouth in the Downtown Eastside
neighborhood of Vancouver, British Columbia, February 11, 2014. Soon before this
image was taken, two vending machines that dispense Pyrex crack pipes for 25 cents
each, owned and operated by the Portland Hotel Society, opened in Vancouver.
(Reuters, permission to author)

had drug addiction rates more than a hundred times those of the general public. Prohibitionists such as the infamous Harry Anslinger of the Treasury
Department, who also spread racist myths about the effects of drugs, cite this
argument to defend their pro-scarcity policies. "We almost never find a lawyer
who plays around with the stuff," Anslinger is reported to have said, "and nobody can tell me that lawyers are more moral or less inclined to get into trouble than doctors or nurses. You can't get away. If people lay their hands on the
stuff, there are always a few who will try." Therefore, if the drug is not available, it will not be abused.[16]

On the other hand, some experts have suggested that the negative effects of
drugs may not be solely a result of chemistry. Other factors, such as the social
context in which consumption takes place, may be involved. As some researchers, like Kleiman, have pointed out, alcohol use is an acute "violence-and-
disorder" problem in Britain, but not in other countries with a large volume of
alcohol consumption, such as Italy. The physician Gabor Maté preaches that
the roots of addiction are found not in genes but in the "early childhood environment." He writes in his memoir: "A hurt is at the center of all addictive
behaviors. It is present in the gambler, the Internet addict, the compulsive
shopper and the workaholic. The wound may not be as deep and the ache not
as excruciating, and it may be entirely hidden—but it's there." Maté's solution
is that addicts need more compassion from society. His critics contend that

his laser focus on childhood traumas is too narrow. Rather, other factors, such as a family's history of "addiction, mental illness and the use of habit-forming pharmaceuticals," need to be taken into consideration.[17]

Johann Hari, in June 2015, gave a TED talk titled "Everything You Know About Addiction Is Wrong." One of his key arguments was that much of addiction is in fact socially determined. He cited the "Rat Park" experiment led by Canadian psychologist Bruce K. Alexander in the late 1970s. The study isolated ordinarily social rats in small cages and provided them with unlimited morphine-laced water. The isolated rats proceeded to drink themselves to death. The scientists then constructed a "rat park," a socially enhanced environment for another group of rats, with the same opium water available. In that setting, the rats largely ignored the drugged water, showing a statistically significant preference for plain water. The implication was that the "real cause" of addiction is social isolation, not the physical composition of the drugs themselves. Hari expands:

> You go from virtually everyone in isolation using loads of it and almost always dying to virtually no one doing that in Rat Park. Bruce [Alexander] began to realize that the right- and left-wing theories of addiction are both wrong. The right-wing theory is that it is a moral failing, that you're a hedonist, you party too hard and kind of fall into it. The left-wing theory is, you know, a brain disease, it takes you over, 'hijacked,' you can't help yourself. . . . Professor Alexander began to think there might be a different story about addiction. . . . What if addiction isn't about your chemical hooks? What if addiction is about your cage? Human beings have a natural and innate need to bond, and when we're happy and healthy, we'll bond and connect with each other, but if you can't do that, because you're traumatized or isolated or beaten down by life, you will bond with something that will give you some sense of relief. . . . The opposite of addiction is not sobriety; the opposite of addiction is connection.[18]

It could, in fact, be the case that addiction depends more on social and environmental factors than it does on drugs. However, activist and recovering addict Andrew Dobbs argues that Hari significantly underplays the chemical element. "If Hari had asked me to call him on my worst days," he writes, "I would have tried to manipulate him for money or other resources until he said no, or until I had borrowed too much to ever pay back. Then I would have been the one cutting him off."[19]

However we may weigh its causes, it is clear that addiction accounts for the vast majority of the ill consequences associated with drug use. These ills stem from the frequency and scale of addicts' destructive behavior, both while under the influence of drugs and while searching for drugs; the quantity of drugs they consume (addicts account for more than 80 percent of the demand for each illegal drug); and the violence of the drug markets they support. Many politically progressive and libertarian critics of the drug war contend that it is really the 10 percent or so of harmful users—as opposed to the relatively benign 90 percent—that make up "100 percent of our official understanding." For Hari, the situation is "as if our only picture of drinkers were a homeless person lying in a gutter necking neat gin. This impression is then reinforced with the full power of the state."[20]

Contrary to popular assumptions, epidemiological research suggests that most addicts resolve their usage "spontaneously," or without formal treatment. This is not to say that self-curing abusers would not benefit from medical and psychological support as they transition away from substance abuse, but rather to point out that most users who might clinically need treatment do not seek it out. Interestingly, users who are legally required to receive treatment respond as well as those who do so voluntarily. Kleiman explains: "In practice, there is no sharp line between voluntary and involuntary treatment, because those who aren't coerced by the criminal justice system often enter treatment under other pressures: from their families, for example, or their employers." Conversely, legal coercion to undergo treatment is often more nominal than real: a majority of drug-related offenders diverted from punishment to treatment either fail to show up for treatment or drop out early.[21]

Drug Policy 101

Hawks and doves will agree that, in some cases, drug use can be very harmful. The key point of contention, then, is what to do about it. When use becomes abuse or addiction, ought the state to try to limit use through prohibition and regulation? Or should it try social pressure, education, and treatment? If the ideological battle over drug policy can be reduced to a single front, this is it. For Hari, who is staunchly opposed to the drug war, one side features the "prohibitionists who believe the tragedy of drug use can be dealt with by more jail cells in California and more military jeeps on the streets of Juarez." On the other side are "the reformers who believe the tragedy of drug use can be dealt by moving these funds to educate kids and treat addicts." The former position, which represents the status quo of American drug policy, assumes that limiting the availability of drugs will reduce consumption. The latter view holds that the current policy of prohibition does not stop our drug problem but rather "piles on another series of disasters on the already existing disaster of drug use."[22]

Of course, the lines in war are rarely so clear, and such a reductionist view doesn't capture the full story. To point to one example, drug war proponents almost always support softer approaches, including treatment and education, alongside other hard-line measures: overseas drug lab busting, domestic law enforcement, and sales and usage prohibition. What's more, as we'll see throughout this book, neither side of the line is entirely right.

So we're left with questions. Principally, how do we design policy that satisfactorily addresses some human beings' demonstrably biological—and arguably biologically inevitable—desire to take drugs? What about issues of social cost and individual freedom and responsibility?

If chronic users steal from their neighbors to finance their expensive habits, are education, rehabilitation, and supply restriction the solution? Or would liberalization lower the price of drugs and thereby reduce users' need to make desperate choices to pay for them? Drug injection spreads HIV and hepatitis C—do we try to keep needles off the streets, or do we give abusers a safe place to shoot up?

The retail drug trade has brought violence to nearly every demographic in the country, from suburban shopping mall parking lots to urban street corners. But is this a result of the restriction of drugs and the resulting black market, or is there something in the nature of the product that produces these externalities?

This book is not going to resolve all of these questions, but by exploring them in fair-minded context, it aims to provide partial answers and the basis for a reasonable way forward. The strict laissez-faire answer—the decision to take drugs is a private choice that falls within the bounds of ordinary social behavior, and any attempt to restrict that choice constitutes an incursion on individual liberty—falls short. It takes a tremendous feat of moral acrobatics to deny the broader social costs associated with drug use. On the other hand, a strict prohibitionist view doesn't work, either. For reasons we will consider throughout the book, almost a century of prohibition has not put a dent in America's drug abuse problem. Illicit drug industries continue to rake in more than $100 billion a year. And on the licit side, there are more than fifteen million individuals with an alcohol use disorder in the United States alone.[23]

It's worth pointing out that our perceptions of various drugs are in part conditioned by the personal and intellectual habits of visible political and social figures. As one scholar put it, the leaders' vices du jour have a way of becoming the official vices, the devil's corollary of *cuius regio, eius religio:* those who control the realm dictate the religion of the realm. Peter the Great, who picked up a tobacco habit abroad, lifted Russia's prohibition of the addictive weed. In 1724, the snuff-addicted Pope Benedict XIII (1649–1730) repealed the global smoking ban set by Pope Urban VII in 1590. The latter had threatened to excommunicate anyone who smoked in sacred locales.[24]

Public use of tobacco and alcohol was ubiquitous throughout the first half of the twentieth century. Winston Churchill, Joseph Stalin, and Franklin Roosevelt smoked and boozed with vigor at Yalta in the waning days of World War II. America's original drug warrior, Harry Anslinger, smoked cigarettes and drank liquor. The more that ministers, teachers, executives, socialites, athletes, and celebrities promoted smoking or drug use by example, the more socially and morally acceptable it seemed.[25]

On the other hand, some scholars have argued that drug policy has been a very effective way for social and political leaders to marginalize and disenfranchise social groups that they dislike. As MIT linguist and prominent public intellectual Noam Chomsky writes, "Very commonly substances are criminalized because they're associated with what's called the dangerous classes, poor people, or working people. So for example in England in the 19th century, there was a period when gin was criminalized and whiskey wasn't, because gin is what poor people drink."[26]

Drug Dealing 101

Selling drugs is a "pure brokerage activity" in which a dealer purchases drugs from a distributor, cuts the volume into smaller amounts, and sells them again on the street to a modest crew of regular customers. The various stages in the distribution process vary in their degrees of risk and profitability. Manufacturing substances like cocaine and methamphetamine can be as simple—and as hidden from drug enforcement authorities—as cooking a casserole. Coordinating smuggling operations across global borders, on the other hand, requires expertise and an extraordinary tolerance for risk.[27]

Drug prohibition and law enforcement made illicit drugs considerably more expensive than they would be otherwise. It's important to remember that these substances are merely "semi-refined agricultural products like flour, tea, or coffee."

In short, illegal drugs are not expensive because their inputs are expensive or because they're difficult to make. They are expensive because they are illegal.[28]

Kleiman and his research colleagues found that in "source" countries like Colombia, cocaine sold on the street for around 1 percent of the street price in the United States. If it were legal in the United States, a kilo of cocaine selling for $1,500–$2,000 in Colombia could be shipped via courier for around $50. "Prohibition and enforcement" bump up the cost of trafficking that same kilo by another $15,000–$20,000. And after making it into America, the coke goes through as many as half a dozen illegal transactions that "collectively drive up the price" to more than $100,000 per kilo. If these drugs were legal, their price in the United States would drop dramatically. Rising "enforcement risk" explains why prices skyrocket as drugs move down the value chain.[29]

Each year, between one and two million Americans are involved in illegal drug distribution; five hundred thousand persons are incarcerated for such reasons at any one time; the average dealer spends a year in prison for every two to four spent out dealing. Taking drug pushers off the streets does deter drug consumption to an extent. It increases risk, which drives dealers to demand higher compensation. These increased "wages" push up the cost of distributing the drugs to buyers, and higher prices cut down drug consumption just as higher prices at the gas pump cut down on driving. Police enforcement can also make it more difficult for a buyer to locate dealers. Police patrolling one drug-ridden neighborhood might "disrupt" the drug market temporarily while the operation works to bypass enforcement. In one telling example cited by Kleiman's team, methamphetamine's street price spiked—and overdoses plummeted—for about a year after each of two series of regulations was imposed on the input chemicals used to make meth. Ultimately, local meth makers found other suppliers, and the majority of the production switched to other countries, where the precursors remained available.[30]

This example points to a key feature of the drug market: the rule of replacement. As courts remove dealers from the market through the criminal justice system, the rule of replacement predicts that newcomers will replace sellers who have been busted. Replacement also helps explain why arresting a small-time dealer—one who sells, say, five kilos a year—does not cut consumption by anything near that amount. However, as the authors of *Drugs and Drug Policy* have documented, there are exceptions to this general rule. LSD, for one, is quite difficult to synthesize outside a laboratory setting. In 2000, the DEA busted a key LSD manufacturer and, U.S. drug agents contended, subsequent rates of the drug's use were half what they'd been the previous ten years.[31]

A Note of Caution

Even a brief overview of the drug trade, as we've seen in this chapter, is enough to dispel some of the myths about drug use, abuse, addiction, trafficking, and enforcement. Although there are clearly two major lines of thinking in the ideological conflict over what to do about problematic drug use, the arguments from both sides aren't quite as clear-cut as they might at first seem.

The discussion has been admittedly general and has only touched the surface of each topic. The next chapters in this section dive into the histories of specific drugs, particularly as they have been distributed and consumed in the United States. In order to make clear decisions about drug policy, we have to start thinking clearly about drugs. To do that, we have to understand the substances themselves.

2 • Alcohol

Order from the best House in Madeira a Pipe of the best old Wine, and
let it be Securd from Pilferers.
—George Washington in a letter to his London agent, Robert Cary &
Company, 1759. (A pipe is 126 gallons.)

Drinking, as Eric Burns writes, was our first national pastime—long
before baseball was invented.
—Susan Cheever, *Drinking in America: Our Secret History*

Starting Early

The story of alcohol is among the most important in any reckoning of the
war on drugs. This might come as something of a surprise, given that alcohol
is one of America's most widely consumed substances; that it remains legal;
and that, in everyday usage, the word "drug" does not immediately bring alcohol to mind. But, as preeminent drug policy scholar Mark Kleiman reminds
us, "Alcohol is not just a drug, but the archetypal drug: the drug most widely
used and the drug that causes the most addiction, disease, and violence."[1]

As far as statistics go, there were eighty-eight thousand alcohol-related
deaths in America each year between 2006 and 2010. According to estimates
from the Centers for Disease Control and Prevention, alcohol accounted for
2.5 million years of potential life lost each year in that same period, shortening
the lives of those who died by an average of thirty years. Excessive drinking,
which includes binge and heavy drinking, caused one in ten deaths among

adults between twenty and sixty-four years. Compared with all other drugs consumed in the United States, alcohol is by far the biggest killer. Further, as many as half of America's inmates had been drinking when they committed the offenses that landed them in prison. As Kleiman notes, "Alcohol shortens time horizons, and people with shorter time horizons are more criminally active because they're less scared of the punishment."[2]

Although the mortality and criminality rates would be cause enough for including alcohol in our consideration of drugs and drug policy, alcohol's story is an interesting one for another reason: it is the only major recreational drug in the United States that has been both prohibited and re-permitted by federal law. Prohibition and its repeal are often cited as "proof" of the inefficacy of our prohibition-centric policies for other drugs. There are flaws in this simplistic analysis, but the history of alcohol in this country does offer several important points of comparison as we think about the arguments for and against legalization of other drugs.

The "chemical soul" in every alcoholic drink is ethanol, a "colorless and highly volatile liquid." Alcohol is classified as a depressant—it inhibits functions of the central nervous system; it is also biphasic, meaning that the nature of its physiological effect changes according to the amount consumed. In larger quantities it causes slowed brain activity, slurred speech, and impaired motor coordination. At high enough doses, the drug will kill.[3]

Ethanol is derived naturally from the fermentation of sugary liquids, such as those found in grains and fruit. All sorts of animals ingest alcohol in the wild and even become drunk. As far back as the prehistoric period, humans have been aware of this natural process and have exploited it to yield potables vaguely like wine or beer. The first known instance of manufactured alcohol dates to around 8000–5000 B.C.E. Archeological evidence that humans were turning their foodstuffs into alcohol comes from the residues of Chinese pots, circa 7000–6000 B.C.E., which contained a fermented beverage made from grapes, honey, rice, and berries. Painted images in Egyptian dynastic tombs from around 3100 B.C.E. depict beer-making, and bookkeeping kept on papyrus scrolls reveals that the workers who slaved to construct the Giza pyramids were given a generous beer ration of 1.5 gallons every day. Ancient Greek city-states and colonies had an important relationship with strong drink, especially wine, which was ubiquitous. "It was used as an offering to their deities; as a currency to buy rare and precious things from distant countries; and it was drunk formally, ritually, as a medicine, and to assuage thirst." In Athens, wine was considered a vital part of civic life. Public *oinoptai* feasts included equal distributions of wine for each citizen—one of the roots of the concept of *demokratia*, or "people power." Homer's two famous epic poems, *The Iliad* and *The Odyssey*, are replete with talk of wine and "the etiquette of its consumption."[4]

"Where There Is a Curse, There Is Drink"

Americans' storied love affair with alcohol dates back to at least the first European settlers. As most seafarers did, the Spanish carried alcohol on their initial voyages to the New World, although they found that Florida's grapes produced bitterer versions of the smooth European wines they were accustomed to. Eventually, the area's indigenous populations developed a taste for wine, the excessive consumption of which contributed to their decimation as early as the seventeenth century.

English settlers on North Carolina's Roanoke Island attempted to make beer from Indian maize in the 1580s. In 1606, the Virginia Company received a royal charter from King James I and sponsored an expedition that sailed for the Chesapeake Bay in 1607. As the colony at Jamestown struggled to sustain itself with rapidly dwindling numbers, the dearth of alcohol received its share of the blame. "To plant a Colony by water drinkers was an inexcusable error in those, who laid the first foundation . . . which until it be laide down againe, there is small hope of health." To address the scourge of impure water, Virginia authorities sought out brewers to cross the Atlantic.[5]

On the fateful *Mayflower* voyage that landed on Cape Cod on November 9, 1620, beer was a coveted cargo, given that the water on board was rancid. And like Virginia colonists who had preceded them by some years, they lamented the lack of "inns to entertain or refresh their weather-beaten bodies." The pilgrims were astounded to discover that the New World water was safe to drink, and "as pleasant . . . as wine or beer." In fact, the Puritan William Bradford, who had replaced the deceased John Carver as governor of the Plymouth colony, defended the settlement in a letter to England in 1624:

> 6th OBJ[ection]: The water is not wholesome.
>
> ANS[wer]: If they mean, not so wholesome as the good beer and wine in London (which they so dearly love), we will not dispute with them; but else for water it is as good as any in the world (for aught we know) and it is wholesome enough to us that can be content therewith.[6]

As Susan Cheever explains in *Drinking in America*, for the Pilgrims, beer was a "good creature of God." Only the "crank-brained" did not partake. Plymouth's first public buildings included a brewery and a tavern. In 1633, a "furnace for brewing" was sent from England. Within years, the Pilgrims had built taverns or public houses across New England that served as centers of civic life. After 1634, communities were required to have inns, or *ordinaries*, for the "receiving, refreshment, and entertainment of travelers and strangers, and to serve public occasions." In Cheever's words, "Often where there is a curse, there is drink, and this was very much the case with the Pilgrims."[7]

By the early 1700s, the British colonies in America were notorious around the world for their drinking. Up to a quarter of the average American's earnings went to drink, and the habit spanned all generations, from infancy to death. In the nineteenth century, Swedish traveler Carl D. Arfwedson noticed a "general addiction to hard drinking." One historian observed a common American welcome: "Come, Sir, take a dram first." It was an offer rarely declined.[8]

On Manhattan Island, the Dutch were as "fond of their booze as the English" and constructed a brewery on "Brouwers Straet." The Dutch colony's last governor, General Peter Stuyvesant, chronicled, "One quarter of New Amsterdam is devoted to houses for the sale of brandy, tobacco, and beer." The Dutch learned, as the Spanish and English had, that the local Indians did not drink alcoholic beverages. As Adriaen van der Donck wrote in his *Description of the New Netherlands,* "They never make wine or beer. Brandy or strong drink is unknown to them, except those who frequent our settlements, and have learned that beer and wine taste better than water. In the Indian languages, which are rich and expressive, they have no word to express drunkenness." This is why, van der Donck concluded, the Indians were not afflicted with "rheumatic gout" and "red and pimpled noses." The problem, though, was that when the Indians got a whiff of booze, they appeared "eager to make up for lost time." A Jesuit living with the Iroquois in the 1640s was told by some of his hosts that they did not like the taste of liquor, but drank it anyway, "simply to become intoxicated—imagining, in their drunkenness, that they become persons of importance, taking pleasure in seeing themselves dreaded by those who do not taste this poison."[9]

Despite the fact that slaves and Indians were largely restricted from taverns, and that myriad laws banning the sale of liquor to Indians were passed, including in New Amsterdam in 1643, Rhode Island in 1654, and New York in 1709, in the end, untold numbers of Native Americans "ruined themselves on the white man's wicked water." Unlike European settlers, who were likely to first encounter wine and beer in childhood, the Indians' first swig was more likely from distilled spirits—more easily shipped to the colonies—"a mouthful or two of which was enough to produce an altered state of consciousness." By the end of the nineteenth century, alcohol abuse was tragically rampant among Native American populations.

Hard Times

One credible explanation for the permissive attitude toward alcohol that persisted through the colonial era and the early years of the United States is its acceptance at the highest levels of leadership. Far from being condemned, both hard and soft versions of the drug were integral parts of the daily life of the American ruling class. They were also important contributors to the fledgling American economy and to the founders' own personal wealth. George Washington was an avid drinker whose preferred libations were Caribbean rum and Madeira wine. American merchants who sold agricultural goods in the Caribbean carried rum on the return voyage to help satisfy the colonists' prodigious appetites. In 1770, the colonies imported four million gallons of the spirit and, for good measure, domestically distilled another five million. Seven-eighths of this supply was imbibed domestically. After the twenty-something George Washington unsuccessfully campaigned to win a seat in the Virginia House of Burgesses, he blamed the loss on his failure to distribute sufficient booze to the electorate. For author Daniel Okrent, "When he tried again two years later, Washington floated into office partly on the 144 gallons of rum, punch, hard cider and beer his election agent handed out—roughly half a gallon for every vote he received." In his day, congeniality by way of dispensing free drinks demonstrated an affinity with the common man. If the candidate got drunk with the people, this revealed upstanding moral character. This perception may well be tied to a more contemporary meme: American voters today often want (or think they want) to vote for a presidential candidate they can imagine sharing a beer with. Historian Robert J. Dinkin's book *Campaigning in America: A History of Election Practices* explained how eighteenth- and nineteenth-century elections swung with a widely used and reliably effective technique known as "swilling the planters with bumbo." In his words, "If a candidate ignored the custom of treating, he often found himself in great difficulty." When James Madison stumped in 1777, his eschewing of "the corrupting influence of spirituous liquors, and other treats" sealed his defeat to a less scrupulous opponent.[10]

General Washington certainly knew how drink could motivate soldiers in battle. "The benefits arising from the moderate use of strong liquor have been experienced in all armies and are not to be disputed." At Valley Forge during the horrible winter of 1777–78, when more than twenty-five hundred men were killed by starvation, disease, and exposure, he doubled his troops' rum ration.[11]

In the period before independence, there were voices of dissent against this copious consumption, even if they were in some sense shouting into the darkness. The writer Kelefa Sanneh has pointed out that hard liquor was banned in some American lands well before the country declared independence in 1776.[12]

Red, White, and Booze

Washington used the years after his presidency ended in 1797 to grow rye and corn at his Mount Vernon estate in Virginia. In 1798, Washington's new rye whiskey distillery was one of the most lucrative ventures on the property—though the father of the nation acknowledged that liquor had become the "ruin of half the workingmen in this country." Washington went on to make brandy with his own fermented grapes and constructed a brewery for beer. A Currier and Ives engraving from 1848 portrayed Washington toasting his officers with a bottle of Madeira. Three decades hence, with the nation in a frenzy over the temperance question, the engraving was reworked to remove the wine glass from Washington's hand; the carafe was turned into his classic tricorne hat.[13]

To be sure, there were dissenting voices to be found among the architects of the nation. Alexander Hamilton, Washington's first secretary of the treasury, the son of an alcoholic father, held a special antipathy for chaos and drunkenness. In his words, "The consumption of ardent spirits . . . is carried to an extreme which is truly to be regretted, as well in regard to the health and morals as to the economy of the community." With small-scale producers popping up on farms across the nation, Hamilton supported the not unreasonable idea to slap a sizable tax on whiskey—on top of extant taxes on rum and molasses—to help finance the nascent government. The tax, which went into effect in 1791, was the first levied by the American government on a domestic product. Northern politicians, such as New Hampshire senator Samuel Livermore, quipped that it was prudent for Americans to be "drinking down the debt."[14]

On the other hand, liquor producers largely in the South and West, who had been especially incensed with the British tax burden that had helped to precipitate the Patriot rebellion, rejected Hamilton's revenue scheme as meddling and unjust. In Georgia, opponents asked for peach brandy to be exempted since it was "a necessary of life . . . in this warm climate." Ironically, even in the federal capital of Philadelphia, tax evasion among distillers was routine; one investigation discovered that in one six-week period alone four large distilleries had paid taxes on only 3,277 of the 5,227 gallons of whiskey they had produced.[15]

In western Pennsylvania, where a quarter of the young nation's stills operated, locals threatened federal marshals with tarring and feathering. In 1794, a few hundred rebel farmers and distillers in the region, calling themselves the "whiskey boys," took up arms and raided the home of tax inspector General John Neville. They even took over the city of Pittsburgh. President Washington dispatched an overwhelming force of fifteen thousand militiamen to Pennsylvania, personally led by the vengeful Hamilton. The rebels eventually abided by the new taxes; two men were found guilty of treason but were quickly pardoned by Washington. Interestingly, the animus against the tax was based partly on class, in that it privileged the more affluent Madeira-drinking aristocracy over the common (whiskey-drinking) man. In the presidential campaign of 1800, Thomas Jefferson, a devoted fan of Italian and French wines, included repeal of the whiskey tax in his platform. He also wrote a letter to James Monroe conveying his sense that Washington had overreacted to the so-called "Whiskey Rebellion." "An insurrection was announced and proclaimed and armed against," he wrote, "but could never be found."[16]

Washington's successor, John Adams, condemned spirits for decades but drank a tankard of hard cider daily and sometimes had beer for breakfast. He tried for years, in vain, to kick his tobacco and Madeira habits. Part of his conflicted opposition arose from his despondency over his sons' alcoholism. In a letter to a friend, the physician Benjamin Rush, Adams wrote bitterly that he was

> grieved to the heart by losses sustained because of alcoholism. If I should then in my will, my Dying Legacy, my posthumous Exhortation, . . . recommend heavy, prohibitory Taxes upon Spirituous Liquors, which I believe to be the only Remedy against their deleterious Qualities in Society, every one of your Brother Republicans and Nine tenths of the Federalists would say that I was canting a Puritan, a profound Hypocrite, setting up Standards of Morality, Frugality, Economy, Temperance, Simplicity, and Sobriety that I know the Age was incapable of.

Adams worried further: "Is it not mortifying that we Americans should exceed all other people in the world in this degrading, beastly vice of intemperance?"[17]

An early abolitionist, the first U.S. surgeon general, and a signatory of the Declaration of Independence, Rush had treated soldiers during the Revolutionary War. His patients included Washington, Adams, Hancock, and Franklin and their families. Rush was a pioneer of public health in America, asking the city of Philadelphia to clean up its refuse to improve its wretched sanitation.[18]

Any heavy drinker, in Rush's estimation, was "in folly . . . a calf—in stupidity, an ass—in roaring, a mad bull—in quarreling and fighting, a dog— in cruelty, a tiger—in fetor, a skunk—in filthiness, a hog—and in obscenity, a he-goat." His essay *An Inquiry into the Effects of Ardent Spirits on the Human Body and Mind* in 1785 presented the idea that drunkenness was an "odious disease." Rush contended that alcoholics were powerless, rather than morally defective—presciently seeing alcoholism for the mental illness that it is. In an especially interesting detail for our story, Rush used beer or wine laced with opium to wean patients off hard liquor.[19]

The brilliant, enigmatic Thomas Jefferson was a connoisseur of wine, later credited with the invention of "the presidential cocktail party." At his residence at Monticello, he invented a dumbwaiter for the purpose of bringing bottles from the wine cellar to the dining room to help lubricate his regular dinner gatherings. The Virginian usually put away two or three times what his guests drank, with seemingly few ill effects, despite political chatter that he was a drunk, which of course he was! He also started a trend: After his investments at Monticello, fine wine cellars and cocktail parties became the sign of

Benjamin Rush, an early abolitionist and signer of the Declaration of Independence, who became an influential physician in the nascent American republic. In 1785 he described alcoholism as a disease. (Library of Congress, Prints and Photographs Division, Washington, D.C.)

political arrival across the country. Like Adams and Washington before him, though, Jefferson feared the prospect of spirits "spreading through the mass of our citizens." In December 1821, a Harvard scholar, George Ticknor, alerted Jefferson about the country's merry ways. "If the consumption of spirituous liquors should increase for thirty years to come at the rate it has for thirty years back we should be hardly better than a nation of sots."[20]

Generally speaking, for all the rancor surrounding hard spirits, early Americans did not consider ales, ciders, and wine to be "intoxicating." In fact, in the years before Prohibition, cider was America's preferred drink. "Up until Prohibition," Michael Pollan writes in his seminal tome *The Botany of Desire,* "an apple grown in America was far less likely to be eaten than to wind up in a barrel of cider." By the mid-nineteenth century,

> virtually every homestead in America had an orchard in which literally thousands of gallons of cider were made every year. In rural areas cider took the place not only of wine and beer but of coffee and tea, juice, and even water. Indeed, in many places cider was consumed more freely than water, even by children, since it was arguably the healthier— because more sanitary—beverage.

As author Howard Means described, "Hard cider was as much a part of the dining table as meat or bread." Frontier settlers spent much of their lives in "an alcoholic haze." On average, they took in about ten ounces of hard cider each day—the same rate at which Americans drank water in 2017.[21]

Drunkard Nation

By 1820, individual alcohol consumption had exceeded today's average. Although women did partake, men made up the lion's share of drinkers. The American Temperance Society reckoned that in the 1820s the three million adult American males downed sixty million gallons of liquor—close to half a pint a day per man—while the nine million children and women drank twelve million gallons. As a *New Republic* piece told its readers in 1979, almost no American abstained. "To refuse a drink was, at best, bad manners, at worst, an insult. A guest at an evening party might be dragged to the sideboard and forced to down glass after glass. A refusal to drink under such circumstances was viewed as proof that the abstainer thought himself better than other people. And refusing could be downright dangerous. A gang of lusty Kentuckians angry with an abstinent comrade allegedly roasted him over a fire." Women who might

have looked unkindly upon liquor as beastly readily imbibed alcohol-based elixirs for "health." "One could swig Lydia Pinkham's elixir for female complaints
(18 percent alcohol) without feeling that one was actually drinking." Thomas O.
Larkin, an American merchant in Alta California, as the southwestern portion
of today's United States was known at the time, observed that the drinking habit
often started with babies. "I have frequently seen Fathers wake their Child of a
year old from a sound sleep to make it drink Rum, or Brandy." In 1829, the U.S.
Army still allowed "habitual drunkards" into its ranks; there may have been little choice, given that perhaps 75 percent of the country's workers drank no less
than four ounces of hard liquor each day. The Delaware Moral Society, for one,
feared that the nation was turning into a "nation of drunkards."[22]

Visiting the United States in 1831, the Frenchman Alexis de Tocqueville
was told that despite the American underclass's prodigious consumption of
liquor, politicos did not want to anger constituents by levying weighty taxes. In
the Frenchman's estimation, which was published in 1835, "the drinking population constitutes the majority in your country, and . . . temperance is somewhat unpopular."[23]

Franklin Pierce became the first alcoholic president when he took office in
1853. Pierce did not permit alcohol at White House receptions, nor was wine
served at state dinners. Behind closed doors, though, the president was more
liberal with his intake. The son of a tavern keeper and an alcoholic mother,
Pierce had been a problem drinker in his days at Bowdoin College in Maine.
His marriage was troubled, and his only surviving son was killed in front of
his eyes in a train wreck outside Andover, Massachusetts, just weeks after his
election in January 1853. (Pierce and his wife Jane both survived.) Pierce no
doubt found comfort in whiskey, but his failed presidency—considered by
historians to be one of the worst in American history—was likely related to his
habitual drinking. Despondent about the looming dissolution of the nation,
he lamented, "What can the next president do but drink?" Pierce succumbed
in 1869 from cirrhosis of the liver and hepatic coma.[24] By the end of Pierce's
presidency in 1857, the seeds of America's first temperance movement had
already sprouted.[25]

Demon Rum

It was in fact in the early 1800s when a variety of "reform-minded ministers" and "pioneer temperance reformers" such as Dr. Justin Edwards
and other evangelical Calvinists associated with the Andover Theological

Seminary in Massachusetts hatched the anti-liquor movement. The effort began with their 1826 establishment of the American Society for the Promotion of Temperance. In the mid-1830s, the group, since renamed the American Temperance Society, began calling for full abstinence. This organizing led to the publication of numerous "militant anti-liquor" pamphlets, whose messages anti-booze ministers shared with their congregations from the pulpit. Regional and state temperance activists set up "moral machines" in villages and towns across the country. As W. J. Rorabaugh explains, an agent arrived in town, "gave a public address in one of the churches, and urged the clergymen and leading citizens to form a temperance society. The agent furnished a model constitution for such an organization, blessed the project, and proceeded to the next town." Temperance pledge signings were often held on July 4, a deliberate effort by proponents to draw a moral link between the anti-liquor mission and the Founding Fathers' struggle. All told, temperance would resonate as one of the nineteenth century's "longest and largest" social movements.[26]

The temperance movement worked to convince or coerce grain growers, distillers, and saloon owners to turn away from "Demon Rum." It also attempted more novel means, such as funding "dry boat lines" on waterways and establishing dry saloons. There were even temperance hotels that might hold worship services or provide guests with religious or temperance literature.[27]

Sanneh writes, "Nineteenth-century temperance campaigners deployed a familiar cast of stock figures: starving children, battered wives, drunks staggering and dying in the streets. (Researchers were just figuring out the science of liver failure, which bloated and killed so many heavy drinkers.)" The goal for these activists was abstinence, not moderation. To an extent, the tactics succeeded: through the middle eighteenth century, temperance grew "less unpopular." In one clear victory for reformers, the temperance activist-cum-mayor of Portland, Maine, pushed through a law prohibiting the production or sale of alcoholic beverages—though the measure was repealed within a decade. He preached, "The traffic in drink tends to more degradation and impoverishment of the people than all causes of evil combined." By the 1840s, pro-temperance parties had helped push through local licensing regimes and, the following decade, state prohibitions.[28]

On April 2, 1840, in Chase's Tavern on Liberty Street in Baltimore, six alcoholic men pledged to not drink again and to spend their lives saving others. A sort of "artisan society" of former drunks, the Washington Movement first worked to reduce alcoholism and alcohol consumption by reaching people individually and founding shelters, known as Washington Homes, for the chronically drunk.[29]

The Washington Movement was outshined by better-organized groups like the Good Templars and the Blue Ribbon Society, but it promoted "temperance," as it was understood to mean then—moderation of quantity, rather than blanket abstinence. This work, however, created a path toward the more unflinching cause of Prohibition half a century later. Indeed, fervent prohibitionists a few decades hence would acknowledge the Washingtonians' spirited influence.

P. T. Barnum wrote in his autobiography from 1855, *P. T. Barnum, Written by Himself,* that he became a strident temperance advocate after listening to a public temperance lecture and signing the "teetotal pledge." "We also saw that large numbers who were saved by these means, fell back again to a lower position than ever, because the tempter was permitted to live and throw out his seductive toils. Our watchword was, 'Prohibition!' We had become convinced it was a matter of life and death; that we must *kill* Alcohol or Alcohol would kill *us* or our friends." Since forever, temperance believers contended, Americans equated drinking with freedom when in fact it was slavery—or as one activist put it, "independence and wealth, in the midst of disgrace and rags." Or for Virginia planter and congressman John Randolph, "Nothing can be more respectable than the independence that grows out of self-denial." As one might expect, many of the temperance organizers were also abolitionists, since both vices were viewed as "economically wasteful as well as immoral." In a sharp reminder of how different this age was from our times, early reformers tended to consider temperance the more pressing issue. As Rorabaugh explains,

> They argued that while slavery encouraged the master to idleness and vice and the slave to ignorance and religious indifference, the effect of drink was worse: a slave had only lost control of his body, a drunkard lost mastery of his soul. The chains of intoxication, declared one reformer, "are heavier than those which the sons of Africa have ever worn."[30]

Reformers aggressively used what might ungenerously be labeled propaganda to disseminate their messages. A New York businessman, Edward Delavan, succeeded in getting former presidents James Madison and John Quincy Adams and incumbent Andrew Jackson to sign a no-liquor pledge, subsequently published on the cover of *Temperance Almanac* in 1837. In 1851 the American Tract Society distributed millions of temperance-pushing pamphlets, a feat facilitated by cheaper production methods. New York aristocrat Stephen Van Rensselaer covered the costs of sending a pamphlet to every post office in the country.[31]

It's worth noting that the early temperance movement still distinguished between hard and soft spirits. In his 1976 history *Deliver Us from Evil*, Norman H. Clark described how the temperance movements in America demarcated liquors, such as gin and whiskey, from "softer" drinks—beer, wine, and cider—that most consumers considered to be part of the normal diet.[32]

"Kind, Unassuming Persuasion"

Despite having opened a tavern in the 1830s in his native Illinois, Abraham Lincoln often abstained from drinking altogether, joking that he would get tipsy after the most modest of sips. After refusing a fine wine proffered to him after he won a seat in Congress, the future president explained: "I promised my precious mother only a few days before she died, that I would never use anything intoxicating as a beverage, and I consider that promise as binding today as it was the day I gave it." In 1842, as a still green-around-the-ears member of the Illinois House of Representatives, Lincoln wittily and presciently described America's deep ambivalence toward drugs and drug abuse in his Temperance Address, delivered at the Second Presbyterian Church of Springfield to members of the Washington Movement:

> I have not enquired at what period of time the use of intoxicating drinks commenced; nor is it important to know. It is sufficient that to all of us who now inhabit the world, the practice of drinking them, is just as old as the world itself—that is, we have seen the one, just as long as we have seen the other. When all such of us, as have now reached the years of maturity, first opened our eyes upon the stage of existence, we found intoxicating liquor, recognized by everybody, used by everybody, and repudiated by nobody. It commonly entered into the first draught of the infant, and the last draught of the dying man. From the sideboard of the parson, down to the ragged pocket of the houseless loafer, it was constantly found. Physicians prescribed it in this, that, and the other disease. Government provided it for soldiers and sailors; and to have a rolling or raising, a husking or hoe-down, any where about without it, was *positively insufferable*.[33]

The American politician urged his listeners to not assume their own moral superiority over drinkers. Rather than chastise Americans into quitting, Lincoln urged a "kind, unassuming persuasion" and dismissed hardline attitudes.

Lincoln aimed much of his address at that branch of the temperance movement inclined toward religious fervor. He was especially critical of attempts to reform alcoholics by threats of damnation, a routine practice for preachers of the day. In special relevance for our examination of America's drug war, Lincoln believed that a republic is threatened when one faction within it becomes the sole bearer of truth. For him, the unreconstructed reformers' use of the "thundering tones of anathema and denunciation," instead of reason and persuasion, was an attempt at cornering that truth. Instead, in his famous conclusion he advocated reason as the solution to alcohol and other ills: "Happy day, when all appetites controlled, all passions subdued, all matters subjected, *mind*, all conquering *mind*, shall live and move the monarch of the world. Glorious consummation! Hail fall of Fury! Reign of Reason, all hail!"[34]

As president, Lincoln focused exhaustively on prosecuting the Civil War, while the alcohol and tobacco industries thrived. The beleaguered president taxed tobacco when cash was required for the war effort; his officers were allowed to drink as long as they could fight. When a temperance group implored him to fire General Ulysses S. Grant for his compulsive drinking, Lincoln cheekily inquired after the general's preferred brand of whiskey so that he could ship a barrel of it to all of his other commanders.[35]

Saloonicide

Before the Civil War, the three essential reform issues in America were temperance, women's rights, and abolition, with the latter ranking as the most pressing. After the war, with the slavery issue ostensibly resolved, temperance and women's suffrage rose to the top of the list—and became increasingly intertwined. It is worth examining the grassroots rise of the temperance movement and its swell toward Prohibition, because it yielded one of the first total federal bans on a drug, the only such ban to be sealed in a constitutional amendment, and the only one to have been subsequently repealed.

Until Prohibition, temperance was considered a women's issue: a core narrative of the time was that men's drinking made women's domestic lives horrible. But women who wanted to support temperance could not do so by voting for it. Still, several key suffragists earned their early activist stripes through their work in the temperance movement: Eliza Thompson, a liquor reformer who became "Mother Thompson"; Susan B. Anthony, who made her first speech to the Daughters of Temperance and pushed for women's rights after the Sons of Temperance would not let her address them; and Amelia Bloomer, who was also barred from a men's temperance meeting. As the eminent publisher Daniel Okrent observed, "One could make the argument that without the 'liquor evil,' as it was commonly known to those who most despised it, the suffrage movement would not have drawn the talents and energies of these gifted women."[36]

In 1875, Frances Willard of Wisconsin helped found the Woman's Christian Temperance Union, a group numbering 250,000 women that "redefined temperance." The WCTU's activism led every state to adopt "scientific temperance instruction" in high school biology curricula by 1902. One early member, Carrie Nation, became a national celebrity for barging into saloons and vandalizing them while singing Christian hymns. The Kansas Constitution prohibited "intoxicating liquors." Nation understood that the police could not arrest her without revealing their own negligence. Sanneh explains: "She was angry at the saloons that were, she held, filling up the jails and the morgues, but her real target was a government that was failing to do what it had promised." Her autobiography reflected upon her first "saloonicide" in Kiowa, Kansas, in 1900:

> There was quite a young man behind the bar. I said to him: 'Young man, come from behind that bar, your mother did not raise you for such a place.' I threw a brick at the mirror, which was a very heavy one, and it did not break, but the brick fell and broke everything in its way. I began to look around for something that would break it. I was standing by a billiard table on which there was one ball. I said: 'Thank God,' and picked it up, threw it, and it made a hole in the mirror. By this time, the streets were crowded with people; most of them seemed to look puzzled. There was one boy about fifteen years old who seemed perfectly wild with joy, and he jumped, skipped and yelled with delight. I have since thought of that as being a significant sign. For to smash saloons will save the boy.[37]

As the temperance movement gained traction, two important influences began to push it in a new direction. First, the ideology became increasingly connected with the late-nineteenth-century Progressive movement, which became a blanket concept for issues from industrial reform and labor rights to voting equality and good government. A "complicated cast of allies" joined Progressives in what was, on the whole, a deeply Christian crusade, "delivering its message in the language of revivalism." The second development was a growing trend toward "medicalizing" alcohol abuse, in some small measure shifting the framing from moral evil to physical illness, a phenomenon echoed

Carrie Nation, a temperance movement radical and bitter opponent of alcohol before Prohibition, smashed up saloons in the early 1900s (Library of Congress, Prints and Photographs Division, Washington, D.C.)

in twenty-first-century attempts to reform the judicial system's approach to abusers of heroin and prescription opioids. The American Association for the Cure of Inebriates was established in 1870 by a host of activists and doctors intent on creating a network of private medical facilities to treat a new kind of disease called alcoholism, named in 1849 by Swedish physician Magnus Huss.[38]

3 · Cocaine

A Simple Little Leaf with a Complicated History

Cocaine is the second most consumed illicit drug in the United States, behind marijuana. Roughly 15 percent of Americans have tried it—five million within the past year, two million in the past month. The drug causes more than five hundred thousand emergency room visits annually.[1]

As of 2018, a gram of pure cocaine on the American street was worth around four grams of gold. Informed estimates place the valuation of the American cocaine market at over $70 billion a year, a number on par with the annual take of Google and double that of Goldman Sachs.[2] The world's demand for cocaine could be met by planting coca on a plantation half the size of Long Island. As journalist Mattathias Schwartz keenly reports, for three decades Washington has, futilely and at great expense, "chased this plantation around the Western Hemisphere."

Cocaine is produced from the leaves of the coca plant, genus *Erythroxylum*, a shrub indigenous to the Andes region. There are more than two hundred *Erythroxylum* species, most of which have some amount of cocaine in them. Most commercial cocaine is derived from two species: *Erythroxylum coca* (primarily) and *Erythroxylum novogranatense*. Coca was one of the first plants domesticated in the Americas. Archeological evidence of coca chewing in the Andes suggests that the practice goes back at least as far as 3000 B.C.E., though hunter-gatherers in the eastern Andes may have begun using coca even earlier to quell hunger during lean times.[3]

One modern scholar, Ronald K. Siegel, described a potshard he discovered in an archeological dig seeking to unearth information about the ancient peoples that preceded the Europeans' arrival in the 1500s:

The unique oval shape suggested it was from the pre-Incan Tihuanaco Empire, perhaps one thousand years old. I brushed the dirt away from the sides to reveal a painted scene. In the center was a cluster of coca branches and leaves. On one side stood a large llama eating the coca. The animal's swollen cheek pouch pictured the ingestion in no uncertain terms. This was Napa, the legendary llama honored in coca ceremonies. On the other side of the coca leaves was an Indian, watching the llama and beginning to reach for the coca with open hands and mouth. Was this the story of coca's discovery in 5000 B.C. by early Andean man? He had apparently observed his pack animals foraging on the plant and perhaps even noticed a certain friskiness to their movements. He copied the coca-eating behavior and soon discovered both the stimulating and nutritious properties of the plant. What a surprise that must have been![4]

The Incan civilization in the fifteenth and sixteenth centuries used coca leaves in religious ceremonies throughout its empire, which roughly comprised present-day Peru, Bolivia, and Ecuador. Indigenous travelers during this period often described a journey in terms of the number of mouthfuls of coca chewed while making the trek. Shamans burned the leaves—which were believed to hold magical powers—to view the future and cleanse places inhabited by evil spirits.[5]

At first, the invading Europeans were underwhelmed with the coca-chewing practice. Here is the nonplussed Florentine explorer Amerigo Vespucci describing an indigenous group his expedition happened upon in 1499:

> All of them had their cheeks full of a green herb that they chewed constantly like beasts, so that they could barely speak. Each one carried around his neck two gourds, one of them full of that herb and the other a white powder that looked like pulverized plaster. They dipped a stick into the powder, and then put the stick in the mouth, in order to apply powder to the herb that they chewed; they did this very frequently. We were amazed at this and could not understand its secret or why they did it.[6]

When Spanish conquistadores seized lands from the native tribes, they imposed a 10 percent tax on coca cultivation. Catholic missionaries considered coca-chewing and the mysticism surrounding it to be impediments to their proselytizing mission. Over time, however, the Spanish began to recognize some of the plant's benefits. In 1609, a Peruvian priest, Padre Blas Valera, the son of Luis Valera, who accompanied Francisco Pizarro on the conquest of the

Incan empire, recorded many of the conquistadores' exploits in his tomes *Vo-cabulario* and *Historia de los Incas*. As he put it,

> Coca protects the body from many ailments, and our doctors use it in powdered form to reduce the swelling of wounds, to strengthen broken bones, to expel cold from the body or prevent it from entering, and to cure rotten wounds or sores that are full of maggots. And if it does so much for outward ailments, will not its singular virtue have even greater effect in the entrails of those who eat it?

Spanish administrators ultimately elected to tolerate the plant's consumption, on the grounds that the leaves boosted labor productivity in the silver mines.

In many respects, coca remains a fundamental element of Andean indigenous peoples' lives. Still today, before giving birth, an indigenous mother chews coca to hasten labor and reduce pain. Relatives celebrate the birth by chewing the leaf together. When a youth wants to wed a girl, he offers coca to her father. Friends and family drink coca tea during a wake and place coca leaves in the coffin before burial.[7]

Bordeaux and Cocaine Concoction

Although an extensive trade for coca developed in New Spain, transatlantic commerce did not follow. For nearly four centuries, the habit simply failed to gain traction in the Old World. It was nearly impossible to ship the raw leaves back to the Europe without their spoiling and losing potency. At the same time, general scientific skepticism toward the plant's medicinal value prevailed. It was only in the mid-1800s that European explorers on the South American continent began to bring the leaves back home in sizable quantities. Over the ensuing decades scientists searched for the active ingredient that made chewing the leaves so invigorating. German graduate student and chemist Albert Niemann at the University of Göttingen recognized the coca leaf's stimulating properties and in the early 1860s described the extraction of the active chemical, cocaine hydrochloride, in his dissertation. Niemann had studied a well-packaged thirty-pound shipment of leaves; at the time, it was the largest quantity of properly prepared coca ever to reach a European lab. Though Niemann died not long after his breakthrough, his work launched a cocaine boom. In 1862, Merck, the German pharmaceutical company, started producing small amounts of cocaine, most destined for research laboratories in Europe and the United States.[8]

In 1884, ophthalmologist and surgeon Karl Koller discovered cocaine's anesthetic properties; the substance rapidly gained popularity as a nerve blocker for dental and eye surgery (the latter application is still used today). As physicians and researchers became more aware of cocaine's psychoactive properties, they dispensed it for anxiety, depression, and addiction. In 1883, Theodor Aschenbrandt, a German military doctor, provided cocaine to Bavarian troops during training to stave off acute fatigue. Victorian-era medical journals touted cocaine as a veritable miracle drug, a cure for flatulence, upset stomach, hysteria, hypochondria, nervous dispositions, and fatigue. Between July and December 1885 alone, the *New York Medical Journal* published twenty-seven articles, notes, and letters on cocaine. By this time, the American Hay Fever Association had adopted the drug as its wonder remedy. William Hammond, a former surgeon-general in the U.S. Army, recommended cocaine for reducing inflammation in mucous membranes and for preventing female masturbation through anesthetization of the clitoris.[9]

Patients clamored for cocaine, and sales exploded. Major drug companies, including Parke-Davis, Merck, and Squibb, began rolling out catalogues of cocaine-based products. In 1885, American manufacturer Parke-Davis sold cocaine in the form of cigarettes, powder, and even a mixture injected directly into the user's veins—with the needle included. The company contended that its cocaine products would "supply the place of food, make the coward brave, the silent eloquent and render the sufferer insensitive to pain."[10]

Therapeutic interest in cocaine soon exceeded the drug's supply. Its expense became, in Sigmund Freud's reckoning in 1885, "an obstacle to all further experiments." The solution to this dilemma triggered a sort of coca gold rush. Parke-Davis, the top American producer, sent Henry Rusby to the Bolivian Amazon to obtain coca leaves and to research other potentially salubrious (that is, profitable) plants. "Brilliant, energetic, stubborn, self-promoting, and racist to the bone," Rusby was the "Theodore Roosevelt of bio-imperialism." On one of his initial half-dozen or so expeditions to South and Central America, he got his hands on twenty thousand pounds of coca leaves. A political revolt, however, prevented him from bringing the leaves back home, and the entire bounty spoiled in the sweltering tropical heat of the Panamanian isthmus. Undaunted, Rusby assembled a motley crew of soldiers of fortune to explore the Amazon, during which venture his outfit gathered approximately forty thousand botanical specimens before reaching northern Brazil "half dead." In part because of this experience, Rusby and other innovators came to understand that extracting crude alkaloid cocaine in the Andes would be far more cost-effective than shipping the leaves for processing in North America and Europe. The race for a more efficient method of extraction was on.[11]

As historian Paul Gootenberg describes in his stellar tome *Andean Cocaine,* on March 12, 1885, pharmacist Alfredo Bignon spent yet another interminable day in the backroom lab of his Droguería y Botica Francesa in Lima's colonial downtown. By combining Andean coca leaf with ubiquitous household chemicals—kerosene and soda ash—he managed to activate crude cocaine. Not long after, he brought his discovery to the attention of the Academia Libre de Medicina de Lima, a distinguished panel of Peruvian physicians and chemists. The reception was warm, to say the least: the Frenchman Bignon had uncovered an "easy and economic preparation in the same place as cultivation." This innovation would bring him both scientific credibility and riches. Native manufacturing would also help his adopted country of Peru meet the booming global demand for cocaine. Drug firms, including Merck of Darmstadt, Germany, could now simply buy the cocaine from Peruvian manufacturers. As Gootenberg shows, in the 1880s Peru was not only the majority world supplier for coca leaf for cocaine production but also the largest exporter of *cocaína bruta,* or semi-refined cocaine. In the early 1900s, the legal Peruvian export industry was sending abroad more than twenty-two thousand pounds of crude cocaine each year, along with more than two million pounds of leaves. Most of the crude cocaine (purity varying from 85 to 95 percent) went to European companies for further processing; the leaves went to the United States. Unlike Europe, the United States was close enough to the Andes to make shipping the raw leaves, once they were bundled and sealed against humidity, viable. Incidentally, coca leaves also happened to enter the country duty-free, while crude cocaine was taxed at a rate of 25 percent. For his part, Bignon would go on to conduct scores of novel studies on cocaine. For Gootenberg, "Turning the humble Indian coca leaf into modern cocaine was to be, Bignon imagined, one of Peru's heroic national endeavors."[12]

Exhilaration and Lasting Euphoria

Sigmund Freud, father of psychoanalysis, was one of the best-known proponents of the pharmaceutical use of cocaine. In fact, Freud's initial contributions to medicine were associated with cocaine, not psychoanalysis. In 1884, the Austrian neurologist published *Über Coca,* in which he made the (now almost amusingly inaccurate) claim that the drug was so efficacious in treating morphine addiction and alcoholism that "inebriate asylums can be entirely dispensed with; in 10 days a radical cure can be effected by an injection of 0.1 grams of cocaine 3 times a day." Of course, Freud's favorite test subject was none other than Freud himself. He expounded on cocaine's effects, using his own experience as principal evidence. He found that the drug cured his upset stomach, dulled his aches, soothed his depression, and produced

> exhilaration and lasting euphoria, which in no way differs from the normal euphoria of the healthy person. You perceive an increase of self-control and possess more vitality and capacity for work. In other words, you are simply normal, and it is soon hard to believe you are under the influence of any drug. Long intensive physical work is performed without any fatigue. This result is enjoyed without any of the unpleasant after-effects that follow exhilaration brought about by alcohol. No craving for the further use of cocaine appears after the first, or even after repeated taking of the drug.[13]

Revealing said euphoria, he forewarned his fiancée Martha Bernays: "Woe to you, my princess. When I come, I will kiss you quite red and feed you till you are plump. And if you are forward, you should see who is the stronger—a gentle little girl who doesn't eat enough, or a big, wild man who has cocaine in his body. In my last severe depression, I took coca again, and a small dose lifted me to the heights in a wonderful fashion. I am just now busy collecting the literature for a song of praise to this magical substance." Freud recommended cocaine to his friend and colleague Ernst Fleischl-Marxow, a Viennese physician addicted to morphine—who wound up addicted to both drugs and died seven years later, at the tender age of forty-five. Freud himself likely kicked the cocaine habit, which he once called his "most gorgeous excitement."[14]

Stimulant for Fatigued or Overworked Body and Brain

The expanding availability of cocaine (alongside other drugs such as morphine and heroin, as we will see) ushered in a new era of consumption: "nonmedical experimentation." As is still the case today, in the first few decades following cocaine's discovery, recreational cocaine use was taken up by popular culture. In 1887, for example, an astute young British physician named Arthur Conan Doyle published his first detective story, *A Study in Scarlet,* a tale that involves Sherlock Holmes injecting himself with cocaine to relax after taxing investigations. It is likely that Doyle's fictional accounts were colored by his voracious reading of the latest scientific and medical literature, including

Freud's *Über Coca,* although Doyle may have experimented with cocaine himself. A memorable scene from his second Holmes novel, *The Sign of the Four,* features this exchange between the detective and his companion, Dr. Watson:

> "Which is it to-day," I asked, "morphine or cocaine?"
>
> He raised his eyes languidly from the old black-letter volume which he had opened.
>
> "It is cocaine," he said, "a seven-per-cent solution. Would you care to try it?"[15]

Coca and cocaine are central to another exemplary work of fiction of the late nineteenth century, *The Strange Case of Doctor Jekyll and Mr. Hyde,* first published in 1886. The savage alter ego of Mr. Hyde seems designed to evoke the human mind on cocaine, at first frenetic and then descending into disquietude. Scottish author Robert Louis Stevenson likely wrote the novel under the drug's influence.[16]

Across the Atlantic, a revered American surgeon named William Stewart Halsted was performing his own experiments with the drug. The first surgeon-in-chief of the new Johns Hopkins Hospital in Baltimore, Halsted pioneered numerous innovations, including the surgical glove, as well as new methods for maintaining sterility in the operating room, safely opening up the body, controlling bleeding, and hastening healing. Having read Freud's *Über Coca* and Karl Koller's subsequent study on the use of cocaine in eye surgery, Halsted hypothesized that the substance could be used as a local anesthetic, a safe alternative to the common but toxic general anesthetics ether and chloroform. Halsted's experiments entailed snorting cocaine as well as injecting it "right to the vein." Soon, Halsted and friends were taking cocaine to fuel social visits outside the hospital environs. Not surprisingly, many of them became addicts. Halsted became such a junkie that he left a screaming patient in the operating room before embarking on a month-long cocaine binge. Halsted committed himself repeatedly to the Butler Hospital for the Insane in Rhode Island. Sadly, much like Fleischl-Marxow before him, the brilliant surgeon became addicted to morphine after it was prescribed to him to kick the cocaine cravings.[17]

As medical historian and physician Howard Markel has deftly chronicled in *An Anatomy of Addiction,* neither Freud nor Halsted, nor for that matter their colleagues, had any foreknowledge of cocaine's potential to dominate and ruin their lives. Freud's and Halsted's attachments to cocaine and morphine represent the "birth of the modern addict"—the user whose excessive consumption causes a loss of control over consumption itself.[18]

Patent Fever

Cocaine distribution surged through the late nineteenth century. In an era in which licensing was lax and legitimate physicians and pharmaceuticals were in short supply, the powder became the ingredient of choice in a host of "patent medicines," a class of remedies that ranged from toothache drops to hemorrhoid plasters. In many places, pure cocaine was available over the counter. It was touted as a remedy for curing shyness in children and as a general panacea for the listless. The *New York Times* in 1885 wrote, "The new uses to which cocaine has been applied with success in New York include hay fever, catarrh, and toothache, and it now being experimented with cases of seasickness. Cocaine will cure the worst cold the head ever heard of." Intrepid Ernest Shackleton and Captain Robert Falcon Scott put these sorts of heady claims to the test when they brought "Forced March" brand cocaine tablets with them on their respective expeditions to Antarctica.[19]

One of the more notable success stories of the era was that of Vin Mariani, a palatable Bordeaux wine and coca-leaf concoction first invented by French chemist Angelo Mariani in 1863. In Mariani's immodest estimation, the drink was "unequaled as a tonic-stimulant for fatigued or overworked body and brain . . . [it] prevents malaria, influenza and wasting diseases." With the patented concoction's promotion cleverly linked to youth, health, and celebrity, Vin Mariani quickly ascended to the level of international sensation. Jules Verne, Henrik Ibsen, Robert Louis Stevenson, Sir Arthur Conan Doyle, a few among a list of the era's celebrities, became enthusiasts, as did Thomas Edison and President William McKinley. Pope Leo XIII, the Roman pontiff himself, was believed to carry around of flask of the concoction regularly and also gave a Vatican gold medal to Mariani.[20]

By the 1880s, Mariani had introduced a variety of cocaine-laced products, including throat lozenges, cigars, teas, and even Mariani margarine. Thé Mariani, a coca infusion, kept former Union general and President Ulysses S. Grant lucid as he was dying of tongue and throat cancer (Grant's habit of smoking around 750 cigars a month in his White House days probably had something to do with this illness). Ron Chernow explains in his biography of the president: "The torment of the inflamed throat never ceased. When the pain grew too great, his black valet, Harrison Terrell, sprayed his throat with 'cocaine water,' temporarily numbing the area, or applied hot compresses to his head. Despite his fear of morphine addiction, Grant could not dispense entirely with such powerful medication." Grant responded to newspaper critics who contended that he was gambling with a new and dangerous drug: "It is not true that they are experimenting on me with a single medicine about which they know little or nothing. . . . The medicine alluded to as the one being experimented with is, I presume, Cocaine. That has never been given to me as a medicine. It has only been administered as an application to stop pain. It is well known that it accomplishes that result without leaving injurious effects behind. It is only applied when much needed." Grant was receiving cocaine as a local anesthetic, but the stimulating psychoactive effects likely did not pass him by. As the disease progressed, his doctor increased the dosage, and Grant's tolerance began to increase. "My mouth hurts me and cocaine ceases to give me the relief it once did. If its use can be curtailed I hope it will soon have its effect again." Cocaine might have been the only thing that kept Grant motivated enough to finish his memoirs. In his final days, Grant received routine morphine injections chased by combinations of morphine and brandy—on top of the cocaine.[21]

It was only a matter of time before Vin Mariani began to see competition. Given America's love-hate relationship with the whiskey bottle, it wasn't a surprise that a Mariani imitator in the States would devise a "dry" tonic that kept in the coca but left out the booze. After the U.S. Civil War, veteran and Atlanta pharmacist John Pemberton began using morphine to dull the pain caused by his wounds and subsequently became addicted. He learned that cocaine could help cure "morphinism," which prompted him to concoct a wine-based tonic that contained cocaine. Pemberton tried and failed to sell "Pemberton's French Wine Coca," a Vin Mariani knockoff that he touted as better than Mariani's.[22]

When Georgia outlawed alcohol as part of the swelling prohibition upswing, Pemberton started mixing cocaine with kola nut extract and soda water, sans alcohol. In 1886, the original formula for Coca-Cola, known at the time as the "temperance drink," contained approximately 2.5 milligrams of cocaine per 100 milliliters of fluid. Pemberton boasted that his "health drink" could "cure impotence and muscle aches." Another pharmacist bought the rights and founded the Coca-Cola Company.[23] The new drink popped. Some southerners were drinking fifty bottles of Coca-Cola a day in order to get a bigger hit of cocaine. An ad for one competitor, Metcalf's Coca Wine, displayed a coca leaf at the center with a brief history of its use in South America. It then detailed the ailments that could be cured if the wine were downed three times a day. Its claims were not immodest: "Elderly people have found it a reliable aphrodisiac superior to any other drink. . . . Athletes, pedestrians and baseball players have found by practical experience that a steady course of coca taken both before and after any trial of strength or endurance will impart energy to every movement, and prevent fatigue."[24]

Historian Grace Hale observes that at the outset, Coca-Cola was popular as the "brain tonic" and "intellectual beverage" for well-to-do white drinkers. But by the turn of the century, Coke was available in bottles, and black customers banned from segregated soda fountains could enjoy the cold, refreshing pick-me-up. Hale expands: "Middle-class whites worried that soft drinks were contributing to what they saw as exploding cocaine use among African-Americans. Southern newspapers reported that 'negro cocaine fiends' were raping white women, the police powerless to stop them. By 1903, [manager of Coca-Cola Asa Griggs] Candler had bowed to white fears (and a wave of anti-narcotics legislation), removing the cocaine and adding more sugar and caffeine."[25]

Today a small quantity of coca leaf is legally turned into pharmaceutical cocaine for use as a local anesthetic in surgeries near masses of fine blood vessels. In the United States, coca leaves are shipped to the Stepan Chemical Company (previously the Maywood Chemical Works) of Maywood, New Jersey, which extracts the cocaine and sells it to pharmaceutical companies. The residue from Stepan's leaves—but not the cocaine—winds up in Atlanta, Georgia, where it remains part of Formula X, the secret recipe for Coca-Cola. In 2003, 419 kilograms of cocaine were produced legally. Indigenous South American advocates point to Coca-Cola's ability to use this coca leaf-based product responsibly as evidence that global anti-coca statutes should be reconsidered.[26]

More Treacherous Than Injecting a Dog with Rabies

Up until the early twentieth century, the federal government essentially left cocaine's production, distribution, and consumption to the free market. This was symptomatic of a general laxity within and around the medical professions. The federal government had little effective control over the licensing of physicians or pharmacists. There were no regulations for the labeling or advertising of compounds. There was no national agency, like today's Department of Health and Human Services or its subsidiary the Food and Drug Administration, to oversee the healthcare industries. Drug producers created what they wished, often with as little training as a line chef at a restaurant; they marketed their tinctures and elixirs as inventively as they wished; and they sold them to whomever they wished. It was up to the consumer to choose the most effective approach to his or her own medical treatment—and this was often dictated more by advertising than by sage professional counsel. In any case, cocaine did well by the system. Given its medical and cultural embrace, it's perhaps not surprising that use spiked in the twilight of the nineteenth century. By 1902, there were an estimated two hundred thousand cocaine addicts in the United States. In 1912, five thousand Americans died of cocaine-related complications. Consumption in 1903 was five times the rate of 1890; much of this was non-medical use among the white, middle-aged, professional class.[27]

Despite this demographic evidence, cocaine became increasingly associated with workers, youths, blacks, and the "urban underworld." By 1900, newspapers across the country were reporting on "Cocaine Alleys"—a moniker for certain impoverished neighborhoods in American cities. That year the *New York Medical Journal* called Chattanooga's Cocaine Alley "a den of vice and filth." One local pharmacist making a night inspection reported seeing hundreds of folks "snuffing" small amounts of cocaine, while others lay around "in every conceivable form state of depravity." In December 1900, a piece in the Illinois *State-Journal* described one section of Springfield:

> "Cocaine Alley," which for several years existed, was some time ago broken up by the police. When this raid was made on the "joints" there were about fifty residents. They moved, but only for a short time, and they returned. There are now probably twenty-five or more persons who congregate in the alley, and day after day they are to be seen roaming about under the influence of cocaine. A nearby drug store daily sells a large amount of the drug to the fiends, and when once with their "leepins" on there is not telling what they will do.[28]

Hyperbolic news reporting fueled distorted perceptions of cocaine use and in some cases went out of its way to paint the issue in racial terms. In 1901 the *Atlanta Constitution* reported, "Use of the drug [cocaine] among negroes is growing to an alarming extent." The *New York Times* described how under cocaine, "sexual desires are increased and perverted . . . peaceful negroes become quarrelsome, and timid negroes develop a degree of 'Dutch courage' that is sometimes almost incredible." Later, in 1914, the *New York Times* published an article with the provocative headline "Murder and Insanity Increasing Among Lower Class Because They Have Taken to 'Sniffing' Since Being Deprived of Whisky by Prohibition" by Dr. Edward Huntington Williams, a physician and dean of Boston University. It included the following reckoning:

For some years there have been rumors about the increase in drug taking in the South—vague, but always insistent rumors that the addiction
to such drugs as morphine and cocaine was becoming a veritable curse
to the colored race in certain regions. Some of these reports read like the
wildest flights of a sensational fiction writer. Stories of cocaine orgies
and "sniffing parties" followed by wholesale murders seem like lurid
journalism of the yellowest variety.

But in point of fact there was nothing "yellow" about many of these
reports. Nine men killed in Mississippi on one occasion by crazed cocaine takers, five in North Carolina, three in Tennessee—these are the
facts that need no imaginative coloring. And since this gruesome evidence is supported by the printed records of the insane hospitals, courts,
jails, and penitentiaries, there is no escaping the conviction drug taking
has become a race menace.[29]

The story of how cocaine became an "underworld" drug is more complicated than reporting at the time might have suggested. As historian Jill Jonnes
has written, southern blacks may have started using cocaine in New Orleans,
where longshoremen discovered that the drug could help them tolerate the
"extraordinarily severe work of loading and unloading, at which, perhaps, for
seventy hours at a stretch, they have to work without sleep or rest, in rain, in
cold, and in heat. . . . Whiskey did not answer and cocaine appeared to be the
thing needed." Anglo bosses freely gave cocaine to (mostly white) workers
"hired for the backbreaking work of picking cotton and building railroads and
levees."[30]

Eventually, cocaine shifted from being a work stimulant to a spark for the
"after-hours high at juke joints and parties." Musicians up and down the Mississippi River picked up the habit, as it fueled late-night gigs and kept up the
energy on grueling tour circuits.[31]

As refinement improved and the price dropped, cocaine also gained popularity in the swelling slums of northern cities. In New York, for example,
Birney's Catarrh Cure (cocaine content: 5 percent) was in high demand—"and
not for its advertised purpose of calming inflamed noses and throats." Working-class boys were another key demographic in this shift. In 1904, Chicago
activist Jane Addams observed children in the surrounding neighborhoods
who were hooked on drugs. She was especially unsettled by one "vivacious boy
. . . animated and joyous and promising. . . . When I last saw him in his coffin,
it was impossible to connect that haggard shriveled body with that I had known
before."[32]

By 1907, American imports of raw coca were twenty times what they had been only a few years earlier. Soon enough, the American Medical Association began to take interest in cocaine's deleterious effects and published several studies exposing the "evil" side of the substance. The American Pharmaceutical Association accused pharmacists of "pandering to this most unfortunate, this man-destroying appetite." As public sentiment shifted, it sparked action. Within a decade, Congress would intervene to ban the non-medical use of cocaine.[33]

4 · Opium

A single custom prevails here among the women at which I was
greatly surprised and really am at a loss how to account for. . . . They
have adopted these many years the Asiatic custom of taking a dose of
opium every morning, and so deep-rooted is it that they would be at a
loss how to live without this indulgence.

—French national St. John de Crèvecœur, *Letters from an American
Farmer*, 1782

Humankind's First Drug

In 1821 Thomas De Quincey, an unknown and downtrodden Englishman,
published a book under the title *Confessions of an English Opium Eater*. The
work disquieted readers with its autobiographical telling of his "tortured love
affair" with laudanum, a tincture of 10 percent opium. As was so often the
case then and is still true today, De Quincey's opioid habit developed from
treating routine physical irritation, specifically rheumatism. Laudanum eased
his rheumatism but also opened up a whole new world.[1]

Sparking a "minor sensation," De Quincey's *Confessions* confronted the
West with a stark description of a novel concept: drug addiction. At a time
when people freely swallowed opium-based remedies for "sundry aches and
pains," De Quincey's account was unexpectedly terrifying. From his first sip
of laudanum, he was taken. "Here was the secret of happiness, about which
philosophers had disputed for so many ages, at once discovered: happiness
might now be bought for a penny, and carried in the waistcoat pocket: portable

ecstasies might be had corked up on a pint bottle and peace of mind could be sent down in gallons by the coach mail."[2]

As is often so true with addiction, De Quincey soon learned that what began as a limitless pleasure soon became an affliction. The drug had "ceased to found its empire on spells of pleasure; it was solely by the tortures connected with the attempt to abjure it, that it kept its hold. . . . I saw that I must die if I continued the opium: I determined, therefore, if that should be required, to die in throwing it off. . . . Think of me as . . . agitated, writhing, throbbing, palpitating, shattered; and much, perhaps, in the situation of him who has been racked."[3]

At the time, the medicinal qualities of the opium poppy, *Papaver somniferum*, had been understood for millennia. In the West, the plant's resin had earned it the moniker "God's Own Medicine." The English clinician Thomas Sydenham stated in 1680, "Among the remedies to which it has pleased Almighty God to give to man to relieve his sufferings, none is so universal and efficacious as opium."[4]

Opium was probably humanity's first drug, cultivated as agricultural civilizations developed alongside bodies of water. Like coca and tobacco, opium poppy is one of "mankind's earliest attempts at genetic engineering," since it was planted as early as five thousand years ago, most likely in the western Mediterranean or the Near East. The Assyrians came up with the practice of cutting and draining the poppy's seedpod, which contains an oozy, alkaloid-rich latex. (The same technique is still applied around the world today.) As far back as 3000 B.C.E. the Sumerians called it the "joy plant." Poppy cultivation passed from the Assyrians to the Babylonians, who imparted the knowledge to the Egyptians. The Indians and the Greeks also grew poppy and used the resin for medical and psychoactive purposes. Homer and Virgil mention potions derived from opium. The ancients turned to the drug as a pain reliever, sleep aid, and euphoria-inducer. Ancient texts also suggest that at least some civilizations were aware that opium resin was habit-forming and mortally poisonous.[5]

Over the centuries, Europeans imported crude opium, either on its own or dissolved in a liquid such as alcohol—and presto, laudanum—and eventually brought it with them to North America. Colonists considered it a reliable pain remedy. In his last years, Benjamin Franklin used laudanum to soften the agony of kidney stones. Before he became president, chronically depressed Abraham Lincoln maintained an account at the Corneau & Diller drugstore in Springfield, Illinois, where during the 1850s he bought brandy and ointments containing laudanum, among other remedies. When he supposedly purchased three sticks of "cough candy" for 25 cents, he likely did not realize that there was opium in each piece. But the gum worked, and the cough disappeared. Despite its wide acceptance, opium's ills were well known. The *American Dispensatory* of 1818 described how the habitual use of opium could lead to "tremors, paralysis, stupidity, and general emaciation." It countered this warning with a proclamation of the incredible worth of opium in mitigating a variety of maladies, including cholera and asthma. One scholar has quipped that given the treatments in vogue at the time—blistering, vomiting, and bleeding—it is not so difficult to understand opium's popularity.[6]

In Asia, where the vast majority of opium was produced, the drug gave rise to a notorious chapter in the European colonial project. Opium was cheap, and the pipe was a rare comfort for Asian workers. Although the British were not the only colonial power to sell Indian opium, they developed an unassailable monopoly system for its sale and production.[7] And the system generated enormous profits for the British Empire.

Most of this product—eventually about 15 percent of total revenue of British India—went to China, against the wishes and policies of the Qing Dynasty. The opium trade in China had been banned by imperial edicts since 1729, and the British conducted business through a complicated scheme of legitimate middlemen, illicit smugglers, and widespread corruption. Private merchant houses smuggling opium into the Middle Kingdom flourished. James Matheson, a partner in the opium, tea, and cotton trading concern Jardine Matheson & Company, became the second-largest landowner in Britain and accumulated enough riches to purchase the Isle of Lewis off the Scottish coast.[8]

As David Courtwright recounts in his superb work *Forces of Habit,* American actors also got in on the opium trade, especially after the War of 1812. In some years, Boston-based Perkins & Company purchased over half of the Turkish opium crop for export to China. The patriarch and grandfather of future president Franklin Delano Roosevelt, Warren Delano II, was director of another American firm, Russell & Company. "I do not pretend to justify the prosecution of the opium trade in a moral and philanthropic point of view," Delano wrote, "but as a merchant I insist that it has been a fair, honorable and legitimate trade; and to say the worst of it, liable to no further or weightier objections than is the importation of wines, Brandies & spirits into the U. States, England, &c." In the opinion of many Chinese, though, Matheson, Delano, and their European counterparts were not businessmen but scoundrels.[9]

The disagreement over whether China should be able to prevent the sale of opium on its own soil generated not one but two wars. In the late 1830s, a

Chinese imperial commissioner named Lin Zexu struck at the opium scourge by arresting dealers, destroying over a million kilograms of opium, and enforcing a blockade across Chinese ports. The British East India Company responded by bringing the empire's military might to bear in 1839 in to order to force China to reopen. Chinese defeat and the Treaty of Nanking in 1842 precipitated what is known in China as "the Century of National Humiliation." A second Opium War took place from 1856 to 1860 between allied French and British forces and the Qing Dynasty. Once again, victory by the foreign powers resulted in another relaxation of trade restrictions and the legalization of Indian opium, among other Qing concessions.[10]

The drug's trade volume, which had topped out at just over six million pounds in 1839, surged to more than fifteen million pounds in 1879. By this point, domestic production exceeded the import market. China was itself making its thirty-two million pounds of opium to meet demand. The majority of this opium came from the southwestern provinces of Guizhou, Yunnan, and Sichuan. Earning two to four times the average take for wheat, opium became the most attractive crop for Chinese farmers. Like tobacco in the colonial Chesapeake, opium served in these regions as a medium of exchange, a source of taxation, and the local drug of choice. As one observer wrote, "Nowhere in China are the people so well off, or so hardy, and nowhere do they smoke so much opium." Yet, the human toll of China's opium scourge was devastating. In 1838, according to one estimate, China had between four and twelve million opium addicts. The same year, officials in Guangdong and Fujian provinces submitted reports to the imperial government indicating that nine out of every ten people in those provinces were addicted. Some scholars have pointed to the soporific effects of opium as a central factor to explain the Chinese military's ineffectiveness against the European powers during this period. By the early 1900s, around half of the adult population was smoking opium at least sporadically. More than sixteen million people (6 percent of the population) were addicts.[11]

A Mix of Clerics, Bohemians, and Street Walkers

At around the time that Goethe was writing *Faust*, a German pharmacist named Friedrich Sertürner working in Paderborn isolated a sleep-inducing alkaloid from opium poppy latex and called it morphine, after Morpheus, the Roman god of dreams. The brilliant but unstable Sertürner was another inventor who became hooked on his own discovery. More powerful than crude opium and a far more effective pain reliever, the new drug gained popularity in the ensuing decades. As author Norman Ohler writes, Heinrich Emanuel Merck, an apothecary in Darmstadt who began commercial production in 1827, used a "business model of supplying alkaloids and other medications in unvarying quality."[12]

At one point, morphine was considered the greatest medical discovery in history. Morphine's use went global thanks to the century's roughly 330 wars and the overwhelming demand for effective painkillers that came with them. The bloody Civil War sparked the cultivation of opium poppies in Virginia, Georgia, and South Carolina. It was during the Civil War, the Franco-Prussian War of 1870, and other conflicts that morphine's power to calm or completely suppress pain became most apparent. The wonder drug transformed field hospitals from shriek-ridden purgatories to silent wards.[13]

Using the sting of the bee as his inspiration, in 1853 a physician in Edinburgh named Alexander Wood invented the hypodermic needle, a far more efficient delivery system than pills or the anal suppositories that were in vogue at the time. Needle injections also enabled more accurate dosing, an important consideration with morphine. Opium was frequently adulterated with "anything from licorice to lead," prompting many users to respond by upping the doses. Accurately measured morphine shots made delivery much more predictable and effective.

Morphine use soared with the adoption of hypodermic medication. Initially, doctors assumed that the needle and pure morphine would not contribute to increased addiction. In fact, given that pain could be controlled with less morphine when injected, they believed it would have precisely the opposite effect. In 1855, Paris hospital patients were given a "scant 272 grams" of morphine; twenty years later, after the new techniques were honed, it was around ten thousand grams.[14] Inevitably, hypodermic injection did make morphine more "potent and euphorigenic" and, by extension, more addictive. Wood's wife, Rebecca Massey, might have been the first known intravenous morphine addict. She died from an overdose delivered by her husband's invention. Roughly a quarter of the first morphine addicts were women. Almost all were middle-class and pursued their habit discreetly. In some chic European salons, though, it became fashionable to shoot up in public.[15]

The beauty and terror of morphine was that it could get at the symptoms of maladies "whose root causes doctors could not treat." For example, in 1886 Jules Verne was shot by a mentally unstable relative—the bullet remained stuck in his foot. A diabetic, Verne could not have endured surgery. With convalescence as the author's only option, Verne's doctors prescribed morphine to ease the recovery. Verne wrote a memorable sonnet to the drug: "Oh, jab me with your needle a hundred times/And a hundred times I will bless you, Saint Morphine." Yet, patients were not the only ones to get morphine. Given their access to the drug, physicians and pharmacists constituted many of the "morphinists"—furnishing another example of how proximity to supply can drive addiction.[16]

Unpardonable Carelessness of Physicians

Chinese immigrants smoked opium in Chinatowns in San Francisco, Los Angeles, New York, and elsewhere. San Francisco passed an ordinance in 1875 banning opium smoking within city limits; by 1900, however, opium dens were commonplace throughout America. In the 1890s newspapers owned by William Randolph Hearst ran stories of white women seduced by Chinese workers and their enticing opium to stoke fears of a "Yellow Peril." In 1886, after a Denver police bust, the *Denver Daily News* started reporting on illicit consumption. It uncovered numerous, and apparently bumping, Chinese-run "joints" and concluded that the "number of slaves to the hop habit in Denver was 145," twenty-seven of whom were women. The story continued: "This habit is principally confined to gamblers and prostitutes, though there are at least six who move in different walks of life." A former "hop-head" confided to a *Daily News* beat writer: "An opium smoker is a peculiar creature. He will pawn the clothes from his back for money to buy the drug. He will do even worse—steal, lie, or betray any confidence for half a dollar which to replenish the empty 'hop toy.' They are a society in themselves and care nothing for the outside world. A fiend full of 'hop' is as happy as a clam at high tide."[17]

Progressive reformers touring New York City's Chinatown in 1901 observed that neighborhood cigar and cigarette stores were often fronts for opium dens. At one brothel on Mott Street in Manhattan, girls could be "seen in nude forms, some of them in their undershirts, others in short silk dresses which come to their knees and then their long stocking, all smoking cigarettes or long pipes which I was informed had opium in them. . . . In all these places the prostitutes have opium and pipes and charge 25 cents for smoking." The reformers also toured one opium den where they found "society women from the uptown districts—some of them were women from families of refinement—were reclining on couches under the influence of opium and generally they had the bosoms of their dress open."[18]

Yet, as is often the case with drugs, the conventional narrative distorts the reality to a certain degree. The infamy of the opium den far outweighed its actual impact. This was in part due to the "imaginative talents" of authors such as Charles Dickens, Sir Arthur Conan Doyle, Oscar Wilde, and Sax Rohmer, who, finding the trope a rich metaphor for underworld activity, milked it. Yes, opium smoking did expand considerably in the 1870s and 1880s, especially in the white underworld. And in the American popular consciousness, opium smoking was certainly associated with Chinese immigrants, in part thanks to the British colonial project. As scholar David Musto has written, this connection was one of the first instances of a powerful concept in the American conception of drugs: associating a certain drug with an outsider group in society. Cocaine was similarly linked with blacks and marijuana with Mexicans in the first decades of the twentieth century. And to a considerable degree, it was these links that drove the regulatory fervor that followed.[19]

The greater share of responsibility for America's first opiate crisis in fact lies with the medical establishment. As Jill Jonnes has written, the typical American doctor in the nineteenth century opened practice after a year of classroom learning. He—in the overwhelming majority of instances doctors

Four men smoking opium pipes in an "opium den" in San Francisco, circa 1921
(Library of Congress, Prints and Photographs Division, Washington, D.C.)

were men—had not trained in an actual hospital, but instead had come across a smattering of illnesses and afflictions during a brief apprenticeship. Little was understood about hygiene or infection, and surgery was very dangerous. One public health official in Iowa, J. M. Hull, blamed the opium abuse problem on "the unpardonable carelessness of physicians" who treated "every ache and pain by the administration of an opiate."[20]

White middle-class American women were especially prone to opium use, given that they could afford to pay for physicians who would treat them with opiates, primarily laudanum and morphine, for painful "female problems" and the "characteristic Victorian complaint," neurasthenia, or nervous exhaustion. Dr. T. Gaillard Thomas, president of the American Gynecological Society, wrote: "For the relief of pain, the treatment is all summed up in one word, and that is opium. This divine drug overshadows all other anodynes.... You can easily educate her to become an opium-eater, and nothing short of this should be aimed at by the medical attendant." Hull opined that most of the addicted were to be found "among the educated and most honored and useful members of society; and as to sex, we may count out the prostitutes so much given to this vice, and still find females far ahead so far as numbers were concerned."[21]

By the end of the century, opiate addiction was rampant, although decades would pass before the condition (then called "chronic opium intoxication") was considered a legitimate illness. Doctors aside, it was easy enough for the general population to access morphine, codeine, and laudanum in the form of patent medicines and over-the-counter compounds. Catch-all medicines marketed as quaint home remedies—Children's Comfort or Carney's Common Sense Cure—were made with opiates. As we saw with cocaine-based pharmaceuticals in the last chapter, opiate patent medicine sales soared in the late nineteenth century from $3.5 million in 1859 to almost $75 million by 1900.[22]

"Foreign Mud"

By the early 1900s British traders were supplying opium to over a quarter of the Chinese population, a rate of drug market penetration unseen before or since. American missionaries who had permeated every part of China after 1860 leveled withering criticism. It was a singular sin for the ostensibly God-fearing British to use the addiction of their colonial subjects to line their already fat pockets. One missionary wrote, "Its history is a Christian sin, a Christian shame. Take away this abnormal, this unnatural ally of heathenism, and we can meet the enemy without doubt of the final outcome." Most of the missionaries' ire was directed at the British government and a public that sanctioned its colonial excesses, although the latter was increasingly opposed to the trade.

The Chinese did not need any sermons to alert them to the depth of the problem. Nationalist leader Chang Chih-tung, governor of Shanxi province, wrote to a friend in 1881, indicating (in probably hyperbolic terms) the scale of the import-driven epidemic. "The real calamity in Shansi is ... the opium. Sixty percent of the country folk, 90 percent of the city dwellers, and 100 percent of the officials, clerks, and troops are addicts." For patriotic Chinese, doing something meant stopping the India trade, "so redolent of barbarian domination," as well as ending domestic production, which the provincial and imperial government relied on for revenue. The Chinese called opium "foreign mud," alongside other terrestrial epithets.[23]

The Qing court finally responded in 1906 with a plan to suppress cultivation and smoking, an effort that was well received in eastern China but not in the opium-abundant southwest. Sichuan officials enacted the reform through the punitive taxation of opium-planted land, which prompted rioters to destroy four tax offices. In 1907, British and Indian officials reached an understanding with the Chinese to phase out exports by 10 percent annually, if the Chinese reduced domestic production at the same rate, which—to the surprise of many observers—they achieved.[24]

This came at a time when British influence in China was already on the wane. The India-China opium trade had been ebbing for years. The Boxer Rebellion of 1899–1901, which targeted foreigners and Christians working in China, proved a decisive blow to European powers' colonial ambitions in the Middle Kingdom. In Britain, the Liberal Party, which was "disproportionately middle-class, temperance-minded, non-conformist, and hostile to the opium trade," took office after the 1906 election and enacted a series of policies to scale back opium ventures abroad.[25]

Lamentably, as soon as a vacuum appeared, another power rose to fill it. Imperialist Japan started "saturating the benighted celestial kingdom" with manufactured opiates such as morphine and heroin. A U.S. Treasury Department attaché passed along this dispirited report from a female missionary in northern Manchuria: "There is a brisk trade springing up in morphine and heroin which is almost entirely run by the Japanese. . . . [T]he country is being flooded with morphine, heroin and opium where little or none existed before." In her small village, she continued, where there had previously been just one or two opium dens, now there were almost fifty, all operated by Japanese and Koreans. American officials believed that this was a game piece in Japan's incipient colonial strategy: flood Manchuria with dope, and Japan would not only reap the revenue, but also shatter the local people's will.[26]

When the Americans acquired the Philippines after the Spanish-American War in 1898, they confronted the opium problem there as well, especially among the seventy thousand Chinese residents. In 1903, the civil governor of the islands, William Howard Taft, reinstated a Spanish-era contract system that taxed opium and used the revenue to help fund a massive public education campaign. Yet the swelling American missionary presence on the island—and the Christian bloc back home—objected. The Methodist Episcopal Bishop of Manila, Homer Clyde Stuntz, believing opium use to be an unmitigated evil, argued that it was immoral for any government to profit through its taxation. Reverend Wilbur Crafts, chief of the International Reform Bureau of the United States, arranged for two thousand protest letters to be sent to the White House. Bishop Charles Henry Brent, an eminent Episcopalian missionary who later served as the president of the Shanghai Opium Commission, also expressed his opposition. Ultimately, Taft abandoned the opium tax plan.[27]

In addition to this organic, religiously driven resistance to the opium industry, another crucial development in the nascent anti-drug movement emerged in the first decade of the twentieth century. The United States reached out to the international community, through multilateral conferences and agreements, to address the opium scourge. Under continued pressure from religious groups, President Theodore Roosevelt convened the first meeting of the International Opium Commission, a diplomatic gathering of fifteen countries, in Shanghai on February 1, 1909. Brent, a key driver behind the meeting, was selected as chair. The American delegation, which included the U.S. State Department opium commissioner Hamilton Wright, Reverend Brent, and another missionary named Charles C. Tenney, had two main goals: to preserve Chinese sovereignty and to open China's markets to American goods. Chinese ire at the abuse of their nationals in the United States had resulted in a boycott of American imports. Wright believed that the anti-opium initiative could be used "as oil to smooth the troubled water of our aggressive commercial policy there." There was an additional motive: in a foreshadowing of the supply-side component of our modern drug war, officials in Washington believed that controlling opium in production countries could help arrest recreational drug use back home.[28]

The Americans found themselves in a delicate negotiating position given the dearth of U.S. domestic anti-drug laws. Even more disadvantageously,

Washington was still earning considerable revenue from taxation on imported opiates, and the opium plague abroad meant less stability and less demand for U.S. exports. The Americans solved this dilemma, as Roosevelt's Secretary of State Elihu Root told it, by passing federal "legislation on this subject in time to save our face." On January 4, 1909, Congress passed the Opium Importation Prohibition, which banned "the importation and use of opium for other than medicinal purposes." The law satisfied Chinese officials ahead of the conference and conferred the additional advantage of placating the temperance activists and missionaries in the American colony in the Philippines.[29]

Even for the reader eager to understand the drug war's early roots, getting into the historical weeds of international laws and conferences in the early 1900s can be a bit numbing. Yet this period is important, because so much of what we understand as the "modern" drug war gained its elemental shape in these white-starched diplomatic events. Almost in the same breath, two big ideas began to take form. First was the realization that drug consumption might be deleterious to personal health and social order; second was the notion that the many-armed apparatus of the American state might have the capacity to identify the sources of the scourge, eliminate them, and thereby solve the problem. Perhaps ironically, the search for a solution began in much the same way it continues today.

In any event, the Shanghai conference failed to produce a treaty. But it represented the beginning of America's outsized role in shaping international anti-drug policies that passed through the League of Nations after World War I and the United Nations after World War II.

Christ's Opium

Germany was able to maintain its lead in new pharmaceutical innovations because it had such a prodigious pool of well-educated chemists. But it was the English researcher Dr. Charles Alder Wright working in London in 1874 who identified a purportedly non-addictive form of morphine when he synthesized a drug he labeled diacetylmorphine. The following decade Heinrich Dreser at the Friedrich Bayer Laboratory in Elberfeld, Germany, reproduced Wright's diacetylmorphine and called it heroin—from *heroisch*, German for "heroic," the term Bayer's employees used to describe its effect when tested on them. Launched with great fanfare that year, the drug sold all over Europe and the United States, usually together with its other popular pain reliever, aspirin, introduced in 1899. A typical Bayer advertisement for heroin showed it as a "respiratory stimulant, sedative, expectorant and analgesic in the treatment of coughs, bronchitis, laryngitis, pneumonia, dyspnea, phthisis, coryza, whooping cough, asthma, hay fever, colds, etc."[30]

Bayer generously distributed complimentary samples to physicians and pharmacists around the world. The pharmaceutical Holy Grail in an era before antibiotics and fundamental public health procedures was anything that worked against pervasive and lethal respiratory diseases, such as tuberculosis, without generating addiction. One of the early advocates in America of heroin was Dr. Morris Manges of Mount Sinai hospital in New York City. His article "The Treatment of Coughs with Heroin," published in 1898 in the *New York Medical Journal,* reported that "the remedy was very prompt and efficacious in a large number of cases." Another attractive feature, Manges added, was that "apparently there was no habituation of the drug." Given the real medical need and Bayer's effective marketing, heroin, like cocaine and morphine before it, surged in popularity. "Heroin" brand cough syrup was soon one of the top-selling legal tonics in America.[31]

Physicians preferred heroin for the same reason they opted for morphine over opium: the same anesthetic effect and a more intense euphoria at much lower doses. Heroin was initially seen as a possible solution to the increasing predicament of morphine addiction; the charity St. James Society championed an effort to mail free samples of heroin to morphine addicts. Impossibly, Western missionaries promoted morphine and heroin to rehabilitate opium addicts in Asia. Even today, morphine is known in China as "Christ's opium." From 1911 to 1914, England exported forty tons of morphine to Asia; Germany exported ten tons of heroin, equivalent to 10,000 tons of Indian opium.[32]

By 1906, the *Journal of the American Medical Association* was warning that with heroin "the habit is readily formed and leads to the most deplorable results." Nonetheless, physicians remained inclined to prescribe it, given that heroin was administered orally, not by syringe, and thus addiction developed more gradually. Even still, heroin addiction rates soared, as they had with cocaine and other opiate narcotics. At this point, the pattern should look familiar: A chemist synthesizes or isolates a drug; widespread unregulated distribution follows with advertising dollars behind it; next comes epidemic addiction and censure by the more (at the time) "progressive" elements of the medical and public-service communities. It was this formula that set the stage for the first federal regulation of drugs.[33]

5 · Cannabis

"Makes People See Demons"

Psychoactive cannabis is the most popular illicit drug in the United States, with ten thousand tons consumed every year. Across racial, gender, and class lines, consumption of the drug "has become such a prevalent, mainstream practice that cannabis users are apt to forget they are committing a criminal act every time they smoke a joint." Cannabis is a resilient and adaptable botanical that thrives in all sorts of climates, from sea level to above ten thousand feet. The plant grows up to twenty feet tall, sprouting serrated, diagonally veined leaves that, for writer Martin A. Lee, "spread like the fingers of an open hand." The gooey resin on the leaves and flower tops holds scores of unique oily compounds; inside our human bodies, they spark neurochemical changes in the brain.[1]

Native to Central Asia, cannabis has been cultivated by humans since the "dawn of agriculture" some ten thousand years ago, making it one of humanity's most ancient crops. Neolithic peoples used every part of the cannabis plant. The stems and stalk made fiber for cordage and cloth. The seeds, full of essential fatty acids and protein, provided food (and they still do: as I write this chapter, I'm sipping a fruit smoothie made with "superfood hemp powder"). The leaves, flowers, and roots were used as medicines and in religious ceremonies.[2]

China claims the first medicinal application of cannabis, dating as far back as 4500 B.C.E. The first written reference to medicinal cannabis dates to 2700 B.C.E., when *ma* (cannabis) was recorded in the *Pen Ts'ao Ching*, the pharmacopeia of Emperor Shen Nung, the father of ancient Chinese medicine. Shen Nung prescribed *ma* to remedy countless maladies, including "female weakness, gout, rheumatism, malaria, constipation, beri-beri, and absent-mindedness." He called *ma* one of the "supreme Elixirs of Immortality." "If one takes it over a long period of time, one can communicate with spirits, and one's body becomes light," the *Pen Ts'ao Ching* recommends. However, over-consumption "makes people see demons." Chinese physicians used a mixture of cannabis and alcohol as a painkiller in surgery.[3]

In 2008, archeologists discovered well-preserved cannabis plants laid on a mummified middle-aged male corpse—likely a shaman of the Gushu culture from around 700 B.C.E.—in the Turpan Basin in the northwest. Here is how *National Geographic* described it to readers: "Thirteen cannabis plants, each up to almost three feet long, were placed diagonally across the man's chest, with the roots oriented beneath his pelvis and the tops of the plants extending from just under his chin, up and alongside the left side of his face." Amazingly, the herb tested positive for tetrahydrocannabinol (THC), the principal psychoactive ingredient in cannabis. In a finding that confirms that marijuana was used for euphoric as well as medicinal purposes long before the birth of Christ, Dr. Ethan Rosso, the team's lead author, determined, "To our knowledge, these investigations prove the oldest documentation of cannabis as a pharmacologically active ingredient. It was clearly cultivated for psychoactive purposes rather than for clothing or food."[4]

The first *suspected* use of cannabis for psychoactive purposes occurred in Central Asia in present-day Mongolia and southern Siberia around 3000 B.C.E. From Central Asia, the diffusion of cannabis proceeded along two separate trajectories. One road moved west from China into northern Europe, likely following the pioneering migrations of the Scythians—"aggressive charioteers in the second millennium B.C." The *Histories* of Herodotus mentions the Asian nomadic Scythians "howling with pleasure" in their cannabis vapor baths.[5]

The second route led south into India, Persia, the Arab Middle East, and Africa. As it moved from region to region, the "pungent plant never failed to ingratiate itself among the locals." In India, where the plant's mind-altering qualities were most coveted, the earliest mention of *bhang*, a mixture of dried cannabis leaves, seeds, and stems, appears in the Atharva Veda, around 2000 to 1000 B.C.E. At times combined with sugar, black pepper, water, or milk, *bhang* was the smoothest of three ancient Indian cannabis preparations. The other two, *ganja* and *charas*, were the real precursors of present-day recreational marijuana preparations; both were made from the dried flowering tops of cultivated female plants and then smoked.[6]

Clearing the Fog

Since *Cannabis sativa* was first classified by Carl Linnaeus in 1753, there has been substantial confusion surrounding its taxonomy. Sometimes the botanists' debate has raged as fervently as the debate over the weed's legality. Generally, the casual term *cannabis* refers to a genus of plant, which, depending on whom you ask, comprises either a few separate species or a few varieties of a single species. Linnaeus originally identified just one, *Cannabis sativa*. In 1785, Jean-Baptiste Lamarck found substantial enough differences in another strain of the plant to name a separate species, *Cannabis indica*. A third, *C. ruderalis*, was identified in the 1940s in Russia, and a possible fourth, *C. rasta*, was discovered in 2005. Today, based on recent genetic evidence, a majority of botanists seem to agree that Linnaeus was right, concluding that there is but one species, *Cannabis sativa*, and that the varieties are best classified as subspecies (*C. sativa sativa, C. sativa indica, C. sativa ruderalis*, and *C. sativa rasta*). But there are some dissenters. And, interestingly, the dispute isn't merely an academic one. In 1975, a convicted pot dealer in California nearly won an appeal on the taxonomic confusion. He argued that the law "refers expressly only to the plant 'Cannabis sativa L.' " and that in his trial there had been "no evidence that the marijuana involved in his case was Cannabis sativa L., as opposed to one of the other species." In keeping with majority opinion, and for the purposes of this book, we'll assume that *Cannabis sativa* is the species and that the real action is happening at the subspecies level.

Grown in warmer climates, the sativa and indica subspecies both produce usefully high levels of THC and are cultivated for their psychoactive effects, for recreational and medicinal use. Grown in the cooler north, sativa tends to produce much less THC and, as Fitz Hugh Ludlow described, "grows almost entirely to fibre, becoming, in virtue of this quality, the great resource for mats and cordage." Ruderalis contains almost no THC but is traditionally used in Russia and Mongolia for fiber and for folk medicine.[7]

The word *hemp*, derived from the Anglo-Saxon word *henep* or *haenep*, refers to northern-grown *C. sativa sativa*. Cultivated for its especially strong fiber, hemp is used in more than twenty-five thousand industrial applications, including rope, paper, fabric, oil, and food. Contemporary books on the history of cannabis—most written by critics of the drug war or proponents of marijuana and commercial hemp—almost invariably report interesting and supposedly powerful facts about hemp, with the aim of normalizing the plant. One good example is *Hemp Bound* author Doug Fine's contribution: Thomas

Jefferson "wrote his Declaration of Independence draft on hemp paper, and Betsy Ross's first flag was made from the plant." The point is accurate, but the authors in this camp generally don't make the necessary distinction between psychoactive and non-psychoactive varieties of cannabis. Though both varieties are from the *Cannabis sativa* species, they are distinct strains with unique biochemical compositions and uses. Non-psychoactive hemp indeed has a long history as a valuable textile crop around the world, including in North America. But it's a long logical leap to suggest that, by virtue of this fact, we ought to have a blanket policy of condoning all types of cannabis. Thomas Jefferson did not, after all, write the Declaration stoned. And while there may well be other reasons to legalize, deregulate, or otherwise permit the plant, the fact that it's been used to make flags and paper—even if they are important flags and paper to our nation—isn't sufficient.[8]

Early Colonial Seeds

Hemp came to America with the first colonists, in the sails and rigging of their ships, and in the form of arable seeds. In 1533, King Henry VIII ordered English farmers to grow hemp or else face a steep fine. Over the next decades, similar edicts applied throughout England's North American colonies. In 1610, only a few years after colonists first planted hemp in Jamestown, the Virginia Assembly required every household in the colony to grow the plant for fabric, paper, and cordage for ships. A number of early pioneers came to North America on contracts to grow hemp in return for their sea passage. In New England, the plant reportedly yielded double what it did in Great Britain. Hemp farming and processing played a key economic role in early American history. Its legacy is manifest in the names of many towns across New England and the Midwest: Hempstead, Hempfield, Hemp Hill, and others. Martin Lee expands, "Early American farmers and their entire families wore garments made from hemp, wiped their hands with hemp towels and hemp handkerchiefs, inscribed words on hemp paper, and sewed with hemp yarn." Hemp's value was perhaps most clearly evident in its role as a substitute for legal tender throughout the colonies in the seventeenth and eighteenth centuries.[9]

Many of America's Founding Fathers, including George Washington, grew hemp and encouraged their compatriots to do so. The future leader of the Continental Army wanted a safe supply so that the colonies would not have to rely on another country for this critical resource. As scholar Ronald Siegel wrote, one who answered this patriotic call was Robert "King" Carter, an early ancestor of President Jimmy Carter. King Carter grew hemp on his vast lands in Virginia, supplying much of the fiber that clothed General Washington's troops. It's ironic, then, that when Americans finally did come across a medical use for cannabis, President Carter's administration was the one responsible for actively eradicating the wild plants whose predecessors were these early colonial seeds.[10]

Thomas Jefferson was also a firm advocate of hemp as a cash crop—one he much preferred over "pernicious" tobacco. "The greatest service which can be rendered by any country," Jefferson wrote, referring to hemp, "is to add a useful plant to its culture." After completing two terms as president, Jefferson retired to his Monticello estate in western Virginia in 1809 to grow fiber hemp, with his estimated six hundred slaves. He ultimately gave up on the effort because it was too labor-intensive. "Hemp is abundantly productive and will grow forever in the same spot," he wrote after his 1815 harvest, but "breaking and beating it, which has always been done by hand, is so slow, so laborious, and so much complained of by our laborers, that I have given it up."[11]

By the mid-1800s, hemp was the young nation's third largest crop behind cotton and tobacco. In the foothills of the California Sierras, James W. Marshall struck gold at Sutter's Mill, near hemp-planted land. The news sparked a flood of prospectors pouring in to look for quick riches. Some of these migrants made the trek overland to California in horse-drawn wagons covered with hemp canvas. In the American West, lynch mobs often dispensed frontier justice with the "hemp collar"—the hangman's noose. Over a century later, cannabis cultivation sparked another "gold rush" in northern California, as high-resin marijuana bloomed into the Golden State's most profitable agricultural crop, "boasting a multi-billion-dollar annual yield despite its proscribed status." Over the second half of the nineteenth century, hemp's value was diminished by the cotton gin and the steamship. At the same time, though, cannabis was gaining currency for another reason: psychoactive cannabis extracts (mostly imported from Asia, North Africa, Mexico, and Central America) were appearing in patent medicines, following much the same path that opiates and coca derivatives first trod to American shelves. Dr. Macalister's Cough Mixture, for one, was a concoction of cannabis, chloroform, and alcohol marketed as "a safe and sure remedy for children and adults." Compounds of cannabis with anything from zinc phosphide to morphine to arsenic were sold to remedy restlessness, as well as "neuralgia, sciatica, and spasmodic pains generally." In 1850, cannabis was registered in the United States pharmacopeia as a treatment for a laundry list of afflictions.[12]

A Vista of Rainbows

In the spring of 1854, a bright and ambitious teenager named Fitz Hugh Ludlow poked his head into one of his favorite shops, Anderson's Apothecary in Poughkeepsie, New York. Smelling of "all things curative and preventive," Anderson's was a welcoming "aromatic invitation of scientific musing," recorded Ludlow, the son of an Abolitionist minister. In his account, *The Hasheesh Eater*, first published anonymously, Ludlow relayed how he had previously experimented with psychoactive compounds such as chloroform and laudanum, an alcohol-based opium tincture. This time, though, he picked up an odiferous, olive-green elixir: Tilden's Extract, made from *Cannabis indica*, Indian hemp, or hashish. On experimenting with an effective dose of the drug several days later, he waxed poetic:

> Ha! what means this sudden thrill? A shock, as of some unimagined vital force, shoots without warning through my entire frame, leaping to my fingers' ends, piercing my brain, startling me till I almost spring from my chair. . . . I spoke; a question was put to me, and I answered it; I even laughed at a bon mot. Yet it was not my voice which spoke; perhaps one which I once had far away in another time and another place. For a while I knew nothing that was going on externally, and then the remembrance of the last remark which had been made returned slowly and indistinctly, as some trait of a dream will return after many days, puzzling us to say where we have been conscious of it before.

Ludlow likened his experience to that chronicled in the *Atlantic Monthly* by the American diplomat and travel writer Bayard Taylor. Taylor's essay on consuming hashish in Damascus was the first to describe for the American general public the psychoactive effects of cannabis. "I was encompassed by a sea of light . . . a vista of rainbows," Taylor wrote. Taylor acknowledged that he also was overcome with panic but did not regret the experience, as it manifested "deeps of rapture and suffering which my natural faculties never could have sounded." Tilden & Company, a pioneer in vending solid and liquid hashish concoctions, recommended *Cannabis indica* for "hysteria, chorea, gout, neuralgia, acute and sub-acute rheumatism, tetanus, hydrophobia and the like." That aside, the "quirky book-worm" Ludlow sought not relief for a malady but inspiration for contemplation. Ludlow's book was well received by critics and readers "from London literary salons to California gold camps" and was eventually regarded as the "preeminent nineteenth century American statement on the subject of mind-altering drugs."[13]

One impressionable young reader was an Ivy League college student named John Hay, who would go on to be Abraham Lincoln's aide-de-camp. Reading Ludlow inspired him to "eat Hasheesh and dream dreams," an evidently much-repeated experience that did not prevent him from becoming both William McKinley's and Theodore Roosevelt's secretary of state. Of particular significance, Ludlow rediscovered an ancient characteristic of this substance: its supposed ability to spark creativity and enhance consciousness, a view that Americans of the Baby Boom generation would embrace with gusto in the 1960s. Even still, Ludlow himself cautioned against the excessive use of hashish.[14]

A literary phenomenon, Ludlow became a freelance reporter in New York City, where he met a group of bohemian artists and writers who frequented Pfaff's, a beer cellar where one might knock glasses with Walt Whitman, Mark Twain, and Louisa May Alcott, the soon-to-be-famous author of *Little Women*. In 1869, Alcott penned a short story, "Perilous Play," that opens with a declaration by Belle Daventry, a dashing socialite: "If someone does not propose something new and interesting, I shall die of ennui!" Dr. Meredith has a solution: giving hashish pastries to Belle and her friends. "Eat six of these despised bonbons," he asserts, "and you will be amused in a new, delicious, and wonderful manner."[15]

Cannabis was also becoming known to intellectuals on the other side of the Atlantic. A French doctor named Jacques-Joseph Moreau studied the drug's effects on his psychiatric patients in the 1840s and found that it reliably suppressed headaches, increased appetite, and aided sleep. Dr. William O'Shaughnessy, an army surgeon who had worked in India, brought the drug to the fore of British medical practice in 1842. Over the next several decades, it became a popular sedative and a remedy for muscle spasms, menstrual cramps, convulsions, and opiate withdrawal. While Friedrich Nietzsche bemoaned the growing impulse in European societies to combat modern alienation with hedonism, intoxication, and the "voluptuous enjoyment of eternal happiness," he did not shy away from the therapeutic applications of cannabis. "To escape from unbearable pressure you need hashish," he wrote in *Ecce Homo*. The future Nobel laureate William Butler Yeats used both hashish and peyote, a hallucinogenic cactus. Recall that at this time, there were no laws against using a wide range of drugs in America and Europe, where any upstanding individual could purchase at a pharmacy a wide array of tinctures and medicines. For many years after the Civil War, Gunjah Wallah Hasheesh Candy ("a most pleasurable and harmless stimulant") appeared in the Sears-Roebuck mail order catalogue. Although the commercial value of hemp had declined with King Cotton's rise, cannabis was quickly growing into its new reputation.[16]

On Marijuana

Among the seemingly infinite terms attached to the cannabis plant, *marijuana* is the most universally recognized and widely used in the English-speaking world—even if, as Martin Booth reminds us, it's not actually an English word. *Marijuana* is a Spanish-language colloquialism of uncertain genesis; it gained traction in the United States in the 1930s, when cannabis prohibitionists used it as a derogatory slur against Mexican immigrants. "Marihuana," spelled with a *j* or an *h*, "quickly morphed into an outsized American myth." Historically and scientifically speaking, "cannabis" is a more appropriate term than "marijuana" or even "pot." The latter term might trace back to Mexican Spanish *potiguaya*, a contraction of *potación de guaya* ("drink of grief")—wine or brandy steeped with cannabis buds. There's some dispute about the truth of this story, and plenty of reason to doubt it. For the sake of sensitivity to popular usage, though, I use *marijuana* and *pot* interchangeably to refer to psychoactive cannabis. I use *hemp* exclusively for the non-psychoactive plant and its related products.[17]

The most popular version of marijuana's origin story as a recreational drug has it beginning not in the United States but in Mexico. Mexican *campesinos* first started smoking *mota,* as they called the plant that grew in abundance across the countryside, for the same reasons that millions of people smoke it today: relaxation and inebriation. One Mexican historian, Isaac Campos-Costero, contends that this wild psychoactive *mota* derived from Spanish hemp crops left fallow after the colonial period. In the 1540s, Madrid mandated the cultivation of fiber hemp across its territories, which stretched from the southern tip of South America to Alta California. Hemp's "extraordinary botanical flexibility" allowed it to propagate beyond the cultivated plantings. In the wild, feral cannabis "underwent trickster-like changes." Exposed to "scorching Mexican sun year after year for centuries," it adapted to the hot climate by "morphing into high-octane marijuana"—becoming something much closer to its THC-rich Central Asian ancestor than had ever been introduced into the Western Hemisphere.[18]

As the conventional narrative has it, recreational marijuana use in the United States remained a niche pursuit among the adventurous literary set until the Mexican Revolution (1910–20), when an "influx of Mexican immigrants introduced the habit." Thousands of Mexicans—and more than a few of Pancho Villa's men—escaped the Mexican Revolution's upheaval by fleeing to Texas border towns such as El Paso and Laredo. Tens of thousands of these immigrants spread out through the United States, taking blue-collar jobs as far from the border as northern California, New York, and Chicago.[19]

Revisionist historians have recently challenged this story, however. In reality, there are few instances of "single-origin" drug trends. The more likely story is that recreational cannabis consumption began with spillover from medical use (as was the case with cocaine and the major opiates); when Mexican pot started crossing the border, the interest was relatively well established. In the decades between 1850 and 1930, Americans consumed cannabis regularly— and not just in medical applications. Vendors sold cannabis at the Turkish Hashish Pavilion during the American Centennial Exposition in Philadelphia in 1876. Over the next several years, hashish dens opened in major U.S. cities. "All visitors, both male and female, are of the better classes . . . and the number of regular habitués is daily on the increase," H. H. Kane wrote in *Harper's Magazine* of a New York City hashish salon in 1883. The essay depicted well-to-do patrons lounging in luxurious, softly lit parlors eating cannabis edibles, smoking hashish, and sipping coca leaf tea. By the time of the Mexican Revolution, cannabis smoking was also spreading out from New Orleans, where sailors had introduced it around the turn of the century.[20]

In fact, the connection between immigrants and cannabis may have been driven, at least in part, by the racial antipathy that marked the first decades of the twentieth century. California banned marijuana in 1913. Henry J. Finger, a vocal proponent of the California legislation, wrote in 1911 to Hamilton Wright, who would later become principal architect of the first U.S. drug policy:

> Within the last year we in California have been getting a large influx of Hindoos and they have in turn started quite a demand for cannabis indica; they are a very undesirable lot and the habit is growing in California very fast . . . the fear is now that they are initiating our whites into this habit. . . . We were not aware of the extent of this vice at the time our legislature was in session and did not have our laws amended to cover this matter.

Four decades earlier, of course, San Francisco officials had targeted another immigrant group, the Chinese, in part by cracking down on the opium trade. The media also stoked the fears surrounding this immigrant plant. A *New York Times* headline from July 6, 1927, read "Mexican Family Go Insane." The story explained: "A widow and her four children have been driven insane by eating the Marijuana plant, according to doctors who say there is no hope of saving the children's lives and that the mother will be 'insane for the rest of her life.' " In 1919, Texas took the idea a step further in its cannabis ban; defending the law, one Lone Star State senator stated, "All Mexicans are crazy, and this stuff [marijuana] makes them crazy."[21]

Free and Easy

It's worth noting that until the 1930s, federal officials and Congress did not view cannabis as much of a concern. As we will see, marijuana was not included in the first federal drug laws. Moreover, the Volstead Act of 1920, which enforced Prohibition and relegated alcohol to the (expensive) black market, helped to make marijuana an "attractive alternative" during the dry 1920s. The nation saw the growth of "tea pads"—by 1930 there were at least five hundred in New York City alone—where frequenters dropped in to buy marijuana for "25 cents or less."[22]

By the 1930s marijuana could be obtained throughout the Southwest and the South, even at remote Civilian Conservation Corps camps. The unfolding cigarette revolution, which taught Americans to "absorb drugs through their lungs," expedited the spread of marijuana smoking, as did the prodigious domestic supply. Planted commercially for seed and fiber, cannabis "grew luxuriantly" around abandoned rope factories and abandoned hemp farms—hence the coinage "weed." The THC content of domestic wild cannabis may have been lower than that of its Mexican counterpart, but it prompted one user to comment, "I'd rather have weed; it do me better than whiskey do." One author described how work-crew convicts in Tennessee dried and smoked the flowering tops of the wild cannabis they mowed along the roads. Inmates at the infamous San Quentin State Prison on San Francisco Bay "grew their own" inside the wall. The abundant supply kept the price low, "from 5 to 50 cents a reefer," well within the budget of an "emerging hip subculture" in U.S. cities.[23]

The story of how cannabis worked its way into this subculture is particularly interesting. One important channel—though probably not the only one—was a single musician, Milton "Mezz" Mezzrow, the "original white Negro," or the "Johnny Appleseed of weed in the hep-cat demimonde." A Jewish boy born in Chicago in 1899, Mezzrow was caught stealing a car with some teenage friends and landed in a reform school, where he befriended a group of black musicians. He learned to play the saxophone, and after his release he became a fixture in Chicago's jazz scene. Mezz first tasted marijuana in 1923, when some New Orleans–sourced "gang" turned up at Chicago's Martinique Club. In his autobiography *Really the Blues,* Mezzrow recounted, "The first thing I noticed was that I began to hear my saxophone as though it were inside my head. . . . I found I was slurring much better and putting just the right feeling into my phrases—I was really coming on. . . . I felt like I could go on playing for years without running out of ideas and energy. There wasn't any struggle; it was all made-to-order and suddenly there wasn't a sour note, or a discord in the world that could bother me. . . . I began to preach my millenniums on my horn, leading all the sinners on to glory."

With nary a dime in his pocket, Mezz arrived in Harlem, the cultural epicenter of black America, not long after the stock market crash of November 1929. Desperate for cash, Mezz started dealing—ten cents a reefer—to acquaintances in the scene, while he continued to gig with a pantheon of jazz legends: Louis Armstrong, Fats Waller, Duke Ellington, Count Basie, Billie Holiday, Cab Calloway. But Mezz was known more for his product than for his playing. In fact, his stuff was so well regarded that "mezz" became a popular slang term for good weed.[24]

Armstrong in particular found cannabis a vital source of creative inspiration. "Satchmo" followed the great exodus of African-Americans from the South, who migrated to northern industrial cities like Chicago in the 1920s looking for a better life. Some bands in Chicago refused Armstrong because his skin was so dark. But he was embraced by the "fraternity of marijuana-smoking musicians—the vipers" at clubs in Chicago. During a set break at the Savoy Ballroom, Armstrong smoked his first stick of "gage." He savored the sweet smell and taste; it calmed his nerves and lifted his feelings. "I had myself a ball," he gushed, "It's a thousand times better than whiskey." Armstrong smoked "Mary Warner" daily, a habit that did not appear to "compromise his musical dexterity" or work ethic, given his schedule of roughly three hundred concerts a year. Over his career, Satchmo often touted reefer's salubrious benefits.[25]

At least as pro-legalization authors tell the story, in November 1930, Armstrong was arrested by two Los Angeles narcotics cops while smoking pot with Vic Berton, a white drummer, in the parking lot of the New Cotton Club. "Vic and I were blasting this joint, having lots of laughs and feeling good, enjoying each other's company," Armstrong recounted, when "two big healthy Dicks came from behind a car nonchalantly and said to us, 'We'll take the roach, boys.' " The two jazzmen spent more than a week in jail before their trial for marijuana possession. They were convicted and sentenced to six months in prison and a fine of a thousand dollars. The judge was persuaded to suspend the sentences with the proviso that Armstrong leave California. Although he was jolted by his run-in with the law, Pops smoked pot for the rest of his life with no apparent ill effects. Armstrong never saw why his beloved reefer was illegal. "It puzzles me to see Marijuana connected with Narcotics—Dope and all that kind of crap," he wrote. "It's actually a shame."[26]

6 · Tobacco

Smoking is a custom loathsome to the eye, hateful to the nose,
harmful to the brain, dangerous to the lungs, and in the black, stinking
fume thereof nearest resembling the horrible Stygian smoke of the pit
that is bottomless.

—James I of England, *A Counterblaste to Tobacco* (1604)

Poisons in the Lungs

One of the most fascinating cases in America's centuries-long love affair
with drugs is tobacco. Although this book is primarily concerned with substances that have been legally prohibited, it is worth spending a moment considering the drug that is almost unmatched in its risks to personal and public
health and yet has remained licit since the colonial era. Like alcohol, tobacco
poses a provocative counterpoint to our understanding of illicit recreational
drugs in the United States. Any reckoning of America's drug war would be
incomplete without at least a topical look at one of the nation's most endur-
ingly popular legal psychoactives. So before we explore the federal government's first earnest efforts to regulate and restrict drug use in the chapters to
come, it's worth spending some time with a drug that has thus far avoided
becoming one of the war's casualties.

Nicotine, the active alkaloid in tobacco, is a psychoactive. As stimulants go,
tobacco is among the most physically gratifying, as millions of users can at-
test. Smoking or absorbing nicotine through the mouth stimulates the production of epinephrine and floods the brain's pleasure centers with dopamine,
yielding the well-known and endlessly sought-after nicotine buzz. Humans in

one lab study rated nicotine's "euphoric qualities" on a par with cocaine, morphine, and amphetamines. When the drug was administered intravenously, said one involved researcher, "nicotine was between five and ten times more potent in producing a euphoric effect than cocaine." Writer Sandra Blakeslee adds, "Nicotine is very different from most other drugs of abuse in important ways. Its effects are felt more rapidly than those of drugs taken intravenously. One-quarter of the nicotine in each drag reaches the brain in seven seconds. The nicotine concentration in the blood peaks at about the time that the cigarette butt is extinguished. The effects then fall off rapidly as nicotine is cleared by the liver and excreted in urine. Within a half hour, many smokers seek a new dose of nicotine. A pack-a-day smoker takes 70,000 drug 'hits' a year."[1]

Like many drugs, nicotine yields both withdrawal (in which physically unpleasant symptoms arise after use ceases and then abate with further use) and progressive tolerance (in which equal doses taken over time yield an increasingly milder effect). Nicotine withdrawal, one report in 1987 said, "often includes anxiety, irritability, difficulty concentrating, restlessness, craving for tobacco, gastrointestinal problems, headaches, drowsiness, decreased heart rate, tremors, and slowed metabolism." In one study of nicotine tolerance of almost eight hundred habitual smokers in their thirties who had seen their daily cigarette use grow considerably, "all respondents indicated a rapid increase in the first few months of smoking followed by a gradual leveling off." Back in the late 1980s, one clinical pharmacologist lamented that the American public had an "exaggerated" view of withdrawal from opioids and had "downplayed" nicotine withdrawal. "If you take away the trappings of how the person looks, you can't tell the difference."

One "astonishing property" of nicotine is that it works as both a sedative and a stimulant. Nicotine dispensed in low doses helps to release the alertness-enhancing neurotransmitter acetylcholine, while higher doses stem this same effect. This is why, in the words of Ovide Pomerleau, who studied behavioral medicine at the University of Michigan, nicotine was the "drug for all occasions." Pomerleau added, "Its variable effects are available on demand and do not outlast the circumstances to which they are appropriate. Unlike other drugs, nicotine does not interfere with normal activity."[2]

This helps to explain the perception of nicotine as a drug that is "less bad," despite the reality that smoking delivers tar, carbon monoxide, and "thousands of poisons into the lungs." It enhances intellectual sharpness, memory, and attention and reduces stress. Memoirist Gregor Hens extolled the psychic virtues of nicotine in a recent book about his lifelong relationship with the drug: "Every cigarette I've ever smoked was a good cigarette. . . . I've smoked because I was glad and I've smoked because I was depressed. I've smoked out of loneliness and out of friendship, out of fear and out of exuberance. Every cigarette that I've ever smoked served a purpose—they were a signal, a medication, a stimulant or a sedative, they were a plaything, an accessory, a fetish object, something to help pass the time, a memory aid, a communication tool or an object of meditation." The journalist Michael C. Moynihan invoked another eminent smoker on the subject:

> The brilliant polemicist Christopher Hitchens, who was rarely seen without a Rothmans between his lips, never wrote a book about smoking. But cigarettes so defined his public persona that several of his books feature him smoking on the cover. After he was diagnosed with esophageal cancer, his mellifluous voice now wheezy and cracked, Hitchens explained to an interviewer that, despite his illness, he still found it easy to index smoking's small virtues: "It stopped me being bored, stopped other people being boring, to some extent. It would keep me awake. It would make me want the evening to go on longer, to prolong the conversation, to enhance the moment. If I was asked, would I do it again, the answer is probably yes."[3]

A Colonial Weed

The use of tobacco, *herba nicotiana,* began among the ancient Mayans and Aztecs in present-day Mexico and Central America. By the fifteenth or sixteenth century, the habit had spread to other American tribes. Europeans first came into contact with the plant in 1492, when two members of Christopher Columbus's crew, Rodrigo de Jerez and Luis de la Torre, observed Taino Indians smoking leaves rolled up into fat cigars. The Spaniards subsequently learned that the Indians also sniffed and chewed the drug—methods of administration that would eventually be copied by millions of Europeans. For roughly the next century, tobacco remained a "botanical curiosity," at most an exotic medicine taken from the New World and sampled by the monarchs and gentry in the Old. Tobacco was simply too expensive to be used by the European masses, although with expansions in cultivation in the colonies, that began to change.[4]

Over the next several decades, sailors and merchantmen brought the smoking habit to the taverns and brothels in countless ports of call. It was initially characterized as a substance that could "clarify the mind and give happy thoughts." In a report from 1588 on the "New Found Land of Virginia," the English mathematician Thomas Harriot chronicled this novel substance:

> There is an herbe which is sowed a part by it selfe & is called by the inhabitants uppówoc. In the West Indies it hath divers names, according to the severall places & countries where it groweth and is used: The Spaniardes generally call it *Tobacco*. The leaves thereof being dried and brought into powder: They use to take the fume or thereof by sucking it through pipes made of claie into their stomacke and heade; from whence it purgeth superfluous fleame & other gross humors openeth all the pores & passages of the body: by which meanes the use thereof, not only preserveth the body from obstructions; but also if any be, so that they have not beene of too long continuance, in short time breaketh them: wherby their bodies are notably preserued in health, & know not many greevous diseases wherewithal wee in England are oftentimes afflicted.

In the late 1500s, the Spanish used a Manila galleon to ship this profitable plant to the Philippines, and by the 1600s, Dutch and Spanish merchants were crossing the Atlantic with their hulls full of tobacco for sale in Europe. In 1611, the Spanish Crown began taxing tobacco's export from Santo Domingo and Cuba. Around 1612, John Rolfe imported Spanish tobacco seeds from the West Indies and planted them experimentally in Jamestown, perhaps not realizing that the indigenous groups around the colony were already avid smokers of the leaf.[5]

Much of the willingness to put up with this obnoxious weed is explained by economics: the plant had a market in Europe. Virginia, Carolina, and Maryland started mass cultivation of tobacco even though the plant depletes even the most fertile soil and demands constant attention. Jamestown's deliverance would come not from beer but from tobacco—a crop that Great Britain coveted, as it was currently in the "grip of a smoking craze. Its poets and playwrights wrote eulogies in praise of tobacco with the enthusiasm they had hitherto reserved for sack and ale." The British even called smoking "drinking tobacco" or "drydrinking"—the newfound habit still lacked language to describe it. In 1620, the first shipment of tobacco sailed to England; seven years later the exports were around twenty thousand pounds a year, a rate that spiked to five hundred thousand pounds in 1627. By the 1630s, more than 1.5 million pounds of tobacco were being shipped from Jamestown annually. A decade later, London was importing roughly that same amount from Virginia. Now

English tobacconists were touting the virtues of America's finest tobacco with verses like this:

> Life is a smoke! — If this be true,
> Tobacco will thy Life renew;
> Then fear not Death, nor killing care
> Whilst we have best Virginia here.[6]

In the early 1600s ships brought tobacco from the Philippines to China, which soon became a country replete with addicted smokers. The Portuguese took the plant to West Africa—in addition to maize, beans, sweet potatoes, and other New World crops—sometime in the late sixteenth or early seventeenth century. The Portuguese also brought it to India, Japan, and Iran. As Courtwright writes, "Like ripples from a handful of gravel tossed into a pond, tobacco use and cultivation spread by secondary and tertiary diffusion: from India to Ceylon, from Iran to Central Asia, from Japan to Korea, from China to Tibet and Siberia, from Java to Malaysia to New Guinea." By the 1630s, tobacco was a global crop.[7]

In 1626 a little-known work by J. Leander, *Tobacco: Universal Panacea*, extolled tobacco's ability to "elevate in ecstasy and create a communication with the gods." A few years earlier Francis Bacon wrote in his *Historia Vitae et Mortis* that the plant gave men "such a secret delight and content, that being once taken, it can hardly be forsaken." In England, prices soared so much that, for a while at least, tobacco was worth its weight in silver. Indeed, in every country where the drug was introduced, addiction-driven demand soared.

Tobacco's takeover of Europe and Asia during the seventeenth century touched all social classes. Rich and poor alike indulged in its attractive pleasures. Tobacco was also able to withstand withering opposition from a variety of powerful actors. At first, many European leaders, including King James I of England, hated the use of this wicked substance, "the smoke from which evokes the horror of an insufferable hell." Even so, James's antipathy did not forestall his crown's taxing, rather than banning, tobacco's importation. In fact, with tobacco such a lucrative crop, King James prohibited it from being planted in England to allow him to control the imported variant.[8]

In the early 1600s, Mikhail Fedorovich, tsar of Russia, decreed that any smoker be tortured until the source of the tobacco was revealed—and also that the noses of two offenders be cut off. In Turkey, Sultan Murad would surprise men smoking, even in the midst of battle, and sanction them with beheading or dismemberment. Chinese emperors had smokers' heads chopped off and impaled on pikes. In 1642, Pope Urban VIII excommunicated anyone who indulged in "such a repugnant abuse in sites adjoining the diocese, and their dependencies." One priest vomited up the Sacrament after dipping tobacco snuff during mass—surely a target for said excommunication. By 1650, any use of tobacco was banned in Bavaria, Saxony, and Zurich; Transylvania, St. Gall, and Sweden would soon follow. In 1639 the director general of New Amsterdam banned smoking. In other areas, bans on smoking in public or use by children achieved little if any result. Indeed, tobacco bans proved futile against the insatiable demand—despite the widespread acknowledgment at the time that tobacco fouled the breath, stained the teeth, and soiled the clothes, not to mention the fact that smoking was rather dangerous in combustible dwellings. The plant's appeal and use marched on, prompting historian V. G. Kernana to call it the most "universal new pleasure man had acquired." As researcher Jack Henningfield put it in a 1987 interview, "Seeing that people would pay almost any price for tobacco, monopolies were started so that government could benefit from the desires of their people. Taxes were implemented, and governments became dependent on revenue generated from nicotine addiction."9

The global demand for tobacco constituted much of the economic impetus behind the first colonies in Virginia and Maryland. America's tobacco exports (up to fifty million pounds annually by the 1750s) grew hand in hand with foreign demand. Indeed, the prodigious tax revenues tobacco has brought to state coffers over the centuries helps to explain why, despite its myriad ill effects, tobacco has been regulated but not banned in the Americas. By the dawn of the American Revolution in 1776, the American tobacco industry was powerful enough to help finance the fledgling war effort. General George Washington, one of the richest tobacco planters of his time, told his fellow Americans how they could help the war effort. "If you can't send money, send tobacco," as its psychoactive wonders improved troops' morale. The British responded by making sure to destroy large stores of cured tobacco leaf (including those stored at Thomas Jefferson's plantation) as they prosecuted the war across the South.10

In the eighteenth century, many punitive sanctions in Europe and Asia were lightened or discarded. Peter the Great stopped torture and mutilations and sold a tobacco license for £15,000 sterling to the British tobacco trust. The Vatican reconsidered its commitment to excommunication. In the nineteenth century smoking once again became fashionable in the salons of Europe. By the 1850s pipes and cigars were outpacing nasal snuff, and the first decades of the twentieth century witnessed the ascension of cigarettes.11

Despite the drug's growing popularity, critics spoke out. "One of the more implacable, Mrs. John Stuart White, objected to smoking during the sinking of the *Titanic*. 'Before we cut loose from the ship two of the seamen with us . . . took out cigarettes and lighted them,' she complained during a Senate inquiry into the disaster. 'On an occasion like that!' " Less breathlessly, a coalition of evangelical and progressive reformers, who blamed "the little white slaver" for corrupting the young and poisoning the race, endeavored to throw up legislative barriers to its progress.[12]

"Just 'Little Cigars,' Right?"

In 1919, a medical student, Alton Ochsner, and his fellow peers observed the autopsy of a person felled by lung cancer. In this era, the malady was "so rare it was thought unlikely the students would ever get another chance." Eighty years later, in November 2012, William Kremer of the BBC World Service noted that over 1.1 million people were killed by the disease each year and that 85 percent of these deaths were the result of tobacco use. Cigarettes killed around 100 million people in the twentieth century. As Stanford University's Robert Proctor put it, cigarettes are the "deadliest artifact in the history of human civilization."[13]

The story of cigarettes' evolution in the United States largely centers on James B. "Buck" Duke, a larger-than-life figure who, as historian David Courtwright had it, "loved business better than anything else." Duke worked furiously until, not yet forty, he had become the "undisputed king" of tobacco and the catalyst behind the "cigarette revolution." Courtwright did not think it outlandish to tout Duke as the "single most important figure in the history of psychoactive commerce." In 1880, twenty-four-year-old Duke became involved in what was then a special market within the larger tobacco trade: "ready-rolled cigarettes." His team in Durham, North Carolina, developed hand-rolled "Duke of Durham" smokes, "twisting the ends to seal them." Soon afterward, Duke collaborated with a young tinkerer named James Bonsack, who invented the cigarette-rolling machine. Together they began mass-producing new, symmetrical cigarettes that were "modern-looking and more hygienic." Bonsack's invention produced 120,000 cigarettes every twenty-four hours—an astounding 20 percent of U.S. consumption at the time.[14]

The upshot, as Jordan Goodman explains in *Tobacco in History*, was that Duke was making far more cigarettes than he had customers for. His solution? Marketing, marketing, marketing. Duke "sponsored races, gave his cigarettes out for free at beauty contests and placed ads in the new 'glossies'—the first magazines. He also recognized that the inclusion of collectable cigarette cards was as important as getting the product right. In 1889 alone, he spent $800,000 on marketing (about $25m in today's money)." The cigarette proved to be the ideal delivery system: "Smokers could inhale cigarette smoke deeply, delivering a powerful dose of nicotine into their bloodstream. The cigarette was to tobacco as the hypodermic syringe was to opiates: a revolutionary technology that permitted alkaloids to work more quickly and with stronger effect on the brain's reward systems." Cigarette smoking increased fourfold from 1885 to 1890, but it was still a relatively minor-league market compared with chewing tobacco, pipes, and cigars. A cigar smoker himself, Duke envisioned an enormous opportunity for cigarettes, which could be smoked in "drawing rooms and restaurants" that were not open to cigars and pipes. As Stanford's Professor Proctor told the BBC, "The cigarette was really used in a different way. And it was milder—and this is one of the great ironies, that cigarettes were widely thought to be safer than cigars, because they are just 'little cigars,' right?"[15]

Over time, smokers took to Duke's "ready-made" cigarettes. "Five to seven minutes with a ready-made cigarette fit the tempo of urban-industrial life much better than a leisurely half-hour with a cigar." Or as one *New York Times* writer put it in 1925, "Short, snappy, easily attempted, easily completed or just as easily discarded before completion, the cigarette is the symbol of a machine age in which the ultimate cogs and wheels and levers are human nerves."[16]

By 1900, Duke's tobacco trust controlled over 90 percent of American tobacco production. Duke's market power was so great that he could determine retail profit margins and wholesale prices for tobacco farmers, who reaped as little as a few cents a pound. In their early iterations, cigarettes had a healthy connotation. They were listed in pharmaceutical encyclopedias until the early 1900s; doctors freely wrote cigarette prescriptions for all sorts of illnesses, including, ironically, coughs. While smoking was surging, opposition to the habit emerged among temperance and religious activists, albeit on moral and social and not health grounds. As a result of their activism, over a dozen states outlawed cigarette production, sale, and use. There were also bans on public smoking by women and near schools. In 1929, Surgeon General Hugh S. Cumming, a smoker, expressed concern about tobacco's effects on young females and the country's "physical tone." Yet Cumming never lined up behind the "more extreme anti-tobacco and temperance reformers" of the era.[17]

"Why Not Light a Lucky?"

Several factors drove the steady rise in smoking through the early twentieth century: World War I, the growth of cities, changing gender roles, and deft advertising. Interestingly, the tobacco industry escaped the ax of the nation's first federal drug-regulation laws, the Food and Drug Act of 1906 and the Harrison Act of 1914, both of which we will examine in more detail in the next chapter. It is worth considering briefly why the leaf was not a target of restriction. For one, smoking enjoyed general social acceptance. Most of its negative health effects had yet to be uncovered. But more germane to this history of the drug war, tobacco thrived for two further reasons: tobacco companies' enormous investments in canny advertising, and the fact that smoking was never associated in mass media with minority or marginalized groups.

The "judicial breakup" of Duke's American Tobacco Company in 1911 led to the creation of four U.S. corporations: American Tobacco, R. J. Reynolds, Liggett and Myers, and Lorillard. To maintain margins, they turned to savvy advertising and public relations firms. As David Courtwright notes, "Their well-paid assistance enabled the tobacco companies to build brand recognition and loyalty, recruit millions of new smokers, improve their products, counter health concerns, and further expand the global cigarette market." In 1948, to pick a year, the Lucky Strike ad account—then worth a massive $12 million—moved to the firm of Batten, Barton, Durstine, and Osborn. The correspondence of Bruce Barton, one of the nation's top admen, reflects the "sheer ingenuity that went into promoting cigarettes and Madison Avenue's sophisticated understanding of their dual nature as psychoactive drugs and as social products." Barton's primary target was the female smoker. In one internal memo he suggested this campaign headline: "Why not light a lucky instead of taking those last few fattening mouthfuls?" In another, "Tension shortens life. . . . Tension makes one grow old faster. Best thing to do when you feel yourself getting tense is to light a Lucky. . . . Amos and Andy coined 'unlax.' Could we coin 'un-tense'? It sounds silly, but probably L.S./M.F.T ["Lucky Strike means fine tobacco," the brand's tagline since 1944] sounded silly when it was first suggested." Barton eventually came up with something different to drive home the brand's association with superb tobacco. "You live only once. Why not live like a millionaire?" His thinking was that "you can't have a Rolls Royce. You can't have a house on Fifth Avenue. You can't spend your summers in Newport. But in one thing, by God, you can be just as well off as the richest man in America."[18]

In 1930, the Tobacco Industry Annual Review reported that American tobacco consumption was at a record high. The report's outlook was rosy: "The
cigarette industry cannot only look forward to annual accretions to its ranks
from the generations of new male smokers but has added the opposite sex to
this group, while continuing its efforts toward those women for whom smoking is still, if not among the taboos, at least a debatable question." Whereas in
1915, cigarette smokers in the United States were in bars and city sidewalks, by
the mid-1950s two-thirds of adult American males smoked frequently. The
shift in American popular opinion regarding cigarettes represents perhaps one
of the most dramatic in the history of the last century. The Irish-born writer
Frank McCourt described his childhood friends in Ireland: "They can't believe
I don't smoke. They want to know if there's something wrong with me, the bad
eyes or consumption maybe. How can you go with a girl if you don't smoke?"
John Updike had a similar experience. "You couldn't get anywhere, in the
high-school society of the late forties, without smoking." Updike wound up
with the habit for three decades.[19]

Big Tobacco's massive global reach and revenues gave it considerable political and social power, expressed through its army of lobbyists, expert witnesses, and lawyers. In one dubious episode, Philip Morris and R. J. Reynolds
paid for almost the entirety of the American Civil Liberties Union's campaign
to secure employees' right to smoke. And while the medical community was
not by and large concerned with smoking, growing voices throughout the
1930s and 1940s had reservations about the outsized, unfounded claims that
cigarette companies were making in their ads. The Old Gold brand touted,
"Not a cough in the carload." The Federal Trade Commission attempted to sue
the companies for their dubious health claims, but lack of regulatory oversight
made these efforts futile. Insurance companies, however, were noticing data
showing a spike in cancer rates over the previous few decades. Two researchers wrote in 1939, "In our opinion the increase in smoking with the universal
custom of inhaling is probably a responsible factor, as the inhaled smoke,
constantly repeated over a long period of time, undoubtedly is a source of
chronic irritation to the bronchial mucosa."[20]

As cautiously worded as the opinion was, the connection that the researchers drew would be the first salvo in a decades-long fight over tobacco's regulatory status in America.

7 • Crackdown

Bill had a sentimental streak about the old days in America,
especially 1910 when you could get morphine in a drugstore without
prescription and Chinamen smoked opium in their evening windows
and the country was wild and brawling and free with abundance and
any kind of freedom for everyone.

—Jack Kerouac, *On the Road* (1957)

No Drug Illegal

The United States in the nineteenth century permitted considerable personal freedom of choice regarding drugs. The idiosyncrasies of the U.S. Constitution—namely a permissive Bill of Rights and the devolution of authority to state governments—helped ensure that potent forms of opium, cocaine, and cannabis remained widely available nationwide. In the American legal system, states were responsible for regulating both medical practice and pharmaceuticals—and until the early 1900s, most state policy was laissez-faire.[1]

In a few cases, states took the initiative to regulate drugs, particularly opium and cannabis, on their own turf. Many of these efforts were part of broader legislative agendas aimed at restricting immigration and limiting the social and political rights of minorities, as was the case with anti-opium laws in California and anti-cannabis laws in the southwestern states. But there's no denying that a major motivation for these laws was the growing recognition in the medical community and political class of health issues associated with drug use and addiction. This manifested in a significant change in the national mood: Americans increasingly believed that the widespread consumption of drugs such as cocaine and opiates was a social ill.[2]

By 1910, most states and several major cities had anti-drug laws. Ritual police raids were a hallmark of the states' haphazard enforcement schemes, as was the case in New Jersey in 1907, when police hysterically arrested scores of dealers after newspapers reported on school kids snuffing cocaine. For the most part, whether state legislatures attempted to control substances by arresting suppliers, levying import taxes, or shuttering opium dens, the users and distribution networks simply went underground. What's more, in an early example of the "balloon effect" that we'll see throughout the book, state crackdowns on opium and cocaine reduced supply, raised prices, and sent the drugs' dependents straight to "another product of the pharmacopeia, one that was still legal and reasonably affordable," namely, heroin.[3]

At the federal level, the first efforts at drug control were designed not to break up underground dealer networks but to regulate the runaway pharmaceutical market. For years, journalists such as Samuel Hopkins Adams had blasted the over-the-counter medicine industry for selling what were often dangerous products under secretive and misleading labels. The muckrakers had also lambasted "red clauses" in contracts between newspapers and patent companies allowing pharmaceutical makers to pull their ads (a chief source of revenue in the news industry) if the paper supported food and drug regulation.[4]

With the outcry of Progressive reformers at peak volume and in the face of sustained resistance from patent medicine producers, Congress passed the landmark Pure Food and Drug Act in 1906. President Theodore Roosevelt signed the bill on the same day he signed the Federal Meat Inspection Act. The reform law created the Food and Drug Administration (FDA) and was intended to rein in excesses and rampant charlatanism in the patent medicine trade. The law did not actually prevent the sale of addictive opiates and cocaine; it simply mandated that certain active ingredients meet standardized purity requirements and forced drug makers to label in a clear way any of ten ingredients considered unsafe. This list included alcohol, morphine, caffeine, opium, and cannabis. The law also created the country's modern prescription system, which made the federal government the watchdog over what "Americans took to make themselves feel better." It thus gave extraordinary powers to the federal bureaucracy to determine which drugs a person was allowed to consume—and in what quantities. Although this law and similar state-level rules did not ban any of the ten substances, specify safe dosages, or provide for effective enforcement, the legislation did mark an important turning point.

For the first time, it codified the opinion that the use of cocaine and opiates outside of normal medical practices was—as one officer of the U.S. Public Health Service neatly put it—a "drug-habit evil."[5]

International Cooperation

In the wake of the Shanghai Opium Conference in 1909, U.S. officials returned to the diplomatic cocktail circuit in order to pursue new anti-drug objectives. In December 1911, suave Charles Henry Brent, who had championed the crusade against opium in Asia, and the State Department drug official Hamilton Wright presided over a conference in The Hague. The following month, a dozen countries signed on to a convention to limit opium and coca leaf production. The Hague International Opium Convention, the first international drug control treaty, mandated that signatories enact domestic laws to limit the drug business. The goal was a world in which drugs were available solely for medicinal use.[6]

For many drug war opponents today, this diplomatic meeting was the Archduke Ferdinand moment, the point when the deeply flawed global drug war began. Dr. Dale Gieringer of the Drug Policy Forum of California wrote that "the Hague convention would lay the foundation for an edifice of further treaties committing the United States and the rest of the world to a century of prohibition, drug wars, and concomitant crime and violence." The treaty also provided the justification for Congress to pass the first federal drug control law, the Harrison Narcotics Tax Act of 1914, a law that permanently changed America's relationship with drugs. The act, named for its sponsor, Congressman Francis B. Harrison of New York, used the federal government's power to tax and regulate those who produced, imported, and sold opium, morphine, heroin, and cocaine. It required these and other narcotics to be dispensed only with a doctor's prescription and limited their over-the-counter sale to "preparations and remedies which do not contain more than two grains of opium, or more than one-fourth of a grain of morphine, or more than one-eighth of a grain of heroin in one avoirdupois ounce." Notably, cannabis, tobacco, and alcohol were not included in the list of drugs that later became regulated (although cannabis still had to be labeled on pharmaceutical packaging under the Pure Food and Drug Act). The narcotics ban passed with surprisingly little public comment or opposition. One congressman commented that "no individual has ever represented to the Committee on Ways and Means that the present extensive traffic in narcotics should be allowed to continue." As we will see, this was in stark contrast to the politically polarizing movement to prohibit alcohol, which was gaining momentum at the same time.[7]

It's worth noting that the Harrison Act was not originally intended to be a prohibition law but rather a relatively limited piece of market-regulation legislation. The act did not ban any drug outright or put drug users under the purview of the criminal justice system. But it effectively became the country's first criminal prohibition statute when law enforcement officials began arresting physicians for prescribing opiates and cocaine to addicts under one of its articles. The act, importantly, failed to recognize addiction as a treatable condition, which led some critics, including the *Journal of American Medicine* to lament that the addict is "denied the medical care he urgently needs, open, above-board sources from which he formerly obtained his drug supply are closed to him, and he is driven to the underworld where he can get his drug, but of course, surreptitiously and in violation of the law." Almost overnight, the Harrison Act created a new connection between drug use and criminality. Addicted patients were left with legitimate withdrawal distress, and many turned to crime to satisfy their cravings for the newly illegal substances.[8]

Drug war opponents, such as Kurt Schmoke, the first African-American mayor of Baltimore in the late 1980s and 1990s, saw the Harrison Act as the second pivotal moment in the drug war's development. "It assumed there would be government regulation, but not blanket prohibition. It assumed that states would be allowed to let physicians distribute drugs. But it was changed over time by the forces of politics and the courts, by J. Edgar Hoover and the early heads of the Bureau of Narcotics." The Harrison Act provided the legal precedent for the much more severe restrictions in the years to come. It set the gears of the drug war in motion and simultaneously initiated an internal logic that has made it nearly impossible to roll back the regulation and restriction of drugs.[9]

Together, the Harrison Act, the Shanghai Conference, and the Hague opium conference helped to position the United States as a global drug regulation leader. The Pure Food and Drug Act and the Harrison Act garnered support from the Western powers as well as China. After World War I ended in 1918, the United States and the United Kingdom added the Hague Convention to the Treaty of Versailles—which bound the peace plan's signatories to enact domestic drug control laws. In the United Kingdom, this led to the Dangerous Drugs Act of 1920, a law often incorrectly attributed to a severe heroin epidemic in Britain. In the years that followed, Washington continued to support international anti-drug treaties and conferences.[10]

"Schoolyards and Candy Stores"

There was at least one other especially significant development in the aftermath of the Harrison Act. The law mandated a strict accounting of opium and raw coca and their derivatives, from arrival into the United States to dispensation to a medical patient. To control this process, the Treasury Department issued licenses to suppliers and levied a small tax at each transfer. Throughout the process, the only actor who did not pay a tax was the patient. The State Department's Hamilton Wright and the Department of Justice contended that this aspect of the act proscribed indefinite maintenance of addiction unless there was a specific and exigent medical justification, such as cancer or tuberculosis. In 1919, the Supreme Court upheld this interpretation. Led by judicial titans Oliver Wendell Holmes and Louis Brandeis, the court declared in a 5–4 decision that indefinite maintenance for "mere addiction" went beyond conventional medical practices—and thus affected a state-level supervision of the medical field. Further, because the patient receiving the drugs for maintenance was not a legitimate patient but a recipient of drugs, the transfer of such substances defrauded the government of tax revenue under the Harrison Act. The decision paved the way for decades of drug-addiction stigma.[11]

The typical nineteenth-century addict was a middle-aged, middle- or upper-class female who abused morphine and opium, in most cases as a result of initial medical use. Jill Jonnes has written, "When the United States first recognized the widespread problem of addiction in 1900, public health officials estimated that one in three hundred Americans was an opiate addict. Adding in cocaine users and assuming a certain overlap, one would have increased that to one in two hundred." If the figures are correct, it reflected an addiction rate that the United States has never seen since. But it wasn't until the Harrison Act passed that two now all-too-familiar drug addiction tropes emerged. In the early 1920s scores of addicts in New York City paid for their habit by sorting through industrial dumps for scraps of copper, lead, zinc, and iron, which they sold to a dealer. *Junkie,* in its first sense, literally meant "junkman." "The term was symbolically appropriate as well, since the locus of addiction had, within a single generation, shifted from the office and parlor to the desolate piles of urban debris." Mass media and government institutions, including the newly minted FDA, increasingly demonized "dope fiends" as deviant and morally repugnant failures. The idea of the junkie stuck and has remained with us for decades. So has another (for the most part) mythical figure that originated in the same era: the heroin pusher who "supposedly worked around schoolyards and candy stores, giving youths habit-forming dope, hoping for future customers."[12]

The stereotypes aside, it's important not to discount the fact that addiction, particularly to cocaine and opiates, can have serious effects on an individual's physical and mental health, which can lead to debilitating patterns of social dysfunction or dependency.[13]

Drugs in Decline

One immediate consequence of the Harrison Act was that it created a spike in the popularity of heroin. The scarcity of over-the-counter opiates drove many addicts toward the drug, which, because of its purity and über-efficient delivery mechanism, tended to be cheaper and easier to distribute at scale on the black market. Heroin had already caught on as a street drug in cities such as New York and San Francisco after citywide crackdowns on opium dens. In 1916, the physician Pearce Bailey wrote in the *New Republic*, "The heroin habit is essentially a matter of city life. . . . The majority are boys and young men who . . . seem to want something that promises to make life gayer and more enjoyable." He continued, "It would almost seem that their desire for something to brighten life up is at the bottom of their trouble and that heroin is but a means."[14]

But even with heroin trending, in the decades that followed the consumption of drugs listed in the Harrison Act declined dramatically. The opium epidemic ebbed over the 1920s and 1930s, with much of the ongoing problem confined to the "periphery of society and the outcasts of urban areas." The Jones-Miller Act of 1922 put additional restrictions on cocaine manufactures, which precipitated an even more significant decline in production and availability. Its street price sky-high, cocaine became an expensive indulgence reserved for the well-heeled set. In the early 1930s, the Mayor's Committee on Drug Addiction in New York City judged that "during the last twenty years cocaine addiction has ceased to be a problem."[15]

One holdout in this overall decline was the entertainment class. Cocaine and opiates continued to be mainstays of Hollywood parties and made appearances in popular mass media. An article in the May 1922 issue of *Vanity Fair*, "Happy Days in Hollywood," exulted:

> With the brightening influence of spring there has been a distinct quickening of the social pace. Drugs are not as much in evidence as during the

more trying days of winter, but they still spread their genial influence at some of the more exclusive functions. Last week little Lulu Lenore of the Cuckoo Comedy Co. gave a small house dance for the younger addicts. "Will you come to my 'Snow'-ball?" read the clever invitations. In one corner of the living room was a miniature "Drugstore," where Otho Everard kept the company in a roar as he dispensed little packages of cocaine, morphine and heroin. The guests at their departure received exquisite hypodermic needles in vanity boxes which have caused many heart-burnings among those who were not invited.

In 1934, Cole Porter invoked coke in his hit song "I Get a Kick Out of You," whose lyrics featured the following: "Some get a kick from cocaine. I'm sure that if I took even one sniff that would bore me terrifically, too. Yet, I get a kick out of you." In the 1936 movie *Modern Times,* Charlie Chaplin's tramp character accidentally consumes heaps of cocaine.[16]

Jill Jonnes writes that at the onset of World War II, "When the U.S. population had almost doubled to 140,000,000, the number of opiate addicts (cocaine had almost disappeared) was about forty thousand, or one in three thousand, a tenfold decline." Some observers, including Jonnes, see this as proof positive of the effectiveness of government regulation in stemming drug abuse and addiction rates. "So successful had government action been against the nation's first drug epidemic that it was virtually forgotten," Jonnes explains. "When illegal drugs reappeared in fearsome quantities again, few remembered the first American experience with habit-forming drugs."[17]

Many commentators in the anti-drug camp have taken up this standard, arguing that it was the U.S. government's quick action that saved thousands, if not millions, of drug addicts. On the other hand, the pro-legalization camp sees the contraction of drug use as a historical anomaly, less a result of government intervention and more the result of other factors. The Great Depression, for one, yielded a paucity of disposable income to spend on drugs. At the same time, an import-supply crash before and during World War II brought fewer kilos of cocaine and opium to U.S. shores. Throughout the war, the government effectively became a monopoly consumer of opiates, amassing large stockpiles for the treatment of combat casualties. Taking these factors into account, some critics of the contemporary war on drugs consider the first crackdowns less an example of effective policy and more the first grunts of a beast that, as it grew, would become ever more destructive.

The Noble Experiment

For American policymakers at the turn of the twentieth century, the most troubling mind-altering substance was not cocaine, or opium, or heroin, but alcohol. In the years following the Civil War, the temperance movement gained steady momentum and an increasingly hardline attitude. They were supported by a brand of journalism that "regularly claimed that booze lay at the root of most of the crime, insanity, poverty, divorce, illegitimacy, and business failures in the United States."[18]

As we consider these early roots of America's war on drugs, it's worth noting a couple of significant ideological mileposts. By the turn of the century, the temperance movement's objective had shifted from moderation to outright prohibition. In the prohibitionist logic, if alcohol was indeed the evil that it appeared to be, then prohibition was the only acceptable action for the U.S. government to take. The Eighteenth Amendment was not the only consequence of this mind-set. It had a resonating—and, as it turned out, enduring—impact on the control of other substances. From here, the federal regulation of drugs progressed with seeming inexorability to a position of—as one *New York Times* article described it in 1921—"no compromise."[19]

Second, the prohibition movement turned the battle over alcohol into a moral struggle. Expressing his support for prohibition on the floor of the House of Representatives, Richmond P. Hobson from Alabama contended that prohibition's aim was "to destroy the agency that debauches the youth of the land and thereby perpetuates the hold on the Nation." The alcohol question was just one of many flashpoints in the broader Progressive movement, the reformist crusade against social ills that had emerged through America's rapid industrialization, urbanization, and immigration. Although the movement's primary aims were to address government corruption and to check the interests of a wealthy and powerful industrial elite, other objectives—prohibition, urban reform, women's suffrage, and early integrationism—came into the movement's fold.[20] On this reading, its association with the Progressives made the campaign against alcohol a struggle to defend the middle class and to lift up the downtrodden. But, as Thomas Feiling reminds us, the temperance movement was also supported by impulses that were less noble. Recent immigrants from Ireland, Italy, and Jewish communities in eastern Europe had been settling in America in unprecedented numbers. Anxiety about rapid urban growth, overcrowding, violence, and the "waning of white Anglo-Saxon Protestants in American cities" manifested, among other dimensions, in suspicion of these groups' drinking habits. It is worth noting that this sort of construed relationship between a psychoactive substance and an outsider group, an underclass, or an "undesirable" segment of society has attended the prohibition of almost every drug in American history. The direction of causality is difficult to assess, but the pattern is revealing.[21]

What all this suggests is that, in the years leading up to Prohibition, the alcohol question morphed into a question about American identity. Advertisements and slogans from the era called alcohol an "Enemy to the Home" because "Alcoholic drinks helped break up 9,228 homes every year." Another read: "Alcohol means death to the nation." Representative Hobson delivered perhaps the most damning line in a speech voicing his support for the prohibition amendment: "A man is a little less of a man after each drink he takes." Alcohol's death knell came well before Prohibition passed, at the moment that it was credibly positioned at the level of federal policymaking as a *moral* ill, a moral danger—as opposed to just a personal habit or a public health issue.

Turning alcohol's status into a question of identity also marked out what would become the contested ground in the drug debate for decades to come. Even today, we talk about drugs in moral terms; we tell narratives and construct worldviews that try to define the contribution of drugs (whether constructive or destructive) to human flourishing; we debate the use and regulation of drugs based on claims we make about their impacts on private and public good. One reason drug prohibition measures have been so tenacious is that since the early 1900s no one has been able to successfully direct the debate over mind-altering substances in a way that extracts it from this moral framing. And it all began with alcohol.[22]

"A New Nation Will Be Born"

Congress ratified the Eighteenth Amendment in January 1919. It then passed the Volstead Act, the enabling legislation that put the law into effect starting January 17, 1920. The legislation didn't ban drinking but rather the sale, manufacture, and transportation of alcohol. Churches and synagogues were allowed ample supplies of wine for religious ceremonies. And medicinal alcohol—basically anything prescribed by a physician—was also exempt. A casual imbiber himself, President Woodrow Wilson vetoed the Volstead Act, arguing, "In all matters having to do with personal habits and customs of large numbers of our people, we must be certain that the established processes of legal change are followed." But Congress overrode the veto before the week

Prohibition officers raiding a lunchroom on Pennsylvania
Avenue in Washington, April 25, 1923 (Library of Congress,
Prints and Photographs Division, Washington, D.C.)

was out. As Daniel Okrent described in *Last Call,* his magisterial social history
of the era, "A mighty alliance of moralists and progressives, suffragists, and
xenophobes had legally seized the Constitution, bending it to a new purpose."
Okrent also reminds us that this was only the second time in history that Congress had signed an amendment to the Constitution delimiting the rights of
individual citizens. The first time they did so, they had abolished slavery.[23]

Prohibition divided the nation along lines that few issues have managed to
draw, before or since. It split the parties; the Democrats had wet factions from
cities in the North and the East and their dry counterparts from the Midwest
and the West. Though Prohibition was an inherently Christian movement,
adherents were active on both sides. Baptists and Methodists saw drinking as
immoral, while Catholics saw the alcohol proscription as an attack on their
culture, "not to mention their Communion wine." The North was "wetter"
than the South, the working class more so than the middle class, and immigrants more so than "Americans with deep roots."[24]

On January 16, 1920, the hilly streets of San Francisco were gridlocked
with cars, trucks, wagons, and "every other imaginable form of conveyance"
crossing the city to finish delivery runs on the final day before such activity
became illegal. At the ritzy Metropolitan Club in Washington, D.C., Assistant
Secretary of the Navy Franklin D. Roosevelt drank wine with friends from
his college days at Harvard. The militantly anti-prohibitionist editorial staff
at the *New York World* breathlessly predicted, "After 12 o'clock tonight, the

Prohibition Administrator Ames Woodcock; H. M. Lucious, secretary of the
Automobile Club of Maryland; and Ernest M. Smith, vice president of the American
Automobile Association (AAA), August 25, 1930. A contemporary publication ran the
photograph, telling its readers, "Stop when you see this sign. This is the new insignia
plate the Bureau of Prohibition has adopted for use by prohibition agents in stopping
suspected automobiles." (Library of Congress, Prints and Photographs Division,
Washington, D.C.)

Government of the United States as established by the Constitution and maintained for nearly 131 years will cease to exist."[25]

In contrast, small-town America welcomed Prohibition's arrival not in saloons but in churches. Thousands of congregations led thanksgiving prayer services for what many considered a victory over the depraved cities. In Washington, D.C., William Jennings Bryan, the controversial orator, outspoken fundamentalist, and three-time Democratic Party presidential candidate, cried to the crowd that had gathered at the First Congregational Church: "They are dead that sought the child's life. They are dead! They are dead!" Not to be outdone, the Anti-Saloon League, arguably the nation's most powerful interest group at the time, declared, "At one past midnight, a new nation will be born."[26]

"One of History's Greatest Opportunities for Creating Illegal Fortunes"

Drug war critics often cite Prohibition as evidence of the counterproductive nature of sweeping and punitive drug bans. Although this book is reluctant to draw generalized conclusions about the present based on a single historical case, there are good reasons to conclude that Prohibition itself was a failure.

On the whole, Prohibition did not keep alcohol out of American bloodstreams. The Volstead Act gained notoriety for the ways that it was sidestepped, but the law itself had all sorts of loopholes. For one, bootleggers sniffed the opportunity in the provision that made alcohol available by prescription. In the thirteen years of Prohibition's reign, the number of registered pharmacists in the state of New York tripled. Attendance spiked at Catholic churches and synagogues across the country. As Sanneh suggested in the *New Yorker* in 2015, this could be taken as a wry foreshadowing of the "suspiciously hale group of patients" who turned up at California medical marijuana clinics in the mid-2000s.[27] Moreover, Prohibition did not have a huge impact on the volume of alcohol that Americans drank. As one comic panel of the time quipped: "Remember the old days before Prohibition, when you couldn't buy a drink on Sunday?" Though it's difficult to measure illegal sales and consumption, some scholars have used proxy data to make reliable estimates. In the early 1900s, average consumption of pure alcohol ran 2.6 gallons per adult per year—around 32 fifths of 80 proof liquor, or 520 bottles of beer. Consumption likely dropped by as much as 70 percent during the first couple of years of Prohibition. It then began to tick upward, as citizens "adjusted" to the new rules. By 1930 the country was drinking illegal booze at almost the same rate as when it was being consumed legally in the early 1900s.[28]

In 1924, journalist H. L. Mencken offered this assessment: "Five years of Prohibition have had, at least, this one benign effect: they have completely disposed of all the favorite arguments of the Prohibitionists. None of the great boons and usufructs that were to follow the passage of the Eighteenth Amendment has come to pass. There is not less drunkenness in the Republic, but more. There is not less crime, but more. There is not less insanity, but more. The cost of government is not smaller, but vastly greater. Respect for law has not increased, but diminished."[29]

One upshot of the law was an uptick in alcohol-related morbidity and mortality. Americans who wanted to drink and were unwilling or unable to quit made their own alcohol or bought "bathtub gin" made by friends and illegal distillers. Some of it tasted like poison; some of it was poison. In America in 1920, fewer than one hundred individuals died from alcohol poisoning. Six years later, in New York City alone, it took almost eight hundred. The national rate in 1924 was over four thousand. Some attribute the problem to a Volstead Act provision that permitted the production of industrial alcohol if it was made undrinkable by the addition of 4 percent methanol, or "wood alcohol." Unfortunately, the toxic additive proved not to be a sufficient deterrent. As satirist Will Rogers quipped, "Governments used to murder by the bullet only. Now it's by the quart."[30]

Before Prohibition, a very strong extract of Jamaica ginger containing 80 percent ethanol by weight had been widely available as a "nerve tonic"; the government outlawed it in 1920 unless it contained enough solid content to make it undrinkable. Much as cocaine dealers concocted "crack" in the 1980s, some unscrupulous bootleggers discovered that adding the plasticizer triorthocresyl phosphate (TOCP) made the tonic legal but not entirely undrinkable. The new brew, nicknamed "Jake," soon became a replacement for liquor. Within months, though, it became apparent that TOCP was a severe, albeit slow-working nerve poison. By the time the extent of the poisoning was understood, some thirty to fifty thousand Americans had suffered horrible and irreversible nerve damage. They manifested a distinctive paralysis of the arms and legs, and an awkward, halting gait: the "jake walk."[31]

The Volstead Act cost the U.S. government an estimated $11 billion in lost tax revenue and an additional $300 million in enforcement. This latter job first fell to the Internal Revenue Service and later to the Justice Department. Paradoxically, Prohibition demanded enforcement from an under-resourced government, too often through ineffective and brutal ends. The new agency inside the U.S. Treasury, the Prohibition Unit, had only three thousand employees, a tiny number to enforce a much-flouted law across the entire territory of the United States. The Bureau of Investigation, predecessor to the FBI, had only six hundred employees. Federal Prohibition agents at times deputized volunteers, including Ku Klux Klan members who saw in Prohibition a movement aligned with their goals of cleansing the nation. In Williamson County, Illinois, in 1923, hundreds of volunteers, many of them Klansmen, violently raided distilleries, bars, and private residences, resulting in hundreds of arrests and at least twelve deaths.[32]

As was often the case in the modern war on drugs in places like Colombia, where narco-guerrillas constructed multi-million-dollar drug submarines to evade detection, booze smugglers showed remarkable ingenuity. Some especially creative crooks built a six-thousand-foot-long "pipeline of beer" through the Yonkers sewer system to bring beer from boats on the Hudson River to local watering holes. Another gang crossed over the border from Canada disguised as priests and were allowed through customs without a search under their robes—until one of them suffered a flat tire. Liquor came into New England from boats anchored beyond the three-mile limit, sneaked onto shore in small vessels. Rum runners brought booze to America's shores in any vessel that could float, from birch canoes to two-masted schooners. One boat landed on Jones Beach, Long Island, stuffed with 400 cases of whiskey and 150 barrels of malt extract. When the mayor of Berlin visited New York in 1929, he asked Mayor Jimmy Walker when the dry laws were to be implemented, so extensive were the violations he had seen.[33]

The law was intended to reduce crime, reduce poverty, and strengthen family bonds. Instead, it replaced legal brewers and distillers with bootleggers and gangsters and generated a violent turf and cash war that the overmatched authorities were never able to control. Undersupply raised the price of a drink threefold over pre-1919 levels, which made the illicit trade even more valuable. Paradoxically, neighborhood criminals, once disorganized and atomized, came together into regional and national criminal syndicates to pursue "one of history's greatest opportunities for creating illegal fortunes." In the brief time that Capone controlled Chicago, shootouts and summary murders were as common as the horrible weather. His racketeers shook down legitimate businesses and created many more illegitimate ones. Capone's gang bought off labor unions and politicians and police officials by the hundreds. For all the many revenue streams his business network eventually relied on, illegal liquor was its bread and butter. The homicide rate skyrocketed to 9.7 per 100,000 persons in 1933, a statistic often cited in today's drug war debate. The record held until 1980, when it reached 10 per 100,000. It's telling that our most familiar symbols of the Prohibition era—mob bosses, bootleggers, rum runners, moonshiners, and revenue agents—refer more to disorder and dependency than to temperance and moral improvement. That's partly because popular history tends to favor conflict over concord. But in this case, criminality and the clash of law and lawlessness actually did have a lot to do with it.[34]

"A Synonym for Corruption and Foolishness"

Almost a century hence, the Noble Experiment continues to be portrayed critically by scholars and journalists. Susan Cheever concludes that "it made people sick, made smugglers and bootleggers prosperous, and created patterns of criminal families and organizations that are still with us today." Okrent deems Prohibition to have been a failure in "almost every respect imaginable." It reduced government revenues, fostered blackmail and official corruption, and sharply limited individual rights. "It also maimed and murdered, its excesses apparent in deaths by poison, the brutality of ill-trained, improperly supervised enforcement officers, and by unfortunate proximity to mob gun battles."[35]

To be thorough, though, Prohibition's fourteen-year embargo did have at least a few positive outcomes. Deaths from cirrhosis of the liver—a standard gauge of heavy consumption by long-term alcoholics—dropped by one-third when drink prices tripled. Although we don't have precise statistics, domestic violence and ordinary drunken murders dropped considerably, even if the more visible and sensationalist gangster violence surged.[36]

Given the prospect that the Noble Experiment had been a national embarrassment, a dramatic reversal was afoot. It was hastened by a new economic urgency. The Great Depression was devastating federal tax revenues, and Washington coveted the millions to be made through taxing alcohol. (Before 1920, around 14 percent of federal, state, and local taxes came from alcohol commerce.) Meanwhile, farmers who had initially supported Prohibition on moral grounds now fought for repeal on pocketbook grounds, given the impact the alcohol ban had had on demand for their grains.[37]

In 1932, Hoover, "the reluctant Prohibitionist," was defeated by Franklin D. Roosevelt, a "reluctant anti-Prohibitionist." On March 22, 1933, when President Roosevelt signed an amendment to the Volstead Act allowing for expanded beer production, he famously quipped, "I think this would be a good time for a beer." The Eighteenth Amendment was repealed on December 5, 1933, with the ratification of the Constitution's Twenty-first Amendment.[38] The Eighteenth remains the only constitutional amendment to have been repealed.

Many Americans feared that the post-dry nation would be awash in cheap booze, but in fact consumption levels remained roughly the same after Prohibition and returned to pre-Prohibition levels by the end of the 1930s. The resumption of standards enabled imbibers to better measure what and how much they were consuming; the death rate from alcohol poisoning eased. Murder rates also fell back, as disputes over distribution and production could now be adjudicated in the courts and not in the streets.[39]

As an illegal drug, booze was an unregulated drug, a phantom. Repeal transformed a laissez-faire ethos into a byzantine system of state-by-state codes, regulations, and enforcement. This new, ostensibly "wet" era came with Sunday blue laws, age limits, and restrictions on where bars and "package stores" could set up. In Okrent's phrasing, "Just as Prohibition did not prohibit, making drink legal did not make drink entirely available."[40]

Rules of the Game

Copious ink has been spilled in trying to tease out why Prohibition was such a spectacular flop. It may be that alcohol's considerable popularity—widely consumed and in certain ways fundamentally rooted in the American cultural identity—made it all but impossible to keep Americans from drinking. However, it's difficult to isolate these well enough to identify any as principal causes. Repeal came because of a combination of factors, among them the facts that demand never ebbed; that this sustained demand had been able to find satisfaction in the black market; that the externalities of this market led to increased pressure on the federal government to counter the violence; that the Depression-era government sorely missed alcohol tax revenues; that the law itself included important structural weaknesses; and that enforcement agencies lacked the resources to fulfill their responsibilities.

Some see many of these factors as universal conditions for any state intervention in a drug market. In their estimation, any punitive or restriction-based drug policy is going to fail to reduce demand for drugs; a black market is inevitably going to emerge; black markets will by nature generate violence; any law will have structural weaknesses that allow people to sidestep or take advantage of it; and enforcement agencies will never have the resources or license to disregard civil rights that their fight requires. In other words, these critics argue, the conditions that brought down Prohibition are in fact the rules of the drug-restriction game. And what these rules ensure is that the policy will fail. At this point, we're not going to try to adjudicate this particular debate; it's enough for now to identify it as one of the signature clashes in the drug war, and let the rest of the story fill the scales.

"The Godfather of America's War on Drugs"

One important consequence of the "extreme stress" of Prohibition, as the historian Lisa McGirr keenly observes, was the establishment of a larger, more sophisticated federal criminal justice system. As she points out, Herbert Hoover, the third Prohibition president, was the first American executive to mention crime in his Inaugural Address, introducing a notion that we often take for granted today: that law enforcement is a vital federal issue. Under President Hoover, J. Edgar Hoover secured unprecedented resources to grow his Bureau of Investigation; overworked prosecutors started using plea bargaining to avoid trials; and the Supreme Court ruled that U.S. agents did not need warrants to conduct wiretaps.[41]

At the same time, Prohibition's ultimate repeal did little to temper Progressives' moralizing fervor, especially when it came to psychoactive substances. The next drug in line was cannabis, which, recall, had escaped regulation at the federal level under the Harrison Act. In April 1937, Representative Robert L. Doughton of North Carolina introduced House Bill 6385, which proposed to restrict marijuana use through a prohibitive tax (around $100 an ounce in an era when you could purchase a spanking new Studebaker for $650). Later that year, Congress overwhelmingly passed the Marihuana Tax Act by a voice vote; there is no recorded vote tally. Signed by President Roosevelt with little public attention, the law went into effect on October 1, 1937. The law required (more modestly than Doughton's proposal) a one-dollar tax stamp for anyone who bought, sold, prescribed, or possessed the drug. Failure to pay the tax could result in a $2,000 fine, up to five years in prison, or both.[42]

The animating force behind the new law was a man named Harry J. Anslinger, director of the recently established Federal Bureau of Narcotics, a diminutive agency in the recesses of the U.S. Treasury Department. But his influence spread far beyond his office. As FBN director, he oversaw the implementation of all laws regulating legal and illegal drugs. Critics of today's punitive drug war denounce Anslinger: "He was the Godfather of America's war on drugs, and his influence on public policy would be felt long after death

Colonel C.H.L. Sharman, chief of Canadian Narcotic Control; Harry Anslinger, U.S. commissioner of narcotics; and Assistant Secretary of Treasury Stephen B. Gibbons, March 24, 1937. A contemporary title for the photograph ran: "Closer cooperation in the control of the use of marihuana weed is expected to be the outcome of a meeting today." (Library of Congress, Prints and Photographs Division, Washington, D.C.)

stiffened his fingers in 1975." As his detractors never fail to mention, Anslinger ran the agency with an "iron fist" over three decades and six presidential administrations. For his part, Anslinger enthusiastically embraced his role as archenemy of American drug users.[43]

Given the signature he left on America's century-long drug war, it is worth spending a moment considering Anslinger's life and career. He was born in 1892, the eighth of nine children in a working-class family in Altoona, Pennsylvania, a locale he described as the essence of small-town America, a "mixture of immigrants, rolling farmlands and new factories, miners, and roadworkers, foremen and factory heads." His Swiss émigré father toiled as a barber before finding reliable work with the Pennsylvania Railroad. Several episodes in Altoona shaped Anslinger's outlook as narcotics commissioner.

One took place when he was twelve years old, during a visit to a neighbor's home: "I heard the screaming of a woman on the second floor. I had never heard such cries of pain before. The woman, I later learned, was addicted, like many other women of that period, to morphine. . . . All I remember was that I heard a woman in pain, whose cries seemed to fill my whole twelve-year-old being. Then her husband came running down the stairs, telling me I had to get into the cart and drive to town. I was to pick up a package at the drug store and bring it back for the woman. I never forgot those screams. Nor did I forget that the morphine she had required was sold to a twelve-year-old boy, no questions asked."[44]

At the end of World War I, Anslinger was working for the State Department on assignment with the American Legation at The Hague. He took subsequent postings in Germany, Venezuela, and the Bahamas. As a junior diplomat, Anslinger specialized in smuggling issues, including, during the Prohibition years, Bahamian rum running. Anslinger's forte was intelligence gathering, an activity that included his successful infiltration of Kaiser Wilhelm's inner circle. In 1930, he abruptly quit the State Department and within three years was an assistant commissioner for the Prohibition Bureau.[45]

The mesmerizing jazz musician Billie Holiday in 1949, before drug and alcohol abuse and associated legal complications helped bring an end to her career. She was earning more than a thousand dollars a week from gigs and blowing it on heroin when Anslinger's agents pulled off a successful buy-and-bust heroin sting. She served more than a year in prison as a result. (Library of Congress, Prints and Photographs Division, Washington, D.C.)

Like most of his own men, Anslinger "cut his teeth battling John Barley-corn" during Prohibition. As an assistant prohibition commissioner, Anslinger endorsed more aggressive punitive enforcement, including jail terms and fines for anyone caught buying alcoholic drinks. Anslinger was criticized for his zealousness, which sometimes came at the expense of judgment. In a dissenting opinion from a U.S. Supreme Court decision that allowed wiretapping to support prohibition enforcement, Justice Louis Brandeis likely had Anslinger in mind when he wrote, "The greatest danger to liberty lurks in insidious encroachment by men of zeal—well-meaning but without understanding."[46]

"Voodoo Pharmacology"

When Anslinger took over at the FBN, there were bans on marijuana in twenty-four states but no federal effort to criminalize the plant. When anti-marijuana activists urged him to take up the fight against pot, he initially resisted. "The plant grew like dandelions in every roadside ditch," he lamented. "You might as well stamp out crickets." It was "a dubious proposition," given that Anslinger had only three hundred agents on his roster. In fact, Anslinger's office was focused almost exclusively on cocaine and opiates until 1934, when, the story goes, the FBN budget was slashed by $700,000 in the depths of the Great Depression. "Then he saw the light and realized that marijuana might be the perfect hook to hang his hat on." Even if Anslinger's real motivations might have been less cynical, he nonetheless ratcheted up a strident campaign to convince the American public and Capitol Hill of the evils of marijuana.[47]

Anslinger drummed up fervor for his campaign in speeches to temperance groups and civic clubs across the nation. On a public radio address, he warned, "Parents beware! Your children . . . are being introduced to a new danger in the form of a drugged cigarette, marijuana." Young people "are slaves to this narcotic, continuing addiction until they deteriorate mentally, become insane, turn to violent crime and murder." Anslinger brought his own racial fears to bear on the marijuana question when he surmised that "reefer makes darkies think they're as good as white men." The FBN's growing power depended in part on a docile yellow press to amplify his views. They all but leapt at the opportunity, publishing unsubstantiated reports that "the killer weed" led users, particularly Mexicans, to commit horrific acts of violence, especially against white women. As William Randolph Hearst's Los Angeles *Examiner* cried in 1933, "Murder

Weed Found Up and Down Coast; Deadly Marihuana Dope Plant Ready for Harvest That Means Enslavement of California Children." Other reports, such as "Mussolini Leads the Way in Crushing Dope Evil," combined Hearst's twin passions for supporting European fascists and fighting drugs.[48]

The narcotics bureau chief also managed to dip his fingers into congressional lawmaking. The text of House Bill 6385, which led to the passage of the 1937 Marihuana Tax Act, was written by none other than Harry J. Anslinger. As the House deliberated the bill, he testified in front of the Ways and Means Committee, presenting an exhibition of pot-crazed killers from his notorious "Gore File," a scrapbook full of Hearst media editorials, racial slurs, and anecdotal accounts of heinous crimes often falsely attributed to marijuana users. In his testimony, Anslinger described pot as "the most violence-causing drug in the history of mankind."[49]

Treasury agents J. W. McDonald and F. E. Walker shovel confiscated heroin blocks into an incinerator, 1936 (Library of Congress, Prints and Photographs Division, Washington, D.C.)

The day after the Marihuana Tax Act was implemented, the FBI and the Denver Police Department arrested Samuel Caldwell, an unemployed farmer from Denver, for selling "marihuana cigarettes" to Moses Baca. Caldwell was booked for unlicensed sale of marijuana. Baca, his twenty-six-year-old buyer, was charged with possession. Harry Anslinger appeared for the trial. Baca served a year and a half; Caldwell was sentenced to four years of hard labor in the federal penitentiary in Leavenworth, Kansas. He died a year after he was released.[50]

From a strictly lexical perspective, the notion that Anslinger was the original author of America's war on drugs is accurate. In the 1940s he promised to wage "relentless warfare" on drugs, becoming the first public figure to invoke an explicitly military metaphor for the anti-drug effort. What is more, that the peak of his work coincided with the rapid expansion of federal law enforcement and criminal justice powers gives this era more than a family resemblance to the modern drug war. As Johann Hari describes, "He pledged to eradicate all drugs, everywhere—and within thirty years, he succeeded in turning this crumbling department . . . into the headquarters for a global war that would last for a hundred years and counting." Anslinger achieved most of this through bureaucratic savvy and stamina; indeed, a great deal of his policy-making success can be attributed to his attention to procedural details. But there is another important contextual factor to consider. After a nearly a century of easy access to nearly any psychoactive substance yet discovered, after multiple addiction epidemics, and after the experiment with Prohibition, Americans were left with a serious ambivalence about drugs. In Hari's words, there was a "deep strain in American culture that was waiting for a man like him, with a sure and certain answer to their questions about chemicals." Had a less zealous crusader filled Anslinger's shoes in the first half of the twentieth century, the war on drugs might look very different today.[51]

8 · Amphetamines

"Pleasurable or Libidinal"

While Harry Anslinger was escalating the war on street drugs, the American pharmaceutical industry was enjoying a period of "hothouse growth." This reflected a broader balance-of-power shift, as industrial might sailed from western Europe to the United States. Most of the first generations of synthetic and semisynthetic drugs had been developed in Germany, the pharmaceutical capital during the late nineteenth and early twentieth centuries. David Courtwright describes how one German firm, Friedrich, Bayer & Company, sold or licensed sedatives and hypnotics including Luminal, Sulfonal, Trional, and Veronal in addition to its two "best-known products," heroin and aspirin. After World War II, it was American firms that would come to dominate the world market. Almost two-thirds of new single chemical drugs introduced between 1941 and 1963 came from the United States, with only 8 percent coming from Switzerland, 6 percent from Germany, 5 percent from Britain, and 3.5 percent from France.

With legislation such as the Pure Food and Drug Act in place, large pharmaceutical companies marketed their new drugs all over the world, because domestic sales alone could not recoup the large costs they now sank into research, development, and regulatory approval. Those drugs that had "pleasurable or libidinal" effects followed a consistent trajectory, seeping from "medical to popular experimentation" and sparking controversy and increased control.

Perhaps no class of drug better exemplifies this pattern than the amphetamines. Amphetamine was first synthesized in Germany in 1887 but remained on the shelf, its psychoactive properties unknown, until 1927. Its close cousin, methamphetamine, was synthesized from ephedrine, an alkaloid isolated from the shrub genus *Ephedra,* by the Japanese organic chemist Nagai Nagayoshi. But methamphetamine too was considered commercially unviable because the process of making it was too complex and costly, until 1919, when another Japanese scientist, Akira Ogata, found a simpler way to make the drug using red phosphorous and iodine.

By the 1920s, methamphetamine was being used to boost blood pressure. In the 1930s, the pharmaceutical heavyweight Smith, Kline, and French started selling the related amphetamine under the brand Benzedrine. The Benzedrine inhaler, a small tube stuffed with a saturated cotton wick, was marketed as a decongestant for colds and allergies. It could be purchased at local pharmacies, without a prescription, to treat thirty-three additional illnesses, including schizophrenia, depression, anxiety, the common cold, hyperactivity, impotence, fatigue, and alcoholism. From the get-go, the drug was welcomed for the "simple fact that it made people feel good."[1]

As those who used the inhaler discovered the "stimulating, insomniac, and anorectic effects" of this formidable drug, doctors pondered possible uses for it as a treatment for fatigue, narcolepsy, obesity, and other conditions. In regular life, word spread that the drug-soaked wicks could be removed and then "dissolved in coffee or alcohol or simply chewed and swallowed," which helped long-shift workers to stay awake—and others simply to get high.[2]

The War Machine

The success of American athletes in the Summer Olympics of 1936 in Berlin, aided in part by the extensive use of Benzedrine, precipitated a quest for stronger substances by the Temmler pharmaceutical company, based near Berlin. The firm's head chemist, Fritz Hauschild, synthesized a form of methamphetamine, which was patented as Pervitin. Temmler sold Pervitin as an all-around stimulant supposedly suitable as a treatment for depression, poor circulation, and low libido in females, among other ailments. The Nazi Party, along with a large swath of the German population, took to the drug. As British academic Antony Beevor explains, "By 1938, large parts of the population were using Pervitin on an almost regular basis, including students preparing for exams, nurses on night duty, businessmen under pressure, and mothers dealing with the pressure of *Kinder, Küche, Kirche,*" a reference to "children, kitchen, church," the realms of life to which the Nazis urged women to restrict their horizons. Pervitin use was considered so normal that it even managed to escape the Nazis' anti-drug propaganda.[3]

As the chief of a defense physiology institute, Professor Otto F. Ranke presciently understood that the substance could solve the fatigue problem that had plagued militaries as long as they had existed. Ranke hatched clinical trials involving Pervitin, Benzedrine, caffeine, and placebos on four distinct groups of troops conducting a range of mental and physical tasks. He found that Pervitin boosted stamina much more than the other substances but also yielded more mistakes in intellectual or computational tasks. For Ranke, these liabilities were trivial compared with the drug's creation of an "artificially stimulated ability to keep going when enemy troops had collapsed from exhaustion." Pervitin, it turned out, made for an exceptional war drug.[4]

As the invasion of Poland unfolded in September 1939, Nazi doctors reported back to headquarters the effect that Pervitin was having on their units. "Everyone fresh and cheerful, excellent discipline," wrote one physician. "Slight euphoria and increased thirst for action. Mental encouragement, very stimulated. No accidents. Long-lasting effect. After taking four tablets, double vision and seeing colors." Before the Nobel Prize–winning author Heinrich Böll ever wrote a novel, he was a conscript in the Nazi military. On June 20, 1940, he sent a letter home with a special favor to ask: "Perhaps you could obtain some more Pervitin for my supplies?" Soldiers on the front came to call the pills "Panzerschokolade" or "tank chocolate." The Luftwaffe gave them to its flyers, who dubbed it "pilot's chocolate" or "pilot's salt."[5]

The Third Reich's health minister became so worried about the way "the entire nation seemed to be addicted" to Pervitin that he mandated prescriptions beginning in November 1939. For the military, though, the German leadership recommended just the opposite. As the Wehrmacht high command secretly planned the invasion of France and the Low Countries via neutral Holland and Belgium for May 1940, it placed orders that forced Temmler to kick up its production to 833,000 pills a day, for a total of 35 million pills between April and July of 1940. General Heinz Guderian, credited with the invention of "blitzkrieg" warfare, admonished his troops in the hours leading up to the strike: "I demand that you do not sleep for at least three days and nights, if that is required." The Wehrmacht's surge across the Ardennes to the Meuse River shocked the French defenders. For the invaders, the "arrogance of victory" was enhanced by the Pervitin rush. Colonel Charles de Gaulle was apoplectic when he got word that invading panzer crews were refusing to take French prisoners. Instead, the Germans told the surrendering troops to put down their weapons and march to the rear of the invading force. As Beevor writes, "These panzer troops appeared to the British and French alike to be armored supermen, even though German ground forces were in fact far less mechanized than their own. It was the Wehrmacht's speed and ruthlessness that defeated the French and British armies, which still acted as if it were 1918. They had no idea how the Germans managed to advance day and night without sleep. The official French report on their defeat described it as a '*phénomène d'hallucination collective.*' "[6]

One physician's report from the Eastern Front in January 1942 detailed how five hundred German soldiers surrounded by the Soviet Red Army attempted to escape through deep snow and frigid temperatures. During the night, the spent men started to fall out of formation, many of them lying immobile in the snow. The commanding officers ordered the troops to take their meth pills, immediately after which "the men began spontaneously reporting that they felt better. They began marching in an orderly fashion, their spirits improved, and they became more alert."[7]

Having joined the Nazi Party in 1936 after the word *Jew* was scratched near his office (he wasn't, in fact, Jewish), skin specialist Dr. Theodor Morell gained notoriety for prescribing "vitamins" bolstered by anabolic steroids or testosterone (for males) and nightshade (for females). By 1936, Dr. Morell was treating Hitler, who was afflicted with intestinal cramps. Between August 1941 and April 1945, Morell interacted with Hitler on 885 out of 1,349 days. He kept exceptionally copious notes out of an understandable anxiety that the Gestapo would seek to punish him if Hitler died. In one effort to treat one episode in 1941, Morell "tried everything he could," including Vitamultin and the other stimulants. He then injected Hitler with derivatives of uterine blood, the sexual hormone Tesoviron, and Orchikrin, pig heart and liver, and cocaine.[8]

The stress of repeated defeats on the eastern front made Hitler insist upon increasingly greater amounts of "Morell's drug cocktails." Morell wrote in his notes that he was using eighty-nine remedies, seventeen of which were psychoactive. Time and again, Morell would write "injection as always." Journalist Norman Ohler concluded in *Blitzed: Drugs in the Third Reich* that Hitler's treatment produced "polytoxicomania," which very likely contributed to Hitler's delusions about maps showing Wehrmacht gains "as he lost all touch with reality on the battlefield." In an interview conducted with the *Chicago Tribune* in 1985, one of Hitler's physicians, Ernst-Günther Schenck, said that the führer had insisted upon injections of "invigorating and tranquilizing drugs," including methamphetamine. It may well have been that Hitler's subsequent and progressive "Parkinson's-like symptoms" and increasingly "derelict mental state" resulted from his methamphetamine habit. A plot to assassinate Hitler in his East Prussian command post in July 1944 missed its mark, but the blast perforated his eardrums, after which Dr. Erwin Giesing administered cocaine fifty times over a two-and-a-half month span.[9]

Temmler continued to produce Pervitin pills for both the East German and West German militaries into the late 1960s. West Germany's military, the Bundeswehr, did not stop using the drug until the 1970s. East Germany's National People's Army used it until 1988.[10]

"The Defining Ideal of American Culture"

It was not only the Third Reich that saw the utility of amphetamines. The U.S. military also distributed more than 180 million methamphetamine tablets to "bomber crews and jungle fighters" to help them cope with the "extreme duress" of their missions. This was in spite of the evidence presented in a U.S. government report from 1939, which said that methamphetamine "had 'psychotic' and 'antisocial' side effects, including increased libido, sexual aggression, violence, hallucinations" and "sadomasochism, inability to reach orgasm, Satanic thoughts, general immorality, and chronic insomnia."[11]

In the postwar years, the use of amphetamines continued to grow in the United States as doctors prescribed it for maladies such as depression as well as chronic hiccups and caffeine dependence. In a world in which the winners were defined by the pace at which they could industrialize, methamphetamine was a kind of miracle, as it suppressed the need for sleep, food, and hydration, all the while keeping workers "peppy," as the ads had it. "Meth" enjoyed wide acceptance in midcentury America. One observer called it the "salt of the earth" for its ability to drive "soldiers, truck drivers, slaughterhouse employees, farmers, auto and construction workers, and day laborers" to work "harder, longer, and more efficiently." Smith, Kline, and French's amphetamine patents expired in 1949, which brought new firms into the market. U.S. amphetamine production, which had leveled out around 16,000 pounds in 1949, spiked to 75,000 pounds in 1958, equivalent to an astounding 3.5 billion tablets.[12]

In this time, U.S. manufacturers urged physicians to prescribe amphetamines, especially to women. The various drugs used a range of amphetamine-family molecules as their active ingredients. A trade advertisement for Dexedrine (dextroamphetamine) in 1950 explained: "Many of your patients, particularly housewives, are crushed under a load of dull, routine duties that leave them in a state of mental and emotional fatigue. Dexedrine will give them a feeling of energy and well-being, renewing their interest in life and living." In ads for Dexamyl (another dextroamphetamine), a woman wearing an apron could be seen "ecstatically vacuuming her living room carpet." Or take Norodin, a methamphetamine-based competitor whose marketers assured doctors that it was "useful in reducing the desire for food and counteracting the low spirits associated with the rigors of an enforced diet." Advertisements for "Methedrine-brand Methamphetamine—For Those Who Eat Too Much and Those Who Are Depressed" were ubiquitous in American magazines through the 1960s. In 1967 alone, thirty-one million legal anorexient (diet pill) prescriptions were written in America. The FDA reckoned that 80 percent of those were written for women.[13]

As the legal market for the drugs grew, a portion of it was siphoned off into the black market. Truck drivers purchased "pep pills" on street corners and in motels. College students and athletes turned to them after participants in clinical studies at the University of Minnesota learned that the drug had utility for "all-night parties and exam blitzes." Word spread quickly, delighting the students at Berkeley, Columbia, Purdue, and elsewhere.[14]

This "democratization of amphetamine" also brought the drug to "high-flying" celebrities. The patient roster of Max Jacobson, the notorious "Dr. Feelgood," included showbiz notables Yul Brynner, Alan Jay Lerner, and Johnny Mathis. Jacobson injected presidential candidate John F. Kennedy with Dexedrine before his historic (and successful) television debate with Republican opponent Richard Nixon. The 1960s witnessed an even more active underground meth market, "feeding off forged prescriptions, bogus wholesale orders, and other diversion tactics" that had started in the 1950s.[15]

Birth of the Meth Lab

Reports first surfaced of users injecting amphetamines (particularly methamphetamine) in the 1950s, but the method—known as "mainlining"—did not gain currency until the following decade. In 1962, San Francisco law enforcement cracked down on pharmacies selling injectable amphetamines. The campaign drew national media coverage to the mainlining craze. It also led to the emergence of clandestine manufacturing facilities, dubbed "speed labs." The majority of these mom-and-pop labs sprouted on the West Coast, and many were run by outlaw motorcycle gangs: the Hells Angels of California and the Sons of Silence from the Midwest.

Two years later, CBS News purchased more than a million amphetamine and barbiturate pills through a fictional company it established with "little more than a post-office box." Its reporting described a "new crop of speed freaks" who were eschewing inhalers and pills for liquid speed scored through the black market or "cooked up" at home. The episode etched a new idea into the American consciousness: that amphetamines were abusable drugs. With legal production soaring (twelve billion tablets a year by the early 1970s), an alarmed federal government imposed strict manufacturing quotas in order to limit "diversion" into illicit markets. What emerged to fill the vacuum would become an icon of present-day American drug culture: the clandestine meth lab.[16]

9 • Alternative Consciousness

I predict that psychedelic drugs will be used in all schools in the very
near future as educational devices—not only drugs like marijuana and
LSD, to teach kids how to use their sense organs and their cellular
equipment effectively, but new and more powerful psychochemicals
like RNA and other proteins which are going to revolutionize our
concepts of ourselves and education.
—Allen Ginsberg, interview in *The Realist*, 1966

"Friendly Conversation and a Little Product"

By the early 1940s, illicit drugs were difficult to obtain in America, and they
were often heavily diluted. World War II saw them virtually disappear as the
legitimate needs of the war wounded took up the majority of supply, especially
pills but also controlled substances. Wartime sea blockades made smuggling
infinitely riskier. One addict reflected, "There were no drugs in New York during World War II, no drugs in Philadelphia, no drugs in Chicago—there were
no drugs on the East Coast. No drugs." For conservative historians such as Jill
Jonnes, this era demonstrates how scarcity leads many users to give up drugs.
Though statistics are spotty, it's certain that scarcity did keep a great many
people from using, and it likely helped some addicts break the habit. But there
are reasons to doubt how generalizable or useful this conclusion is. One is the
fact that, since the end of World War II, there hasn't been anything like it. The
conditions that limited the supply of drugs in this country—the massive diversion of resources toward a single national effort, the militarization of almost

every major sea passage, an extremely limited supply of private aircraft and navigable international airspace, to name a few—haven't returned since the 1940s and may well never occur again. Moreover, hard addicts still found fixes even amid the shortage of street opiates and cocaine—a notable source being Benzedrine, the synthetic amphetamine initially prescribed for chest complaints like asthma, distributed to American GIs to keep them alert, and eventually made available on the American black market. This holds with a pattern still in evidence today: The most committed drug users readily jump to another solution when the preferred drug is unavailable. A third reason is the existence of a substance that did remain plentiful throughout the lean war years, one that many non-addicted recreational drug users found to be an acceptable substitute for scarce narcotics. That substance was cannabis.[1]

After the war, cannabis became a potent fuel for the countercultural awakening that began to spread across the nation. Here is how author Bruce Barcott described that arousal: "In the rich loam of the Mississippi Delta, the hustlers' alleys of Times Square, the nightclubs and pool halls of Chicago, Denver and Detroit, and the bohemian flats of San Francisco, buds and shoots emerged. They sprouted in jazz clubs, radio stations, art galleries and bookstores and along the nation's growing interstate highways. These first iterations appeared as ideas, attitudes, songs, novels, jokes and poems." And in almost every place these things sprouted, so did cannabis. All the while, Harry Anslinger's FBN continued to wage a mostly futile war against the weed.[2]

The longer version of this story starts in Harlem. In the 1940s, a new generation of bebop jazz players—Lester Young, John Coltrane, Charlie Parker, Miles Davis, Thelonious Monk—followed their predecessors to Mezz Mezzrow's haunts for "friendly conversation and a little product." The neighborhood's jazz clubs and theaters attracted a diverse clientele after the war, becoming, among other things, unlikely seedbeds for racial integration. One of the white "slummers" who enjoyed the sounds at Minton's Playhouse in Harlem was a young writer named Jean-Louis Lebris de Kérouac. His buddies called him Jack. Kerouac had dropped out of Columbia University after a disagreement with the football coach but continued to hang around Morningside Heights with a new friend, "a spindly Jewish kid with horn-rimmed glasses and tremendous ears sticking out." This was the eighteen-year-old Allen Ginsberg, a "bright, mixed-up" student from New Jersey who aspired to be a labor attorney. Ginsberg's dad was an amateur potter, high school teacher, and leftist; his mom was a devout Communist and a sometime inmate at mental institutions. Blessed with a capacious and curious mind, Ginsberg was "oddly systematic."

Preternaturally fascinated with novelty, he recorded drink-by-drink his first experience of getting drunk—just one of umpteen experiments he conducted on his mind during his life.[3]

In 1946 the cash-short Ginsberg read Mezzrow's autobiography cover to cover while standing in Columbia's bookstore. The book confirmed Ginsberg's sense that Mezz had emerged as an earlier version of himself, a brainy kid who studied literature and found creative expression and authenticity by fashioning for himself the life of an outsider. Before too long, an older, trust-funded Harvard graduate, William S. Burroughs, joined their scene.[4]

Over the next decade, Ginsberg, Kerouac, Burroughs, and a growing cohort of "writers, poets, musicians, queers, junkies, misfits, dropouts, idiots, and geniuses" would cultivate an American bohemian scene to rival that of Paris in the 1920s. With a "manic cat from Denver," Neal Cassady, the crew passed the time getting "jagged and loose on bennies [Benzedrine] and pot, yakking nonstop about philosophy, literature, art, drugs and sex and laughing madly into the early morning of the night. The bebop blowing at Minton's expressed everything they sought but rarely found in postwar America: improvisation, freedom, creativity, surprise, nonconformity and discordance."[5]

Ginsberg experimented with all sorts of drugs in the 1940s, but pot was the first one to unleash his consciousness. "It was the first time I ever had solid evidence in my own body that there was a difference between reality as I saw it myself and reality as it was described officially by the state, the government, the police and the media," Ginsberg revealed in an interview with Larry Sloman in the 1970s. "To a few of us in the '40s," he continued, "that experience of marijuana catalyzed a reexamination of all social ideas, because if one law was full of shit and error, then what about all those other laws?" Out of this question came rebellious works of art. In the fall of 1955, Ginsberg debuted his poem "Howl" at the Six Gallery in San Francisco, sparking a different sort of buzz in the literary world with his vision of an unseen America. *On the Road*, Jack Kerouac's answer to "Howl," was published in September 1957, six years after he first submitted the manuscript in its initial version written as an uninterrupted single-spaced paragraph of ninety thousand words on a scroll of drawing paper the author had cut to fit in his typewriter. The book told of restless young misfits searching for meaning in an America they had rejected, and it irretrievably vaulted the white hipster subculture into the mainstream, horrifying older folks and mesmerizing the young. In the process, it "invented a counterculture."[6]

A New Intoxicant

The Beat-driven imperative to "divorce oneself from society, to exist without roots, to set out on that uncharted journey into the rebellious imperatives of the self," as Norman Mailer described the project in his essay "The White Negro" in 1957, happened to coincide with another trend: burgeoning scientific inquiry into the stimulation of alternative states of consciousness via psychoactive substances.[7] Humans had been consuming plant-based psychoactives for millennia. Mescaline, occurring naturally in the peyote cactus, was used by both Mayans and Aztecs in today's Mexico for at least 5,700 years. It is still possible to encounter living shamanic cultures for which vision-inducing plants are at the core of their spirituality and customs. In *Breaking Open the Head*, Daniel Pinchbeck notes that for some tribes in Africa, Siberia, and North and South America, music, medicines, cosmology, and capacious botanical knowledge are all linked to psychedelic visions.[8]

The classification "psychedelic" itself is vague: many psychedelic drugs are not very closely related in terms of their effect on human physiology, and the full set resists precise categorization. Nevertheless, the term is generally taken to mean a class of substance that primarily affects cognition and perception. Psychedelic alkaloids such as psilocybin, LSD, DMT (*N,N*-Dimethyltryptamine), and mescaline bind to serotonin receptors thought to regulate sensory input and interpretation. With "normative" levels of serotonin, Pinchbeck writes, the brain experiences "consensual reality," something akin to the "local pop radio station." By substituting a psychedelic compound for serotonin and other neurotransmitters, "suddenly you begin to pick up the sensorial equivalent of avant-garde jazz." These alkaloids operate mostly outside the dopamine pathways through which opioids and cocaine work, which might help to explain psychedelics' far lower (and in some cases nonexistent) addiction rates.[9]

The modern history of psychedelics begins in 1886, when a Berlin toxicologist named Louis Lewin crossed the southwestern United States and acquired some *muscale* buttons taken from the peyote cactus. Peyote had spread north of the Rio Grande in the aftermath of the U.S. Civil War and had achieved "ritual status" among tribes like the Kiowa and the Comanche. As Jay Stevens recounts in *Storming Heaven*, back in his Berlin lab Lewin isolated several peyote alkaloids and tested them on animals but desisted from "self-experimentation." That "risky adventure" fell to, among others, Arthur Heffner, a colleague who took each alkaloid in turn, until he isolated the significant one, which he christened *mescal*. Although Lewin's research waned in prominence, it provided the groundwork for a group of English researchers in Canada in the early 1950s to develop the "psychedelic model" of hallucinogens.[10]

In 1955, the English politician Christopher Mayhew participated in an experiment for the BBC television program *Panorama* in which he ate 400 milligrams of mescaline under the supervision of a psychiatrist, Humphry Osmond. The film was deemed too controversial to air. Mayhew later called it "the most interesting thing I ever did."[11] The British novelist Aldous Huxley first took mescaline in 1953. Huxley had been fascinated with mysticism long before he was aware of psychedelics. His 1931 novel *Brave New World* was a prescient vision of a high-tech authoritarian future; the book featured an invented narco-hallucinogen, Soma, the "ideal pleasure drug." The same year Huxley published an article addressing the need to kill the quotidian drudgery of modern existence. "If I were a millionaire, I should endow a band of research workers to look for a new intoxicant." The author committed the last years of his life to drugs, including mescaline and LSD. His work *The Doors of Perception* in 1954 was destined to become the "most famous volume on the psychedelic bookshelf." Had an ordinary hack written a book prescribing mescaline as "an estimable value to everyone and especially to the intellectual," wrote the *Reporter's* Marvin Barrett, it would have been dismissed as the "the woolgathering of a misguided crackpot. But coming . . . from one of the current masters of English prose, a man of immense erudition and intellect who usually demonstrates a high moral seriousness, they deserve more scrutiny."[12]

On roughly the same timeline, Dr. Albert Hofmann, a chemist, began investigating another naturally occurring compound under the aegis of the chemical company Sandoz in Basel, Switzerland. Hofmann joined the firm in 1927, shortly after his graduation from the University of Zurich. Sandoz had recently been bolstering its traditional product line of herbicides and dyes with drugs, "sifting the chemical possibilities like archeologists working adjacent digs" to find a better antibiotic, a safer headache pill, a more forceful cough suppressant. Sandoz had placed a bet on *Claviceps purpurea*, better known as ergot, a fungus that grew on diseased rye kernels. According to Stevens, while ergot had been used in childbirth to expedite uterine contractions, the fungus was best known as the cause of St. Anthony's Fire, or what doctors called dry gangrene: "swallowing ergot-contaminated rye caused one's fingers and toes to blacken, then drop off, as a prelude to a particularly nasty death."[13]

In charge of the ergot project for eight years, Hofmann had diligently synthesized one ergotamine molecule after another. "A peculiar presentment," is how Hofmann subsequently described the sense that shrouded him after he ingested the twenty-fifth compound of the lysergic acid series, lab notation "LSD-25." Here is a subsequent report from his published account, *LSD: My Problem Child*.

> Last Friday, April 16, 1943, I was forced to interrupt my work in the laboratory in the middle of the afternoon and proceed home, being affected by a remarkable restlessness, combined with a slight dizziness. At home I lay down and sank into a not unpleasant intoxicated-like condition, characterized by an extremely stimulated imagination. In a dreamlike state, with eyes closed (I found the daylight to be unpleasantly glaring), I perceived an uninterrupted stream of fantastic pictures, extraordinary shapes with intense, kaleidoscopic play of colors. After some two hours this condition faded away.

A few days later he took a much stronger dose.

> By now it was already clear to me that LSD had been the cause of the remarkable experience of the previous Friday, for the altered perceptions were of the same type as before, only much more intense. I had to struggle to speak intelligibly. I asked my laboratory assistant, who was informed of the self-experiment, to escort me home. We went by bicycle. . . . On the way home, my condition began to assume threatening forms. Everything in my field of vision wavered and was distorted as if seen in a curved mirror. I also had the sensation of being unable to move from the spot. Nevertheless, my assistant later told me we had traveled very rapidly.[14]

Hofmann had isolated the most potent psychoactive chemical then known, five to ten thousand times more powerful than an equivalent dose of mescaline, the substance LSD-25 most closely resembled. Hofmann and his colleagues tested the compound on mice, cats, chimpanzees, and spiders. All weathered massive dosages without suffering apparent physical harm, although they presented significant behavioral anomalies. Spiders, for example, spun webs of heightened complexity. One researcher injected LSD into a lab chimp, and then reintroduced the animal to its colony. The chimp appeared to have forgotten all of the social norms of colony life.[15]

For Good and Ill

LSD was well received by scientists following its introduction into the United States in 1949. As author Martin A. Lee found, over the next decade the compound gained an esteemed position among psychiatrists. By 1960, more than a thousand clinical papers had been published on the subject, encompassing some forty thousand patients. The drug was found to mitigate the physical and psychological stress of terminal cancer patients by helping them deal with the anguish of death. Scores attested to psychedelics' utility for treating clinical depression, obsessive-compulsive disorder, and alcoholism. In fact, the very word *psychedelic*—meaning "mind-manifesting"—was coined in this wave of enthusiastic research. Research uncovering the drug's therapeutic prospects helped mitigate concerns about its safety. One study surveyed a sample of five thousand individuals who had taken LSD twenty-five thousand times. It found an average of 1.8 psychotic episodes per one thousand ingestions, 1.2 suicide attempts, and 0.4 completed suicides. The clinician Sidney Cohen concluded, "LSD is an astonishingly safe drug." The U.S. government began funding LSD programs at the Palo Alto Veterans Hospital, the San Mateo County Hospital (where I was born in 1971), and Napa State Hospital.[16]

In his decade of self-experimentation, Huxley surmised that LSD and other psychedelics might "help the psychiatrist in his battle against mental illness, or they may help the dictator in his battle against freedom. More probably (since science is divinely impartial) they will both enslave and make free, heal and at the same time destroy."[17] During World War II, America's wartime intelligence service, the Office of Strategic Services, sought a drug to break the will of interrogation subjects and compel them to give up information. An OSS team field-tested several compounds, including mescaline and scopolamine, at St. Elizabeths Hospital in Washington, D.C. In 1953, the six-year-old Central Intelligence Agency diverted $300,000 to fund Project MK-ULTRA, a series of human psychological experiments intended to identify and develop drugs and procedures of potential use in interrogation. MK-ULTRA researched drugs from nicotine to cocaine, but LSD became the central focus. In fact, the CIA is alleged to have considered LSD so promising that in November 1953 it dispatched two men to buy up Sandoz's entire supply, which was then around ten kilograms. To conduct the tests, the agency turned to the psychology field, especially to labs that were already investigating LSD and mental illness. One CIA-funded experiment involved seven drug addicts at a hospital in Lexington, Kentucky, who were given LSD over six weeks, their dosages doubled and quadrupled as tolerances increased.[18] Some of those commissioned, including the Caltech-educated chemist Sid Gottlieb and his colleagues, appeared to take the opportunity to finance their own LSD journeys: they "were taking LSD regularly, tripping at the office, at Agency parties, measuring their mental equilibrium against those of their colleagues. Turn your back in the morning and some wiseacre would slip a few micrograms into your coffee." The CIA's active involvement with LSD ended in 1958.[19]

"Social Fabrication"

In May 1957, R. Gordon Wasson, a vice president at J. P. Morgan Bank, published a photo essay, "Seeking the Magic Mushroom," in *Life* magazine's Great Adventure series. A seventeen-page spread with color photographs, the article chronicled Wasson and his wife Valentina's worldwide trek to learn about the role of toadstools in indigenous societies. Their adventures led them to the isolated highlands of Mexico, where they met a medicine woman who served them *teonanácatl*, the "divine flesh." As he chewed the astringent fungus, Wasson was determined to resist its effects and give an objective account of the changes that unfolded in his mind. As he explained to a million *Life* readers, his willpower "soon melted before the onslaught of the mushrooms."

> We were never more awake, and the visions came whether our eyes were opened or closed. . . . They began with art motifs, angular such as might decorate carpets or textiles or wallpaper or the drawing board of an architect. They evolved into palaces with courts, arcades, gardens—resplendent palaces laid over with semiprecious stones. . . . Later it was as though the walls of our house had dissolved, and my spirit had flown forth, and I was suspended in mid-air viewing landscapes of mountains, with camel caravans advancing slowly across the slopes, the mountains rising tier above tier to the very heavens. . . . The thought that crossed my mind: could the miraculous mobility that I was now enjoying be the explanation for the flying witches that played so important a part in the folklore and fair tales of northern Europe? These reflections passed through my mind at the very time I was seeing the visions, for the effect of the mushrooms is to bring about a fission of the spirit, a split in the person, a kind of schizophrenia, with the rational side continuing to reason and to observe the sensations that the other side is enjoying. The mind is attached as by an elastic cord to the vagrant senses.[20]

Wasson's article piqued the curiosity of a young professor named Timothy Leary. As a youth, Leary had passed on an opportunity to study at a Catholic seminary, then dropped out of West Point after refusing to resign over an alleged honor code violation. He enrolled in the ROTC program at the University of Alabama in 1941 to study psychology but was expelled after being caught in a girls' dormitory. After a short stint in the military, Leary received his doctorate in psychology from the University of California at Berkeley. At the time of Wasson's *Life* essay, Leary was directing clinical research at the Kaiser Foundation Hospital in Oakland, California, near the Berkeley campus. He had already written an acclaimed psychology textbook and invented a personality evaluation, "The Leary Interpersonal Behavior Test," that was being used by the CIA and other organizations to test prospective employees.[21]

His reputation and career both soaring, in 1959 Leary started a new position as a lecturer in clinical psychology at Harvard University, where for several years students had served as guinea pigs for CIA- and Pentagon-funded LSD experiments. In the summer of 1960, Leary, then thirty-nine years old, was on holiday in the spa town of Cuernavaca, Mexico, when a friend gave him *teo-nanácatl*. The professor was dubious; nevertheless, he chased down the mushrooms with a few slugs of a local beer. As is not uncommon for those who experiment with psychedelics, Leary's first trip was deeply moving. "It was above all and without question the deepest religious experience of my life," he later observed. "I discovered that beauty, revelation, sensuality, the cellular history of the past, God, the Devil—all lie inside my body, outside my mind." He concluded:

> For most people it's a life-changing shock to learn that their everyday reality circuit is one among dozens of circuits which, when turned on, are equally real, pulsing with strange forms and mysterious biological signals. . . . Since psychedelic drugs expose us to different levels of perception and experience, use of them is ultimately a philosophic enterprise, compelling use to confront the nature of reality and the nature of our fragile, subjective belief systems. . . . We discover abruptly that we have been programmed all these years, that everything we accept as reality is just social fabrication.

Leary went back to Harvard and, along with associates such as Richard Alpert (later known as Ram Dass), set up the Harvard Psilocybin Project with the support of Dr. Harry Murray, who chaired the Department of Social Relations. They administered psilocybin, the active alkaloid in mushrooms, obtained through Sandoz, to hundreds of graduate students, artists, and other test subjects. In 1962, Leary was paid a visit by a portly Englishman named Michael Hollingshead, who brought with him a mayonnaise jar holding several thousand doses of LSD. Leary initially demurred but finally sampled the product, which propelled him light years beyond the "cozy, know-thyself psilocybin."

LSD "detonated his ego." It was clear to Leary that, after LSD, he would soon have to leave Harvard—and American society—behind.[22]

To bring the story back around, as *New Yorker* writer Louis Menand describes in his article "Acid Redux: The Life and Times of Timothy Leary," in December 1960 Allen Ginsberg and his longtime partner, the actor Peter Orlovsky, met at Leary's house in a suburb near Cambridge, Massachusetts. Leary handed them each a pill containing psilocybin. After a moment of queasiness, Ginsberg and Orlovsky stripped off their clothes and paraded through the house. Ginsberg was filled with messianic emotions. "We're going to teach people to stop hating. . . . Start a peace and love movement." Ginsberg tried to get John Kennedy, Soviet Premier Nikita Khrushchev, and Mao Tse-tung on a phone call in a cosmic conversation that would rid them of their trivial obsessions with war. This proving unworkable, he called Jack Kerouac, who was then living with his mother in Northport, New York. When the operator answered, Ginsberg identified himself as God wanting to speak with Kerouac. He repeated his name, spelling it out: G-O-D. On reaching his friend, he implored him to take mushrooms. "I can't leave my mother," the author of the bible of the Beat generation told him. Ginsberg urged him to bring his mother along. Kerouac told him he would have to pass this time.[23]

The "quintessential egalitarian," Ginsberg wanted everyone alive to experience the drug's mind-expanding wonders. The time had come to launch a psychedelic crusade—and, for Ginsberg, there was no better leader than Leary. It was ironic, Ginsberg observed, "that the very technology stereotyping our consciousness and desensitizing our perceptions should throw up its own antidote. . . . Given such historic Comedy, who should emerge from Harvard University but the one and only Dr. Leary, a respectable human being, a worldly man faced with the task of a Messiah." Avatars of this embryonic psychedelic movement believed that psilocybin and LSD could change the individual—and thus, the world—by "deconditioning" him or her from limiting beliefs and neuroses. Harvard dean David McClelland, an erstwhile support of Leary's work, had another opinion: "It tears my heart out to see what's happened to them. They started out as good scientists. They've become cultists."[24]

Nonetheless, an energized Ginsberg returned to New York City from Massachusetts with a stash of psilocybin. At the Five Spot in Greenwich Village, he gave the pills to Thelonious Monk, the piano jazz legend. A few days later Ginsberg dropped by Monk's apartment to see how he was faring. Monk received Ginsberg with an ear-to-ear grin. Ginsberg also "turned on" trumpeter

Dizzy Gillespie and, later, saxophonist John Coltrane, who reported that he had "perceived the inter-relationship of all life forms."[25]

Back at Harvard, Leary's research activities were getting tangled up with reports that sugar cubes laced with LSD (street price reckoned to be about five dollars) were circulating on campus. There were also rumors about wild LSD parties and undergraduates pushing acid scored on the black market. The frenzy prompted two Harvard administrators to publish a letter in the *Crimson*, the campus newspaper, warning that LSD and psilocybin "may result in serious hazard to the mental health and stability even of apparently normal persons." Accounts favorable to Leary (as most tend to be) usually attribute his dismissal from Harvard in 1963 to his missing an honors committee meeting. It is more likely that the university took action after it discovered that students had been given psychedelic drugs in nonclinical settings. Whatever the cause, the inimitable Leary maintained that LSD was "more important than Harvard."

Inspired by Ginsberg but above all driven by his "own flashy temperament," Leary opted for the mass market to spread his mind-expansion gospel. Whether the psychedelic movement would have spread without Leary is, of course,

Allen Ginsberg, Timothy Leary, and Ralph Metzner, in the late 1960s. The three are standing in front of a ten-foot plaster Buddha, preparing for a "psychedelic celebration" at the Village Theater. (Library of Congress, Prints and Photographs Division, Washington, D.C.)

impossible to know, but he unquestionably defined its public image, cranking out pamphlets, books, and records that "equated LSD with the discovery of fire and the invention of the wheel." The redoubtable professor also started a retreat in upstate New York, where he hosted scores of young professionals eager to experience the Other World. In September 1966 he founded the League for Spiritual Discovery, whose purpose, he explained, was to "change and elevate the consciousness of every American within the next few years. Slowly, carefully, and beautifully, you can learn to drop out of American society as it is now set up." Hence the League's soon-to-be-famous slogan: "tune in, turn on, drop out."[26]

The Rise and Fall of the Acidhead

In the autumn of 1958, twenty-four-year-old Ken Kesey, a stocky, blue-eyed former high school wrestling star, arrived in Palo Alto, California, to study at the Stanford Writing Program. He grew a beard and strummed folk songs on his guitar; he got drunk, something he'd only done a few times before; he ate his first pot brownie, none of which seemed to diminish his "cornball enthusiasm" for life and sport. In the spring of 1960, Kesey wrestled in a "close but fruitless bid" for a spot on the U.S. Olympic team.

Like Ginsberg and his associates, Kesey was turned on to LSD by means of a federally funded research program. He earned seventy-five dollars a day as a guinea pig in a study of "psychomimetic drugs" in the Menlo Park lab of Dr. Leo Hollister, one of the scientists the CIA had contacted when it decided to delegate its MK-ULTRA program to independent researchers. Hollister gave Kesey psilocybin and, later, LSD. Kesey found them terrific. The young writer soon started working at the veteran's hospital as a psychiatric aid. He worked the graveyard shift when the ward was empty; luckily for him, the medicine cabinet where the psychotomimetic drugs—LSD, mescaline, Ditran, and a mysterious chemical known only as IT-290—were stored was "wide open for anyone who wanted to borrow an experimental chemical or two." The drugs gave him insight into the patients he had hitherto overlooked. "Before I took drugs," Kesey explained, "I didn't know why the guys in the psycho ward were there. I didn't understand them. After I took LSD, I suddenly saw it. I saw it all. I listened to them and watched them, and I saw that what they were saying and doing was not so crazy after all."[27]

When Kesey tried peyote, he had a vision of a weird, primitive face. It was the image of a Native American, Chief Broom, who would become a character in his first novel, *One Flew Over the Cuckoo's Nest*. Gradually, with the aid of these federally funded trips, the book that would make him an American literary sensation bloomed in Kesey's mind. Kesey accomplished much of his writing high on LSD or peyote. The book was met with sensational reviews and bestowed a "curious legitimacy" on this nascent psychedelic science. Now, it seemed, "one could have one's cake (LSD) and write the great American novel, too."[28]

Soon enough, the drugs Kesey filched in the middle of the night from the hospital ward were circulating among his friends on Perry Lane, the district Tom Wolfe called "Stanford's bohemian quarter" in *The Electric Kool-Aid Acid Test*. The Perry Lane community changed as more and more of its denizens started turning on to psychedelics and psychotomimetics. A party scene developed around Kesey's legendary venison chili, a spicy dish laced with a liberal dosing of LSD. Guests who shared "electric" meals included the artist Roy Seburn, the dancer Chloe Scott, a young musician named Jerry Garcia, and the writers Larry McMurtry and Hunter S. Thompson.[29]

Kesey used the royalties from his big-splash novel to purchase a place in the coastal mountain hamlet of La Honda, about an hour's drive south of San Francisco. There, he finished his second novel, *Sometimes a Great Notion*. His spread became a destination for "beatniks, college professors and a new breed of doper—the acidhead." Amplifiers anchored in the trees blasted rock and roll. Acid was of course consumed liberally.[30]

The shenanigans at La Honda evolved into Kesey's notorious Merry Pranksters, a nouveau-bohemian troupe association that landed somewhere between cross-country caravan and performance-art project. The Pranksters bought a 1939 International Harvester school bus and outfitted it with bunks, shelves, a refrigerator, a sink, and a liberal supply of LSD and other drugs. They punched a hole in the roof so that passengers could ride on top and play music. They painted the bus with bright, swirling designs to create the first "psychedelic motor transport." The back end bore a sign that read, "Caution: Weird Load." There were about two dozen folks on board, dressed in elaborate costumes and painted with Day-Glo, all ready for the "great freak forward." Kesey's sassy mantra said it all: "Get them into your movie before they get you into theirs."

What was the purpose of the psychedelic experience they were proselytizing? "To learn the conditioned response of people and then to prank them," Kesey contended. "That's the only way to get people to ask questions, and until they ask questions they're going to remain conditioned robots." As they arrived in any location, loudspeakers blaring Bob Dylan or the Beatles, the Pranksters were fully aware they appeared to straight citizens like Martians.

During the 1964 presidential campaign the Pranksters passed through Phoenix, waving American flags and demonstrating with a large sign that said, "A Vote for Barry Goldwater is a Vote for Fun."[31]

The bus's intrepid driver, the aforementioned Neal Cassady, an "aging beat avatar" in an era characterized by its heady avatars, had not long before been released from San Quentin State Prison after serving two years for marijuana possession. San Quentin had tested his ebullient nature, but Cassady's signature attitude remained the "mad exultation in the moment," his taste for velocity even more uncontrollable after he'd swallowed amphetamines.[32]

By age thirty, Kesey had published two well-received and commercially successful novels, a "literary debut unmatched since the days of Hemingway and Fitzgerald." But he gave up literature to shape, through psychedelics, a new art form—what he called the "acid test." A latter-day Johnny Appleseed, he roamed up and down the California coast throwing multimedia drug fests. The most significant of them, the Trips Festival, took place in 1966 when thousands of "psychedelic revelers" partied over a few nights in San Francisco's Longshoreman's Hall.[33]

Jay Stevens points out that Kesey and Leary were not the only ones "beating the psychedelic drum." In 1966, *Time*'s cultural section detailed the proliferation of "oddball cult groups," colorfully clad college-educated philosophers who discussed LSD and mushrooms with the types of pious fervor "last heard in the West during the high Middle Ages." These "acid heads," *Time* told its readers, were everywhere. In pop culture, the Beatles were singing, "Turn off your mind, relax, float downstream," this last a phrase that they had pinched from one of Leary's books and that he had originally borrowed from the *Tibetan Book of the Dead*. By the 1960s, the counterculture had become mainstream. Disenchantment with the Vietnam War, suburban materialism, and racial segregation became a dominant mood—and as this happened, psychedelics, cannabis, and other drugs became symbols of rebellion for millions of high school and college students.

Ginsberg also kept up the pace. In one episode in 1966, he recommended to a church congregation in Boston that "every man, woman and child American in good health over the age of fourteen . . . everybody including the President and his and our vast hordes of generals, executives, judges and legislators of these States go to nature, find a kindly teacher or Indian peyote chief or guru guide, and assay their consciousness with LSD." The logic implicit in the psychedelic movement was simple: drop acid and change yourself—change yourself and you can change the world.[34]

Party Over

By the mid-1960s, a social and cultural backlash was brewing. As early as 1965 the federal government was beginning to close LSD clinics across the country. In March 1966, *Time* reported that America was mired in an LSD epidemic. "The disease is striking in beachside beatnik pads and the dormitories of expensive prep schools; it has grown into an alarming problem at UCLA and on the UC campus at Berkeley. And everywhere the diagnosis is the same: psychotic illness resulting from the unauthorized, nonmedical use of the drug LSD-25." The parents of all the acid-dropping youths sensed that something horrible was afoot. LSD did not expand your consciousness, the newspaper and television spots now urged; it made you insane. But the kids were not listening. If you want a staid life of sanity, they retorted, then give me crazy. It was a perspective that led many older Americans to revise their "estimate of Godless communism as America's number-one enemy."[35]

Senator Thomas Dodd of Connecticut chaired subcommittee hearings in 1966 to examine the drug craze, eventually supporting "stamping out" such use through criminalization of these substances. Timothy Leary, one of the several witnesses to testify, told the senators, "The challenge of the psychedelic chemicals is not just how to control them, but how to use them." When subcommittee member Senator Ted Kennedy of Massachusetts asked Leary if taking acid was "extremely dangerous," Leary answered, "Sir, the motor car is dangerous if used improperly . . . Human stupidity and ignorance is the only danger human beings face in this world." Leary's recommendation that LSD use be regulated and limited to adults fell on deaf ears; on October 6, 1966, LSD was banned in California. Two years later, a bill sponsored by Dodd and Harley Orrin Staggers of West Virginia made LSD possession illegal in every state.[36]

But by then, LSD had already "shed its lab coat" and moved to the streets, where it has remained ever since. In a span of just a few years, LSD had gone from a miracle drug to a horror drug via what one journalist labeled the "moral panic" of the early 1970s, whereby any rational considerations about it had vanished. Even though study after study had found LSD to be remarkably safe when used in a clinical setting, it was now associated with emergency room visits, suicide attempts, "blown minds, wasted potential, and social chaos." The campaign to truncate the spread of these drugs among the American public also squelched the nascent field of psychedelic research (although, as we will see, after a hiatus of several decades, scientific research on psychedelic pharmacology and therapy has quietly resumed). Amazingly, until the mid-

1960s, there were somewhere around forty thousand research subjects for studies using psychedelics, one thousand published studies, and half a dozen global scientific conferences on LSD, a stunning endorsement of the chemical's seeming potential.[37]

One final footnote on Timothy Leary, whose life stands as a sort of dubious symbol for the wonder and occasional absurdity that are part of the broader story of America's drug war. Leary's first encounter with the police came in late December 1965, when he took his two kids, Jack and Susan, and his girlfriend, Rosemary Woodruff, to Mexico. On their return, U.S. agents discovered a small amount of marijuana in Susan's underwear. Leary, taking responsibility for the pot, was convicted of possession on March 11, 1966, under Harry Anslinger's Marihuana Tax Act of 1937. His sentence included a $30,000 fine, mandatory psychiatric treatment, and thirty years in prison. While appealing the decision, Leary was arrested a second time on December 26, 1968, in Laguna Beach, California, for possession of a couple of "roaches." Leary was again convicted, despite contending that the arresting officer had planted the drugs to frame him. Less than a year later, in *Leary v. United States*, the Supreme Court overturned Leary's earlier conviction from 1965 and declared the Marihuana Tax Act unconstitutional. The same day, Leary announced his candidacy for the governorship of California against the incumbent Republican, Ronald Reagan. In January 1970, in the midst of his political campaign, Leary was sentenced to ten years in prison for the 1968 Laguna Beach offense. Upon his arrival in prison, he was submitted to a battery of psychological tests. As he had created some of these tests himself, he shaped his responses to appear a congenial and law-abiding person with a deep interest in gardening. As a result, he was assigned to a low-security prison with outdoor work duties. The inimitable Leary, once labeled by President Richard Nixon "the most dangerous man in America," staged a dramatic escape and fled overseas, spending time in Algeria and Switzerland before being captured in Afghanistan in 1973 and brought back to California. He spent three more years in U.S. prisons before he was pardoned and released by Governor Jerry Brown in 1976.[38]

10 • Nixon's War

We knew we couldn't make it illegal to be either against the war or
blacks. But by getting the public to associate the hippies with marijuana
and blacks with heroin, and then criminalizing both heavily, we could
disrupt those communities.

—John Ehrlichman, White House aide to Richard Nixon

The Class of Grass

Over the course of the second half of the twentieth century, drug use again
became commonplace among the American middle class. The federal crackdown in the Progressive era—with the Harrison Act and Prohibition—and
Harry Anslinger's ensuing anti-drug crusade made it easy to forget that Americans had ever before flirted with mind-altering substances. This has led
some observers to believe that the 1960s drug boom was strictly the result of
fringe habits and subcultures—things born in Chinatown opium dens, Baltimore ghettos, Harlem jazz clubs, Texas border towns, northern California
communes—leaking into Middle American homes. Such is the analysis offered by Jill Jonnes, who concludes that for white middle-class Americans pursuing the suburban good life, illicit drug use before the late 1960s was a
"remote and irrelevant vice." Jonnes argues that drugs were simply not part of
growing up white and upwardly mobile.

Take Milford Mill High School in Maryland, for example. In the 1950s and
1960s the perennial worries about underage drinking and premarital sex occupied people's attention, but in the fall of 1967, students recalled a "happy ignorance." One student reflected, "When I first came into high school I had never

heard of drugs." One teacher, Robert Rivkin, acknowledged, "I had heard of marijuana and heroin from stories I'd read in magazines and newspapers. But it was
definitely all thug-underworld stuff to me at the time." On Jonnes's reading, all
of this changed in the cultural upheaval that hit the nation in the late 1960s. Suddenly, drugs seemed to be everywhere. The Milford senior class of 1968 was
called the "Class of Grass," partially because the athletic field had been reseeded
that year but mainly because of the students' prodigious pot smoking. Popular
music reflected a "new normal" of mind-altering drugs, from the Beatles' *Sgt.
Pepper's Lonely Hearts Club Band* to Jefferson Airplane's "White Rabbit."[1]

That's one part of the story, certainly, but when we consider it in full historical context, the proliferation of drug use in the three decades after World
War II looks less like an unprecedented and precipitous moral decline than
another phase in a cycle of shifting social attitudes toward drugs, with multiple, periodic ebbs toward acceptance and permissiveness and flows toward
vilification and restriction.

The New War on Addiction

The federal government, spurred by Anslinger, met the rising tide of drug
use with resistance. While Richard Nixon is usually associated with the advent
of the war on drugs, his efforts were only one part of a "postwar presidential
tradition." The issue was already on the Oval Office desk as early as the 1950s.
On November 2, 1951, President Harry S. Truman became the first chief executive to sound the alarm on drugs, declaring them a subject "of grave concern to me." Truman backed the Boggs Act of 1951, a little piece of legislation
that turned out to have big consequences. It was the first federal law to require
mandatory sentences for drug convictions. The key target was marijuana, the
possession of which could now land a person in jail for a minimum of two to
ten years. Truman also appointed an interdepartmental committee on drugs
by executive order, to be led by none other than Harry J. Anslinger. Truman's
successor, President Dwight D. Eisenhower, paused his Thanksgiving golf vacation in 1954 to announce a "new war on narcotics addiction at the local, national, and international level," a bellicose phrasing that echoed Anslinger's
pledge of "relentless warfare."[2]

It is significant that the focus of Eisenhower's concern was drug addiction,
much of which was concentrated at this point among war veterans. The medical
kit distributed to field infantry soldiers in Europe and the Pacific contained an
infamous "quarter grain of morphine sulfate," and some of that quantity eventu-

ally made its way into the black market. As historian Kathleen Frydl explains, "because soldiers' (non-medical) use of morphine remained a quiet (and disquieting) subject for many years after the war, soldiers themselves were left as lone witnesses to illicit morphine use. And recreational use of opiates was by no means a sequestered or individual activity: one World War II soldier recalled that, after being pierced in the lung by a bayonet wielded by a Japanese prisoner of war, he was boosted with morphine in the hospital and, shortly after that, he sought it on his own, making contacts among his fellow soldiers." Eisenhower convened a special cabinet committee to coordinate a national anti-narcotics initiative; its mandate was to run a "national survey of both addiction and law enforcement needs." Two years later, he signed a bill that authorized treatment of regular opiate users in the District of Columbia. "This measure, for the first time, made a civil procedure for the commitment of narcotic drug users in hospitals for treatment and rehabilitation rather than terms in a prison. Eisenhower believed that this was the first step toward addressing the problem of drug addiction."[3]

Eisenhower's acknowledgment that addiction might be a medical condition to be treated rather than a criminal behavior to be reformed was a significant countervailing force against the rush toward stricter law enforcement and punishment in midcentury drug policymaking. Despite these efforts, drug trafficking and use as well as addiction rates continued to rise through the late 1950s. Commissioner Anslinger assured the White House and Capitol Hill that the solution lay in one direction: tougher mandatory sentences.

In another key development, in 1961, the United Nations, in session in New York City, passed the Single Convention on Narcotic Drugs. Despite its banal title, the Single Convention was a milestone in the history of multilateral anti-drug efforts. The agreement codified many prior international treaties and extended existing bans to include the cultivation of plants grown as the raw material for drugs. The convention's ambitious overarching goal was to limit the production, distribution, and possession of drugs to exclusively medical and scientific uses and to combat drug trafficking through international cooperation. While officially multilateral, this was a Washington-crafted agreement that came at a time when most, but certainly not all, ardent drug prohibitionists were Americans. The convention obligated its signatories to cut the supply of illicit drugs, to treat and rehabilitate addicts, and to crack down on traffickers. The range of banned substances was expanded to include coca leaves and cannabis—seemingly minor additions that will play into our story later on. Peru and Bolivia, for instance, were now expected to end coca leaf cultivation within twenty-five years.

Following through on a campaign promise, in late September 1962, President John F. Kennedy launched the first White House Conference on Narcotics and Drug Abuse, a two-day seminar attended by five hundred people, "from cops to governors to psychiatrists." In 1968, Lyndon B. Johnson reinforced the status of narcotics as a law-enforcement concern when, by executive order, he created the Bureau of Narcotics and Dangerous Drugs, transferring all administrative responsibility for drug law from the Departments of the Treasury and Health, Education, and Welfare to the Department of Justice. Like the Harrison Act and the U.N. Single Convention, these seemingly insignificant bureaucratic adjustments had enormous significance for the war on drugs. They would not be, by any stretch of the imagination, the last such moves. Interestingly, Johnson's last attorney general, Ramsey Clark, responded with a more humanitarian approach tilted toward public health. In 1966, when he was still deputy attorney general, Clark pressed Johnson to support the Narcotic Addict Rehabilitation Act passed by Congress that year, which allowed addicts to serve civil sentences under health worker supervision and provided $15 million in funding for drug research and local treatment centers.[4]

At this point, it's worth asking what, exactly, was driving this ramp-up against drugs. The metastasis of Ken Kesey and Timothy Leary's psychedelic utopianism into middle-American youth culture explains some but not all of it. There was another issue at play. Contrast Baltimore's Milford Mill High School, described by Jill Jonnes above, with Charlotte Street, a three-block neighborhood in New York's South Bronx. In 1961, the 41st Precinct recorded eighteen murders, 183 robberies, and 667 burglaries. The prime culprit in this urban decay, according to some observers, was heroin. One resident recalled, "On Charlotte and Minford they sold drugs like they were groceries. They used to carry the drugs in a baby carriage." In 1967 a beat cop described the neighborhood's addicts as a plague of locusts, destroying whatever lay in the swarm's path. "So many people OD'd, we used to get them all the time in the hallways and vacant lots." In 1971 the same precinct saw a fivefold jump in murders and a fifteenfold increase in robberies.[5]

The French Connection

Given its few medical benefits compared to its high risk of addiction, heroin might have passed into history after its initial discovery and experimentation in the late nineteenth century. Instead, it replaced morphine on the streets. The second major wave of opiate addiction in America began with the return of morphine-hooked veterans and the emergence of hipsters and beat-niks in urban centers. Heroin flourished because traffickers discovered that it was stronger, easier to make, and cheaper than morphine. Heroin's highs and lows, too, came faster and with more intensity than those of other opiates. For addicts, the drug cravings were an all-day affair; they needed steady doses to function physically. This made them fantastic customers.

The early heroin world, perhaps best captured in William S. Burroughs's underground classic *Junky*, was a castoff America: homosexuals, artists, itin-erant con men, and jazz musicians.[6] Yet author Sam Quinones points out that, despite its infiltration into hip subcultures, heroin was never just about the "romantic subversion of societal norms." It was also about the squarest of American things: cold, boring commerce. Heroin lent itself to the underworld business model. Dealers organized their heroin distribution networks almost precisely according to business school principles of franchising and trust; it worked, as long as the dealers didn't use the product. It didn't hurt that their customers were "slaves to a take-no-prisoners molecule."

Unlike marijuana, most of which came in from Mexico, heroin was almost exclusively supplied by the vaunted "French Connection," a cooperation be-tween the Sicilian Mafia and Corsican gangsters in Marseilles, France.[7] World War II had disrupted global supply routes such that by the end of the 1930s, heroin was virtually nonexistent on America's urban streets, as we learned earlier. Addicts were substituting "all manner of intoxicants" in its stead.

Mafia boss Charles "Lucky" Luciano and his underworld associate Meyer Lansky had built a thriving heroin distribution network in New York and its environs, supposedly modeled on the licit model of John D. Rockefeller's Standard Oil Trust. Luciano was arrested in connection with a prostitution ring in 1936 but continued to run his operation from prison, until the ambi-tious scheme began to implode under the weight of wartime scarcities and disruptions. An added complication was that American officials were begin-ning to crack down on suspected Fascist subversion around U.S. ports and were more aggressively monitoring the docks where the mob was active. This tense situation gave rise to a quid pro quo, in which the mob bosses gave U.S. intelligence operatives access and ordered their own men to identify German spies or sympathizers, and in return, the feds allowed the mob to attack union organizers who were agitating at the ports. During the wartime years, scores of dock laborers were killed, their cases never solved.[8]

Luciano also bolstered communication between exiled Sicilian gangsters in America and Old World connections to retrieve intelligence that was used to plan the U.S. invasion and occupation of Sicily in 1942. U.S. officials "expressed [their] gratitude" by installing mob bosses as leaders of occupied Italy, from which positions the beneficiaries murdered Communist rivals and resumed the heroin trade. New York governor Thomas Dewey even freed Luciano in January 1946. Later that month, Luciano was deported as a condition of his parole to Sicily, where he reportedly set up shop as the head of a "worldwide dope syndicate."[9]

In 1950, Italian authorities intervened to prevent a pharmaceutical firm from legally selling heroin to Luciano. The move was backed by Anslinger's FBN. In an early example of the perennial "balloon effect," the crime boss simply joined forces with the Corsican mob, which was already involved in the heroin trade and, it just so happened, had muscled its way into the Marseilles market. The French Connection was born. It would supply almost all of America's heroin over the next two decades. In the same period, the network suffered not a single major bust. The reticence might have stemmed from the CIA's preference not to crack down on the Corsican mob for Cold War–related national security reasons. As is often the case, drug war concerns are often subsumed by larger domestic and foreign policy considerations.[10]

New York City was now ground zero in the growing heroin trade. First sold on the streets of Manhattan, junk would be "distributed by endlessly replenished immigrant or black gangs" up and down the East Coast and into the heartland. Quinones explains that heroin, unlike marijuana or wine, is a "commodity, like sugar, and usually varies solely in how much it's cut—that is, diluted—or how well it's been processed and refined." Dealers quickly learned that they needed to pursue forceful marketing tactics to differentiate what was a largely uniform product. A new generation of Italian mobsters pursued just such a strategy after seizing a large share of the trade in the 1950s. As is often the case with new drug markets, they got their start by giving away free samples to potential buyers. The rest, they say, was history: "Their weak dope made injecting it popular. Injecting heroin sent what little heroin was in the dose directly to the brain, maximizing euphoria. Injecting begot nasty public health problems—among them, later, ferocious rates of hepatitis C and HIV." In 1961, a heroin shortage sent usually discreet heroin users "ricocheting around the city" searching for drugs—bringing what had been a private vice out into the public domain and quite suddenly making it very difficult for authorities to ignore.[11]

One of the Foremost Social Problems in the United States

The Vietnam War and the half million U.S. soldiers deployed to the Indo-chinese Peninsula made up the central campaign issue of the 1968 presidential election. But for a "Silent Majority" of Americans who had watched almost two dozen cities set ablaze in the 1968 summer race riots and who had been led to believe that drugs were everywhere, domestic order was the greater worry. Conditioned by several years spent in New York City outside of public service, Republican candidate Richard Nixon believed "that the narcotics problem and the high crime rate associated with it had become one of the foremost social problems in the United States and had to be stopped, whatever the cost." The assessment rang true for just enough voters to give Nixon a plurality of less than a percentage point in the popular vote. Upon taking office, Nixon set out to deal with drugs not as a tangential or cynical campaign promise but as a central policy objective. What had been "middling priorities" in the Johnson administration—getting France to clamp down on heroin, Turkey and Mexico on opium—was now an priority for the executive branch.[12]

Jill Jonnes observed that had heroin not been freely available only in the "crumbling netherworlds of urban America"—places like the Bronx's Charlotte Street—it is unlikely that the Nixon administration would have been so exercised about the drug scourge. Yet, as Senator Harold Hughes of Iowa, a leading congressional expert on addiction, observed, when heroin "moved out of the ghettos and into the suburbs and small towns and it moved right next door, that's when it became a crisis." As we'll see, the 1970s heroin outbreak was not the last time that an opiate problem would spread from marginal communities to whiter, wealthier parts of the nation—and then magically become a political priority on a national basis.[13]

Grass Intercepted

On July 14, 1969, President Richard M. Nixon announced with much fanfare his "national attack on narcotics abuse." One reason for the alacrity on the drug issue was that Nixon had a campaign promise to uphold. Back in September 1968, just two months before the presidential vote, he had spoken in southern California's conservative Orange County, where he told the largely white, middle-class audience that as president he would "move against the source of drugs."[14] The July 1969 message to Congress decried the explosion in drug use—juvenile arrests for drug possession had surged by 800 percent between 1960 and 1967—as a "growing menace to the welfare of the United States." The president continued, "It is doubtful that an American parent can send a son or daughter to college today without exposing the young man or woman to drug abuse." Indeed, Nixon was convinced that illegal drug abuse in America had reached epidemic levels. He blamed the surge on myriad sources: Vietnam, paraphernalia shops, sympathetic media coverage, and "youthful disenchantment with mainstream culture." Marijuana and heroin were the main culprits; cocaine was quietly making a comeback from its Victorian-era peak but still remained out of reach of most drug users.[15]

Along these lines, Nixon's cabinet-level Special Presidential Task Force Relating to Narcotics, Marihuana, and Dangerous Drugs reported that Mexican-supplied cannabis traffickers were "largely responsible for the marihuana and drug abuse problem" in the country. In a harbinger of the "supply side" war on drugs, the task force recommended "a concerted frontal attack on the illegal importation into and subsequent illegal sale and use of marijuana, narcotics and dangerous drugs into the United States."[16]

On September 21, 1969, the backup of cars and trucks at the San Ysidro Port of Entry in San Diego, California, stretched for miles into the Mexican desert. Ordinarily, U.S. Customs officials would have waved through nineteen out of twenty vehicles without an inspection. But this day was different. They searched everyone, looking for a particular psychoactive substance. Similar searches were conducted all along the two-thousand-mile border with Mexico. This was day 1 of Operation Intercept—the kind of name American officials compulsively give to substantial law enforcement campaigns. The goal: reduce the amount of marijuana smuggled into the United States from Mexico. As has been the case in many succeeding efforts, there were initial positive results. That day 493 drug runners were apprehended at the border. A few weeks later, the program's name was changed to Operation Cooperation, reflecting the Mexican police's coordinated effort to torch marijuana plants in northern Mexico.[17]

Yet the blowback from the three-week operation was immediate: economic disruption on both sides of the border and major logistical headaches for commuters and legitimate import-export traders. What is more, marijuana traffickers in the United States simply turned to other source countries, Thailand in particular, to meet American consumer demand. They simultaneously began importing hashish, concentrated cannabis oil, from North Africa and the Middle East to substitute for the Mexican sinsemilla. And, ironically, tougher border inspections had the long-term consequence of sparking new sinsemilla cultivation north of the border, a situation that even today helps to make agriculture one of northern California's primary industries. What's more, the Mexican and U.S. media had a field day deriding Intercept's Keystone Kops–like elements. *Time* magazine titled its account "Operation Impossible."[18]

Doubling down, in 1970 Nixon signed the Comprehensive Drug Abuse and Control Act, which superseded all other federal anti-drug laws. More than any other, this piece of legislation is responsible for shaping the domestic drug war as we know it. The law produced a new framework for thinking about drugs that has remained the dominant model for policymakers and for much of the American public. This framework was called scheduling. The Controlled Substances Act, a section of the 1970 comprehensive law, classified drugs into "schedules," with distinctive regulations, controls, and penalties at each level. Drugs were placed into one of five schedules depending on the government's estimation of the potential for abuse, the accepted medical use and safety, and the potential for physical and physiological dependence. Heroin, cannabis, and most hallucinogens were judged to be unsafe and to have a high level for abuse with no known medical application. In August 1970, a senior federal public health official named Roger O. Egeberg urged that marijuana be classified as a Schedule I substance, a designation it kept over the next half-century. Here is how Egeberg explained his decision: "Since there is still a considerable void in our knowledge of the plant and effects of the active drug contained in it, our recommendation is that marihuana be retained within schedule I at least until the completion of certain studies now underway to resolve this issue." In subsequent decades, drug war critics would often contend that there was in fact scientific evidence for safe medical use of cannabis—as the La Guardia Committee report of 1944, for instance, detailed—and that scheduling made it unnecessarily difficult to conduct potentially beneficial research. Today, mescaline is thought to have potential as a treatment for alcoholism and depression, but its Schedule I listing limits its availability to drug researchers. As with LSD, only a few studies testing mescaline's potential therapeutic effects have been conducted since the early 1970s.[19]

Cocaine, amphetamine, and opium were among the drugs placed in Schedule II: they had high potential for abuse but accepted medical benefits. Tobacco and alcohol remained unscheduled. All told, by 1970 more than fifty federal drug laws (not including alcohol laws) had been passed to tighten the Harrison Act; state legislatures enacted hundreds of others. America's punitive drug war was now in full swing—even if it was being waged more aggressively at home than abroad.[20]

Drug scheduling did not arise out of the blue. Two species of drug use were flourishing at rates the United States hadn't seen since the late 1800s: recreational consumption and full-time addiction. And the reports coming in from the field looked dire. In predominantly African-American urban settings, 10 percent of males were using heroin. As an example, according to a 1973 report, in certain especially vulnerable neighborhoods in Washington, D.C., the percentage of males born in 1953 who became addicted to heroin exceeded 25 percent. A present-day study of one East Harlem block in New York City reported that one-third of teens interviewed for a study in 1965 had subsequently become heroin addicts.[21]

The urban heroin epidemic was rivaled by another pernicious drug abuse scourge: heroin use among American GIs in Vietnam. The infamous "no. 4 heroin" was everywhere, sold by teenage girls at roadside stands on the key highway that connected Saigon to the U.S. Army base at Long Binh. In Saigon, pushers peddled hits of 95 percent pure heroin for the numerous GIs in the city. These aggressive sales efforts led to predictable results. In late 1970 Army doctors surveyed a few thousand soldiers and learned that almost 12 percent had tried heroin since arriving in Vietnam, and 7 percent were still using it regularly. As was recorded in Alfred McCoy's seminal account *The Politics of Heroin in Southeast Asia*, the U.S. Army estimated that 10 to 15 percent of the soldiers deployed in Vietnam, an astounding 25,000 to 37,000 men, were regular heroin users.[22]

A U.S. congressional delegation returning from Vietnam warned that a similar number of troops were actually addicted to heroin. Here is how Major Richard Ratner, a New York City psychiatrist treating addicts at the Long Binh base, described the drug crisis. "Vietnam in many ways is a ghetto for the enlisted man," he said. "The soldiers don't want to be here, their living conditions are bad, they are surrounded by privileged classes, namely officers; there is accepted use of violence, and there is promiscuous sex. They react the way they do in a ghetto. They take drugs and try to forget. What most of them say when they come into the center, however, is that they took to heroin because of the boredom and hassle of life here."[23]

Celerino Castillo III, a former U.S. Drug Enforcement Administration (DEA) agent from Texas and a Vietnam veteran, recalled the effects heroin abuse had on American troops and ways they dealt with the stateside moral shame of GIs succumbing to this potent drug. "If the [heroin-overdosed] soldier was well liked, someone would pump a bullet in his body, and the family would be told he'd died a hero's death. If the consensus was that the dead soldier had been an asshole, he would be sent home with nothing more than needle pricks in his arms." A former gang member, Luis Rodriguez, described the impact on local communities. "A lot of poor working-class kids were sent to war, and they came back traumatized, addicted to heroin and knowing how to kill people. And they contributed to the gangs [in California], making them better organized, and probably a little nuttier." The American media's breathless coverage of the heroin crisis in South Vietnam fueled a perception that the situation was out of control and that it was only a matter of time before the GI heroin zombies would return home. In May 1971 the *Washington Post* ran a front-page article headlined "GI Sales in Vietnam: Cheap, Fast, Ignored by Police," in which soldiers laughingly affirmed that heroin was still as plentiful as ever. "You can go anywhere, ask anyone, they'll get it for you. It won't take but a few seconds."[24]

As has been widely written, much of the U.S. military's heroin epidemic in South Vietnam was an unforced error. In the cause of "cultivating anticommunist allies in the byzantine world of Southeast Asia," the CIA established ties with warlords in the Golden Triangle, where Laos, Burma, and Thailand come together. These dons expanded their poppy cultivations and sent potent heroin throughout Southeast Asia, using helicopters and airplanes to "supplant mules and sampans." By 1970 Golden Triangle heroin had inundated South Vietnam, addicting first the GIs and then the Vietnamese.[25]

The King Helps Out

With domestic drug use becoming mainstream, the Nixon administration pondered how it might respond to this multifaceted dilemma. The evolving drug culture debate certainly had its surreal moments. One of these came on December 21, 1970, when Elvis Presley visited the White House. The previous day Presley had appeared at the exterior gates of the White House complex to deliver a handwritten letter addressed to Nixon in which he stated his unequivocal opposition to "the drug culture, hippy elements, and Black Panthers." He added that he wanted nothing but to "help the country out" and requested to be designated a "federal agent-at-large" the following day. Elvis met Nixon in the West Wing and gave him a gift of a World War II–era Colt .45 pistol. The iconic photograph of the two star-crossed men shows Nixon in his suit and tie and Elvis in tight purple velvet trousers, a purple jacket tossed over his shoulders, and a large belt buckle framing his middle. The two men agreed that "those who use drugs are in the vanguard of American protest."

Two weeks later, Nixon wrote Elvis a note thanking him for the Colt .45, but declining to recruit the pop star in the war on drugs. Subsequent private correspondence among Nixon's staff suggests some ambivalence surrounding Presley's utility. In an interoffice memo crafted on the morning of Presley's visit, White House aide Dwight Chapin suggested that if the president wanted to meet "bright young people outside the government, Presley might be the one to start with." In response, H. R. Haldeman, Nixon's chief of staff, scribbled, "You must be kidding." Elvis Presley died from heart failure in 1977. The coroner could not ascertain the causes of death, but many have hypothesized that the ten drugs found in his bloodstream at the time of death may have contributed. Elvis was known to use Dilaudid, Percodan, Placidyl, dexedrine, biphetamine, Tuinal, Desbutal, Ecatrol, Amytal, quaaludes, Carbital, Seconal, methadone, and Ritalin. Thus were the paradoxes and hypocrisy of the drug war manifest in this tragic American soul.[26]

Quantum Leap

What is especially remarkable about Nixon's aggressive approach to the drug issue is how quickly his administration brought it to the highest levels of domestic and foreign policymaking, even though the nation was mired in a tragic and unpopular war. Drugs were not being dealt with by anonymous White House aides or assistant secretaries of state or defense but by the administration's most senior servants: the president, National Security Adviser Henry Kissinger, Secretary of State William Rogers, Secretary of Defense Melvin Laird, Attorney General John Mitchell, and presidential adviser Daniel Patrick Moynihan.[27]

In 1969 Nixon ordered the State and Justice Departments to prepare a policy recommendation for combating heroin trafficking from abroad, "regardless of foreign policy consequences." When the young Moynihan swept through Paris in August 1969, he informed the U.S. embassy's chargé d'affaires of Washington's decision to make international drug trafficking the highest of priorities, which elicited cooperation and puzzlement. The American diplomat knew virtually nothing about the subject and had no inkling that the White House was worried about it. Moynihan later reflected, "There was a quantum leap in the amounts of money, executive energy, and White House concern with the problem after 1969."[28]

The American ambassador to France, Sargent Shriver, soon raised the heroin question with Paris. Secretary of State Rogers discussed opium poppy numbers with his Turkish counterpart. American officials met with Mexican authorities to discuss the ill-fated Operation Intercept. In the fall of 1969, Attorney General Mitchell suggested to Nixon a series of "recommendations for an intensified international heroin control program." Kissinger directed the White House Task Force on Heroin to "prepare a detailed diplomatic scenario." Nixon reached out to recently elected president Georges Pompidou in France. Pompidou agreed to cooperate, even if he disputed Nixon's belief that over three-quarters of the world's heroin passed through his country.[29]

Nixon remained anxious about the lack of progress at home, as well as the unfolding "drug mess in the quagmire" of Vietnam. In a protracted meeting on June 3, 1971, he gave a tongue-lashing to several cabinet members and White House staffers. One participant's notes from the meeting recorded, "President told group . . . crapping around will not be tolerated. . . . [We] have tried to persuade our allies, Turkey and France, of the importance of heroin traffic to the US. We will be tough with our allies now and will put more emphasis on solving the problem, than on diplomatic niceties. . . . [The] president expressed concern that some of the public, especially some employers, view the Vietnam veteran as a ruthless killer and a junkie, and therefore he cannot get a job." Days later Nixon led a similar "laying-down-the-law meeting" for CIA director Richard Helms and U.S. envoys to Turkey, France, and several Southeast Asian nations.[30]

There were some modest victories. As most heroin was thought to have originated in Turkey, the Nixon administration pressured the Turkish government to ban opium cultivation. Ankara agreed to act in 1971, but only in return for $27 million in compensation to farmers. A euphoric Nixon called Prime Minister Nihat Erim to Washington to "share the limelight" when the news was made public. However, Turkish politics led to a rescinding of the ban, which provoked plenty of chatter from Capitol Hill about unreliable allies. Tighter oversight by Turkish authorities did drive a steep drop in heroin production in that country, but there were other weak links in the chain. Despite American pleading, Paris had not closed a single heroin laboratory in Marseilles for several years, and heroin was still "pouring out of [the city]."[31]

NORML

It was in 1971 that Nixon most dramatically turned up the rhetorical volume on the drug crisis. Before Congress and the American public that year, Nixon called drug abuse a "national emergency" and "public enemy number one." He implored Congress to furnish the "authority and the funds to match our moral resources." For Nixon, the question was "not whether we will conquer drug abuse, but how soon."[32] This escalation led to at least one interesting ideological development. It pushed several prominent conservative thinkers to come out in favor of drug liberalization. At the beginning of the decade, Nixon appointed a National Commission on Marihuana and Drug Abuse, chaired by former Pennsylvania governor Ray Shafer. In 1972, the commission made waves when it issued a 1,184-page report, "Marihuana: A Signal of Misunderstanding," that concluded that "the existing anti-cannabis law are excruciatingly anachronistic." It further argued that while "marihuana was not an innocuous drug," intermittent pot use "carries minimal risk to public health." The commission recommended removing cannabis from the Schedule I designation and decriminalizing possession. It was so sensational that Signet books hurried a condensed 223-page paperback edition to press. Nixon told the press, "I read it and reading it did not change my mind." The Nixon White House quietly ignored the commission's work. "The line against the use of dangerous drugs is now drawn on this side of marijuana." Nixon declared. "If we move the line to the other side and accept the use of this drug, how can we draw the line against other illegal drugs?" Yet this did not prevent others from acting on its findings.[33]

The redoubtable William F. Buckley Jr., the "most influential conservative public intellectual in the country at the time," endorsed the report. Concerned that anti-cannabis conservatives were alienating the youth vote, Buckley and his magazine, *National Review,* came out in support of legalization. They took the libertarian view that if people self-medicated with drugs and it didn't harm others, then it was none of the government's damned business. In 1972, *National Review* ran an edgy cover story by Richard Cowan, the Ivy League–educated director of the right-wing student organization Young Americans for Freedom. Cowan argued that marijuana proscription insulted core conservative principles: "The hysterical myths about marijuana . . . have led conservatives to condone massive programs of social engineering, interference in the affairs of individuals, monstrous bureaucratic waste."[34]

Interestingly, Cowan was also an early advocate of the National Organization for the Reform of Marijuana Laws (NORML), then as now the preeminent cannabis legalization outfit in the United States. NORML was hatched in 1970 by an attorney named Keith Stroup with a $5,000 gift from the Playboy Foundation. The organization's advisers included pediatrician Benjamin Spock, former deputy director of the Bureau of Narcotics and Dangerous Drugs John

Finlater, and Harvard Medical School faculty member and psychiatrist Dr. Lester Grinspoon. Though it later expanded, NORML was first a legal effort to get cannabis taken off the list of Schedule I controlled substances so that it could be prescribed by physicians.[35]

Another group that took issue with Nixon's war was Legalize Marijuana (LEMAR), an unlikely alliance between the radical left and libertarians. In 1964, Lowell Eggemeier, a "lone crusader," had sparked up a joint in front of San Francisco's police headquarters, telling the officers who swarmed to arrest him, "I am starting a campaign to legalize marijuana smoking. I wish to be arrested." Eggemeier's "puff-in" got him a felony drug possession charge and just under a year in prison. Arch-libertarian attorney James R. White III got wind of the episode and promptly asked the California Supreme Court to release the "Haight Ashbury peacenik." White contended that the standing

Allen Ginsberg leading a group of demonstrators outside the Women's House of Detention in Greenwich Village, January 10, 1965, demanding the release of prisoners arrested for use or possession of marijuana (Library of Congress, Prints and Photographs Division, Washington, D.C.)

legal penalties, based on the designation of cannabis as a banned drug, contra-
dicted the constitutional proscription on cruel and unusual punishment. That
same year, Eggemeier established LEMAR. The organization began publishing a "hip zine," *The Marijuana Review,* where readers could get "detailed
reports on the price of pot, what was available on the street, legal and scientific developments, activist campaigns, and other examples of reefer rabble-
rousing." Allen Ginsberg helped create a local LEMAR chapter in New York.
"The universal fear of marijuana was so great that no one would talk openly
about it on a bus," Ginsberg reflected. "You couldn't talk about changing the
law, much less about smoking grass, for fear you would be arrested." Ginsberg wrote an article in the *Atlantic Monthly* titled "The Great Marijuana Hoax:
First Manifesto to End the Bringdown." In the piece, Ginsberg argued that the
Federal Narcotics Bureau had perpetrated an "insane hoax on public consciousness" and linked the prohibition on marijuana to the "suppression of
Negro rights."[36]

Narcotics agents pose with more than four hundred pounds of marijuana hidden
in suitcases, 1963 (Library of Congress, Prints and Photographs Division,
Washington, D.C.)

In 1972, NORML held the inaugural "People's Pot Conference" at a church on Capitol Hill. The hundreds of "delegates" included "an unusual mix of long-haired leftists, suit-and-tie liberals, and conservative libertarians, underscoring that marijuana law reform was a 'big tent' issue whose time had arrived." By the end of the 1970s, twelve states would decriminalize simple cannabis possession, though some of these rules would subsequently be rolled back under pressure from parent advocacy groups in the Reagan era.

The War on Drugs

In 1973, Nixon made an announcement that most observers today consider America's official declaration of war on drugs: by executive order he unveiled the Drug Enforcement Administration to lead the federal effort in an "all-out global war on the drug menace." Harry Anslinger's unyielding logic from the 1950s aptly described what the DEA would be all about. In his words: "We intend to get the killer-pushers and their willing customers out of selling and buying dangerous drugs. The answer to the problem is simple—get rid of drug pushers and users. Period."[37] A bureaucratic behemoth formed from the union of several federal agencies, Nixon's DEA embodied the idea that we could win the drug war at home by disrupting production and transportation abroad. For many observers, this was a crucial bridge to cross in the ideological battle over drugs—it opened the gates for a slew of, at the best of times, cooperative multilateral efforts, and at the worst of times, interventionist policy debacles. Nixon himself likely could not have imagined that his metaphorical war would span five decades, cost a trillion dollars, and be met with as much skepticism and controversy as any policy initiative in American history. The DEA launched in July 1973 with 1,500 personnel and an annual budget of $75 million; in 2016, those figures were, respectively, 5,000 agents and $2.7 billion. DEA agents were active in sixty-three countries.

By the mid-1970s, Mexico had replaced Southeast Asia as the main producer of heroin destined for the U.S. market. Overcoming its initial reluctance, Mexico City in 1975 gave the United States sweeping authority to assist with Operation Condor, an aggressive poppy and marijuana eradication campaign. Foreshadowing operations in Colombian coca fields three decades later, thousands of Mexican soldiers were deployed into cultivation areas, accompanied by the Mexican Federal Police and U.S. DEA agents. Drug fields were mapped with imagery from U.S. surveillance planes and satellites and then eradicated by aerial spraying of chemical defoliants. Troops leaped out of helicopters to secure the areas and destroy any remaining crops. In Mexico, the program was known as the "la campaña permanente," or the permanent campaign. Operation Condor initially looked like a victory: in the United States, heroin's purity and overdoses dropped as prices increased. Soon enough, though, poppy cultivation in Iran, Burma, and Afghanistan picked up the slack. This was not enough to preclude Condor from becoming a model crop eradication program for other source countries, including Bolivia, Peru, and Colombia, in the decades to follow.[38]

In another ultimately ephemeral triumph, the heroin epidemic peaked in the mid-1970s. This was likely due to the combination of overseas supply reduction, which included banning opium in Turkey, spraying fields in Mexico, and breaking up the vaunted French Connection trafficking route. The chief of preventive medicine at New Haven's Department of Health wrote in *U.S. News & World Report:* "We have arrived at a turning point in the heroin epidemic. In New Haven, as in many other cities, overdose and death due to this drug have become a rarity, and the number of persons coming under care for detoxification is showing a sharp decline." The number of addicts had plunged across the nation, from 300,000 to 150,000 in only a few years. The data did suggest a remarkable success. In 1973, the rates of overdose deaths, drug-related hepatitis, and property crimes—all indicators of heroin addiction—fell throughout most of the country. Mission accomplished, it seemed.[39]

Just as only a staunch anticommunist could have presided over détente with the Soviets and the opening of Red China, only a "law and order Republican" could have spearheaded the soft approach to America's drug use and addiction crisis. Nixon appointed Dr. Jerome Jaffe, a Chicago specialist in addiction and treatment, to take charge of the "demand" side of the drug crisis as the new White House Special Action Office for Drug Abuse Prevention. Dr. Jaffe's central belief was that if sufficient treatment was available, "no one could say he committed a crime to get drugs because he couldn't get treatment. I believed that only this way would our society make the distinction between the habitual criminal who happens to use illicit drugs but who would be involved in crime anyway, and those who in the absence of drug use and the high price of illicit drugs might have achieved a law-abiding if unconventional social adjustment."[40]

The boldest and most controversial of Nixon's progressive demand-side policies involved legalizing a controversial and addictive member of the opiate family, the synthetic opiate methadone, and then making it available to addicts through government clinics, the first of their kind since the 1920s.

German scientists first synthesized methadone in an effort to make the Nazi war effort medically self-sufficient. The Allies took the patent following the war; Eli Lilly and Company introduced the drug into the American market in 1947. In searching for ways to aid heroin addicts, Dr. Vincent Dole, an addiction expert at the Rockefeller Institute in New York City, noticed that methadone was the only opiate available whose addicts did not demand more doses every couple of hours. They were simply content with the same dose once a day, carrying them through the next twenty-four hours. And unlike heroin addicts, methadone addicts seemed to be able to talk about more than where their next fix was coming from. Dole concluded that addicts could be "maintained" on methadone indefinitely; one dose a day and they could function as regular citizens. In New York City in 1970, Dole established the first methadone clinic for heroin addicts.[41]

Concerned about returning Vietnam vets, the pragmatic Nixon administration supported efforts to set up drug clinics that included methadone as a treatment option. Nixon's spending backed this up: treatment dominated federal anti-drug spending from 1971 to 1975. Federally funded treatment centers grew from sixty to four hundred, with some eighty thousand methadone "slots" opening up across the country. The clinics showed how a powerful narcotic could be dispensed in a safe, clinical environment. Methadone stabilized an addict and allowed him to find employment or repair strained relationships. As Sam Quinones writes, "There were also no dirty needles, no crime, and addicts couldn't be robbed at the clinics." Methadone undercut street dealers, replacing their trade in an often impure and dangerous substance with a safer and more reliable product.[42]

Yet, methadone maintenance was not the magic bullet first envisioned, in part due to growing public opposition to maintaining addicts on methadone indefinitely. At first, methadone was typically dispensed with the intent to eliminate the addiction, dose by dose. Problems arose when the clinics became "for-profit affairs" and restricted the counseling and therapy that might have helped the patients kick the opiate addiction entirely. Critics came to see some clinic owners as drug dealers, "stringing patients out for years, and charging twenty and thirty times what the drug actually cost," which came to about fifty cents a dose.[43]

A racial component came into play as well, as most heroin users and methadone patients were African-American. Some activists denounced the treatment program as a white plot to keep blacks permanently addicted. The U.S. General Accounting Office would find in the early 1990s that around 50 percent of clinics provided substandard care. As Quinones explains, methadone clinics nationwide maintained core populations of opiate addicts on too-small doses and without necessary therapy. Meanwhile, addicts who did not receive doses that were strong enough craved another opiate later in the afternoon when the clinics were closed. They turned to the street to score a hit, and thus returned to the heroin underworld. Incredibly, at clinics that combined low doses and insufficient therapy, "addicts took to using methadone and heroin interchangeably."

Before that came to light, in the mid-1970s, a few years after my birth in 1971, Americans had good reason to believe that foreign interdiction and domestic treatment were winning the battle against heroin. Sadly, I wrote this book at a time when the nation was enduring yet another—and this time even deadlier—heroin plague.[44]

11 · Reagan's War

"The Champagne of Drugs"

If the first half of the 1970s was the drug war's infancy, the second was its coming of age. The Haight-Ashbury counterculture burned out or straightened out. The nation witnessed a second heroin epidemic that terrified politicians and tore open the social fabric of inner cities across America. And yet, societal acceptance and use of drugs continued to grow. The National Household Survey on Drug Abuse began using a new metric in the early 1970s that included a question about drug use in the "last month." Slicing the respondents pool into four age cohorts, it asked about tobacco, marijuana, heroin, psychedelics, even some inhalants. In its first report in 1972, 7 percent of the youngest cohort (twelve- to seventeen-year-olds) had used either marijuana or hashish in the previous month, jumping to 12 percent in 1976 and just under 17 percent in 1979.[1]

In this increasingly permissive context, cocaine made its grand reentry. Recall that a century earlier, a three-decade "cocaine frenzy" in the United States had culminated in the country's first comprehensive drug law, the Harrison Act of 1914. Now, cocaine supplied by enterprising and ruthless Colombian traffickers came to grip America like no other drug before it.[2] Mainstream magazines like *Newsweek* began characterizing cocaine as "the status symbol of the American middle-class pothead." Even a senior official in Chicago's Bureau of Narcotics advised, "You get a good high with coke and you don't get hooked." The Haight-Ashbury Clinic in San Francisco reported that "in its pharmacologic action, cocaine . . . reinforces and boosts what we recognize as the highest aspirations of American initiative, energy, frenetic achievement, and ebullient optimism even in the face of great odds." In an "uncanny repeat" of a *New York Times* editorial comment of 1885, the paper's *Magazine* in 1974 ran an article, "Cocaine: The Champagne of Drugs," describing how "for its devotees, cocaine epitomizes the best of drug culture—which is to say, a good high achieved without the forbiddingly dangerous needle." One observer likened it to "flying to Paris for breakfast"; another called it "God's way of saying you've got too much money."[3] Coke was "currency, energy, excitement, power itself." It enabled a frenetic pace of work life and nightlife "when people went out night after night until late in the morning and then somehow had to show up for jobs the next day."[4]

Urban Americans' social tolerance of the drug continued to surge in the latter half of the seventies. Moviegoers burst out laughing when Woody Allen sneezed into a mound of cocaine in his movie *Annie Hall* in 1977. The offensive line of the Pittsburgh Steelers partied the night away with a cocaine dealer two days before playing (and winning) the Super Bowl in 1979. Two years later, *Time* ran a cover article that named cocaine the "all-American drug," calling it the "drug of choice for perhaps millions of solid, conventional and often upwardly mobile citizens." It was too expensive to be more than the occasional indulgence for anyone other than wealthy users. The poor could not afford the drug, and addicts were virtually nonexistent as late as 1976, the year that a book co-authored by Harvard Medical School psychiatrist Lester Grinspoon cast aspersions on earlier research showing cocaine's deleterious effects: "The most significant fact about cocaine today is that it is rapidly attaining unofficial respectability in the same way as marijuana in the 1960s. It is accepted as a relatively innocuous stimulant, casually used by those who can afford it to brighten the day or evening."[5] The hype caused the drug's price to skyrocket, from fifty dollars for a single gram in the 1970s to three times as much in the early part of the next decade. The "white lady" produced billions in profit, inestimably more than marijuana or heroin. And most of these ill-gotten gains went to Colombia.

Kings of Coke

Longtime Miami residents sometimes speak of the 1970s and 1980s in almost nostalgic tones. In a 2005 memoir, Carlos Suárez de Jesús, a former waiter at the Mutiny Hotel, a notorious drug joint, writes of cocaine's takeover: "Around town the lure of easy cash was leading friends to dabble in the drug trade's quick-strike opportunities. Guys I knew who were perennially broke and literally stealing food from the backs of parked Holsum bread trucks weeks earlier would drop by my job in brand-new BMWs, waving their Rolexes in the

air. Some had been driving coke shipments to New York or Chicago for their
employers, others had been unloading boats by moonlight. It was remarkable
how they shrugged off the risks and bragged only of the money."[6]

Miami Herald crime reporters Guy Gugliotta and Jeff Leen reported in their
riveting book *Kings of Cocaine* how the longstanding balance of power between
Colombian suppliers and Cuban middlemen in south Florida had managed to
keep violence at bay. Colombians purchased the leaf and semi-processed base in
Bolivia and Peru, turned it into cocaine in their own country, and then shipped
it north. Sometime in the mid-1970s, the Colombians started cutting out
the middlemen, and within a few years their mobs controlled nearly all of the
Miami market. With this shift came a new dynamic. Surging demand kept the
profits soaring. A kilogram of cocaine, the standard unit of measure in the illicit
business, sold for $51,000, up from $34,000 a year earlier. Miami became "a
boomtown, and cocaine was its currency, filling its banks with laundered cash
and its nightclubs with Latin men." That year, illegal cocaine imports were reckoned to be Florida's biggest source of revenue, estimated around $10 billion
wholesale. The following year, the U.S. Customs Service and the IRS jointly
launched Operation Greenback, targeting the pocketbooks of Colombian traffickers. Greenback succeeded in nabbing a young Colombian woman at Miami
International Airport "trying to smuggle $1.5 million in cash out of the country
in six Monopoly boxes." That amount of money seemed significant then.[7]

Another upshot of the Colombian takeover was an uptick in violent crime.
Weapons were ubiquitous. More than two hundred thousand firearms were
sold in the city in the late 1970s. In 1980, a quarter of the city's murders were
committed with machine guns. The *Miami Herald* story that followed the sensational headline "Shoot-Out at the Cocaine Corral" detailed a string of extraordinary drug-driven executions: victims shot to death while "sitting in noontime
traffic" and bullet-ridden bodies dumped in the Florida Everglades. Each year
the body count set new records, from 349 in 1979 to 569 in 1980 to 621 the
following year. This continued into the 1980s. For several years, Miami-Dade
County ("Miami-Dead," according to the gallows humor of the time) was the
murder capital of the country.[8]

The Dawn of the "War on Drugs"

When I was in middle school in 1985, my mother volunteered as a chaper-
one for one of my older brother's high school graduation dances. Over breakfast the following morning she calmly relayed to me how one of the security

guards at the dance hall in San Francisco had discovered a discarded vial of cocaine outside one of the bathroom stalls and had apparently tried to shut down the party. Though not a drug user herself, my mother was nonetheless convinced that the guard had totally overreacted to a minor incident. My mom probably was not yet aware of the fact that cocaine was once again the source of a major public health problem.

As cocaine use exploded, it produced an equal and opposite counterreaction. Young and middle-aged workaholic Wall Street executives and bond traders with no previous medical history turned up at drug clinics in droves, begging for help with their coke habits. Many were turned away on the assumption that cocaine was not addictive. But high-profile cases, such as comedian Richard Pryor's near death from burns incurred while freebasing cocaine in 1980 and actor John Belushi's death from a "speedball" overdose in 1982, brought new attention to the drug's risks. Bestselling novels like *Bright Lights, Big City* and *Less than Zero* chronicled a young generation wasting itself on "Bolivian marching powder." After having promoted cocaine just a few years before, that well-known arbiter of Baby Boomer coolness *Rolling Stone* magazine ran the headline, "How to Get Off Cocaine." It warned readers that the substance "has enjoyed a far better reputation than it deserved. There is now a belated recognition that the drug is addicting. While cocaine doesn't produce the physical symptoms of narcotic withdrawal, continued use—by snorting, smoking and shooting—can lead to severe dependency."[9]

In December 1981 several prominent Florida industrialists—including Eastern Airlines chairman Frank Borman and Knight-Ridder newspapers chairman Alvah H. Chapman Jr.—made a trip to Ronald Reagan's White House in the manner of a "cow-town sheriff calling on the U.S. marshal." These civic leaders had joined together to form Miami Citizens Against Crime.

Early the following year, the Reagan administration established an executive branch task force chaired by Vice President George H. W. Bush to confront the south Florida trade. The president correctly identified Miami as the nation's central spot for illegal drugs from abroad. A "federal posse" comprising hundreds of officials from DEA, Customs, FBI, IRS, and other agencies would come to the beleaguered region's rescue. The task force beefed up the number of judges, prosecutors, and police in Miami, as well as military radar and surveillance tools—which "until we changed the law, could not be done." The Pentagon contributed Vietnam War–era U.S. Army Cobra helicopters and U.S. Navy Hawkeye E2-C surveillance planes to aid in the search for illicit maritime trafficking. South Florida appeared to welcome the federal help. "U.S. Cavalry Is Coming, and It's About Time," trumpeted the *Miami Herald.*[10]

On October 2, 1982, Reagan used his national radio address from Camp David to expound his goals for the drug war. He complained that "for too long the people in Washington took the attitude that the drug problem was so large nothing could be done about it. Well, we don't accept this sit-on-your-hands kind of thinking." Reporting on the Miami task force, he declared, "The important thing is that we're hurting the traffickers. It's true that when we close off one place they can move somewhere else. But one thing is different now: We're going to be waiting for them. To paraphrase Joe Louis, they can run but they can't hide."[11]

Reagan's next move was to repeat his south Florida programs in a "hot pursuit" strategy for the entire country. One of the first major initiatives was to coordinate the nine departments and thirty-three agencies in the executive branch that had "some responsibility in the drug area," but had until then operated in their own silos, to launch a "planned, concerted campaign." Previous administrations, he explained, had put together drug strategies but had failed to build the necessary bureaucratic structure to implement them. "We now have that structure," he said. Reagan ended the speech with a call to arms: "Drugs are bad, and we're going after them. As I've said before, we've taken down the surrender flag and run up the battle flag. And we're going to win the war on drugs."[12]

Make no mistake: It was Nixon who was first responsible for the rhetorical and programmatic elements that we now recognize as the modern war on drugs. But Reagan's use of the phrase was the first by an American head of state. In any case, Reagan took the further step of establishing a new agency, the Drug Abuse Policy Office, which became the White House's Office of National Drug Control Policy (ONDCP). Reagan's initial DAPO head was a "curious character" named Carlton Turner, a lab scientist who had built his career growing research-grade cannabis under federal contract at the University of Mississippi. One of the country's foremost researchers of cannabis and a former president of the American Council on Marijuana's Scientific Advisory Board, Turner "grew pot, studied pot, and hated pot smokers." Another warrior in the nation's culture wars, he once declared that pot smoking was a "behavioral pattern that has sort of tagged along during the present young-adult generation's involvement in anti-military, anti-nuclear power, anti-big business, anti-authority demonstrations." What's more, he said, marijuana was (contemptibly, in his view) associated with "people from a myriad of different racial, religious or otherwise persuasions demanding 'rights.' " Keep in mind that during the presidential campaign, Reagan, who loathed pot and pot smokers, pronounced that "leading medical researchers" believed marijuana was "probably the most dangerous drug in the United States."[13]

The early Reagan years held intimations of how aggressive the domestic side of the war would become. In 1984, for example, the Reagan administration supported the DEA's new campaign, Operation Pipeline, which tasked more than three hundred state and local law enforcement agencies with escalating "pretextual traffic stops" and "consent searches," in which officers used a minor traffic violation such as a broken taillight to stop a motorist and then "leverage" consent to a search for drugs. Over the next fifteen years the DEA trained over twenty-five thousand officers in Pipeline strategy. In her bestselling work *The New Jim Crow*, anthropologist Michelle Alexander cited a legal expert who argued that Operation Pipeline was "exactly what the Framers meant to prohibit: a federally-run general search program that targets people without cause for suspicion, particularly those who belong to disfavored groups." Pipeline enabled authorities to stop "staggering" numbers of motorists, sweeping up "extraordinary numbers of innocent people" in the process. According to one estimate in California, the approach yielded no drugs 95 percent of the time. As one California cop framed it, "It's sheer numbers. . . . You've got to kiss a lot of frogs before you find a prince."[14]

Brought On by Crack Use

In the mid-1980s, the price of powdered cocaine on American streets plunged. In Miami, ground zero of President Reagan's enforcement strategy, a kilo of cocaine cost about $42,000 from 1974 to 1984. In 1984, the price of even purer product had dropped to less than $14,000. (In less than a year, prices would double, mostly due to increased interdiction in Colombia.) Stuck with plummeting revenues, drug runners in the Bahamas crafted a cheap new product: freebase cocaine in rock form.[15] The Bahamians figured out how to derive the base cheaply by processing powdered cocaine with water and sodium bicarbonate; this yielded a crystal that could be smoked or dissolved and injected: crack. (The label "crack" derives from the crackling sound the rock makes as it is heated.) Crack typically has more impurities than freebase or powder cocaine due to its makeshift production, and it tends to be more powerful and more addictive. Traffickers began selling crack exclusively on American streets, at $10 to $20 a vial. In this way, they were able to turn $100 worth of powder cocaine into twice that in revenue. As one report dryly noted, "The strategy worked extraordinarily well for the cocaine industry."[16]

The drug's entry into urban neighborhoods came with a decline in cocaine's social cachet, from chic clubs and corporate executive bathrooms toward "abandoned lots and burnt-out cars." Crack was the "fast food of drugs." It came in ready-to-smoke pieces "shaped like French fries, wrapped like dime store candy, or aspirin-size tablets with the brand name 'Easy Access.' " Its prevalence also sparked devastating violence and social disruption. Young, often minority males became the central flywheels in crack's brilliant distribution network. Especially in the early years, battles erupted over distribution turf on streets from New York to Detroit to Compton. And with crack-driven crime and violence came increased legal sanctions for cocaine sales and possession. In turn, American jails and prisons swelled with dealers, distributors, and users. Within three years, crack had replaced heroin as the primary illicit "problem drug" in America.[17]

A regular user might purchase a $10 vial three to four times a day. More than half of New York City's crack addicts were spending a thousand dollars a month on the drug—often funded by their own drug sales or crime. The Justice Department recorded drug tests for 4,847 nondrug felony arrestees in Manhattan in 1984. Around 42 percent tested positive for cocaine, 21 percent for opiates, 8 percent for methadone, and 12 percent for PCP. In 1986, a repeat sample had 83 percent of arrestees testing positive for cocaine, while the other drugs remained flat. The National Cocaine Hotline started up in the early 1980s. In September 1985, it did not receive a single crack-related call. Less than a year later, the center's founding physician reckoned that a third of the year's calls were for crack addiction. "It's a true epidemic," he said.[18]

"Just Say No"

First Lady Nancy Reagan was visiting a school in Oakland, California, in 1982 when a student asked her what to do if she were offered drugs. "Well, you just say no," she replied. This phrase generated the "Just Say No" campaign that was launched that same year. By 1989, more than twelve thousand "Just Say No" clubs had been formed across the nation and world. The Reagan Presidential Library's website claims that cocaine use by high school seniors over this time dropped by a third, to the lowest rate since the previous decade. "Just Say No" was more than a series of clubs: it was both partial cause and symptom of American hysteria on the drug issue in the 1980s.[19]

For the first lady, the solution was not simply to say no but also to ensure that others didn't partake. In her opening speech for the White House Conference on a Drug-Free America in 1988, she explained to two thousand passionate anti-drug activists: "The casual user may think as he takes a line of cocaine or smokes a joint in the privacy of his nice condominium, listening to his expensive stereo, that he's somehow not bothering anyone. But there's a trail of death and destruction that leads directly to his door." Her message was unequivocal. "If you're a casual user, you're an accomplice to murder."[20]

Nancy Reagan's critics have contended that her approach succeeded in nothing so much as reducing the discussion about how to deal with drug use in America to a single word: No! At one rally in 1984, Nancy Reagan led the youth audience in yelling "No! No! No!" to drugs. "That's wonderful," she affirmed. "That will keep the drugs away." This sort of passion was rich fodder for those who dismissed the upbeat rallies as a "collective exorcism of moral corruption." Other drug war critics were equally scathing. As Bruce Barcott has written, "Nixon saw drugs as a political issue and a police matter. The Reagans expanded it into an all-out cultural war."[21]

"Just Say No" was only one of several outspoken anti-drug movements to emerge in this period. In 1977 a group of families in Atlanta, Georgia, founded the anti-drug organization Families in Action (FIA). Their goal was to battle "extremely youthful drug culture" enabled by the idea of "responsible use." Families in Action first gained traction in local schools and then turned up the heat. In the early 1980s, they managed to persuade the Georgia legislature to pass laws that shut down paraphernalia shops around the state.[22] By the mid-1980s, over four thousand grassroots anti-drug groups existed across the country. In the early 1990s, federal anti-drug officials credited FIA and related organizations with a two-thirds reduction in "past-month" drug use among teenagers. Although reported past-month drug use among teenagers has never returned to the peak level of 1979, after 1992 the rate increased considerably and then held constant for the next three decades.[23]

"Threaten to Fire Him"

The Reagan White House's visible advocacy was matched by numerous anti-drug media campaigns to educate Americans on the dangers of substance abuse. The largest and most influential was the Partnership for a Drug-Free America run by the American Association of Advertising Agencies. The three-year, $500 million drive was the biggest public service campaign since World

War II. Its budget was larger than the annual advertising budgets of Coca-Cola and the Chrysler Corporation. Said one ad executive, the goal was to "convince people that drug usage is not chic, not acceptable, and is plain stupid." The messages did not mince words. "Do crack while you're pregnant and your baby may be doing it for life," as one had it. Another stated: "In a few days a lot of pot smokers will forget they read this." One showed a photo filled with conventionally wholesome-looking kids and the big, bold headline: "Can You Find the Drug Pusher in This Picture?" Another segment depicted a dark-skinned hand holding crack vials with the line: "Addiction is slavery." And a ubiquitous workplace poster urged, "Help an Addict. Threaten to Fire Him."[24]

The partnership's first television ad—one that scared the daylights out of me when I was a kid—appeared in 1987 and featured actor John Roselius standing in an otherwise empty apartment. In the spot, Roselius asks whether there are any viewers out there who don't understand the harms of drug use. Then he holds up an egg and says, "This is your brain," and points to a sizzling frying pan. "This is drugs." He cracks the egg and drops it in the pan. "This is your brain on drugs. Any questions?" *TV Guide* named it one of the best 100 commercials in the history of television; *Entertainment Weekly* listed it as the eighth best commercial ever aired. The American Egg Board was less enthusiastic.[25] It is worth mentioning that during the Reagan years the healthcare and accident-related costs of tobacco and alcohol were almost $500 billion and $116 billion, respectively—an order of magnitude greater than the estimated $60 billion in lost productivity, medical treatment, and law enforcement related to illicit drugs. And despite all the media efforts, by the end of Reagan's presidency, cocaine was cheaper and more widely available than ever.[26]

"Instantly Addictive"

The national media both reflected and fueled the fear of drug abuse—and of crack cocaine in particular. In 1986, CBS aired the much-viewed hour-long special *48 Hours on Crack Street*, while NBC ran *Cocaine Country*. Images showed Senator Alfonse D'Amato of New York and the U.S. attorney for the Southern District of New York, Rudolph Giuliani, purchasing crack undercover in the Washington Heights neighborhood of New York City. That same year, *Newsweek* called crack the biggest story since Vietnam and Watergate. *Time* labeled crack the "issue of the year." Mayors of inner-city communities and African-American pastors were holding street vigils in cities all over the Northeast, calling out cocaine a "new form of genocide."[27]

Subsequent observers have dismissed this as a demonization campaign. Michelle Alexander shows that as late as 1989 the media continued to "disseminate claims that crack was an 'epidemic,' a 'plague,' 'instantly addictive' and extraordinarily dangerous—claims that have now been proven false or highly misleading." Alexander is correct in identifying the hyperbole and ignorance surrounding crack. At the same time, it very much was an epidemic, if only in the sense that it was a widespread public-health phenomenon. And it's also been proven that crack cocaine is much more psychologically addictive than powder cocaine, which entails a higher likelihood of chronic heavy use and abuse. The drug's particular "downscale" one-rock-at-a-time distribution model also meant that it brought more violence to American streets than any drug that had come before it.[28]

Nothing better captured the decade's hysteria than the "crack babies" mania that began in 1985. A series of news accounts cited an article in the *New England Journal of Medicine,* in which a small study of two dozen women had found an association between crack use and premature births, miscarriages, and "depression of interactive behavior" in newborns. Despite warnings from the researchers that their findings were not conclusive, CBS News aired a story on a baby in the throes of "cocaine withdrawal." The network's correspondent Susan Spencer urged viewers, "If you're pregnant and use cocaine, stop." With that line, a "mad dash" to document crack babies began. Within months a new consensus was emerging on the effects of crack on infants: low birth weight, learning disabilities, a lack of "normal human feelings," constant crying, and "Alzheimer's-like symptoms." The U.S. Department of Health and Human Services predicted that a hundred thousand crack babies would be born annually, at a cost of $20 billion. Within months, news reports were forecasting 375,000 crack babies born each year. According to this take, America would soon have to reckon with a "biological underclass whose inferiority is stamped at birth."[29]

In the 1990s however, an Emory University researcher noticed that all of the women studied in the preliminary *New England Journal of Medicine* study also drank alcohol and smoked cigarettes. Their babies, she concluded, might well have been suffering from fetal alcohol syndrome. In another ten-year study published years later, Dr. Deborah Frank, a pediatrician at Boston University School of Medicine, conducted longitudinal studies of the developmental and behavioral outcomes of children exposed to crack and powder cocaine in the womb. It concluded that the "biological thumbprints of exposure to these substances" were identical. She added that babies exposed to powder or crack cocaine experienced small but identifiable effects and that the effects were similar to those associated with prenatal tobacco exposure. Further research has found similar results, and the balance of evidence now suggests that the crack baby epidemic was a media-instigated falsehood. Even the liberal *New York Times* editorial page stoked the hysteria of the "damaged generation" theory by reporting whopping sum of $700 million to treat stricken youth in the state of Florida alone—a sum, the paper acknowledged three decades later, "clearly drawn from myth." For the chastened *New York Times* editors writing in January 2019, the idea that cocaine was "uniquely and permanently" harmful to unborn babies was etched into "social policies and the legal code." In this telling, "The idea of a mentally impaired 'crack baby' resonated with long-held views about black Americans. It captured the imaginations of reporters, politicians, school officials and others who were historically conditioned to believe just about anything about the African-American poor."[30]

Just Criminalize It!

In 1985, eight million Americans reported having used cocaine within the previous month. The National Household Survey on Drug Abuse found that between 1985 and 1988 there was a 33 percent spike of people using cocaine or crack once a week or more. In 1986, Reagan called drug abuse "a repudiation of everything America is" and urged the nation to join a "national crusade against drugs." Pollsters routinely ranked drugs as the public's number one concern, above nuclear war, one of the top anxieties of the era. Stories of cocaine and crack addiction continued to pour in. Amid all of the hysterical media coverage and political demagoguery and racist implications of Operation Pipeline's search and seizure tactics, the fact remained that crack took a massive toll on American communities. The personal testimonies are powerful. Vic Graziello, a junkie for almost a quarter century on the Lower East Side of Manhattan, "used every conceivable drug in the pharmacopoeia" before picking up the crack pipe. In his words: "One hit and I was gone. . . . What was there about the high that was so addictive? It was so instant, so instant! When that pipe would get red hot, I knew it would have to cool off, but I could never wait and would always burn my hands. Even though my heart was going too fast and felt like it was going to explode, I couldn't get enough and had to hit it."[31]

In 1986 the Reagan administration began to reconsider its tack on the drug question. A series of internal debates inside the White House yielded a striking decision. In April that year, Reagan signed National Security Decision

Directive 221, declaring drugs crossing U.S. borders to be a national security threat. For many contemporary observers, this was the moment that launched the "supply side" of the drug war. The directive meant that drugs had officially shifted from a domestic social problem to a matter of foreign policy, all but ensuring a permanent role for the Pentagon in the policy response.[32]

That September, Reagan issued Executive Order 12564 covering the "Drug-Free Federal Workplace," which mandated that every federal agency establish procedures for mandatory drug testing. Only a month earlier Reagan, Vice President Bush, and a number of White House staffers had demonstrated their support for this home-front campaign by taking "voluntary" urine tests. While they might not have been able to predict it at the time, the workplace drug testing initiative would give birth to a hundred-million-dollar industry.[33]

In Congress, both Republicans and Democrats scurried to draft amendments with stiffer sanctions. The result was the (hastily passed) Anti-Drug Abuse Act of 1986, which Reagan signed into law on October 27 after it was approved overwhelmingly on Capitol Hill, 392 to 16 in the House and 97 to 2 in the Senate. The law included sizable increases for domestic and international anti-drug programs and operations. This marked a major change in the prosecution of the drug war abroad. On the domestic front it also made several unprecedented moves that would become deeply controversial. For one, it sanctioned the U.S. military's participation in domestic drug-eradication efforts. It also required mandatory minimum sentences for drug offenses. Michael S. Gelacek, who served on the independent and bipartisan U.S. Sentencing Commission established by Congress in 1984 to develop fair federal sentencing guidelines, explained the zeitgeist: "We wanted honesty in sentencing. We wanted the public to no longer worry about how long somebody actually went to jail for. If they got a ten-year sentence, they did ten years. What we wound up with is a sentencing system that's based on quantity and conspiracy in the drug area, and that leads to enormously lengthy sentences. You can go to jail for life in this country very easily." The mandatory minimum provision not only ensured a sharp uptick of prison terms for drug-related offenses but also stripped judges of the power of discretionary sentencing.[34]

It's worth noting that the legislation included much harsher punishment for crack offenses than for powder cocaine offenses. The idea was simple: everyone who uses or deals drugs goes to jail, and those who deal or use crack go to jail for longer. On a weight basis, the infamous ratio was 100–1 powder to crack. That is, distributing five grams of crack (the weight of two pennies, about $80–$140 on the street) earned a five-year mandatory sentence. It took five hundred grams of powder cocaine to land the same sentence. The official reasoning behind the differential sentencing cited crack's greater potency and higher addiction rates, as well as the turf battles and other violence that accompanied its distribution networks. Critics jumped on the differential as an example of racially discriminatory rule-making. It is likely that the bill's supporters in Congress sincerely believed that crack was more addictive and destructive than powder and that its low cost and ease of manufacture guaranteed higher rates of problem use and addiction. But what many accounts overlook is the extent to which differential sentencing was simply the upshot of congressional political gaming. Here is how one staffer described the bill's negotiations: "They looked at it and said: 'OK, well if the Democrats have a sentence of five years to 20 years, let's up it to 10 years to 40 years. And if the Dems say 20 grams, we'll make it 5!' Nobody looked at the proper ratios based on how harmful it was. It was completely detached from science. Nobody could say that crack was 100 times more dangerous than powder."[35]

There was additional controversy over the ways in which law enforcement prosecuted the refreshed domestic drug war. Arrests often came through undercover "buy-bust" setups. Said one police official, "Were we effective at putting a dent in the narcotics trade? No. We were effective at putting dope on the table, and we were effective at arresting people. It didn't matter how many people you arrested. For every one you arrested, there were two fighting to take his place."

All told, between 1982 and 2002, the number of arrests for drug offenses in the country more than doubled. By 2006, the police were making 1.88 million arrests annually. The DEA's budget doubled between 1985 and 1990; by 1994 it would be more than $1 billion.[36]

Potent Economic Incentives

Congress acted again two years later when it passed the Omnibus Anti-Drug Abuse Act of 1988. This "zero-tolerance" law made it an official U.S. policy objective to create a "drug-free America by 1995." Sanctions for drug violations became significantly steeper. Some observers believe that the death of Maryland basketball phenom Len Bias in a 1986 freebase overdose alone was responsible for the legislation's harshness: "Hundreds of thousands of people would never have gone to jail if Len Bias had not died." The legislation created a five-year mandatory minimum and twenty-year maximum sentence for simple possession of five grams or more of crack cocaine. The maximum penalty for possession of five hundred grams of powder cocaine or any amount of another drug remained fixed, at one year in prison. One upshot of this stricter differential was this: imagine that a major trafficker sold 499 grams of powder cocaine to a middleman, who cut it and sold one-ounce bags of powder to a few street dealers. One of these dealers then turned a small amount of powder cocaine into a 5.01-gram rock of crack. If the street dealer were arrested and charged, he would now face a mandatory minimum sentence of five years for crack possession. The trafficker one level up on the distribution chain, by contrast, would still get at most one year.[37]

Together with more aggressive prosecutorial and investigative policies, mandatory minimums increased the severity of actual federal prison sentences. By the early 1990s the median time served for drug offenses in federal penitentiaries had jumped to more than six years, up from two in 1980. This was the equivalent of 4,500 "cell years" in 1980, which grew to more than 85,000 cell years in 1992 and 135,000 cell years in 2001. On the state side, in 1980 fewer than 20,000 drug offenders were in state prisons, a rate that shot up to a peak of over 250,000 in 2016.[38] The average sentence for a crack cocaine offense in 2003, according to the ACLU, was just over ten years, three and a half years longer than the average sentence for a powder-related offense.

Because of crack's relatively low price, it was more accessible to poorer Americans, who were disproportionately African-American. Critics howled that mandatory minimum sentencing and differential sentencing for crack cocaine "unjustly and disproportionately" penalized black defendants for drug trafficking on the same scale as that of white defendants. African-Americans were indeed more likely to be convicted of the harsher crack cocaine offenses, while whites were more likely to be convicted on powder cocaine charges. The ACLU reported that in 1986, before the federal mandatory minimum for crack cocaine began, the median federal sentence for blacks was 11 percent higher than for whites. In 1990, the average federal sentence for blacks was 49 percent higher.[39]

The Omnibus Anti-Drug Abuse Act also allowed public housing authorities to evict tenants who allowed drug-related crime to take place on or near public housing premises. It also cut myriad federal benefits, such as student loans, for individuals convicted of drug offenses. The Congressional Black Caucus was divided on the legislation, as some believed that harsher penalties were needed to stop the crack scourge in its tracks. In any case, the law resulted in a quarter century of disproportionately negative outcomes for "defendants who were disproportionately black."[40]

Senator John McCain of Arizona explained the political imperative of supporting this anti-drug legislation: "This is such an emotional issue—I mean, we're at war here—that voting no would be too difficult to explain. By voting against it, you'd be voting against the war on drugs. Nobody wants to do that." Reagan's top justice officials also continued to press the agenda. In 1985, Attorney General Edwin Meese, a noted drug hawk, judged that to use drugs was to "deal in terror, torture, and death." He urged defense attorneys to inform on clients who were facing drug charges. "Constitutional freedoms," he suggested, "should not be used as a 'screen' to protect defendants who engaged in the evils of drugs."[41]

Over Reagan's two terms, critical voices did emerge in the administration ranks, despite the overwhelming consensus to get tougher on drugs. A senior Navy officer, Admiral Carlisle A. H. Trost, predicted, "The economic incentives are so potent and the network of communications from farm to market via thousands of boats and small planes is so extensive. . . . The only way we are going to stop this immense flow of illegal narcotics into this country is to shut off the demand for it." Reagan's own Commission on Organized Crime concluded in 1983 that despite "continuing expressions of determination, America's war on drugs seems nowhere close to success." The commission's report noted that the previous seventy-five years of federal efforts to reduce drug supplies and related social, economic, and criminal justice problems had failed. The reason: "continuing and overwhelming demand for drugs."[42]

Given that a stated goal of the drug war was to drive up the price of drugs by constricting supply, it was distressing that the street prices of all major drugs dropped over the course of the decade. Heroin's price, for one, plunged by a third between 1981 and 1991. The DEA began measuring crack numbers only in 1986, but the price dropped by 50 percent between then and 1991. The cost of methamphetamine in rural counties dropped by 25 percent from the early to mid-1980s. In fact, the only major scheduled drug of any significance to increase in price during the 1980s was cannabis.[43]

Race

Was the Anti-Drug Abuse Act a racist law? A lawyer who worked on the draft legislation offered the following in a 2011 interview: "There were all of these mythologies about how Congress did this intentionally because powder was only used by whites. The way it was put together wasn't racist, it just wasn't thought out." One research study reported that blacks made up 15 percent of the country's drug users but represented 47 percent of those convicted and 74 percent of those receiving prison sentences for drug offenses. In 2003, whites were less than 8 percent and African-Americans more than 80 percent of the defendants in cases under the new crack cocaine laws, despite whites constituting more than two-thirds of crack users. In 2000, there were more African-American men in prisons and jails (791,600) than there were enrolled in higher education (603,032).[44] Driven in good part by the mandatory minimum sentences, between 1994 and 2003 the average time black drug offenders spent in prison rose by 77 percent; for white drug offenders it rose only 28 percent. African-Americans served roughly as much prison time for drug offenses, 58.7 months, as whites did for violent offenses, 61.7 months.[45]

For civil rights organizations like the ACLU, that African-American defendants received mandatory minimum sentences more often than white defendants, who were equally eligible, further corroborated the "racially discriminatory impact" of the penalties. For drug war critics, including the ACLU, these statistics were proof positive that the approach to criminalizing drug use was "a major contributor to the disruption of the African American family." To be sure, by 2005, one in every fourteen African-American children had a parent in prison or jail; the proportion was nine times lower for whites. Another 1.4 million African-American males—13 percent of the entire adult population—were disenfranchised because of felony convictions. Civil rights activists concluded that mandatory minimums for felony convictions, particularly for "very-low level involvement with crack cocaine," were "devastating, not just for the accused, but also for their entire family."[46]

Congress explicitly stated that the mandatory minimum penalties for crack were designed to target "serious" and "major" drug traffickers. Yet the evidence suggested that the opposite was largely the case. Mandatory penalties for crack offenses usually applied to low-level drug dealers. The Sentencing Commission reported that 75 percent of crack defendants (note that this is not same group as *convicted* crack defendants, a distinction often overlooked, intentionally or otherwise, by mandatory minimum opponents) were "street dealers, couriers, and lookouts."[47]

Keep in mind that the drive to "lock 'em up" was pervasive even among the minority communities most affected by the violence. Blacks were as willing to support "rough, 'Dirty Harry'-style justice as were suburban whites." The African-American *Los Angeles Sentinel* demanded that pushers be "tarred and feathered, burned at the stake, castrated." Jesse Jackson Jr., son of the prominent civil rights activist and Democratic presidential candidate of the era, said in 1988, "No one has the right to kill our children. I won't take it from the Klan with a rope; I won't take it from a neighbor with dope." U.S. Attorney Eric Holder Jr., who later became attorney general under President Barack Obama, said, "Did Martin Luther King successfully fight the likes of Bull Connor so that we could lose the struggle for civil rights to misguided and malicious members of our own race?"

Assembling the evidence, Stanford Law School professor Richard Thompson Ford suggests that the prison population spike driven by mandatory minimums was a "profound social and *racial* injustice." But, he adds, many civil rights leaders and African-American politicians were willing to "countenance" it, suggesting that it was not "simply an instrument of white supremacy, motivated by racial hostility and indifference to black suffering."[48]

Weed the People

Aside from crack, Reagan renewed a war on domestic cannabis, especially in its traditional horticultural refuge of northern California. The area encompassing Humboldt, Trinity, and Mendocino counties is nicknamed the Emerald Triangle for being the largest cannabis-producing region in America. What began as a side hustle for pioneering organic farmers and hippies in coastal northern California in the 1960s became an "economic lifeline" for 100,000 to 150,000 commercial cannabis growers sprinkled across the country by the mid-1980s. For boosters like Barcott, growing sinsemilla made financial sense for those American farmers who started planting pot to save their farms from foreclosure in a bleak rural area made worse by Washington's rigging the game "in favor of a few agribusiness giants."[49]

President Reagan decided to smash pot by taking the fight to northern California. The Emerald Triangle soon became a "combat zone, a key battleground of the newly militarized war on drugs." The Campaign against Marijuana Production (CAMP) began during the 1983 harvest, when U-2 spy planes and military helicopters started flying sorties over the region. Two years later, on August 5, 1985, federal officials launched Operation Delta-9, the biggest anti-pot mission in American history, with more than two thousand federal, state, and local law enforcement officials working across the fifty states. Delta 9 eradicated 250,000 pot plants in just seventy-two hours.[50]

Locals opposed to the aggressive new eradication programs organized themselves to defend their civil liberties. They monitored and videotaped what they saw as CAMP abuses and sued in court to "thwart the de facto military occupation of their communities." They printed bumper stickers that demanded, "U.S. Out of Humboldt County." Drug war critics believe that the Emerald Triangle's decidedly radical affiliation with leftist causes might have been one reason that it was "singled out for selective, paramilitary overkill." Former Reagan-era congressional staffer Eric Sterling described the "visceral hostility towards those people that could now be vented."[51]

Pot seizures continued to rise in subsequent years, from 2.5 million plants in 1982 to 7 million in 1987—a haul that roughly equaled the government's previous estimate of the *entire* domestic cannabis crop. By 2001, the U.S. government reported that 120 million plants had been destroyed by 1989, half a billion by 2001.[52]

Federal laws following the Anti-Drug Abuse Acts of 1986 and 1988 made it easier for police to seize the property of cannabis-growing suspects. Mandatory minimum sentences stipulated that growers would get five years for growing one hundred or more plants. This combination of factors pushed pot cultivators to move their operations to public lands and to indoor grow houses. The paradox was that the "success" of interdiction made the incentives for farmers to grow cannabis even greater, since the return was so lucrative. As author Martin Lee lucidly explains, "No matter what the U.S. government did, marijuana wouldn't go away. By targeting overseas supplies, the Reagan administration provided a substantial boost for domestic pot farmers. Uncle Sam's assault on outdoor ganja gardens triggered a rapid increase in the number of indoor grow-ups. Nearly every major technological development that improved marijuana cultivation was driven by law-enforcement intervention."[53]

Gangster Crack

When crack appeared in L.A.'s ghettos in the mid-1980s, the "New Gang Godfathers"—Tootie Reese, Wayne Day, Michael "Harry O" Harris, and "Freeway" Rick Ross—were "the most violent in the nation." Although some considered the Godfathers to be folk heroes for bankrolling large street parties, covering funeral charges, and distributing cash to the poor and desperate, they also thrived in a hard business ruled by drugs, cash, and guns. The most menacing of the bosses was Day. One clandestine video showed Day lecturing hundreds of Crip gang members in a Compton neighborhood stadium on how to effectively carry out a drive-by execution. When the DEA went after him and he had to slow his drug business, a competing dealer tried to exploit the temporary vacuum. As a former special crime unit detective with the Los

Angeles Police Department reported: "They found the guy nude with his balls and his dick cut off and stuffed in his mouth and a great big cucumber sticking out of his ass, and that just terrorized everybody. From then on, nobody challenged [Day]." Rick Ross's estimated net worth, in 2016-adjusted dollars, was $2.5 billion in gross sales and $850 million in profit. At his apex, it was said that he sold $30 million in crack in a single day.[54]

By the end of the decade, the FBI, DEA, and LAPD had taken out the New Gang Godfathers. After that, "thousands of wannabes on the streets" were in the game. They included one young member of the Rolling Twenties Crips named Calvin Broadus, who later became world-famous as the rapper Snoop Dogg. As he wrote in his 1999 autobiography, *The Doggfather*, Broadus got into the trade with "three ounces of decent-quality rock" (street value of $5,400) fronted to him by the Insanes, a Crip gang. It did not hurt that crack was a volume business with a seller's market. Customers sought him out "twenty-four-seven, three hundred and sixty-five, with those big bills clenched in their sweaty hands and their eyes all beady and bright and that rasp in their voice that's about halfway between a whisper and a scream." Dealing brought real-world lessons home to Snoop Dogg: "Selling rock is the best way I know to get a good look at human nature on the flip side, down and desperate, with none of the fake bullshit that's supposed to make us civilized. A white man in a Mercedes and a two-thousand-dollar suit is no different than a nigger in a Hyundai and three-day-old sweats when it comes to getting high. They're both ready to do what it takes, pay what it costs, and take any risk just to draw down on that rock one more time."[55]

The life that Snoop Dogg chronicled was encapsulated in terms like *gangsta*, *thug life*, and *the hood*. The money was usually not enough to escape a world of grinding poverty and lack of opportunity, but it did allow for "fancy wheels for their cars and big-link gold chain necklaces"—and more and more weapons, including Uzis, MAC-10s, AK-47s, and all sorts of heavy-caliber handguns. Killings and related drug-violence became "terrifyingly mundane on the streets." As Martin Torgoff describes, "A whole new word, *drive-by*, would enter the popular glossary to describe the payback killings done from passing automobiles by groups of young men in their corn-rowed braids, G'ed up in their low-slung baggy shorts and Nikes, two-toned ball caps, and do-rags, all of them strapped with their gats purchased with drug money."

The tension and anger rising in these Los Angeles neighborhoods finally ignited on April 29, 1992, after a jury acquitted four Los Angeles Police Department officers of using excessive force against an African-American motorist, Rodney King. In what became known as the Los Angeles Riots, a series of protests, lootings, and arsons seized Los Angeles County for almost a week. Fifty-five people were killed, and another two thousand were injured. Property damage totaled more than a billion dollars. As one leader of the Crips gang, Sanyika Shakur (a.k.a. Monster Kody Scott), put it, "The scar of over twenty years that had been tucked out of sight and passed off as 'just another ghetto problem' burst its suture and spewed blood all over the belly of America."[56]

Snoop Dogg, at least, eventually left the drug trade. "Cocaine is poison, straight up," he later wrote, "and if you're looking for what brought life in the ghetto down to a dog-eat-dog level, then you've sure enough got your culprit." His solution: "We've got to stop killing each other. We've got to turn our rage and righteous anger on the target where it belongs—the system that keeps us oppressed and down and addicted to crack and attacking in the dead of night like wild animals tearing at each other's throats." Snoop put his "body and soul" into a new vocation. Retreating to an "old toolshed filled with busted mowers, he would go from sunup to sundown finding rhymes in time and sound that that would become his essence." Over a three-decade career, he went on to sell thirty-five million albums worldwide.[57]

PART 2:
SUPPLY-SIDE CRUSADE

12 • Supply Side

There is no match for a united America, a determined America, an
angry America. . . . Victory—victory over drugs—is our cause, a just
cause. And with your help we are going to win.
—President George H. W. Bush, "Address to the Nation on the
National Drug Control Strategy," September 5, 1989

Full Fury

The tough-on-crime approach to politicking inaugurated in the Reagan era
reached its apogee in the 1988 presidential contest, when Republican candidate George H. W. Bush turned the tide of the race by criticizing his opponent, Massachusetts governor Michael Dukakis, for furloughing murderers.
A television spot funded by a pro-Bush PAC introduced Americans to the
African-American inmate William Horton, a convicted murder with a life sentence. Under Dukakis's criminal justice policy, the ad went, Horton was
"allowed to have ten weekend prison passes," during one of which he committed another heinous rape and murder. In the presidential debates that followed, Dukakis gave a "bloodless, and politically catastrophic, answer" after
CNN's Bernard Shaw asked whether he would support the death penalty if his
wife were raped and murdered. "No, I don't, Bernard," he said, "and I think
you know that I've opposed the death penalty during all of my life. I don't see
any evidence that it's a deterrent and I think there are better and more effective ways to deal with violent crime." His answer failed to impress a majority
of American voters.[1]

When Bush took office on January 20, 1989, the nation was in "full fury" over drugs, with the alleged crack epidemic the focus of greatest ire. That same year, a record 64 percent of Americans told a *New York Times*/CBS poll that drugs were the most pressing problem in the country. On September 5, 1989, Bush took to network television to warn the American public of this national emergency, using as a prop a baggie of crack that the DEA had managed, at the behest of the commander-in-chief, to purchase near the White House three days earlier from a teenager with no previous criminal record. Sitting in the Oval Office for his first prime-time speech, the president described this heinous substance. "It's as innocent-looking as candy. But it's turning our cities into battle zones. And it's murdering our children." Delaware's Joe Biden, the chairman of the Senate Judiciary Committee, offered the Democratic televised rebuttal. "Quite frankly, the president's plan is not tough enough, bold enough, or imaginative enough to meet the crisis at hand," Biden told the nation. "The president said he wants to wage a war on drugs. But if that's true, what we need is another D-Day, not another Vietnam; nor another limited war fought on the cheap and destined for stalemate and human tragedy."[2]

The media both reflected and contributed to this impression. The *Washington Post*, to pick one major daily newspaper, ran more than 1,500 articles on the "drug scourge" between October 1988 and October 1989. The newspaper's ombudsman, Richard Harwood, later admitted that the paper had lost a "proper sense of perspective" on what proved to be a "hyperbolic epidemic."[3]

An often overlooked but bureaucratically and politically significant component of Reagan's Omnibus Drug legislation in 1988 was that it mandated the formation inside the White House of a single agency to manage federal anti-drug efforts. The Office of National Drug Control Policy was tasked, among other things, with crafting an annual National Drug Control Strategy with "quantifiable long-term and short-term goals." It was to be led by what the press called the president's "drug czar." Early into his tenure, Bush appointed the hard-charging conservative commentator William Bennett, who had just served as Reagan's secretary of education, as his first ONDCP chief. The new drug czar made no apologies about his hawkishness: "Two words sum up my entire approach: consequences and confrontation. Those who use, sell, and traffic in drugs must be confronted, and they must suffer consequences." Staking his side in the ongoing Baby Boomer cultural battle, the incoming Bennett echoed Progressive-era reformers in once again framing the question about substance use in terms of American moral identity. For Bennett, drugs represented a "crisis of national character," a question of "right and wrong." "Somewhere along the way," he wrote, "in the late 1960s and 1970s, part of America lost its moral bearings regarding drugs." And it was not just the hard-core addicts that were the problem, he argued; it was the "highly contagious" casual users who were "willing and able to proselytize" drug use to an otherwise innocent America.[4]

The solution? For the nicotine-addicted Bennett, who reportedly smoked up to two packs of cigarettes a day, the strategy was simple: reduce drug use at home. "The highest priority of our drug policy," he wrote in his first annual strategy, "must be a stubborn determination further to reduce the overall level of drug use nationwide—experimental first use, 'casual' use, regular use and addiction alike." A "massive wave of arrests" was the policy prescription— making a point by hitting users hard. Bennett went on to lament that drug suspects were entitled to due process and fair trials, which "kind of slow things down." He publicly endorsed beheading drug dealers. "Morally, I don't have any problem with that."[5]

The American public seemed to be behind him. In February 1990, one survey reported that 65 percent of Americans agreed with Bennett that taking illegal drugs solely for intoxication was morally wrong. A roughly equivalent number of Americans said they would forfeit "some freedoms" to fight the war on drugs. Bennett promised a 10 percent reduction in the number of Americans using drugs by 1991 and a 50 percent drop by 1999. Interestingly, while drug use rates had in fact been dropping in the 1980s, they increased dramatically during and beyond Bennett's watch, almost doubling over the next twenty years. Further, between 1990 and 2007, the street price of cocaine and heroin, which Bennett sought to drive up in order to deter new users, plunged by up to 80 percent. The falling prices were not due to reduced enforcement: During the same period, the DEA's budget tripled.[6]

Some voices on the right took issue with Bennett's strident anti-drug line. The Nobel Prize–winning economist Milton Friedman wrote in the *Wall Street Journal*, "Your mistake is failing to recognize that the very measures you favor are a major source of the evils you deplore." Friedman, a giant of the Reaganite free-market caucus, was a powerful advocate for legalizing pot. He lambasted prohibition as "an attempted cure that makes matters worse." His warning to Bennett was categorical: "The path you propose of more police, more jails, use of the military in foreign countries, harsh penalties for drug users, and a whole panoply of repressive measures can only make a bad situation worse." Gary Johnson, the Republican governor of New Mexico and a visible proponent of libertarianism, echoed Professor Friedman in calling the drug war an "expensive bust" and in pressing for the legalization of marijuana.[7]

The Andean Initiative

The late 1980s and early 1990s are the period in which the United States most forcefully brought the drug war to "source countries." The logic was: If you want to kill the bees, you have to destroy them at the hive. In the case of the global drug war, the hives were the poppy, coca, and cannabis fields of Peru, Bolivia, Colombia, and Mexico. During his presidential campaign, George H. W. Bush stated that he supported taking military action in other countries to interrupt drug production. After taking office—and only weeks after the reformist and anti-drug Colombian presidential candidate Luis Carlos Galán was brutally murdered at a campaign rally—Bush signed National Security Directive 18, allocating more than $250 million in military, intelligence, and police assistance to fight drugs in the Andes over the next five years. Just days later, Bush authorized sending a U.S. Special Forces team to Colombia to train its police and military in quick-reaction tactics. Within the month, Bush announced the Andean Initiative, designed to effect a "major reduction in the supply of cocaine." Bush explained the stakes to journalists: "The rules have changed. When requested, we will for the first time make available appropriate resources of America's armed forces." That June, Bennett effectively endorsed using U.S. military force to kill the Colombian kingpins, declaring, "We should do to the drug barons what our forces in the Persian Gulf did to Iran's navy."[8]

In 1989, Congress approved President Bush's $2.2 billion five-year Andean strategy to hit drug cultivation and trafficking at the source. The approach represented a major escalation of the militarized supply-side strategy initiated by Reagan with National Security Decision Directive 221 in 1986. Colombia was the source of more than 80 percent of the cocaine pouring into the United States. As critical sources of raw coca production, Peru and Bolivia were also likely targets. The strategy had three pillars. The first two leaned on brute force: eradicating coca crops and "decapitating" the cartels, which were turning leaf into cocaine and smuggling it into the United States. The third took a softer approach: so-called alternative development, whereby the United States would fund programs to help farmers transition from coca to licit crops such as cacao, citrus, or hearts of palm. Critics anticipated the turbulence in these efforts. "Nibbling around the edges of the leaf market is terribly inefficient," said a scholar at the University of California. As we'll see throughout this section of the book, the results were mixed. Michael Reid, a correspondent for the *Economist,* wrote: "Two decades and several billion dollars later," drug war-riors could "point to a series of tactical victories, in particular places and times," but the flow of coke to America was "never seriously interrupted."[9]

Our Man in Panama

At times, the "supply side" of the drug war has yielded highly intervention-ist policy decisions, the scope of which has extended far beyond eradication and crop-substitution support. During the first years of the George H. W. Bush source country strategy, the U.S. government launched what remains the single most intrusive drug-driven intervention in a foreign state. On De-cember 20, 1989, twenty-four thousand U.S. troops descended on Panama to decimate the country's military dictatorship and apprehend its leader, Manuel Antonio Noriega. At the time, the invasion represented the largest U.S. mili-tary operation since the Vietnam War. It was also the first invasion of any country after the fall of the Berlin Wall in 1989.

While a host of historical factors, path-dependencies, and prior policy fail-ures ultimately led to the military campaign, it is important to emphasize the centrality of drugs in this story. During the 1970s and 1980s, successive U.S. administrations viewed Noriega as an unsavory but efficient ally and regional intelligence source. But by the mid-1980s, Noriega's increasingly problematic behavior, above all his involvement in the international narcotics trade, made him a liability to the United States, especially at a time when the American public's concern about illegal drugs was reaching its peak.[10]

Back in 1967, Noriega took classes at the U.S. School of the Americas in the Panama Canal Zone, quickly ingratiating himself to U.S. officials with his seemingly unparalleled intelligence-gathering capabilities. Contrary to the im-pressions that some observers have, Washington did not support Noriega ex-plicitly to create an American puppet in Panama City; rather, the reason was more quotidian. The United States was looking for a reliable intelligence source to provide timely and accurate information on growing leftist guerrilla insur-gencies, Cuba, and the increasingly important issue of narcotics trafficking.[11]

Noriega did all of that and more. Indeed, Noriega worked for the Ameri-cans, but he also worked for the Cubans and the Colombian drug lords and whoever else was willing to pay the price. In 1980, former Costa Rican presi-dent José Figueres was visiting Fidel Castro when Figueres commented that Castro was the best-informed man in the region. Castro responded, "No,

Noriega is the best informed man. He knows everything the left and right are doing." Some State Department officials called Noriega "rent-a-colonel," and he was known in the drug underworld as the "Caribbean Prostitute."[12]

By the early 1970s, Noriega had become chief of G-2, the Panamanian National Guard's intelligence service. The United States helped train Noriega in intelligence and soon put him on the payroll. Over the next decade, Washington paid Noriega hundreds of thousands of dollars to report on the seedy Central American intelligence world. He had become such a cherished resource to the U.S. intelligence community that by 1976, when the American Ambler Moss took over as ambassador, he discovered that Noriega was the liaison for the CIA, FBI, Customs Service, and several military intelligence agencies. During the 1970s and 1980s, Noriega established working relationships with high-ranking U.S. policymakers such as the CIA director William Casey and the National Security Council staff member Oliver North. In December 1976, Noriega even met with the CIA director at the time—George H. W. Bush—at a private lunch hosted by the Panamanian ambassador in Washington. A 1978 letter from President Carter's DEA director, Peter Bensinger, highlights the value that Noriega provided to the intelligence-gathering efforts, gushing that the DEA "very much appreciates all of your support and cooperation which you have extended to our agency during the last year" and wishing Noriega "very best regards for a happy and successful new year." The DEA continued to send Noriega letters of support, known as "attaboy" letters, up until just a few years before the invasion.[13]

While the notion of working with Noriega seems outrageous today, in the context of the times the dealings are more understandable. For example, Noriega continued to arrest drug traffickers and send them to the United States. Since he was also working for Cuba, Noriega was deemed a good source of information about a country that had been difficult for U.S. intelligence agencies to penetrate. Even through the mid-1980s, U.S. intelligence agencies continued to believe that Noriega's benefits outweighed his costs. As late as March 1987, Noriega was cooperating in major bilateral money-laundering investigations. The 1987 annual report of the State Department's narcotics division certified that Panama had "fully cooperated" with anti-narcotics matters.[14]

Things Fall Apart

In August 1981, Panama's de facto dictator Omar Torrijos died in a plane crash that has not been fully explained to this day. In March 1982, Noriega and two other officers ousted Colonel Florencio Flores, who had succeeded

Torrijos as commander of the National Guard. In a remarkable feat of duplicity, Noriega did not back his co-conspirator, Lieutenant Colonel Rubén Paredes, in the elections that followed; instead, he threw his support behind Nicolás Ardito Barletta, a former vice president at the World Bank. Paredes's campaign withered, and he was soon ousted from the Guard. Noriega stood alone at the top of the Panamanian military. Before long, he had promoted himself to the rank of brigadier general and changed the name of the National Guard to the Panamanian Defense Forces (PDF).[15]

In a highly irregular election, Barletta defeated the octogenarian Arnulfo Arias by fewer than two thousand votes out of six hundred thousand counted. Despite clear evidence of foul play, Reagan's secretary of state, George Shultz, attended Barletta's inauguration, and President Reagan received him at the White House. An administration that was deeply concerned about the spread of communism in the isthmus now had a government in Panama that it could work with. Barletta was a widely known technocrat, and Noriega was the undisputed king of intelligence. In 1985, however, Noriega ousted Barletta and replaced him with Vice President Eric Arturo Delvalle, slated to serve until 1989. For the next five years, Noriega dominated all aspects of Panamanian life from his position as commander of the PDF. With no need to appoint himself president, Noriega instead allowed political figures to fill the post, lending a veneer of democratic legitimacy to his rule.[16]

Meanwhile, certain members of Congress who had been observing Noriega's illicit activities began to raise an alarm. Freshman Massachusetts senator John Kerry and his conservative colleague Jesse Helms of North Carolina quietly pressured the Reagan administration to do something about Noriega. Helms directed Congress's attention toward the regime in March and April 1986, when he conducted hearings on Noriega's dirty work and the Reagan administration's support. Helms wanted to demonstrate the regime's unsuitability for controlling the strategically important Panama Canal, which the United States was slated to hand to the Panamanians in 1999. According to one of Helms's aides, "We want to turn the canal over to a viable, stable democracy, not a bunch of corrupt drug runners."[17]

Soon after Helms's hearings began, Kerry started his own investigation into drug trafficking in Panama. Over the course of the next two years, Kerry's Foreign Relations Subcommittee on Terrorism, Narcotics, and International Communication was the epicenter for congressional scrutiny of Noriega's dealings. What emerged from the investigations was an entire series of revelations about Noriega's dealings with Cuba, the Contras in Nicaragua, and Colombian drug kingpins and guerrillas and about Panama's position as the money-laundering capital of the region.[18]

A front-page article in the *New York Times* on June 12, 1986, by investigative reporter Seymour Hersh amplified Congress's scrutiny of Noriega. Hersh, who made his name uncovering the My Lai massacre during the Vietnam War, wrote the article to coincide with a visit to the United States by Noriega, where he was presented with a Panamanian medal of honor at the Inter-American Defense Board. Hersh argued that Noriega was tied to the grisly killing of prominent regime critic Hugo Spadafora and that, "for the last fifteen years, he had been providing intelligence information simultaneously to Cuba and the United States."[19]

The spotlight put pressure on the Reagan administration to do something about Noriega. The intelligence value he provided, as was becoming clear, was now outweighed by the damage he was doing to Reagan's credibility in Panama and in Washington. What's more, the growing drug concern in the United States meant that any national politician with aspirations for the future had to demonstrate that he or she was doing something about drugs. For President Reagan, this meant removing Noriega. The administration began outlining classified scenarios for his ouster.[20]

The quiet plans to dislodge the Panamanian strongman received a jolt on February 5, 1988, when two grand juries, one in Tampa and the other in Miami, announced indictments against Noriega. The twelve-count Miami indictment accused Noriega of helping Colombia's notorious Medellín cartel ship more than two tons of cocaine through Panama in return for a payment of $4.5 million. One Miami attorney stated that, "in plain language, he utilized his position to sell the country of Panama to drug traffickers." The three-count Tampa indictment charged Noriega with attempts to smuggle more than one million pounds of marijuana into the United States. It also alleged that Noriega had agreed to allow more than $100 million in profits from drug sales to be laundered through Panama banks. The cumulative sentences for Noriega, if convicted, were for 145 years in prison.[21]

Noriega's close working relationship with the Colombian narcos ensured it was "no coincidence" that Escobar and company scooted to Panama after they ordered the assassination of the Colombian justice minister Rodrigo Lara Bonilla in 1984. As one account of this large-scale relocation had it, the cartel moved 120 people to Panama, including "accountants, bodyguards, lawyers, and families. Noriega provided them housing, advice, and even Panamanian passports." When Medellín's Jorge Ochoa was apprehended months later, he and his family were traveling with Panamanian diplomatic passports. The cartel bosses who most needed security and secrecy rented U.S. officers' homes at Fort Amador, which had reverted to Noriega under the terms of the Panama Canal Treaties. Some were booked in "plush suites atop" the Caesar Park Marriott Hotel.[22]

The cartel felt safe about Panama because the Colombians had been giving Noriega hundreds of thousands of dollars "each time a planeload of cocaine used a Panamanian airstrip" since the early 1980s. In 1983 Medellín had agreed with Noriega to build a massive cocaine lab in Panama's El Sapo mountains in the inhospitable Darién region adjacent to Colombia. Here is what happened next:

> This just completed facility [was] raided, by Noriega's Panamanian Defense Forces no less, and now twenty-one cartel members were in Panama jails! . . . Complaints by local Indians had filtered back to the U.S. embassy. Noriega, working every side of the aisle, had decided to placate the DEA by giving them the cartel's new lab. Pablo Escobar was infuriated at the double-cross. He tried to contact Noriega, but the president conveniently had taken off to Europe and Israel on official business. Stymied, Escobar threatened to murder Noriega if he didn't make good. And, of course, by now, no one underestimated such threats.[23]

Although they might have had cosmetic appeal in terms of the war on drugs, the indictments were poor foreign policy. Critically, the United States did not have an extradition treaty with Panama, which meant that there was no ready legal mechanism to get Noriega to Florida. Furthermore, the sanctions were not universally applied, and many U.S. corporations easily found ways to keep doing business with the Noriega regime. As expected, Noriega responded to the indictments with his usual scorn, calling them "a joke and an absurd political movement." Panama's gross domestic product did fall by 17 percent in 1988 and 8 percent in 1989, prompting National Security Adviser Colin Powell to declare that the sanctions were having a "telling effect." But even as the sanctions certainly hampered Panama's economy, Noriega was buoyed by seemingly limitless drug revenues. He was able to continue paying his 15,000 PDF members, the key factor in his political survival.[24]

On May 11, 1988, the White House announced that the judicial indictments would be dropped, in return for Noriega's retirement. It was something of a Hail Mary pass. However, bargaining with America's "number one drug thug" proved politically damaging for Republican presidential candidate George H. W.

Bush, still vice president under Reagan, who was slipping in the polls against Democratic contender Michael Dukakis. Dukakis slammed Bush for his supposed longtime connection to Noriega. "How about telling us who in this administration was dealing with Noriega. Who was paying Noriega? Who was ignoring the fact that we knew he was dealing in drugs and making millions and we're still doing business with him?"[25]

Congress was also almost uniformly opposed to the idea. On May 17, the Senate passed a nonbinding amendment stating that no negotiations by the United States with Noriega should be made that "involve the dropping of the drug-related indictments against him." Republican senator Robert Dole of Kansas said that the White House was sending the "wrong signal" on drugs. In his mind, with the indictment, "we have said that under certain circumstances we'll negotiate with leniency for those who are responsible, directly or indirectly, for the addiction and death of our children." Republican senator Pete Wilson of California opined that a deal with Noriega was akin to cutting "a deal with the devil." By the end of May, the White House quietly withdrew the offer.[26]

With Noriega still in power and the sanctions proving ineffective, during the summer of 1988 a rupture emerged inside the administration about how to proceed. The State Department believed that a more muscular approach was needed and that Washington should start considering a plan for a military intervention, namely a commando-style raid, to nab the strongman. The Pentagon, on the other hand, was more cautious; the generals worried that a military operation could easily lead to a hostage situation. According to one White House official who participated in the discussions, "The diplomats wanted a muscular military policy. The soldiers, who would have to do the fighting, wanted negotiations with Noriega."[27]

Mounting Pressure

By mid-1988, the United States was involved in a low-intensity conflict with Noriega's forces. From February 1988 to May 1989, more than six hundred incidents involving harassment of U.S. civilians and troops were reported, including several instances when U.S. servicemen were detained and beaten. U.S. policymakers were becoming concerned about the potential for a Tehran-style hostage situation. At the same time, the CIA supported several unsuccessful attempts to oust Noriega.[28]

In 1989, newly inaugurated President Bush faced a difficult situation. Among his first acts as president was the approval of several covert operations against the Panamanian strongman. He also supported Congress's move to transfer $10 million through the National Endowment for Democracy to the opposition groups and candidates who were planning to run against Noriega's handpicked candidate in the May 1989 presidential elections.[29]

That election unfolded amid rampant fraud, protests, and violent attacks by PDF "Dignity Battalions" against opposition candidates and their supporters. They led to Noriega annulling the election and installing his crony Francisco Rodríguez as president. Bush responded by declaring that the United States "will not recognize or accommodate a regime that holds power through force and violence at the expense of the Panamanian people's right to be free." Ambassador Arthur Davis was immediately recalled. Bush also ordered an additional two thousand troops to Panama, a move that Joint Chiefs chairman William James Crowe Jr. agreed to only reluctantly. Bush then announced a seven-point plan intended to remove Noriega through a combination of pressure and incentives. The points included greater regional diplomacy with the Organization of American States (OAS), more diplomatic and economic sanctions, and preventive measures such as encouraging U.S. companies to send dependents back to the United States.[30]

Over the course of 1989, the National Security Council's Policy Coordinating Group met regularly to discuss Panama policy. There was a growing sentiment that more forceful action was needed. While some top officials still preferred the commando-style option or no operation at all, a full-scale invasion was becoming increasingly popular. Pressure mounted that October, when a military coup failed, and Noriega narrowly escaped with help from the elite PDF force Battalion 2000. The three months following the revolt were by far the most intense in U.S.-Panama relations since the public feud with Noriega had begun two years earlier. In early November, Bush approved an additional $3 million to fund covert operations in Panama, though he blocked the CIA from attempting to assassinate Noriega. Noriega responded to the coup in his own way: by cracking down on domestic opposition. Political opponents were jailed, tortured, and killed. American and PDF troops continuously traded shots inside the Canal Zone.[31]

Then, on December 15, in a surprise move, Noriega removed Rodríguez as president and installed himself as the "Maximum Leader of National Liberation." Noriega then declared before the Panamanian legislature that Panama was in a "state of war" with the United States. Wielding a machete, he opened his speech with a "word of praise and thanks to the just and merciful God of the universe, as Jehovah, as Allah, as Yahweh, as Buddha, as the universal conscience of the soul." He continued that the U.S. military had "launched psychological attacks and have carried out a plan to poison minds by inventing all sorts of lies and trying by every means to win the minds of the weakest. We have resisted, and now we must decide to advance in our land to strengthen our internal front to improve our resistance and advance toward an offensive of creativity and development in the generational project of the new republic. . . . Render unto Caesar what is Caesar's, to God what is God's, and to the Panamanians what is Panama's."[32]

The Invasion of Panama

On December 17, 1989, the day after Noriega's forces shot and killed an unarmed U.S. soldier in the Panamanian capital, President Bush called a meeting with his senior advisers to decide among three military options. Bush apparently ended the meeting with these words: "This guy is not going to lay off. . . . It will only get worse. Ok, let's do it." Two days later, a full-scale invasion, Operation Just Cause, was ready to go.

Just Cause had several objectives: protect American lives and installations; capture Noriega and eliminate the PDF; replace Noriega's regime with the democratic government of May's jilted presidential candidate, Guillermo Endara; and rebuild the Panamanian military. The invasion began in the early morning of December 20, with Special Forces attacks and bombing runs on key PDF installations. By daylight, 10,000 American troops had joined the others already in the combat zone. The Americans secured the U.S. embassy and overran the PDF headquarters on the first day. All told, 23 American soldiers were killed and 323 wounded; around 300 PDF troops and roughly 300 Panamanian civilians were killed (although around 200 of these were reckoned by some counts to have been part of the Dignity Battalions). Although two days of chaos and widespread looting in the capital followed, the relative ease of the military operation enabled the Joint Chiefs chairman Colin Powell to focus on the political side, in particular installing Endara and eliminating the PDF. This campaign began on December 22, when the 96th Civil Affairs Battalion landed in Panama with the task of establishing a police force, distributing emergency food, and supervising Panamanian contractors cleaning up the city. It was also charged with the sensitive task of helping to develop "grassroots" efforts to sell the Endara government to the Panamanian public. On December 22, Endara formally abolished the PDF and announced the creation of an organization called the Fuerza Pública.[33]

At this point, however, the American command faced one particularly acute embarrassment: U.S. forces had still not located Noriega. The fugitive had learned about the invasion while he was spending the night with a prostitute at a hotel near Panama City and fled. Over the next five days, more than forty Special Forces operations across the country were conducted with the goal of apprehending Noriega. All of them failed, even after the Bush administration placed a $1 million bounty on Noriega's head.[34]

On Christmas Eve, officials at the Vatican embassy in Panama City sent a car to meet Noriega at a secret location and bring him back to the embassy. The deposed strongman appeared to have decided that an attempt at political asylum was his last hope to escape a prison cell in the United States. Noriega entered the embassy dressed in running shorts and a T-shirt and carrying two AK-47 rifles. When Vice President Dick Cheney was informed that Noriega had just surfaced at the Vatican embassy, he apparently told Powell not to "let that guy out of the compound." The State Department immediately contacted the Vatican in Rome and requested that it not grant political asylum to Noriega. Near the embassy, Major General Marc Cisneros negotiated unsuccessfully with Vatican officials to broker a deal that would lead to Noriega's leaving the compound peacefully.[35]

Over the next week, a surreal scene unfolded outside the compound. The U.S. commander on the ground, General Max Thurman, ordered rock music—songs such as "I Fought the Law" and "Voodoo Chile"—to be blasted at the embassy around the clock. Panamanians congregated around the clock to shout slogans against Noriega—"Death to Hitler" or "Justice for the Tyrant"—and to hand flowers to Americans keeping watch. After over a week in the embassy, Papal Nuncio Monsignor José Sebastián Laboa convinced Noriega that there were no other options but to give himself up. On January 3, dressed in his military uniform and carrying a Bible, Noriega walked out of the front of the embassy, where U.S. troops immediately apprehended him and put him on a plane to the United States. Significantly, it was not military but U.S. DEA agents who escorted the strongman to Miami. On the flight, Noriega is reported to have given his autograph to some of the U.S. agents. That same night, thousands of celebrating Panamanians packed the six-lane Calle Cincuenta in Panama City. Just a few days before the invasion, this extradition might not have been a viable move, owing to the Posse Comitatus Act of 1878, a law that forbade U.S. military personnel conducting police work both in the United States and abroad. However, a few days before the attack, the administration had released a "clarification" that would allow the military to arrest persons overseas wanted under a U.S. warrant. As it turned out, this small jurisprudential edict would become a core part of U.S. drug enforcement strategy in Latin America over the coming decades.[36]

In the aftermath, the Bush administration wanted the invasion to be seen as a victory in the war on drugs. William J. Bennett, Bush's drug czar, told reporters that Panama "has been used as a sanctuary, a vacation spot, a banking center for traffickers, a place to go when the heat is turned up. I believe Panama is unlikely to be used in that capacity in the future." On Thursday, January 4, 1990, Noriega appeared before a federal judge in Miami and was charged with narcotics racketeering.[37]

Considerable ink has been spilled debating the consequences of the U.S. invasion of Panama, and the extent to which the United States was justified in removing a repressive dictator from a nearby state. The substance of this debate lies outside the scope of this book, but there is one angle that is germane to present purposes: the impact of the invasion on the supply of drugs reaching the United States was negligible. The devastating blow to the international drug-trafficking business that Noriega's removal was expected to deliver never came.[38]

Manuel Noriega, January 1990. This iconic booking photo was taken by U.S. Drug Enforcement Agency agents after the Panamanian strongman surrendered to the U.S. military in Panama. (Reuters, permission to author)

Poppin' Fresh

One reason for this flaccid result was that the Colombian cartels simply found other places to hide their cash—and themselves, when the time came. This is a prime example of a phenomenon that we will see repeatedly through the drug war's history: the "balloon effect." This is a well-worn metaphor for the process by which drug trafficking activity moves around in response to crackdowns in one or more particular geographical areas. Apply pressure to a balloon, and it will swell on the opposite side. As long as the drug war has been waged, it has spun off witty phrases to describe this phenomenon. The "Pillsbury Doughboy effect" is another. As Rand Beers, an undersecretary in the Department of Homeland Security (DHS) put it, you "stick your finger in one part of the problem, and the Doughboy's stomach just pops out somewhere else." In *Life and Death in the Andes*, Kim MacQuarrie writes, "Efforts thus far to stamp out cocaine production in the Andean republics . . . is known as *la cucaracha*, or 'the cockroach,' effect: just as you call kill a cockroach in one part of a room only to have another pop up somewhere else, the efforts of local and/or foreign governments to stamp out cocaine production have resulted only in cocaine production rising an equivalent amount in another."[39]

A related phenomenon is blowback—the unwanted and deleterious consequences of any policy action. For instance, as we will see, coca eradication programs under the Andean Initiative pushed coca farmers in several areas in rural Colombia to join forces with the Marxist guerrillas who were waging war on the Colombian state. Blowback, of course, isn't just limited to guerrillas. In April and May 1999, Laurie Anne Hiett, the spouse of the top-ranking U.S. Army colonel in Colombia, used the U.S. embassy's special mailing privileges to mail to New York six packages stuffed with just under sixteen pounds of pure cocaine (street value roughly $230,000). The U.S. Customs form she filled out listed the pouch's contents as books, candy, coffee, and candles. At the time, the federal charge of conspiracy to possess cocaine with the intent to distribute carried a sentence of ten to twelve years in prison. Colonel James C. Hiett voluntarily stepped aside after the news broke and eventually pleaded guilty to failing to report his wife's crimes, and served a term in federal prison.[40]

In a similar incident, on March 28, 2005, when I was working on Western Hemisphere policy at the National Security Council, five American soldiers flew a U.S. military aircraft loaded with over fifteen kilos of cocaine—retail price $300,000—from the Gómez Niño Apiay Air Base in southeastern Colombia to El Paso, Texas. The central conspirator, Army staff sergeant Daniel Rosas, confessed that he had been shipping more than 100 pounds of the drug to the United States between 2003 and 2005.[41]

The balloon effect and blowback will play important roles in the chapters that follow. Indeed, they will become the central metaphors for the complex interdependencies that the supply side of U.S. drug policy has never managed to escape.

13 • Kingpin

"En la vida se presentan dos o tres ocasiones de ser héroe, pero casí
todos los días se presenta la occasion de no ser cobarde." [In our lives
we have two or three opportunities to be a hero, but almost every day we
have the opportunity not to be a coward.]
—Colombian National Police officer to a friend in the U.S. DEA, 1986

The Medellín Cartel

Colombia's sweet-smelling cannabis was ubiquitous, from the countryside
to interior cities such as Medellín. In the early 1970s, the export-grade product
became the global gold standard for pot. Savvy Colombian kingpins first
shipped cannabis northward, sometimes using American pilots, who would
land at remote airstrips to pick up hundreds of kilos at a time. Cocaine, by
contrast, was at this point leaving Colombia only a kilo or two at a time.
Brought across by paid (or, sometimes, unwitting) smugglers known as
mules, imports of the white powder to the United States totaled maybe six
hundred kilos a year, according to U.S. drug agencies' reckoning.[1]

An oft-repeated but unconfirmed story describes how Colombian cocaine
went from an almost incidental tag-along with cannabis to America's drug du
jour. It began in the early 1970s, in the Federal Correctional Institution in
Danbury, Connecticut, where Carlos Lehder Rivas, then a "humble automobile parts smuggler," shared a cell with a young pot dealer. As the writer Robert Stone described, "The hippie kept holding forth on how grand and festive
the day of his release would be. His girl would be there, his good buddies,
some mellow sounds. And there would be coke, cocaine . . . and if God ever

made anything better, He never let on. Except of course for heroin. Colombian journalist and author Gabriel García Márquez picks up the story: 'Caramba!' says Lehder, 'If cocaine is what you like, we have it lying around on the ground in my country.' " Next, Lehder and the flower-child inmate "took to importing cocaine, a drug whose use had hitherto been confined to fringe characters like Minnie the Moocher, and, using the old methods of smuggling emeralds or marijuana or orchids, grew vastly rich—and the rest is very, very bad history."[2]

Soon enough, a major shift on the "demand side" irrevocably changed Colombia's fortunes: during the mid-1970s the American pot generation found cocaine. Pure cocaine bought for $2,000 a kilo in Colombia started selling for more than $55,000 in the United States. These incredible profit margins attracted a motley assortment of characters. José Gonzalo Rodriguez Gacha was an emerald dealer before he got into the cocaine game. The Ochoa brothers, Fabio, Juan David, and Jorge Luis, trained horses and set up restaurants before setting up a "brutal, million-dollar business smuggling drugs" around the world. With Lehder running logistics, they formed a small price-fixing cartel centered on Medellín. Another organization formed in Bogotá, the nation's capital. And the Rodríguez Orijuela brothers, Jorge, Gilberto, and Miguel, busied themselves building the Cali cartel.[3]

At the height of Colombia's cocaine boom in the 1980s, as much as 80 percent of the cocaine in the United States could be traced back to one source: the Medellín cartel. And at the center of this storm of greed, violence, and excess, there was one man: Pablo Escobar.

Pablito

The third of seven children, Pablo Escobar was born on December 1, 1949, in Rio Negro, less than thirty miles from Medellín. His mother was an educator; his father worked a farm. Escobar's maternal grandfather bootlegged moonshine, among other illicit goods. Escobar came of age in the midst of an ongoing civil war between factions of Colombia's dynastic, hierarchical Liberal and Conservative parties, a period of wanton violence so horrific and "empty of meaning" that it is known simply as La Violencia.[4]

Fleeing the interparty violence in the countryside, the Escobar family relocated to the bucolic township of Envigado, next to Medellín. Pablo was a good student who loved playing soccer, but he eventually dropped out of high school. He started smoking marijuana daily as a teenager and slept late, habits he kept for the rest of his life. But he set his sights high. As he once told his cousin and friend Gustavo Gaviria, "I want to be big."[5]

Pablo Escobar's first arrest is believed to have occurred when he was twenty-four, on September 5, 1974, when Medellín police booked him for snatching an automobile. Just two years later, Colombian authorities arrested him and five associates for smuggling dozens of kilos of cocaine through Medellín hidden inside the gang's vehicle. Escobar served only three months of his jail term, when his arrest order was mysteriously withdrawn. Less than three months later, police arrested him again, but he was freed on bail within weeks.[6]

At the time, Escobar was processing cocaine in a "grungy, ill-kept" apartment as a side hustle. He got to know another Medellín trafficker, Fabio Restrepo, who was running a few dozen kilos of cocaine northward annually. He wanted in on Restrepo's lucrative business. But the seasoned player was unimpressed by the "small, soft-spoken man" and his minor drug operation. Within a few months of their meeting, Restrepo was dead, and it was clear to everyone that Pablo Escobar meant business.[7]

Colombia's security service arrested Escobar in the aftermath of Restrepo's murder. Within a few weeks, after his associates made the appropriate payments, Escobar was sprung from prison. In his memoir, his brother Roberto Escobar described his plans for the two narcotics agents who had arrested him: "Pablo promised, 'I'm going to kill those motherfuckers myself.' . . . I have heard from others that Pablo had them brought to a house, made them get down on their knees, then put a gun to their head and killed them." Whether Pablo actually executed the men himself or delegated the job to his hired guns, shortly after his release, Medellín newspapers reported the discovery of the bodies of the two agents of the Departamento Administrativo de Seguridad riddled with bullets.[8]

In 1975 Escobar organized a scheme in which he and his business partners used several French Renault sedans outfitted with secret storage containers to smuggle coca paste from Peru to Colombia. Escobar personally drove one of the cars. Within the year, Pablo, "who had once processed a single kilo of *pasta básica* in his own bathtub[,] was soon sending forty to sixty kilos of refined cocaine to Miami by small plane *per week* and earning roughly $8 million of profits per month." The preferred route was an established marijuana pathway: a short flight over the Caribbean Sea to Florida, where packages were dropped into the Everglades, snagged by launches, and whisked over to Miami.[9]

The young runner was also quickly earning a reputation for "casual, lethal" violence. Pablo established a hallmark way of dealing with local and federal officials: *plata o plomo*. You either took Escobar's *plata* (silver) or his *plomo* (lead). He exacted revenge by killing his enemies—or their friends and families. Not infrequently, he tortured his victims before delivering the coup de grâce. The strategy carried him to a position of such power and infamy that it made "even Italian Mafia bosses shudder."[10]

By late 1975, Escobar and the consolidating Medellín cartel were shipping multiple hundreds of kilos at a time, a fact confirmed by a Colombian police raid that uncovered six hundred kilos in a single aircraft. Escobar used his prodigious revenues to vertically integrate his business. He traveled to Peru, Bolivia, and Panama to establish direct business links with the *pasta básica* producers. He invested millions in protecting his intermediate processors and distributors. He built a cartel organization that set prices and funded its own security, while largely operating as a franchise. Escobar commanded large percentages from his associates. He charged his fellow runners not just for the cost of trafficking but also for what he called "my struggle." The overhead was not insignificant.[11]

Bribes were the oil that lubricated the machine. When people could not be bought—or when others betrayed them—Medellín called in the guns. The word *sicario* comes from the Latin *sicarius,* or "dagger man," referring to a "self-defense splinter group" of Jewish guerrillas who resisted Roman control of ancient Judea. By the mid-1980s, the cartel relied on multiple thousands of *sicarios,* who more often than not were teenagers. The signature *sicario* execution was a motorcycle drive-by shooting. For his part, Escobar preferred that his men use two bullets to the forehead. "A person might survive *one* of those bullets, Escobar advised, but never *two*."[12]

Escobar's ingenious methods for moving product northward became legendary. For example, he used radio-controlled "narco-subs" that could carry two thousand kilos of coke from Colombia's northern Pacific coast to a rendezvous location in the Caribbean. Men used scuba gear to locate the craft and remove the cargo and then carried the shipment to southern Florida by boat.[13]

The profits were almost incomprehensible. Between 1976 and 1980, bank deposits in Colombia's three largest cities, Bogotá, Cali, and Medellín, roughly doubled. At the peak, Medellín was likely pulling in $60 million *every day*. There was so much cash that the cartel began burying it in secret locations around the country. By the mid-1980s, the cocaine trade was the fastest-growing and most profitable industry in the world. A 1988 story in *Fortune* magazine made waves when it estimated Colombian cocaine exports at more than $4 billion annually. This was more than the country's coffee and oil exports combined. *Fortune* marveled at the Medellín cartel's business acumen. The entity had customs agents, industrialists, bankers, ranchers, military brass, cops, and, not least, politicians pitching in. Pablo's billions were the "sum total of every furtive transaction, his risk was the sum total of all his users' petty risks." At the end of a long chain of illegal dealing was Pablo Escobar, the man who "ran the Big Risk and reaped the Big Reward."[14]

The Revolutionary Armed Forces of Colombia

Had Pablo Escobar and the cartels been the only players in Colombia's cocaine game, the country might have avoided many of the horrors of the decades that followed. But besides the drug gangs, there were scores of other players.

Among the most pernicious were two unlikely candidates, Colombia's oldest guerrilla insurgency, the FARC (Revolutionary Armed Forces of Colombia), and the right-wing paramilitary groups that fought them. If one were to consider these actors on purely ideological grounds, their involvement in the drug trade might seem counterintuitive. The FARC, for one, preceded Colombia's illicit drug boom by several decades and until the 1980s eschewed the trade as crassly bourgeois. The paramilitaries were often driven by a staunch social conservatism that opposed drug use entirely. Yet, these movements became inextricably tangled in Colombia's biggest industry.

These dynamics can get complicated fast, so a bit of key background is warranted. Colombia has a population of more than 40 million in a country larger than Texas, New Mexico, and Louisiana combined, with several distinct zones: the sweltering Caribbean and Pacific coasts with their plantation agriculture; the Andes mountain range, split by the lowland Magdalena River; the vast Llanos Orientales, grasslands that stretch east through the border with Venezuela; and Amazonia, the Amazon basin, extending southeast to the Amazon River and the border with Brazil. During colonial times, the Magdalena River connected the north coast with the remote inland capital of Bogotá. In the twentieth century, the Magdalena River valley, like some grotesque version of Mesopotamia, became the birthing ground not only for Escobar's Medellín cartel but also for the FARC and its major paramilitary opposition.[15]

The story of these latter groups begins in the cruel era in the 1940s and 1950s known as *La Violencia*, when enmity between the country's two hereditary parties, the Liberals and the Conservatives, erupted into open violence. *La Violencia* lasted until 1957, when the Liberal and Conservative elites brokered a power-sharing agreement they called the National Front. Meanwhile, armed bands of Liberal-aligned *campesinos*, who had fled to remote mountain lairs during the worst of the fighting, had begun to organize—and to get religion, in the form of revolutionary Marxism. As the National Front's quasi-democracy took its shaky first steps, these groups continued raiding and terrorizing wealthy landowners in the hills and mountains around the Middle Magdalena. These politicized, Robin Hood–like *bandidos* became heroes to their undernourished and disenfranchised countrymen.[16]

One of these outlaws, based in the department of Tolima in the upper Magdalena valley, was a teenaged salesman named Pedro Antonio Marín. Having left home at the tender age of thirteen, Marín was a prodigy military tactician; his skill as a rifleman earned him the nickname "Tirofijo" (Sureshot). In the early 1950s, he assumed the nom de guerre Manuel Marulanda, honoring a slain labor organizer and took to dressing in trademark *campesino* garb: long-sleeved plaid tops, white T-shirt, pants tucked into high rubber boots, a white towel over one shoulder, machete and pistol holstered around the waist. Thus equipped, Marulanda would become one of the most consequential guerrilla leaders in Latin American history.[17]

After Fidel Castro seized power in Cuba in 1959, the National Front government in Bogotá was increasingly eager to dispense with these lingering communist bands. In 1964, after the Colombian military razed the hamlet of Marquetalia, Marulanda and his comrades were convinced that only armed revolution could overthrow the oligarchic central government and install a Marxist state. Later that year, Marulanda founded the FARC.

In these early years, the front had but several hundred poorly armed men and women in its ranks. They fought a typical guerrilla war in the mountains and jungles, operating according to a strategic plan that emphasized the need to control key segments of the rural population. This they accomplished through a tremendous dispersal of guerrilla forces into regional "fronts" and "blocs" across Colombia's vast and often inhospitable territory. Further to this end, the insurgents aggressively deployed propaganda to indoctrinate the rural poor and selectively threatened and killed members of the propertied class—mostly large-scale farmers and cattle ranchers. One FARC tactic that was a particular source of consternation was *pesca milagrosa* (miracle fishing). Insurgents would set up roadblocks throughout the country and demand national identity cards from motorists they saw. When they hooked a "big fish"—anyone who appeared to have financial means—they kidnapped him or her.

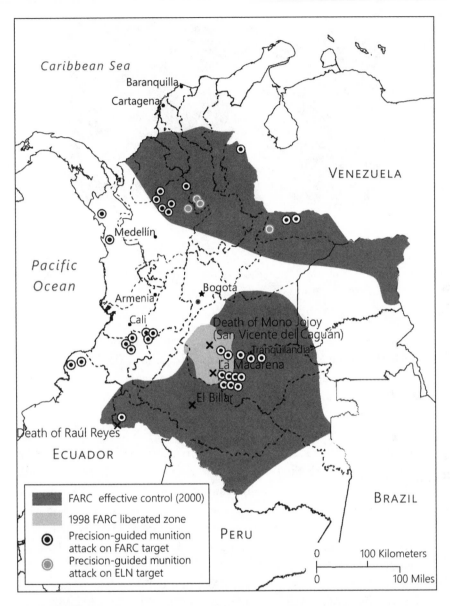

Map of Colombia. The Revolutionary Armed Forces of Colombia (FARC) was Latin America's largest and strongest Marxist insurgency. At the height of its power in the early 2000s, the Leninist narco-guerrilla force had a presence in more than a third of the national territory. (University of Wisconsin Cartography Lab)

Manuel Marulanda (known as "Sureshot"), circa 2000. He was born to a poor farmer
around 1930 in Colombia's lush western Andean coffee region. (Marcelo Salinas,
permission to author)

By the end of the 1970s, FARC guerrillas held dominion over the Middle
Magdalena. Yet the FARC leadership deduced that total victory in Colombia
would also require developing a serious political force to seize power in the
cities—*la combinación de todas formas de lucha* (the combination of all forms
of struggle). As part of a series of peace talks that ultimately foundered in the
early 1980s, the FARC created a legally constituted political party, the Unión
Patriótica (UP, or Patriotic Union). Between 1984 and 1988, when support for
the party was at its peak, the FARC added around a dozen new military fronts,
doubling in size. Not coincidentally, a strong share of these new fronts arose
around cities in which the UP had control of the mayor's office. Some reckoned that municipal funds were making their way into rebel coffers to finance
the new units. It also happened that many UP strongholds were also bastions
of coca production.[18]

The problem, though, was that the FARC and UP's clandestine plans conflicted with those of a "similarly ambitious project." The country's drug lords
and their private armies viewed the relatively stateless territory of the Magdalena Valley as their dominion as well. Medellín and their Cali counterparts
started using their exorbitant profits to buy up cattle ranches and other rural
properties. In the end, they owned more than 2.5 million acres, or one-twelfth
of Colombia's farmland, much of it in the Middle Magdalena. The investment
allowed the traffickers to launder the cocaine money and to gain a semblance

of social status, which Colombia's old-money elites had not permitted them to share. Escobar's most extravagant contribution to the land grab was the sprawling, seven-thousand-acre Hacienda Nápoles. The ranch boasted a palace that could house a hundred guests at a time, a zoo stocked with hippopotamus and elephants, and—mounted "as if it were a national monument," in Gabriel García Márquez's inimitable prose—the small plane used to smuggle the cartel's first cocaine load. By the mid-1980s Escobar and others were the richest "landowners" in the Andean nation's checkered history. Like the guerrillas, the narcos desired greater and greater isolation to operate the cocaine business.[19]

Perhaps unsurprisingly, the guerrillas saw the newcomers as cash cows. In 1981, the FARC kidnapped the father of a two-bit drug and emerald dealer named Fidel Castaño. It was an everyday operation for the Marxist rebels to finance their war machine, but it would have "fateful consequences." According to one account, Castaño's father, "who had been held to a tree by a long rope for many days, slammed his head against the tree trunk until he dropped to the ground and there was 'left to die' by the guerrillas, presumably of a heart attack." Then, on November 12, 1981, a smaller leftist guerrilla group known as M-19 kidnapped Marta Nieves Ochoa, the youngest sister of Jorge Ochoa and the daughter of drug lord Don Fabio Ocho. The guerrillas' demands included a ransom of more than $10 million. Despite grave worries, the Ochoa family refused to cooperate with the captors.[20]

Instead, in early December 1981, a small airplane "described lazy circles in the Sunday afternoon sky" above a stadium in Cali as soccer fans were gearing up for the tense match between local side América and a rival Medellín-based team. Just as the opening half began, the plane dropped leaflets that described a recent "general assembly" in which a group of prominent Colombian businessmen, drug traffickers, and military officers agreed that they had had enough of the guerrillas. These men had each committed treasure as well as their reputations to establish a paramilitary death squad, Muerte a Secuestradores (death to kidnappers), saying in a statement, "The basic objective will be the public and immediate execution of all those involved in kidnappings beginning from the date of this communiqué." The guilty "will be hung from the trees in public parks or shot and marked with the sign of our group—MAS." Guerrilla kidnappers already in jail would be killed as well. If this failed, "our retribution will fall on their closest family members."[21]

After scores of M-19 guerrillas and their family members had been killed, the chastened rebels made a pact with the traffickers never to kidnap them or their relatives again. Escobar 1, Guerrillas 0. Journalists covering Colombia's drug war at the time concluded that MAS represented a new era in Colombia's drug history. It was the first time that the drug cartels had ever taken a coordinated public position on a particular matter. The original MAS soon unraveled, but it had two broader effects. First, it galvanized the Medellín cartel to take a more active political stance. Second, it spawned a generation of paramilitary groups in the Middle Magdalena Valley.[22]

Though MAS effectively chastened M-19, the FARC proved more intransigent. In 1983, the Castaño sons avenged their father's death. A group of men under orders from son Fidel descended on villages around Segovia, where Castaño *pater* had been held captive, "pulling babies out of their mothers' arms and shooting them, nailing a child to a plank, impaling a man on a bamboo pole, hacking a woman to pieces with a machete." Twenty-two villagers were dead before the killers relented. The murders were but the first in what became a decades-long assassination campaign by *grupos de autodefensa comunitaria* or, more commonly, *autodefensas* or *paras*. The *paras* were exterminators, paid by the cartels or otherwise self-deputized to purify the Middle Magdalena of Marxist guerrillas and their suspected sympathizers. As Alma Guillermoprieto writes, the paramilitaries "sprang up, like soldiers grown from dragons' teeth," and quickly found support in a familiar class of actors. Narco-landowners, including Escobar and the especially bloodthirsty "El Mexicano," funded the *paras* to make the FARC problem disappear.[23]

A Decade of Living Dangerously

In a system in which the cartels owned or rented law enforcement, from villages and barrios on up to the military leadership, the bosses faced only one real threat: extradition. In 1979, under Presidents Jimmy Carter and Julio César Turbay, the United States and Colombia signed a treaty that proscribed international drug trafficking as a crime against the United States. It said that Colombian traffickers could be extradited to the United States and, if convicted, imprisoned there. (On cue, Escobar had denounced the treaty as an infringement of Colombian "national security.") U.S. authorities were confident that the treaty, backed by $26 million in foreign aid, would usher in a lasting era of bilateral anti-drug cooperation. This hope was set back when President Belisario Betancur, who took office in 1982, refused to extradite Colombian nationals as a matter of principle.[24]

The *capos* celebrated an apparent victory. For his part, Escobar exploited an especially nationalistic mood to run for national office as a Liberal Party candidate. He was elected an "alternate" congressman. Whenever his partner on the congressional ticket, Jairo Ortega, was absent, Escobar substituted for him in the Chamber of Representatives. The position came with automatic judicial immunity, so Escobar could no longer be prosecuted for crimes under Colombian law. He was also entitled to a diplomatic visa and diplomatic immunity, allowing him to travel to the United States. In May 1980, his family visited Disney World and Washington, D.C., where he had a family picture taken in front of the White House. Meanwhile, Pablo's illicit cocaine continued to flow northward. In fact, his mules were coming back to Colombia with so many hundred-dollar bills that the Medellín accountants found it easier to weigh the bills than to count them by hand.[25]

With his status officially legitimized, Escobar "installed lights at soccer fields, built roller-skating rinks, spoke at public events, and handed out money." He started a social agency called Medellín without Slums, funded a radio show, *Civics on the March,* and made plans to construct the immodestly named Barrio Pablo Escobar, a massive apartment complex for the city's desperate poor. Thanks to these charitable efforts, Escobar and his colleagues enjoyed total impunity and even a certain social prestige. Don Pablo also employed a gaggle of publicists and paid reporters to burnish his public persona. For two or three years they did a reasonably good job casting Escobar as a philanthropist determined to give back to the poor barrios where he began. The conservative Catholic Church in Medellín supported Don Pablo's social programs. However, the Colombian police continued to eye him, suspecting that, whatever his political and social ambitions, he was still the same ruthless and vengeful enforcer he'd always been. More to Pablo's dismay, his quest for respectability was never accepted by "polite Colombian society." A blue-blood Medellín country club, Club Campestre, denied his application to join.[26]

The congressional seat turned out to be the high-water mark for Escobar's political ambitions. In August 1983 Colombia's young justice minister, an ambitious member of Luis Carlos Galán's reformist New Liberal movement named Rodrigo Lara Bonilla, revealed Escobar's not-so-well-kept secret. Pablito was no real estate tycoon, Bonilla told the nation, but the world's biggest cocaine trafficker. "The more I learn," Lara Bonilla said, "the more I know of the damage that the *narcos* are causing the country. I will never again refuse the extradition of one of these dogs." To rub it in, an embarrassed Bogotá promptly seized more than a hundred of Pablo's exotic animals at Nápoles, citing illegal importation. Days later, the influential daily *El Espectador* ran new pieces touting Escobar's mid-1970s drug trafficking arrest, alongside the now infamous police mug shot from the same arrest, with Pablo wearing a knowing smile. The New Liberals ejected the cocaine baron from the party, along with his seat, his immunity, and his diplomatic visa.[27]

Lara Bonilla also authorized the DEA-assisted Colombian National Police's raid of March 10, 1984, on a massive cocaine-processing lab in the hamlet of Tranquilandia, on the Yarí River in the southern jungle. This sprawling facility consisted of nineteen scattered camps and utilized scores of laborers who lived in dorms. The security forces confiscated an astounding twenty-seven thousand pounds of cocaine. Marxist guerrillas were suspected to have served as guards. This so-called grandfather lab, the largest known to exist in Colombia at the time, was producing five thousand kilos of refined cocaine per week, at a street value of $1.2 billion.[28]

With his licit cover blown and political aspirations extinguished, Escobar, now humiliated, no longer needed to pretend that he was anything other than a ruthless criminal. In retaliation, Escobar declared war on the Colombian state. Political kidnappings, assassinations, and bombings surged. The key objective for the *paisa* cocaine baron was to force Bogotá to rescind its extradition treaty with the United States. A summary phrase is often attributed to Escobar: "Better a tomb in Colombia than a jail cell in the United States."[29]

Lara Bonilla became Escobar's obsession. Escobar first tried to smear him with outlandish accusations, which Lara Bonilla countered by denouncing Escobar in a congressional session. Terrified, Lara Bonilla accepted the U.S. embassy's offer to relocate his family to the United States under assumed names. On April 30, 1984, an ex-convict *sicario* on a red Yamaha motorcycle hit Lara Bonilla's car with a spray of bullets. Seven of them struck the justice minister.[30]

The Conservative president, Betancur, refused to jettison Lara Bonilla's "crusade" against the drug barons and the gringo aid that came with it. During Lara Bonilla's memorial, the Colombian president declared "war without cease-fire"; he signed a state of siege and ordered the National Police to seize the estates of the *capos* and other illicit assets. He extradited jailed drug lords to the United States, thirteen in total from 1984 to mid-1987. The top DEA official in Bogotá, John Phelps, told the *New York Times* he was confident that Betancur's swift measures would pay dividends: "If the campaign continues at this pace, it is going to have a major impact on trafficking in Colombia and to the United States and Europe." A recent increase in wholesale cocaine prices indeed seemed to indicate that the policies, including the bust of the mega-lab in Tranquilandia, were having the desired impact. Short-lived as this might have been, for much of the 1980s Pablo Escobar was tortured by the notion of extradition: it was "spoiling his pursuit of the good life."[31]

Don Pablo's War

Lara Bonilla's killing marked the onset of the nation's "decade of living dangerously." Pablo Escobar hastily departed from Medellín to Panama City, where his business partners Carlos Lehder Rivas, José Rodríguez Gacha, and the Ochoa brothers were already hiding out at a country club residence, compliments of a character we've already spent time with, General Manuel Noriega. From their headquarters-in-exile, the Medellín cartel waged a war of incredible intensity against the Colombian state and anyone else they perceived as threatening their business. Medellín-hired *sicarios* tracked Lara Bonilla's successor, Enrique Parejo, all the way to Budapest. One of the assassins shot the minister in the head, though not lethally. A federal judge, Tulio Manuel Castro Gil, was killed by *sicarios* in July 1985 while hailing a cab, soon after he had indicted Escobar and other Medellín cartel leaders as conspirators in Lara Bonilla's murder.[32]

On November 6, 1985, M-19—the very same group that had kidnapped Marta Nieves Ochoa and spurred the "Death to Kidnappers" campaign—raided the Palace of Justice in the heart of Bogotá. Guerrillas held hostage the Colombian Supreme Court justice and aides and ritually placed President Betancur on trial for not having brokered peace. They also demanded that the government reverse the 1979 extradition treaty. Refusing to negotiate, Betancur ordered the military to storm the palace. After a fiery ten-hour battle, ninety-five people were confirmed dead, including nine of twenty-five judges and Chief Justice Alfonso Reyes Echandía. The raid undermined Colombia's legal system and effectively terminated Betancur's peace moves with the FARC and M-19. Also believed to have been destroyed in the standoff were thousands of criminal records, including the casework against Pablo Escobar. The unconfirmed theory is that Escobar and other kingpins paid M-19 as much as a million dollars to carry out the mission.[33]

Escobar's war took the lives of scores of judges, politicians, and journalists as well as hundreds of police officers and ordinary Colombians. The decade made Bogotá more willing to accept American aid and training, as the *capos* became a more existential threat. President Virgilio Barco, elected in 1986, intensified the cartel war, first issuing a sweeping set of temporary but pervasive state-of-siege decrees that placed Colombia under martial law.

In 1987, Colombian authorities extradited Carlos Lehder Rivas to the United States. On July 20, 1988, the thirty-eight-year-old trafficker, believed to have a net worth of $2.5 billion, was sentenced in a U.S. court to life in prison without parole, plus an additional 135 years. At his sentencing hearing, Lehder characterized himself as a political prisoner persecuted by an overzealous American judicial system. The American judge himself had words for Lehder that also shed valuable light on our broader story of America's war on drugs. "The truth of the matter is your main goal was to make money, and you did so at the expense of others. Your conspiracy burned a path of destruction and despair from the coca fields of South America to the streets and byways of this country. Accordingly, Mr. Lehder, the sentence I impose on you today is meant to be a message for drug smugglers who control large organizations, for importers of cocaine, and for street pushers. . . . This sentence is a signal that our country will do everything in its power and within the laws to battle the drug problem that threatens the very fabric of our society."[34]

The Kingpin Strategy

The cartels responded with a spate of bombings in the capital and at least one commercial airline. On August 18, 1989, a *sicario* murdered pro-extradition presidential candidate Luis Carlos Galán. President Barco responded to the carnage by sending more than twenty suspected traffickers to the United States. He established three special operations police units, one of which, the Bloque de Búsqueda (Search Bloc), he assigned the single task of getting Escobar. Within two weeks of the Search Bloc's existence, more than two dozen of its men had fallen.

The violence also alarmed Washington, especially after cartel operatives were busted attempting to purchase over a hundred Stinger anti-aircraft missiles in Florida. The Bush administration released a Justice Department opinion concluding that deploying U.S. military abroad to hunt narco lords would not violate the Posse Comitatus Act's restrictions on military involvement in civilian law enforcement matters; this was the same "clarification" that facilitated the extradition of Noriega from Panama that year.[35]

It was in this atmosphere that a new side of the U.S. war on the supply of drugs emerged. Robert Bonner, a former federal prosecutor and judge before becoming head of the DEA, is credited with developing the "kingpin strategy," whose aim was to "decapitate" the cartels by targeting their leaders for execution or capture. In journalist Andrew Cockburn's assessment, the strategy assumed that the United States faced a "hierarchically structured threat that could be defeated by removing key leadership components." In this, Bonner echoed a traditional U.S. Air Force doctrine: that any enemy system must contain "critical nodes," the destruction of which would lead to the enemy's collapse. The balance sheet on this particular assessment is still being filled out.[36]

The birth of the kingpin strategy was an important moment for American law. American agents, or the domestic forces they supported in source countries, could now legally kill foreign nationals for their involvement in drug trafficking. It was also a major moment for the DEA. Now, as never before, Bonner's agency had teeth, and it was able to draw on the resources of the CIA, the NSA, and the FBI to pursue anti-drug aims. Not since the days of Harry Anslinger had an executive drug agency carried so much weight.

President Bush also allocated $250 million in emergency enforcement assistance to combat drug operations in the Andes and deployed a Special Forces team to train their counterparts in the Colombian armed forces and national police. That this was primarily *counternarcotics* aid is telling for our broader story. It was not the last time that Washington would attempt to "save" Colombia through fighting drugs. Within weeks of Galán's assassination, U.S. assets began to arrive in Colombia: two C-130 transport planes, five UH1H helicopters, eight A-37 Dragonfly light attack aircraft, and all sorts of other matériel. In February 1990, Bush escalated the rhetoric during a visit to Colombia, declaring, "We have committed ourselves to the first common, comprehensive international drug control strategy." He backed the words with $2 billion in American aid over five years.

In 1990 Escobar began kidnapping prominent journalists and society scions, a shrewd political and psychological calculation given how close these individuals were to the ruling class. Among the victims was Maruja Pachón de Villamizar, sister-in-law of the assassinated presidential candidate Luis Carlos Galán and wife of the prominent Liberal politician Alberto Villamizar, who had spearheaded the extradition legislation. Another was Marina Montoya, sister of politician German Montoya. Diana Turbay, a television executive and daughter of the former Liberal Party head Julio César Turbay, was captured on the same day as Francisco Santos, editor-in-chief of the influential newspaper *El Tiempo*. Sadly, there was little the Colombian justice system could do to bring Escobar and his cadre to account. Judges and magistrates, "whose low salaries were enough to live on, but not enough to pay for the education of their children," faced an awful dilemma: sell themselves to the traffickers or be killed. *Plata o plomo*. Many of them chose death.[37]

Meanwhile, the new president, César Gaviria, and his top aides and ministers were attempting to negotiate Escobar's surrender, an effort that was now tied up with the hostages. In late May 1991, Escobar indicated that he was ready to give himself up in exchange for lenient punishment and immunity from extradition. Impossibly, Gaviria dispatched Alberto Villamizar to Medellín to meet with Escobar to hammer out the details of his surrender and the release of the hostages. Villamizar was not only the husband of Escobar's highest-profile hostage but had also been the victim of at least one assassination attempt, allegedly at the hands of Escobar's *sicarios*. He revealed to one of Gaviria's national security aides: "Imagine how I feel. First he threatens me. Then he makes an attempt on my life, and it's a miracle I escape. He goes on threatening me. He assassinates Galán. He abducts my wife and my sister, and now he wants me to defend his rights."[38]

Escobar held out until the constitutional assembly approved a prohibition on extradition—a move vehemently opposed by Washington. Then he turned himself in through a deal brokered between his lawyers and the government. At the time of his surrender, Escobar faced ten indictments for drug trafficking and murder in the United States. Escobar admitted to having been present at the meeting when the decision to kill Galán was made but denied ordering the politician's murder. "The fact is that everybody wanted to kill Dr. Galán," he said.[39]

After almost a year in captivity, Francisco Santos and Maruja Villamizar were released in May 1991, soon after Escobar's surrender. Santos was sympathetic to the plight of his captors. "They were boys from the Antioquian countryside who had emigrated to Medellín, lost their way in the slums, and killed and were killed with no scruples. As a rule they came from broken homes where the father was a negative figure and the mother a very strong one. They were used to working for very high pay and had no sense of money." Two other hostages had not survived their ordeals. Diana Turbay had been inadvertently killed by the National Police during a rescue operation on January 25, 1991. Marina Montoya, sixty-five, had been summarily executed.[40]

As the *New York Times* told an incredulous global audience, Mr. Escobar's new home on a wooded hilltop on the edge of Envigado consisted of a "cluster of red-tiled bungalows with private baths and panoramic views of the Andes." Surrounding the perimeter was a menacing eighteen-foot-high electrified fence. Arguably, the prison, dubbed La Catedral, was designed more to keep Escobar's enemies out than to keep him and his crew in. The surrender contract even prohibited police and soldiers from entering the two-and-a-half-acre compound. But this was also the entire premise of the surrender deal: Escobar would never have agreed to come in from the cold if he could not count on his own security.[41]

Pablo's Escape

Escobar continued to run his empire from La Catedral. International media covering Escobar's surreal surrender commented that Bogotá's efforts had already disrupted Medellín's cocaine trafficking significantly. One report suggested that the "preeminence in the drug trade has passed to the quieter, more businesslike traffickers based in the city of Cali." But U.S. officials at the embassy were getting reports that Escobar was still collecting a $500,000 "war tax" from traffickers on the outside. There was also intelligence documenting lascivious parties with prostitutes and incessant unchecked visitors. In mid-1992, Escobar invited several of his former associates, including Fernando and Mario Galeano and brothers Gerardo and William Julio Moncada, to La Catedral, ostensibly for a business meeting. Instead, Escobar had them killed for hoarding millions of dollars they "did not feel like turning over to El Patrón."[42]

Rattled and more than a little embarrassed by the revelations, Gaviria swiftly approved an operation to snag Escobar from his "prison" and move him to a higher-security facility. Escobar likely learned of Gaviria's plan on television news. Assuming that the government's real plan was either to kill him or to ship him in chains to the United States, he came to the conclusion that it was time to find a safer locale. In July 1992, under the noses of the five hundred troops surrounding the compound in preparation for the emergency transfer, Escobar and his closest confidants walked out hours before the operation was slated to begin. The security forces they almost certainly encountered were either "too friendly or too intimidated" to stop them.[43]

Now on the run, Escobar quickly realized the enormity of his miscalculation and pleaded with Gaviria to "repeat the favor of imprisoning him" through an unconditional surrender. Being Escobar, he matched this carrot with the stick of a ferocious terrorist bombing offensive. Gaviria defiantly ignored his proposals, and an epic manhunt began.[44]

Only days after Escobar fled La Catedral, Ambassador Morris Busby requested American military support from Foggy Bottom, which passed it along to the National Security Council. After consulting with Chairman Colin Powell of the Joint Chiefs of Staff, President Bush told Secretary of Defense Richard Cheney to give the U.S. embassy anything it wanted. With this green light from the top executive branch officials, a mad rush of men and weapons stormed to Colombia to aid the hunt.

The force included at least one elite U.S. Army Delta Force unit (usually composed of a dozen operators) active in Bogotá and Medellín. The Air Force dispatched Boeing RC-135 reconnaissance jets, Lockheed C-130 Hercules cargo planes, Lockheed ultra-high-altitude U-2 planes, and Lockheed SR-71 Blackbirds. The Navy sent Lockheed P-3 Orion maritime surveillance planes. In a precursor of the postmodern military and intelligence drone, the CIA dispatched a Schweizer SGM 2-37, a fixed-wing surveillance glider that could hover stealthily over a target for hours. The operation required ten C-130s just to deliver the contractors and maintenance staff for all of the equipment. At one point, seventeen American spy planes were in Medellín airspace at one time, so many that the Air Force had to put a Boeing E-3 Sentry in the air just to monitor them.[45]

Despite the scale of the deployment, the greatest difficulty for Colombia's elite Search Bloc and its American counterparts proved to be simply finding Escobar. He was in home territory, a city in the "center of terrorism." Colombian intelligence estimated that more than two thousand individuals were working in the slums for Escobar. Even still, Pablo delegated little. He served as "his own military commander, his own head of security, intelligence, and counterintelligence, an unpredictable strategist, and an unparalleled purveyor of disinformation." Under especially intense pressure, he changed his eight-person team of bodyguards each day. He used state-of-the-art communications, wiretapping, and tracking devices. When law enforcement gave out two phone numbers for submitting information on his location, Escobar "hired whole schools of children" to create a wave of phone calls that would ensure the line remained busy. When Escobar realized that his phone calls were being tapped, he spoke into his radio phone: "Colonel, I'm going to kill you. I'm going to kill all of your family up to the third generation, and then I will dig up your grandparents and shoot them and bury them again. Do you *hear* me?"[46]

Los Pepes

In late January 1993, an explosion rocked Medellín, this time from a car bomb that demolished one of Escobar's family residences. A shadowy outfit calling itself People Persecuted by Pablo Escobar (or Los Pepes) claimed responsibility. It was the first of scores of operations. The Pepes located and killed attorneys working for Escobar, torched his antique car collection to "molten rubble," and "bombed and burned" several of his properties. On February 3, the corpse of Luis Isaza, a Medellín cartel member, was dropped off in a city neighborhood with a sign around his neck reading, "For working for the narco-terrorist baby-killer Pablo Escobar. For Colombia. Los Pepes." On April 16, police found the tortured body of Pablo's most prominent lawyer, Guido Parra, alongside his teenage son, Guido Andrés Parra, in the back of a vehicle near a Medellín social club. A stern message was painted nearby: "Through their profession, they initiated abductions for Pablo Escobar. Los Pepes." And as a postscript, "What do you think of the exchange for the bombs in Bogotá, Pablo?" In June, Los Pepes kidnapped and shot one of Pablo's brothers-in-law. The reprisals were proving more effective in hunting the fugitive Escobar than the efforts of either the Colombian or the U.S. government. This led Alma Guillermoprieto to reflect in the pages of the *New Yorker*, "If it weren't for Los Pepes, it is unlikely that the government could have Escobar so cornered today."[47]

U.S. officials were ebullient, believing that courageous civilians were finally fighting back. "We thought it was a citizen group that had finally reached the stage where they were going to straighten things up." But before long, U.S. intelligence—and just about everyone else in Colombia—understood that Los Pepes were a creation of the Cali cartel. U.S. officials were further discouraged to learn that Los Pepes were even paying Colombian police officers to kill Escobar's allies, effectively turning the force into "assassins for Cali interests." Said Joe Toft, DEA agent-in-charge in Bogotá, "We knew that Cali had a better game plan and were smarter, and that they would try to capitalize on Escobar's problems. But I don't think anyone understood how fully they were to take advantage of the situation until the process was well underway."[48]

Killing Pablo

By 1993, Pablo Escobar's world had changed. Allies who could have helped him now had little reason to do so. A fortune once estimated at $3 billion was largely lost to his protracted war. There was no place his family could live "where they would sleep without nightmares." Escobar himself could not spend more than six hours in a single location. He continued to offer to turn himself in, the last time in October 1993, in a message conveyed to the mayor of Medellín.[49]

On December 2, 1993, Escobar "couldn't resist the temptation" of speaking on the telephone for several minutes with his son, Juan Pablo. This gave a team of Colombian and U.S. specialists in a surveillance van in Medellín time to confirm his exact location in the middle-class neighborhood of Los Olivos. A little after three o'clock that afternoon, a team of twenty-three special plain-clothes police cordoned off the immediate area and forced their way to the second floor.

Escobar spoke his last words to Juan Pablo on the phone: "I'm hanging up because something funny's going on here." Minutes later, Search Bloc officers shouted and called superiors. "Viva Colombia! We have just killed Pablo Escobar!" A chase that endured for sixteen months and involved six separate U.S. agencies was over. In the years to come, a rumor would endure that a U.S. Delta Force soldier had delivered the fatal shot, but evidence for this alternative scenario is scant.[50]

Post-Pablo

Thousands of sobbing *paisas* mourned Escobar's death as his casket was drawn through the streets of Medellín before arriving in a "muddy hilltop cemetery." A *New York Times* headline encapsulated the scene: "A Drug Lord Is Buried as a Folk Hero." The journalist Mark Bowden keenly observed: "A man of lesser ambition might still be alive, rich, powerful, and living well and openly in Medellín. But Pablo wasn't content to be just rich and powerful. He wanted to be admired. He wanted to be respected. He wanted to be loved." In the ensuing years, his grave become a tourist attraction—or, for some, a spiritual pilgrimage.[51]

For their part, American anti-drug officials were confident they could see the light at the end of the tunnel. "We felt like it was one down, fifteen to go," recalled John Carnevale, director of planning and budget for the ONDCP, to a *Rolling Stone* interviewer in 2007. "There was this feeling that if we got all 16 [of Colombia's top drug lords], it's not like the whole thing would be over, but that was a big part of how we would go about winning the War on Drugs."[52]

14 • Plan Colombia

Atomization

American and Colombian anti-drug officials celebrated Pablo Escobar's "decapitation" as proof positive that the kingpin strategy was on its way to eradicating cocaine trafficking in Colombia. What these authorities did not fully anticipate, however, was how quickly other criminal actors would fill the vacuum. After Escobar's killing, Medellín's drug bosses met to discuss business, apparently in an underground parking garage in the neighborhood of Envigado, the same barrio where Escobar had gotten his start. From this meeting emerged the so-called Envigado Office, with a man known as Don Berna at its helm. Don Berna, born Diego Fernando Murillo, was a formidable Medellín drug trafficker and an erstwhile member of the Marxist Popular Liberation Army. He had at one point collaborated with Pablo Escobar before turning against the *capo* and joining the rival gang that helped lead authorities to him.[1]

Not content to be just another kingpin in a city full of them, Don Berna began turning his enmity toward his former comrades-in-arms, most notably the FARC. In a turn that dramatically complicated the drug war and broader U.S. policy in Colombia, Don Berna joined an alliance of right-wing militias that targeted such leftist groups, not so much because of their political position but because they were now rivals in the drug trade. These attacks came as a shock to the guerrillas, who were used to facing a far less formidable garrison-style military. Soon, Don Berna was commanding more than three thousand of these paramilitaries, as they came to be known.[2]

The Envigado Office was never as powerful as its Medellín predecessor had been. That honor now went to the Cali cartel, an association of four billionaires who managed a worldwide cocaine monopoly, controlling everything from production in Peru and Colombia to sales in the suburbs and cities in the United States and around the globe. The organization ended up so cash-rich that it began buying aging 727 jets at a few hundred thousand dollars a pop, stuffing them with hundred-dollar bills, and then flying them to clandestine runways in Colombia's remotest regions, where they left them to rust.[3]

Yet, in contrast to Medellín's violence and gaudy displays of narco wealth, the drug traffickers of Cali considered themselves both subdued and sophisticated. One Cali city official told me in an interview: "They have highly educated people, degrees from American schools. They followed the Italian mafia concept of threatening and bribing, rather than killing—unless they had to." They spent millions of dollars building community projects, including local police stations and a hospital and library. This being Colombia, they even owned the city's professional soccer team.[4]

Yet the contrast can only go so far. Before Escobar's death, the Cali capos paid more than $1 million to a team of British mercenaries to attempt to murder their Medellín counterpart. They also employed a skilled team of sicarios to enforce discipline and compliance in its diffuse organization. American drug enforcement agents called the cartel's intelligence unit the "Cali KGB." And, like Medellín, Cali engaged in liberal bribery to buy the soul of the Colombian government. Its payment network included police offices, senators, and even members of the elite counternarcotics force. A revolving door of former politicians constituted the cartel's "lobbying wing," which arranged meetings between kingpins and government officials—all in an effort to spread the word that "the gentlemen of Cali would be generous to friends." Cash, cars, women, luxury vacations, and, of course, cocaine were some of the incentives. As one Colombian told me in the mid-1990s, the Cali cartel was the cocaine version of the American sugar lobby: low-profile but incredibly effective.[5]

The Cali cartel's secret multi-million-dollar contributions to Ernesto Samper's presidential campaign coffers became the subject of a bitter dispute with Washington while Samper was in office from 1994 to 1998. In fact, in March 1995, the United States formally decertified Colombia as a full partner in the drug war. It lumped Colombia, one of America's oldest allies in South America, with rogue states such as Afghanistan, Burma, Iran, and Syria—though Washington ultimately opted not to impose sanctions. The irony was that Samper went on to preside over the decimation of the very Cali cartel that had likely tried to buy him off.

During the mid- to late 1990s, the Cali cartel suffered the same fate as its Medellín competitor. But rather than falling to a hail of police bullets, the Cali heads were arrested or turned themselves in. It appeared that the kingpin strategy was working. Within a few years the remaining dozen-plus cartel bosses were either dead or in Colombian and U.S. prisons. The problem, though, was that the successful "decapitations" of the Medellín and Cali cartels simply atomized cocaine production and trafficking into smaller entities that were much harder to track and interdict. Former ambassador Busby acknowledged in a 1996 interview that the long-term success of U.S. drug policies was lacking. "We, the United States, put tremendous effort into the drug war, and arguably haven't made a big difference," said Busby. "We scored, I scored, major, significant successes, but I have got to tell you, did it make a difference here at home? I don't think it did."[6]

After the Cali cartel imploded in the mid-1990s, the entire Colombian cocaine industry atomized. Smaller cartels, mom-and-pop operations, paramilitaries, and guerrilla organizations all took a share of the illicit trade. In some instances, Colombian players would sell the cocaine to Mexican buyers before the product even left the country. Not surprisingly, this shift in the production chain wreaked havoc on a region that was already suffering from dire political and social vulnerability.[7]

One prominent domestic player that emerged was the Norte del Valle Cartel (NDVC), based in the northern part of the Valle del Cauca department, which includes Cali and the Pacific port of Buenaventura. As the esteemed nonprofit outfit InSight Crime reported, NDVC built a number of key trafficking routes that were still in use at the time of this book's publication in 2020, many of which use high-speed boats and fishing vessels to smuggle cocaine from Colombia's Pacific coast to Mexico. In 2005, the DEA reckoned that NDVC exported more than five hundred tons of cocaine—valued at $10 billion—over the course of a decade. At its highest point, the cartel was responsible for roughly 60 percent of the cocaine entering the United States. Like the Cali cartel, the NDVC established a broad network of bribery and influence that involved police forces, intelligence agencies, and prosecutors. The NDVC also linked up with paramilitary forces to protect its cocaine laboratories and distribution routes.

But, as fate would have it, the NDVC did not become the most powerful drug player to fill the vacuum left by the cartels. That honor would fall to a rather more surprising organization.

Farclandia

During the cocaine frenzy of the late 1970s and early 1980s, the Medellín traffickers had discovered that the coca they were shipping in from Peru and Bolivia also grew exceptionally well in Colombian soil. The cartels' operatives in rural agricultural regions in the Amazonia region encouraged farmers to increase their plantings. Soon enough, a poor *campesino* could raise his paltry income by a factor of ten by switching from licit crops to coca. Cultivation soared, and cash piled up in these hitherto desperately poor regions.

The Cali and Medellín cartels controlled this domestic coca-growing industry, dictating the terms of trade and sending buyers into jungles to purchase semi-refined paste. But, beginning in the 1980s, the FARC began to establish a more forceful presence in these reaches. Ironically, for much of its existence, the FARC had considered the drug business counterrevolutionary and feared that drug money would corrupt its adherents. Yet, with money always in short supply, the FARC leadership finally switched tacks in 1982 and began taxing drug producers and smugglers, starting at 10 percent per kilogram of coca base. The rebels also collected fees for every drug flight that left the areas under their control. As the FARC gained a foothold in other parts of the country, they extended the tax to marijuana and opium poppy growers. When they took the southeast, the FARC levied a fee on coca plantings. This virtually limitless revenue source fueled a two-decade-long military expansion.[8]

Decapitating the Medellín and Cali cartels left the FARC as the only major player left. The erstwhile revolutionaries enjoyed effective dominion over the first stages of the cocaine production chain. And the atomized organizations that emerged in the cartels' absence turned to the guerrillas for security. At the same time, the relative success of U.S.-supported crackdowns in Peru and Bolivia drove the illicit agricultural production over the border into rural Colombia. There, thanks to the lawless conditions engendered by ceaseless fighting among leftist guerrilla groups, rightist paramilitaries, and the Colombian military, coca production in Colombia outpaced that of Bolivia in 1995 and Peru in 1997, much of it in the FARC-controlled Llanos and Amazon, making the star-crossed nation the world's largest supplier of coca leaves. Once covering only a few thousand acres, Colombia's coca plantings spiked to four hundred thousand acres annually by 2000, producing at least 680 tons of cocaine. For the FARC, this was a gift made in white gold. The insurgency was at one point believed to reap $500 million a year from the drug business.[9]

Swollen with these revenues, the FARC in the mid-1990s launched a vicious new stage of its revolutionary war. In August 1996, guerrillas attacked and destroyed a military base in the remote jungle region of Putumayo. Casualties included fifty-four Colombian soldiers killed, seventeen wounded, and sixty taken prisoner. In late December 1997, the FARC bombed a military intelligence base, taking eighteen soldiers captive and once again embarrassing the political elite and military brass in Bogotá. Then, in a stunning move, in March 1998 the FARC decimated an entire elite army unit in Caquetá department, after villagers relayed the soldiers' whereabouts to guerrilla spies. Within forty-eight hours, 154 soldiers were killed.[10]

Emboldened by this success, FARC commander Manuel Marulanda imagined seizing larger cities, including Bogotá, and from there, the entire country. To strike fear in the Colombian nation, the guerrillas started bombing electrical towers to cut off electricity in Bogotá. The situation was so dire that in 1998 the U.S. Defense Intelligence Agency secretly estimated that the FARC and its drug-trafficking allies would be able to overthrow the central government and convert Colombia into a "narco-state." While this scenario was unlikely, the important thing for the FARC leadership was that the Colombian people believe such a proposition was possible.[11]

With the nation paralyzed by the offensives, Conservative presidential candidate Andrés Pastrana campaigned in 1998 on peace. He promised to negotiate an end to the conflict with the FARC. In May, his Liberal opponent, Horacio Serpa, won a plurality, but not a clear majority, and a second round was scheduled for June. A few days before the decisive national election, media outlets were abuzz with the image of Pastrana's peace adviser "somewhere in the wilderness, deep in conversation with the perennial and aging" Marulanda. The putatively clandestine meeting established Pastrana's bona fides. The FARC, it appeared, had indicated which of the two candidates it would make peace with. Less than a week later, on June 21, 1998, the Colombian people elected Pastrana with a strong majority. Pastrana's and the electorate's bet that the FARC wanted peace was not unreasonable. As I found while I was working on human rights in Colombia before writing my doctoral thesis on U.S.-Colombian relations, the FARC knew that it had maximized its military influence and now had the most leverage it would ever have with the government.[12]

As a precondition to peace talks, the FARC made an unbelievable demand: a demilitarized zone of more than sixteen thousand square miles, about the size of Switzerland. Pastrana granted the request, much to the outrage of his political opposition in Bogotá. The official *zona de distension* (easing zone) was often referred to as "El Caguán," given its location in the Caguán River basin. Others called it *el despeje,* or the clearing. But the most popular and enduring name for this state-within-a-state by far was simply Farclandia.[13]

In January 1999, Pastrana took the risky step of traveling to a FARC stronghold in the eastern part of the Andes to inaugurate peace talks with Marulanda. The newly elected head of state, in effect, was being received by a legitimate belligerent force in its own territory. But the FARC leader failed to appear, and Pastrana, humiliated, was left sitting next to an empty chair. Formal peace talks did finally kick off two days later, but the FARC suspended them again, noting that rightist paramilitaries had increased their offensive maneuvers. That May, Pastrana decided to reauthorize the *despeje*, against the advice of his defense minister, who promptly resigned, and the seventeen generals and dozens of colonels who "threatened to follow him."[14]

Pastrana's increasingly impotent administration returned to the *despeje* repeatedly to negotiate, while the FARC launched brazen attacks across the country. In July 1999, more than four thousand FARC troops left El Caguán to assault military bases and isolated towns in five regions. The following year, FARC commandos killed Diego Turbay, head of the Congressional Peace Committee. As the months dragged on and a deal receded further out of sight, it became increasingly evident that the FARC was not interested in peace. It had used the negotiations as a clever blind to buy time while they exploited the *despeje* for a massive expansion of coca growing and cocaine processing. Meanwhile, they invited luminaries, including the CEOs of AOL and the New York Stock Exchange, to observe a carefully curated selection of the FARC's activities in the region and to pressure Bogotá into ending the war on favorable terms. In other parts of the autonomous zone, it later became clear, bomb-making experts from the Irish Republican Army were teaching FARC operatives how to make crude gas cylinder bombs. The FARC was also busy deepening ties with Mexico's Tijuana Cartel and Brazilian cocaine smugglers. In 2001, to take just one example, an incarcerated Brazilian drug trafficker, Luiz Fernando Da Costa, revealed to Colombian agents that the FARC had assisted him in smuggling more than two hundred tons of cocaine to Brazil the previous year, levying a "revolutionary tax" of $500 per kilo and $15,000 per drug flight.[15]

Paras

Ironically, in addition to creating room for the FARC to move, decapitating the Medellín and Cali cartels effectively orphaned the paramilitary outfits that had grown up alongside them. Paramilitary leaders wasted no time in getting themselves deep into the cocaine trade. By 1997, like-minded paramilitary groups throughout the country were united under the umbrella Autodefensas Unidas de Colombia (United Self-Defense Forces of Colombia). At its height, the AUC had more than thirty thousand well-armed and -trained soldiers in its ranks. It became the FARC's biggest competitor in the cocaine game, and it behaved much as its rivalrous predecessors, the cartels, had done. In classic scorched-earth counterinsurgency fashion, the AUC struck back by targeting not the FARC but its suspected civilian sympathizers among the local leftist student, labor, and political organizations. Yet, as the anthropologist Aldo Civico writes in his indispensable book, *The Para-State: An Ethnography of Colombia's Death Squads,* the paramilitaries added an extra dimension of predatory complexity: like venomous snakes hidden in the weeds in these vulnerable communities, the paramilitaries established a "perverse intimacy with their prey," which they terrorized in return for "submission, respect, and a twisted form of envy."[16]

For the next several years, and at times with the tacit or explicit consent of the armed forces, the AUC committed rampant murder and other atrocities against civilians. Between 1997 and 1999 alone, AUC fighters killed an estimated nineteen thousand Colombians, the vast majority of whom were noncombatants.

The Colombian state and military were often willing to turn a blind eye, given that the paramilitaries appeared to be the "enemies of their enemies," namely the leftist guerrillas. In 1998, while I was working with Catholic Relief Services in Colombia, I visited a community that had just endured a paramilitary attack. In the words of one resident: "Where is the state? The military? Without them, we live in the Wild West. . . . There are many bandits but no sheriff." That year, a paramilitary faction around the city of Barrancabermeja in the Middle Magdalena killed sixty civilians. In June, they slaughtered another twenty-five hostages they had been holding for weeks. I had recently visited Barrancabermeja to support my colleagues on the ground there. It was several weeks before the Colombian state acknowledged the attack—and confirmed that my colleagues had not been among the victims.[17]

In February 2000, three hundred AUC soldiers, guided by captured FARC guerrillas, killed about ninety suspected FARC sympathizers in the town of El Salado. The AUC troops "sang and danced in the church square while they tortured the villagers and slit their throats one by one." In total, forty-four civilians, all suspected of guerrilla sympathies, were killed during the four-day rampage.[18]

Human rights groups working in the country accused Colombian security forces of supporting and even jointly conducting operations with paramilitary units. One *para* fighter interviewed by Civico described a peculiar relationship between the drug-trafficking paramilitaries and local police in the Bajo Cauca region. Every few months, the police would announce a seizure of a few tons of cocaine as a demonstration of the progress they were making against "drugs and thugs." The secret, though, was that the *patrón* himself had handed over the drugs as a kind of appeasement. Meanwhile, another eighty tons, perhaps, had left the country with law enforcement's blessing. Civico described the extent of the *paras'* cocaine connection via an interview with a "soldier" named Jader:

> Here there are more paramilitaries than civilians. . . . Everyone in town lives off the cocaine industry. "Everyone" means *everyone*. In fact, the farmer lives off cocaine. The collector lives off cocaine. The stores make a living out of cocaine. If I am a collector, I need to go to a shop and buy stuff. And where is the money coming from? From cocaine. . . . [I]f the boss is sending fifty tons of cocaine and it gets lost, we are left without uniforms, food, money—that is, with nothing. We are left naked, because money comes from cocaine. That's how we eat. That's how we can wear new uniforms. Without cocaine, there are no armed groups—no guerrillas, no paramilitaries, no nothing. In fact, the FARC and the self-defense groups would not fight over a banana plant or a yucca. No. They fight over coca plants, which here might not cost much, but in another place might be worth millions of dollars. That's why they fight against each other.[19]

In this tyrannical rentier system, the drug *patrón* became the local despot; paramilitaries served as his private police, ensuring that the merchandise was not lost or stolen. It was a monopoly "enforced with a violence that tolerates no competition or any form of cheating." Civico came to believe that cocaine and the "desires, fantasies, and profits attached to it" were the central organizing principles of towns like Tarazá. "Like a god, it possesses the powers of life and death over its residents," he writes. "Cocaine is the substance that sustains their dreams of better lives, that fuels their desires and offers the illusion of someday fulfilling them." In regions like Bajo Cauca, he concluded, the "law of the *patrón* . . . replaced the law of the state."[20]

International observers, the U.S. embassy in particular, put pressure on the Colombian government to crack down on the *paras'* human rights abuses. The campaigns of violence by the *paras* were significantly hampering the Colombian government's ability to rein in the FARC and as a result compromised efforts to slow down the production and export of cocaine.

Plan Colombia

On February 25, 1999, three American indigenous rights activists working with the U'wa Indian tribe in the northeast department of Arauca were abducted. Their bodies were found two weeks later. The FARC eventually took responsibility for the killings, although uncertainty remained regarding who within the insurgency's hierarchy had given the order. The FARC subsequently announced that it would conduct an internal investigation and punish those responsible, but this was not enough for the U.S. and Colombian governments, who demanded that the FARC hand over the perpetrators. The FARC never met this demand, and the case of the three murdered American activists brought a tougher attitude toward the rebels from the Clinton administration. The murders also fueled a growing perception in Washington that President Pastrana's peace strategy was more naive and less credible than it had first appeared and that the FARC was not going to negotiate in good faith.[21]

Doubts about the guerrillas—both the FARC and Colombia's second-largest guerrilla group, the Ejército de Liberación Nacional (National Liberation Army)—were compounded when, on April 12, 1999, the ELN hijacked an Avianca Airlines flight from the provincial city of Bucaramanga to Bogotá. A few weeks later, the ELN struck again, kidnapping 143 churchgoers from the La María cathedral in the southern city of Cali.[22]

By the summer of 1999, the combination of murdered Americans, stalled peace talks, frequent guerrilla attacks and kidnappings, and an explosive increase in coca cultivation (especially in the southern department of Putumayo, where the FARC was extremely active) made Colombia a "crisis" for the United States. Much as President George H. W. Bush had concluded at the height of Escobar's power, the Clinton administration judged Colombia's instability a serious risk to U.S. national security. The first indication that U.S. officials were considering a drastic adjustment to Colombia policy arrived on July 13, when the office of drug czar Barry McCaffrey, director of the Office of National Drug Control Policy, leaked a State Department memo that called for a massive increase in assistance to the embattled state, to the tune of more than $1 billion.[23]

Because McCaffrey was well liked by President Clinton, he had the influence to force the issue. A billion dollars became the benchmark for Clinton's spending on Colombia in the coming year. McCaffrey's call for such an unprecedented aid increase also took the wind out of the sails of Republican critics in the House of Representatives, who had been claiming for years that the Clinton White House was not doing enough to fight the drug war. Thus, the Clinton administration outflanked the drug hawks in Congress. In early August 1999, Under-Secretary of State Thomas Pickering became the highest-ranking U.S. official to visit Colombia for several years. Pickering returned convinced that the United States needed to do more to stop the bleeding. The solidified Pickering-McCaffrey partnership formed the basis of the Clinton administration's new policies toward Colombia.[24]

The idea of a new strategy was matched by Andrés Pastrana's willingness to take up U.S. funding. The fix that came out in the following months was "Plan Colombia," a robust program designed to "save" the imperiled country by drastically escalating counternarcotics efforts. In fact, Pastrana presented Plan Colombia as his own idea, a $7.5 billion plan to revive the Colombian economy, promote social development, eradicate illicit crops, and jump-start the stalled peace talks. The plan called for the Colombian government to allocate $4 billion, with the remaining $3.5 billion furnished by the international community.

In truth, the ostensibly "Colombian" Plan Colombia was actually devised by the U.S. government and delivered to the Pastrana administration, a fact that U.S. officials publicly admitted later on. A Spanish-language version of the plan did not even exist until months after the first English copy had been drafted. That Pastrana issued the initial public announcement allowed the Clinton administration to act as if it were merely addressing the request of a reliable hemispheric ally.[25]

On January 11, 2000, the Clinton administration announced a $1.6 billion package to fund Plan Colombia, with roughly $1 billion of the total slated for military and police aid. The military component consisted principally of a combination of Huey and Black Hawk helicopters designated for anti-drug operations. The proposal also called for the creation of two more Colombian counternarcotics battalions, to be deployed in Putumayo, where drug cultivation had increased in recent years. To hasten congressional approval, the Clinton administration emphasized the time-critical nature of the package.[26]

Concern that Plan Colombia would lead the United States into "another Vietnam" created the potential for congressional opposition. To avoid this, the Clinton administration presented the plan as an anti-drug scheme above all else. This placed any opponents in the awkward position of appearing to be soft on the drug war. At the same time, the Clinton White House mollified more liberal members of Congress who believed Plan Colombia was overly militarized by vastly increasing "soft side" (social and economic) assistance. The administration also took pains to distinguish *counternarcotics* from *counterinsurgency* initiatives. As the assistant secretary of defense for special operations Brian Sheridan testified in September 2000, "The targets are the narco-traffickers, those individuals and organizations that are involved in the cultivation of coca or opium poppy and the subsequent production and transportation of cocaine and heroin to the U.S. Only those armed elements that forcibly inhibit or confront counterdrug operations will be engaged, be they narcotraffickers, insurgent organizations, or illegal self-defense forces. I know that some are concerned that we are being drawn into a quagmire. Let me assure you, we are not."[27]

Plan Colombia Becomes Policy

Plan Colombia represented a typical Beltway response to solving a foreign policy crisis. Debate over how to intervene was driven less by on-the-ground realities and sober foreign policy calculations than by politicians attempting to score political points in their home districts. Members of Congress bickered over the actual composition of the assistance package. Much was made of the unprecedented sum of money allocated for "Colombia," but the reality was that most of the funds were destined for domestic defense contractors to construct and deliver the war matériel. One dispute erupted over the awarding of helicopter contracts to defense manufacturers Bell-Textron, headquartered in Texas, and Sikorsky, based in Connecticut. Even a longtime Latin America policy dove, Connecticut senator Christopher Dodd, got into the act, making sure the package included one hundred Sikorsky-made Black Hawks and exactly zero Bell-Textron Hueys. All of this led one observer to quip, "This was supposed to be Plan Colombia, not Plan Connecticut."[28]

Despite several months of spirited debates and last-minute compromises in Congress, the bill passed easily. On July 13, 2000, Clinton signed the legislation. In addition to the $329 million that had been approved for Colombia in fiscal year 2000, this bill provided $862.3 million (including a few million reserved for anti-drug assistance for Bolivia, Peru, and Ecuador). Colombia would receive roughly $1.1 billion over two years. Passage of the bill represented a victory for the White House. What's more, given that Republicans were more enthusiastic about the package than the Democrats, the Clinton White House successfully preempted any criticism that it was not doing enough to fight the war on drugs.[29]

The package signaled several more material changes in U.S. policy. First, in the time of Andrés Pastrana's isolated predecessor, Ernesto Samper, the U.S. government had worked almost exclusively with the National Police on anti-drug efforts. Now it would be working with Colombian military, in particular the new counternarcotics battalions. Second, the package revealed Washington's weariness with Pastrana's peace process. Only $3 million was approved to support it. Washington's official line on this was that the civil conflict and the peace process were both too close to the counterinsurgency side of things to be palatable. Third, significant increases in assistance for human-rights enforcement, judicial reform, and alternative development assistance enabled the White House to deflect criticism that the assistance was strictly military. The bill provided $51 million for a broad range of human-rights issues, including programs to protect human-rights workers and establish human-rights units within the Colombian military. The language proposed by the Senate required the State Department to certify the military's performance on human rights before the aid could be delivered. The Senate's final bill was loosened to include a presidential waiver option, on national security grounds.[30]

Even if Plan Colombia did account for a substantial increase in soft-side programs, they were never the focus. Like counterinsurgency, democracy and human rights weren't big-ticket items for the Clinton administration. To the extent that concern tracked money, helicopters and interdiction seemed to matter a great deal more. All that said, policy priorities do tend to evolve over time. The popular impression was that Plan Colombia basically entailed Washington footing the bill for Colombia's defense spending. However, even at its height, U.S. assistance represented only 6 percent of Colombia's annual military budget. And as Colombia developed and institutionalized the capacity of its military and police forces, Plan Colombia money—eventually totaling more than $8 billion—shifted more toward economic development assistance.[31]

The Hookup

Plan Colombia's immediate impact was a dramatic increase in the amount of military hardware used to fight the drug war, from high-tech helicopters to night-vision goggles. For years, Washington had provided the Colombian government with helicopters, training, and private contractors (mostly to pilot the aerial spray flights and to provide intelligence and security). Under Plan Colombia, these programs swelled to $350 million annually. Of course, this isn't a metric we can use to evaluate the success of a policy initiative, although at times it has been used that way inside the Beltway. In the peculiar logic of militarization, dollars spent sometimes become not just a proxy measure for commitment to the drug war but a measure of those very dollars' effectiveness.[32]

All of the new hardware meant that the Colombian armed forces had to dramatically increase training. In the aftermath of September 11, 2001, Washington decided to allow Plan Colombia aid and training to be used for counterterrorism, in addition to drug war operations. Funds could also now go to

Aerial eradication of coca plants in the department of Arauca in Colombia, circa 2000. Largely targeting coca plantings but also poppy (the raw material for heroin), these spraying operations were a hallmark of the U.S.-led counternarcotics efforts in the Andean country. (Marcelo Salinas, permission to author)

training police forces, in addition to soldiers. It was a fateful decision, although no one understood it as such at the time. Freed from the narrow narcotized restrictions of the original Plan Colombia, the more expansive post-9/11 authorization enabled U.S personnel to engage in much broader activities with the Colombian military. The training, in so many instances, proved to be far more significant than the equipment.[33]

Spray, Spray, Spray

Since the Reagan years, aerial crop eradication had been a central pillar of the supply side of the drug war. The operation, known as a "spray package," involved small propeller planes that crop-dusted coca plantings with glyphosate, the active herbicide in the commercial product Roundup, while helicopters manned by Colombian police officers provided protection. In 1999, spray

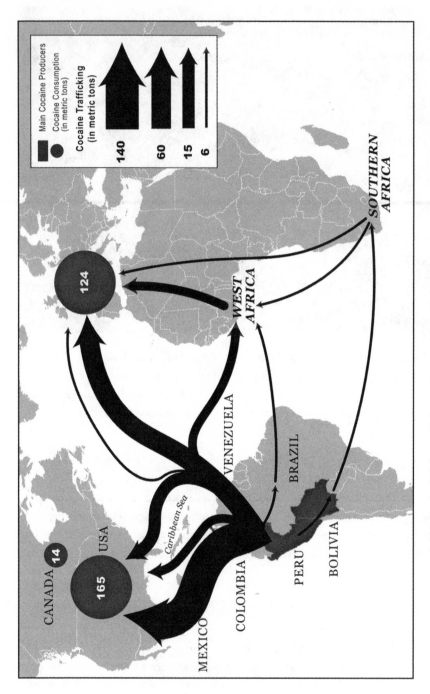

Global supply and demand for cocaine (University of Wisconsin Cartography Lab)

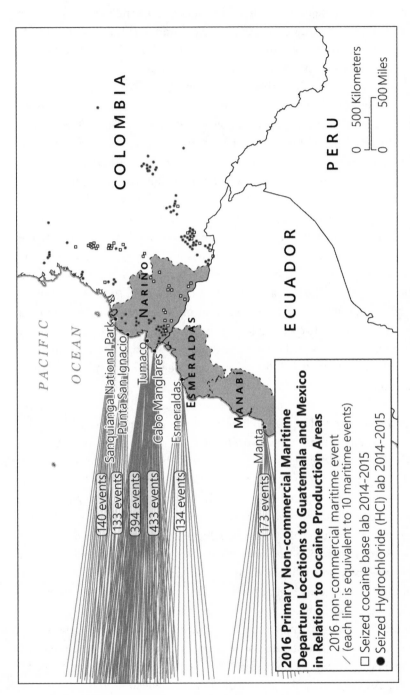

2016 Primary Non-commercial Maritime Departure Locations to Guatemala and Mexico in Relation to Cocaine Production Areas

2016 non-commercial maritime event / (each line is equivalent to 10 maritime events)

□ Seized cocaine base lab 2014-2015

● Seized Hydrochloride (HCl) lab 2014-2015

COLOMBIA

PERU

ECUADOR

PACIFIC OCEAN

NARIÑO

ESMERALDAS

MANABI

Sanquianga National Park
Punta Sanignacio
Tumaco
Cabo Manglares
Esmeraldas
Manta

140 events
133 events
394 events
433 events
134 events
173 events

0   500 Kilometers
0   500 Miles

Antidrug officials refer to intelligence images like this as "spaghetti slides," given the display of a seemingly overwhelming number of potentially illicit drug routes (University of Wisconsin Cartography Lab) packages became a major budget line in Plan Colombia and in U.S. assistance efforts throughout the Andes. By 2004, the program was fully operational. At the peak, at least 85 percent of the U.S. anti-drug budget in Colombia supported aviation-based operations.[34]

In late 2000, as Plan Colombia was just getting off the ground, I paid a visit to the U.S. embassy in Bogotá to talk with a variety of counternarcotics agents. I was a young scholar studying U.S. policy in Colombia. The U.S. mission's chief military official told me in quiet tones that they were soon going to unleash a ferocious campaign of aerial spraying in southern Colombia.

What was different this time, I asked, given the dubious results in previous aerial eradication efforts? His answer was that coca cultivation had been "finally cornered" in southern Colombia. That is, the success of coordinated spraying efforts across the Andes meant that there was nowhere else for the plant to grow. Dispersed cultivation in Bolivia and Peru was largely gone. As far as intelligence showed, most coca was now being grown plantation-style in one localized part of Colombia. All that was needed now, some American officials believed, was a massive aerial spray effort that would finish off the coca once and for all. With coca withering in the fields, traffickers—especially "narco-guerrillas" such as the FARC—would be robbed of their key revenue source. The campaign that followed my interview with the military official would become the vaunted "push into southern Colombia."[35]

The aerial coca-spraying campaign became a hallmark of the tenure of the U.S. ambassador to Colombia William Wood, who repeatedly argued that the drug trade would be infinitely worse if eradication were to cease. (Interestingly enough, Wood was later dispatched to run the embassy in Afghanistan to replicate his apparent drug successes in Colombia.) Indeed, the push into southern Colombia demonstrated beyond a shadow of a doubt that the United States could eradicate massive amounts of coca in Colombia. The aerial program destroyed a volume of coca that would have resulted in the production of 150 metric tons of cocaine with an estimated street value of $15 billion; given that a single spray only kills the plant for one harvest, reported annual spraying numbers are typically higher than reported annual coca cultivation.[36]

U.S. drug officials made much of the fact that Colombia's cultivation dropped from 420,000 acres in 2001 to 280,000 acres in 2003. Deputy Secretary of State John Negroponte was technically correct when he claimed that the "exponential growth in Colombia's cocaine production has been stopped." But on closer inspection, the picture didn't look quite so promising. For one thing, coca cultivation had concomitantly spiked in Bolivia and Peru. And where it was once "cornered" in Colombia, it was now suddenly dispersed. At the onset of Plan Colombia, the U.S. government's maps of Colombia indicated that almost all of the coca cultivation was concentrated in the southeastern section of the country along the border with Ecuador. In subsequent years, the same map looked like a Jackson Pollock painting, with green splattered all over Colombia, with coca displaced to far more locales in the country. As expected, the FARC and other violent groups followed the coca production into parts of the country that, up until this point, were relatively pacific.[37]

Other factors also complicated the spray strategy. If coca farmers received warning that a spray operation was imminent, they quickly harvested their fields. If the plants were hit by spray, farmers would immediately pick them to save as much of the crop as possible. Glyphosate is a relatively benign herbicide, which meant that new plants could be seeded even one day after a field had been sprayed. Alternatively, growers often quickly pruned the compromised plants down to the stems, destroying the current crop but saving the plant. Ironically, the subsequent regrowth resulted in a much larger and more productive plant. This led at least one U.S. narcotics official to lament, "It's working as fertilization, not fumigation."

To add to the complexity, the aerial spraying efforts were dogged with claims that they degraded the environment and the health of local populations. The U.S. government lost the public relations battle on this sensitive question. One embassy official told me, "I think the term fumigation has been introduced by critics for political purposes. You fumigate a house to kill cockroaches, but you aerially spray crops with a herbicide."

And yet, aerial spraying remained a popular policy option. Why? For one, it was low in risk. According to one U.S. drug official, "Unlike some of the stuff we do, spraying is not particularly bloody, dirty, nor nasty." Busting a cocaine lab was messy. Thugs with powerful guns and an equally powerful disregard for the law stood ready to defend the operation. Spraying did not require boots on the ground. In fact, the spray program was so risk-averse that if a plane reported taking fire, the entire operation had to be called off.

Equally important, spraying was quantifiable. It was infinitely easier for U.S. officials to appease an impatient Congress by reporting success through increased spraying than to suggest and approve an alternative approach. It wasn't a lie, after all, to claim that the spraying efforts were destroying coca crops that could have been turned into cocaine. But the incentives ultimately reduced evaluation of U.S. drug efforts in Colombia to this kind of report: "Last year, we sprayed X acres, this year we sprayed Y acres, and next year we plan to spray Z acres." Such reports were factually accurate, but they did not reflect the full truth: that action does not necessarily imply effectiveness. In fact, some American counternarcotics officials on the ground in Colombia privately contended that money and manpower would be much better spent going after processing labs and "transit points" such as coastal shipping hubs, whose destruction would take a larger bite out of trafficking organizations' bottom lines.

15 • Catastrophic Success

Kidnapped

Between 1999 and 2002 another series of peace talks between the Pastrana administration and the FARC began and stuttered, with the guerrillas alternately leaving the table and submitting counterproposals before withdrawing completely. A "furious and demoralized" Pastrana had had enough. In January 2002, he ordered twelve thousand troops to encircle the demilitarized zone. He then appeared on television to inform the FARC they had forty-eight hours to evacuate five key towns in El Caguán. Predictably, the FARC ignored Pastrana's threat. The Colombian president ordered the military to retake the region, and "the war returned to full intensity."[1]

In mid-February 2002, three presidential candidates met in FARC territory, where they urged the guerrillas to terminate the conflict. The delegation included presidential hopeful Ingrid Betancourt, a half-French "spitfire senator from Bogotá." Sitting near Betancourt in full FARC military uniform was the FARC's ideological chief, Simón Trinidad. With national news media in full array in the remote community of Los Pozos, "campesinos clambered for a view" of the candidates and FARC leaders together. Betancourt pleaded with the rebel leaders. "When each of you decided 'I'm going to the mountains to fight' what was your intention? Was your intention to take water and electricity from the people whom you wanted to defend?" She forcefully concluded by imploring the rebel leaders to make a "unilateral gesture toward peace: no more kidnappings. No more kidnappings. . . . Stop kidnapping, and free the hostages."[2]

In these years the guerrillas were taking thousands of new hostages each year. To deal with this "population boom," the FARC built primitive prison camps where they kept the captives for months and sometimes years. With the escalated fighting throughout the country, there were more FARC soldiers in Colombian prisons as well. Back in 1997, Marulanda had suggested an exchange of prisoners and requested that the Colombian Congress pass a "law of exchange." Now, the guerrillas considered any political actor who came into their controlled territory as "exchangeables," a distinct class of hostages who wouldn't be ransomed and could only be released through a swap.[3]

On February 23, 2002, fiercely clinging to a longshot campaign, Betancourt and her aides ventured to a "steamy jungle town" on the edge of the demilitarized zone. When they reached a rebel checkpoint in an attempt to cross into the *despeje* itself, the guerrillas on duty calmly informed Betancourt and her team that they were now hostages of the Revolutionary Armed Forces of Colombia.[4]

"War First, Peace Later"

At the time of Betancourt's kidnapping, the FARC had become the de facto state in most coca-growing regions in southern Colombia. The guerrillas were up to their ears in drug revenues; rough estimates suggest that in the early 2000s, the group brought in about $100 million a year from the cocaine business alone—a number that eventually grew by a factor of ten. And that did not factor in revenue from kidnapping, extortion, and other criminal activities. The enormous war chest funded a dramatic increase in the FARC's fighting capabilities.

In 2002, voters turned out in droves to elect the rightist candidate Álvaro Uribe, who pledged to use all the tools of the state, especially the military tools, to protect citizens from illegal violence. Back in 1983, the FARC had killed Uribe's father after a bungled kidnapping. Many on the left feared that the Uribe administration would become a "violent four-year vendetta." During the campaign, the FARC attempted to assassinate Uribe on multiple occasions, including detonating a bomb next to his presidential motorcade. Uribe was not injured, but three others were killed and thirteen wounded. FARC commandos attacked the inauguration ceremony at the presidential palace with crude gas-cylinder bombs. The bombs missed their target and landed in a nearby area to the south, killing nineteen of the capital city's homeless population and wounding sixty.[5]

President Uribe took office in 2002 on the promise that his government would establish security in all areas of the country. This was a bold claim. Since its founding in the early nineteenth century, the Colombian state had never effectively governed extensive swaths of its national territory. Uribe used Plan Colombia funding and matériel to double down on the insurgency. Colombian military convoys began opening up key highways by deploying an armed soldier at every kilometer marker. Enhanced air mobility allowed the security forces to chase FARC bands across high mountain ranges and thick jungle. The message to Colombians was unequivocal: The Colombian state will protect you; you will no longer be a prisoner in your own country.

Not surprisingly, Uribe's hardline approach was controversial. Critics believed that it simply used violence to fight violence. The most stringent of these accused Uribe of employing paramilitaries, primarily and most heinously the AUC, to do the government's dirty work. Over the next eight years, these accusations would build into a scandal that exposed deep connections between the paramilitaries and the political system. As far as the U.S. government was concerned, Uribe's priorities did not always match those of the anti-drug effort—either in terms of human rights or in the impact on Colombian cocaine entering the United States. But in the early years of his administration, few Colombians believed that the FARC would negotiate a settlement, so Uribe's "war first, peace later" stance made sense to a political majority disabused of excessive hope.[6]

The Contractors

As the authors of *Hostage Nation* tell the story, in the morning hours of February 13, 2003, a squad of FARC commandos was patrolling the Andean foothills of southeastern Colombia. Hearing an all-too-familiar propeller buzz above, they assumed it was one of the reconnaissance or spray planes that frequented the coca-rich vicinity. One guerrilla, nicknamed "La Pilosa" (the smart one) requested permission to act. "There is a bug flying by here, very low. . . . Hey, if it's a fumigator, can we burn it?" Her superior, El Paisa, head of one of the most feared blocs of the FARC, responded, "[If] it's low, burn that tail."[7]

The aircraft in question, a Cessna 208, had taken off from an airstrip in Bogotá 250 miles to the north, en route to a base near the border with Brazil; it was conducting a surveillance operation, imaging coca plantings. There were five crew members on board, including four Americans and a Colombian intelligence officer. A mechanical snafu that had forced the single-engine plane to lower altitudes despite the jagged Andean peaks surrounding them suddenly got worse. Keith Stansell, the technician seated in the back, had radioed to base: "Magic worker, Magic worker, Mutt 01 is declaring Mayday. We have lost engine." Tommy Janis, a veteran American military pilot, frenetically attempted an emergency landing in a small clearing in the middle of the dense forest.[8]

Unaware of the engine outage, the guerrillas opened fire on the descending plane. Janis put the craft down roughly two hundred yards from the guerrillas' location. La Pilosa radioed El Paisa to [mistakenly] claim the shoot-down. "We knocked it down. . . . These gringos fell to us from the sky." By this time, more than fifty guerrillas were assembled at the crash site. Keith Stansell attempted to surrender. "No armas! No armas!" he cried, meaning that they had already ditched their weapons.[9]

The guerrillas summarily executed "at close range" Janis and the Colombian Army intelligence officer, Sergeant Luis Alcides Cruz. Janis was the first U.S. government employee to be killed by the FARC in the decades-long Colombian conflict. Understanding from experience that the gringos would have called in their position before the crash, the rebels forced the three remaining Americans—Thomas Howes, co-pilot; Keith Stansell, first technician; and Marc Gonsalves, second technician—to leave the site in custody. The march turned out to be a punishing three-week trek. Other guerrillas searched the aircraft and took anything valuable that wasn't already destroyed. They planted land mines around the site to harry the Colombian rescue troops who would certainly be arriving.[10]

And arrive they did. The Colombian military dispatched more than two thousand soldiers into Caquetá department, where the FARC had carried out kidnappings and drug-financed guerrilla operations for years. U.S. soldiers and intelligence experts using reconnaissance aircraft were also involved. President George W. Bush sent an additional 150 American soldiers to assist in the search, putting the total over 400. The search effort included the use of Black Hawk helicopters provided as part of Plan Colombia. Janis's body was found about a mile from the crash site. Republican congressman Thomas M. Davis III of Virginia issued a dire warning: "I don't think there's any question that this precipitous action by the FARC is going to meet with very strong retaliation," he said. "Precisely what happens is being discussed as we speak, but they've made a very grave error." FARC commanders, by contrast, immediately declared the three Americans "prisoners of war" who would only be handed over as part of a larger *canje* (prisoner exchange) with Bogotá for some or all of the three thousand rebels then in prison.[11]

Stansell, Howes, and Gonsalves were officially employed by a subsidiary of the defense contractor behemoth Northrup Grumman. They were part of an $8.6 million contract to obtain intelligence on drug production and trafficking, overseen by U.S. Southern Command in Miami. In their own words, "Our targets were FARC-controlled and -operated drug labs, one of which we knew to be under the command of Mono JoJoy, one of the FARC's major players." This often proved difficult, given that they were flying at five thousand feet, looking down at an "endless sea of green." After almost two decades of fumigation operations, growers had adapted to the aerial surveillance by covering their small labs with vegetation or by building them next to their small residences.[12]

This multi-million-dollar contract was but one grain in the beach of sand that was U.S. anti-drug spending on Colombia. The official U.S. policy objective in this instance was to help the Colombians interdict drugs and narco-terrorists. When this policy was operationalized, though, it became quite a bit more complicated. Most policy implementation entails lucrative private contracts, typically engaging American companies. Contractors could also be accurately called mercenaries, except that their work is considered legal under U.S. law. All of this can be seen as part of a "military-industrial-narcotics complex," an iteration of the defense spending trend that the departing president Dwight D. Eisenhower warned the nation about in 1961.

When I would come down from Washington to Colombia during my time in government, most of the anti-drug officials I met were in fact retired U.S. military and Foreign Service officers, who had transferred into a "second career" as contractors doing very similar work—and earning some very good coin. Whenever our discussions turned to Capitol Hill or the White House's reduced funding for spraying and other expensive anti-drug operations, they would give me all the reasons that this work was essential. I would keep quiet, remembering that I first started getting these same "spray, spray, spray" pep talks two decades before.

The FARC kept most of their political hostages in a large prison camp deep in Farclandia territory. But given the three Americans' extremely high value, they were held in even more remote and primitive conditions. With no radio or newspapers and limited contact with other prisoners, they were clueless about what was going on in the outside world—including the rescue efforts conducted on their behalf. At what the captors labeled New Camp, the three men were forbidden to talk to each other and suffered from insufferable loneliness. They did not have contact with anyone but their captors until July, when an intrepid Colombian journalist, Jorge Botero, arrived and made a proof-of-life tape. His description of the captives stunned viewers. "I had never seen so much sadness in one place. . . . Some were walking like zombies, ignoring reality; others clung fanatically to prayer, raised their arms to heaven, and asked for clemency, compassion freedom . . . their spirits had collapsed. Their souls were empty."[13]

More than a year after the crash, the Bush administration refused to engage the FARC directly, instead publicly supporting whatever Uribe said on the matter. A year later, in November 2004, President Bush visited Colombia but made no mention of the hostages. As later become clear, however, quite a bit more was happening behind the scenes. Prize-winning reporter Dana Priest wrote a painstakingly researched and documented *Washington Post* investigation of secret U.S. assistance to Colombia in the early 2000s. This assistance never appeared in the Plan Colombia books, but it was one of several "enhanced intelligence initiatives" in "countries where drug cartels have caused instability" that "escaped public notice" in the years following the 9/11 terrorist attacks. Within the executive branch, it was justified by two presidential "findings." The first, which allowed clandestine efforts against terrorist groups, was cited to justify CIA and Joint Special Operations Command (JSOC) intelligence work against al-Qaeda. The second, which allowed intelligence services to target drug traffickers abroad, had been in place since the Reagan years and had authorized the CIA and JSOC to hunt down Pablo Escobar.[14]

Now, the Bush administration drew on the findings to authorize a "new covert push against the FARC." After the American flyers were taken captive, Bush apparently "leaned on" his CIA director, George Tenet, to locate the three American captives—and give the FARC a bloody nose. The CIA subsequently deployed secret U.S. operators, who had just been "at the forefront of locating and killing al Qaeda," to conduct training and reconnaissance missions to help find and rescue the three American hostages. At one point, more than nine hundred American military personnel were deployed to Colombia, even though legal stipulations capped the permitted number at eight hundred. A "legal loophole" pertaining to the search for the Americans enabled more military men to continue their fight against the FARC.[15]

Coincidentally, I started my new job as director for Western Hemisphere Affairs at the National Security Council on the same day that President Bush visited Colombia in 2004. I was not part of the special committee that met to discuss the three hostages' situation, but I talked almost daily with one of its members in what is called "the interagency," the regular policy meeting of the alphabet soup of executive branch agencies, including the State Department, the CIA, and the Department of Defense. I will never forget commemorating the second anniversary of the abductions in early February 2005. I kept thinking to myself that I couldn't believe that they were *still* out there. In my role, I discovered that, aside from geopolitics, one of the largest factors complicating the contractors' rescue was simply the density of the triple-canopy jungle. Even if the hostages were located, a typical commando-style rescue mission would struggle to get through the impenetrable landscape to reach them.

In 2007, Jorge Botero traveled out to the hostage camps to make another report. His video showed that at various times the Americans and the Colombian politician Ingrid Betancourt had been in the same place. Betancourt's emaciated, corpse-like appearance was disturbing to see, "skin gray and stretched over the bone, and her hair plunging to the waist." After almost six years in captivity, including a hunger strike protesting her conditions and numerous death threats from her jailers, Betancourt had given up. "Here nothing is one's own," she wrote. "Nothing lasts, uncertainty and precariousness are the only constant."[16]

Trinidad

On January 2, 2004, with CIA assistance, Colombian and Ecuadoran security operatives in Quito seized a FARC commander named Ricardo Palmera Piñeda, known universally by his guerrilla handle, Simón Trinidad. The rebel *comandante* was in Ecuador, he claimed, to coordinate the swap of around fifty FARC-held prisoners for hundreds of jailed FARC-istas. A year later the Colombian government extradited Trinidad to the United States to face charges of "conspiracy to take hostages" and "supporting terrorism." At this point, the whereabouts of the three hostages were still unknown. On December 31, 2004—nearly two years after the FARC had captured the three American air surveillance crewmen—a "stocky middle-aged man, bald and bespectacled, sat handcuffed and shackled" on official U.S. aircraft en route north to the seat of the *Yanqui* empire. He was guarded by five FBI agents and one DEA agent. Before boarding the plane, the fifty-four-year-old Trinidad, the highest-ranking FARC member ever to be captured, raised his hand defiantly and shouted, "Viva las FARC! Viva Manuel Marulanda! Viva Simón Bolívar!"[17]

In early 2005, Trinidad pleaded not guilty to the five charges leveled against him, which included hostage taking (one count for each American), conspiracy to commit kidnapping, and supporting a terrorist organization. Almost two years later, on November 21, 2006, the court declared a mistrial due to a hung jury. U.S. prosecutors then arranged a new trial, which began in early June 2007. Ken Kohl, a veteran Justice Department prosecutor, made clear the government's objectives as it made a second attempt at conviction: "As prosecutors on the case, we felt that the best thing for Marc, Keith, and Tom would be to make their hostage taking as costly as possible for the FARC, so that the FARC would recognize that kidnapping Americans is counterproductive."[18]

Interestingly, as the CIA and U.S. military attaché in Bogotá were developing plans to rescue the hostages, Trinidad was the strongest and certainly the most public leverage that the George W. Bush White House had against the FARC. John Crabb, assistant prosecutor, gave the opening argument: "The FARC is led by a small group of men. One of their leaders, in fact one of the FARC's most important leaders is here today. [Here, Crabb aimed his finger at the defendant.] It's that man, Simón Trinidad. Now Simón Trinidad didn't order that Marc, Keith, and Tom be taken hostage. But this is what he did do. Once they were taken hostage by the FARC he tried to exploit the situation for the FARC's benefit. . . . Ladies and gentlemen, Simon Trinidad tried to use Tom Howes, Keith Stansell, and Marc Gonsalves as get-out-of-jail-free cards for FARC criminals that are in Colombian jails." Both Kohl and Crabb were confident this time around, given that the jury in the first trial had stalled out at 10–2 for conviction.[19]

During Trinidad's retrial, Kohl asked me to serve as an expert witness in the case. He and Crabb wanted to establish that, contrary to Trinidad's testimony, the FARC were not a bunch of misunderstood and heroic freedom fighters but rather violent insurgents up to their ears in drug money. I was willing to participate, first, because, after reviewing all of the evidence and testimony, I was certain that Trinidad was guilty at least of the kidnapping conspiracy. Second, the FARC by then was Colombia's largest drug player. If the trial had taken place two or three decades earlier, I would have testified that the FARC did in fact have legitimate ideological claims and enjoyed significant political support. But the insurgency in 2007 was a vastly different beast, and only the most credulous observers could overlook the cynicism and cruelty that had been their ideology over the previous decade.

On July 9, 2007, a jury declared Trinidad guilty of the charge of conspiring to hold the three U.S. citizens hostage. The FARC Secretariat was shocked by the verdict, having assumed that they would be able to trade Trinidad for the three Americans. At the sentencing in early 2008, Kohl requested the maximum penalty of sixty years. A life sentence was off the table; the option had been revoked as part of the extradition agreement with Bogotá. But everyone knew that sixty years was an effective life sentence for the fifty-nine-year-old guerrilla. A separate indictment charged Trinidad with drug trafficking, with a separate trial to follow, in September 2007. The jury was hung in this third trial, as well as the fourth. In May 2008, the drug charges were formally dismissed. It was remarkable to me that the U.S. officials still decided to go after Trinidad on drug trafficking, given that he'd been convicted on the kidnapping conspiracy in the earlier trial and would spend the rest of his life in solitary confinement prison. It is a sign of the uncompromising tenacity that has come to characterize the war on drugs.[20]

Parapolitics

Still unable to rescue or even locate the hostages, a beleaguered Uribe could do little to placate a frustrated Washington. At the same time, he was facing his own political crisis, which had emerged from revelations of his government's connections to paramilitaries. He managed to deflect some of the criticism by reaching a peace agreement with the AUC and ushering in a Justice and Peace Law to administer the paramilitaries' laying down their arms. (The *New York Times* editorial board called it the "Impunity for Mass Murderers, Terrorists and Major Cocaine Traffickers Law.") In 2006, the AUC "demobilized and reintegrated" the vast majority of its thirty-thousand-strong force. Uribe faced further setbacks, though, when, in the process of confessing their own war crimes, paramilitary commanders exposed their ties to the hardline president's "allies and relatives." In one damning revelation, in March 2007, the *Los Angeles Times* reported that the head of the army had authorized joint missions with paramilitary groups to eradicate leftist guerrillas. The country's Supreme Court, tasked to investigate public officials, began a tireless "parapolitics" inquiry, which connected several members of Uribe's political network, including the Colombian foreign minister, the national police chief, a state governor, and dozens of legislators, to the paramilitaries. As the scandal unfolded, more than a hundred national legislators were removed from office. By 2008, the much-derided Justice and Peace process had registered some two hundred thousand victims. Paramilitary fighters had confessed to thousands of crimes, and a roughly equal number of mass graves had been discovered.[21]

On May 12, 2008, Uribe made an unexpected move. In the middle of the night, he had fourteen "paramilitary heavyweights" imprisoned in various parts of Colombia transferred to Bogotá and loaded onto a U.S. government plane to face drug charges in the United States. Until this point, Uribe had refused to extradite paramilitary bosses, despite Washington's demands; indeed, the offer of immunity had been a critical piece of the landmark peace agreement in 2006. The captives sat in collective shock and "stony silence," as the reality dawned on them that Uribe, despite his presumed "shared ideology," had broken his pledge.[22]

These unprecedented extraditions came as a surprise even to the American diplomatic and counternarcotics establishment. Few could deduce what had driven Uribe to act so precipitously. The president's public justification was drugs. He accused the warlords of continuing to run their drug operations from their prison cells, much as Escobar had run the Medellín operation from La Catedral. "Most of the top bosses are there," Interior Minister Carlos Holguín said on Colombian radio. "In some cases, they were still committing crimes and reorganizing criminal structures." Many Colombians were outraged. Uribe's move conveyed a pessimistic view of the integrity of Colombia's justice system, a sticking point throughout the countries' star-crossed diplomatic history. But more than that, as journalist Deborah Sontag explained, "the United States–led war on drugs seized priority over Colombia's efforts to confront crimes against humanity that had scarred a generation." If Uribe's aim was to bring justice to the perpetrators of violence in Colombia, the extraditions were an admission of defeat.[23]

It was a windfall for Washington. Latin American human rights activist José Miguel Vivanco explained, "The driving policy during the Bush administration was cooperation on anti-narcotics efforts. Not human rights, not atrocities, not to make victims of crimes against humanity committed by these bastards have a day in court in Colombia." He added, "So what do you do if overnight you get as a gift from the president of Colombia 14 guys wanted for narcotics? You just welcome them."[24]

Uribe's legions of critics, though, countered that the president was trying to keep the paramilitary bosses from revealing their longstanding ties to Uribe's conservative political coalition, as well as the president's own family through their participation in the Justice and Peace Law–driven testimonials. That is, he was silencing them through a long stay in a gringo prison. A victims' rights group equated the move to exporting "fourteen Pinochets," in reference to the infamous rightist Chilean dictator. The fourteen men had been accused of atrocities in an imperfect yet hugely significant transitional justice process. While the men now faced "lengthy sentences" in the United States for drug trafficking, their wanton crimes in Colombia would go unpunished.[25]

Sontag concluded that, all things considered, the paramilitary leaders "received relatively lenient treatment for major drug traffickers who were also designated terrorists responsible for massacres, forced disappearances and the displacement of entire villages." Most were "handsomely rewarded for pleading guilty and cooperating with the American authorities." Salvatore Mancuso, for one, was implicated in the murders of more than a thousand citizens. He was described as "one of the most prolific cocaine traffickers ever prosecuted in a United States District Court." With his plea agreement, Mancuso received thirty years to life in prison.[26]

A character we've met before, Diego Murillo Bejarano, alias Don Berna, was another of the extradited bosses. He had become head of the Envigado Office after the decapitation of the Medellín cartel. He eventually commanded a force of three thousand paramilitary fighters that fought the FARC and its alleged civilian sympathizers with particular viciousness. After turning himself in to Colombian law enforcement in 2005, Don Berna remained Medellín's chief drug boss behind bars, although other elements in the Envigado Office challenged his hold. The infighting caused Medellín's murder rate to spike, reaching six per day in 2011, up from just two per day in 2007. In 2009, Don Berna was sentenced in a U.S. federal court to thirty-one years in prison for conspiring to smuggle cocaine into the United States. The drug-para boss testified that he had helped finance President Uribe's first presidential campaign.[27]

Perhaps the greatest problem of all in Uribe's justice and peace process was that a number of middle-ranking combatants did not give up their weapons even after seeing their commanders locked up or extradited. Hundreds of AUC fighters "tasted the uncertainties of their future" and opted for the "certainties of life as cocaine mercenaries." New, shadowy groups with exotic names like Águilas Negras (Black Eagles), the Rastrojos, and the Urabeños began operating in the same areas theretofore under *para* rule. Known collectively as "Bacrim" (the Spanish acronym for *bandas criminales*), they took control of the country's strategic drug trafficking routes. The groups often specialized in one element of trafficking and offered their services to the highest bidder—even to their erstwhile sworn enemies, the Marxist guerrillas. Within two years of demobilization, there were roughly thirty Bacrim active across the country.[28]

A debate emerged regarding the Bacrim's official status. Were the groups simply recycled AUC actors, or were they—as the government in Bogotá contended in order to bolster the credibility of the demobilization process—an entirely new phenomenon? Most likely, the truth was somewhere in the middle. Perhaps a quarter of the "demobilized" paramilitary fighters joined Bacrim. Like their predecessors, the Bacrim sowed terror, killing prostitutes and petty crooks, imposing curfews, and enforcing civil order through a warped code of vigilante justice. Unlike their predecessors, they tended to

shun publicity, seldom wore military fatigues, and denied any coherent political ideology.[29]

Bombs on Foreheads

As the *para* saga was unfolding, the FARC was still hard at work consolidating the Colombian drug business. The insurgents were no longer simply taxing
coca growers and cocaine production. Now they were selling cocaine to gangs
in Mexico and Central America, often dispatching their own units to traffic it
overland across the porous borders into Panama, Venezuela, and Ecuador—
and then onward to the prized destination market, the United States. In 2008,
Sergio Jaramillo, Colombia's vice minister of defense, told hemispheric colleagues at an OAS meeting that the FARC "controlled most of Colombia's drug
trade," at that point about 90 percent of the global cocaine supply. The research
outfit Insight Crime concluded that when military capacity, territorial control,
and earnings from the cocaine chain (an astounding $1 billion a year) were
factored in, the FARC was "one of the most powerful drug syndicates in Colombia, and perhaps the world."[30]

Despite Uribe's aggressive approach, the Colombian military struggled to
secure a definitive advantage against the FARC until March 2008. Then, the
military embarked on what American advisers dubbed a "bombs-on-foreheads"
campaign, using precision-guided missiles to directly target FARC commanders. A key element in this program—covertly supplied and funded by the
United States—was an inexpensive $30,000 GPS guidance system, which
converted a "less-than-accurate 500-pound gravity bomb into a highly accurate
smart bomb." The system enabled artillery operators to determine the exact
location of targets under the triple canopy jungle.

Bombs on foreheads was a strategy born not in Colombian jungles but in
the Afghan desert. The Bush White House evidently concluded that the same
legal justification that had authorized precision strikes against al-Qaeda and
other "lethal operations" in Pakistan, Yemen, and Somalia could also be used
in Colombia. Killing FARC leaders with smart bombs would not be "assassination," since they both threatened Colombia's stability and posed "a threat to
U.S. national security."

In the effort's first mission, the Colombian Air Force bombed a FARC
camp just over the border in Ecuador. The raid was controversial in that it vio-
lated Ecuador's sovereignty, but it killed Raúl Reyes, the FARC's second-in-
command. As one report had it, "The smart bombs' guidance system turned

on once the planes reached within three miles of Reyes's location. As instructed, the Colombian pilots stayed in Colombian airspace. The bombs landed as programmed, obliterating the camp and killing Reyes, who, according to Colombian news reports, was asleep in pajamas." In the ensuing raid, Colombian forces recovered three laptop computers, external hard drives, and USB memory sticks, on which Reyes had stored files, some of which dated back decades, including records of strategies, meetings, and correspondence. It was a treasure trove of the FARC's past and present. Most sensationally, the documents revealed the FARC's longstanding political and military involvement with Colombia's two most important neighbors, Ecuador and Venezuela. To list just a few of the highlights: the FARC expected to receive upward of $250,000 from the Venezuelan government of Hugo Chávez; the guerrillas directly contributed $100,000 to the campaign of then Ecuadorean president Rafael Correa; and they likely helped round up an additional $300,000 for Correa's candidacy from sympathetic leftist sources. Few were surprised that the FARC had sought ties with sympathetic neighboring governments, given the countries' porous borders and ample sanctuaries.[31]

Checkmate

Only four months after the raid, U.S. military and intelligence personnel assumed the role of "unused understudy" on another dramatic operation inside Colombia. In June 2008, the commander of the FARC's First Front, a seasoned guerrilla known as César, received a message from his commandant, Jorge Briceño, a.k.a. Mono Jojoy, who controlled more than twenty fronts in the FARC's Eastern Bloc. Mono Jojoy wanted to know how the "cargo" was doing. "The cargo is good," César replied. César then relayed the geographic locations of three groups of hostages under his command. They included the three Americans, Ingrid Betancourt, and eleven Colombian military and police officers. A week or so later, Mono Jojoy ordered César to act. "Reunite all of the cargo. Create the conditions to receive an international mission in a safe place. When you are ready, send a message. Saludos, Jorge." Seventy-two hours hence, César got another message from Jorge: "Keep plan secret. Do not include people who are not under your command. How is everything going? Your mission is to guarantee the life of the prisoners." César responded through his radio operator, "Comrade Jorge, everything's going well. We are moving slowly to guarantee the secret. In days we will all be together and we will communicate. Saludos, César."[32]

In truth, César was speaking not with Mono Jojoy but with the Colombian military. The same was true of Mono Jojoy. A team of Colombian intelligence officers had broken the FARC code and interposed agents who brilliantly mimicked the voice of each of the guerrillas. Colombian intelligence operatives wondered how far they could take this already bold gambit.

In late June, mission planning began. Military strategists made up a non-governmental organization, the Misión Humanitaria Internacional, to provide a cover story. Colombian majors, medics, lieutenants, and a nurse who had no former military intelligence experience prepared for roles through a crash course on acting. One would pose as an Australian humanitarian worker "with beach-blond hair, who spoke no Spanish." There would also be a doctor, three nurses, and two guerrillas wearing Che Guevara T-shirts. They even created and memorized fake life histories, perfected foreign accents, and scrubbed all traces of "military training from their speech and physical demeanor."[33]

For transportation, the military painted the exteriors of two Russian Mi-17 helicopters white, with the bright orange trim of the imaginary humanitarian organization. The radio impersonators ordered César to have the hostages wear white shirts to be more easily spotted from the air. Mission planners decided to have only one of the helicopters land at the rendezvous site so that the other could hover above, creating noise and confusion.[34]

On July 2, Operation Jaque (meaning "Check," as in chess) went ahead. The helicopters headed to a site near the Apaporis River, where César had assembled the three groups of hostages. The first helicopter landed. An imposter television crewman distracted the scores of rebels guarding the hostages. The mission nearly hit a snag when some of the hostages refused to be handcuffed before boarding the helicopter. The "blond Australian delegate" walked the Americans out of earshot and spoke to Howes in English. Howes asked, "Are you U.S. Army?" "We're Colombian army," he responded. Then Howes announced, "Okay, we're going," and agreed to be handcuffed with plastic ties. Astoundingly, the actors convinced César and his subordinate in charge of the hostages, Enrique, not to bring their weapons on a humanitarian mission. They boarded the helicopter unarmed.[35]

The helicopter lifted off. Moments later, a team member grabbed César, and the man playing the doctor jabbed him with a hypodermic needle. Within seconds, César was unconscious. Enrique was also taken down.[36]

The hostages were free. Marc Gonsalves wrote, "One of the aid workers grabbed me, kind of put his arms around me and put me down, and he said. 'We are army. We are army.' And that's when I found out I was free." Howes was similarly beyond belief. "You're suddenly free. I was dazed by it. The second thing I thought was, Man, I'm in a Russian helicopter. I hope this thing doesn't crash, because I wanted to make it through to enjoy this freedom." Betancourt was worried that all of the celebrating would bring down the chopper: "Be still! Calm down! Sit down!"[37]

Less than sixty minutes later, the helicopter touched down at the military base in San José de Guaviare, where Betancourt spoke to her mother for the first time since she had been kidnapped more than six years earlier. "Mama, I'm alive! I'm free! Mama, the army rescued me . . ." The three Americans were flown to Bogotá, where they were met by Ambassador William Brownfield and other U.S. officials before transferring to a medical facility in Texas.[38]

Not a single shot was fired during the entire operation. A few days later the FARC released a communiqué: "The escape of the 15 prisoners of war last Wednesday, July 2, was the direct result of the despicable conduct of [Gerardo Aguilar] 'César' and [Alexander Farfán] 'Enrique' who betrayed their revolutionary principles and the confidence placed in them."[39]

The U.S. military did play a role in Operation Jaque. For months, American military personnel had been working with small Colombian reconnaissance teams in San José del Guaviare, just a few miles away from the Jaque rescue site. American authorities were notified of the plan a week before the undertaking, and, if Dana Priest's reporting in the *Washington Post* is accurate, a "JSOC team, and a fleet of U.S. aircraft, was positioned as Plan B, in case the Colombian operation went awry." This contingency plan aside, American involvement in the actual rescue was likely limited to intelligence, planning, and operating surveillance and emergency signaling technology.[40]

César and Enrique both went to prison in Colombia. In February 2009, the Colombian Supreme Court refused to extradite Enrique, since the crimes he was accused of had been committed on Colombian soil. That July, however, it allowed César's extradition on drug trafficking charges in U.S. federal court. U.S. Department of Justice officials wanted the charges to include the kidnappings, but the Colombian judicial authorities refused. César was sentenced to twenty-seven years in at a medium-security prison in California on drug trafficking conspiracy.

Swan Song

With the success of Jaque and other aggressive military operations, the FARC forces were on the run. Not surprisingly, life as a "FARC-ista" became far less enjoyable. FARC soldiers, most of whom had been forcibly recruited into the guerrilla ranks in the first place, began to jump ship. In a sign that even some diehard revolutionaries were losing faith, Bogotá reported that a large proportion of the deserters had spent ten to fifteen years with the rebel group. (It's no fun becoming middle-aged in the jungle, it seems.) Some of the revolutionary fervor had likely already begun to wither after the group's original leader, Manuel "Sureshot" Marulanda, died of a heart attack in 2008, just two months before Operation Jaque.[41]

At times, the Colombian military debriefed deserters and then reinserted them into the FARC ranks without the guerrilla commanders' even noticing they had left. These "moles" provided critical on-the-ground intelligence to the Colombian security forces. In some cases, they actually planted homing beacons in the FARC commanders' headquarters, to guide smart missiles to their targets. Not only were its ranks diminished, FARC's finances had also been reduced, as illicit trade revenues plummeted from perhaps $500 million to $250 million by the end of the decade.[42]

In 2010, Uribe's hardline defense minister, Juan Manuel Santos, was elected president. That September, he authorized a raid against the FARC's now second-in-command and chief military strategist, Mono Jojoy. Employing thirty planes, twenty-seven helicopters, and more than thirty tons of explosives (including fifty precision-guided munitions), Operation Sodom ended in the death of the most feared man in the country, wanted for more than a hundred separate crimes. Colombian defense minister Rodrigo Rivera characterized Jojoy's thousand-foot-long hideout, equipped with Viet Cong–like tunnels and escape routes, as "the mother of all FARC camps." President Santos ebulliently called the strike a "turning point" and "the beginning of the end for the FARC."[43]

Indeed, the security forces' manpower, hardware, and intelligence forced the FARC onto a self-described "strategic defensive." From its peak force of twenty thousand men, women, and children, the FARC now numbered well below half that figure. Yet, FARC diehards vowed not to give up their revolutionary struggle. They began laying thousands of landmines to slow pursuing soldiers and to intimidate police officers who were manually eradicating the guerrillas' coca fields. From 2000 to 2009, seven thousand Colombians were killed or wounded by mines, most of which were planted by FARC combatants. The FARC also continued to bomb oil pipelines, causing sizable local environmental disasters and lost revenue for the national and local governments. In a further sign of desperation, the FARC reportedly lowered its recruiting age to twelve. To maintain its war chest, the insurgency expanded its cocaine trade activities. It built and commanded "narco-subs" that carried drug shipments through the Caribbean. All this said, the FARC was able to wreak only a fraction of the havoc it had in earlier decades.[44]

Backed into a corner, the FARC Secretariat returned to the negotiating table in September 2012. The parties finally reached an agreement four years later, on August 24, 2016. However, a referendum on October 2, 2016, that had been stipulated in the terms failed to ratify the deal, with 50.2 percent of Colombians voting against, 49.8 percent in favor. Scrambling, the government and the FARC hastily signed a revised agreement on November 24 and sent it to Congress for ratification, rather than risking another plebiscite. Congress passed the accord in the last days of November. This marked the end of a fifty-year conflict that had killed more than 220,000 people and forced nearly 7 million more from their homes, earning Colombia the world's highest rate of "internally displaced people" (IDPs).[45]

Under the treaty, over the next several years the seven thousand remaining FARC combatants would be disarmed and demobilized. The FARC would become a legitimate political party, and its members would be allowed to run for election. The pact also made much of the process of "transitional justice." Interestingly, shortly after the deal was signed, FARC leader Carlos Antonio Lozada confessed that, "like his colleagues, he had come to regret the FARC's ties to the narcotics trade. 'We know that it helped delegitimize us, and we have concluded that without a doubt it did us great harm.' Despite this, he said, his revolutionary ideals allowed him 'to live with peace of mind.' "[46]

All told, the FARC's submission to negotiated peace was a direct outcome of an exacting military campaign substantially supported by U.S. military and financial assistance. But we have to look at this, too, with a critical eye. The beginning of wisdom here is the recognition that the Colombian military never fully defeated the FARC. Rather, "victory" entailed a negotiated settlement predicated on the FARC laying down its arms in return for the political legitimization of its socio-ideological point of view. Even more, as many as a third of the "former" guerrillas would continue to be involved in narcotics trafficking, illegal mining and logging, and other criminal ventures.

"The Only Risk Is Wanting to Stay"

Several years ago, the Colombian government launched a witty advertising campaign: "Colombia—the only risk is wanting to stay." The ads were aimed at luring foreign tourists and investors who had shunned the country because of its reputation for drugs and violence. Having not long ago held the dubious distinction of being the kidnapping and IDP capital of the world, Colombia was changing for the better. By the measure of the country's overall political stability, the narcotized U.S. policy strategy can arguably be considered a success (even if we might debate how large an impact U.S. efforts actually had).

In 1999, there were approximately two thousand terrorist attacks and three thousand kidnappings in Colombia. The country's murder rate was 60 per 100,000 residents. (For comparison, the murder rate in gang-riddled Mexico in 2012 was only 24 per 100,000.) In 2013, kidnappings had dropped by 95 percent to about two hundred per year. Murders were down by half, tracking a rate last seen in 1984. In 1999 almost two hundred of the country's thousand-plus municipalities had mayors who would not go to their offices for fear of leftist or rightist threats. By 2011, each municipality had a police force and a mayor who showed up for work. Senior Colombian defense officials privately said that the country might be on the cusp of "catastrophic success." In other words, the country was approaching maximum feasible achievement, although this had come at extremely high cost.[47]

Colombian authorities began to move beyond counterinsurgency to good government. President Santos, for one, was determined to achieve a sort of humanitarian revolution. Government agencies and citizen groups began openly talking about and pursuing real justice, restitution, reconciliation, and even the taboo subject of land reform. Colombians were slowly but decisively adapting to life in a "normal" country. In increasing numbers, they were taking domestic vacations, traveling from rural towns to provincial cities without the fear of kidnapping or disappearance. Bolstered by a dynamic economy—part of the ongoing peace dividend—more than a million Colombians moved out of poverty. Another million arrived in the middle class.

Citing these trends, U.S. counternarcotics officials often bristled at criticism of the Colombia strategy. Yet the fact that there is a "soft side" to the war on drugs in Latin America does not automatically justify the overall strategy, which remained punitive and prohibitionist. We have been using the U.S. Navy, the Coast Guard, the Border Patrol, and the DEA to enforce policies that bring about these softer outcomes for so long that it has become routinized and almost beyond the power of reflection to change it.

Moreover, human rights violations, absence of the rule of law, and economic deprivation remained an inescapable part of life for many Colombians, who still cited security as their overarching concern after the FARC peace agreement. Very likely, part of this concern involved the optics of memory. Another very substantial part of it involved the Bacrim. Working in bands of up to a few hundred fighters, the narco-gangs continued to terrorize rural towns and villages, driving civilians from their homes, demanding narco-taxes, and serving as guns for hire. For many Colombians, this was a bitter reminder of the Bacrim's predecessors, who settled domestic family disputes and national political contests with a bullet to the back of the head.[48]

A further setback to peaceful transition came in the form of the "False Positives" scandal. In the early 2000s, President Uribe offered rewards to soldiers who handed over the bodies of guerrillas they had killed. Thus incentivized, they began killing civilians in remote reaches of the country, dressing them in guerrilla rags, and reporting the deaths as FARC kills. By June 2012, more than 3,300 false-positive cases had been raised in the court system.[49]

The Impact on Drugs

Even though Colombia's security situation improved radically in the 2010s, the illicit drug front offered a more mixed picture. Coca cultivation was down by about half from its late-1990s peak, but Colombia remained the world's primary producer of cocaine, with much of the product winding up in the United States, western Europe, and, increasingly, Brazil, as that country grew richer and its tastes grew fancier. In this sense, ironically, Plan Colombia could be considered a success for Colombia's security but not for the war on drugs.[50]

For some, this is a difficult conclusion to swallow, but it is the one that seems to follow from the available evidence. On its own core metrics—the production and flow of drugs—the counternarcotics side of U.S. policy in Colombia failed. Whatever its other positive externalities, whenever the policy succeeded in suppressing drug activity in Colombia, it merely migrated to other countries. The total supply reaching the United States—crudely measured through the retail street price—did not change very much. In 1994 the street price of a gram of cocaine was around $200. In 2008 it had dropped to under $140, before returning to 1994 levels by 2010. According to the U.S. government, during roughly this same period domestic cocaine use remained roughly the same—around 1.5 million users per month.[51]

For this reason, when I left government for the last time in 2011, I was more confused about what the U.S. government was doing in the war on drugs than I had been when I came in. Part of the problem, in my mind, is an awe-inspiring lack of coordination among the dozens of agencies, administrations, and services that execute the thousands of functions of drug policy. To take just one example, in the Secretary of Defense's Office, there are "Western Hemisphere" people and "counternarcotics" people, whose spheres of concern mostly overlap but who have their own policy programs and funding stovepipes and authorizations. In my position, I routinely traveled to Colombia to meet with my foreign counterparts to discuss a range of policy issues. I would meet with a roster of Colombian generals who took me on helicopter rides to eradication zones and showed me the progress they had made. On most trips, I would inevitably discover that one Pentagon colleague or another, of similar rank but in a different bureau, had been down to Bogotá recently, a fact of which I'd had no idea. My colleagues had their own generals, who took them on their own helicopter rides. And while I was trying to create and promote my agency's policies with multi-billion-dollar authorizations, they were doing the same, sometimes at cross-purposes.

The End of an Era?

For the sake of counterargument, a potential cause for optimism arose with Operation Martillo ("Hammer"), unveiled in 2012, in which the U.S. Joint Interagency Task Force and Colombia's navy and air force pursued transnational criminal groups exploiting the sparsely populated and rarely monitored coasts of Central America. After years on the defensive for the apparent failure to significantly affect the cultivation of coca and the amount of processed cocaine leaving Colombia, U.S. officials now contended that they were making real progress via innovative multinational operations. They cited statistics such as the estimated decrease in coca cultivation from 100,000 acres in 2007 to as low as 64,000 acres over a few years. Colombian authorities echoed these claims, stating that they had achieved record drug seizures: in 2012 they captured roughly 240 tons of cocaine, believed to be nearly 70 percent of the total amount produced in the country. Most critically, Colombian officials contended, there was a 72 percent drop in pure cocaine production capacity in the country, from an estimated 700 tons in 2001 to 195 tons in 2011. Back in the United States, advocates of the drug war cited evidence of decreasing purity and rising retail prices as reflecting a reduction in the supply of cocaine as a result of these efforts.

However, a familiar problem attended these claims of victory: the violence stemming from Colombia's drug trade had simply moved north, to Mexico and Central America. Increased maritime interdiction operations in the Caribbean and the Pacific made overland transit across Central America preferable. This route now carried an estimated 85 percent of all U.S.-bound cocaine. Suddenly, the praise attending Operation Martillo sounded a lot like the hype surrounding the big push into southern Colombia in the early 2000s. We thought we'd finally cornered it, but yet again, we'd just squeezed the balloon.

In May 2015, the Santos administration announced that it was halting the aerial glyphosate spraying, citing environmental and health worries. This surprised many observers, because Santos had been such a staunch proponent of counternarcotics efforts, and aerial fumigation in particular. Spraying had peaked in 2006, with 405,000 acres covered; in 2014, only 137,000 acres were hit. One former Colombian defense ministry official predicted disaster. "If the spraying is stopped, the income of the drug traffickers, the criminal gangs and the guerrillas will go up substantially and so will the number of dead and wounded," he said. "Coca and cocaine production would also go up, and there would be more addicts and more people will die." What was missing in this argument was the fact that spraying had never yielded anything like a long-term victory over coca production.[52]

Two years later, Bogotá resumed use of the herbicide to eradicate coca, but this time only with manual eradicators, not spray planes. In 2017, Colombia's estimated coca production was 188,000 hectares—up almost 20 percent from two years earlier and the largest annual volume in more than two decades. One of Colombia's leading security analysts put the effort in perspective, "We have been fumigating these illegal fields for 20 years and we have not achieved great results."[53]

16 · Our Man in Lima

The M Word

U.S. policy in Colombia may have been all drug war through the 1990s and 2000s, but the drug war was not confined to Colombia. It's worth spending at least a few chapters on other hot spots in the Andes. First landing: Peru. On May 11, 1996, there was a sizable but certainly not unprecedented cocaine seizure in Lima, Peru's capital, nestled in the arid hills next to the Pacific Ocean. Peruvian authorities happened upon 174 kilograms of cocaine hidden inside the fuselage of a Douglas DC-8 jet belonging to the Peruvian Air Force. The plane was slated to fly to Russia—via the Canary Islands and Bordeaux—to have aviation parts of Soviet make repaired. Adding to the intrigue, just a few months earlier this DC-8 was in use as the executive plane for the Peruvian president Alberto Fujimori. Interviewed on the topic for local television, Fujimori declared that he had started an investigation to get to the bottom of the unacceptable incident—"even if generals fall." Fujimori might have wanted to be more careful with his words, given that in the several years leading up to 1996, 240 Peruvian police officials and forty from the military had been linked to drug trafficking.[1]

One security analyst, Javier Zavaleta, told a Spanish-language daily soon after the discovery that the National Intelligence Service (SIN), Peru's military intelligence arm, acted with alacrity to pressure military brass to reveal which officials had been scheduled to be on the flight to Russia. It is still not clear who was behind the shipment or to whom it was going to be delivered. One news investigation speculated that the Peruvian military had conducted multiple routine smuggling flights in the past.[2]

Only a few months after the DC-8 sensation, the notorious drug traffickers Demetrio Chávez Peñaherrera, called "El Vaticano," and Abelardo Cachique Rivera named three generals involved in their trafficking network. El Vaticano also testified that he had bribed Peruvian military officials on multiple occasions so that his drug ring could operate with impunity. Then he dropped a bomb. He had also successfully bribed the de facto chief of the SIN, Vladimiro Montesinos. After his conviction, Peñaherrera told reporters that Montesinos had once confessed to him that he had conducted "some work" for Pablo Escobar.[3]

Vladimiro Lenin Ilich Montesinos Torres was born in 1946 in the southern provincial city of Arequipa. His parents, devout Communists of Greek origin, named their son after their ideological hero. In 1965, just shy of twenty years old, Montesinos graduated as a military cadet from the U.S. Army's School of the Americas in the Panama Canal Zone. The following year he graduated from a military school near Lima. Montesinos became a middle-ranking military officer in the 1970s, but in 1977 he was sentenced to twelve months in prison after being convicted of, ironically enough, informing U.S. intelligence sources, possibly the CIA, about Soviet weapons sales to Peru. Upon leaving prison, Montesinos "began a fresh career" in Lima as a private drug attorney. His clients included "leading Colombian traffickers" and other shady actors under legal scrutiny.[4]

Montesinos got to know the future Peruvian presidential candidate Alberto Fujimori while representing him in a real estate fraud case. When the "unknown mathematician and university official" threw his hat into the 1990 presidential campaign, he drew Montesinos into his inner political circle. Rumor has it that Montesinos also "fixed" the election by confirming Fujimori's eligibility with a dubious birth certificate, which showed that the candidate had been born in Peru, not Japan. As it turned out, Fujimori won a stunning upset victory over the world-renowned Peruvian novelist Mario Vargas Llosa. He appointed Montesinos as the effective head of the SIN, a job that included anti-drug cooperation with the U.S. embassy. In fact, as investigative journalists wrote at the time, American diplomats acknowledged that the CIA and State Department's narcotics and law enforcement directorate had helped to create and fund the SIN's anti-drug unit.[5]

Montesinos was instrumental in the ultimately successful victory over the pernicious Maoist guerrilla group known as the Shining Path, although this effort was dogged with accusations of extrajudicial killings and disappearances. His power surged after Fujimori's "self-coup" in April 1992, when the president shuttered Congress, suspended the constitution, and assumed other autocratic powers. The spy chief pursued relationships with U.S. counterparts, presenting himself as the "president's emissary," and reopened a channel with the CIA. Montesinos's initial intelligence "proved to be true, and his reliability was confirmed." Keep in mind, though, that not every American agent or agency was enthusiastic about the relationship, given sustained rumors about Montesinos's role in the 1992 self-coup and extrajudicial murders. But for most of the 1990s, the CIA "repeatedly argued successfully" in interagency deliberations that Montesinos was an important source inside Fujimori's government. Speaking anonymously to Karen DeYoung of the *Washington Post,* one U.S. agent explained that working with someone like Montesinos involved a "deliberate decision balancing the nature and severity of the . . . abuse against the potential intelligence value of continuing the relationship." In this instance, he contended, the balance favored continuance.[6]

Following the Shining Path's defeat in the mid-1990s, Washington's attention in Peru was once again on drugs. Peru and Bolivia at this point were the world's two largest producers and exporters of coca leaves and coca paste. According to Karen DeYoung's keen reporting, the increased focus on Peru's cocaine trade meant that Montesinos "had come to be seen by many U.S. officials, even outside the CIA, as indispensable to U.S. counter-narcotics efforts" as well as Washington's broader relations with Fujimori's government. Between 1990 and September 2000, the CIA sent a minimum of $10 million as well as "high-tech surveillance" gear to Montesinos's SIN anti-drug shop. "Confronted with bureaucratic roadblocks or squabbles among officials, U.S. officials would ask the CIA station in Lima to seek the assistance of the man they called 'the doctor' and the problems would disappear," DeYoung wrote.[7]

At the same time, Montesinos was also weaving a "vast web" of illicit operations, including graft, gunrunning, and drug trafficking. This clandestine activity allowed him to stockpile more than $250 million in Swiss, U.S., and Cayman Islands banks. It does not take much imagination to conclude that at least some of this money came directly from CIA coffers. As one U.S. official told an investigative reporter, "It was an agency to agency [CIA to SIN] relationship with Montesinos as the intermediary. . . . Montesinos had the money under his control."[8]

U.S. agents acknowledged that they privately suspected that Montesinos was skimming some of the cash, but the CIA was directed to continue working with him. The justification was that Montesinos was "Peru's designated chief of counternarcotics and the only game in town." Another official privately revealed, "If we moved against [Montesinos], Fujimori would cut us off and tell us to go home." Indeed, Montesinos was considered "key to Washington's drug war in the Andes." The thinking carried the echo of a line President Franklin Roosevelt had supposedly conjured to describe the Nicaraguan strongman Anastasio Somoza García: "Somoza may be a son of a bitch, but he's our son of a bitch."9

Through the DC-8 incident and El Vaticano's court revelations in 1996, the "Montesinos connection" found its way into the public light. But given that most of the accusations came from drug traffickers' post-arrest revelations, Washington still had reason to doubt them. In October 1996 the shadowy Montesinos made a "surprise appearance" at President Fujimori's meeting with the Clinton administration drug czar Barry McCaffrey in Lima, an encounter that provoked protests from the U.S. embassy and U.S.-based human rights groups. A year and a half later, McCaffrey attended a meeting in which Montesinos presented a briefing. A Peru television channel controlled by the increasingly autocratic Fujimori regime aired a video clip from the meeting to intimate that Montesinos had been the "main attraction" for the drug czar. Despite the CIA's quiet protests, McCaffrey told the press that he was "offended" by the effort to "rehabilitate [Montesinos's image]. . . . I would not want to characterize Mr. Montesinos nor really associate myself with his work."10

In these years, Montesinos was using the SIN to corral political opponents and the media, through a deft combination of bribery and intimidation. Soon, Montesinos controlled not only the SIN for his own enrichment and his boss's political use; he also controlled the media, the military, and the courts. In 1997, the State Department cited Montesinos's illicit activities in its annual human rights report. Over the next two years, the Senate Appropriations Committee "repeatedly expressed concern about U.S. support for the Peruvian National Intelligence Service" and requested that it be "consulted prior to any decision to provide assistance to the SIN."11

Ten Thousand AK-47s, Courtesy of Vladimiro

In 1998, operatives under the direction of Vladimiro Montesinos posed as Peruvian military officers to buy fifty thousand Soviet-era surplus AK-47 assault rifles from Jordan. These weapons were delivered to Peruvian authorities in 1999. The broker was Sarkis Soghanalian, a "rotund arms trafficker and occasional U.S. intelligence informant." He was known as the "Merchant of Death" for his long career supplying weapons to dictators like Iraq's Saddam

Hussein. At a ritzy ocean-side social club in Lima, Montesinos expressed his thanks to Soghanalian for arranging the deal.[12]

The catch, though, was that more than ten thousand of those AK-47s were then smuggled via parachute drop to FARC guerrillas across the border in southern Colombia. Montesinos and Fujimori countered press reports about the illegal and politically catastrophic transfer with an official story that, in its brazenness and cynicism, ranks among the worst ever examples of state spin. On August 21, 2000, Montesinos and Fujimori "announced with great fanfare" that the SIN had busted the very "gun running scheme" that Montesinos had orchestrated. Soghanalian was shocked to learn that the SIN chief had accused him of being part of the crime ring. "The weapons I sold went to the Peruvian government," the dealer contended. "None went to the Colombian side. If any illegality occurred, it was on the side of the Peruvians." The Jordanian government also criticized the Peruvian account, countering that this had been a legitimate government-to-government sale. Yet, facts came to light—possibly leaked by military officers incensed by Montesinos's expanding power—that demonstrated incontrovertibly that Montesinos had actually "orchestrated the gun-running operation rather than dismantling it." Given that Washington considered the FARC to be narco-guerrillas and public enemy number one in the drug war, the Montesinos gambit put the American intelligence community in an awkward spot. The "AK-47s for the FARC" scandal quickly spelled the end of Montesinos's favorable treatment by U.S. officials. And it once again put the CIA and State Department in a bind over how to bust drugs and thugs in "source countries" like Peru.[13]

Los Vladi-Videos

It was not until 2000, when intelligence emerged that Montesinos was behind Fujimori's illegal attempt at a third term in office, that the Clinton administration publicly turned against him. This decision came in the face of continued CIA resistance. This "internal U.S. dispute" became moot in September 2001, when Fujimori called for new elections. He withdrew himself from the contest and committed to tearing down Montesinos's intelligence network. Fujimori's sudden announcement followed the leak of a sensational video that showed the SIN chief bribing an opposition congressman to ditch his party and join Fujimori's congressional coalition. Over the ensuing weeks and months, hundreds of "Vladi-videos" surfaced showing Montesinos and his associates bribing powerful Peruvians, from politicians to media bosses.

Some of the videos further documented Montesinos's machinations in the FARC AK-47 deal.[14]

Fujimori received Montesinos's resignation and applauded him for his service to Peru. As the Fujimori administration imploded, Montesinos vanished and turned up in Panama claiming political asylum. In November 2001, holed up in a hotel in Japan, Fujimori resigned from office. Despite the millions Washington had banked for his services, Montesinos was now persona non grata in Peru. With the help of the U.S. authorities, the former SIN chief was apprehended in Caracas on June 23, 2001, and returned to Peru to face charges. At trial, one arrested arms dealer said that Montesinos had recruited him to hatch the AK-47 deal and that the gun runners were "tortured to prevent them from implicating the spy chief." His story was reinforced by other testimonies, including those of Peruvian military officers. In late September 2006, Montesinos was sentenced to twenty years for "masterminding" the Jordan-FARC arms deal. As the *Washington Post* noted, Montesinos "appeared impassive" as the judge announced the sentence, bringing to a close a "nearly three-year trial that has heard testimony resembling a spy thriller."[15]

Writing in 2000, DeYoung identified a core message of the U.S.-Montesinos saga: "The story of Montesinos's relationship with Washington—at least from the American side—is a familiar tale of conflicting U.S. priorities in Latin America. Montesinos is the most recent in a long line of intelligence assets, including Chilean intelligence chief Manuel Contreras and Panamanian strongman Manuel Noriega, who ended up behind a changing policy curve."[16]

Air Bridge

As the Montesinos empire fell, the U.S. policy priority for this Andean nation remained the same: stopping the flow of coca to cocaine processing sites, mostly in Colombia. As far back as 1989, under the senior President Bush's Andean Initiative, the federal government had earmarked $2.2 billion in economic and military assistance for the Andean Region—Colombia, Bolivia, Peru, and Ecuador—to be spent through 1994. The program's ambitious aim was to reduce the amount of cocaine reaching the United States by 60 percent before the turn of the century. Peru also received a big assistance boost with the passage of Plan Colombia—roughly $450 million of the plan's total $1.1 billion budget went to Peru and other Andean states.[17]

One of the chief objectives in the campaign in Peru was shutting down what Beltway officials called the "air bridge." Until the mid-1990s, almost all of the coca that became cocaine was harvested in Bolivia and Peru, turned into base, and flown in small planes via the uncontested "air bridge" into Colombia for final processing and "re-export" to consumer markets northward. Shut down the air bridge, the thinking went, and the game would be over for the drug suppliers. Much as the kingpin strategy was supposed to break the drug trade's business model by eliminating its leadership, blocking this vital transportation artery would disrupt its primary supply chain. In 1995, President Clinton authorized the CIA to set up the clandestine Air Bridge Denial Program in coordination with the Peruvian military. Relying on CIA intelligence, between 1995 and 2001 Peruvian Air Force jets shot down scores of aircraft suspected of trafficking drugs. By the early 2000s, American officials pointed to the Air Bridge Denial Program as an unmitigated success. Of course, one reason it was so successful was that the program played hardball, a fact that did not sit well with many observers. Indeed, some critics contended that many of these "shoot-downs" could not possibly have been verified drug hits, as they happened without any warning and only within a couple of minutes of the targets' being identified.[18]

On April 20, 2001, the hitherto secret CIA program erupted in controversy when Peruvian jets opened fire on a single-engine Cessna that they assumed was a drug flight. American missionary Veronica Bowers and her infant daughter Charity were killed. Her husband, Jim Bowers, and their six-year-old son Cory miraculously survived without injury. The pilot Kevin Donaldson was "seriously wounded" but managed to pull off an emergency crash landing on the Amazon River. After the incident, it emerged that the Cessna had been tracked by CIA surveillance aircraft flown by American contractors, who passed along the intelligence to the Peruvian Air Force. Perhaps influenced by a desire to deflect culpability away from the agency, a CIA investigation laid blame for the politically delicate tragedy at the feet of the Peruvian Air Force. The air force, the report claimed, had "misidentified the plane as involved in drug trafficking and engaged the aircraft over the objections of CIA personnel." At the same time, acknowledging "problems with the program," the report noted that more than a dozen CIA officers had received "administrative punishment." The program was suspended and then reopened in 2003 on the Colombian side of the "bridge."[19]

Aside from its questionable means, the Air Bridge Denial Program had at least one other strike against it: it did little to stop coca production. As we have already seen, when the cost of shipping from Peru became high enough, Colombian traffickers simply started planting coca inside Colombia, particularly

Dressed in heat-reflecting suits, Peruvian firemen hold up a bag of cocaine before incinerating it, November 14, 1995. The total amount of drugs to be burned totals some 4.5 tons and includes cocaine, marijuana, and opium. The drugs had been confiscated earlier that month in the Peruvian Amazon jungle.
(Reuters, permission to author)

in the sparsely populated Llanos and Amazon regions to the east. Given the rise of rightist paramilitaries and Marxist guerrillas in the same areas, the campaign's local success yielded a financial bonanza for these illegal actors.[20]

Postscript

Between the mid-1990s and 2000, the amount of cocaine leaving Peru dropped by an estimated two-thirds. Roughly twenty years later, when I was working on this book, Peru was once again the world's number one producer of coca. (By the time I finished the manuscript, however, Colombia had jumped back in front.) According to U.S. and Peruvian anti-drug officials, "new" threats that came with this shift were "narco flights." Up to a dozen times a day, small civilian aircraft left Peru's coca hotbed in the Apurimac, Ene, and Mantaro river valley region (known in Peru as the "VRAEM") laden with cocaine and "associated intermediate products." Unlike their air bridge–era predecessors, these contemporary narco-flights were ferrying drugs to Bolivia and Brazil, rather than to Colombia, where U.S.-supported enforcement was more active.[21]

As security analyst Evan Ellis explained, the contemporary Peruvian drug trade was run by "family clans" with connections to potent drug syndicates such as the Sinaloa cartel in Mexico, the Urabeños in Colombia, and the First Capital Command in Brazil:

> These family clans buy the coca leaf from local farmers, smuggle precursor chemicals to production sites, produce intermediate products and cocaine itself, and arrange the transportation of those products out of the region, via persons on foot ("mochileros"), in hidden compartments of vehicles, via river, and with light aircraft from clandestine airstrips "rented" from local landowners. Throughout the process, with the financing of the external organizations that are their clients, it is the family clans who pay "protection money" to both [drug-trafficking remnants of the] Shining Path and local guards, and manage other details of the local operation and its security.

In this chain, Ellis reported, the families would hand over the product to the Mexican, Colombian, or Brazilian organizations at ports or airstrips just before it left the country. In March 2015, the Peruvian Congress unanimously enacted a law permitting the country's armed forces to interdict—by forced landing or shoot-down—aircraft suspected of transporting drugs in its airspace. *Plus ça change.*[22]

17 • Bolivian Backlash

There are countries in the world where the history has been so
brutal, so humiliating, and so unreconciled, that it has become
part of the national iconography—sometimes to a degree that can
startle foreign visitors.
—Jon Lee Anderson, writing on Bolivia for the *New Yorker*

Cocalero to Presidente

Not a day over twenty years old but with a sun-weathered face that suggested he was twice that age, the bus driver on my visit to Bolivia in 2007 was
a former *cocalero* (coca farmer) from the Chapare region, on the eastern front
of the central Andes. He had abandoned the land a few years earlier to find
stable work in the capital city, La Paz, after the Bolivian government sought to
eradicate the only lucrative crop he had ever grown. My driver had the physical
features of an indigenous Bolivian, but his dress was Western, a combination
that marked him as one of the millions of Bolivian *cholos*—people of mixed
Amerindian and European descent. In conversations that ranged widely as we
traveled from La Paz to Lake Titicaca, he echoed the feelings of many of his
long-excluded compatriots in expressing his support for the radical government of President Evo Morales. Morales, an indigenous Bolivian, had risen to
power in 2005 and was best known to Americans for his efforts to modify the
country's long-standing anti-drug programs.[1]

Bolivia's age-old social and political instability had been on full display in
the years leading up to the ascendancy of Morales. Apart from his tenure,
there were five presidents in the new century's first five years; two had been

ousted in popular revolts that teetered on civil war. As the wise observer Alma Guillermoprieto described the pre-Evo era: "Dozens of people were killed; and even in areas not involved in the conflict, roads were blocked for weeks on end and commerce was virtually paralyzed." Guillermoprieto wondered, as did many students of the landlocked nation's fraught history, whether the "old tensions" between the "impoverished *altiplano*"—the Andean plateau where Evo's indigenous base resided—and the "tropical east"—the resource-rich region where "most of the country's self-described white people live"—would erupt into violence. A "water war" in the provincial city of Cochabamba was only the initial conflict in a string of revolts and protests that led to the sweeping electoral victory of Morales in 2005.[2]

The words and actions of U.S. ambassadors and policymakers still carried enormous weight in determining the course of events here—but often not in the way Washington wanted. A case in point occurred in mid-2002 when U.S. ambassador Manuel Rocha told the Bolivians that the United States would have to reconsider its sizable counternarcotics assistance if the Bolivians elected a candidate who was soft on the drug question. Many took Rocha's remark to be a veiled jab at Morales, an Aymara coca grower who was now a presidential candidate. Rocha's comments boosted the vote total for Morales in what ended up as a narrow loss. Morales was only half-joking when he later quipped that the ambassador had been his "best campaign manager."[3]

In December 2005, Morales did win the presidency in a historic landslide after campaigning on a fiercely anti-American and anti–drug war platform. Upon his inauguration, the new chief of state became a highly controversial figure in Latin American politics, one with options few Bolivian leaders have ever possessed. Within two years of taking office, Morales nationalized Bolivia's massive natural gas reserves and renegotiated lucrative extraction and distribution contracts with U.S. and Brazilian energy entities.[4]

During his campaign in 2005, Morales promised that as president he would end the controversial practice of forced coca eradication. Calling his policy "*coca sí, cocaína no*" (coca yes, cocaine no), Morales contended that there was no reason Bolivia could not cultivate copious amounts of coca for licit products and still successfully combat narcotics trafficking. Efforts to promote legal coca production were but one part of Morales's attempt to "re-found" the country along "socialist" (that is, Venezuelan and Cuban) lines. As one might expect, skeptical U.S. officials worried that the new approach by Morales would reverse the progress they had made in crop eradication. After Morales took office, coca production indeed ticked up considerably.[5]

"Coca Gold Rush"

This was not Bolivia's first coca boom. The global demand for cocaine in the early 1980s sparked a massive spike in cultivation, particularly in the scrappy and moist Chapare, a region straddling the area between La Paz and the eastern city of Santa Cruz. Almost overnight, coca came to represent up to 4 percent of Bolivia's national income. Desperately poor, predominantly indigenous Bolivians living in the highlands migrated to the Chapare to take part in the "coca gold rush." An estimated 7 to 13 percent of Bolivia's workforce became involved in coca cultivation, and annual production soared from five thousand to about forty thousand hectares per year. As expected, the excess production fed directly into the cocaine industry. My ex-*cocalero* bus driver told me as we drove through a village near Lake Titicaca during a research trip in 2010: "Back in the 1980s in the Chapare, you would walk into a market and see what you thought were piles of flour. But it was cocaine. It was all perfectly legal. Ah, the good old days."[6]

Beginning in the late 1980s, Washington responded to Bolivia's coca boom by pressuring successive governments to implement rigorous anti-drug programs. This was part of the advent of the supply-side drug war in the Andes. Programs like the semi-clandestine Operation Blast Furnace (July–October 1986) combined alternative crop development programs, voluntary and forced coca eradication drives, and the interdiction of processed cocaine. I recall a senior U.S. counternarcotics official in La Paz who summed up to me the logic behind the carrot-and-stick approach: "The whole idea is to get people to switch to, say, hearts of palm. But these crops can never compete with coca because the narcos will always pay top dollar for it. Folks only switch when there is the threat of losing their entire coca crop." But while these programs were focusing on the Chapare, in 1988 the Bolivian government passed Law 1008—also known as the Coca and Controlled Substance Law—which permitted twelve thousand hectares of coca for "traditional" use to be grown in another region, the Yungas, near La Paz. Passed under pressure from the United States, Law 1008 outlined the distinctions between "traditional" coca usage and cultivation for the production of coca derivatives, particularly cocaine. In addition to restricting and defining coca cultivation within Bolivia, the law imposed harsh penalties for consumption and possession of controlled substances—i.e., cocaine.[7]

In the late 1990s, the Bolivian government agreed to step up its forced eradication initiatives in the Chapare via Operation Dignity Plan, which aimed to eradicate coca in the region by 2002. This "zero coca" strategy cost the

Chapare more than $700 million in annual income. Not surprisingly, *coca-leros* in the region did not take "zero coca" lying down. They organized a series of major strikes that often turned violent, resulting in the deaths of scores of *cocaleros* and several police officers. After years of conflict, President Carlos Mesa resolved the crisis by informally allowing 3,200 hectares of coca production in the Chapare. Sensing that all available alternatives would be much worse, the U.S. government did not publicly oppose the compromise.

Despite the violence, the zero coca strategy in the Chapare did achieve its objective. By the early 2000s, there was almost no commercial coca production there, aside from the 3,200 "compromise" hectares, plus the twelve thousand legal hectares in the Yungas. (Recall, though, that in 2000 the "push into southern Colombia" had just begun, in small part because of this region's coca cultivation increase due to "successful" developments in Peru and, especially, Bolivia. In classic [reverse] balloon effect manner, within the next four

Bolivian police officer guards bags of confiscated cocaine in Santa Cruz, Bolivia, August 2, 2003. In the load, which was destined for Spain, Bolivian authorities discovered three tons of cocaine (street value $300 million) inside a huge shipment of instant mashed potatoes. (Reuters, permission to author)

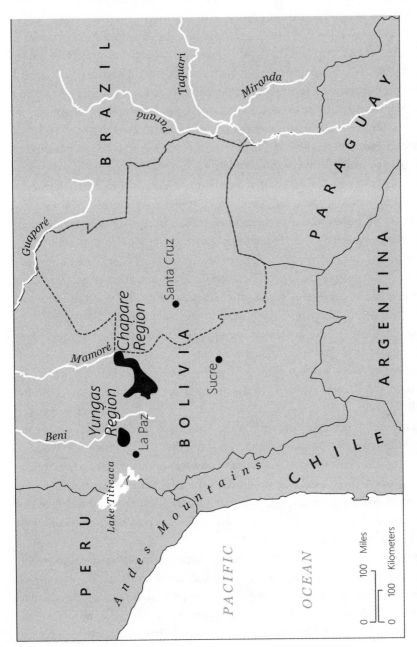

Map of Bolivia showing the Yungas and Chapare coca-growing regions (University of Wisconsin Cartography Lab)

years, aerial spraying efforts in Colombia would spark an overall increase in coca cultivation in Peru and Bolivia.)[8]

In addition, after more than a decade of arduous effort and hundreds of millions of dollars, alternative-development assistance projects—funded mostly by the U.S. government—began to bear fruit. Chapare's licit agricultural production rose to roughly $25 million in 2002, up from nearly zero a few years earlier. In the decade that followed, funds from the U.S. Agency for International Development built critical infrastructure and provided technical assistance that have allowed Chapare farmers to tap into the global market. Chapare-grown bananas became widely available in Europe. As my colleague and friend Ramiro Orias, a noted development expert in La Paz, told me: "It took almost twenty years, but there [were] tremendous successes."[9]

By 2008, however, the gains had been rolled back. During the coca boom, the *cocaleros* created labor "federations" based on the model they had used for generations as miners in the high Andes. In 2008, six coca federations covered distinct geographic areas within the Chapare, and Morales was the leader of them all. As one Bolivian analyst characterized it, "Evo was the maximum authority in the Chapare." It was easy to see why: Disaffected coca growers found in Morales, with his anti-U.S. and pro-coca rhetoric, a committed representative of their economic interests. To confirm his allegiance to the Chapare *cocaleros,* Morales made a former Chapare coca leader, Felipe Cáceres, his "drug czar." Cáceres regularly met with his American counterparts, both formally in bilateral meetings and informally over beers. But few on the U.S. side trusted the Morales government on the drug issue, and there was ample reason for suspicion. Morales announced soon after taking office that while he would still support the standing limit of one "cato" (one sixth of a hectare) per coca grower, there would be no limit on the number of coca growers in the Chapare. Not surprisingly, the "one cato" policy encouraged an influx of new *cocaleros* into the region, and coca production shot up around 10 percent there in the year after the announcement.[10]

Morales's continued leadership of the Chapare coca federation allowed him to reach peaceful agreements on coca production levels in this region. Yet most *cocaleros* in the Yungas regarded him as a frontman for the Chapare growers. Yungas farmers feared that Morales was cagily using punitive eradication efforts toward them while allowing farmers in the Chapare to plant coca with abandon. Some observers suggested that the endgame for Morales was to eliminate the Chapare's main domestic competitor. Unlike the Chapare, the Yungas received scant alternative development assistance, and there was growing alarm that increased eradication would leave farmers in that region broke.

In February 2017, the Bolivian government passed the General Coca Law, expanding the legally allocated land for coca production from 12,000 hectares (as regulated by Law 1008) to 22,000 hectares. The rationale behind the Morales administration's push for reform was the supposed increase in traditional usage of coca, which had been believed to have entailed 3.3 million people out of a nation of only 12 million. While ostensibly standing up for cultural heritage and indigenous rights, the passage of the law also represented a strong stance against cooperation in coca eradication and drug control efforts, an attitude in line with the general anti-drug war posturing of the Morales presidency.

Morales's policy innovations left international observers—particularly those in Washington—wondering where Bolivia's excess Chapare coca crop was going. And many, not incorrectly, deduced that it was bound for the illicit cocaine market. Without mounting a strong defense against this suspicion, Morales contended that the solution to unaccounted-for excess coca was not to limit cultivation but rather to expand the range of its licit uses. The Bolivian government's term for this was *industrialización*. Morales floated ideas about coca being used for toothpaste, hemorrhoid cream, flour, and even wine. The Morales administration also raised the possibility of sending five hundred thousand tons of coca leaf to China for medicinal uses. In the end, though, little emerged from these unorthodox designs.[11]

Most experts remained dubious about the prospects for *industrialización*. As one U.S. official succinctly put it, "Coca flour costs three times as much as normal flour and it tastes like shit." Similarly, a Bolivian academic wondered, "Why can't Evo understand that people like to drink wine made from grapes, not coca?" Furthermore, many observers were convinced that, even if it were practical, developing new licit coca markets in the region would do little to reduce the amount of the crop supplied to cocaine producers. *Industrialización* was complicated by the fact that coca was a banned substance under a United Nations treaty, making it illegal for signatory countries to import coca products. Morales made several attempts to get coca removed from the U.N. list, but Venezuela was the only country to support him.[12]

Morales may have been sincere in his hope that Bolivia would be able to grow as much coca as possible and that all excess production would be seamlessly "industrialized" for sale in foreign markets. Bolivian police, trained via U.S.-funded programs and by U.S. personnel, would interdict any residual cocaine. Yet given the apparently insatiable international demand for the drug and the discouraging prospects for legal coca products, it was natural to wonder whether Morales's policy of *coca sí, cocaína no* would inevitably become *coca sí, cocaína sí*. And whether Morales himself already understood this.

Bringing Back the Stick

Although the U.S. embassy in La Paz had been eager to show patience toward Morales's evolving coca policies, some U.S. officials in Washington and several members of Congress worried about a looming Bolivian "narco-democracy." The State Department's Western Hemisphere Bureau won a fierce bureaucratic fight in the fall of 2006 to keep Bolivia off the "uncooperative" list in the drug war, a ruling that could have resulted in the cessation of nearly all U.S. economic assistance and the forfeit of the leverage within La Paz that went with it.[13]

An intensifying debate in Washington over Bolivia reflected the seismic shift that U.S.-Bolivian relations had undergone since Morales took office. Those who urged decertification contended that Washington shouldn't "reward bad behavior." Morales's routine denunciations of "American imperialism" certainly frustrated those U.S. officials who advocated patience and engagement with the Bolivian government. Still other critics urged the George W. Bush administration simply to ignore Morales, since, in fact, very little Bolivian cocaine reached the United States. (Most of it ended up in Brazil, Argentina, and Europe, a development that understandably made these governments pay more attention to Morales.)[14]

Despite these acerbic disagreements, almost all U.S. officials privately acknowledged that U.S. influence in Bolivia was sharply diminished. Unlike in years past, when threats to cut off development assistance instantly resulted in compliance with American wishes, Bolivia's leadership now had Venezuela, Cuba, and perhaps even China as alternative aid markets. As one American diplomat asked, "What's to prevent Evo from saying, 'Forget it. Take your toys and go home'?" And that is more or less what happened. Over the next several years, Morales kicked out the DEA, USAID, and the American ambassador.[15]

Congress and the Obama administration finally pulled the plug on what little remained of State Department counternarcotics funding and programs in Bolivia in 2013. Ultimately, Washington had concluded that precious antidrug dollars were better spent in more cooperative places, such as Peru or Colombia. This is one of the difficult realities of the war on drugs—that U.S. counternarcotic efforts and development assistance don't always go where they are needed but rather where they are welcome. Contrasting the story of Colombia with that of Morales-era Bolivia, one reason U.S. policy became so "narcotized" in the former may be simply that Colombia was willing to bear it. In any case, the news gave Colombian, and, increasingly, Mexican and Central American narco-bosses yet one more reason to relocate their business to Bolivia.[16]

The Evo Way?

In 1949, the chief of the embryonic U.N. Commission of Inquiry on the Coca Leaf, Howard B. Fonda, explained the logic behind banning coca chewing. "We believe that the daily, inveterate use of coca leaves by chewing . . . not only is thoroughly noxious and therefore detrimental, but also is the cause of racial degeneration in many centres of population, and of the decadence that visibly shows in numerous Indians. . . . Our studies will confirm the certainty of our assertions and we hope we can present a rational plan of action . . . to attain the absolute and sure abolition of this pernicious habit." In 1964 the Bolivian military government's signing of the U.N. Single Convention on Narcotic Drugs of 1961 meant that Indian communities lost the right to chew coca leaves for twenty-five years. When this interim period ended in 1989, the issue was left "under dispute."[17]

Five decades after the signing of the U.N. Single Convention on Narcotic Drugs, in 2011, Morales announced that Bolivia was withdrawing from the single convention. The following year it became the first country in half a century to pull out of the global anti-drug accord. Morales's government simultaneously requested to be readmitted to the treaty if the U.N. scrapped the language classifying coca as illegal. Morales contended that the 1961 statute conflicted with the country's 2009 constitution, which committed the state to "protect native and ancestral coca as cultural patrimony" and stated that coca "in its natural state . . . is not a narcotic."[18]

A significant international dispute was the immediate result. Bolivia's new status could only be checked if more than one-third of the close to two hundred signatory countries opposed Morales's decision. The conventional view was that both Washington and London—as well as Rome, Stockholm, Amsterdam, and Moscow—were "frantically lobbying" other signatory nations to block the effort by Morales. One activist at the Transform Drug Policy Foundation supported La Paz, stating, "The Bolivian move is inspirational and ground-breaking. It shows that any country that has had enough of the war on drugs can change the terms of its engagement with the UN conventions." In 2013, Morales's government "re-adhered" to the Single Convention but won a reservation to exclude traditional coca chewing.[19]

The controversy only heightened when, in the lead-up to his visit to Bolivia in July 2015, Pope Francis "specifically requested" to chew coca to help stave off altitude sickness. The Bolivian minister of tourism and culture Marko Machicao told the press, "We will be waiting for the Holy Father with the sacred coca leaf." (In the end, the Pope told the press that he had declined to try it.)[20]

For many drug war observers and activists, the "Bolivian model" suddenly became an appealing alternative. Morales remarked, "We in Bolivia, without U.S. military bases and without the DEA, even without the shared responsibility of drug-consuming countries, have demonstrated that it is possible to confront drug trafficking with the participation of the people." A column by the *New York Times* editorial board in September 2016 contended that Morales's gentler approach, based on consultation with the coca growers, represented a viable alternative to Washington's reflexive prohibitionist war on drugs.[21]

> This stands in stark contrast to the strategy the United States has long financed in the region—a combination of aerial herbicide spraying, manual eradication and the prosecution of drug kingpins in the United States. The inadequacy of this approach is most obvious in Colombia, which has been Washington's closest ally in Latin America on counternarcotics.[22]

Having read the editorial, I was eager to see these policies in action when I took a dozen of my students on a ten-day field trip to Bolivia in October 2016. Although I did not make it back to the Chapare as I had when I toured it in an official capacity in 2010 alongside drug czar Cáceres, I spoke to anyone I could about the country's drug situation. Just about all of them were adamant that narcotrafficking was rampant in the country under Evo. In fact, they contended, the frenetic construction boom in La Paz was fueled by kingpins looking to launder their illicit gains into legal properties. Every now and then the government would announce a "massive" bust, demonstrating that it was diligently prosecuting the illicit trade. But the Americans' assessment on the ground was that the Morales government was tolerating the narcos, as long as they stayed low-profile and kept the violence to a minimum.

There were also, for the first time in recent memory, reports of dozens of rustic airstrips under construction in the remote jungles and low plains; their intended use, it was hard not to conclude, was to help ensure that Bolivian marching powder continued to make its way into foreign noses. In power for fourteen years, Morales resigned on November 10, 2019, in the aftermath of highly dubious presidential election results the previous month. Calling the removal a "coup," Morales fled to Mexico, where he was granted political asylum.[23]

18 · El Narco Mexicano

Pablo Escobar is like a Boy Scout compared to the Mexicans.
—U.S. Army veteran

We're going to give them a one-year warning, and if the drugs don't
stop, or largely stop, we're going to put tariffs. And if that doesn't stop
the drugs, we close the border.
—U.S. President Donald Trump, April 4, 2019

The wanton violence that laid waste to Mexico in the first years of the twenty-first century was often so extreme that it seemed like a horror film; what made it genuinely terrifying was that it was, indeed, real. Mexico's decades of living dangerously were at least in part fueled by the U.S. war on drugs. The cultural shifts that normalized drugs such as cocaine and heroin in the United States in the 1960s and 1970s had ripple effects in Mexico, from the opium fields of the Sierra Madre to the government agencies of Mexico City. Colossal demand across the border prompted Mexican entrepreneurs to get into the drug business, as it had throughout Latin America. Struggles for control of the trade led to the concentration of power in the hands of a small number of gangs and cartels on the Pacific and Gulf coasts, in border states such as Chihuahua, and in sparsely populated and lightly policed Sinaloa. For decades leading up to the 1980s, Mexican gangs smuggled "homegrown marijuana and heroin" to their northern neighbors. As David Luhnow and Jóse de Córdoba explained in the *Wall Street Journal*, "These groups, notorious for their shifting alliances and backstabbing ways, have fought for years for control of trafficking routes. Personal hatreds have marked fights over market share with barbaric violence."[1]

Cocaine's hype in the 1980s created a wild price surge, from $50 for a single gram in the 1970s to $150 in the next two decades, producing billions in profit. In the 1970s, most of these ill-gotten gains made their way back to Colombia. That began to change, however, as Mexico gained a foothold in the cocaine trade as a relatively "safe" transit country.[2]

Cocaine destined for the United States in the early years followed a path through the Caribbean islands, into Florida, and out across American cities to the north. But as the United States pursued more aggressive interdiction strategies in the Caribbean, the Colombians began searching for other ways into the North American market. They found one in Mexico, where an elaborate network of criminal organizations and drug distributors was already in place. As one DEA agent explained, the Colombians told Mexican bosses, "We are going to provide cocaine and you are going to deliver it from somewhere in Mexico to somewhere in the United States, and you are going to turn it back over to us, our cartel emissaries."[3]

With the business established, billions of cocaine dollars poured into Mexico. Mexican smugglers served as independent contractors, exacting a fee from the Colombian suppliers to move the cargo. The Caribbean route's eventual demise forced the Colombians to begin paying the Mexican traffickers not in cash but in product. And more than anything else, it was this transition that realigned the power dynamics along the narcotics supply chain in the Americas, because it allowed the Mexicans to "stop serving as logistical middlemen and invest in their own drugs instead." The Colombians' markup had been enormous: a kilogram of cocaine was worth $25,000 in the United States but cost only $2,000 to produce. The Mexicans realized that it was far better to have the Colombians' drugs than their money. Instead of making one or two million dollars a shipment, Mexican cartels could now make twenty or even forty million dollars at a time. Ironically, America's focus on Colombian traffickers, particularly the extradition of kingpins, improved the Mexican underworld's hand. Soon Mexican gangs controlled 90 percent of the cocaine entering the United States, at an estimated $70 billion a year. This was before adding the figures for marijuana and another gringo drug of choice, methamphetamine. In the United States, it was difficult to obtain the precursor chemicals needed to synthesize this popular drug. Not so in Mexico: small laboratories hidden away in remote stretches of mountainous desert produced 80 percent of the crystal meth sold in the United States.[4]

Guns crossed the border in the opposite direction. Around 70 percent of the firearms recovered from crime scenes in Mexico originated in the United

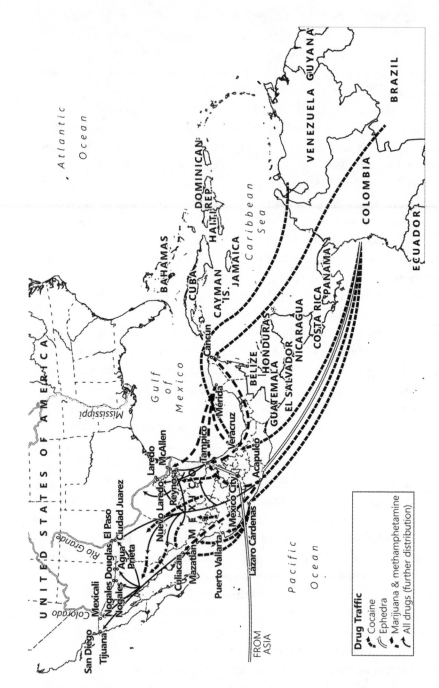

Mexican drug routes (University of Wisconsin Cartography Lab)

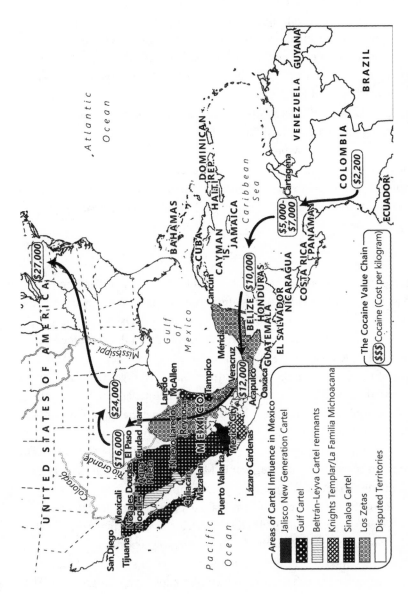

Mexican drug cartels, areas of influence (2008–2015) and the cocaine value chain from Colombia to New York City (University of Wisconsin Cartography Lab)

States. This confluence of criminal markets turned Mexico into one of the most dangerous countries in the world.[5]

The Mexican cartels were also involved in human trafficking, the exploitation of immigrants, kidnapping, murder, money laundering, and general corruption. Their money and power undermined the legal system and subverted the government. Campaigning politicians and investigative journalists were assassinated with impunity, while the general population was intimidated by the gang members' ruthless violence. Mexican assassins took notes from their Colombian counterparts, recruiting from the slums of provincial cities and even adopting the name *sicarios*. They further imitated the Colombian habit of ambushing targets in moving vehicles, but where their tutors preferred motorcycles and pistols, the Mexican assassins used SUVs and AK-47s. As Mexico's drug violence intensified, ambushers routinely pumped dozens of rounds into their victims, leaving piles of spent shells on the ground nearby.[6]

Gang Wars

The rags-to-riches rise of the drug kingpin is by now a familiar trope in the drug war saga, so much so that it is often immortalized in *narcocorridos,* folk ballads about the industry's heroes and their exploits. Osiel Cárdenas Guillén's path to infamy began humbly. An auto mechanic in the provincial city of Matamoros in the state of Tamaulipas, Cárdenas began running drugs as a member of the Gulf cartel then run by Juan García Abrego. In 1996, García was arrested and, after some inevitable middle-management infighting, Cárdenas seized control by killing his friend and rival, Salvador Gómez—an act that earned him the moniker "El Mata Amigos" (the friend-killer).[7]

In a sign of his growing power, Cárdenas began to intimidate the U.S. officials who were overseeing the drug war in Mexico and along the border. (Washington and Mexico City had been coordinating anti-drug efforts since Operation Condor in 1976, albeit often with mutual suspicion. Over the following decades, U.S. drug agents remained active in varying levels of quantity and velocity south of the border.) As the *Houston Chronicle* reported, in May 1999 Cárdenas threatened to murder an undercover sheriff's deputy of Cameron County when the latter refused to produce 988 kilograms of marijuana. That November, DEA agent Joe DuBois and his FBI colleague Daniel Fuentes had a run-in with Cárdenas, while an informant from a Mexican newspaper was touring them around drug hot spots in Nuevo Laredo. Cárdenas appeared toting a "gold-plated AK-47" and a Colt pistol with a gold grip tucked into his belt.

The drug boss "calmly asked" DuBois and Fuentes to hand over the snitch. Smiling, Fuentes displayed his U.S. badge. Cárdenas retorted that he didn't give a damn who they were and that he'd shoot them if they did not give up the target. DuBois told Cárdenas, "You don't care now, but tomorrow and the rest of your life, you'll regret anything stupid that you might do right now. You are fixing to make 300,000 enemies." Eventually, Fuentes and DuBois and their informer were released, and they scooted back to Brownsville, Texas. For the gringo law agencies, the "damage had been done," and they pressured Mexico City to get Cárdenas. DuBois and Fuentes received "exceptional hero-ism" badges from the U.S. attorney general, and as of 2017 they were still at their jobs.[8]

By the early 2000s, Cárdenas was running a "vast drug trafficking empire" responsible for bringing thousands of kilograms of cocaine and marijuana into the United States. According to the FBI, drug ledgers seized in Atlanta in June 2001 revealed that Cárdenas's Gulf cartel had made more than $41 mil-lion in drug sales over a three-and-a-half-month span in that city alone. In 2003, Cárdenas appeared on the FBI's list of ten most wanted fugitives, with a $2 million bounty for his apprehension.[9]

Under increasing pressure from rival cartels, Cárdenas began recruiting deserters from the Mexican army's elite Grupo Aeromóvil de Fuerzas Especia-les (GAFE, Special Forces Corps) to form Los Zetas, his "private mercenary army." Cárdenas was almost certainly not aware that in doing this he was molding the next generation's most lethal drug cartel. Between 2001 and 2008, the Gulf cartel and Los Zetas were collectively known as La Compañía. In March 2003, Cárdenas was busted in Matamoros after a shootout between Mexican military troops and Zeta sicarios. He was then placed in a maximum-security prison, La Palma, where he continued to run his operation. From his cell, Cárdenas expanded the reach and power of Los Zetas. Beyond simply de-fending the Gulf cartel leaders, the enforcers began to carry out kidnappings, levy taxes, collect debts, run protection schemes, and, inevitably, take hold of cocaine trafficking routes known colloquially in Mexico as plazas (zones). The gang also began killing rivals, "often with grotesque savagery."[10]

The Gulf cartel's chief rival, the Sinaloa cartel, responded by forming its own "heavily armed, well trained enforcer group," Los Negros, though they never rivaled Los Zetas in size, reach, or excess. Some drug war experts con-sider this development the beginning of the Mexican drug war, pointing to a clash between Los Zetas and Los Negros in the border city of Nuevo Laredo as the conflict's opening shots in 2004.[11]

Just across the Rio Grande from Laredo, Texas, Nuevo Laredo had long been Mexico's largest inland port and a key trucking hub. In the 2000s, it was also the point where almost 80 percent of Mexican-trafficked cocaine and crystal meth passed through on its way to the United States. At the time, the Gulf cartel controlled this *plaza,* but the Sinaloa cartel, under the leadership of Joaquín Guzmán, attempted to muscle its way in following the arrest of Cárdenas. Guzmán, better known as "El Chapo" (Shorty), had brokered and killed his way into a position as one of Sinaloa's top *jefes.* Now he dispatched a young deputy to seize control of Nuevo Laredo.[12]

While he remained behind bars, Cárdenas relied on the Zetas, as well as "most of the Nuevo Laredo police," to check El Chapo's power grab. Now the "rival cartels were fighting it out with machine guns, grenades and bazookas in broad daylight." The violence reached such a Baghdad-esque peak that it forced the U.S. Consulate to close. As foreign and Mexican press painfully chronicled, the region neared a state of anarchy. From late 2004 to mid-2005, thirty American citizens were killed or kidnapped in the city. In 2006, not a single one of the town's officially recorded 4,500 murders was solved. The fighting quickly spread as these two rival drug gangs "fought for dominance all over Mexico's northern border." One eyewitness to a battle in 2006 reported seeing "men with assault rifles throwing bodies into the backs of trucks and SUVs. The corpses were disposed of on the outskirts of the city, where they were dissolved in vats of acid, minced up and fed to animals or incinerated with gas so all evidence of them disappeared. Sometimes there was a very public murder to make a point. The dead body of Dionisio 'El Chacho' Ramón García, leader of the local *Los Chachos*—'The Lads'—gang ... was left out on public display dressed in women's underwear."[13]

With the ruthlessness of Los Zetas, the Gulf cartel eventually got the upper hand. They imposed a *Pax Mafioso* in which they administered the city by terrorizing police, journalists, and public officials and extorting money from licit businesses. As one intrepid human rights activist, Raymundo Ramos Vásquez, explained, "There has been a truce, I don't know the details, and I don't want to know them, but the Gulf cartel has won, and the Sinaloa cartel has lost, and they have reached an accord. I can only guess that Guzmán pays some kind of tax to use the corridor, if he uses it at all. The Gulf Cartel controls the corridor again, and the federal army patrols every block of the city, twenty-four hours a day, three hundred and sixty-five days a year." In 2009, the DEA labeled the Zetas "Mexico's most organized and dangerous group of assassins."[14]

The bodies of seven men arranged in chairs in Uruapan in the Mexican state of Michoacán, March 23, 2013. The placard on the right reads: "Warning! This will happen to thieves, kidnappers, sex offenders, and extortionists." (Reuters, permission to author)

Rats on People's Front Doors

In late 2006, in the gritty border metropolis of Ciudad Juárez, the sixty-nine-year-old Francisco María Sagredo Villareal had finally had enough with the dead bodies discarded outside his home. So he hung up a sign that read, "Prohibited: Littering and Dumping Corpses." The bodies continued to pile up until October 2008, when a group of men shot Sagredo outside his front door. Two months later, a gang killed his daughter Cinthia and dumped her body under the sign. The following day a group of men fired twenty AK-47 bullets into his other daughter and her friend as they drove in Cinthia's funeral procession. In a separate count, in August 2010 cartel-linked gunmen entered a barn in the state of Tamaulipas and shot seventy-two Central and South American immigrants in cold blood.[15]

These grisly episodes were but two in an extraordinarily violent drug war that began in earnest in late 2006, when the country's president, the right-of-center Felipe Calderón, declared his intention to put an end to the drug scourge. Although the drug violence had been worsening before his tenure, Calderón's declaration of war amounted to kicking the hornet's nest. Launching what he dubbed the *mano dura* (firm hand) approach, he deployed the normally barracks-bound Mexican military to Tamaulipas. The operation spread across various states, with 7,000 troops deployed to Acapulco and 3,300 to Tijuana.

While observers debate to this day whether Calderón's decision was a wise or necessary one, it is certain that horrific violence was one of its results. Much as the Medellín cartel waged war against the Colombian state under Presidents Betancur and Barco, the Mexican cartels launched a bloody campaign of terror. Between late 2006 and early 2010, Mexico witnessed more than thirty thousand drug-related murders. And while most of the shocking statistics did involve "narco-on-narco" killings between the Zetas and the Sinaloa cartel, civilians were increasingly caught in the crossfire. Between 2000 and 2016, more than seventy journalists were murdered. Fifteen others disappeared between 2010 and 2016. One reporter described what often happened to those killed by the cartels: "All that is left is your body destroyed in a vacant lot, hanging from a highway overpass, or locked in the trunk of a car. Your name is severed, cut off, and discarded. The history that remains attached to your body is that of your particular death, bullet holes, burns, slashes, contusions, limbs removed. The executioners of this killing ground destroy each person twice. First they obliterate your world; if you are lucky, they do so with a spray of bullets. But then, once you are gone, they will turn your body from that of a person into that of a message."[16]

The battle of Los Zetas with Sinaloa and its allies spread to half a dozen states. Suddenly, cartels that had been fighting one another to facilitate drug trafficking were instead trafficking to fund a war. The gangs were reckoned to have about ten thousand gunmen each. The Zetas were especially successful at locating "fresh recruits" in Monterrey's slums. Both sides were making snuff videos and putting beheaded corpses on public display. In one episode, La Familia Michoacana, a gang working with the Zetas in Michoacán State, rolled five human heads onto a dance floor. In another, Zetas fighters laid a note next to some of their rivals' corpses: "Chapo Guzmán and Beltrán Leyva, send more *pendejos* [pubic hairs, a popular Mexican slur] like this for us to kill." The numbers attached to this violence were staggering. At the end of the first year of Calderón's presidency, dozens of known decapitations had been reported. Over the next few years there would be hundreds. Between 2008 and 2016, more than fifty-five thousand people were killed. The number of disappearances probably ran somewhere between the official figure of six thousand and the unofficial estimates of twenty thousand or so.[17]

Once it became clear that the Mexican government could not contain the violence, a smattering of self-defense militias, or *autodefensas,* arose in the country's most lawless areas. A desperate government began to incorporate them into the state apparatus. Yet despite their good intentions, the *autodefensas* did not live up to the advance billing: as the militias expanded, they became less selective and more easily corrupted by the cartels. While the *autodefensas* were not likely created as part of some grand cartel-led conspiracy, they certainly did more to worsen cartel violence than to eliminate it.[18]

The (Gringo) Cavalry Arrives

In 2008, the George W. Bush administration began sending the Mexican government some $400 million a year for gear and training to fight the cartels. U.S. officials contended that the plan was to smash the cartels into smaller organizations, like "breaking down boulders into pebbles," as one U.S. agent put it. That this very same atomization had been an unintentional consequence of the kingpin strategy that ultimately made it *harder* to stop the flow of drugs out of the Andes seemed to be lost on the new generation of policymakers. But, even more, it reflected a certain resignation in the face of almost unimaginable violence. President Calderón's hawkish anti-drug government had long given up thinking "they might one day eliminate the drugs trade altogether." Jorge Tello, a drug war adviser to Calderón, colorfully defined the new thinking: "It's like a rat-control problem. The rats are always down there in the sewers, you can't really get rid of them. But what you don't want are rats on people's front doors."[19]

The funding package, known as the Mérida Initiative, eventually became a $2.3 billion plan to help Mexico confront threats to its national security, in part (à la Plan Colombia) through promoting judicial reform and providing military equipment and intelligence support. The plan was enthusiastically executed under President Obama's watch. In a turn that would have seemed unfathomable some years earlier, given Mexico's reflexive mistrust of its northern neighbor's intentions, U.S. Army Special Forces started training their Mexican army counterparts. The U.S. Marine Corps also launched an exchange program with the Mexican Marine Corps equivalent to share urban warfare tactics honed in Iraq and Afghanistan. Given Mexico's longstanding history of public corruption, especially among the police and military, this embrace did not come without its risks.[20]

Topolobampo, Mexico, January 25, 2007. A Mexican marine lifts a package of marijuana, part of a consignment of about four tons of marijuana, located in the northwestern Mexican state of Sinaloa. The lot was later incinerated at a naval base here. (Reuters, permission to author)

Nor did it escape criticism. As one writer noted, much of the money intended for Mexico under the Mérida Initiative would never cross the border. The taxpayer-funded money went to private U.S. contractor corporations for surveillance "software, computers, ion scanners, gamma-ray scanners, satellite communication networks, and other goods and services." A significant share of the initial budget was for aircraft and included just over $100 million to Textron, Inc., for eight Bell Helicopters to transport troops and support counternarcotics missions, $100 million to the Connecticut-based Sikorsky Aircraft Corporation for three Black Hawks, and $10 million to cover the delivery of three single-engine aircraft "for surveillance of drug trafficking areas and for a wide range of surveillance missions."[21]

Corruption: The Secret to Success

Although the overwhelming share of the narco war's violence was inflicted on gangsters, the conflict actually posed a significant threat to the Mexican state. Here is one account from the *Wall Street Journal* in 2009:

Last year alone, gunmen fired shots and threw a grenade, which didn't explode, at the U.S. Consulate in Monterrey. The head of Mexico's federal police was murdered in a hit ordered by one of his own men, whom officials say was working for the drug cartels. Mexico's top antidrug prosecutor was arrested and charged with being on a cartel payroll, along with several other senior officials. One man in Tijuana admitted to dissolving some 300 bodies in vats of acid on behalf of a drug gang. Every day brings a new horror. In Ciudad Juárez on Friday, gunmen killed a police officer and a prison guard, and left a sign on their bodies saying they would kill one officer every two days until the city police chief resigns. He quit late Friday.[22]

The status of law enforcement and justice systems was particularly telling. Cartel gunmen killed more than 2,200 policemen, 200 soldiers, judges, mayors, a gubernatorial candidate, a leader of a provincial assembly, and scores of federal officials. Mexican gangsters routinely attacked police stations with

Shootout in Tijuana, January 17, 2008. A policeman carries a child away during a gun battle in the Mexican state of Baja California. The violence, which erupted after police agents moved in on a drug cartel group, left four people injured and forced the emergency evacuation of a school in Tijuana. (Reuters, permission to author)

guns and grenade launchers, conducted mass kidnappings of officers, and left mutilated corpses on public display. Narcos murdered one mayor by stoning him in front of stunned onlookers. According to one investigative story, of the 120,000 people that soldiers and police detained in the years after Calderón's drug war began, prosecutors brought charges against only 1,300 for connections to the drug trade.[23]

Experts inside Mexico and in the United States feared that Mexico was on the verge of becoming a narco-state. Others contended that the risk was not so much that Mexico would collapse or be taken over by the gangs but that it would become something like Russia, "a state heavily influenced by mafias." The incoming Obama administration seemed to take the dimmer view. I had been at my Defense Department appointment for only a few weeks when the Pentagon listed Mexico as a country facing a significant risk of its government suffering a "swift and catastrophic collapse."[24]

Indeed, as was the case in Colombia, Mexico's cartel wars were inextricably linked to the country's incomplete transition to democracy. Mexico had a rapidly growing middle class and roughly fifteen years of electoral democracy under its belt, following seven decades of authoritarian rule under the Institutional Revolutionary Party (PRI). The drug trade put Mexico's fledgling democratic institutions under siege. Drug exports helped to stabilize the peso and directly or indirectly provided thousands of jobs, many in underserved regions desperate for a way out of poverty. As illicit profits spilled over into just about every other industry—hotels, cattle ranches, racehorses, music labels, football teams, and film studios—in many regions out of the central government's reach, gangs took over essential local and regional administrative functions. Mexicans described the traffickers collectively as *El Narco*, a ghost whose income swept in around $64 billion every year.

Journalist Patrick Radden Keefe reported on an internal survey of the DEA's top fifty snitches, who were asked to cite the most critical factor in a successful drug business. The overwhelming response? Corruption. One retired police officer from Juárez, Jesús Fierro Méndez, admitted that he had worked for the Sinaloa cartel. "Did the drug cartels have the police on the payroll?" a lawyer asked him. "All of it," Fierro Méndez responded. When Keefe added it all up, he concluded that bribery might have been the "largest line item on a cartel's balance sheet." In 2010, Genero García Luna, the country's chief of public security, estimated that the cartels shelled out over $1 billion to municipal police alone. Even Noe Ramírez, President Calderón's top anti-drug official, was alleged to have accepted $450,000 a month. "Presumably, such gargantuan bribes to senior officials cascade down, securing the allegiance of their subordinates."[25]

The Green Monster

Discouragingly, a small but significant number of U.S. anti-drug officials also succumbed to the drug trade's temptations. North of the border, U.S. agents were pressured by the cartels to look the other way or to get into the game directly. As journalist Alfredo Corchado noted, scores of agents across the DEA, the FBI, and Immigrations and Customs Enforcement (ICE) have been implicated in the corruption. From 2004 to 2012, there were just under 140 indictments or convictions of such behavior. One cause of this activity might have been the swift growth of border enforcement after the creation of the Department of Homeland Security in the aftermath of 9/11. "In their hurry to fortify the U.S.-Mexico boundary with uniformed personnel, it seems, officials may have made allowances on background checks and screenings. In some instances, job offers have been extended to the immediate relatives of known traffickers." With the Anti-Border Corruption Act in 2010, Congress made polygraph testing obligatory for new employees, but many bad apples were already on the inside. As President Obama's drug czar and Customs and Border Protection (CBP) commissioner Gil Kerlikowske explained, "Polygraphs have made it so we don't hire people with significant problems. The bigger problem is what happens to people who are already on board." In early 2017, an investigative story in the *Atlantic* contended that two-thirds of CBP applicants failed the polygraph test. In another damning statistic, an average of one CBP agent was arrested each day between 2005 and 2012.[26]

In one notorious episode from 2013, a Border Patrol agent named Ivhan Herrera-Chiang, assigned to Yuma, Arizona, was outed as an informant for drug traffickers. He had leaked sensitive intelligence including maps and the coordinates for clandestine underground sensors. Mr. Herrera-Chiang acknowledged he had been bribed with $45,000.[27]

After the arrest of one crooked CBP employee, former senior official James Tomsheck said that the agent was "not one bad apple" but rather "one part of corruption that exceeded that of any other U.S. federal law-enforcement agency." A DHS communiqué in May 2015 concluded that corrupt Border Patrol agents "pose a national security threat." Rotten agents in the pay of the cartels "waved tons of drugs" and unknown thousands of unauthorized immigrants across the border in return for millions of dollars. By 2018, bent agents were believed to total roughly 1 to 5 percent of the CBP's sixty-thousand-strong complement.[28]

Corruption aside, the simple issue of CBP's size and mission was troubling in its own right. Between 2001 and 2017, Washington's outlays for border and immigration enforcement totaled $100 billion—more than the total budgets of the FBI, the Secret Service, the U.S. Marshals, ATF, DEA, and the New York City Police Department combined. As Garrett Graff of *Politico* magazine pointed out in his aptly titled piece "The Green Monster," this load of cash paid for not only the sixty thousand agents but "a fleet of some 250 planes, helicopters and unmanned aerial vehicles like the Predator drones the military sent to Iraq and Afghanistan, making CBP both the largest law enforcement air force in the world and equivalent roughly to the size of Brazil's entire combat air force."[29]

A Washington Suit Heads to El Paso

In the summer of 2009, just a few months into my stint in Obama's Department of Defense, I arrived in El Paso with a senior delegation of Pentagon officials to see our Border Patrol and U.S. military policies in action. One question facing the incoming Obama administration was whether we would continue Bush's hardline approach to border enforcement, which had sent six thousand National Guard troops to the border through Operation Jump Start in 2006. While I was in El Paso, I met a genial CBP agent who informed me that his team had just busted a motorist with bricks of cannabis stashed in the chassis of his vehicle. He led my colleagues and me over to a sort of holding pen, where I could see an elderly Latino male. Imagine your average *abuelo,* or grandfather.

The scene was a near-perfect synecdoche for the border war, its motives, and its realities. First, there were the (for the most part well-intentioned) Washington suits, like me, who had taken time off from our cushy political or civil servant jobs inside the Beltway to get an "unvarnished" look at the front lines. Next, there were the local agents, ever eager not to upset Washington and lose precious budgetary allocations, making a convincing case that the work they were doing was both vital and successful. Over there in the holding pen was the bad guy. And here were the drugs. "Dr. Crandall," the border agent asked me, "would you like us to take a picture of you holding the cannabis?"—as if it were a big-game trophy. It was difficult to avoid the sense that this whole scene was scripted, that what we were all doing down there was going through a set of rote procedures that existed primarily because it existed, mostly irrespective of whether it would ever fulfill the mandate for which it was created. In my role as a good politico, I now needed to return to the federal cocktail circuit to talk about what it was like facing down narco-giants in El Paso and Juárez.[30]

If anyone had asked me at the time, I would have candidly said that my visit to the border was qualitatively different from the average CBP tour, given that it was contributing to official and patently vital government work. That is, I was seeing and doing things that others outside the U.S. policy apparatus were not. I am now amused and a bit embarrassed to know how similar my visit was to those of countless journalists, scholars, and others who are hosted by the U.S. agencies responsible for guarding the border. To take one example from late 2013, *New York Times* journalist Lawrence Downes described an experience almost identical to my own: "Through night-vision binoculars, I watched two figures silhouetted on a rise against the glow of lights from the Mexican side, crouching and running but keeping their distance. It was impossible to know what they carried—contraband or merely hopes for a better life." In 2017, House Speaker Paul Ryan was treated to the same show on his first official visit to the Texas border: "a helicopter tour, a horse patrol demonstration, the boat ride, a stop at a United States Customs and Border Protection operating hub, and a meeting with local leaders."[31]

Yet, as easy as it is to heap criticism on a struggling system, a more balanced view would take into account the fact that U.S. public servants were often doing their best under difficult circumstances. As many observers have commented, CBP agents constantly save the lives of migrants who would otherwise fall victim to brutal weather, harsh terrain, and the predation of gangs and coyotes.[32]

As it turned out, Obama's new DHS secretary, Janet Napolitano, announced in late March that additional National Guard troops would indeed be sent to the border. What wasn't reported as thoroughly at the time, though, was that most of these reinforcements were assigned to civilian tasks like manning traffic posts, rather than actively patrolling the line. But why send in the troops if they're not actually troops? As far as I could tell from my Pentagon perch, it was all about symbolism. Everyone, including Napolitano, a former governor of Arizona, wanted to look tough on the border.[33]

"A Satanic Cult"

After their schism with the Gulf cartel, the Zetas made a bid to become the dominant players in the Mexican game. Where they exceeded the reputations of their predecessors was in their wanton application of torture, extortion, arson,

Printouts of Ayotzinapa Rural Teachers' College students abducted and eventually executed near the Mexican city of Iguala in the volatile, gang-ridden state of Guerrero, late September 2014. A mass grave full of charred human remains was subsequently located. (Reuters, permission to author)

and assassination. Seasoned scholar George Grayson suggests that the reputation for "sadistic treatment of foes and friends" was a legacy of the Zetas' two leaders: Heriberto "The Executioner" Lazcano Lazcano and Miguel Ángel "Z-40" Treviño Morales, who delighted in such pathological practices as castration and *guiso* (stew), in which he dropped victims into large barrels, showered them with gasoline, and set them on fire. The Zetas also cannily used PR stunts from Facebook campaigns to public hangings in order to intimidate their way to power. The brutal tactics allowed them to establish effective control across numerous Mexican states.

Much like Colombia's *paras*, when the Zetas took over a *plaza*, they took over just about everything. The gang managed retail stores, distributed pirated films, and served as dubious migrant guides. In the areas where they operated, "whoever want[ed] a job, any kind of job," had to work for them. The border stronghold at Nuevo Laredo gave them ready access to the United States to purchase weapons, establish licit businesses, and recruit teenagers.[34]

Alliances with other gangs and syndicates increased the Zetas' penetration into illicit networks. Early on, they capitalized on "situational alliances" with the Beltrán Leyva Organization, an enforcer gang that had splintered off from its own erstwhile Sinaloa overlords. In Central America, the "invaluable confederates" of the Zetas were Los Chulamicos, who provided arms, informants, assassins, and safe houses. Zetas even contracted with U.S.-based gangs such as Houston's Tango Blast to "collect debts, acquire vehicles, carry out hits, and sign up thugs."[35]

On October 7, 2012, Mexican marines killed Lazcano after a "withering gun battle," which began while he was "nonchalantly watching a baseball game" in the northern state of Coahuila. Treviño (Z-40, or "El Cuarenta") quickly ascended to the top spot. Mike Vigil, a former DEA chief, described him thus: "Miguel Treviño is 100 percent more violent than Lazcano ever was." El Cuarenta had a $5 million reward on his head courtesy of the *yanqui* government and a $2 million bounty from the Mexican government, not to mention that his own cartel rivals were gunning for him. So he took Pablo Escobar's seemingly unsurpassable paranoia to new levels. Z-40 frequently traveled in ambulances or low-flying planes. He slept inside his car, where he carried hundreds of thousands of dollars to bribe any authority who got too close. He was protected by some two hundred hit men, plus corrupt cops and officials who helped form a circle of fifteen levels of security around him—and also reportedly maintained a vigilant distrust of everyone in this circle except his brother, Óscar Omar "Z-42" Treviño Morales. His organization would have been difficult for anyone to penetrate, but it was especially so for a government whose intelligence was often compromised.[36]

In his arresting book *Midnight in Mexico,* dogged Mexican-American reporter Alfredo Corchado describes Treviño as "a madman." The chief's second nickname, "Muerte" (Death), spoke volumes. His pithy encouragement to associates was, "If you don't kill someone each day, you're failing." On some accounts, the Zetas under El Cuarenta's command became a "satanic cult," providing the "blood and hearts of victims to the devil in return for their protection." Z-40 was known for "removing a victim's heart—while the person was still alive—and taking a bite out of it. He believed it would make him invincible." A U.S. agent witnessed so much barbarity in the aftermath of Cuarenta-signed attacks that on his trips to Mexico City he would "slip into the Basilica de Guadalupe to pray to the Virgin for peace and strength. . . . On Sundays he went to confession, where, he reported, one priest asked him, 'Why do you rejoice at news of the killing of some big drug kingpin?' He responded: 'Because that kingpin was the closest thing to the devil.' "[37]

Corchado broke the story of Treviño's apprehension by the Mexican navy on July 14, 2013. Atypically, no shots were fired in the operation. Authorities believed that Z-40 was succeeded by his brother, Z-42. Then in the early morning hours of March 4, 2015, Z-42 was apprehended in a wealthy Monterrey suburb, again without violence. A few weeks later, a possible successor to Z-42, Ramiro Pérez Moreno ("El Rana," the Frog), was captured.[38]

Shorty

To the west of the Gulf cartel's strongholds in Tamaulipas lay the 1,500-mile-long Sierra Madre Occidental, for decades the veritable cradle of Mexican drug trafficking. The scratchy, arid mountain range stretches from Arizona to the "Golden Triangle," an area comprising the states of Chihuahua, Sinaloa, and Durango, so named for its vast narcotics output. The mountains are rugged enough to hide an entire army, as U.S. General John Pershing discovered in his 1916 pursuit of revolutionary bandit Pancho Villa, who eluded American forces in the Sierra after carrying out a raid on Columbus, New Mexico. Although many gangs have originated in the Triangle, one formidable narco organization stands out: the Sinaloa cartel.[39]

On one dusty Sinaloan road, in a remote mountain pueblo in the "lumpy green mountains" of the Golden Triangle, stood the childhood home of Joaquín Guzmán. Born in 1957 and equipped with only an elementary school education, Guzmán struggled with literacy as an adult; one account had him using a ghostwriter to "compose letters to his mistress." Despite his humble start, by the 1970s Guzmán was working diligently under some already infamous drug lords: Amado Carrillo Fuentes, known as the "Lord of the Skies" for his fleet of drug-hauling aircraft, as well as "El Padrino" (the Godfather), a former cop and head of the Guadalajara cartel.[40]

In 1980, Guzmán struck out on his own and founded the Sinaloa cartel. By the 2000s, he had become one of Mexico's wealthiest businessmen, with an asset value estimated at $1 billion and counting. American federal agents considered him the biggest drug trafficker of all time (although Pablo Escobar might have disputed that claim). The Chicago Crime Commission named Guzmán Public Enemy Number One, a testament to the quantum reach of drug violence, considering that the Mexican kingpin may have never set foot in the Windy City. The first criminal to earn the title had been Al Capone in 1930.[41]

In 1989, El Chapo's mentor El Padrino was apprehended, and the Guadalajara members still standing met in Acapulco to discuss "which smuggling route each capo would inherit." It was ostensibly a rendezvous among allies. But the remnants of El Padrino's Guadalajara cartel would soon become the seeds of others—Tijuana, Juárez, Sinaloa—and "these onetime colleagues would soon become antagonists in a cycle of bloody turf wars."[42]

In 1992, Guzmán's *sicarios* turned up at a bustling nightclub in Puerto Vallarta on the Pacific coast. The hitmen sliced the phone lines so that no one could call for aid, "then walked inside and opened fire on the dance floor," killing six revelers. El Chapo's intended targets, Tijuana cartel members whom Sinaloa was trying to oust from Baja smuggling routes, were apparently in the bathroom when the hit went down and escaped. A few months later, Tijuana kingpins plotted to get El Chapo at Guadalajara's main airport. Yet the gunmen instead killed Archbishop Juan Jesús Posadas Ocampo, whom they likely mistook for Guzmán. The Sinaloa boss escaped the fracas and sought shelter in a nearby neighborhood. From there, over the course of the next several days, he made his way to Guatemala.[43]

The Posadas killing stirred a "political uproar" across the nation that sent the military and police on a months-long manhunt. From his Guatemalan exile, Guzmán was eventually apprehended, returned to Mexican authorities, and convicted of drug trafficking and other crimes. Yet, while he was interned at Puente Grande, the Mexican penal system's equivalent of a "supermax" facility, he ordered his meals from a menu that included lobster bisque and filet mignon. He ran his drug business by cell phone and had frequent visits from prostitutes.[44]

In January 2001, eight years into Guzman's twenty-year sentence, a prison guard peered into the boss's cell and announced, "He's escaped!" Patrick Radden Keefe details: "A subsequent investigation determined that Guzmán had hidden in a laundry cart pushed by a paid accomplice. But many in Mexico speculate that he didn't have to bother with subterfuge. Guzmán controlled Puente Grande so thoroughly by the time of his exit that he might as well have walked out the front door. Criminal charges were eventually brought against seventy-one people who worked at the prison, including the warden." El Chapo returned to Sinaloa, his drug operations, and his wars with other organizations.[45]

Soon enough, the Sinaloa cartel underwent its own version of organizational mitosis. Much as the Gulf cartel had done with the Zetas, Sinaloa outsourced its security and enforcement dirty work to an affiliated organization headed by Marcos Arturo Beltrán Leyva and his four brothers. Their breakaway was precipitated by the capture of one of the brothers, Alfredo, known as "El Mochomo" (Desert Ant), by Mexican authorities on January 21, 2008. The brothers blamed

El Chapo for the betrayal. The Beltrán Leyvas quickly formed an eponymous cartel and agreed to an alliance with the Gulf cartel and Zetas—pre-schism.[46]

In 2009, after a months-long search, Mexican commandos cornered Marcos Arturo at a Christmas party in Cuernavaca. Mexican Special Forces surrounded the building, but their mark narrowly escaped. Authorities seized almost $300,000 in cash, sixteen AK-47 and AR-15 assault rifles, and 1,700 rounds of ammunition. But Beltrán Leyva's luck had run out. Naval intelligence tracked the gangster to another residence. Once more, scores of marine commandos infiltrated the property. Unlike Guzmán, who would later go out with a whimper, Beltrán Leyva fought like "Al Pacino in *Scarface*," firing rounds and throwing grenades at the soldiers before he and five of his bodyguards were killed. The marines decorated his corpse with dollar bills discovered in the raid, and photographers were invited to record the scene.[47]

In revenge, gunmen loyal to Beltrán Leyva assaulted mourners at the wake of a marine killed in the battle, murdering his mother, brother, sister, and aunt. Beltrán Leyva was buried by his family at Culiacán's Jardines del Humaya, a cemetery "packed with the grandiose tombs of generations of Sinaloan narcos." A few weeks later, the head of a man in his thirties was found on the grave.[48]

The killing of Marcos Arturo Beltrán Leyva was initially a big score for the Calderón administration. Yet violence in Mexico only escalated as local outfits fought over his lucrative markets. As for El Chapo, it brought him out of his strictly enforced self-isolation, perhaps because he had decided it was "better to lead one good year than ten bad ones." As Keefe wrote in a masterful *New Yorker* article in May 2014, "By early 2012, the DEA had homed in on Guzmán's BlackBerry, and could not only monitor his communications but also use geolocation technology to triangulate his signal."[49]

In 2014, fresh intelligence, evidently gleaned from Guzmán's captured bodyguards, suggested that he had been making clandestine trips to Culiacán, the capital of Sinaloa state, and the Northern Pacific resort of Mazatlán. In the early hours of February 22, 2014, ten pickup trucks carrying Mexican marines pulled up at the Mazatlán condominium where Guzmán was believed to be staying. After breaking down its steel-reinforced door, the soldiers found him in bed with his wife, a former beauty queen. Guzmán may have been visiting Mazatlán for only a day or two to see his twin baby daughters, who were also present, before planning to return to safer confines in the mountains. Although he did tussle with his captors, Guzmán made no attempt to use the machine gun that rested near his bed. No shots were fired in the raid, but agents confiscated ninety-seven rifles and machine guns, thirty-six handguns, two grenade launchers, a rocket launcher, and forty-three vehicles, many of which were armored. Having beaten Guzmán and dragged him outside to confirm his identity, the marines transported their prisoner to Mexico City and, finally, to a federal detention center. Shorty had been on the run for thirteen years. Now that they had him in their hands again, Mexican authorities went out of their way to make sure he stayed in custody.

Like Tony Soprano

Guzmán's capture in 2014 came amid a wave of high-level takedowns of key cartel leaders, including Los Zetas' Z-40. Drug enforcement officials' hope that the Sinaloa cartel would implode without Guzmán was short-lived. His handpicked successor took over with minimal fanfare. And given the vast revenues that drugs still brought in, it was almost inevitable that ambitious new actors would step in to seize a share of the market. On June 25, 2015, U.S. officials sent a formal extradition request to Mexican justice officials. The Mexican government had long disdained the idea, preferring to keep El Chapo in chains on its own turf as a demonstration of national sovereignty. Six months earlier, the previous attorney general, Jesús Murillo Karam, had made this point emphatically: "El Chapo must stay here to complete his sentence, and then I will extradite him. So about 300 or 400 years later—it will be a while."

Such displays of bravado did little but deepen the dismay when El Chapo broke free yet again, in plain view of the video camera in his cell. This time he fled through a series of sophisticated tunnels that led from the floor of his cell's bathroom to a spot his henchmen had purchased seventeen months earlier, a mile away from the prison. In the game of chase that had come to mark the drug war's moments of highest intensity, it was one point for the mouse. Two private jets carried El Chapo back to his Sierra Madre stomping grounds, where he promptly returned to work. President Enrique Peña Nieto had told the nation following Guzmán's 2014 arrest in Mazatlán that another escape "would be unforgivable." Journalist Azam Ahmed wrote in the *New York Times* that Guzmán's second escape "cast a lurid spotlight on the incompetence and corruption that has long dogged the Mexican state, driving many to view the government on a par with criminals."[50]

In a bizarre twist, in October 2015, El Chapo sat for a seven-hour interview with the American actor Sean Penn for *Rolling Stone* magazine. In the interview he admitted, "I supply more heroin, methamphetamine, cocaine and marijuana than anybody else in the world. I have a fleet of submarines, airplanes, trucks and boats." At the same time, he told his interlocutor, "Look, all I do is defend myself, nothing more. But do I start trouble? Never." Mexican military forces narrowly missed capturing Guzmán in an operation just hours after the liaison.[51]

In early 2016, six months after his last prison break, Mexican marines in the coastal city of Los Mochis, in the northern part of Sinaloa, finally caught up with their quarry. They cornered Guzmán in a safe house under construction where he had been squatting, likely since the previous October. Before dawn on January 8, seventeen Mexican Special Forces marines raided the house, killing five of Guzmán's bodyguards, but missing the capo yet again. They found him just hours later, driving a stolen car out of town. Here is Keefe's humorous take: "As he was duck-walked before the cameras, bedraggled in a grubby tank top, he looked not so much like Chapo Guzmán as like a man wearing one of those rubber Chapo Guzmán masks that were popular on both sides of the border last Halloween, his pale and hairless shoulders out of proportion with the big, familiar, square-jawed face and the improbably black mustache." In January 2017 Guzmán was extradited to the United States to stand trial in Brooklyn in a federal drug case that had begun almost two years earlier, culminating in a jury finding him guilty on ten criminal counts. The mesmerizing trial provided an inside glimpse into the "inner workings of the Sinaloa drug cartel, complete with tales of gruesome murders, diamond-crusted pistols, caches of cocaine smuggled in cans of peppers and, at the center of its all, a defendant who twice escaped from prison." In July 2019, Guzmán was sentenced to spend the rest of his life in a U.S. maximum security penitentiary. (In 2017, the United States assured Mexico City it would not pursue the death penalty as part of the extradition.) U.S. District Judge Brian Cogan explained why leniency was not warranted: "The overwhelming evil is so severe." Reading written comments through an interpreter, Guzmán claimed "there was no justice" in the trial and condemned the "psychological, emotional, mental torture, 24 hours a day."[52]

"Bathed in Blood"

In December 2012, the recently inaugurated Mexican president, Enrique Peña Nieto, had announced a new campaign, probably in response to Calderón's sobering attempts to defeat the cartels, that emphasized soft efforts to counter the drug trade, such as social investment, crime prevention, and the strengthening of public institutions. He proposed a government commission that would spend $9 billion over the next few years in more than two hundred

Drug tunnel, Tijuana, Mexico, October 30, 2013. U.S. authorities shut down a secret underground tunnel equipped with electricity, ventilation, and a rail system for smuggling drugs between Tijuana and a San Diego industrial park. At the rented warehouse where the passageway ended on the U.S. side, border control and drug enforcement agents seized more than 7,700 kilograms of marijuana and 147 kilograms of cocaine from the tunnel, arresting three men. (Reuters, permission to author)

of the most violent municipalities. The campaign included longer school days, drug-addiction treatment programs, and public-works projects. The Peña Nieto administration also announced a greater focus on disrupting the street gangs and criminals hired by the cartels, a departure from Calderón's emphasis on killing the top drug traffickers.[53]

Yet, in keeping with the malignant dynamics of the war on drugs since Nixon began this struggle almost half a century ago, the gains were eventually replaced by further setbacks and suffering. By 2017, violence in rural Mexico was surging again, thanks to the new foothold Mexican cartels had gained in the heroin market and the continuing boom days for methamphetamine. As of this writing, Mexico supplied 90 percent of the heroin reaching the United States, compared with the 10 percent it provided in 2003. Between 2013 and 2016, according to a DEA report, Mexican opium poppy cultivation tripled. In 2017, U.S. Customs interdicted more than fifty-four thousand pounds of crystal meth crossing into the United States from Mexico, also a threefold increase since 2012. As Joshua Partlow reported in the *Washington Post,* "The opioid epidemic that has caused so much pain in the United States is also savaging Mexico, contributing to a breakdown of order in rural areas." A *Wall Street Journal* article in 2017 documented that Mexican armed forces were unable to keep up with all the new poppy plantings. The Pacific coast state of Guerrero was leading the way in producing "more and stronger heroin and market[ing] it more aggressively" to a gringo market that favored the drug "over more costly opiates like oxycontin." The blowback in pueblos and provincial cities across the state was considerable. Guerrero saw entire villages abandoned. José Díaz Navarro, a retired schoolteacher and courageous social activist monitoring the violence, described his community of Chilapa in central Guerrero as "bathed in blood." A hundred and fifty were slain in the first six months of 2017 alone. "We don't know who is involved with whom," he said, "but the criminals kill anyone for whatever reason." Journalist Dudley Althus put the violence in perspective: "The fight to supply surging U.S. demand for heroin has poured jet fuel on long-smoldering political and social tensions. Complicit or cowed, local officials and police have proved unable to contain the violence and sometimes abet it, activists say." Embattled Guerrero governor Héctor Astudillo even floated the notion of legalizing poppy cultivation "as a way of lessening the gangland rivalries." In some towns, citizens responded by organizing militias, which in the most extreme cases replaced the absent state with a system of vigilante administration, complete with extrajudicial killings, "purges," and the accession to authority by "whoever has the guns."[54]

With more than two thousand murders recorded, May 2017 became Mexico's deadliest month since 1997, when statistics were first compiled. Several by now predictable pressures had contributed to the devastation: successful aerial spraying of poppy plantings in the Andes; similar drug eradication programs in Afghanistan and other parts of Central Asia; the paralysis of the Mexican state; and the breakdown of the rule of law in rural areas. In short, it was classic balloon effect. But this time, the outcome was compounded by new factors. One was that more and more drugs were actually staying in Mexico. Between 2006 and 2016, reported illegal drug use doubled among Mexican men and women between ages twelve and sixty-five. One U.S. drug official explained the mechanism: the cartels were producing more opiates and meth than distributors could carry across the increasingly restricted border, "so mid- and lower-level distributors push it out into the local markets." Another new factor was the unprecedented surge in demand for opiates in the United States, driven largely by the overprescription of opioid painkillers. A third was the elimination of one of the cartels' principal revenue streams: as more and more American states relaxed their restrictions on domestic cannabis production and consumption, grass from Mexico just wasn't selling like it used to.[55]

19 • Fear and Loathing in Central America

Gangster Warlords

Like a parasite, the species of criminal organization known as a gang keeps its host, the state, alive just enough to feed off of it. As Berkeley scholar Nils Gilman wrote in his seminal essay "The Twin Insurgency," gangs aim to "carve out *de facto* zones of autonomy for themselves by crippling the state's ability to constrain their freedom of (economic) action." In Latin America, gangsters took advantage of the vulnerability of the states they operated in to such a degree that they frequently became shadow powers. Thriving in conditions of conflict that were not quite civil war but much more extensive than typical criminal violence, these groups terrorized their host societies, using corruption, extortion, and bullets as their weapons of choice. Thirty-four of the fifty most violent cities in the world were in Latin America—in 2017, San Pedro Sula, Honduras, held the top spot. That year the region had just 8.5 percent of the global population but 27 percent of its murders. These statistics were almost exclusively a result of the impunity enjoyed by the region's criminal organizations, primarily those with ties to the illicit drug trade.[1]

A gang's origin story often began with the members of a marginalized class, such as the aggrieved residents of slums or the former political prisoners of a military dictatorship, channeling their anger into associations with strict codes of conduct and a deep, even mystical air of camaraderie. As the journalist Ioan Grillo documented in his gripping book *Gangster Warlords,* many justified their participation in the drug game by arguing that it was a means of redistribution: taking from wealthy gringos and elites in their own countries and putting that money into the pockets of poor families and neighbors. In slums, where the state failed to provide much of anything, drug gangs often served as the de facto administrator of social services. They were an armed neighborhood watch program, public works department, welfare system, and drug distributor all rolled into one. Whether they were paving roads, sponsoring football clubs for kids, hosting block parties, or donating to local charities, Latin American gangster warlords gave back to the community—though of course with the quid pro quo of silence and cooperation.[2]

The shining example of the modern drug gang was the transnational organization Mara Salvatrucha, known as MS-13. In the 1970s and 1980s, hundreds of thousands of Central Americans, a majority of them Salvadorans, fled dictatorial repression and ideological violence in their home countries and landed in the United States. In Los Angeles, Salvadoran youths at the mercy of predatory gangs from other Latin American countries organized the first iteration of MS-13, which expanded across the United States and then inevitably sent feelers back to El Salvador. There, in the absence of an effective state, the organization sprouted like a weed.[3]

Whereas in the United States MS-13 included a few thousand members and was just one element in a multifaceted criminal gang ecosystem, in El Salvador the organization came to occupy a central role in society. At one point, 14 municipalities out of 262 were considered under effective Mara control. More than three hundred thousand people—almost 6 percent of the population—were financially dependent on an estimated sixty thousand gang members. And for several years, the Massachusetts-sized country of 6.3 million people had one of the world's highest homicide rates: fourteen per day, just behind neighboring Honduras. Gangsters all across the region exploited the weakened institutions meant to rein them in. Alarmingly, many groups grew out of the penitentiary system or were strengthened during their members' prison stints. Prisoners in El Salvador received frequent visits from associates and prostitutes, and some were even permitted to carry firearms. Incarcerated leaders continued calling the shots—often literally—for organizations on the outside. Guards had little control or leverage over their inmate populations. In some cases, the prisons actually became the gangs' headquarters. So dire were conditions that the president of El Salvador declared a state of emergency, barring visitors and confining prisoners in their cells.[4]

Reporting in 2015 and 2016 confirmed that MS-13 and similar gangs had become "vicious occupying forces" in much of the "Northern Triangle," which includes El Salvador, Guatemala, and Honduras. In reporter Douglas Farah's description: "The scruffy, rag-tag teens of years past were violent, brutal, and often stoned, but could only afford homemade pistols and the rare AK-47 or hand grenades left over from the 1980s. Now many of the *clicas,* or neighborhood gang organizations, had assault rifles, vehicles, safe houses, and encrypted satellite phones. Some factions were even able to deploy drones to monitor the movements of the police or rival gangs."[5]

In the 2010s, the Northern Triangle became mired in a gangland conflict as pervasive and destructive as the worst days of revolution and counterinsurgency that scarred the region through the 1970s and 1980s. As Dagoberto Gutiérrez, a former commander of El Salvador's former Marxist FMLN insurgency, lamented in an interview: "We are living in the worst war of our history, but no one wants to acknowledge it as a war." The statistics were numbing. Between 2012 and 2015, slightly fewer than fifty thousand citizens were murdered in Guatemala, Honduras, and El Salvador, making the Northern Triangle the most violent region in the world outside of declared combat zones. Over this same time span, the three countries achieved convictions in 2,295 cases, or about 5 percent of all homicides. El Salvador's homicide rate of 105 inhabitants per 100,000 was the world's highest; Guatemala and Honduras ranked in the top five. In El Salvador, an astounding 10 percent of the population was involved in gang activity. Life in gang-run regions was a daily horror. Girls as young as eleven were taken as *jainas,* or sex slaves, and boys were forcibly recruited into the gangs. The gangs extorted protection payments from businesses to the point of bankrupting them. An estimated three hundred thousand Salvadorans were forced from their homes in 2014. MS-13 and its gang allies and blood enemies were by no means the only criminal elements contributing to the Northern Triangle's deterioration. Mexico's bloodthirsty Sinaloa and Zeta cartels, also active in the region, collaborated with local gangs to traffic drugs, persons, and weapons.[6]

MS-13 and affiliates attacked the Salvadoran National Police 400 times in 2015, compared to 200 in 2014 and 140 in 2013. *Mareros,* as members are known, attacked police stations with grenades, assassinated more than twenty off-duty military officers, and used improvised explosive devices against public agencies, including a car bomb detonated outside the Treasury Building in September 2015. Gang-control police started wearing balaclavas to conceal their identities, hoping to keep themselves and their families alive. In the first seventy-three days of 2016, 1,688 people were murdered in El Salvador, more than twice the number from the same period the previous year.[7]

El Salvador's gangster woes had their surreal aspects as well. One was the booming business in coffin making and funeral services. In San Pedro Perulapán, a nondescript town not far from El Salvador's capital, reporters investigated the town's funeral home bonanza. A funeral home employee go-ing by the pseudonym Rogelio told a reporter, "We are selling coffins like hot bread!" Funeral home workers had even coined a verb, *muertear*, meaning to search the streets for dead bodies. Given the surging demand, Rogelio had grown accustomed to the particular challenge of preparing bullet-riddled ca-davers. One gang member's body arrived at the funeral home with twenty-three gunshots in his chest, five in one hand, and several more in the face. Rogelio attributed the spike in business to the violence that had riven his town and the surrounding countryside, where locals lived at the whim of MS-13's chief rival, Barrio 18, or "La 18," as it is often called in Central America. Barrio 18 started in the 1980s as a small-time street gang in Los Angeles. One of its greatest infamies was its involvement in the riots that erupted in Los Angeles after the acquittal of the police officers who had clubbed and beaten Rodney King. Its membership initially consisted primarily of Mexican immigrants in the City of Angels, but Barrio 18 expanded its recruitment and footprint, even-tually taking the show—via the same surge in deportations of unauthorized residents with criminal records—to their native (Central American) lands in the 1990s.[8]

"A Pact of Silence"

Across the border in Honduras, on December 8, 2009, the country's high-est anti-drug official, Julián Arístides González Irías, was shot after dropping off his daughter at school. González was a retired general "distinguished for his rectitude and efficiency." The official investigation into the murder lasted only three weeks. In 2016, *New York Times* reporters Elisabeth Malkin and Alberto Arce broke a story implicating the senior ranks of the Honduran po-lice force in a cover-up of the assassination. Malkin and Arce described a "glar-ing example of top-level government corruption and collusion" with drug gangs. The main suspects were a "cell of high-ranking police commanders working hand-in-hand with drug traffickers." Honduran journalist Thelma Mejía revealed that police officials had agreed to a "pact of silence" to prevent any of them from informing on their colleagues.

On the night before González was killed, more than a dozen officers had met at the Honduran National Police headquarters to discuss the plot. "One of them clicked open a briefcase, and bundles of American dollars were distributed among the police officers." As the men departed the room, a few senior officers spoke on the phone with Wilter Blanco, who ran a drug cartel in the Caribbean.

One police official told Blanco, "Keep watch over the news tomorrow, sir. We'll do it all in the morning." Some time earlier, González had broken up Blanco's plot to hire police officers to steal around 150 kilos of cocaine from another gang. Evidently, killing González was revenge. The conspiracy apparently reached "all the way to the chief of police."9

Two years later, another counternarcotics czar, Alfredo Landaverde Hernández, was also assassinated, a short while after he "publicly accused" police leadership of allowing narco gangs to work with cops. A swift investigation determined that the main suspects were the very same police commanders. A comprehensive report was sent to the police chief, but it was not made public. The *New York Times* coverage painted a "chilling portrait of impunity at the very top of Honduras's police hierarchy: the unchallenged power to carry out assassinations and force a cover-up of the investigation." Aside from its devastating impact on the credibility of the Honduran state, the revelations created a dilemma for Washington. In an effort to bolster the very public institutions needed to enforce the rule of law in this gang-riddled nation, the United States was spending millions to "overhaul" the Honduran police force. Vermont senator Patrick Leahy put the issue in perspective. "Despite good intentions, I think our own officials, especially in the past, have sometimes been naïve in the way they have supported the Honduran government's actions and inactions." Congress ditched the effort when it came out that, in the wake of the assassinations, "only a handful of officers had been fired."10

Two migrants from Guatemala sleep on train tracks in Arriaga, Mexico, August 8, 2014 (Reuters, permission to author)

Antinarcotics police officers destroy bundles of confiscated drugs (just under
12,000 kilograms of cocaine) before incinerating them in Panama City, Panama,
November 22, 2013 (Reuters, permission to author)

"Mara-land"

In the summer of 2014, tens of thousands of children from the Northern
Triangle streamed across the U.S. border with Mexico. This was the peak of a
migration boom that had taken off in the early 2000s. In 2000, about 1.5 million people born in Honduras, Guatemala, and El Salvador were living in the
United States. By 2013, there were 2.7 million. That represented an exodus
of 10 percent of the Northern Triangle's 30 million citizens in that period of
time. The overwhelming number of desperate migrants created an array of
moral and logistical challenges in the United States. Most of those who came
through official asylum-seeking channels at the border were first processed by
CBP officers, whose task was to triage migrants as asylum seekers, those seeking alternative forms of legal protection, and all other categories. The vast
majority were turned away. As Sarah Stillman reported in the *New Yorker*, by
2013, "more than eighty per cent of deportations were nonjudicial, with the
result that life-or-death decisions now routinely rest in the hands of immigration authorities at the border." In February 2016, Senate minority leader

Harry Reid condemned the policy, saying, "Deportation means death for some of these people."[11]

For the most part, American media and the public paid scant attention to the structural issues driving the migrant crisis. In some ways, this was consistent with the usual American news cycle: U.S. media outlets tend to show interest south of the border only when developments abroad merge with a salient issue in domestic politics—immigration, drugs, trade deficits, gang violence. But this was arguably an instance of arriving late on the scene, given that Mexican and Central American gang activity had already spilled into the United States.[12]

As policymakers trudged up and down Capitol Hill, members of Mara offshoots were running prostitution rings, selling drugs, and extorting fellow Central American migrants less than ten miles away in the Maryland suburb of Langley Park. The *Washington Post* described Langley Park neighborhoods "plagued by MS-13 drug dealing, prostitution, robbery, extortion and murder." Maras were charging residents sometimes as much as $1,500 for protection— from the Maras, of course. Around 4,500 unaccompanied Central American minors landed in Prince George's County, where Langley Park is located, during 2014's "summer of living dangerously." A portion of them fed directly into the gang. Indeed, some parts of Maryland began to look more like "Maraland." And the Maras were not the only gang to make it in America. Jamaica's Shower Posse dominated crack cocaine sales all across the country in the 1980s, and Mexican cartel bosses kept safe houses full of cash and cocaine in some of the wealthiest suburbs of Texas and California.[13]

Operation Anvil

If U.S. media weren't paying sufficient attention, the dysfunctional U.S. foreign policy apparatus was. The Departments of State, Defense, and Homeland Security had been aware for several years of the Northern Triangle's descent into a gangster hellhole and were increasingly vocal about trying to reverse it. One of the first efforts in this regard was an increase in American advisory missions and joint operations with Central American military and law enforcement. American agents had been on the ground in Central America since 2004, when the Bush administration created the Foreign-deployed Advisory and Support Team (FAST) program. The program had started up when the DEA began providing investigative expertise to U.S. Special Operations Command hunting Afghan drug lords linked to the Taliban.

Part "special forces manhunters, part detectives," FAST knew how to "kick down doors, work informants, and collect evidence." In 2009, a FAST team assisted in a bust that captured an Afghan drug lord and recovered a ledger recording over $250 million in heroin sales. In the same year the DEA asked Congress for two additional FAST teams to be used in "ungoverned spaces" and "possible terrorist havens" in the Western Hemisphere. One of the spaces named in the request was Honduras.[14]

In 2012, a FAST team worked with members of the Honduran National Police's Tactical Response Team in Operation Anvil to surveil drug organizations, seize shipments, and apprehend smugglers. (Their work found that an astounding 87 percent of the small planes carrying cocaine to the United States transited through the thinly populated northern coast of Honduras.) On one mission, Honduran security officials shadowed by U.S. agents accidentally killed four civilians, including two pregnant women, in the country's remote and now drugs-and-thugs-infested Mosquito Coast. Just a few weeks later, an American drug enforcement agent shot and killed a suspected drug trafficker during a raid on a smuggling operation.[15]

These tragic episodes were a chilling reminder of how little the drug war had changed in its essence over the past quarter century. Indeed, Anvil was a twenty-first-century successor to supply-side U.S.-led counternarcotics operations with colorful names like Blast Furnace, Ghost Zone, Snowcap, and Zorro. As journalist Mattathias Schwartz writes, Anvil, like its predecessors, combined the "legal framework of a police action with the hardware and the rhetoric of war." Honduras and other source and transit zones were "often referred to as 'downrange'; drug traffickers are 'the enemy'; the Mosquito Coast is a 'battlespace.' " Schwartz was accurate in his assessment of how closely Anvil followed past efforts: "In a broad sense, FAST was nothing new. What is remarkable is how many times the U.S. had tried such militarized counter-narcotics programs and how long it has been apparent how little they amount to."[16]

Obama Responds

With the crisis in Central America deepening, in January 2016, Vice President Joe Biden published an op-ed essay titled "A Plan for Central America" in the *New York Times,* in which he correctly stated that the "security and prosperity of Central America are inextricably linked to our own." The new executive decisions that followed ostensibly marked one of the most significant shifts in policy toward Central America, and in the war on drugs, in several years. There is an important difference, however, between rhetoric and action when it comes to policymaking. On closer inspection, the reengagement with Central America looked less like a correction of course than an amplification of programs that had already been running, for the most part unsuccessfully, for years.[17]

What were these policies? First, the Obama administration announced a budget request to nearly double aid to the Northern Triangle to $750 million, in support of the region's multi-billion-dollar Alliance for Prosperity Plan. What the White House's statements and Biden's op-ed did not mention is that between 2008 and 2015 the United States had given the region just over $1 billion through the Central America Regional Security Initiative (CARSI), an extension of the George W. Bush administration's Mérida Initiative to support Mexico's war against drug gangs. As far as any objective observer could tell, the differences between the Bush and Obama administrations' aid-based approaches to the problem were nonexistent.[18]

The Obama administration also doubled down on a longstanding policy of deporting MS-13 and Barrio 18 criminals from U.S. prisons back to the Northern Triangle—essentially the reverse of the kingpin extradition strategy deployed in Colombia and Mexico. U.S. authorities deported around twenty thousand criminals to Central America between 2000 and 2004. Between 2010 and 2012, they repatriated another hundred thousand. In El Salvador, the conservative, Amherst College–educated president, Francisco Flores, met the American deportation policy with Plan Mano Dura, unveiled in July 2003. The plan escalated police and military sweeps, criminalized gang membership, and allowed suspected gang members to be arrested on the basis of their physical appearance alone. The hardline approach led to the capture of many criminals: Over the next four years, the number of imprisoned gang members doubled from four thousand to eight thousand. By the end of the decade, it was estimated that close to half of El Salvador's gang members were in prisons, which were filled at an alarmingly high 300 percent of capacity. Flores's successor and fellow conservative Antonio Saca unveiled Super Mano Dura in 2006, an approach intended to complement the hard fist with gang prevention and rehabilitation programs and legal and institutional reform. As a result of this hard-nosed approach, roughly twenty-six thousand people were imprisoned in El Salvador in 2011, about four times as many as a decade earlier. Unfortunately, moving a problem around does not qualify as solving it. Given the inability of the Northern Triangle states to manage this deluge of criminality, it was no coincidence that violence spiked. In fact, the deportation program arguably strengthened the gangs' power in their home countries. The gangs ruled with impunity both inside the prisons and across large swaths of the country.[19]

In addition to returning immigrants and criminals caught in the United States to what amounted to failed states, the United States enlisted the Mexican government to the same end. Urged on by Washington, Mexico apprehended 70 percent more Northern Triangle migrants in 2015 than in the previous year. Mexico's more muscular stance likely accounted for a precipitous drop in Northern Triangle apprehensions along the U.S. border. However, the push-pull dynamic set in motion by the deportation of criminals caused a rebound. A new wave of seventeen thousand Northern Triangle minors fleeing violence hit the border in the summer and fall of 2015. All told, between 2010 and 2016, the United States and Mexico apprehended more than a million Northern Triangle immigrants, deporting eight hundred thousand of them, including forty thousand children.

In fairness, there had been a few bright spots. The Obama administration enlisted the United Nations to open screening centers for migrants hoping to reach the United States, thus offering an alternative to the arduous journey out of their native lands through cartel-infested Mexico. In 2016, Honduras ranked third among Northern Triangle countries sending unaccompanied children to the United States, down from first place in 2014. Its murder rate dropped precipitously in the same period. Part of this, as Sonia Nazario reported, came as the result of a joint effort between the U.S. and Honduran governments to mobilize local communities in violence-prevention efforts. In 2014, USAID and the Bureau of International Narcotics and Law Enforcement Affairs set up neighborhood outreach centers, which, among other activities, provided vocational training and mentors for unemployed residents.[20]

In late March 2019, President Donald Trump announced that he was stopping $500 million in economic assistance already approved by Congress for El Salvador, Honduras, and Guatemala. "I'm not playing games," said Trump. "We were paying them tremendous amounts of money and we're not paying them anymore because they haven't done a thing for us."[21]

Cutting the Cord

And what of the Northern Triangle countries' own policy efforts? A brief moment of hope came in El Salvador in 2012, when the popular FMLN president Mauricio Funes, with the help of the Catholic Church, quietly managed to broker a truce between the gangs. Overnight the murder rate dropped to only five per day—the average for Central America. The gangs also put the brakes on recruiting youth. Experimental "peace zones" were set up on former killing grounds, where social programs helped reinforce and maintain the ceasefire. The Funes government moved gang leaders to lower-security prisons and supported new initiatives that provided jobs in bakeries and farms for recently rehabilitated convicts. Estimates vary, but anywhere between two thousand and five thousand Salvadorans are alive today thanks to the agreement.

But although the murders dropped, the truce proved not to be a political winner for Funes, who later took pains to distance himself from the accords. Part of this was no doubt thanks to the truce's deep unpopularity among ordinary Salvadorans. A poll in 2014 showed dissatisfaction running as high as 80 percent. This made a certain amount of sense. The truce effectively enhanced the gangs' standing in society. Imprisoned gangsters began appearing regularly on television for media interviews as if they were upstanding community organizers. Furthermore, discoveries of mass graves in 2014 suggested that both MS-13 and Barrio 18 had simply replaced broad-daylight murders with kidnapping and secret execution—a grisly return to the dark days of the civil war years in the late 1970s and 1980s. And finally, the public was frustrated that while the gang-on-gang murders might have dropped, general public security had not greatly improved, nor had the gangs ceased their extortion and larceny rackets. The mass exodus later that summer gave credence to this analysis.[22]

Funes's successor, the former leftist guerrilla President Salvador Sánchez Cerén, came under intense pressure to crack down on the Maras. The president's spokesman told the press in August 2015, "We will not speak to or reach any kind of agreement with these criminals." Days later, the Supreme Court ruled that the gangs should be considered terrorist groups, laying the political and legal groundwork for legal actions against them. The former director of the national police force, Rodrigo Ávila, soberly indicated, "We have to cut the cord that connects the kids to the gangs." Ostensibly funded by a tax on cellular phones and cable television, the Salvadoran government's hallmark $2.1 billion five-year initiative of that year, "Secure El Salvador," was intended to promote security and development by boosting the state's presence in the country's most violent towns and regions, bolstering public institutions including prisons, and ensuring better treatment for crime victims.[23]

Like the Obama White House's Northern Triangle strategy, the Salvadoran initiatives proved far more difficult to implement than to design. At the beginning of 2015, Sánchez Cerén's government transferred high-level gang leaders back to maximum-security prisons from which they had been relocated as part of the prior government's truce dialogue. This hardline initiative precipitated yet another bloody wave of violence.[24]

Despite this setback, the government continued to explore various approaches, such as capturing key gang leaders not already in prison while more effectively isolating those already incarcerated. As crime scholar Evan Ellis reported, in the handful of prisons in which gangs were concentrated, the government installed devices to block cell phone signals. This helped to curtail the bribing and threatening of prison guards. San Salvador also announced plans to build three new minimum-security prisons that would relieve the intractable overcrowding through the transfer of ten thousand low-risk prisoners who were not gang members.[25]

Fundamentally Flawed

One inference we can draw from the saga of the past two decades is that state responses to narcotics trafficking and other forms of organized criminal activity in Central America and beyond were severely lacking. State weaknesses promoted, either directly or indirectly, the work of gangs and criminal bands, wreaking havoc on the lives of the citizens caught in the middle. If a state's security forces, prisons, and politicians are unable to limit the violence, what is to be done? The drug war's failure to answer that fundamental question meant an ongoing horror story, not only for millions of innocent people in Latin America but for the United States and the rest of the world as well.

20 • The Global War

It is spring that determines how a year turns out, according to an
Afghan proverb. And if the Helmand poppy fields this spring are any
indication, the Taliban will have a very good year.

—*New York Times* correspondents Taimoor Shah and Mujib Mashal, 2016

Trafficking in Terror

In the post-9/11 "Age of Terror," U.S. anti-drug enforcement achieved a
fully global reach. Opaque anti-drug missions first piloted in Latin America
were exported to Thailand, Canada, Africa, Europe, and the Middle East, at
times without the knowledge or cooperation of the governments concerned.
In 2006, Congress passed a landmark piece of legislation that dramatically
expanded the scope of American officials' presumptive license abroad. The
new rules gave U.S. counternarcotics agents legal standing to "pursue narcotics and terrorism crimes committed anywhere in the world" if the drug activity could be linked to terrorism. Here is how Republican congressman Henry
Hyde of Illinois explained the scope of this new escalation in the global war on
drugs: "This bill makes clear that, even without direct U.S. nexus, if these
drugs help support or sustain a foreign terrorist organization, the producers
and traffickers can, and should, be prosecuted for material support of terrorism, whether or not the illicit narcotics are ever intended for, or enter, the
United States." A key impetus behind the legislation was an explosion in cocaine consumption in Europe over the first fifteen years of the twenty-first
century. Indeed, during that period Europe's cocaine use doubled. Shipments
typically came directly from the Andes into hub cities like Madrid or London

smuggled aboard commercial airlines, or they followed a long, tortuous path from Colombia, Peru, and Bolivia via Brazil and West Africa to southern Europe. This latter route took the goods through areas controlled by Islamist groups, including Al-Qaeda in the Islamic Maghreb (AQIM), who were eager to get a piece of the pie.[1]

In December 2009, U.S. federal agents indicted three Malian nationals who had been arrested in their home country and extradited to the United States under the 2006 rule. The men, who claimed to be linked to al-Qaeda, thought they were working with FARC operatives to build a cocaine transit route through western Africa and the Sahara toward Spain. According to the *New York Times,* "Federal officials say the case promises to peel back what they contend are increasing ties between drug traffickers and Al Qaeda as the terrorist group seeks to finance its operations in Africa and elsewhere." For the U.S. agents, the sting made an airtight case. However, according to a remarkable report by investigative journalist Ginger Thompson published in the December 14, 2015, issue of the *New Yorker,* several key witnesses appeared as the Mali trafficker-terrorist case evolved. As Thompson explained, "The defendants emerged as more hapless than hardened, childhood friends who believed that the D.E.A.'s informants were going to make them rich. 'They were lying to us. And we were lying to them,' [one of the defendants] told me from prison." In fact, Judge Barbara Jones found that "there was no actual involvement by the defendants or the undercovers . . . in the activities of either Al Qaeda or the FARC." For Jones, the problem was that the case relied on evidence that the DEA obtained "using agents or informants who were paid hundreds of thousands of dollars to lure the targets into staged narco-terrorism conspiracies." The DEA countered that such methods were essential to combating a breed of criminality that was unprecedented in both reach and opacity. Said one official, "Almost all of our investigations are proactive." One former American Foreign Service Officer, Russell Hanks, who had a "firsthand look" at some of the DEA's handiwork in West Africa, had this to say: "The DEA provided everything these men needed to commit a crime, then said, 'Wow, look what they did.' This wasn't terrorism—this was the manipulation of weak-minded people, in weak countries, in order to pad arrest records." This may have been motivated by the agency's own existential worries, contended one former DEA official. "What is going on after 9/11 is that a lot of resources move out of drug enforcement and into terrorism. The DEA doesn't want to be the stepchild that is last in line." Prosecuting narco-terrorism, whether real or manufactured, became an "expedient way for the agency to justify its existence." It was perhaps no coincidence that the DEA's funding for global missions jumped by three-quarters in the seven years after 9/11.[2]

As Thompson reported, the DEA continued to run operations similar to the 2009 Mali-FARC ruse. In a counterpoint to the claim that the targets of DEA narco-terrorism busts were hapless dupes, in 2013, high-level government and military officials in the West African nation of Guinea-Bissau were implicated in a drug trafficking scheme that neatly followed the Mali setup. Indictments alleged that Antonio Indjai, the armed forces chief of staff, had agreed to be an intermediary for cocaine dealers he believed to be Colombian FARC members. In reality, he was dealing not with Marxist narco-guerrillas but undercover DEA agents. Indjai said he would help the "Colombians" obtain weapons and safe passage in exchange for a slice of the cocaine profits. Another ensnared official was Guinea-Bissau navy chief José Américo Bubo Na Tchuto, whom the DEA arrested in 2013: "The DEA team, which had been alerted to alleged planeloads of cocaine flying from Venezuela into the hands of Na Tchuto and his military, tricked the navy boss into coming aboard a 'chic' 115-foot luxury yacht produced by the DEA. He'd been lured by the promise of an [sic] long term relationship with the fake FARC, and an offer of $1 million per ton of coke coming through Guinea Bissau under his protection." The bust landed Na Tchuto in prison in Brooklyn, New York.[3]

Around the same time, a DEA sting used intermediaries connected to the Lebanese insurgent group Hezbollah acting as Mexican traffickers to ensnare the son of the president of Suriname. In September 2015, two Pakistani nationals were extradited to the United States for selling drugs and weapons to DEA informants posing as FARC traffickers. Mark Hamlet, the chief of the DEA's special-operations unit, stated that the arrests "illustrate once again that drug trafficking and terror conspiracies often intersect."[4]

The Colombia Option

Over the dozen years following the overthrow of the Taliban in Afghanistan in late 2001, the U.S. government made a "mammoth investment" of blood and treasure—the latter amounting to roughly $8 billion—to combat the country's drug trade. The effort included opium poppy eradication, drug addiction treatment, the creation of an anti-drug police corps, and justice reform. Writer David Brown thought that this might well have been "money well spent," given that Afghanistan was responsible for more than 90 percent of the world's opium. "No effort to build a stable nation there can succeed amid the hurricane forces of financial and institutional corruption that come with a thriving drug trade," he wrote in 2014.[5]

In 2002 and 2003, the first full years of the occupation, American anti-drug policy was limited to "sweep and destroy" missions to eradicate poppy fields. By 2007, the strategy had proved insufficient, as opium production and its associated revenues had only grown. That year, the ragged nation witnessed an especially large opium harvest, whose bumper revenues funded a significant Taliban offensive against the U.S.-backed government in Kabul. U.S. officials doubled down on their efforts to persuade the ostensibly allied government of President Hamid Karzai to allow spraying of the herbicide glyphosate, the same chemical used to kill opium poppy and coca plantings in Colombia. President George W. Bush, Secretary of State Condoleezza Rice, National Security Adviser Stephen Hadley, and drug czar John Walters each raised the issue with Karzai over a two-year period. But glyphosate's most outspoken advocate of all was the U.S. ambassador in Afghanistan, William Wood.[6]

Ambassador Wood had made his name as a diehard proponent of the U.S.-led drug war during his four-year ambassadorial tenure in Bogotá. He considered glyphosate to be indispensable to the effort. (Wood once claimed that he would submit to being doused with the chemical to prove its safety.) The strategy's apparent success in Colombia, about which this book has already raised doubts, prompted the George W. Bush administration to ship Wood to Kabul to reproduce his magic. British diplomats dismissed him as "Chemical Bill"; other American officials were more bullish. Said one diplomat, "There is absolutely no evidence that spraying causes harm to people or cattle. Everyone has seen the rise in the poppy harvest, and obviously the current policy is not working." Antonio Maria Costa, a senior U.N. drugs and crime agency official, optimistically predicted that with a spray campaign, "We may be able to create a corridor, or an area ranging from Pakistan in the southeast to Turkmenistan in the northwest" that would be opium-free. The corridor could be critical for the broader international mission in Afghanistan, potentially even allowing U.N. and Afghan forces to "slowly regain control of the other provinces."[7]

In 2009, U.S. officials admitted failure. President Obama's special envoy for Afghanistan and Pakistan acknowledged that the poppy eradication efforts had been counterproductive: "They did not result in any damage to the Taliban, but they put farmers out of work and they alienated people and drove people into the arms of the Taliban."[8]

So U.S. policymakers went back to the drawing board. The result was a "more sensible" policy. Following the "soft side" of Andean Initiative and Plan Colombia programs, the United States allocated funds to help farmers pursue alternative crops such as saffron and grapes. Funding and personnel were also assigned to assist Afghanistan with setting up its own version of the DEA as well as with "forensic accounting" to get hidden Taliban funds. U.S. and Afghan troops set up security cordons in villages and towns in the opium corridor and set up rehabilitation clinics for addicts. As Brown explained in a 2014 article detailing the strategy, the United States "led a full-spectrum effort to provide a better life for the average Afghan, which would in turn make poppy cultivation less appealing." By 2014, though, there were more acres dedicated to poppy than there had been in 2001, when U.S. forces ousted the Taliban. In fact, Afghan farmers were planting more opium poppies than "any other time in modern history."[9]

By 2016, the United States had spent more than $7 billion to fight the runaway poppy production that made Afghan opium the world's biggest brand. According to journalist Azam Ahmed, "tens of billions more went to governance programs to stem corruption and train a credible police force. Countless more dollars and thousands of lives were lost on the main thrust of the war: to put the Afghan government in charge of district centers and to instill rule of law." The dispatches of foreign correspondents were gloomy: "Multiple visits to Afghan opium country over the past year, and extensive interviews with opium farmers, local elders, and Afghan and Western officials, laid bare the reality that even if the Western-backed government succeeds, the opium seems here to stay." Lamented one U.S. official active in the Helmand's poppy-rich Garmsir District, "In the case of the opium trade, they [the Taliban] try harder. There's just too much money to ignore it." Making matters worse, Afghan authorities tended not just to tolerate poppy but even to rely on it as a revenue source, much as the Taliban had. The state's collusion in the illicit trade was not novel: "Power brokers, often working for the government, have long operated behind the scenes, producing, refining and smuggling opium or heroin across one of the many porous borders of Afghanistan. That kind of corruption has been seen nationwide." In the words of Hakim Angar, former police chief of Helmand province, "Over the years, I have seen the central government, the local government and the foreigners all talk very seriously about poppy. In practice, they do nothing, and behind the scenes, the government makes secret deals to enrich themselves."[10]

Correspondents Taimoor Shah and Mujib Mashal have described how the spring opium harvest of 2016 brought "high yields" for farmers in areas such as the Zhari district of Kandahar Province. On top of that, the Afghan government canceled eradication campaigns for the year. The news did not bode well for

Afghan drug war optimists. The harvest weeks were a veritable "recruitment drive" for the Taliban, with "thousands of men" coming from all reaches to look for work. Senior Afghan official Abdul Jabar Qahraman put it bluntly: "The war in Afghanistan is not a war of ideology, it is a war of financial benefits. The poppies support the Taliban financially. The commanders of the Taliban stuff their pockets with cash. Once they receive the cash that makes their stomachs oily, they prepare themselves for fighting." As Shah and Mashal wrote in the *New York Times,* the Taliban "collect the opium tax they impose on the local level, as well as stick around for the additional 10 percent Islamic tax on farm produce, called *ushr.* Those proceeds are supposed to go to the needy, but often end up going to the Taliban." The United Nations found that the insurgency was now reaping $3 billion a year in the illicit trade. And owing to changes in battlefield balances, most of Helmand province was once again under Taliban control.[11]

Perhaps inescapably, given what often feel like the scientific laws of the drug industry, opium production in Afghanistan contributed its share to the unraveling of the nation's social fabric. In 2010, to pick a year, more than eight hundred thousand Afghans were using heroin, opium, or other drugs—all sharp increases from the previous decade. A U.N. report from the same year concluded that the country had one of the world's highest rates of heroin use. As Antonio Maria Costa suggested, "Many Afghans seem to be taking drugs as a kind of self-medication against the hardships of life." Demographic research established that 7 percent of the country's fourteen million adults were regularly using hard drugs, of which over 90 percent described themselves as needing treatment.[12]

U.S. Marines patrol a poppy field in a village in the Golestan district of Farah province, Afghanistan, May 5, 2009 (Reuters, permission to author)

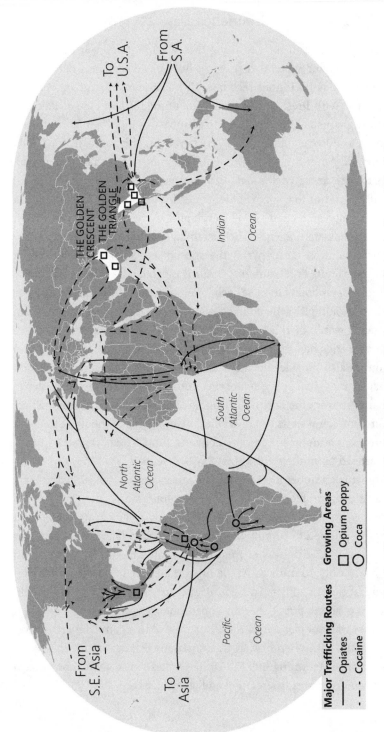

Major Trafficking Routes
— Opiates
- - - Cocaine

Growing Areas
☐ Opium poppy
○ Coca

THE GOLDEN CRESCENT
THE GOLDEN TRIANGLE

To U.S.A.
From S.A.
From S.E. Asia
To Asia

Indian Ocean
South Atlantic Ocean
North Atlantic Ocean
Pacific Ocean

Global trafficking routes and cultivation regions (University of Wisconsin Cartography Lab)

Groundhog Day

One could be forgiven for assuming that Washington's war on drugs in South Asia began after September 11, 2001. But we had been here before. Back in the mid-1980s, as Jill Jonnes recounts, Vice President George H. W. Bush traveled to meet with President General Mohammed Zia ul-Haq of Pakistan. Along with Afghanistan, the South Asian country was then "a major source of heroin going to Europe and America" via family organizations in Iran. Pakistan had allowed American operatives to use their territory as a staging ground for efforts to back anti-Soviet *mujahideen* insurgents in neighboring Afghanistan. The problem was that some of these guerrilla groups—notably the fundamentalist Hekmatyar faction—were developing a major heroin industry in collusion with Pakistani agents. The instability generated in Afghanistan by the Islamic revolution in 1979 and the subsequent Soviet invasion created ideal conditions for its development. "Opium cultivation became important for the war effort for its ability to raise cash," Jonnes writes. "Guerrillas, peasants and criminals would plant the poppies, and prune, irrigate, and harvest them. The by-product would then be smuggled across the porous Pakistani border." Now both countries had their share of home-grown regional and global traffickers. Jonnes also provides details from a September 1985 report in a Pakistani newspaper: Afghan police do not check official Pakistani vehicles entering into Afghanistan from the northwest frontier. Some observers were convinced that Washington knew of its putative allies' involvement in the illicit trade but kept it quiet even as domestic enforcement and supply-side programs in Latin America ramped up in the frantic "Just Say No" years.[13]

Like Afghanistan under the Taliban in the next century, Pakistan developed a "noticeable drug problem." With refineries proliferating, the drug became cheap and easy to score. The addict count, holding steady around five thousand in 1980, jumped to seventy thousand three years later. At its peak, the number of heroin addicts was estimated at 1.3 million—in a country whose population was only 70 million. At the time, the United States had five hundred thousand heroin addicts in a country of 250 million. As a senior Pakistani anti-drug agent put it, heroin consumption was "completely out of hand." Jonnes was not pleased with the outcome of this game of narco-driven realpolitik: "This same heroin that was enslaving Pakistanis in unheard of numbers was also streaming into the United States. Once again, our putative allies were sending a steady stream of addictive drugs our way."[14]

PART 3:
THE HOME FRONT

21 • The War over the War on Drugs

History shows that successfully diminishing the drug culture (as
America did before World War II) requires complete societal
commitment. That is why the re-stigmatization of drugs is so important.
—Jill Jonnes, *Hep-Cats, Narcs, and Pipe Dreams: A History of
America's Romance with Illegal Drugs*

If the drug war goes away, I might be unemployed.
—U.S. counternarcotics agent

"No Silver Bullet"

Returning to the home front, there is another kind of conflict raging, one
that I call the war over the war on drugs. This idea of a secondary, derivative
war is not only a useful framing device for understanding the question of
drugs in the United States over the past two decades; it is also an ideological
war in a very real sense. It is over whether the fight against drugs has achieved
its objectives; whether it can plausibly achieve them in the future; whether the
moral, political, economic, and personal costs of protracted policies of drug
prohibition outweigh those of alternatives such as liberalization; and whether
we ought to continue prosecuting our longest war as we have in the past. The
stakes are high. Far from a dry, clinical academic debate, the conflict's outcomes have a material impact on millions of people, and, given that its language so often invokes markers of individual and collective identity—class,
race, economic opportunity, and the moral character of the nation, to name a
few—it also evokes strong emotions.

Consider the positions of two commentators on opposite sides of the drug war divide. First is John Walters, director of the White House Office of National Drug Control Policy under George W. Bush. Speaking a few months after the terrorist attacks of September 11, 2001, he recruited core American values to defend the drug war, at the same time according it the same status as another hot policy issue: "If you use drugs, you are standing against the rule of law. You are standing against freedom. You are standing against those who fight terrorism." On the other side is philosopher Sam Harris, who wrote in 2011: "The war on drugs has been lost and should never have been waged. I can think of no right more fundamental than to peacefully steward the contents of one's own consciousness. The fact that we pointlessly ruin the lives of nonviolent drug users by incarcerating them, at enormous expense, constitutes one of the great moral failures of our time."[1]

What stands out in these two examples—aside from each author's unwavering belief in his own rightness—is their readiness to cast the debate in moral terms and to rely on principles drawn from the ideological camps they represent. It is not unusual for weighty policy issues to be framed in moral terms: we're often conditioned by political leaders and media to consider the debate about health insurance as a contest between an individual's right to accessible medical care and a countervailing right to choose how to spend one's money. What's unusual in the case of the drug war is how little the terms have changed in the past century.

The conservative view on drugs today essentially reiterates that of the Temperance and Prohibition movements, which were themselves part of the Progressive reform wave that swept the country at the turn of the twentieth century. On this argument's logic, if you use drugs, you're a condemnable person; pervasive drug use in America is a signal of moral decline, and prohibition is the only solution. The other, critical view still speaks the language of 1960s counterculture. From the left, drug use is inevitable and benign in the overwhelming majority of cases; prohibition is an assault on civil liberties and a malign attempt by the privileged to terrorize already marginalized groups of people. There's not much middle ground available between these two poles. And, yet, both seem willfully blind to historical facts that don't suit their own arguments but that could actually lend the discourse considerable substance and subtlety.

There have been attempts in the past to change the terms of the debate. One effort in this direction was to eschew the term "war on drugs" itself. As *Rolling Stone* magazine reported in 1994, "The Clintonites, Attorney General Janet Reno and White House drug policy director Lee Brown most adamantly among them, recoil from that once capital phrase: war on drugs. 'You won't hear us using the metaphor "drug war," ' Brown says. 'We should help those who need help and arrest those who are trafficking in drugs. But I don't think we should declare war against our own people.' " In 1997, Clinton's second drug czar, General Barry McCaffrey, a recently retired hero of Operation Desert Storm, made a similar point. "If you want to fight a war on drugs, sit down at your own table and talk to your children," he declared. He further explained to Congress, "Wars are relatively straightforward. You identify the enemy, select a general, assign him a mission and resources and let him get the job done. In the struggle against drug abuse, there is no silver bullet, no quick way to reduce drug use or the damage it causes." High-minded as the idea was, it ultimately proved unconvincing. The Clinton White House still allocated two-thirds of the federal anti-drug budget to interdiction and domestic law enforcement. His ramp-up of supply-side programs in Latin America, such as aerial spraying and the heavily militarized Plan Colombia, further belied the rhetoric. Yet it set a tone for Presidents George W. Bush and Barack Obama, who both shied away from using military metaphors for the drug question, even if much of the actual war, especially abroad, continued unchanged.[2]

Unraveling

Until the early 2000s, a remarkable consensus held in Congress, among presidents, and in Beltway policy circles on the ends and means of drug policy. The answer, always, was prohibition. The reigning logic was that we must go after both supply and demand if we're ever going to have even a remote chance of success. Departure from this bipartisan line risked creating the perception of being soft on drugs, which, for elected officials and bureaucrats alike, always carried the potential to become a career-ending label. However, as the remaining chapters demonstrate, the first two decades of this century witnessed the unraveling of this consensus.

There are many explanations for how and why the cracks emerged. One was the sheer financial cost of the war. Forty years in, Washington and state governments had shelled out north of a trillion dollars to combat drugs at home and abroad. That kind of outlay might be justified by clear strategic successes or negligible moral costs. But the realities on both counts failed to satisfy an increasingly vocal group of critics. For opponents, the drug war's evils far outweighed its advantages and even the harms of drugs themselves. Critics of the supply side cited ills like the shocking waves of violence that washed over Mexico in the 2000s. More than eighty thousand people had been killed in Mexico since President Calderón kicked the hornet's nest in 2006 by vowing to crack down on the cartels. Further evidence was available in the de facto war zones in countries such as Honduras, Guatemala, and Belize and in the resulting migrant crises at U.S. borders. According to the objectors, these phenomena were directly attributable to prohibitionist drug policies. On the domestic front, the critical camp cited incarceration-related injustices and soaring addiction rates. In 2015, there were roughly 208,000 people incarcerated in federal prisons, 48.6 percent for drug-related offenses. Of the 1.3 million in state prisons, about 16 percent were there for drug crimes. The numbers disproportionately represented black, Latino, and low-income populations compared with overall national demographic distributions. Add to that the highly reported resurgent opioid epidemic that racked the rural U.S. beginning in the early 2000s. According to Margaret Talbot, writing for the *New Yorker,* "between 2000 and 2014, the number of overdose deaths in the

Noelle Bush, daughter of Florida governor Jeb Bush, departs Orange County Court with her attorney, Peter Antonacci, in Orlando, November 8, 2002. The presiding judge sentenced her to ten days in jail for violating the terms of her treatment after she was caught in September with a small amount of crack cocaine by workers at the Center for Drug-Free Living. (Reuters, permission to author)

United States jumped by a hundred and thirty-seven per cent." At least ten people per hundred thousand died from opioid overdoses in 2016; by comparison, the peak rates that attended the next most recent heroin epidemic in the 1970s and the crack epidemic in the 1980s were 1.5 and 2.0 per hundred thousand, respectively. In early 2016, Obama asked Congress to spend an additional $1.1 billion to fight prescription painkiller and heroin abuse.[3]

Further, to cite two basic measures, the drug war had yielded no sustained reduction in the overall volume of drugs entering the United States and no long-term change in the street price of drugs in real terms (an increase in price would suggest a possible diminishment of supply, but that was not happening). For detractors, these numbing statistics pointed to a deeper truth: despite a fistful of short-term tactical victories, the punitive, prohibitionist war on drugs had failed. And the criticism from without eventually insinuated itself into the machinery of official thinking in Washington.[4]

National Football League Hall of Famer Lawrence Taylor leans over to consult with his lawyer Angelo Ferlita after pleading no contest to drug charges in Pinellas County Court in Clearwater, Florida, November 30, 1999. Taylor entered the plea shortly after a police informant testified at a court hearing that he sold the New York Giants legend fifty dollars' worth of crack cocaine at a beach resort hotel in the St. Petersburg area in 1998. (Reuters, permission to author)

Protesters from the "Support, Don't Punish" group wear masks depicting former
U.S. president Richard Nixon to demonstrate against the criminalization of drug use
in London, June 26, 2013 (Reuters, permission to author)

The Portugal Option

It was not only in the United States that the consensus was crumbling.
Leaders around the world became more outspoken in their criticism of the
drug war and of prohibitionist drug policies in general. The pedigree case was
that of Portugal. Beginning in the 1980s, Portugal suffered an especially pernicious epidemic of problematic heroin use and addiction. The government
initially responded with the standard prohibitionist repertoire of ramped-up
interdiction, apprehension, and punishment, none of which did much more
than deepen the problem. The crisis, which had originated among marginalized homeless and unemployed sectors, soon extended through every stratum
of Portuguese society.[5]

Desperate for a solution, Lisbon appointed a broad and eclectic array of
experts—physicians, academics, attorneys, community activists—to a committee to study the phenomenon and prescribe solutions as part of a renewed
national project. After almost a year of work, the commission's report stunned
the global drug enforcement community in recommending the decriminaliza-

tion of both hard and soft drugs as the path of least resistance to reducing drug abuse. The report also suggested that "drug users should be treated as full members of society instead of cast out as criminals or other pariahs."[6]

Contrary to the chorus of skeptics who predicted that the commission's report would be ignored or ridiculed, the Portuguese Parliament debated it extensively and, in 2001, passed almost all of the recommendations into law. Selling and trafficking drugs remained a crime, but it became permissible to possess any drug in a quantity equivalent to ten days' worth of personal consumption. People found in possession of amounts within the limits were ordered to appear before a "dissuasion commission," which could recommend fines, treatment, or noncriminal penalties. The panel emphasized that the power of decriminalization itself should not be overestimated. It was an intervention of limited force, which made it easier for "dependent users" to seek treatment and lowered the penalties for citizens who wanted to help those in need of intervention. So it was less about "giving the green light" to drug use and more about "reducing harm, stopping useless punishment, and achieving better control over the drug problem." Some, however, were dubious, predicting that this soft approach to the epidemic would only make a bad problem worse. Others worried that the country would become a "drug paradise."[7]

In the ensuing two decades, the number of people using drugs in Portugal did not increase dramatically; it even fell among some age groups and drug types. Most notably, the Portuguese Ministry of Health reported that the number of "problematic users" had plunged from one hundred thousand to fifty thousand; overdoses were "reduced significantly." The Harvard political theorist Danielle Allen contended in a *Washington Post* op-ed column: "The number of people seeking treatment increased by 60 percent between 1998 and 2011, and adolescent drug use has decreased since the law's passage. At the same time, the percentage of people in prison for drug violations fell from 44 percent in 1999 to 24 percent in 2013. And the overall quantity of illicit drugs seized actually increased, possibly because public-safety resources could be directed to targets higher up the supply chain."[8] In addition, the number of citizens with drug-related morbidities like HIV and Hepatitis B and C decreased. A major factor in this reversal, according to one Portuguese official, was a change in the social perception of drug addiction. Heroin users now being treated more like alcoholics than like stereotypical "junkies."

Interestingly, at the same time that Portugal's heroin addiction rate was rapidly falling, it was increasing by almost the same rate in America. This led drug war reformers to posit that "all the available evidence" from the Portugal option showed that it was a better choice than prohibition. As former president and vocal drug reform advocate Fernando Henrique Cardoso wrote, "By decriminalizing the consumption of all drugs, Portugal broke with a global paradigm. Instead of insisting on repressive measures that are, at best ineffective, at worst counterproductive, it chose a bold approach that favors more humane and efficient policies."[9]

Yet as much as we might be willing to acknowledge the advantages of the Portugal Way, we should also be circumspect about their generalizability. Portugal was unique in at least one dimension: the "sheer scale" of the 1990s heroin scourge in Portugal ensured that families and communities were desperate for any remedy, however extreme. As Johann Hari writes, it was "almost impossible to find one Portuguese family that had no problems inside the family or in the close neighborhood." At the time of writing in 2018, the United States was not yet up against such a wall. More significantly, it was not at all clear that a majority of Americans were ready to accept radical decriminalization—and, again, this reversal of social perception and judgment was a potentially decisive factor in the Portuguese case. Be that as it may, the Portugal option continued to receive largely positive media coverage years after it launched.

Latin America Stands Up

Until the mid-2000s, most Latin American governments either tolerated or endorsed the gringo view that an aggressive supply-side counternarcotics strategy was the only effective way to address the drug scourge. Doing nothing on the interdiction side was simply not an option. Official dissent in the "backyard" began with Bolivia's Evo Morales, whose policy of "coca sí, cocaína no" led a wave of radical reconsiderations of zero-tolerance approaches. This was followed by increased resistance from other regional leaders, some of whom had been among the most hawkish supporters of the U.S.-led war in their own countries.[10]

In November 2011, the U.K.-based Beckley Foundation published an open letter titled "The Global War on Drugs Has Failed." Signers included current and former heads of state and cultural figures including George Shultz, Sting, Yoko Ono, and Noam Chomsky. The letter contended, "The drug-free world so confidently predicted by supporters of the war on drugs is further than ever from attainment. The policies of prohibition create more harms than they prevent. We must seriously consider shifting resources away from criminalizing tens of millions of otherwise law abiding citizens, and move toward an approach based on health, harm-reduction, cost-effectiveness and respect for human rights. Evidence consistently shows that these health-based approaches deliver better results than criminalization."[11] Remarkably, the letter's signatories also included Colombian president Juan Manuel Santos and Guatemalan president Otto Pérez Molina. It was a highly unusual move, given how supportive Santos had been of the war on drugs throughout his presidency.

Along with other Latin American counterparts, Santos and Molina again pushed back against criminalization at the April 2012 Summit of the Americas in Cartagena, Colombia, denouncing what they now considered overly militarized and criminalized drug war strategies for creating havoc in their fragile democracies. Santos told an American journalist that it was time for a new approach: "There's probably no person who has fought the drug cartels and drug trafficking as I have. But at the same time, we must be very frank: after 40 years of pedaling and pedaling very hard, sometimes you look to your left, you look to your right, and you are almost in the same position. So you have to ask yourself: Are we doing the correct thing?" Santos qualified his support for decriminalization with the claim that Colombia could not lead such an effort.[12]

It was unclear whether Santos might go the Portugal route and decriminalize all narcotics or begin with softer drugs such as cannabis before implementing broader measures. A tentative answer came in June 2016, when Bogotá granted an initial license to a private Canadian firm, PharmaCielo, to produce cannabis for the medical market at a facility located, ironically, just outside Medellín. The Colombian national legislature had legalized medical marijuana earlier that same year. César Gaviria, president of Colombia from 1990 to 1994 and a strong advocate of drug-law reform, argued that in light of the "persecution" of farmers in producer countries, Colombia should consider fully legalizing marijuana. But he also noted that although regulatory systems work better than criminalization, it was still "too early to talk about the legalization of cocaine."[13]

In response, President Barack Obama opened the drug war as "a legitimate topic for debate" and welcomed a "conversation about whether the laws in place are ones that are doing more harm than good in certain places." What he left out of his short remarks was the great irony that the United States, which had created and aggressively pushed for massive militarized drugs-interdiction efforts across the region, was at the same time becoming an incubator for experiments in legalizing narcotics. In the November 2012 general election, voters in the states of Colorado and Washington approved the legalization of marijuana for personal recreational use. When asked whether he would enforce federal laws that still took precedence over the outcomes of these referendums, Obama dryly observed that he had "bigger fish to fry." (As we will see, the relaxation of marijuana restrictions in these states was followed by similar decisions in Oregon in 2015 and several other states in the years that followed; as of the summer of 2019 eleven states and the District of Columbia have legalized the recreational use of marijuana.)[14]

The inconsistency was not lost on Latin American politicians. Mexican congressman Fernando Belaunzarán of the Party of the Democratic Revolution introduced a marijuana legalization bill exactly one week after the 2012 U.S. elections. Belaunzarán voiced the question on so many people's minds: "What sense does it make to keep up such an intense confrontation, which has cost Mexico so much, by trying to keep this substance from going to a country where it's already regulated and permitted?"[15]

Joining the parade on December 10, 2013, sleepy Uruguay became the clearest example yet of Latin American countries' drift away from Washington's supply-side campaign when it established the state regulation (and effective legalization) of marijuana. In some ways, Uruguay was an unexpected drug war apostate, given that, unlike Colombia or Mexico, it has historically not been deeply involved in the supply-side drug war in the region. The force behind the shift was the country's idiosyncratic president, José Alberto "Pepe" Mujica, a former leader of the Tupamaro urban guerrillas. As a young adult Mujica was jailed by the ruling military dictatorship for fourteen years, ten of them in solitary confinement. Mujica proposed legalizing the sale of marijuana, with the government as sole licit vender. Framed as an anti-crime measure, the legislation was intended to channel the estimated $750 million that Uruguayans spent on the drug each year into public coffers. Mujica argued that the traditional interdiction approach hadn't worked, and that "someone has to be the first" to try this new method. This view was echoed by Eleuterio Fernández Huidobro, Mujica's defense minister and onetime Marxist guerrilla, who claimed that spiraling drug violence and the cost of incarceration had created a bigger crisis "than the drugs themselves."[16]

Touting its quarter century–long editorial advocacy of legalizing drugs, the *Economist* eagerly asked Mujica if his decision to legalize cannabis was motivated by security or concern for individual liberties. Mujica's response?

> Look, it began essentially as a security issue. We have spent many years repressing and spending money to fight drug-trafficking. We have had glorious successes, but trafficking continues to increase. . . . We came to the conclusion that this is an addiction, you have to treat it on the one

hand through the police, but then you have to treat it as an illness. You can't treat an illness in [conditions of] illegality. In Uruguay there must be 150,000 sporadic consumers, but they are clandestine. We oblige them to be clandestine. When we can treat them it's already late, it's often irreversible; and moreover frequently they have committed related crimes to get money. It is pure loss for society.

What are we proposing? We are proposing a market logic: if we can't beat them through policing, we are going to try to steal the market from them so that this ceases to be a business. But we're not trying to foster an addiction. We have no truck with the idea that planting marijuana is good and that it's less harmful than cigarettes and all of these things that are said. No, no, I believe that no addiction is good. . . . This is the question, to be able to limit [consumption] to a certain quantity, and when they go over that to consider them as having an illness and treat them.[17]

In short, Mujica's government was implementing not radical reform but a "sober anti-crime measure." The government's hope was that the new program would starve the black market and allow police to focus on more serious illicit drugs like cocaine.[18]

Passed by the Cámara de Senadores (Chamber of Senators) in a 16–13 vote after earlier approval by the lower house, the Cámara de Diputados (Chamber of Deputies), the 2013 law marked the most liberal national pot legalization approach in the world to date. Consumption of pot had been decriminalized in Uruguay since the 1970s. Now the government was growing marijuana and distributing it to licensed pharmacies; the retail price ceiling was $1 per gram, roughly 30 percent below the current black market rate. Uruguayans were allowed to grow up to six plants of their own, as well as to join fifteen- to forty-five-member "clubs" that could harvest larger amounts of plants each year. Interestingly, foreign tourists are ineligible to purchase the stuff, in an effort to avoid the opprobrium of becoming the Amsterdam of the Southern Cone.[19]

It is worth noting that, despite the 2013 amendment, Uruguayans themselves mostly opposed legalization, citing fears that the country would see more crime or become a tourist destination for drug users. One public opinion poll before the pot law passed reported just 29 percent approval. But this was up from only 3 percent a decade before. Not unexpectedly, legalizing cannabis did not completely end the trade in illicit marijuana and other drugs. In 2013, prior to the legalization measure, just under 750 individuals were indicted for drug offenses, a number that jumped to more than 1,200 in 2015. Cannabis remained the most frequently seized substance, at over two and a half tons between March and December 2015. An estimated 40 percent of marijuana users did not cooperate with the new state regulations, including registration. One obstacle was the inefficiency of the state operation: "slow, bureaucratic, and in a certain way improvised." This points to a critical issue in the war over the war: it's not just *whether* to legalize drugs that matters, but *how* to do so.[20]

In 2017, *Washington Post* reporter Josh Partlow identified a regional trend toward cannabis liberalization: "Uruguay has fully legalized weed for sale. And a large chunk of South and Central America, including Brazil, Peru, Chile, Colombia, Ecuador and Costa Rica, have made marijuana more available in varying ways, whether it is for medical or recreational use." That same year, President Enrique Peña Nieto of Mexico, an erstwhile opponent of drug legalization, signed a decree that opened the way for legalizing medical marijuana. Mexican senator Armando Rios Peter called the law a "tiny step" toward addressing a failed war on drugs. As in Uruguay, one survey found that around two-thirds of Mexicans opposed the legislation. The Roman Catholic Church also came out sharply against it. The online publication *Desde la Fe* published an editorial that argued, "A drug is a drug even if it's sold as a soft medicinal balm. Bad Mexican copycats emulate the actions of the neighbors to put on the table of 'sane democracy' a bleak, absurd and counterproductive debate. Recreational marijuana is a placebo to ease the pain of social destruction in which we irremediably wallow."[21]

Stay the Course

In 2014, thirteen years after Clinton drug czar Barry McCaffrey left the White House, the general appeared at an on-the-record Council on Foreign Relations panel discussion about the current state of the war on drugs. Domestic drug abuse, he reported, had gone down drastically, maybe by as much as half, from its height in 1979. The U.S. military had transformed from an institution "significantly impaired" by drug abuse in the late 1970s—when around 50 percent of troops tested positive for pot, 25 percent for other drugs—to one in which "we're positive testing one, two percent" (the latter statistic was from 2001). What was moving in the wrong direction, McCaffrey thought, was the number of adolescents who were now abusing pot, ecstasy, and alcohol. He had an explanation: the "growing normalization of the use of marijuana." The chief culprits were the medical marijuana establishments—"400 in Denver; Los Angeles 800 or 900; nobody really knows"—proliferating across the country. In his estimation, the message that these places sent to impressionable youth was, "If it's medicine, how could it be dangerous?"[22]

Supporters of the punitive drug war make a wide range of arguments in its defense. Most hinge on the idea of a rising consumption curve. In this view, eradication and interdiction on the supply side and punitive law enforcement on the demand side keep drug use and violence indisputably lower than they otherwise would be. On this view, legalization would only make the situation worse. For Jonnes, "To envision America with more easily and cheaply available heroin and crack, just imagine even larger armies of homeless." At his Council on Foreign Relations talk, McCaffrey added interesting subtlety to this line of thinking, explaining that legalization is "a stalking horse for a more Darwinian approach, in which drugs in general are viewed as not my problem, my community. It's somebody else; it's black people, brown people, poor people, west coast people, somebody besides me." Legalization, in other words, would effectively institutionalize a race- and class-motivated NIMBYism (that is, the widespread feeling citizens have that the negative externalities of government policies should occur "not in my back yard"), freeing well-off Americans from the obligation to assist communities that suffer the worst harms of drug abuse and addiction. The right approach, then, was to hold the course, following the same model that the punitive drug war had followed at a steadily increasing scale since its inception.[23]

"We Don't Have Good Ideas"

By Obama's second term, the war over the war on drugs was in full fury. "People see a war as a war on them," Gil Kerlikowske, the current drug czar, told the *Wall Street Journal*, in 2009. "We're not at war with people in this country." In August 2013, the Department of Justice advised federal prosecutors not to consider possession of small amounts of marijuana an "enforcement priority," even though it remained a federal crime. A majority of U.S. citizens supported decriminalizing marijuana for recreational use, and by the summer of 2019, eleven states and the District of Columbia had legalized recreational cannabis, and a majority of states had elected to permit medical marijuana. The Obama administration at least initially removed legal restrictions on providing federal funds for needle-exchange programs and shrinking sentencing disparities between crack and powder cocaine. Before leaving office, President Obama commuted the sentences of eight inmates who had been convicted of crack cocaine offenses, perhaps signaling a new approach; still, more than 320,000 people remained incarcerated on drug charges.[24]

Reading between the lines, the question that emerged was whether Obama was subtly urging the nation to reconsider how we fight drugs. And would this mean forgoing the inertial logic that had hitherto underpinned America's drug war? Some, like former Seattle police chief Norm Stamper, believed that the answer was yes. "We pay dearly for a vindictive system that often serves to make matters worse—much worse." Even William Brownfield, a redoubtable public servant and at the time the State Department's top "drugs and thugs" official, told a Senate subcommittee weighing counternarcotics assistance to Mexico, "If the endgame is perfection, we'll never get there. At least, not in this world." The measure of success, he told the senators, needed to move from "inputs" (aircraft, equipment, and training) to "outputs" (homicide rate, conviction rate, interdictions).[25]

Having driven much of the war on drugs in the late 1980s and 1990s, many on Capitol Hill were also experiencing a change of heart. "There is great fatigue surrounding our drug programs in the Western Hemisphere," a congressional staff member told the *New Yorker*. "We don't have good ideas. We don't have good answers. We don't have good anything. But we also know that doing nothing is a problem. So the whole thing is on autopilot. When you're in the machine, it's very difficult to say anything other than 'Keep shooting. Keep decapitating the cartels.'"[26]

22 • Law Enforcement and Incarceration

Buy-and-Bust

On April 4, 2016, the *New York Times* published a report by journalist Joseph Goldstein that revealed many of the competing goals and attitudes in the post-1980s era of aggressive drug enforcement. The article described, among other examples, a situation involving a fifty-five-year-old crack addict, Reginald J., who was standing outside a liquor store in Harlem one evening. Mr. J., who asked that only the first letter of his surname be published, was approached by a fellow down-and-out who asked him to help buy some drugs. Perhaps hoping for a "pinch," Reginald found it difficult to say no, so he accepted cash from the stranger to purchase crack or heroin from a local peddler and was immediately arrested on felony drug-dealing charges. The person who requested and funded Reginald's drug purchase was an undercover narcotics officer with the New York Police Department. "For him to put the money in my hands, as an addict, let me tell you what happens," Reginald told Goldstein. "I like to think I could resist it, but I'm way beyond that. My experience has shown me that 1,000 times out of 1,000 times, I will be defeated."[1]

Brian McCarthy, the assistant chief in charge of the Narcotics Division of the New York Police Department, defended such buy-and-bust tactics as a necessary response to community complaints. Undercover buy-and-bust officers were "going to a location where there are prior incidents," he explained. McCarthy also noted the fluidity in the line between user and dealer: "It is common that the people we arrest are also using the narcotics they are selling. . . . I believe that we attempt to do our jobs in a planned manner with the utmost integrity where we do get people who are selling narcotics." Getting the bigger dealers was still the larger goal, yet, in these small-scale stings, narcotics cops typically did not pursue or arrest the dealers who sold drugs to the addicts, preferring instead to use the intelligence they gathered to assemble cases for larger drug-enterprise takedowns.[2]

Criminal charges in the Big Apple involving small amounts of heroin and crack were not infrequent in the 2010s: almost five thousand were handed down in 2015, and slightly over six thousand the year before. A majority of the charges for drug dealing concluded in plea-bargaining agreements; in many of the cases that did go to trial, jurors were left wondering why the police and prosecutors would so "aggressively pursue troubled addicts." One juror said: "The big underlying question is why a nine-person buy-and-bust team did not follow him to the dealer where he got it from. Everyone was scratching their heads, wondering what the heck is wrong with our system." Criminal practice activist Tina Luongo, quoted in Goldstein's article, underscored one of the major hypocrisies in the system: "We all talk a lot in this city about the public health crisis of drug addiction, and yet we take a very regressive approach to locking people up."[3]

The buy-and-bust policy was a significant flashpoint in the nascent war over the war on drugs. For its defenders, the policy was an effective way for police to hit their arrest quotas. But for critics, it was just one of a number of punitive anti-drug strategies that unfairly target people based on their race, neighborhood of residence, and income class, while contributing to the "age of mass incarceration." The punitive and incarceration-driven domestic drug war has indeed generated substantial challenges for law enforcement and for broader social policy. This chapter offers a close reading of some of those challenges, but we will also complicate the conventional critical picture, highlighting new sociological evidence that suggests that the thorniest problems may derive from a somewhat different set of issues.[4]

Tough on Crime

When Bill Clinton ran for the presidency in 1992, he was determined to demonstrate his tough-on-crime bona fides. Through the Reagan and Bush Sr. years, Democrats had come off looking soft compared with "zero-tolerance" Republicans. Considerable public support across racial lines had attended the unprecedented anti-drug and anti-crime legislation of 1986 and 1988, which, recall, introduced mandatory minimum sentences for drug crimes and led to the 100-to-1 guideline for crack offenses. In the weeks leading up to the crucial

New Hampshire Democratic primary, Clinton decided to head back to Arkansas to oversee the execution of Ricky Ray Rector, a mentally handicapped African-American "who had so little conception of what was about to happen to him that he asked for the dessert from his last meal to be saved for him until the morning." After the execution, Clinton burnished his anti-crime image, saying, "I can be nicked a lot, but no one can say I'm soft on crime." Clinton won New Hampshire, solidifying his electoral pathway to the White House the following year.[5] In the first year of his presidency, violent crime affected almost eleven million Americans; thirty-two million endured thefts or burglaries. Such staggering numbers draped many American communities, especially in urban centers, in an asphyxiating pall of fear. "The death yesterday of a 41-year-old armed security guard from Long Island was not an uncommon occurrence in East New York," the *New York Times* chronicled on December 20, 1993. "Indeed, it followed 13 other killings in the 75th Precinct in the last nine days."[6]

In 1994, Congress enthusiastically passed a severe $30 billion law called the Violent Crime Control and Law Enforcement and the Federal Death Penalty Act. The largest crime-control bill in American history, the new legislation added an additional sixty offenses to the roster of capital crimes. It also offered almost $10 billion in incentives to states to construct more penitentiaries if they adopted "truth in sentencing" policies designed to enforce "harsh punishments and limit parole." It added new mandatory minimum sentences to those already on the books, as well as new protocols for habitual offenders, generally known as "three-strikes laws," wherein a defendant convicted of a severe violent crime following two prior convictions automatically received a mandatory life sentence. It even went so far as to ban assault weapons. On the softer side, the Violent Crime Control bill prescribed community policing initiatives and dedicated $6.1 billion to drug prevention and treatment programs "designed with significant input from experienced police officers." The bill also institutionalized drug courts as alternatives to incarceration, although this point is often overshadowed by the prominence of punitive programs in the law's budget.[7]

Every Democratic senator but one supported the legislation. A majority of African-American congressional leaders voted in favor. The Congressional Black Caucus even requested further punitive provisions that never made it into the final legislation. Professor Michael Fortner of the City University of New York provided one explanation for this outpouring of support: "There was grassroots mobilization of the community, particularly by black pastors. There was a group of influential black pastors who signed a letter encouraging the Congressional Black Caucus to support the bill. And then later, on top of that, black elected officials, who portrayed themselves at various points as un-comfortable with some of these laws, went along anyway because of pressure coming from their communities, and because they also realized the problem was so bad."[8]

Clinton signed the sweeping anti-crime bill to cheers from both sides of the congressional aisle. A year later, with the optimism typical of drug war presi-dents, he declared, "All of this is beginning to work. For the first time in a very long time, crime has decreased around the country." He went on to announce, "We are putting 100,000 police officers on America's streets. We banned as-sault weapons because America doesn't want drug dealers to be better armed than police officers. We are helping schools to rid themselves of guns, and we are also helping schools to prevent teenage drug use by teaching children about the dangers of drugs and gangs." In the eyes of the Clinton administra-tion, the struggle was far from over: "We cannot stop now. We have to send a constant message to our children that drugs are illegal, drugs are dangerous, drugs may cost you your life—and the penalties for dealing drugs are severe. I am not going to let anyone who peddles drugs get the idea that the cost of doing business is going down." Clinton upheld stiff penalties for crack of-fenses despite recommendations by the U.S. Sentencing Commission, which had concluded by the early 1990s that there was no "scientific basis" for the 100-to-1 ratio in crack and powder cocaine sentences, and recommended equalizing them to remedy what it contended was an unfair disparity.[9]

Still, Clinton continued to pursue the drug war policies of the past. In his State of the Union address in 1996, the president warned: "From now on, the rule for residents who commit crime and peddle drugs should be one strike and you're out." This was followed by an initiative colloquially dubbed the "One Strike" policy, which banned convicted violent crime and drug offenders from public housing assistance. Many observers subsequently saw these moves as counterproductive and even racist. There was soon a surplus of "one-strikers," now indigent and homeless, "locked out not only of main-stream society but their own homes."[10]

One residue of the anti-crime fervor was record-setting incarceration rates. From 1980 to 2002, the number of people in prisons and jails shot from 300,000 up to two million. The probability that an arrest would lead to felony charges doubled from 1994 to 2008—and not necessarily for crimes specified in the 1994 federal law. When the rate peaked in 2007 at 767 per hundred thou-sand, it towered over that of any other developed country and even outpaced

Bill Clinton being applauded by lawmakers after a ceremony in the White House
Rose Garden where he signed three crime-related bills, October 3, 1996
(Reuters, permission to author)

those of repressive regimes like China, Iran, and Russia. More than seven million Americans—one in every thirty-one adults—were in prison, in jail, on probation, or on parole. The United States held in prison a larger percentage of its
black citizens than South Africa had at the apex of apartheid in the 1980s.[11]

By 2015, the rate had ebbed somewhat, to 670 per hundred thousand, although the total number of incarcerated persons in this country still exceeded
the number of internees in Stalinist gulags. In 2016, the Prison Policy Initiative counted "more than 2.3 million people in 1,719 prisons, 102 federal prisons, 942 juvenile correctional facilities, 3,283 local jails, and 79 Indian County
jails as well as military prisons, immigration detention facilities, civil service
commitment centers, and prisons in the U.S. territories." In two decades, 250
million arrests put 77.7 million people—one-third of U.S. adults—in the FBI
master criminal database. Four of ten males were arrested at least once before
turning twenty-three. The statistic for African-Americans was just under 50
percent; for Latinos, 44 percent. Annual spending per inmate exceeded
$30,000. Between 1980 and 2013, according to Holly Harris, executive direc-
tor of the nonprofit Justice Action Network, federal penitentiary spending
spiked by a factor of seven; state facilities swelled from $10.6 billion in 1987
to $50.9 billion in 2015, an inflation-adjusted increase of 380 percent.[12]

Over the subsequent decades, there was a precipitous drop in violent crime.
To illustrate this, in April 2018 the *New York Times* ran a headline about the

identical crime-savaged neighborhood it had covered in 1993; the city's overall number of homicides was just under 300 in 2018, down 85 percent from 1,960 in 1993. By one reckoning, if the 1993 rate had continued over the proximate quarter century, 49,000 people would have killed instead of 15,000, making a net of 34,000 New Yorkers still alive. For the entire country, this net would be 150,000. For one observer, "Those were the teenagers who *did* come home that night, the mom or dad or sibling who *wasn't* missed at dinner. It's one of the most impressive social achievements of the past 30 years." So while no one was contending that crime rates had not plunged, a robust debate focused on the causes. Keep in mind that the 1994 crime bill overlapped with a sustained economic expansion and the ebbing of the crack epidemic and, according to some, was also the accidental beneficiary of legalized abortions "eliminating thousands of would-be criminals before they had a chance to be born." For proponents like the columnist Bret Stephens, the crime bill was a shining but restive bipartisan example of moving the country to a better place: "of more policing and tougher enforcement and a powerful refusal to continue defining criminal deviancy down in the face of those who said we just had to take it." The central takeaway from all the crime bill's legacy? For the conservative Stephens, it was a "vastly safer country" and an "act of moral clarity married to political possibility, which is what statesmanship is all about."[13]

Militarization

A hallmark of the tough-on-crime era was the militarization of domestic law enforcement, especially on the anti-drug front. Special Weapons and Tactics (SWAT) teams were first formed from police ranks in the 1960s to handle extreme cases such as mass shootings and hostage situations. But by the 1990s their hallmark mission was serving narcotics warrants through "forced, unannounced entry." In 1972, there were a few hundred SWAT squad raids. There were thirty thousand in 1996; forty thousand in 2001; and fifty thousand in 2015.[14]

For more than a hundred years, federal law prohibited the military from being deployed inside the United States against American citizens. Over the past several decades, that line has become blurred. In 1988, Congress created the Edward Byrne Memorial State and Local Enforcement Assistance Program in honor of an NYPD officer killed on duty at the residence of a drug case witness. The changes were intended to encourage local police forces to apply for federal grants to assist them in anti-drug enforcement.[15]

A decade later the Pentagon began donating military weapons to local governments. Observers such as journalist Dexter Filkins documented tens of billions of dollars of military matériel, "all of which [was] designed for combat," procured by domestic police departments through donations or using grant money from the Departments of Defense and Homeland Security. This included armored personnel carriers like the $20 million mine-resistant, ambush-protected vehicle (MRAP), M16 assault rifles, grenade launchers, infrared sight guns, even bayonets. Critics like Filkins hypothesized that using the SWAT teams and their military equipment for routine police operations encouraged the police to act in ways they otherwise would not.[16]

In one instance in 2014, the sheriff's department of Richland County, South Carolina, deployed its SWAT team to raid a "home in a run-down neighborhood" where the residents were suspected of holding cannabis. The team members, dressed for full combat—"black fatigues, helmets, and assault rifles"—smashed the doors and windows, entered the home, and arrested the owner's son. They confiscated $837 in cash that the son claimed he needed to manage his landscaping business. For their trouble, the officers seized a gram and a half—a trace amount—of marijuana. As critics saw it, the 780 cases of flawed paramilitary raids that reached appellate courts between 1989 and 2001 were clear evidence that "community policing" had become "military policing."[17]

Narcotic-Prison-Industrial Complex

Another consequence of the tough-on-crime policies and the wave of incarceration that followed was a "prison building boom the likes of which the world has never seen." America's federal prison population swelled by almost 800 percent between 1980 and 2013, a rate that far outpaced the ability of the Federal Bureau of Prisons to accommodate inmates in its own facilities. The undersupply led the bureau in the 2000s to broker deals with private prison operators to confine federal inmates. In 2013, the bureau recorded thirty thousand inmates, or about one-sixth of all federal prisoners, in private facilities. In 2014, the country's fifth-largest prison system, after those of the federal government and the three largest states, was operated by one private prison outfit, the Corrections Corporation of America (now named CoreCivic).[18]

There is no disputing that the prison boom opened up fantastic business opportunities. But it also raised significant ethical questions. Whereas for states there tended to be financial and political incentives to reduce recidivism, for private prisons recidivism meant repeat customers. Equally, there are profit incentives for private companies that limit or eliminate spending on myriad inmate services that for a public institution might seem advisable or even obligatory. The less Corrections Corporation had to spend on food, education, vocational training, medical care, and rehabilitation, the better the bottom line. Given that almost all of these firms were not publicly traded—save the publicly held private prison operators Corrections Corporation of America and the GEO Group—getting accurate information on their business practices was "nearly impossible." In 2016, *New Yorker* investigative journalist Eric Markowitz reported that Corizon Health, the nation's largest prison health care entity, treated over three hundred thousand inmates and brought in $1.4 billion each year in revenue. Corizon was also the subject of numerous investigations and lawsuits and was named as a defendant in hundreds of malpractice suits. Many of the private outfits gave state and local entities a slice of their sizable revenues—one company stated in its public relations materials that it had paid $1.3 billion in state "commissions" over the previous decade.[19]

It was perhaps not surprising that these same companies lobbied hard for three strikes and other tough-on-crime measures. In 2011, the two largest private prison companies donated almost $3 million to politicians and hired 242 lobbyists nationwide. Less noted but nonetheless telling, the food industry also lobbied to keep prisons full, as wholesalers knew that a captive market of 2.2 million Americans was "powerless to protest if much of the food delivered to them is well past its sell-by date."[20]

Jim Crow Justice

Critics characterized the crime laws of the 1990s as part of a national frenzy to put low-level criminals in prison, which, as one writer put it, "ravaged poor communities, taking a particularly devastating toll on African-Americans that political leaders are only now working to reverse." Proponents of this view correctly pointed out that the federal drug budget topped $17 billion in 1998, a tenfold increase over 1981, and that the percentage of drug arrests resulting in prison sentences (as opposed to dismissal, community service, or probation) quadrupled in the years that followed the Clinton crime laws. For some, such as the prominent lawyer and author Michelle Alexander, there was a clear and ready causal connection to be drawn between the drug war, the "incarceration state," and the private prison phenomenon. This now orthodox view of the critical camp can be summarized this way: "The root cause of incarceration is the racist persecution of young black men for drug crimes, which overpopulates the prisons with nonviolent offenders. Then mandatory-sentencing laws leave offenders serving long prison sentences for relatively minor crimes. This hugely expanded prison population, one that tracks in reverse the decline of actual crime, has led to a commerce in caged men—private-prison contractors, and a specialized lobby in favor of prison construction, which in turn demands men to feed into the system." In evidence, Alexander listed U.S. cities where upward of 80 percent of young African-American men had criminal records and states in which African-American males were admitted to state prisons on drug charges at rates twenty to fifty times higher than whites. Given that repeated studies had demonstrated that people of all races used and sold drugs at similar rates, the difference in incarceration outcomes revealed "stark racial disparities."[21]

On top of this, the 80 percent of drug defendants who were poor often lacked competent legal assistance from public defenders. Many defendants were encouraged or pressured to take plea deals to avoid draconian sentences if convicted—even, of course, if they were innocent, which perhaps 2 to 5 percent were. The *Los Angeles Times* quoted a public defender who described the scene: "They are herded like cattle into the courtroom lockup, up at 3 or 4 in the morning. Then they have to make decisions that affect the rest of their lives. You can imagine how stressful that is." The severe sentencing law also encouraged individuals to snitch and plead guilty to face lighter sanctions. At the same time, possibly reflecting a "changing public mood," district attorneys became more likely to pursue felony charges and long sentences.[22]

In the first decades of the twenty-first century, more people began to speak out against the costs of these policies. Some of the harshest criticism came directly from the judiciary. Federal judge Lawrence Irving, a Reagan appointee, said upon retiring, "If I remain on the bench I have no choice but to follow the law. I just can't in good conscience, continue to do this." Another Reagan appointee and notorious "tough sentencer," Judge William W. Schwarzer, admitted to feeling unsettled when he sentenced a first-time offender, Richard Anderson, to ten years in prison without parole for giving a drug dealer a ride to a meeting that was actually with an undercover drug agent. One judge refused to take on more drug cases in light of his dismay about "much of the cruelty I have been party to in connection with the 'war on drugs.' "[23]

In 2003, Supreme Court justice Anthony Kennedy made headlines when he addressed the American Bar Association and argued: "Our prison resources are misspent, our punishments too severe, our sentences too loaded. I can accept neither the necessity nor the wisdom of federal mandatory minimum sentences. In all too many cases, mandatory minimum sentences are unjust." Judges and prosecutors on drug cases across the board came out against mandatory minimums, contending that such sanctions were arbitrary and excessive. Judge Robert Sweet of the U.S. District Court for the Southern District of New York opined that the 100-to-1 guideline in crack cases "has resulted in Jim Crow justice." Paul G. Cassell, U.S. district judge for the District of Utah, blasted the legal disparity between crack and powder cocaine, contending that "apparent inequality in the sentencing guidelines produces actual injustice to the crack-cocaine defendant." Several judges, all of whom had previously served as U.S. attorneys, wrote a letter to the U.S. Senate and House Judiciary Committees declaring, "It is our strongly held view that the current disparity between powder cocaine and crack cocaine, in both mandatory minimum statutes and the guidelines, cannot be justified and results in sentences that are unjust and do not serve society's interest."[24]

Action followed. In 2010, Congress passed the Fair Sentencing Act, which raised the drug quantities that triggered minimum sentencing and lowered the crack cocaine ratio from 100-to-1 to 18-to-1—reduced but still not *equal*. In 2019, Joe Biden, exploring a campaign for the presidency in 2020, addressed a Martin Luther King Jr. Day crowd where he stood next to the seasoned civil rights activist Reverend Al Sharpton. "I know we haven't always gotten things right," said Biden, the former vice president and head of the Senate Judiciary Committee in the late 1980s and early 1990s. "Rev, it was with your help back in 2010 that Barack [Obama] and I finally reduced the disparity in sentencing, which we'd been fighting to eliminate, in crack cocaine versus power cocaine." The sentencing disparity "was a big mistake when it was made. We were told by the experts, that 'crack, you never go back,' and that it was somehow fundamentally different. It is *not* different, but it has trapped an entire generation." Some experts were not convinced by Biden's "recent crack mea culpa." Jasmine Tyler at Human Rights Watch excoriated the Democratic Party icon: "His legacy didn't trap *a* generation. If you think about the children, and if you think about the impact on those children's children—we're talking about *three* generations. A century of slavery, 60 years of Jim Crow, followed by Biden's policies of mass incarceration of the drug war."[25]

A few years after the 2010 fair-sentencing legislation, liberal Democratic senator Patrick Leahy of Vermont teamed up with the libertarian Republican Rand Paul of Kentucky to introduce legislation that would end federal mandatory minimum sentences in drug cases. In 2014, Barack Obama's attorney general Eric Holder sent a memo detailing how his agency was "refining" its guidelines to address "unduly harsh sentences" for "low-level, non-violent drug offenses." Some of the supposed reforms, however, were useless. The governor of Iowa, for example, commuted the entire roster of life sentences of the state's juvenile defendants but only made them eligible for parole after sixty years.[26]

The public debate became increasingly unified in asking how this could have happened. A *Washington Post* investigation in 2016 explained that everyone from "Congress to the Koch brothers" had apparently lost their appetite for the tough-on-crime policies that had seemed so imperative in the 1990s. The article cited a Pew survey showing that in 2001 Americans were split on the "virtues of mandatory minimums for nonviolent drug crimes" as well as a 2014 version of the same poll, which showed Americans opposing them by a two to one margin. Respondents agreed that the country had too many people in prison and that many were staying for too long. Half of American prisoners were in jail for nonviolent crimes. The number of prisoners serving life sentences was 160,000, or twice the entire incarcerated population in Japan.[27]

In 2014, President Obama announced a plan for federal prisoners serving overly punitive sentences to have their terms commuted by executive writ. The program solicited petitions from prisoners (1) who had already served ten years for nonviolent offenses; (2) who under present laws would have received significantly lighter sentences for the same crime; and (3) who had demonstrated good behavior in prison. What President Obama did not do, though, was issue an amnesty to broad categories, as his predecessors Gerald Ford and Jimmy Carter had done for draft resisters after the Vietnam War. Before Obama left office, the executive office had received 33,149 petitions through the program; Obama's 1,715 commutations amounted to more than all of those issued by his seven predecessors combined. One round of commutations on August 30, 2016, included 111 federal inmates, all booked on nonviolent and overwhelmingly drug-related charges; thirty-five of them had received life sentences. The policy provoked minimal criticism; indeed, the most strident called on the president to let even more people go free.[28]

In August 2016, in another signal of the swelling bipartisan reform movement taking hold, Deputy Attorney General Sally Q. Yates sent a memorandum to the Bureau of Prisons instructing it to take the "first step" in the process of "reducing—and ultimately ending" the federal government's use of private prisons. Even if private prisons accounted for only a small fraction of total inmates and the $80 billion that the American public spent that year on corrections, the Department of Justice's decision was considered a "modest victory" for criminal justice reform advocates.[29]

Rejoinder

Interestingly, as these reforms were beginning to take hold, the orthodox critical view that attributed the rise of the incarceration state to racial discrimination, the drug war, and corporate greed also came under fire. Scholars such as Fordham University law professor John Pfaff, for one, critiqued the drug war angle of what he called the "Standard Story." Based on extensive analysis of sociological data, Pfaff concluded that about half of new sentences in federal and state systems during the "great wave" followed violent crime convictions, while only one-fifth followed nonviolent drug convictions. Even if all those in federal and state facilities on drug charges were set free, Pfaff argued, the U.S. incarceration rate would still be four times that of the early 1970s. Pfaff dramatically discounts the impact of mandatory minimum policies, countering that prison sentencing for violent crimes far outpaced sentencing for the relatively low-level crimes that would trigger mandatory minimums.[30]

Pfaff reaches a different conclusion to explain Michelle Alexander's insight that incarceration rates rose as violent crime fell in the 2000s. For Pfaff, the decisive variable in the incarceration surge was not drug sentencing rules, such as mandatory minimums, but "discretionary prosecutorial decisions." On his alternative interpretation, "Prosecutors in the nation's three-thousand-plus counties charged arrestees with felonies at a higher rate even as the crime rate itself declined. Ultimately, more punitive exercise of prosecutorial discretion fed a steady net influx of convicts to state prisons. District attorneys were motivated by tough-on-crime politics and enabled by cost-shifting economics: Counties pay for police and prosecution, but imprisonment comes out of the state budget." While Pfaff does find fault in the disproportionate representation of racial minorities and the economically marginalized in America's prisons, in his view, reforming drug sentencing is not the way to fix it.[31]

Another perspective comes from conservative writer Heather MacDonald, who contends that high incarceration rates were driven simply by high rates of offense. The murder rate in the United States in the 2000s was seven times the average of almost two dozen Western countries and Japan. The gun homicide rate was just under twenty times the average. MacDonald's take is that "prison is a bargain when compared with the costs of crime" and that attempts "to find evidence proving that the overrepresentation of blacks in prison is due to systemic racial inequity" have "always come up short."[32]

A third camp disputes both this conservative view and the orthodox critical view. Citing a 50 percent drop in violent crime since the 1990s, Democratic legal counselor David Yassky contended that Clinton-era policies "set in mo-tion" a reversal of the dismaying crime rates. Moreover, he adds, the people who overwhelmingly benefited from the reduced crime levels came from poor urban neighborhoods. Yassky also pointed out that even white Americans were locked up far more frequently than before—totaling more than four times the number of prisoners in multiethnic France. Yassky contended that two decades of mass incarceration might indeed have inflicted "massive harm" on African-American men and their families, but "to lay mass incar-ceration and the damages to black communities on the doorstep of the 1994 crime act was historically inaccurate."[33]

Although it is true that violent crime declined after the 1994 legislation passed, this may have been the delayed effect of an effort that began decades before. Some research suggests that the trend toward increased incarceration had actually started in the early 1970s with an array of changes to state and federal criminal justice policies that toughened penalties. For Pfaff, the critical insights were that tough sentencing policy should be considered on a much longer timeline than the roughly two decades after 1994 and that violent crime may well have already topped out before the 1994 law went into effect.[34]

A Double Reversal

In 2015, the Department of Justice reported, the incarceration rate dropped to one in 115 adults, down from one in 110 adults in 2007. Then by 2019 we had learned that the decade between 2007 and 2017 had witnessed a 10 per-cent decline in incarceration. Observers began to wonder if the great wave of incarceration might be coming to an end. In particular, the push to address mass incarceration precipitated a dramatic decline in new prisoners from cit-ies. Between 2006 and 2014, prison admissions plunged 69 percent in Los Angeles County, 93 percent in San Francisco, and 36 percent in Indianapolis. Part of this turnaround came from cities' more flexible stances on drug of-fenses, including greater use of alternative drug courts, treatment, and proba-tion. There was also the simple but critical factor of less crime, which plunged 19 percent from 2007 to 2017. For the first time in almost half a century, the once-assumed intractable racial discrepancies in U.S. prisons began to re-verse. Stanford University scholar Keith Humphries reported that incarcera-tion of African-Americans dropped continuously faster than incarceration of whites between 2000 and 2014. The rate of new African-American prisoners dropped by a quarter from 2006 to 2013 and the rate for Latinos by a third.[35]

But another kind of reversal attended these shifts. A story by the *New York Times* in 2016 described how, despite the overall downward trending numbers, overwhelmed by a malignant heroin epidemic, and anxious about what released prisoners might do in their communities, significant parts of rural and suburban America were actually sending *more* defendants to prison than they had in the prior two decades. The gap, the *Times* reported, did not appear to be due to changes in crime rates, which had fallen in rural and urban areas at similar rates. Rather, it resulted from a disagreement about "how harshly crime should be punished." In contrast to cities, these rural heartland communities—mostly white and politically conservative—were administered by prosecutors and judges who still held great sway over "who goes to prison and for how long." Many had little desire to reduce their prison populations. Dearborn County, Indiana—97 percent white—was a poster child for the new spike in rural imprisonment. Ten percent of the county's adults were in prison or jail or on probation. "I am proud of the fact that we send more people to jail than other counties," Aaron Negangard, the elected prosecutor in Dearborn County, said in 2015. "That's how we keep it safe here." He added, "My constituents are the people who decide whether I keep doing my job. The governor can't make me. The legislature can't make me."[36]

It is startling how closely such efforts in rural America resembled the aggressive campaigns against crack in the 1980s and against drugs and violent crime in the 1990s. For drug hawks such as Negangard, the solution to the opioid problem was more aggressive enforcement and imprisonment, not less. "If you're not prosecuting, then you're de facto legalizing it," Negangard declared. Cops pursued low-level drug offenders, routinely offering to throw out drug possession charges in return for information on acquaintances or family members who were dealing. Probation was also strictly monitored with frequent drug testing; hundreds of violators were sent to state prisons. In Cincinnati, by contrast, city policy sent more and more drug offenders to outpatient treatment programs. If an offender completed the program, the charge would be dismissed. In a bizarre twist, Cincinnati police occasionally helped lure suspected dealers over to Dearborn County, where they could be arrested and punished with great severity. To address the increased number of inmates, Dearborn County officials paid $11.5 million to double the size of the local jail and allocated $11 million more to expand the county courthouse.[37]

In many rural counties, prisons were the only sufficiently funded source of social services for drug-addicted populations. An estimated 225 of the 250 inmates in the Dearborn County jail were addicted to one or more drugs. Rehabilitation programs could handle only forty of them. Negangard acknowledged that he wished that his county could locate more funds for treating these patient-inmates. But maybe one in two of the addicts in prison, he reckoned, were hardened criminals who were likely to commit additional crimes whether they received addiction care or not. (That this reasoning introduced troubling questions about the practice of pretextual imprisonment did not seem to worry the prosecutor.) He concluded, "We can't just let the bad guys go."[38]

In a sign that the policy and cultural debate had not abated, in May 2017 President Trump's attorney general Jeff Sessions ordered the Justice Department to have federal prosecutors charge suspects with the most serious provable crimes, thus moving away from the Obama-era easing. The shift provoked heated debate on both sides of the congressional aisle. Senator Mike Lee, Republican of Utah, expressed unease, writing on Twitter, "To be tough on crime, we have to be smart on crime."[39] Lee himself was one of two lead sponsors of a broadly bipartisan bill in 2017 known as the Smarter Sentencing Act, which was designed to "modernize federal drug sentencing policies by giving federal judges more discretion in sentencing those convicted of nonviolent drug offenses." On December 21, 2018, President Trump signed into law the First Step Act, which had received overwhelming bipartisan support in Congress even though Republicans have previously balked at backing a similar Obama-era legislative initiative. Among other reforms, the bill changed the infamous "three strikes" sanction for narcotics felonies from life imprisonment to twenty-five years, and made retroactive the 2010 Fair Sentencing Act's reduction of the discrepancy between powder and crack cocaine penalties—thereby affecting thousands of disproportionately African-American inmates who had been convicted before the 2010 law and could now petition for a review of their cases. Although it did not apply to state prisons and jails, the reform was estimated to cut a "collective 53,000 years off the sentences" of federal prisoners over the next decade. Trying to counter predications that supporting the bill would make Republicans appear soft on crime, Georgia representative Douglas A. Collins countered, "I stand before you as a son of a Georgia state trooper. I know this bill will help in the long run. . . . We're helping law enforcement do their job." On the left, Representative Cedric L. Richmond of Louisiana warned against overestimating the legislation's reach. "Does [this bill] address the criminalization of poverty? No," the Louisiana congressman said on Capitol Hill. "It leaves many sentences, unjust sentences, in place. However, there is no doubt in my mind that this bill is a positive step in the right direction."[40]

23 · Cannabis Revisited

Mountain Sweep

In late August 2012, U.S. federal, state, and local anti-drug agencies launched a two-month effort called Operation Mountain Sweep, targeting large illegal marijuana cultivations on public land in seven Western states: Arizona, California, Idaho, Nevada, Oregon, Utah, and Washington. Marijuana cultivation on public lands, especially in the American West, had grown immensely in the previous few years, so the more aggressive response from anti-drug elements came as no surprise. Alongside Mexico, the United States itself had emerged as one of the largest marijuana producers in the Americas; Mexico supplied about half of all the cannabis consumed in the United States; much of the remaining portion came from domestic production. Interestingly, concerns about the environmental impact of cannabis cultivation on delicate ecosystems served as a major catalyst for the operation. Cultivation-driven environmental degradation in the United States was eerily similar to that in cocaine source countries, where growers slashed virgin rainforest to make way for coca plantings. Domestic pot growers often destroyed thirsty mature trees to allow more sunlight into the sites and diverted streams from natural flows to irrigate the plants. The DEA reported that each outdoor cannabis plant required around 1,200 gallons of water. Half a million plants would use up to 600 million gallons—enough to supply San Francisco for three weeks. U.S. officials contended that Mountain Sweep had resulted in the eradication of almost seven hundred thousand marijuana plants across the seven states with an estimated street value of almost $1.5 billion. The operation had also collected enormous volumes of trash, irrigation pipes, fertilizer, and pesticides. All evidence pointed to the fact that the growing phenomenon was not "Smokey Bear" sprouting a few plants in a national park but the work of sophisticated commercial enterprises. Pressure from U.S. domestic eradication efforts forced growers to abandon large outdoor marijuana plantings in favor of indoor cultivation—easier to disguise and much harder to interdict.[1]

ONDCP chief Gil Kerlikowske's office singled out Operation Mountain Sweep in its annual National Drug Control Strategy as an example of success in the decades-long drug war. Ironically, however, the aggressive campaign concluded only weeks before Washington and Colorado citizens voted to legalize recreational marijuana use. That turned out to be only one of two ironies. The state decisions also clashed with the punitive drug war the U.S. government was continuing to escalate abroad, especially in Latin America, but increasingly in West Africa and South Asia. That European tourists were now visiting Denver to get stoned before their ski vacations did not sit particularly well with foreign drug war allies. As the war over the drug war raged, some observers denounced these kinds of disconnects as the absurd contradictions of a nonsensical policy program; others considered them the bad consequences of diminishing resolve in an effort that was as justified and necessary as it had ever been.

Pot Legalization and Medical Marijuana Movements

The peculiar status of cannabis in the 2010s was the cumulative result of several factors, the most important of which were the persistent, and in many respects overlapping, pot legalization and medical marijuana movements. Martin Lee's *Smoke Signals,* arguably the most exacting account of these movements to date, attributes their success to a handful of outsized figures. He recounts how in 1976 Robert C. Randall, a young academic in Washington, D.C., made "medical and legal history" by successfully suing the U.S. government to obtain cannabis to treat his glaucoma. Randall was often unable to procure an adequate supply of his "herbal medicine" from the street, so he started growing plants in his yard. One day he returned home to find his crop destroyed and his house turned upside down. On a table were a search warrant and a note from the D.C. cops telling him to head to the police station. Randall could have pleaded guilty to a misdemeanor possession charge and paid a fine. Instead, he became the "Rosa Parks" of the medical pot movement by fighting the charges on the basis of "medical necessity"—the legal notion that permits breaking the law when compliance would cause greater harm. Randall spent more than a week at UCLA undergoing "rigorous testing" by a medical doctor who determined that large doses of smoked marijuana lowered Randall's intraocular pressure into a normal range. At the trial, Randall contended that it was entirely reasonable to break the law to save his eyesight. Randall was acquitted of the charges.[2]

Energized by the legal victory, Randall filed a petition requesting the federal government to provide him with sufficient cannabis to meet his medical needs. U.S. authorities reluctantly agreed. Lee explained, "First he was told he could use marijuana only in a hospital under a doctor's supervision. He said no way. Then he was told that he had to keep his pot at home in a 750-pound safe. Yeah right. When Randall tried to get a letter from the DEA indicating that he was legally allowed to smoke marijuana—in case he was ever stopped by the police—the DEA refused." But the redoubtable activist eventually pushed the FDA to create a "Compassionate Investigational New Drug Program," which supplied patients, "if they were persistent and lucky," with government-sourced cannabis grown on an experimental farm at the University of Mississippi. For the next quarter century, Randall smoked legal pot cigarettes each day—and never lost his eyesight.[3]

Lee's second outsize actor was psychologist Tod Hiro Mikuriya. Dr. Tod, as his patients called him, explained to a small northern California daily that cannabis "had been available to clinicians for one hundred years until it was taken off the market in 1938. I'm fighting to restore cannabis." In the mid-1960s, Mikuriya ran an addiction treatment center in Princeton, New Jersey. By 1967, he was conducting marijuana research for the National Institute of Mental Health but resigned due to what he contended was an institutional bias against cannabis. Regarded as the "grandfather of the medical marijuana movement," Mikuriya eventually moved to California and spent the next several decades pushing the medical marijuana political and research agenda.[4]

Mikuriya was an important force behind California's groundbreaking Proposition 19. This November 1972 measure was the first attempt to decriminalize marijuana through the ballot box. It was defeated resoundingly, 67 percent to 33 percent. But on Lee's reckoning, the vote mobilized a "sizable but hitherto unrecognized" political coalition. Politicians did not overlook this; in 1976, the California State Assembly passed the Moscone Act, which changed minor cannabis possession from a felony to a misdemeanor punishable by a maximum fine of $100. Pot proponents considered this not only a moral victory but a solid step forward fiscally, given that it would save the state over $100 million annually in law enforcement expenses.[5]

The third figurehead in the medical marijuana movement was Dennis Peron, a resident of San Francisco's Castro District who developed a close working relationship with cannabis in the 1990s as he procured and administered the drug as a palliative for his partner, Jonathan West, who was dying of AIDS. His answer was to turn marijuana dispensation into a patient service. He pushed for a citywide ballot initiative, Proposition P, which recommended that the state of California and the California Medical Association legalize medical-use "hemp preparations." Proposition P passed in November 1991 with an astounding 80 percent of the vote.[6]

Not long after, Peron created the San Francisco Cannabis Buyers Club. For Peron, the club was the medical marijuana movement's "coming out" moment. Enjoying the moral but not legal support of city government, the Cannabis Buyers Club soon became a "San Francisco institution." Similar buyers clubs were organized in dozens of other U.S. cities. But, unlike in San Francisco, these "green cross" centers were not sanctioned by local governments. Nonetheless, tens of thousands of sick patients broke the law "every day by consuming the forbidden herb."[7]

Lee's fourth player was Mary Jane Rathbun, or "Brownie Mary," who baked more than fifteen thousand pot-laced brownies a month in the late 1980s and passed them out to the AIDS patients dying in Ward 86 at San Francisco General Hospital. Her grandmotherly manner made Rathbun the "Florence Nightingale of Medical Marijuana." Perhaps more than any other figure, Rathbun "changed the face of marijuana activism." Her work had started earlier, in the 1960s and 1970s. She perfected her pot brownie recipe in a tiny home kitchen in a city housing project while holding down a waitressing gig at IHOP. Later on, she discovered that her brownies seemed to alleviate inflammation and nausea in cancer patients. This eventually led to her visits to the AIDS wards. Police agents raided her house in 1981 and seized fifty-four of her "magically delicious" brownies along with eighteen pounds of cannabis. The fifty-seven-year-old told the cops, "I thought you guys were coming." Sentenced to five hundred hours of community service, Rathbun completed them in a record two months through volunteering at a hospice, a gay thrift store, and a soup kitchen, while still managing to keep up her rounds on Ward 86. Brownie Mary went on to help Peron found the San Francisco Cannabis Buyers Club.[8]

Largely thanks to these four somewhat unassuming Californians, by the mid-1990s the medical cannabis movement had become a formidable political entity. On two occasions, the California assembly approved legislation legalizing medical marijuana; both were vetoed by Republican governor Pete Wilson. Peron and other activists decided to put the issue directly to the citizens via a ballot initiative in the 1996 election. They drafted a bill called the Compassionate Use Act. Dr. Tod Mikuriya was one of the measure's architects. Getting a

measure on the ballot was a laborious process that required 443,000 signatures. The way advocates tell the story, with the signature submission deadline
looming and tens of thousands of signatures still to go, billionaire financier
and longtime drug war foe George Soros and other rich allies found out about
the measure and took out their checkbooks. Petitioners appeared in droves
across the state, and Proposition 215 went to the voters.[9]

The proposition's advocates were especially careful to frame their communications in terms of "patients' rights, treatment options and compassion"
and to avoid "anything that smacked of hippies in tie-dyed T-shirts." One ad
showed an oncologist who told viewers, "Morphine works. Marijuana works.
Let us physicians treat you with every medicine that can help."[10]

Opposing Prop 215 was a formidable assortment of groups and individuals
that included scores of police chiefs, sheriffs, and fifty-seven of fifty-eight district
attorneys (San Francisco's being the lone exception). Also included were former
presidents Jimmy Carter and Gerald Ford, California senators Barbara Boxer
and Dianne Feinstein, former surgeon general C. Everett Koop, and a host of
high-level Clinton administration officials. Opponents cast the initiative as a
gimmick that cynically used sick and desperate patients as a backdoor to legalizing recreational pot. They cited a statement by former NORML frontman Richard Cowan: "The key is medical access, because once you have hundreds of
thousands of people using marijuana under medical supervision, the whole
scam is going to be brought up again. . . . Then we will get full legalization." Indeed, it is entirely conceivable that the rise of medical marijuana was not a historical accident but a calculated event. NORML's founders presciently recognized
that establishing the drug's medical usefulness would be the most efficient strategy for achieving the broader goal of legalization. In other words, medical use
was the soft spot in drug scheduling's armor. Seen from the perspective of two
decades later, it is remarkable how prescient Cowan's words proved to be.[11]

Perhaps the most dogged and formidable opponents proved to be California
attorney general Dan Lungren, a conservative Republican, and drug czar Barry
McCaffrey, who visited the Golden State several times before the vote to speak
out passionately against the measure: "There is not a shred of scientific evidence
that shows that smoked marijuana is useful or needed. This is not science. This
is not medicine. This is a cruel hoax." McCaffrey warned Californians that medical legalization would lead to "increased drug abuse in every category."[12]

As the November vote approached, public support for Proposition 215 continued to grow. At the same time, Lungren coordinated with the DEA, the state
narcotics bureau, and the San Francisco Police Department to hatch an opera-

tion to "infiltrate and destroy" the San Francisco Cannabis Buyers Club. According to author Martin Torgoff, Lungren expected that arrest would expose Peron as "nothing but a dirty drug dealer." On the morning of Sunday, August 4, 1996, more than a hundred police officers in "heavy black body armor" wielding "pistols, shotguns, and assault weapons," used a battering ram to smash open the club's front door. The authorities seized around 150 pounds of marijuana, eleven thousand patient records, and "tens of thousands of dollars in cash." The raid proved to be a public relations disaster. Three months after the Buyers Club raid, California voters approved Prop 215, with 56 percent voting in favor.[13]

Ironically, marijuana arrests spiked in California in the aftermath of Prop 215's passage. In fact, authorities nabbed pot users, "many with valid medical recommendations," at the unprecedented pace of almost sixty thousand arrests in 1997. McCaffrey also tasked the medical research arm of the National Academy of Science to conduct a thorough study of the scientific literature on medical cannabis. Not unreasonably, he assumed that the positive results would be disproved. However, the report stated that the science confirmed the "potential therapeutic value" of cannabinoid drugs, mainly THC, for "pain relief, control of nausea and vomiting, and appetite stimulation." The report added that cannabis also proved efficacious in suppressing epileptic seizures and reducing intraocular pressure in glaucoma patients. The main downside, the institute found, was in the method of delivery. Smoked cannabis was a "crude THC delivery system that also delivers harmful substances" including benzene, toluene, naphthalene, carbon monoxide, and tar. As one author summarized, "That is, the same inhaled nasties that came with tobacco cigarettes."[14]

Far from acting on the report, McCaffrey and Attorney General Janet Reno vowed to arrest doctors and revoke their licenses if they even suggested to a patient that cannabis might be a treatment option. They committed to prosecuting doctors who prescribed the Schedule I drug as well as subjecting law-breaking doctors to IRS audits. At the same time, McCaffrey's office pumped millions of dollars into a clandestine program to include anti-drug messages in television shows. Between 1998 and 2000, the ONDCP spent up to $25 million to ensure that pot users were portrayed as losers on programs like *Beverly Hills 90210*, *Chicago Hope*, and *The Drew Carey Show*. McCaffrey responded unapologetically to a *Salon* magazine exposé: "We plead guilty to using every lawful means to save America's children."[15]

In early 1997, in an especially unvarnished editorial, the vaunted *New England Journal of Medicine* chastised Washington's efforts to go after physicians on medical marijuana. Dr. Jerome Kassirer, the editor-in-chief, stated, "I be-lieve that a federal policy that prohibits physicians from alleviating suffering by prescribing marijuana for seriously ill patients is misguided, heavy-handed and inhumane." Despite the increased enforcement, on November 4, 1998, five additional states—Alaska, Nevada, Oregon, Washington, and Arizona—voted in favor of legalizing medical cannabis.[16]

When George W. Bush assumed the presidency in 2001, he reinforced the legal and police efforts against medical pot. In fact, the administration took a tougher approach than its Democratic predecessor had, "filing criminal charges instead of lawsuits." Attorney General John Ashcroft targeted dispen-saries, activists, and "grow-ops" across the state. "I want to escalate the war on drugs. I want to refresh it, relaunch it," he said. Over his four years in the na-tion's top law enforcement spot, Ashcroft instructed federal prosecutors to note when federal judges opted for lesser punishments for drug convictions than federal sentencing guidelines directed. Bush's drug czar, John Walters, sent a memo to every prosecutor in the country "urging them to make canna-bis crimes a high priority and to fight efforts to weaken drug laws." Walters repeatedly called cannabis a "poison" and supported longer prison sentences for marijuana users. He claimed that "marijuana use, especially during the teen years, can lead to depression, suicide, and schizophrenia." Walters solic-ited the support of church-based youth organizations to help with his anti-drug campaign. A Roman Catholic himself, Walters tasked John DiIulio, director of the White House's Faith-Based Initiatives office, to permit religious organiza-tions working on anti-drug efforts to receive federal support. With Bush's ap-proval, Walters unveiled "Faith: The Anti-Drug," a program intended to get religious communities to promote cannabis abstinence. Echoing his predeces-sors' comments on Capitol Hill, Walters described the crackdown on cannabis, and the broader war on drugs, as a "conservative cultural revolution."[17]

A Frivolous Foible

A decade hence, the conservative view still held the day, as far as federal policy was concerned. As we saw in the last chapter, federal prosecutors and the judiciary continued to press marijuana convictions through the early 2010s, further extending the Clinton-era tough-on-crime numbers game. Campaigns continued against grow operations at home—such as Operation Mountain Sweep—and abroad in Jamaica, Mexico, and Afghanistan. Mari-juana remained a Schedule I substance. The plant appeared "alongside some of the most dangerous and mind-altering drugs on earth, ranked as high as heroin, LSD, and bufotenine, a highly toxic and hallucinogenic toad venom that can cause cardiac arrest." By contrast, cocaine and methamphetamine ranked a notch down on the government's rankings, in Schedule II. But under the federal statute, Americans could be arrested, prosecuted, and punished for selling, holding, or growing cannabis.[18]

But a steady process of erosion was also undeniably under way at the state level. In November 2012 Colorado handily approved Amendment 64, 55 percent to 45 percent; the bill outpolled President Obama in Colorado by almost two hundred thousand votes. In Washington state, the margin was slightly greater—56 to 44 percent. Both bills decriminalized the possession and consumption of marijuana for recreational purposes up to certain maximum amounts and created a licensed and regulated industry for production and distribution similar to many state alcohol control regimes.[19]

Colorado permitted some registered producers to grow up to 10,200 pot plants; the federal penalty for growing more than one thousand plants was a minimum of a decade in prison and fines up to $10 million. Needless to say, this created intense administrative uncertainty in which growing, selling, and possessing pot legally in the two states still entailed culpability under federal sanctions. What eventually emerged was a "laissez-faire" approach that permitted states to run their legal cannabis markets with little federal meddling.

As has been the case for all of the ebbs and flows that make up America's history with drugs, much of the explanation for this gradual loosening up on pot lies in changing public perception. Indeed, the attitudes of a substantial and growing proportion of Americans toward cannabis were undergoing a dramatic shift in the first decades of the twenty-first century, on a scale not seen since the brief flame of 1960s counterculture. In January 2016, the *Washington Post*'s Wonk Blog reported a "growing sentiment that perhaps pot wasn't so bad after all." The overwhelming message that Americans who came of age in the Reagan era of "Just Say No," when anti-pot programs initially appeared to coincide with a drop in pot use, had heard was that drugs were evil and cannabis was among the worst; far from a risk-free recreational activity, smoking or ingesting marijuana was the "gateway" to a lifetime of drug abuse and social deviance. But public disapproval of cannabis use "significantly declined" in the first decades of the twenty-first century, particularly among adolescents. In 2014, just one in three twelfth-graders saw regular pot use as harmful—an almost 20 percent drop from a decade earlier. The number of American college students who said they had used cannabis in the previous year went from 30 percent in 2006 to 36 percent in 2013. Among the broader population, Gallup polls in the early 2000s showed that just one in three Americans supported legalization. That number had jumped to 44 percent by 2009 and 64 percent by 2018, including a majority of Republicans.[20]

The shift in one American city, Nashville, Tennessee, is particularly illustrative. In 1980 Nashville police chief Joe Casey publicly declared that marijuana was causing people to commit murder and crimes and that those convicted of growing or selling the substances three times should be executed. In 2016, "the Buckle of the Bible Belt" joined a long list of U.S. cities that decriminalized cannabis, approving an ordinance that gave the police an option to refrain from arresting and charging those caught holding a half-ounce or less. Nashville-based folk singer Todd Snider told the press that the routine references to cannabis in country music were a good indication of where the middle of the country stood on the issue. "That's the barometer. Those guys don't say stuff that mom don't tolerate. And mom's like, 'Ah, pot's not so bad anymore.' " Reporter Richard Fausset concluded that the very fact that the decriminalization effort seemed likely to pass in Nashville—the "promulgator of heartland values in song"—spoke volumes about the steady erosion of the fear of marijuana.[21]

Among American police officers, cannabis appeared to be less of a "major threat to communities," taking a 2015 DEA survey as evidence. Indeed, marijuana finished last, with only 6 percent of respondents listing it as the biggest drug threat, a rate that had been "declining steadily" since the 2000s. Heroin and methamphetamine together accounted for around 75 percent of police departments' number-one votes. However, arrests for pot possession remained steady. The *Washington Post* explained that this was at least in part because pot was low-hanging fruit: Cannabis was "by far" the most widely used illegal drug, and more users meant more possible arrests. In 2014, around 620,000 persons were arrested for "simple marijuana possession"—around 1,700 each day, or over one per minute, for an overall ratio of one in every twenty arrests. By contrast, in 1990 the total number of cannabis possession arrests was roughly 200,000. The ACLU reckoned that "the typical marijuana arrest . . . costs about $750," so with 620,000 arrests it estimated that state governments were spending around half a billion dollars to arrest people for pot possession. What some cannabis legalization proponents do not always mention is that only a tiny fraction (perhaps 1.5 percent) of those arrested for pot actually spend any time in prison. It is also true that, in many cases, simple marijuana possession does lead to imprisonment if associated with, say, a parole or bail infringement on a separate conviction.[22]

Another barometer was the way in which presidential candidates addressed their personal experience with cannabis. (It was a delicious irony that candidates' pot smoking became a staple of political campaigns—and often a subject of some amusement—after the drug war began in full.) In 1992, Democratic candidate Bill Clinton told an audience that he had tried marijuana as a Rhodes scholar: "When I was in England I experimented with marijuana a time or two, and I didn't like it. I didn't inhale it, and never tried it again." Barack Obama readily described his youthful pot exploits in his bestselling memoir *Dreams from My Father* in 1995. As a teenager, "Barry" and his buddies called themselves the Choom Gang—"chooming" being slang for smoking pot. A 2012 biography by David Maraniss shows Obama as an enthusiastic practitioner of a theory of smoking marijuana called "total absorption," or "TA" for short. As Maraniss writes, "When you were with Barry and his pals, if you exhaled precious *pakalolo* (Hawaiian slang for marijuana, meaning 'numbing tobacco') instead of absorbing it fully into your lungs, you were assessed a penalty and your turn was skipped the next time the joint came around." In the 2008 election, vice presidential candidate Sarah Palin admitted that she had smoked grass but emphasized that she opposed legalization. In a 2016 debate, Republican presidential contender Jeb Bush cut off Senator Rand Paul to make it clear that he had smoked weed. "So 40 years ago I smoked marijuana, and I admit it. I'm sure other people might have done it and might not want to say it in front of 25 million people. My mom's not happy that I just did." Moments later, the Bush campaign team tweeted a message: "Sorry Mom." Pro-legalization Democrat Bernie Sanders, who challenged Hillary Clinton for the 2016 nomination, noted, "I smoked marijuana twice, but it did not quite work for me. It's not my thing, but it is the thing of a whole lot of people."[23]

For pro-cannabis activists, identifying a change in public attitude was one thing; translating it into federal policy was a far more onerous undertaking. The first attempt to move cannabis from Schedule I to Schedule II came in 1981. Other bills appeared in Congress over the years. Democratic congressman Barney Frank, in fact, introduced a medical marijuana bill in every Congress between 1995 and 2010; every single one of them failed. In 2011, Frank and Ron Paul of Texas introduced legislation to take cannabis off the schedules entirely. The bill died before a roll call vote took place. In August 2016, as the Obama administration was winding up its second term, the DEA "denied" two congressional petitions that asked the agency to reschedule marijuana. Drug liberalization activist Mason Tvert of the Marijuana Policy Project called the Obama decision "intellectually dishonest and completely indefensible." He added, "Not everyone agrees marijuana should be legal, but few will deny that it is less harmful than alcohol and many prescription drugs." A hastily organized protest was scheduled in front of the White House; it included "Tone Deaf Karaoke" to ridicule President Obama's often shifting stances on the topic.[24]

But even if the policy hadn't changed, the shift in national mood was finding its own reflection in the rhetorical output of the executive branch. President Obama said that he had better things to do when asked in late 2012 about his planned response to the Washington and Colorado referenda. Obama's attorney general Eric Holder hinted at support for movement on the Schedule I designation when he said, "I think it's certainly a question we need to ask ourselves, whether or not marijuana is as serious of a drug as heroin." In August 2013 the Justice Department produced a memorandum advising Colorado and Washington that it would not stymie the states' legalization policies if they managed to meet certain conditions, such as preventing sales to minors and prohibiting export of the drug beyond state borders. In 2014, America reached a "tipping point": for the first time since the 1930s—the era when Harry Anslinger and "Reefer Madness" relegated weed to the nation's back alleys—a majority of U.S. citizens lived in states with some form of "marijuana legality."[25]

The United States of course is a populous country, so a rough estimate of 45 million adults smoking pot appears to be a massive number on its face. But one of the ironies of the rapid shift in the perceptions of marijuana was that it remained a drug that, playing with the statistic above, 85 percent of American adults did not use in 2017—even once. Put this rate side by side with alcohol, where 70 percent had one drink or more that year.[26]

Given that a strong share of Americans do not smoke pot at all, skeptics and outright critics of cannabis liberalization have argued that the growing acceptance of the drug is fueled by "decades-long lobbying by marijuana legalization advocates and for-profit cannabis companies." It is the interested parties, argue authors like the former investigative journalist Alex Berenson, author of the alarmist book *Tell Your Children: The Truth About Marijuana, Mental Illness, and Violence* in 2019, who have "shrewdly recast marijuana as a medicine rather than a toxicant." For these skeptics, the pot proponents have "squelched discussion" of science study–based health effects generating "far more negative" results. Of particular concern: heavy pot use and greater risk of developing schizophrenia—than a few decades earlier. And this, of course, does not take into account the fact that THC levels in marijuana had increased significantly, from around 5 percent in the 1960s through the 1980s, to usually 25 percent more recently. (Of course, users could be smoking less of the vastly more potent strains.) For Berenson, the new science on pot's ill effects should have been dismaying to the American public—but instead openness to legalization doubled in the first two decades of the twenty-first century. Another key question in the raging debate was whether cannabis was a gateway to opioids and cocaine, among other drugs. It could be that marijuana indeed "activates certain behavioral and neurological pathways" that facilitate "the onset of more serious addictions." At the same time, it could also be true that pot "offers a safe alternative" to more dangerous alternatives like opioids and cocaine. So, as the polymath Malcolm Gladwell has pointed out, you might begin smoking joints to treat a knee injury but then "you never graduate to opioids." As Gladwell reasonably speculated, "Maybe cannabis opens the door to other drugs, but only after prolonged use. Or maybe the low-potency marijuana of years past wasn't a gateway, but today's high-potency marijuana is."[27]

Wonder Drug?

While states relaxed their marijuana penalties, cannabis advocates redoubled their efforts to highlight the drug's medical usefulness. A study published in 2014 found a surprising negative correlation in medical-marijuana laws and opiate-related mortality. States that had legalized medical marijuana reported 25 percent fewer opiate overdose deaths between 2006 and 2010 than states that had not. Cornell psychiatry professor Richard Friedman speculates that this outcome may have had to do with the use of cannabis as a comparatively safe painkiller. "Having legal access to cannabis as another option for pain relief," he writes, "may actually reduce consumption of opiates."[28] In September 2015, the *New Republic* magazine published a cover article by Elizabeth Bruenig titled "The Wonder Drug." The article zeroed in on cannabidiol, an active compound that occurs naturally in the cannabis plant but doesn't produce the psychoactive effects of THC. Research conducted in the 1970s indicated that plant-derived CBD reduced the frequency and severity of seizures. Anecdotal evidence and early, informal clinical studies suggested that CBD could be a miracle cure for intractable forms of childhood epilepsy— seizure disorders that for centuries have ruined lives and shattered families. And since CBD is "plant-derived and native to the brain's own chemistry," it seemed to be an especially appealing natural treatment option. "In online forums and news articles," Bruenig writes, "CBD has been hailed as a new frontier in epilepsy treatment, with parents testifying that it managed to stop their children's seizures when nothing else could." As Bruenig notes, between 2013 and 2015 seventeen states passed legislation legalizing CBD to allow patients to get the medication "without fear of prosecution from local authorities."[29]

In 2013, after a CNN documentary titled *Weed* profiled CBD's effectiveness with seizures, demand for "hemp oil products exploded." In fact, CNN's senior medical correspondent, Dr. Sanjay Gupta, announced on the air that, in the course of researching for the documentary, he had shifted his stance on pot. Only a few years earlier, Gupta had published a piece in *Time* titled "Why I Would Vote No on Pot." Now, he said, "I am here to apologize. I mistakenly believed the Drug Enforcement Agency listed marijuana as a Schedule I substance because of sound scientific proof." In fact, Gupta explained, despite the DEA's denials, pot had "very legitimate medical applications." At times marijuana is the "only thing that works."[30]

Bruenig contended that CBD's potential for treating some illnesses was "yet another argument in favor of legalizing the entire cannabis plant." Taking cannabis off the Schedule I designation would allow scientists to research its "full medical potential." It would also allow pharmaceutical entities to develop cannabis-based drugs and eventually get them approved by the FDA and on the market. Regulated laboratories could test products like hemp oil for quality. And lastly, "Doctors could prescribe marijuana-based medicines with full knowledge of potential side effects and drug interactions, and without fear of losing their medical licenses or being thrown in jail."[31]

In August 2016, the DEA, in coordination with findings issued by the secretary of health and human services, denied two congressional petitions to reschedule marijuana because it "did not meet the criteria" for currently accepted medical use, had a high potential for abuse, and was unsafe in medical application.[32]

Referenda

All told, twenty-three states permitted marijuana use for one or more purposes in 2016, often through referenda.[33] Republican presidential candidate Donald Trump's stunning upset victory over Democratic rival Hillary Clinton on November 8 largely overshadowed those pro-cannabis state referenda. Yet when recreational legalization measures passed in California, Nevada, and Massachusetts that night, the proportion of Americans living in states with legal recreational pot jumped from 5 to 20 percent. California came out in favor of recreational use by a solid 56 percent. This nearly matched an unprecedented Gallup poll showing that 60 percent of voters in America supported legalization. The *New York Times* reminded readers that in the late 1960s only about one in ten Californians had backed pot legalization and that the 2016 ballot results reflected the "culmination of decades of campaigning by proponents."[34]

Some critics believed that the fault lay with these tireless public-relations efforts. Kevin Sabet, of the anti-legalization organization Smart Approaches to Marijuana, lamented that legalization in states like Colorado had made pot appear safe. Moreover, he saw another motive behind the campaigns: "There's a lot of money to be made if marijuana is legal, not a lot of money to be made if it remains illegal."[35]

Legalization activists, on the hand, touted the moves as steps toward greater personal freedom, social justice, and fairness—given the disproportionate arrests and convictions of minority populations in drug cases. *New York Times* columnist Timothy Egan concluded that, while "not without its problems," cannabis legalization had been "mostly no big deal" and overall an important step toward a more sensible drug policy.[36] And certainly the subsequent successful recreational and medicinal legalization campaigns in a slew of states— including deep red ones like Utah and Oklahoma—reinforced the apparent shift to a nation of "red, white, blue, and green."[37]

There is merit to both perspectives. Cannabis has a clinically documented medical use, and further research is likely to reveal more. The drug is not nearly as onerous in its physical, emotional, and social harms as opiates or amphetamines. Given the ubiquity of its consumption in the United States, its outright prohibition as a Schedule I substance is heavy-handed, and the punitive consequences attached to it have caused disproportionate and often unnecessary harm to individual lives and communities, especially among racial minorities and the economically disadvantaged.

But the topic is not quite so one-sided as that. Cannabis does have both psychoactive effects and a potential for abuse that make some sort of regulation appealing on commonsense grounds. The general scientific consensus is that somewhere between 5 and 10 percent of cannabis users report the drug causing problems at home, school, or work or a "reduction in social, occupational, or recreational activities." Addiction expert Roger Hoffman at the University of Washington described it this way: "Most people who use pot occasionally do not become dependent. But that doesn't mean it's impossible to become dependent on pot." He continued, "There are many excellent reasons to legalize marijuana. But it is not a harmless drug."[38]

For many centrist observers, the shifts in public opinion and state law regarding cannabis in the first decades of the twenty-first century seemed to show that marijuana prohibition had "broken down, probably beyond repair." Whether this was indeed the case (or rightly the case), one thing that was in-disputable was that legalizing pot on a state-by-state basis was increasing dis-parities among the states themselves. It remained a troubling contradiction that a licit activity in California or Massachusetts "could lead to life-ruining consequences for somebody just across the state line."[39]

California Haze

In states that legalized, ceaseless press reports touted "happy days" for the weed industry. In Colorado, sales jumped from an estimated $1.5 billion in 2013 to $2.7 billion a year later. One study reckoned the sum would hit $35 billion by 2020. *National Geographic* ran a sympathetic cover story in June 2015 titled "Weed: The New Science of Marijuana." One reporter described the "green rush" as "the next great reversal of history." The *Wall Street Journal* sent reporter Zusha Elinson to the "piney" Mendocino town of Albion, which local growers had begun to call the "Bordeaux of cannabis." Elinson's front-page article described the setting to *Journal* readers. "The cool, marine air that blankets the Mendocino coast gives the marijuana here a distinctive 'fresh, earthy taste.' " Cannabis growers were applying to their own efforts the notion of "terroir," the idea that "unique climate, soil and farming practices influence agricultural crops. It stretches back centuries to the grape-growing monks of Burgundy, France, who, legend has it, tasted the soil in an effort to demarcate different wine regions."[40]

Farther south, the "rough-edged community" of Adelanto in the high des-ert northeast of Los Angeles was hoping to become a "very different type of pot mecca." As the California recreational referendum loomed in the fall of 2016, Adelanto mayor Richard Kerr anticipated rows of "high-tech grow houses" rising in the "flat expanse of desert" and producing more than a hundred tons of cannabis—bringing with it an estimated $10 million in tax revenue, equal to the city's current budget. All told, in 2019 legal cannabis was one of the fastest-growing industries in America—employing as many as 300,000 peo-ple in total—with jobs spanning from harvesting plants on farms to executive management.[41]

On the cutting edge of medical cannabis in the 1990s, California was now attempting to "pull marijuana out of the black market." California's medical marijuana sales in 2015 alone were $2.7 billion—accounting for about half of all legal pot sales in America and already the world's largest legal pot market. In

2016, the DEA estimated that as much as 60 percent of the cannabis consumed in the United States, legally or otherwise, was grown in California. Some observers expected recreational legalization to cause the market to double by 2020.[42] The *New York Times* had this to say about the looming green gold rush:

> After decades of thriving in legally hazy backyards and basements, California's most notorious crop, marijuana, is emerging from the underground into a decidedly capitalist era. The opening of the marijuana industry here to corporate dollars has caused a mad scramble, with out-of-state investors, cannabis retailers and financially struggling municipalities all racing to grab a piece of what is effectively a new industry in California: legalized, large-scale marijuana farming.[43]

Desperate to hit tax pay dirt, cities like Adelanto were scrambling to issue permits for commercial marijuana production. Land prices "tripled almost overnight" as investors bought "every inch" of real estate where cannabis production would be permitted. In Desert Hot Springs, California, a medical cannabis holding company, CalCann Holdings, expected to bring "modern agricultural techniques" to the high desert to spur the production of eight thousand pounds of pot annually. Here is how one CalCann employee explained the new dynamics: "We're transitioning out of the complete free-for-all, wild West. It will be like alcohol—you can't just set up a still and produce it in your garage. You have to apply for permits and pay taxes." Tommy Chong, one half of the "Cheech and Chong" stoner comedy franchise, was talking to a company in Adelanto about how to "mass produce" his brand of cannabis, "Chong's Choice." Chong, seventy-seven, told the *Times*, "If conglomerates come in, my answer is: God bless 'em—it saves me the hassle." At the same time, recreational pot legalization was not the panacea that some reform advocates had predicted. As the sixth such state to implement recreational cannabis, in early 2019, a year into the experiment, California was estimated to annually consume 2.5 million pounds of pot, while still producing a whopping 15.5 million pounds—with the excess, roughly a dozen times Colorado's annual growth total, being "smuggled eastward" to more lucrative markets in the eastern half of the country (one pound of legal pot was selling for $1,183 in the Golden State, while it fetched just over $3,000 in New England). Pot proponents, to be sure, see this California plant exporting not as a bug but a benefit of legalization, with supply meeting demand in a legal and regulated market.[44]

Such corporatization of weed opened up a Pandora's box of new regulatory questions. One was related to the environmental impact of large-scale cannabis plantings—exactly one of the concerns that had motivated Operation Mountain Sweep just four years earlier. Scientists from the California Department of Fish and Wildlife studying northern California's Emerald Triangle found that marijuana cultivators required more water than streams could provide during "low-flow" seasons in three major watersheds. Moreover, illicit cultivators frequently used banned pesticides and fertilizers, which ended up in local streams and rivers, decimating fish populations. Environmental regulators were soon tasked with defining criteria for issuing water permits to licit growers. In 2015 California passed the Medical Marijuana Regulation and Safety Act, which required various state agencies to create lists of requirements for regulations related to their spheres of governance.[45]

But these more mundane policymaking concerns were soon overshadowed by a major reversal at the federal level. On January 4, 2018, Trump's attorney general Sessions rolled back the Obama-era "bigger fish to fry" approach to dealing with state-level legalization in a memorandum that advised, "In deciding which marijuana activities to prosecute under these laws with the Department's finite resources, prosecutors should follow the well-established principles that govern all federal prosecutions." Those principles, he averred, "reflect Congress's determination that marijuana is a dangerous drug and that marijuana activity is a serious crime." In March 2017, Sessions had told an audience of law enforcement officials that marijuana was "slightly less awful than heroin" and that "using drugs will destroy your life."[46]

The upshot was that federal prosecutors now faced a political imperative to shut down grow operations and state-sanctioned distribution facilities and to enforce federal possession laws that had generally been back-burner priorities for DAs and law enforcement alike. Legislators on both sides of the aisle swiftly condemned the move, with one staunch Republican calling it "regrettable and disruptive" and another, "heartless and cold." The *Washington Post* (perhaps hopefully) conjectured that "the end result of this policy could well be to *accelerate* the liberalization of the nation's marijuana laws," given that more than 60 percent of Americans favored legalization in the latest Gallup poll. While many observers believed that the ruling was "unlikely to result in arrests of small-time marijuana users," it seemed almost inevitable that crackdowns would push a now far more robust and well capitalized market underground.[47]

24 • Big Tobacco

Thirteen hundred people die from smoking every day. Imagine three jumbo jets crashing every single day with no survivors. But because this happens slowly and quietly, thirty or forty years after people start smoking, we no longer notice and we no longer care.
—Dr. David Abrams, College of Global Public Health, New York University

Tobacco's Discontents

If the modern regulatory history of cannabis has a mirror image, it is that of tobacco. It is our central objective in this chapter to see the uneven, cynical, and outright hypocritical evolution of this legal but still addictive and harmful drug. What's more, seeing how citizens and politicians have combatted the tobacco scourge will give us valuable context for other campaigns against other substances. Lastly, Big Tobacco's legacy as a once wildly successful corporate special interest in an industry dedicated to a single product that killed many of its users—who used it as intended—provides further insights.

To get started, jump back in time a half century. After a consumption peak in 1963, the year when Americans smoked a record 523 billion cigarettes, evidence began to stack up against the industry. Medical research over the previous two decades had found correlations between tobacco and low birth weight, emphysema, and heart disease, to name some of the more pernicious maladies. Scientists demonstrated that cigarettes were much more addictive and dangerous than cigars. Following the first reported connection between smoking and lung cancer in 1939, the critical causal link emerged in 1957 in the

United Kingdom and several years later in America. Stronger medical evidence linking cigarettes to lung cancer began to appear throughout the 1950s. As David Courtwright explains, the industry did not take the news well: "Tobacco executives hated the pioneer cancer researchers. They hated them for selfish reasons, because they threatened their profits, but also for sentimental ones, because they spoiled the 'innocent' pleasure people took in cigarettes. America in 1950 was a smoker's paradise. The haze was so thick in New York's legendary Birdland nightclub that the canaries behind the bar died within weeks of its opening. Social custom and the millions invested in advertising over the years had fostered an ideal mind-set for smoking." As late as 1955, a physician in New York City contended that there were "no scientific grounds for believing smoking harmful. All I can say is, if I had a spare $2,000 kicking around, I would still invest it in cigarettes." In the 1950s Americans were buying nearly fifteen thousand cigarettes each *second*. And global production totaled over eight billion pounds each year.[1]

On January 11, 1964, Surgeon General Luther L. Terry, M.D., published the innocuous-sounding first report of the Surgeon General's Advisory Committee on Smoking and Health. Here is the report's central contention: "Pathologists and laboratory scientists confirmed the statistical relationship of smoking to lung cancer as well as to other serious diseases, such as bronchitis, emphysema, and coronary heart disease. Smoking, these studies suggested, and not air pollution, asbestos contamination, or radioactive materials, was the chief cause of the epidemic rise of lung cancer in the twentieth century." The contention was based on research published in thousands of medical articles, mostly over the previous decade. The report determined that smoking caused lung cancer in men and was a "probable cause" for lung cancer in women. It called for "appropriate remedial action" but did not list specifics. In 1958, 44 percent of Americans believed smoking caused cancer; by 1968 that figure had leaped to 78 percent.[2]

The following year, Congress acted by passing a law requiring cigarette boxes to carry a health warning; four years later Congress outlawed cigarette ads on television and radio. On the Centers for Disease Control and Prevention (CDC) website, one finds the plausible claim that the ensuing anti-smoking campaign was a success "with few parallels in the history of public health."[3]

It is likely that 1964 marked the inflection point for tobacco consumption in the United States; the rate declined from half a pack per adult each day in the 1960s to a third of a pack in the early 1990s. Tobacco companies were forced to look for new markets to stay afloat. In addition to expanding abroad, tobacco companies also sought out adolescent smokers to replace those who had quit or died. Although the industry denied it pursued this strategy, skeptics contended that confidential internal correspondence proved the contrary. One R. J. Reynolds memo from 1975 stated: "To ensure increased longer-term growth for CAMEL FILTER, the brand must increase its share penetration among the 14–24 age group, which have a new set of more liberal values and which represent tomorrow's cigarette business." Brown and Williamson, a large U.S. tobacco company, counseled one cigarette manufacturer: "To the best of your ability (considering some legal restraints), relate the cigarette to 'pot,' wine, beer, sex, etc. Don't communicate health or related points."[4]

The early 1970s witnessed the arrival of a grassroots movement to advocate for smoking abstinence. These activists drew inspiration from the 1960s civil rights movement and environmental protection organizations in their claims about "innocent victims of tobacco smoke" and the "right to breathe clean air" versus the "right of the smoker to enjoy a harmful habit." Interestingly, at this time there was little documented medical understanding of the harms of secondhand smoke. Groups like Smoke Watchers, Quit Now, and Control of Smoking promised smokers a path out of their wicked, costly habit. The sheer popularity of smoking at the time made public health advocates "reluctant to portray smokers as addicts or as presenting a threat to society." Or as Richard Nixon's public health aide, Jerome H. Jaffe, pointed out, "The major difference between tobacco dependence and other drug addictions is tobacco's social acceptability." Nevertheless, in part as a response to activism, the federal government restricted smoking to the rear 20 percent of buses and to distinct smoking sections on domestic aircraft. In 1973, Arizona became the first state to pass bans on smoking in public.[5]

Joseph Califano Jr., President Jimmy Carter's secretary of the Department of Health, Education, and Welfare, labeled cigarettes "Public Health Enemy Number 1" and "slow motion suicide." Writing in a 1979 report, Califano cast a new emphasis on the financial cost associated with the habit, "Why, the reader may nevertheless ask, should government involve itself in any effort to broadcast these facts and to discourage cigarette smoking? . . . Why, indeed? For one reason, because the consequences are not simply personal and private. Those consequences, economic and medical, affect not only the smoker, but every taxpayer." As the evidence and official government pronouncements reinforced the linkage between smoking and cancer (including through secondhand exposure), the tobacco industry labored to undermine the findings and recommendations. One "orchestrated campaign" designed to discredit a

Japanese study on secondhand smoke involved "arranging critical letters to the editor of the *British Medical Journal,* which published the paper, commissioned research with the intent of obtaining findings that would point to bias in the study, and even newspaper advertisements discrediting such findings."[6]

Tobacco Siege

A further point of contention between the industry and would-be regulators had to do with tobacco's addictiveness. For most of the twentieth century, tobacco companies had successfully promoted the idea that cigarette smoking was "no different than compulsive potato chip eating." But in 1988, the surgeon general issued an unequivocal judgment in a 618-page report: "The short answer is that cigarettes are addicting." In reality, the industry had known this was the case for several years, based on its own internal research. (William I. Campbell of Philip Morris later testified that on multiple occasions he had worked to prevent publication of a study on rats that indicated nicotine's addictive properties.) In 1987, Scott Stath, a representative of the Tobacco Institute in Washington, D.C., dismissed tobacco's addictiveness with a flourish: "The idea that cigarette smoking is more addictive than cocaine or heroin is ludicrous. The term 'addiction' is a debased coin worth nothing at all. You even see references to viewing sports as addictive." Even so, the report presented a dilemma for manufacturers. The industry launched an effort to discredit the report, while repeating the claim that people became habitual smokers under their own volition.[7]

By the late 1980s, five hundred thousand people were dying prematurely every year from tobacco-related health problems. A key development that attended this damning statistic was the advent of successful personal injury lawsuits against tobacco companies. One salient case, *Cipollone v. Liggett Group, Inc.,* involved a smoker in New Jersey who developed lung cancer. The plaintiffs relied on internal tobacco company files to demonstrate that Liggett had kept what it knew about the cancer link from the public eye. In pursuit at the same time were state governments seeking to be compensated for Medicaid expenses related to treating sick smokers. In 1988, after five years of litigation, the Tobacco Master Settlement Agreement (MSA) was finalized between the four largest American tobacco companies (Philip Morris Inc., R. J. Reynolds, Brown & Williamson, and Lorillard) and attorney generals from forty-six states. The legal process resulted in "tens of millions of pages" of "internal memoranda, reports, and other tobacco company documents" made available to the public. The agreement required tobacco companies to pay, in perpetuity, annual payments to cover smoking-related health expenses. The MSA tab for Big Tobacco for the first twenty-five years alone was $200 billion. The MSA also added more restrictions, such as a ban on billboard advertising.[8]

The backlash against the tobacco industry culminated in a series of congressional hearings in which senior executives struggled against the limits of credibility to keep up the company line. A headline in the *New York Times* on April 15, 1994, read, "Tobacco Chiefs Say Cigarettes Aren't Addictive." While the top executives from all of the half-dozen or so largest tobacco firms testified that they did not believe their product was addictive, they acknowledged that they would prefer that their own children abstain from using it. After one CEO stated that all sorts of products like candy or soda were addictive, Democrat Henry Waxman, who chaired the House Subcommittee on Health and the Environment, jumped in, "Yes, but the difference between cigarettes and Twinkies is death." Waxman also asked, "How many smokers die each year from cancer?" James W. Watson of R. J. Reynolds replied that he couldn't be sure, as the numbers were "generated by computers and are only statistical." Waxman asked Lorillard Tobacco Company's Andrew H. Tisch if he was aware of the link between cancer and smoking. "I do not believe that," was his response. Waxman continued the inquisition: "Do you understand how isolated you are from the scientific community in your belief?" Indeed, by the late 1990s, the science overwhelmingly attested that smoking tobacco was the "most widespread and lethal form of addiction in the world." And, in contrast to many other substances, there was no way to remove the danger.[9]

From the perspective of the drug war, what's noteworthy about this attack on tobacco is that the drug's critics claimed little desire to ban cigarettes entirely. Instead, they emphasized, "some way ought to be found" to use regulation to mitigate cigarettes' myriad harms. Press accounts cited anonymous tobacco industry leaders who acknowledged a willingness to allow for certain restrictions, such as capping the amount of tar and nicotine permitted in each cigarette. A decade later in 2006, the U.S. Department of Justice won a court ruling (*United States v. Philip Morris*) that concluded that "the industry had marketed and sold their lethal products with zeal, with deception, with a single-minded focus on their financial success, and without regard for the human tragedy or social costs that success exacted." As one researcher noted, Big Tobacco became the only legal industry to have been "pursued and convicted under federal racketeering statutes." To soften the impending blow, tobacco companies such as Philip Morris publicly supported federal regulation and in doing so managed to secure seats at the negotiating table to help guide legislation on the industry's governance. In 2009, the FDA assumed regulatory oversight of all tobacco products in the United States.[10]

"It's Like There's Two Worlds Now"

In the latter half of the twentieth century, tobacco consumption dropped dramatically among the educated classes in America and western Europe. Following the regulatory sweep in the 1990s, between 1995 and 2015 the U.S. smoking rate dropped from 25 percent to 15 percent. And this reduction translated into a 37 percent decrease in cigarettes sold. In 2017, half of all Americans who once smoked had kicked the habit, although 45 million continued to light up. Ironically, the United States, headquarters to many of the global tobacco conglomerates, had become a "nonsmoking island in a worldwide ocean of puffers."[11]

American tobacco companies responded to this demand shock in at least three ways. For one, they expanded abroad, particularly in developing nations. British American Tobacco, the top British exporter (originally formed as a joint venture between Duke and Britain's Imperial Tobacco), was "growing aggressively" in these regions, including in the former Eastern bloc. The fall of the Berlin Wall, wrote BAT's Sir Patrick Sheehy, sparked "the most exciting times I have seen in the tobacco industry in the last 40 years." American firms were not apt to be left behind. The most aggressive of the American lot, Philip Morris, started selling twice as much tobacco abroad as at home. At the turn of the century, each year more than 1.1 billion smokers—a third of the population over age fifteen—smoked 5.5 trillion cigarettes. In 2015, the World Health Organization predicted that unless drastic preventive measures were adopted, more than 100 million individuals worldwide would die from tobacco-related disease over the next three decades.[12]

Deftly, the tobacco giants vigorously pursued the remaining "demographic bases" in America that resisted the anti-smoking shift: non-urban, low income, and less educated. These groups continued to smoke at rates of over 40 percent. Meanwhile, richer and better-educated Americans were "largely spared the cost and deadly effects of the vice." It appeared that, in a more unequal American society, smoking was a symptom of deeper societal problems in this age of the Great Unraveling. Residents in upscale enclaves from Santa Monica to Brooklyn might go several days without seeing a smoker. But in, say, rural Martinsville, Virginia, cigarettes were everywhere. As William Wan described, "People smoke on their morning drive to work and on weekends mowing their lawns. Tobacco stores line the strip malls, and cigarette ads are in the windows of every gas station and convenience store." A local social worker, Debbie Seals, offered an explanation: "People down here smoke because of the stress in their life. . . . They smoke because of money problems, family problems. It's the one thing they have control over. The one thing that makes them feel better. And you want them to give that up? That's the toughest thing in the world." Meanwhile, nonprofits and the CDC released advertisements contending that Big Tobacco was targeting the poor, minorities, Native Americans, and even the mentally ill—thus making the tobacco question an issue of social justice.[13]

Finally, American tobacco companies widened their margins by *increasing* their prices by about 32 percent, pumping up revenue by a roughly equivalent amount, as in 2016, when tobacco companies added an additional $93.4 billion to the bottom line. The price of a pack of cigarettes averaged $6.42 that same year, an increase from $3.73 fifteen years earlier. An article on the front page of the *Wall Street Journal* on April 24, 2017, explained how a "flurry of consolidation" had cut the American tobacco industry from seven "big players" to only two: Altria and Reynolds American, Inc.—which now held 80 percent of the domestic market. Incredibly, despite the financial setbacks of the massive punitive legal settlements, the industry's operating profits swelled by over 75 percent between 2006 and 2016, to $18.4 billion. While the six-dollar pack came with a bite of 40 percent in taxes, the rate was well below that in other countries, such as Britain, where an 82 percent tax put the per-pack cost just under $11. The industry also benefited from First Amendment protections that shielded it from having to publish the more aggressive, graphic—and thus effective—warnings that other countries mandated. In Britain, Peru, and Australia, to name a few, cigarettes were sold in somber packs with graphic images and warnings about health implications from cancer to blindness to impotence. For the consolidated firms, the American market was "attractive again." In 2016, this country's smokers funded the world's second most profitable tobacco market—just behind China's state-run system.[14]

Back during the big settlement, the keenest industry observers had concluded, logically, that the U.S. tobacco industry "may be teetering . . . on the edge of distress, if not bankruptcy." As Phil Angelides, the California state treasurer who led the state's public employee's retirement fund tobacco divestment effort, contended, Big Tobacco "was on its knees." Yet the settlement also cemented a floor for American tobacco's legal liabilities—and thus sharply cut fiscal risk. In total, the tobacco industry coughed up just under $120 billion. The industry realized that it could pass along a significant share of its settlement obligations to current and future customers—to the tune of about 69 cents a pack.[15]

Big Tobacco Tells People to Quit Smoking

As I was researching this chapter in 2017, I went to the Philip Morris International website. I wasn't sure what sort of branding I'd come across, but I did not expect to see a large banner claiming that the company was "Designing a Smoke-Free Future." The official website's home page touted a "common-sense approach for Public Health."

It seemed that the industry saw an opportunity in alternative delivery systems for nicotine—perhaps owing to regulatory uncertainty and steadily diminishing demand. (By 2019, electronic cigarettes and related vaporizers—basically nicotine delivery devices without "the tar, the carbon monoxide, the garbage mouth, the smell" of a cigarette—was a multi-billion dollar market, even though it was still dwarfed by its cigarette cousin. Contrary to what we often assume, nicotine does not cause cancer. For cigarettes, it is the arsenal of carcinogenic substances that kill us.) For its part, Philip Morris had been hard at work in its research center in Switzerland to find, as one British news account put it, "cigarette substitutes that will sell—but not kill." It was a worthy ambition indeed, considering that smoking still killed about six million people a year. Of course, the industry continued to rely on "old-fashioned cigarettes to sustain their profits" and fund the R&D program. Philip Morris's CEO Andre Calantzopoulos reinforced the gradual conversion strategy: "We can't stop cold turkey." Not surprisingly, many critics were not convinced that Big Tobacco and its $770 billion worldwide industry had mended its ways. According to the chief of the U.S.-based Campaign for Tobacco-Free Kids, "Given their history, no one should ever trust what a tobacco company says it intends to do."[16]

25 • Psychedelics 2.0

Barriers to Entry

Psychedelics were another emerging front in the war over the war on drugs in the mid-2010s. Most psychedelic substances, including LSD, mescaline, MDMA, and psilocybin, had been Schedule I–listed since 1970, when a blanket prohibition in the Controlled Substances Act criminalized the use, possession, and sale of hallucinogens. The scheduling imposed significant barriers to scientific research on the substances and their effects, through stringent security requirements, FDA approval, and expensive DEA licensing fees for institutions working with the drugs. For decades, researchers found it virtually impossible to secure licenses. In 1989, the FDA created the Pilot Drug Evaluation Staff, which made it easier for the scientific community to liaise with the administration. One of the first researchers to take advantage of the opening was Dr. Richard Strassman, who managed to get a research protocol involving DMT and psilocybin off the ground. He defended his work by arguing that hallucinogens "elicit a multifaceted clinical syndrome, affecting many of the functions that characterise the human mind, including affect, cognition, interoception, and perception. Characterising hallucinogens' properties will enhance understanding of important mind-brain relationships. . . . Second, naturally occurring psychotic syndromes share features with those elicited by these drugs. Understanding effects and mechanisms of action of hallucinogens may provide novel insights and treatments in endogenous psychoses." Yet, just as the drugs' scheduling seemed to show little signs of change in the twenty-first century, the same held true for overall public perception. Only 0.5 percent of respondents in the National Survey on Drug Use and Health in 2013 said they had used hallucinogens in the previous month.

In public opinion polls, Americans remained strikingly unreceptive to hallucinogens as late as 2014, with more than 60 percent opposing the legalization of all psychedelics and only 9 percent favoring legalization of LSD.[1]

Indeed, among the many battles of the drug war, psychedelics represented a minor skirmish. Nevertheless, it bears some scrutiny, given trends in clinical research with these substances that indicated potential grounds for reconsidering their medical relevance. Although it was far too early to draw any conclusions about a new status of psychedelics in the American consciousness, it is good to remember that the shift on cannabis began in medical research labs.

"Xanax Isn't the Answer"

Dr. Roland Griffiths carved out an expertise in the field of abuse potential in drugs. His reputation in working with mood-altering substances helped win approval to conduct psychedelic experiments that had been banned for thirty years. One government-sanctioned study, which began in 2001 and came out in 2006, involved dozens of volunteers, whom Griffiths asked to recline "on a comfy couch in an architecturally challenged building on Johns Hopkins' stark medical campus in North Baltimore." He then instructed each volunteer to ingest a pill; for some the pill contained a negligible placebo dose for experimental control. For others, the capsule contained up to 30 milligrams of psilocybin. Griffiths later described to Tom Shroder the reactions of subjects: "What I wasn't prepared for is people would come in two months later and I would say, 'Well, so what do you think of the experience?' And they'd say . . . 'It was one of the most important experiences in my life.' " More than 70 percent of the volunteers, Griffiths concluded, considered the psychedelic trip one of the most important moments in their lives; fully a third believed it was the most meaningful moment of their lives. Griffiths said, "My initial response was kind of disbelief. It just doesn't sound right, does it?" His conjecture is that psilocybin acts as a kind of "inverse P.T.S.D."—"a discrete event that produces persisting positive changes in attitudes, moods, and behavior, and presumably in the brain."[2]

As the sage food writer Michael Pollan explained in an extended essay in the *New Yorker* in 2015, clinical trials using psilocybin were a key segment of a "renaissance of psychedelic research." Another study had demonstrated that cancer patients treated with psilocybin experienced an easing of their dread of death. A former researcher at Johns Hopkins told Pollan: "A high-dose psychedelic experience is death practice. You're losing everything you know to be real, letting go of your ego and your body, and that process can feel like dying." Pollan expanded, "Yet patients do not die. On the contrary, some patients come to believe that consciousness may somehow survive the death of their bodies." Researchers sense that the "psychedelic experience" aids users by reducing the dominance of an imperious ego and the "rigid, habitual thinking" it demands. In this telling, the ego can be one's own devil, a phenomenon most apparent in depression, "when the self turns on itself and uncontrollable introspection gradually shades out reality." Pollan met with researchers from New York University who seemed unusually surprised and excited about the study results. Dr. Stephen Ross revealed, "I thought the first ten or twenty people were plants—that they must be faking it. They were saying things like 'I understand love is the most powerful force on the planet,' or 'I had an encounter with my cancer, this black cloud of smoke.' People who had been palpably scared of death—they lost their fear. The fact that a drug given once can have such an effect for so long is an unprecedented finding. We have never had anything like it in the psychiatric field."[3]

Another researcher called the preliminary results "mind-blowing." "People don't realize how few tools we have in psychiatry to address existential distress. Xanax isn't the answer. So how can we not explore this, if it can recalibrate how we die?" As we learned earlier in the book, psychedelic research flourished in the 1950s. After tens of thousands of doses of such drugs were administered, a medical consensus formed that these substances could be "of utmost value in psychotherapy." After extensive recreational use outside the clinical laboratory in the 1960s sparked a government crackdown, a tiny community of researchers still held on to the "belief that psychedelic drugs were too potentially valuable to be discarded."[4]

Pollan explained that many of the clinical volunteers report psychedelic experiences that differed from normal dreams:

> For one thing, most people's recall of their journey is not just vivid but comprehensive, the narratives they reconstruct seamless and fully accessible, even years later. They don't regard these narratives as "just a dream," the evanescent products of fantasy or wish fulfillment, but, rather, as genuine and sturdy experiences. This is the "noetic" quality that students of mysticism often describe: the unmistakable sense that whatever has been learned or witnessed has the authority and the durability of objective truth. "You don't get that on other drugs," as Roland Griffiths points out; after the fact, we're fully aware of, and often embarrassed by, the inauthenticity of the drug experience.[5]

Steve Jobs considered "dropping acid" one of the most indispensable experiences of his entire life. "LSD shows you that there's another side to the coin," he said, "and you can't remember it when it wears off, but you know it." It might have even been a source of Jobs's brilliance, "a way of decoding inputs and stimuli that allowed him to—as the billboards used to say—'think different.' " In 2015, Daniel Kottke, a friend of Jobs, recalled their LSD trips as actually fairly quotidian—basically just two "monk-wannabes" who would, say, go on long walks to discuss higher beings.[6]

The Drug of Choice for the Age of Kale

A 2016 profile of the explosion in Americans experimenting with naturally occurring psychedelics suggested that if cocaine manifested the "speedy, greedy ethos of the nineteen-eighties," then ayahuasca—a drug also listed Schedule I since the Controlled Substances Act of 1970—reflected the present "Age of Kale." As the writer Ariel Levy put it, "It is a time characterized by wellness cravings, when many Americans are eager for things like mindfulness, detoxification, and organic produce, and we are willing to suffer for our soulfulness." Levy cheekily told her readers that ayahuasca, "like kale, is no joy ride." The drug is prepared as a tea brewed from the *Banisteriopsis caapi* vine native to Amazon rainforests; its active ingredient is *N,N*-Dimethyltryptamine, or DMT. Ayahuasca became a subject of clinical curiosity in the 1970s after Harvard biologist Richard Evans Schultes, one of the originators of the field of ethnobotany, received a few specimens of the plant from one of his graduate students. As one devotee tells it, "Ayahuasca takes you to the swampland of your soul."[7]

Here is Vaughn Bergen, a twenty-seven-year-old art gallery professional in New York City describing one of his trips: "I came home reeking of vomit and sage and looking like I'd come from hell. Everyone was trying to talk me out of doing it again. My girlfriend at the time was, like, 'Is this some kind of sick game?' I was, like, 'No. I'm growing.' " And the next trip was ethereal. "I got transported to a higher dimension, where I lived the whole ceremony as my higher self. Anything I thought came to be." Bergen told Levy that almost all of the "ceremonies" he participated in were disturbing, but he expected to use ayahuasca for his remaining time on earth. "He believes that it will heal not only him but civilization at large."[8]

Bergen was not alone is his fervor. One "self-help guru" in San Francisco explained ayahuasca's ubiquity in his city. "Ayahuasca is like having a cup of coffee here. I have to avoid people at parties because I don't want to listen to their latest three-hour saga of kaleidoscopic colors." A researcher at the University of Washington School of Medicine, Leanna Standish, asked the FDA for permission to conduct a "Phase I" clinical trial related to the drug's ability to treat cancer and Parkinson's disease. "I am very interested in bringing this ancient medicine from the Amazon Basin into the light of science," she said. "It's going to change the face of Western medicine." Even still, in 2018 the drug's swelling use constituted a "vast, unregulated global experiment."[9]

A Little Green Capsule

Upon returning from Iraq in 2006, veteran Jon Lubecky discovered that his wife had permanently left him, taking his dog and his motorcycle with her. Shattered, Lubecky drank heavily and battled insomnia each night. Veterans Administration doctors prescribed conventional anti-depressants that failed to treat the horror show of his post-traumatic stress disorder. He attempted suicide five times. In the last of these gruesome episodes, Lubecky "put the muzzle of his Beretta to his temple and pulled the trigger." Fortunately, the gun failed to go off. And in that "microsecond after the hammer fell," the Army vet was overtaken by a surreal sense that everything would turn out okay. A few weeks later, Lubecky enrolled in an experimental trial in which he took a "little green capsule" that ended his suffering.[10]

The brains of patients taking a pure dose of MDMA experience a surge of the neurotransmitters serotonin, dopamine, and norepinephrine: "A loved one's touch suddenly feels like it transmits their love directly through your skin. Rhythmic beats and aesthetically pleasing sights become completely enthralling." This unparalleled ability to "flood users with intense feelings of euphoria" is what made MDMA the in-house designer drug at club parties. But, as emerging clinical studies showed, the drug could also be an effective aid in unraveling the tangle of combat-induced PTSD. More specifically, the flood of neurotransmitters allowed users to engage traumatic memories more fully. As Sara Chodosh has written, "Biologically speaking, every time you engage a memory, you're re-experiencing it. The set of neurons that encodes that memory are all firing the same way they did when the memory formed. But that means you might have an opportunity to revise the memory every time you recall it: because the original neurons are firing, they're more susceptible to making new connections or strengthening old ones. A fearful memory will stay fearful if you experience the same fear all over again whenever you recall it. MDMA could help rewire that memory. While high on ecstasy, patients don't feel the same pain when resurfacing a scarring memory."[11]

In 2017, the FDA approved MDMA as a "breakthrough therapy," which fast-tracked the testing and review process that all drugs must go through before they can be prescribed and marketed. It was a little curious that a substance with a primarily party-drug reputation and the DEA's most restrictive designation was being touted as a potential miracle therapy. As retired Brigadier General Loree Sutton, the army's highest-ranking psychologist until 2010, explained, "We're in this odd situation where one of the most promising therapies also happens to be a Schedule 1 substance."[12]

Like cannabis, psychedelics have their institutional advocates. The psychedelic analogue to NORML is the Multidisciplinary Association for Psychedelic Studies (MAPS), founded by Rick Doblin in 1986 to promote research on the substances' use in mental-health applications. Doblin, who enjoyed tripping on acid as a "rebellious, long-haired college freshman" in the 1970s, was eager to spread the LSD gospel via therapeutic applications but was stymied by the drug's illegal status. He intentionally selected PTSD as the most strategically promising case for ending the ban on psychedelics. "If you were to design the perfect drug to treat PTSD," the former hippie said, "MDMA would be it. We wanted to help a population that would automatically win public sympathy. No one's going to argue against the need to help them."[13]

MAPS, now headquartered in Santa Cruz, California, started out as Doblin's "one-man band" before swelling to twenty-five staff members. MAPS sourced millions of dollars in seed money from fellow travelers in nearby Silicon Valley. Doblin told the *Washington Post* that it took him decades to see the shortsightedness of the earlier approach to social change on drugs. "The flaw of the early psychedelic movement," he said, "was that they made it countercultural, a revolution. Culture is dominant. Culture is always going to win."[14]

MAPS sponsored a raft of studies on PTSD. Findings from several of those studies were revealed in April 2017 at the Psychedelic Science Conference in Oakland, California. One study assessed participants on a widely accepted scale of self-reported and clinician-observed symptoms, and found that "after two or three sessions of MDMA-assisted therapy, about 67 percent of participants no longer had the illness." The trend held for more than a year after the sessions.[15]

Conclusions

It is impossible to overstate how undeveloped this new phase of psychedelic research still was at the time of writing. Its conclusions, while promising for some patients in certain medical applications, were far from definitive—even if drug war critics and not a few prominent media outlets were quick to jump on these reports as suggesting a new path forward for dealing with drugs. In 2017 and 2018, studies were being developed for Phase III clinical trials, the last step of FDA approval before a drug can be prepared for market. If those results confirm MDMA's effectiveness, they could not only make a valuable therapy available but also clear the way for further investigation into the effects of other psychedelics. This latter development might give the attentive reader pause. If the stories of drugs such as cocaine and synthetic opiates—stories that also originated in clinical labs—have any wisdom to offer, it is that there is always good reason to wonder about the latest "wonder drug."[16]

Aftermath

Admittedly, before I started writing a few years ago I had little, if any, understanding of the surge in clinical research on psychedelics and the myriad illnesses described above. If you had asked me in my twenties or thirties my opinion on whether LSD or magic mushrooms should be legalized, I would have said no—that the harm to brains, especially the adolescents who often experiment with these drugs, was too unknown and too potentially devastating. I mean, just remember all those well-meaning, mostly privileged middle-class kids in the 1960s and 1970s who "turned on, tuned in, and dropped out" and wound up acid heads for years, if not the rest of their lives. Indeed, very much a Generation X kid coming of age in the "Just Say No" era of the Reagan/Bush 1980s, I was an intellectual victim of the Boomer cultural war's catfight era, one that so often seems to seep into our current era. In high school, my mom anxiously urged me to read a wrenching magazine essay of a father mourning the death of his teenaged daughter, who had somehow overdosed on, if I recall correctly, LSD. Although it is still a profound tragedy, I of course know now that it is extraordinarily difficult to overdose from the drug, even if more commonly someone might ingest a different (and more dangerous) substance thinking that it was acid. What's more, even as recently as 2013, writers like the New Yorker's Dorian Rolston were penning pieces titled "A Trip That Doesn't End," reminding readers that "psychedelic lore is littered with cautionary talks." Make no mistake, however, just because you can't overdose on LSD—or any other psychedelic—doesn't mean it's a miracle cure or even that it's safe, especially when made and distributed clandestinely.[17]

This is all a way of saying that not until I read the current research, including Michael Pollan's inimitable meditations and even personal experiences on a variety of psychedelics, did I consider taking one of these drugs for my own chronic PTSD, going back almost two decades. For the first decade or so I did not realize I had the disease, and it only continued to worsen. Over the past five years or so, generally positive strides in my well-being were achieved through, in many fits and starts, a treatment consisting of daily meditation, weekly or monthly psychotherapy, and pharmacological SSRIs (selective serotonin reuptake inhibitors) like the brand-name Zoloft. The use of the latter put me in the company of one in roughly eight Americans over the age of twelve who used an anti-depressant—a 65 percent jump from 1999 to 2014. My treatment also included self-medication with low, irregular doses of psychoactive cannabis and high, daily doses of nonpsychoactive but amazingly powerful CBD oil.[18]

It did not take me long to decide on psilocybin, the naturally produced chemical in certain mushrooms (and the psychoactive ingredients isolated by Albert Hofmann in 1958) as the likely best chemical for my particular type of PTSD. So the first question was where the heck I would find magic mushrooms or a synthesized cousin. (Interestingly, it took over a half century before researchers at Germany's Friedrich Schiller University of Jena discovered how to synthesize it in 2017.)[19]

I signed up for the waiting list for a clinical study at Johns Hopkins—coincidentally, my graduate school alma mater—but no dice in the end. With the Johns Hopkins option no longer on the table, in 2019 I eventually visited a clinic in southern Mexico where I was able to receive three rounds of treatments with increasingly larger doses of psilocybin. At the retreat center, the mostly American and Canadian "facilitators"—including a single feisty female shaman from Seattle—were entirely committed to their vocation of using "plant medicine" to heal people. Throughout the entire experience, there was not even a single intimation that what guests were doing was somehow about partying or getting high. Each round of medicine was consumed as a hot tea mixed with a hunk of raw ginger (to help ease the stomach) in a ceremony filled with music, light, and incense that lasted three to five hours. The methodology was all about letting each participant take the journey privately with love and support all around. It all feels very New Age and hippie, and is thus easy to lampoon, but for me and I think just about everyone one else in my place, the experience was deeply profound and impressive.

Before our group began the first ceremony, I was astounded by the variety of backgrounds and conditions we expressed to each other. There was a young couple from the Pacific Northwest where the wife had severe and recently suicidal depression from her work as a physician's assistant at a pain clinic that was ripping off its mostly indigent patients left and right. A U.S. Army Iraq combat veteran in his thirties wanted to get help with his stress linked to strenuous activities with other PTSD-suffering vets or, as he put it, "men who were simply broken." At least two others described their years of alcoholism before sobriety, including a now seventy-year-old who had first gotten drunk at fifteen but had been off booze since 1985. Remarkable to me, these former alcoholics did not appear to have any interest in drinking or partying whatsoever. But most of them—unlike the vet and physician's assistant who were psychedelic rookies—had taken mushrooms, LSD, or ayahuasca over the years, especially recently. And they were taking these psychedelics because they too had no doubt that the medicines made them more alive, not less.

All three psychedelics were powerfully liberating and reassuring. I saw the stereotypical "light shows" of brilliant colors and images and did not fear them at all. At times I joined in with these dancing bears or Mickey Mouse–like, Technicolor-esque animations, all asking me to be joyous. And as we were reminded, there is nothing wrong with fear, given that confronting this is often where breakthroughs happen. I also knew right then and there that I was going to be "Okay!" and that whatever trauma was in my life and in my mind was part of me and what my life needed to be. The entire retreat's mantra was "the plant is medicine, but everything here and in your life is medicine," which I very much believed. I was also astounded about how, right after the ceremonies would end, I had a feeling of absolute sobriety, a deep clarity of mind and purpose. I had never felt more relaxed in my life, and I was able immediately to dig into a book, meditate, or even journal my novel, life-changing experiences. There was no sense of a booze hangover, or the sense of having three or four beers in an evening when one or two would have been better. I also could not help but wonder about my experiences over the previous several years trying one SSRI after another, suffering their invariably strong side effects (for me at least) of unpredictable fits of sleepiness and chronic gastrointestinal irritation.

In my post-retreat reflections, I had to admit fully that I had indeed greatly benefited from using both psilocybin, a drug illegal in the United States (it was "unenforced for native use" in Mexico), and cannabis, also a key part of my treatment cocktail. What's more, back in North Carolina, I was unable to escape the whiff of irony and even hypocrisy for I—the onetime drug policy warrior (although always with personal doubts about aspects of the drug war)—had come to believe in the healing power of medicinal plants (at least, this medicinal plant). My subsequent course of treatment was to use "micro-doses" of mushrooms, basically 10 percent of a normal dose, which kept me lucid but also calm and energized. As I review the copyediting of this manuscript in late 2019, I am planning on taking the most potent dose yet in a couple of weeks.[20]

Make no mistake, as the proud father of three young boys, I was uncomfortable revealing my newly found medical plant (cannabis and mushrooms) insights and treatments with them—even if they were indispensable to me—lest it somehow make them more inclined to try such drugs, especially recreationally, as youths—which, needless to say, would not be a prudent choice.

In May 2019, by a razor-thin margin of 50.6 to 49.4 percent, Denver became the first city to decriminalize psilocybin.[21]

26 • The Most American Drug

As Long as God Allows It

One of the most chilling scenes in Matthew Heineman's Oscar-nominated documentary *Cartel Land* shows a crew of Mexican methamphetamine cooks standing around a few steaming plastic barrels. One of the cooks explains to the filmmakers his motivation for working in this illicit trade. Here is my translation: "If we were doing well, we'd be just like you. Traveling the world or doing good clean jobs like you guys. But if we start paying attention to our hearts, then we'll get screwed over. It's reacting. . . . We will do this as long as God allows it. As long as He allows it, we will make drugs. And we will make more because this is not going to end, right? What do you think, guys? The good stuff is about to begin."

Until opioid addiction grew into a full-fledged crisis, the scourge drug of twenty-first-century middle America was indisputably methamphetamine. Well into the 1980s, methamphetamine was still widely prescribed and misused across America under brand names like Methedrine and Norodin. A related compound, methylphenidate, was quickly becoming one of the most popular ways to treat attention-deficit disorder and hyperactivity in rambunctious American children—in the form of Ritalin. In the 1990s, more than 15 million Ritalin prescriptions were written, amounting to over 350 million daily doses; 80 percent of those were for children. Meanwhile, illicit meth had remained popular with underground lab cooks and users since the days when it flowed through the counterculture of postwar New York and San Francisco. Critics cheerfully pointed out the hypocrisy of describing Big Pharma manufacturing and selling *legal* amphetamine as capitalism in action, but biker-gang speed as a scourge.[1]

While there are very convincing reasons to believe that doctors overmedi-
cated multiple generations of Americans with amphetamines, the comparison
does trade on a serious misunderstanding. Not all amphetamines are created
equal. Molecularly, methamphetamine and methylphenidate, for instance,
both share an amphetamine "backbone," which sets off a massive release of
the neurotransmitters dopamine and norepinephrine, which in turn causes
spikes in body temperature, heart rate, and blood pressure, producing "heightened alertness, wakefulness, and loss of appetite." However, methamphetamine produces significantly stronger euphoric effects, inducing a much more
intense high and increased addictiveness. Methamphetamine also happens to
be extremely neurotoxic. Extended use can lead to depression, paranoia, and
even some of the "jittery symptoms" associated with Parkinson's disease. As a
result, meth is generally prescribed in lower doses and only after other, safer
therapeutic approaches have been ruled out. Moreover, there is a divergence in
the way that the drugs are taken. Home cooks produce a raw form of meth
designed for injecting, snorting, or smoking. These delivery methods shoot the
drug almost directly into the bloodstream toward the brain, "delivering a bigger, faster rush" than orally ingested pills, which must first pass through the
stomach, the intestines, and the liver, journeys that "take time and dilute the
power of the high."[2]

The popularity of clandestine crystal meth surged in the 1990s, thanks to
two notable properties. "Even as it helps people work hard," as Nick Reding
has written, "whether that means driving a truck or vacuuming the floor, meth
contributes to a feeling that all will be okay, if not exuberantly so." One leading
expert on addiction, neuropharmacologist Stanley Koob, considers methamphetamine to be "way up there with the worst drugs on the planet." Hard
work and euphoria conspire, Koob has explained, to bolster a drug's "social
identity"—the background context guiding its acceptance. "Add to this the
fact that ours is a culture in which the vagaries of hard work are celebrated as
indicators of social worth, and the reasons to do crank are in fact quite often—
initially, at least—more numerous and compelling than the reasons not to do
it." But then comes the kicker: meth's most dangerous physical and psychological effects don't emerge until after a user is addicted. The side effects of
meth use are manifold, including, as Reding recounts, "bleeding skin sores as
your pores struggle to open and expel the drug, which often become infected;
internal organs shrunken from dehydration; vast areas of the brain that according to CAT scans are completely depleted of neurotransmitters: a sense
that a person is literally falling apart from the inside out."[3]

The first state to be hit by the burgeoning meth scourge was Hawaii in the mid-1980s. It then spread to California and, over the next two decades, moved readily eastward "at a pace unrivaled by any other drug in recent times." By the new century, up to a quarter of Americans had used some illegal form of the drug. In his arresting and indispensable book *Methland,* Reding places the development of the meth crisis in the context of a set of profound social trans-formations. Heartland towns, which "for one hundred years had been places of great prosperity," began to unravel with the farming crisis of the 1980s and the concomitant loss of jobs. As traditional centers of livelihood faltered, meth "moved from the controlled environment of corporate campuses to the under-ground production sites of bikers and outlaw chemists. The new form of meth, a drug that has always been popular among men and women doing hard labor, became both purer and vastly more available."[4]

Another factor that made methamphetamine seem almost custom-fit for small-town America was its ease of manufacture. Local cooks typically made meth in small batches, often no more than a few grams at a time. The process required a lithium strip extracted from a battery, a bit of Coleman lantern fuel, anhydrous ammonia (nitrate-rich chemical fertilizer ubiquitous in rural Amer-ica), pseudoephedrine extracted from cold medications like Sudafed and Con-tac, and a "ninth-grade knowledge of chemistry." Lab sites could be set up anywhere from a gas station convenience store to a motel bathroom. Small-time makers relied on what might well have been the least sophisticated supply chain in the history of drug production:

> The first order of business . . . is to amass quantities of cold pills. To do this, cooks generally hire people who will work in exchange for a portion of the product. These people stereotypically ride together in vans from one town to the next, piling into gas stations, Wal-Marts, grocery stores, and pharmacies in order to steal or buy as much cold medicine as they can. They might do one county today, and another tomorrow. If they've been particularly active lately around Oelwein [Iowa], they might run up to Caledonia, Minnesota, hit Decorah and Kendallville, Iowa, on the way, then rob their way home via Prairie du Chien, Wisconsin. Cops across the country, playing on the van element and the fact that the peo-ple riding in them are apt to be acting funny, call the process of amass-ing pills "Smurfing."
>
> Depending on how successful the cook is, he might have his own supply of anhydrous ammonia, which is generally to say that he gets it from a farmer who takes a cut of the profit. For small-timers, though,

stealing is the order of the day. It's dangerous work and a common source of injury. For use as a fertilizer, anhydrous is highly diluted; for use in making crank, it must be gotten in its concentrated form, which is largely done at night and surreptitiously. One common and incredibly hazardous way of getting anhydrous from the heavy, thick-walled steel tanks in which it is stored is to prop the tank legs on bricks and then drill holes just above the settling line of the anhydrous, easily identified, like studs in drywall, by rapping one's knuckles along the tank and listening to the pitch.[5]

Making meth is an extremely dangerous endeavor. Anhydrous ammonia can burn human tissue to the bone. Adding lithium to anhydrous can produce "explosive boiling" if done incorrectly. One method of production involves adding blue iodine to red phosphorous, often producing phosphine gas, "toxic enough to cauterize lung and throat tissue." And, once it's made, meth residue has an uncanny ability to "bind to food, countertops, microwave walls, sink basins, and human lung tissue for days after being synthesized." One Iowa school district famously stopped bake sales after children manifested symptoms from consuming meth-tainted cookies.[6]

By 2005, small-town residents across the country were clamoring for a harder approach to combating the meth scourge. Cheered on by residents, local cops began pulling over male drivers on the smallest pretext in order to find meth. Some citizens pushed back, contending that the police were trampling on civil rights when they ought to be busting the meth labs, which "regularly caught fire in residential neighborhoods, sending toxic plumes of smoke in whatever direction the wind happened to be blowing."[7]

"A Nationwide Epidemic"

By 2005, drug authorities in Washington considered methamphetamine to be the "nation's most serious local drug problem." A federal task force reported that meth was the "most widely used and clandestinely produced synthetic drug" in the country. Meth-related emergencies had surged 420 percent in just a few years. Democratic state representative Brady Wiseman of Montana said, "It is now clearly a nationwide epidemic, and anyone who thinks it isn't hasn't studied the issue." Almost two-thirds of five hundred regional police agencies said that methamphetamine was their most severe drug issue; almost 90 percent cited an increase in meth-linked arrests over the previous three years. Over five thousand "foul smelling, highly toxic and potentially explosive" meth labs in 2004 were located in the three states of Iowa, Missouri, and Tennessee alone. The toxic fallout from meth labs prompted the DEA to train fifteen thousand local and regional law officers in hazardous-material mitigation strategies.[8]

Skeptics pointed out that while meth use might have been increasing (up to 1.3 million Americans in 2003), this was still dwarfed by cocaine (6 million) and marijuana (25 million). Moreover, teen meth use was down 10 percent since the late 1990s. In an interpretation of the drug war we've heard earlier in this story, the head of the nonprofit Law Enforcement Against Prohibition, Jack Cole, said the meth horror story "sells a lot of newspapers, gets a lot of politicians voted back into office and raises money for police departments." Allison Colker at the National Conference of State Legislatures (NCSL) asserted that the "almost hysteria" surrounding meth labs had taken on a life of its own. "The idea that you could go camping and not know there are chemicals there [left over from a meth lab] has really captured people's attention." The DEA countered that meth was still an epidemic for the velocity at which the drug was spreading and the destruction it was doing to users and families and communities. A DEA spokesperson said in 2005, "Meth is the No. 1 drug threat to rural America, and in many places is the No. 1 threat—period."[9]

The Same Band-Aid

In 2004, Oklahoma became the first state in the country to enact a tough new anti-meth law after three police officers were killed by users. Cold medicines containing pseudoephedrine (rescheduled as a Schedule V controlled substance) now had to be purchased from a pharmacist, and restrictions were placed on the number of tablets individuals could purchase. In the year after the law went into effect, meth lab busts plunged by 85 percent. For proponents, this was evidence of success.[10]

Oklahoma's move helped push many other states to adopt similar legislation. The George W. Bush White House and Capitol Hill followed with a similar approach at the national level. One sponsor of federal legislation based on the Oklahoma model, Democratic senator Dianne Feinstein, argued that the most efficacious way to battle the epidemic was to "make it harder for criminals to get the key ingredient in the production of this deadly drug." Republican senator Jim Talent of Missouri, the state with the largest number of meth labs uncovered (2,707 in 2004), was even more emphatic: "This legislation is a dagger at the heart of meth manufacturing in America."[11]

The Combat Meth Act of 2005, signed into law by George W. Bush on March 9, 2006, immediately put quantity-based restrictions on the sale of cold medicine containing pseudoephedrine, one of meth's infamous "precursor chemicals." As the bill was making its way through Congress, lobbyists for the National Association of Retail Chain Stores (acronymized, impossibly, NARCS), which represented drug chains like CVS, Target, Rite-Aid, and Walgreens, claimed that such "stop-buy" regulations would force the pharmacists to act as cops. Why not, they countered, simply supply the purchase information to law enforcement so that they could take appropriate action?[12]

The bill also permitted the State Department to cut foreign aid to countries that did not take measures to stop the diversion of pseudoephedrine and ephedrine to illicit markets, and it imposed quotas on the quantity of pseudoephedrine and ephedrine that U.S. pharmaceutical companies could import.

The following year, the White House's annual anti-drug strategy included support for Mexico's crackdown—restricting raw ephedrine and pseudoephedrine imports from Asia—and a multi-agency campaign to go after processed meth at the U.S.-Mexico border. In other words, the very same supply-side strategy that had dominated the approach to Colombian and Andean cocaine cartels was now in action on meth.[13]

Interestingly, these quotas actually did reduce the amount of pseudoephedrine that reached the black market and subsequently reduced meth imports. Pfizer, the world's largest cold-medicine producer and the maker of Sudafed, started using the chemical phenylephrine, which cannot be made into methamphetamine, in half of its cold products. Pfizer's switch forced nine companies that produced a significant share of the world's supply of pseudoephedrine to drastically decrease production. This, in turn, further diminished the availability of pseudoephedrine for illicit meth makers. Simultaneously, Mexico cut its own pseudoephedrine imports in half. Between September 2003 and November 2004 alone, Mexican and U.S. officials confiscated 67 million pseudoephedrine tablets.[14]

Total meth imported into the United States dropped by three-quarters between 2004 and 2006; the drug's purity also plunged, from 77 to 51 percent— a sign that considerably less meth was being produced. "Mom-and-pop" meth production dropped both domestically and in Mexico. In September 2004, DEA deputy chief Michele Leonhart lauded the "successful culmination" of Operation Brain Drain, a joint DEA–Canadian Mounted Police operation that eliminated "a major source of U.S. meth." The bounty? Ninety arrests, five of which nabbed "major traffickers"; just under 100 pounds of methamphetamine; 1.7 million ephedrine pills; and two super labs.[15]

These encouraging statistics are likely what helped lead President George W. Bush's drug czar, John Walters, to tell the *Oregonian* in an August 2006 interview that America was "winning" the war on meth. "Was meth an epidemic in some parts of the country? Yes. . . . Is it the worst drug problem? Is it an epidemic everywhere? The answer is no." Walters stopped short of declaring "mission accomplished," but he did put the epidemic squarely in the past tense.[16]

Sinaloa Rears Up

As if Walters had been right, the American media effectively lost interest in the methamphetamine question in the last half of the decade. They took the closure of American labs as the "sole indicator" that the epidemic had ebbed. However, while domestic production dropped, the number of users in the country remained relatively steady, with approximately 1.2 million nonmedical users "in the last year" in 2013. And the initial drop in imported meth proved to be a temporary blip, most likely an artifact of disruption on the production side that was quickly erased when supply operations reconsolidated.[17]

Indeed, beginning in 2008, meth production in Mexico surged—and that country's drug trafficking organizations (DTOs) grabbed a large share of the market. Mexican gangs promptly adjusted to the disruption of reduced legal pseudoephedrine imports by purchasing it from middlemen in China and Africa. The DTOs also started using phenylacetone, an organic compound banned in the United States but available in Mexico. This, as it turned out, allowed them to manufacture purer methamphetamine, up from 39 percent to 100 percent. Now American users who had been getting home-cooked crank—maybe 15 to 25 percent of all users—were increasingly conducting business directly or indirectly with Mexican DTOs. The transition was so swift that by the end of 2011 up to 85 percent of the meth consumed in America was coming from Mexican-run labs. For organizations like the Sinaloa cartel, meth was a miracle product: unlike cannabis, it could be manufactured, and unlike cocaine, it could be manufactured right in Mexico. As expected, the DEA reported a rise in meth seizures along the U.S.-Mexico border between 2008 and 2013. According to U.S. Border Patrol statistics, in 2012, 3,430 pounds of methamphetamine were seized, compared to 1,838 pounds the previous year.

One popular smuggling trick involved dissolving crystal meth in a solution and hiding it in the washer-fluid reservoir of a car, then later re-crystallizing it for distribution on U.S. streets. In Arizona, in one notorious episode, a woman had meth molded into the shape of the bra that she wore as she attempted to cross the border.[18]

In the 2010s the Sinaloa cartel's profits reached the stratosphere. "They were so confident of the purity and quality of their meth that initially they used to include batches of the 'product' with cocaine and marijuana for shipments that had already been ordered—they sent it for free. They were convinced the foreigners would be hooked." The gambit worked. In an ironic inversion, the Mexican cartels also discovered that they could manufacture meth on U.S. soil. U.S. authorities busted a Mexican meth gang whose network spanned from the Mexican state of Michoacán into Texas, California, and Oregon. In 2015, a DTO allowed a British news team to shadow their "super lab" meth operation after eight months of back-and-forth discussions:

> Inside a heavily-guarded factory, men in overalls and wearing gloves and face masks mix together a series of chemicals into huge drums. There is an instant reaction, sending clouds of foul smelling, toxic and highly explosive gas into the air. . . .
>
> The "super lab" is made up of a number of different locations. We crossed town to another secret building where we found 10 men in masks and gloves sitting around tables laden with crystal meth.
>
> For the next 48 hours they will pack the powder into tiny capsules before it is shipped abroad. There is a quarter of a million pounds-worth of drugs on the table and the gang leader told me he can produce that amount once a week.
>
> "We are making [$18 million] a year profit and we are a medium-sized operation. It all goes to the U.S. because it sells for more; the product goes directly to the United States," the kingpin said, adding that the value of the drugs increases nine times by the time they get to Europe.[19]

A drug official at the U.S.-Mexico border summed up the new reality: Meth was up; cocaine was down. "We started noticing the increase with meth in fiscal year 2014," he said, "so we noticed an increment on crystal meth and obviously it all starts from the demand, you know. They're demanding this drug." It was remarkable to see how closely the drug policy bureaucracy's response to the meth uptick resembled its response to periodic spikes in cocaine and heroin over the previous three decades. It was Groundhog Day all over again, and the best that U.S. law enforcement could do was to throw more money and manpower at interdiction.[20]

The Crisis to Come

According to the National Institutes of Health, there were 1.2 million illicit meth users in America in 2012, almost exactly the same number as roughly a decade earlier, when the perception of a meth epidemic was most acute. In contrast to opioids, there was no demonstrated medical treatment available for methamphetamine addiction beyond clinical detox. And because of the physiological damage long-term use of the drug does to the brain, there were more limits to the effectiveness of psychological counseling and therapy for meth addiction than for dependency on other substances. These factors, along with meth's short-onset rate of addiction, made it particularly difficult for policymakers to manage the drug's demand side.[21]

In some ways, the methamphetamine crisis of the 2000s anticipated the opioid addiction crisis to come. As we will see, at the same time the pharmaceutical industry and medical community began to stream opioids into the market, many of the same sociological and economic factors that drove epidemic meth addiction persisted in heartland towns and rural areas and in fact extended into more and more corners of middle-class America.

Distressingly, some states began to see a resurgence of meth addiction at the same time that opioid addiction rates were skyrocketing. FBI agent John Kumm noted that his office was seeing cases of meth users switching to "heroin to take the edge off their highs, and heroin addicts who turn to meth because there's less chance of an overdose." As NBC reporter Jon Schuppe noted in July 2017, "Some states are fighting both epidemics at once."[22]

27 • Opioid Nation

There was a stigma about being gay. There is also a stigma about
being addicted to drugs. The entire society is suffering and the
government can't seem to get their arms around this [opioid]
epidemic. If it's an epidemic, treat it like an epidemic.
—Luke J. Nasta, drug treatment official, Staten Island, New York

Narcotics such as morphine, derived from chemical compounds in poppies, have been part of the American pharmacopeia since the early nineteenth
century. The nation's first opiate-addiction epidemic developed in the context
of an extensively unregulated market for these new compounds, which physicians prescribed for ailments from menstrual cramps to the common cold. As
federal and state governments cracked down on the runaway market in the
early 1900s, researchers synthesized new opioids, such as hydrocodone and
oxycodone, with the expectation that these new molecules would prove less
habit-forming. In the 1970s the elusive quest for a non-addictive painkiller
produced two new substances, Percocet and Vicodin, which combined semisynthetic opiates with acetaminophen. For the greater share of the century,
American doctors resisted prescribing such heavy-duty anesthetics except in
cases of severe pain, reserving them for cancer treatments and post-operative
recovery.[1]

In the 1980s and 1990s, however, this norm started to shift. Pain was increasingly described not "only as a symptom but as an illness in itself." The
American Society for Pain Management Nursing started operating in the early
1990s, financed mostly by the Baxter Company, a medical supply and anesthetic manufacturing giant; within a few years the association had more than

two thousand members. In 1996, the Veterans Health Administration adopted pain as a fifth vital sign, so that the subjective, patient-reported experience of pain came to rank among pulse, blood pressure, body temperature, and respiration as the basic clinical measurements used to assess a patient's physiological functioning. Tens of millions of Americans, it now appeared, suffered from untreated pain. One public opinion survey around the turn of the century found that half of respondents could not recall what it meant not to feel pain; only a fraction of these had been treated for their torments. By the early 2000s, aggressive pain management formed part of a new medical consensus; it was "unacceptable for patients to be in pain," one expert suggested. Hospitals were increasingly evaluated on how well they "assessed and treated" a patient's pain. Congress declared the first decade of the century to be the "Decade of Pain Control and Research."[2]

This shift opened an important question: If new classes of opiates could alleviate needless pain, was it immoral not to administer powerful painkillers to end an "unnecessary epidemic"?[3] Sam Quinones describes what ensued: "Doctors were urged to begin attending to the country's pain epidemic by prescribing these drugs. Interns and residents were taught that these drugs were now not addictive, that doctors thus had a mission, a duty, to use them. In some hospitals, doctors were told they could be sued if they did not treat pain aggressively, which meant with opiates." Within a decade, a "culture of aggressive opiate use" had emerged, supported by a number of key sectors: pain specialists, medical school professionals, the Joint Commission on Accreditation of Healthcare Organizations, pharmaceutical companies, and even hospital attorneys.[4]

The cynical side of this story, as Quinones and others have documented, is that it was largely the result of a concerted marketing onslaught by pharmaceutical companies. Big Pharma dollars helped to drive the perception that pain was no longer "something that had to be endured."[5]

Some physicians and medical associations expressed concerns about the new approach. Even for a meticulous doctor, it was very difficult to differentiate between a "desperate patient who is genuinely suffering and a manipulative patient who's seeking out drugs." As now seems inevitable, doctors and hospitals "overshot" on pain. Painkillers were distributed gratuitously for small or invented ailments. In the 2000s, Vicodin could be bought and sold through online pharmacies. Pain treatment centers "advertise[d] like car dealerships." "Well-meaning general practitioners," urged on by aggressive sales campaigns, prescribed opiates by the dozen.[6]

The upshot was an American addiction epidemic more extensive and more destructive than any that had come before it.

Oxy

In 1984, the privately held pharmaceutical company Purdue Pharma, based in Norwalk, Connecticut, developed a long-term pain reliever called MS Contin. The time-release formula put an anesthetic opioid into a user's bloodstream continuously over the course of several hours. After MS Contin's patent expired, Purdue Pharma brought to market another time-release pill, OxyContin, in 1996. Both pills contained a single drug: oxycodone, a painkiller German scientists first synthesized in 1910s from thebaine, an opium derivative similar to heroin and morphine. Alleviating pain over a ten- or twelve-hour span, the medication was a godsend for millions of patients. But it also contained large doses of oxycodone—40 and 80 milligrams. Purdue Pharma aggressively marketed the new drug to general practitioners who generally accepted the company's claim that OxyContin was less addictive than Percocet or Vicodin. Purdue Pharma used its swelling national sales force to convince doctors that OxyContin could and should be used for "bad backs, knee pain, tooth extraction, headaches . . . as well as football, hockey, and dirtbike injuries."[7]

Purdue Pharma sent doctors and pharmacists on underwritten trips to ritzy resorts across the American southwest for "pain management seminars." It recruited physicians to join its national speakers network to address the use of oxycodone at medical conferences and hospitals in locales like Boca Raton, Florida, and Scottsdale, Arizona. The company gave doctors OxyContin swag from baseball caps to a pedometer that read, "OxyContin . . . A step in the right direction." The DEA later attested that this was the first time in history that a company had used these kinds of marketing techniques for a Schedule II drug—that is, a substance believed to be addictive but with demonstrated medical usefulness. Purdue Pharma also founded the American Pain Foundation, which touted the use of opiates for both "acute and chronic" pain. One nonprofit media investigation reported that the American Pain Foundation had supported Purdue Pharma in a class-action suit from 2001, brought on behalf of patients in Ross County, Ohio, who claimed to have gotten hooked on Oxy.[8]

The drug company compiled databases of doctors inclined to prescribe OxyContin and increased its solicitation of this cohort. In 1996, Purdue

Pharma doled out $1 million in bonuses to Oxy salespersons; by 2001, that sum had swelled to $40 million. Unsurprisingly, this coincided with a pharmaceutical sales representative boom: the ranks of sales reps—sometimes called "feet on the street"—grew from 35,000 in 1995 to 110,000 in 2005. Some Purdue Pharma reps—particularly in southern Ohio, eastern Kentucky, and other regions "first afflicted with rampant Oxy addiction"—were reported to have made up to $100,000 in annual bonuses—in a few cases, even *quarterly* bonuses—hawking this blockbuster painkiller.[9]

In 2002, U.S. doctors were prescribing several times more OxyContin than they had in 1997. Prescriptions for chronic pain swelled from under seven hundred thousand in the mid-1990s to more than six million in 2002. Scrips for cancer pain went from 250,000 to more than a million over the same period. By 2003 or 2004, over half of OxyContin prescriptions came from primary-care physicians who were little versed in pain management and who lacked the time to properly diagnose vague and highly subjective symptoms of discomfort. The global manufacture of oxycodone jumped from two tons in 1990 to 135 metric tons in 2009, with over two-thirds of this production occurring in the United States. Vicodin, Percocet, OxyContin, and other semisynthetic opiates became the most commonly prescribed medications in America. Sales of OxyContin represented 80 to 90 percent of Purdue Pharma's revenues—more than a billion dollars in 2001 and 2002 alone.[10]

But the bonanza was predicated on one crucial piece of misinformation: that OxyContin and other synthetic opioids were not addictive when used as prescribed. As it turned out, they *were* addictive. The Sackler family owned Purdue Pharma, the maker of OxyContin, in its entirety; in 2015 the family was worth $14 billion, which made it one of the nation's wealthiest families. *Forbes* ran a story calling the Sacklers the "Oxycontin Clan," noting that they had amassed enough Oxy-driven wealth to take the place of "storied families like the Busches, Mellons, and Rockefellers."[11]

Painkiller Tourism

By 1999, towns like Chillicothe, Ohio, were "awash in hundreds of patients" addicted to OxyContin. Overfilled rehabilitation clinics were turning away people on "spectacular doses" of the drug—300 milligrams a day or more. The crisis seemed to have descended overnight. At one point, Dr. Carl "Rolly" Sullivan, who ran a drug rehabilitation clinic at the University of West Virginia in Morgantown, was contacted by Purdue Pharma, which asked him to address the addiction question with its sales reps. Sullivan met with twenty Purdue Pharma sales reps in Charleston, West Virginia. He detailed the "foot traffic at his clinic, the amounts of their drug that addicts, some of them former pain patients, were consuming." As one sales rep said, "We were told this was safe." Sullivan brought along an addict recovering from her OxyContin habit. A Purdue Pharma sales rep asked her how long it would take her to score OxyContin on the streets outside the hotel. "About twenty minutes," she responded. "But that's only because I don't drive." A few months later the woman died of an OxyContin overdose.[12]

Mark Kleiman reminds us that it was among the populations "largely untouched by heroin" where pain pills penetrated most deeply. In many cases, the scourge originated with pain management clinics—pill mills, as they came to be called. Staffed by doctors writing hundreds of prescriptions a day, the clinics became "virtual ATM[s] for dope." Kleiman explains, "Rising supplies of prescribed opioids helped create a black market. Patients exchanged and sold unused pills; burglars stole them. Drug dealers began to recruit people to pose as patients and secure high-dosage prescriptions from as many physicians as possible. Drug-seeking patients learned that they usually could get a prescription just by rating their pain at seven or above on an arbitrary ten-point scale."[13]

It did not take users long to figure out that grinding up the OxyContin capsules compressed the time-delay effect and produced an intense and more immediate high. Seniors and disabled workers began selling their prescribed pills on the street. Addicts visited medical practice after medical practice with elaborate characterizations of pain. Street dealers who had been selling cocaine or meth added Oxy—"hillbilly heroin"—to their lineup. All told, the number of Americans using opioids for nonmedical purposes jumped from roughly 200,000 to 2.4 million between 1992 and 2012.[14]

Controversially, then and now, as this epidemic continued to grow, Purdue Pharma declined to pull the drug. Several states and numerous citizens sued the company, "which fought with tobacco-company-like determination," but eventually it gave in. In 2007, in a lawsuit brought by the U.S. Department of Justice, Purdue Pharma pleaded guilty in a federal court to felony charges of misleading the public about OxyContin's risk of addiction. The company was fined $634.5 million, and three Purdue Pharma executives pleaded guilty to criminal charges. Although Purdue Pharma had long held that it was not aware of the potential for abuse, news reports in 2018 explained that the Department of Justice believed the pharmaceutical entity knew about "significant" abuse of OxyContin soon after the 1996 launch of the drug but did not disclose this finding. These federal prosecutors came across more than a hundred in-company correspondences between 1997 and 1999 including the words "street value," "crush," or "snort." Purdue Pharma responded in a statement: "Suggesting that activities that last occurred more than 16 years ago are responsible for today's complex and multifaceted opioid crisis is deeply flawed." It was now clear that crushing the pills, and then snorting or a heroin-like injection turned each pill into "essentially an instantaneous double dose of oxycodone." In September 2019, the corporation, long accused and now legally guilty of malfeasance, declared bankruptcy to adhere to the settlement with thousands of litigants, including twenty-three states and two thousand counties and cities. If the massively complex deal does not fall apart, it would mark the only time a drug corporation had been found "accountable for their role in the opioid epidemic."[15]

An Epidemic of Despair

Yet the fury of the addiction and overdose epidemic was far from over. As abuse of prescription opiates began to drop somewhat, rural America turned to heroin. Heroin cost twenty dollars for an average dose, compared with twice that for a single OxyContin pill. So now a prescription drug epidemic was becoming a street drug epidemic. And as we know, heroin has been used (and abused) for more than a century and was strictly regulated in the United States with the Harrison Narcotics Tax Act of 1914. Quoted in a searing *Atlantic* piece, a thirty-eight-year-old drug rehab patient named Kevin sought treatment for a "transition to heroin" precipitated by a "decades-long relationship" with Vicodin and Percocet. As he related, "The only time I touched heroin was whenever I couldn't find pills," he recalled. "There were times where I did it for a couple days at a time until I found pills, then I would just do the pills." Eventually, though, the harder drug took over. The Centers for Disease Control reported that from 2002 to 2012, nearly 80 percent of new heroin users had previously abused prescription painkillers.[16]

Heroin busts at the U.S.-Mexico border surged from 556 kilos in 2008 to 2,100 kilos in 2012. I remember receiving a briefing from anti-drug officials at the U.S. embassy in Bogotá back in the mid-2000s showing that poppy cultivation in Colombia had been all but eliminated. But it had started up again, and Latin America was producing 90 percent of the heroin consumed in the United States. The typical Latin American supply chain mimicked that of

Colombian cocaine during its peak. Colombian farmers grew the raw opium, followed by clandestine processing in jungle or high Andean labs. Mexican gangs carried it through the Caribbean or across the U.S.-Mexico border. And then dealers—Dominicans, more often than not in this era—would "package it, stamp it with brands like Breaking Bad or Government Shutdown, and sell it to street dealers." American and Mexican anti-drug officials reported that Mexican opium production shot up roughly 50 percent in 2014, in large part due to the "voracious American appetite."[17] Production also spiked in Afghanistan: the U.N.'s annual World Drug Report indicated that Afghanistan's poppy cultivation had grown by a third from 2012 to 2013. Global poppy cultivation was at its highest level leading up to World War II.[18]

Although heroin wasn't usually more addictive than OxyContin, it was more unpredictable. One research physician explained, "Ten milligrams of Oxy is always ten milligrams of Oxy." With heroin, by contrast, "impurities and contamination can make a dangerous drug even more deadly." One of the highest-profile cases was the accidental overdose death of the actor Philip Seymour Hoffman, whose prescription opiate addiction had led him to a raft of other drugs, including heroin. In late February 2014, Hoffman's body was discovered in the bathroom of his New York apartment with a syringe still in his forearm and fifty bags of heroin nearby. Cocaine, heroin, benzodiazepines, and amphetamine were found in his system.[19] Another question was whether the heroin epidemic was a *supply* case of the drug being manufactured and thus sold to soon-to-be addicted customers or a *demand* case of, say, originally prescription drug addicts now seeking out a new, more potent, and cheaper alternative.[20]

For local law enforcement across Appalachia, the drug was now their "number one problem." The U.S. attorney for the Northern District of West Virginia, William Ihlenfeld, explained to journalist Olga Khazan, "It's affecting all segments of society. . . . All levels of income. All neighborhoods. It's everybody." The big factor, it seemed, was the status of opioids as "the ultimate escape drugs." Dr. Judith Feinberg at West Virginia University explained, "Boredom and a sense of uselessness and inadequacy—these are human failings that led you to just want to withdraw. On heroin, you curl up in a corner and blank out in the world. It's an extremely seductive drug for dead-end towns, because it makes the world's problems go away." This was one reason that economically sclerotic—though often tight-knit—rural communities were so vulnerable. As one West Virginian put it, "If the lady next door is using, and so are the neighbors, and people in your family are, too, the odds are good that you're going to join in." Treatment in the state remained woefully

unavailable to most addicts. In 2000, West Virginia opened up its first methadone clinic to treat painkiller addicts; by 2003, there were six more, a number
that held steady through the 2010s. West Virginia remained one of seventeen
states where methadone was not covered by Medicaid. "Chances of getting
treatment in West Virginia is ridiculously small," said a local addiction treatment expert.[21]

A November 2015 headline story in the *Washington Post* cited a new study
in which four in ten Americans said they knew someone who had been addicted to prescription painkillers. In 2015, four times as many Americans died
from drug overdoses as died from guns, and one and a half times as many as
died in car accidents. Opioids were also a contributing factor in many fatalities
with more proximate causes, "deaths of despair" involving alcohol, drugs,
mental health issues, and suicide. For thousands of Americans, especially in
the heartland, this epidemic excised a central tenet from the American Dream,
that children enjoy longer lives than their parents.[22]

Manufactured Death

In March 2015, the DEA alerted Americans to the lethal risks of yet another
synthetic opiate, fentanyl. Until then, few Americans would have recognized
the name. By 2014, a national warning described a "killer heroin" cut with
fentanyl, but little federal action was taken, even if anecdotal reporting from
morgues in locales like Providence, Rhode Island, were showing an alarming
frequency of overdoses caused by this novel opioid. Incredibly fast-acting, fentanyl could be fatal even at minuscule doses. Though the warning glossed over
this detail, it was also known to "induce a state of extreme relaxation and euphoria." Physicians had legally administered fentanyl since it was first synthesized in 1960 and introduced under brand names like Actiq and Sublimaze to
treat patients in extreme pain. In 2015, physicians wrote 6.64 million legal
fentanyl prescriptions. At first, fentanyl appeared on the street laced into heroin, but it was increasingly sold on its own—without the buyer's knowledge.
In Massachusetts in 2013, state police crime lab investigators discovered pure
fentanyl, not mixed in with other illicit drugs, in half a dozen overdose cases;
two years later, the lab identified 425. Street names for the drug included:
Apache, China Girl, China White, Dance Fever, and TNT. The extent of fentanyl's prevalence was not initially apparent because of its resemblance to
heroin, as special toxicological testing is required to detect the drug.[23] By
2017, the epidemic had spread across the nation, especially in urban areas.

Firefighters wearing hazmat protection remove items from a vehicle in which several
drug overdose victims were found in Chelsea, Massachusetts, as well as a powder
believed to be fentanyl, August 4, 2017 (Reuters, permission to author)

Here is how the *Washington Post* described Philadelphia resident and addict
Art Gutierrez's situation:[24]

> Most days, in the early mornings, Gutierrez gets his first hit of heroin
> free. Heroin has been sold in Kensington for decades, and the neighbor-
> hood, known colloquially as the Badlands, has a reputation for offering
> the purest kind. The introduction of fentanyl has led to increased com-
> petition, and dealers now aim for the best price and the highest potency.
>
> Some give away a little product as an enticement, but the samples
> come with a deadly catch, Gutierrez said. One bag out of the batch usu-
> ally contains a lethal dose of fentanyl. If word of an overdose from the
> lethal bag spreads, drug users seek out the dealer—because they know
> that dealer has the strongest product, the best fix for the money.
>
> Gutierrez said his friend overdosed and died in an abandoned build-
> ing earlier this year from a lethal sample.
>
> "They hit him with a hotshot," he said. "The boy died instantly. He
> took his last breath sliding down the wall."

Gutierrez returns here because he has to. The pain of withdrawal is unbearable.

"Every bone in your body hurts," he said. "You get hot and cold sweats. It is 90 degrees out here, but you'd be freezing with goose bumps. There is no middle ground."

But as people die around him, he wonders why he survives.

"Some of the best kids come out here and do one bag and die. They don't deserve it," he said. "Why am I still alive?"[25]

As is often the case with novel drugs, fentanyl seemed to come out of no-where. In one raid in 2015, police located over thirty pounds of fentanyl and heroin (retail price $2.2 million) in a single residence in Lawrence, Massachu-setts. Police then confiscated sixty-six pounds of fentanyl-laced heroin, with a street price of millions of dollars, in nearby Tewksbury. One middleman would buy a hundred "fingers" (ten grams) of fentanyl for $400 apiece and resell each finger for $750 in New Hampshire and Maine, a weekly profit of $35,000.[26]

Fentanyl works so quickly that there is usually little if any time to adminis-ter the life-saving drugs that can reverse the effects of an overdose. "At least with heroin, there is a chance that if someone relapses, they can get back into recovery," said the head of a Massachusetts nonprofit helping families coping

A used needle on the ground in a park in Lawrence, Massachusetts, where individuals were arrested earlier in the day during raids to break up heroin and fentanyl drug rings in the region, May 30, 2017 (Reuters, permission to author)

with addiction. Lawrence police reported that the opioid epidemic was so per-vasive that it was "no longer a shock" to witness drug users collapsing in pub-lic spaces. It was also increasingly common to see addicts "buying drugs, getting high and passing out with their children in tow." Lawrence police also reckoned that children were nearby in roughly 10 percent of their drug cases.[27]

Because the drug war is a story of eternal return, a novel substance was once again "transforming the face of the drug crisis." Between April 2015 and September 2017, fake prescription pain pills containing fentanyl were inter-cepted by police in forty states; they were the proximate cause of death in no fewer than seventeen overdoses. The *Washington Post* quoted the DEA's top New England official: "If anything can be likened to a weapon of mass destruc-tion in what it can do to a community, it's fentanyl. It's manufactured death." In some cities like Baltimore, fentanyl, cheaper and easier to make, appeared to have pushed aside heroin—a narcotic with a wrenching history in these in-ner cities—at least for a while.[28]

As should be clear by now, the opioid crisis of the early twenty-first century did not conform to many of the patterns of the modern war on drugs. Most notably, this wasn't a case of Latin American kingpins shipping powdered tickets to Wall Street parties or getaways from modern life; this was a phenom-enon that began squarely within the American healthcare industry. At best, it was the result of the parasitism of loosely regulated pharmaceutical manufac-turers; at worst, it was the inevitable consequence of the American healthcare system's basic structure. If the contemporary epidemic bore a resemblance to any previous drug crisis, it was the first opiate scourge in the late nineteenth century, which affected about a tenth as many people and which, as we saw, gave rise to the nation's first regulatory regimes for psychoactive drugs.[29]

What's more, the illicit drug trade found itself in the rare position of having to play catch-up with the sanctioned pharmaceutical market. Soon enough, though, Mexican cartels found a way in. They started by smuggling fentanyl from China and later developed processes for making it on their own in clandestine labs. They integrated the drug into the same U.S. supply chain that drove the heroin trade. In predictable balloon-effect fashion, the broadly effective crackdown on prescription painkillers pushed the street price of oxycodone and other opioid pills up. This drove demand for heroin, as discussed, but it also made fentanyl—synthesized "without the hassle of growing poppy"—a very lucrative alternative.[30] In a press interview, Maura Healey, the attorney general of Massachusetts, indicated that fentanyl had be-come the Mexican cartels' "drug of choice," outshining cocaine, marijuana, and cannabis in profitability. "They have figured out a way to make fentanyl more cheaply and easily than heroin and are manufacturing it at a record pace," Healey said. A Mexican government raid on a remote and primitive landing pad in Sinaloa in 2015 seized twenty-seven kilos of fentanyl, including almost twenty thousand fentanyl tablets disguised as oxycodone. Two of the men arrested were "high ranking members" of El Chapo Guzmán's Sinaloa cartel.[31]

The economics of fentanyl were staggering. A $6,000 kilo of Colombian heroin might bring in $80,000 wholesale inside the United States. A $5,000 kilo of, say, pure Chinese fentanyl, by contrast, was powerful enough to be diluted into twenty-plus kilos, with cutting agents like heroin or caffeine added in. Each "kilo" of fentanyl was sold for around $80,000, bringing home a whopping profit of roughly $1.5 million—twenty times heroin's take. In May 2018, in a single bust Nebraska police confiscated 118 pounds of fentanyl—or enough to kill twenty-six million people. In Arizona in late January 2019, U.S. Border Patrol agents made the largest-ever fentanyl bust: 254 pounds (pills and powder form, enough for more than a hundred million lethal doses and a street price of $3.5 million) stashed under cucumbers inside a truck driven by a twenty-something Mexican national attempting to cross into the United States from Mexico at the Nogales, Arizona, port of entry.[32]

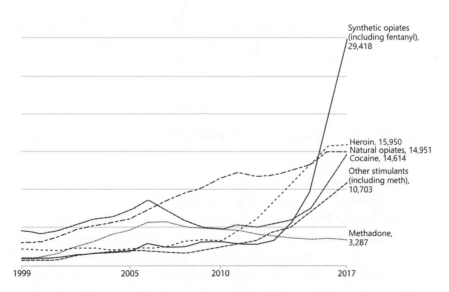

U.S. drug overdose deaths, 1980–2018 (University of Wisconsin Cartography Lab)

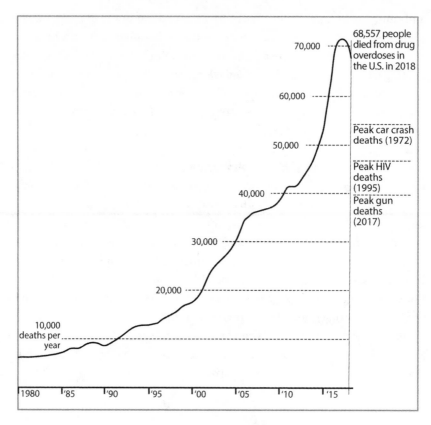

Annual U.S. overdose deaths involving selected drugs, 1999–2017. Many overdose fatalities result from a cocktail of drugs. (University of Wisconsin Cartography Lab)

Alternatives and Antidotes

In 2015, a Staten Island, New York, paramedic described a call he'd been on the year before:

We received a call for an unresponsive person in the courtyard of an apartment building, early morning, around three or four o'clock, on a night shift last February. The unresponsive person, a lady in her sixties, was slumped over on a bench, in like a robe or a housecoat. Near her we found a pill bottle for painkillers, almost empty, and I saw on the label that it had been filled only a week before. She was not breathing, lips blue, pupils miotic—pinpoint-size—all symptoms of opioid O.D. We put her head back, secured a breathing passage. I took the Narcan injector and sprayed a milligram of the naloxone solution in each nostril, and about a minute later she coughed and started breathing again. My partner that night, Henry Cordero, and I were, like, "O.K.! We figured it out!" We put her on the stretcher and brought her to the hospital, and they took over from there.[33]

The woman's case was one of thousands in which an almost certainly fatal overdose was reversed by naloxone, an inhibitor of the body's opiate receptors. In 2014, emergency responders averted 829 more deaths with naloxone—likely a small proportion of the total lives saved, as many naloxone doses were administered by other drug users and went unreported. With no "psychotomimetic effects" and no clear potential for abuse, naloxone was a seeming miracle overdose treatment. In short, "anybody can use it to revive an overdose victim with little fear of causing injury." As Ian Frazier wrote in his *New Yorker* essay "The Antidote," "If there ever was a *primum non nocere* drug, naloxone is it." In 2017, all but three states had passed legislation easing access to naloxone. That said, it wasn't without its critics: the drug causes withdrawal, making the user "dope sick," craving more heroin. Some officials lamented that naloxone might be creating conditions of moral hazard. The availability and success rate of the antidote mean that it has not been resulting in permanent changes in addicts' behavior. And even despite the "miracle drug," seventy-eight people in the country were dying each day from drug overdoses. Another dilemma exists when someone *does* overdose on opioids but people around them are reluctant to call 911. Studies concluded that the overriding reason for not calling 911 was fear of criminal charges—a sanction that dates back to the late 1980s crack era, especially the Anti-Drug Abuse Act co-authored by Senator Joe Biden. The law's central premise was to steepen sentences of drug dealers who "destroyed the lives of addicted people." Yet the law unwittingly turned "accidental overdoses into homicides" and thus served as a powerful deterrent to calling for emergency responders. In the depths of the national opioid epidemic, prosecuting authorities in hard-hit regions relied on this "Len Bias law" to go after drug overdose victims—or, as one observer put it, "the lowest hanging fruit in the drug supply chain." From 2015 to 2018, prosecutors in over a dozen states pursued more than a thousand "drug-induced homicide cases."[34]

At the 2016 Democratic National Convention in Philadelphia, New Hampshire senator Jeanne Shaheen called for all emergency responders to carry naloxone, eliciting applause from the audience. Separately, Pennsylvania governor Tom Wolf said that the only serious answer to the swelling epidemic engulfing the Keystone State was to make naloxone widely available and in-crease treatment. "This is a disease, not a moral failing," the governor said.[35]

There was also much greater talk among Republicans about dealing with drug users through treatment rather than incarceration. New Jersey governor Chris Christie routinely compared treating drug addicts for their psychologi-cal dependency to treating smokers for cancer. Referring to his mother, a for-mer smoker and cancer patient, he told a small gathering of voters in New Hampshire, "No one came to me and said, 'Don't treat her; she got what she deserved.' We need to start treating people in this country, not jailing them." Jeb Bush and Carly Fiorina, both candidates for the Republican presidential nomination in 2016, called for more sympathy. "I have some personal experi-ence with this as a dad, and it is the most heartbreaking thing in the world to have to go through," Bush said at a primary campaign event in Merrimack, New Hampshire. His daughter, Noelle, had been jailed twice while in reha-bilitation after being busted with prescription pills and accused of possessing crack cocaine. The first question Hillary Clinton was asked at a presidential campaign event in New Hampshire in April 2016 concerned not the economy or health care but heroin. Clinton led other discussions on drugs and addic-tion in well-attended forums. Not coincidentally, she released a ten-year $10 billion plan to combat and treat drug addiction.[36]

Public opinion surveys showed that the opioid crisis had skyrocketed to the top of voters' list of priorities in many of the same areas of the country—rural states, suburbs, the early voting state of New Hampshire—that were hot spots in the presidential electoral landscape. This predominantly white, middle-class-to-affluent demographic was well organized and vocal. Michael Botti-celli, President Obama's second drug czar and a recovering alcoholic who had been sober for almost thirty years, explained, "They know how to call a legisla-tor, they know how to get angry with their insurance company, they know how to advocate. They have been so instrumental in changing the conversation."[37]

Yet with these rhetorical shifts also came a redoubling of familiar tough-on-crime interventions in the illicit market. State and federal prosecutors ramped up charging distributors caught selling pills. The media uproar surrounding the crisis induced prosecutors and judges to press for maximum penalties, resulting in decades- and life-long sentences for opioid dealers caught with even small doses. In some districts, prosecutors began charging friends and relatives who had bought drugs for overdose victims with manslaughter and even, in a few cases, homicide. Fifteen states introduced legislation that man-dated harsher penalties for dealers whose drug sales resulted in overdose deaths; the laws passed in at least two. All the while, quasi-legitimate pain clinics continued to distribute the same drugs with a free hand.[38]

The Addict Next Door

In April 2016, the *New York Times* ran a piece from Vancouver, British Columbia, that suggested what a new policy approach to opioid addiction might look like. It described a local resident, Dave Napio, who had begun using heroin more than forty years earlier, when he was eleven years old. Mr. Napio had spent nearly half of his fifty-five years in prison. These days, he was getting three daily doses of the drug at the only medical clinic in North America currently allowed to prescribe heroin. As the *Times* explained, "Instead of robbing banks and jewelry stores to support his habit, Mr. Napio is spending time making gold and silver jewelry, hoping to soon turn his hobby into a profession." Said Napio, "My whole life is straightening out. I'm becoming the guy next door." Napio and around a hundred other addicts had prescriptions for diacetylmorphine hydrochloride, heroin's active ingredient.[39]

Sergeant Randy Finchman of the Vancouver Police Department explained the logic behind this radical shift. "We tried to arrest our way out of it and that didn't work. Clogging up our courts and jails was not the solution." At the prescription clinic, addicts did not have to worry about the purity of their heroin. Vancouver's publicly financed program cost around $21,000 per participant per year. One academic study concluded that a single "untreated severe opioid user" cost governments a minimum of $35,000 a year in emergency medical care, incarceration, and other expenses.

In 2020, there were more than a hundred safe injection facilities across ten European countries and Canada. To date, no one has ever died from an overdose at one of these centers. The Vancouver clinic's success made headlines in the United States. A rare kind of political bipartisanship emerged in support of legislation that would fund treatment for addicts and overhaul mandatory minimum sentences of convicted drug users and sellers. But such efforts met with resistance from some of the stauncher drug hawks in Washington. For these critics, the clinic approach failed to address the "thefts, prostitution, and other criminal behavior" that surrounded drug use. Even as medical experts across the United States attempted to establish overdose prevention facilities, they faced legal headwinds as the Trump administration, citing the "crack-house statute" of the Anti-Drug Abuse Act of 1986 co-sponsored by Senator Joe Biden, sued a nonprofit organization to prevent it from opening

such a clinic in Philadelphia. In fact, the Trump administration began insisting on the conservative view that the opioid crisis was principally a law-and-
order problem. Commenting on a report by an administration commission,
Donald Trump reiterated, "The best way to prevent drug addiction and overdose is to prevent people from abusing drugs in the first place." Although it
was still too early to see what the Trump-era drug war would look like, these
initial rhetorical plugs suggested: more of the same.[40]

From a different perspective, some skeptics of the new righteousness on
addiction questioned whether this "relatively humane response to the opiate
epidemic" was driven more by the identities of the victims than by an even-
handed moral regard for citizens. Heroin use had grown among all demographic slices, but especially among whites, who made up 90 percent of
first-time users between 2005 and 2015. The current crisis, centered in the
nation's middle-class suburbs and rural areas, was generating calls for compassion and clemency, whereas the 1970s heroin outbreak and the 1980s
crack frenzy, which devastated minority neighborhoods in inner cities, had
sparked media hysteria and expedited mass incarceration.[41]

Whether or not the new rhetorical stance reflected an enduring change of
position on opioids at the federal level, several states did take their own steps
toward managing the crisis—much as they had during the first opiate crisis,
around the turn of the twentieth century. In late May 2017, Ohio attorney general Mike DeWine sued a number of opioid producers—including Purdue
Pharma—for covering up the dangers that prescription painkillers presented
to users. "Like the tobacco companies, defendants used third parties that they
funded, directed, and controlled to carry out and conceal their scheme to deceive doctors and patients about the risks and benefits of long-term opioid use
for chronic pain," DeWine wrote in the suit. DeWine also lambasted the companies for paying prominent doctors and medical groups to advocate for the
drugs' expanded use. The suit cited a record 3,050 overdose deaths in the state
in 2015. Eventually, a legal battle that began in a small number of states blos-
somed into a more than $200 billion settlement. In January 2019, Massachu-
setts presented documents in court that it contended demonstrated how, long
after the deleterious effects were well known, the Sackler family not only knew
about the illicit and uncouth operations at Purdue Pharma but in fact pushed
them personally. Here is a sample of some of the damning language used by
Richard Sackler, then a vice president with the corporation, in a private email:
"We have to hammer on the abusers in every way possible. They are the culprits and the problem. They are reckless criminals." A few weeks later, at the

Sackler-funded Guggenheim Museum in New York City, multi-generational activists led by a recovered opioid addict, the renowned photographer Nan Goldin, launched a protest, tossing flyers "swirling like snow as they descended the six stories. Within minutes the floor was coated white." Each was a prescription written by "Robert Sackler, M.D." to be taken once an hour each day. They also tossed around medicine containers with stickers: "Prescribed to you by the Sackler Family. Oxycontin. Extremely Addictive. WILL KILL. . . . Rx# 400,000. . . . Side effect: Death." Hastily hung banners proclaimed, "200 Dead Each Day" and "Take Down Their Name" in reference to the family's philanthropic affiliation with the museum.[42]

By Any Other Name

When I first envisioned this book in the early 2010s, I planned to write about America's unprecedented prescription painkiller outbreak. By the time I started writing, heroin was the story's protagonist. In 2016, it was fentanyl and the anti-overdose drug naloxone. As I first drafted this chapter in 2017 and 2018, another synthetic drug, carfentanil, had been popping up in batches of street heroin in Cincinnati and southern Indiana. A staggering ten thousand times more potent than morphine, carfentanil is used to tranquilize elephants and other large animals. At least fifteen carfentanil overdoses, one fatal, struck two adjacent counties in Indiana. The drug was linked to as many as 189 overdoses in the two states. It takes a far greater dose of naloxone to reverse a carfentanil overdose, and it's rare that a life-saving hit can be administered in time. Mass overdoses are often associated with one supplier. In Columbus, Ohio, a single batch of pure carfentanil was linked to eleven overdoses and two deaths. Melvin Patterson, a DEA spokesman, told the *Cincinnati Enquirer* that in a few instances, carfentanil had been linked to Chinese producers who smuggled it through Mexico into the United States. "It's such a restricted drug there's only a handful of places in the United States that can have it," said Patterson.[43]

Around the same time, in Georgia patients were turning up in hospitals with a perplexing set of symptoms—"multi-organ failure, mimicking stroke, sepsis, all at the same time," according to one emergency room physician in Macon. The culprit? A rogue batch of synthetic opioids, including U-47700, seven times more potent than morphine. They had been combined and pressed into fake Percocet pills and sold to unsuspecting buyers on the street. The *Washington Post* correctly surmised that state and federal crackdowns on licit painkiller clinics were partly to blame for the proliferation of counterfeit pills: As states enforced new limits on prescriptions and tracked the activities of doctors, the result was that not as many painkillers were available. The balloon effect struck again.[44]

Given the inevitable delay between a policy's introduction and its effects, it was still too early to tell whether the crackdowns on illicit opioids were having a sustainable impact on the drugs' overdose and death rates. For my part, I have little doubt that by the time this book arrives in readers' hands, this epidemic will have been eclipsed by something else. The names and nature of America's crisis drugs will continue to change. What endures, it seems, is the drive that compels Americans to use them.

Concluding Thoughts and a Tentative Way Forward

"Still Hammering Away"

By 2020, the drug war had achieved few, if any, of its stated objectives. Despite the billions of dollars spent on prevention, treatment, law enforcement, and interdiction, as of the writing of this book almost 23 million Americans between the ages of twelve and sixty-five were illicit drug users (and 120 million to 225 million globally). Roughly three-quarters of these Americans were using marijuana. Marijuana use among Americans over the age of twelve in the previous thirty days was increasing steadily, from 13.9 percent in 2016 to 15.9 percent in 2018, and nationwide drug use had been steadily ticking up by roughly 15 percent. The United States was also buckling under an enormous drug abuse and addiction problem, with 15 million troubled users of alcohol and several million others regularly abusing illegal drugs. In addition, on average each day 3,900 Americans began "nonmedical" use of opioids; another 580 tried heroin for the first time—a quarter of these going on to become addicted. The criminal trade in illicit psychoactive substances earned around $50 billion per year, although the $6.7 billion legal marijuana market in several American states (heady projections predicted a swell to over $20 billion by 2021) certainly put a dent in this sum.[1]

Less than a year after I left the Western Hemisphere bureau of President Obama's National Security Council in 2011, the United States and roughly a dozen partner countries, from the United Kingdom and France to Honduras and Guatemala, unleashed Operation Martillo. An official Pentagon profile titled "Operation Martillo Drops the Hammer on Smugglers" detailed progress on the new initiative, which was designed to interrupt the Florida/Caribbean channel that South American kingpins were using as a funnel to North

America in order to "flood the market and streets with massive amounts of white powder." Based on the Pentagon report, one might be impressed by Martillo's successes in its first year: 339 arrests, 101 vessels confiscated, 152,000 kilos ($3 billion) of cocaine interdicted, and 47,000 pounds ($44 million) of marijuana discovered. The article quoted air force general Douglas Fraser, head of the U.S. Southern Command: "More than 80 percent of the cocaine destined for U.S. markets is transported via sea lanes, primarily using routes through Central America." I had the privilege of working with General Fraser during my stint at the Pentagon, and he is a public servant of the highest order and capacity. But his comments in 2012 could just as easily have described conditions in 1992 or 2002 or, really, any year through 2050, probably. For the Pentagon, the win was "largely attributed" to the utilization of "naval aviation aircraft in spotting, tracking and intercepting these vessels." The problem, as we know all too well from this book, is that these sorts of tactical wins have never translated into an enduring strategic victory. Predictably, four years later in 2016, the Pentagon's official website headline touted Martillo as "still hammering away" at drug trafficking.

In August 2017, George W. Bush's drug czar, John Walters, and his conservative think-tank colleague David W. Murray co-authored an opinion piece in the *Wall Street Journal* titled "Trump Can Save Lives by Stopping Illegal Opioids at Their Source." Walters and Murray argued that addiction therapy and overdose-reversal drugs would prove futile if the United States did not also "make suppressing the supply of drugs its leading priority."[2] The essence of their case was that the solution to drugs was more law and order, more lab busting, more border enforcement. What Washington needed to do, Walters and Murray urged, was to repeat the success of the sustained interdiction efforts against cocaine. Here is the story they tell:

> After a brief remission in the 1990s, cocaine from Colombia began to flood U.S. streets. Some six million Americans used cocaine in 2006, according to the National Survey on Drug Use and Health. Then something unprecedented happened. Between 2006 and 2011, cocaine users dropped rapidly, to under four million. . . . During this time cocaine-positive workforce drug tests declined more than 60%. Meantime, cocaine treatment admissions fell from about 268,525 a year in 2005 to 143,827 in 2011. Cocaine-related drug overdose deaths fell 44% between 2006 and 2010.
>
> Treatment rescued many, and prevention slowed initiation. Yet during this time demand-reduction policy didn't change, nor did funding

increase. The driving factor was the decline of cocaine production in Colombia. Military progress against cocaine-producing rebel groups and crop-eradication programs, joined with development efforts, led supply to shrink from an estimated 700 metric tons in 2001 to 210 metric tons by 2012. Data showed a decline in cocaine purity on U.S. streets, and a corresponding surge in price.[3]

The authors also found supporting evidence in the significant decrease in confiscated cocaine—from 26,908 kilograms to 7,143 kilograms—from 2006 to 2011 along the border with Mexico. What Walters and Murray missed, however, was that the drug's street price had been dropping overall since the 1980s. The DEA's success nabbing shipments and traffickers should have resulted in a spike in the price, but cocaine remained 74 percent cheaper than it had been three decades earlier, at the height of the *Miami Vice* cocaine bonanza. An alternative explanation—and one embraced by drug war critics—is that after its peak, cocaine's popularity cycle had run its course. It is possible that the disappearance of cocaine in early 2012 in cities like Baltimore, Houston, and Chicago was a result of lower *demand,* not lower *supply*—and that the market of erstwhile cocaine users had decided that the drug's costs outweighed its benefits and given it up. This demand-side factor also helps explain lower drug prices in spite of interdiction. Yet this picture is not complete either, for the "wins" on cocaine were quickly supplanted by the country's worst opioid epidemic to date. It is likely that some cocaine users simply switched over to cheaper, more available opioids. One interpretation could be that the upward trend in opioid use was itself supply-driven, as the painkiller industry and medical establishment prescribed enough synthetic opioids "for every American to be medicated around the clock for three weeks."

This speaks to another factor contributing to the drug war's failure: the balloon effect. Given inelastic demand and product substitutability, it is also relatively easy for drug production to shift to new locations and new products when regulatory efforts "squeeze the balloon" in a given dimension. When the kingpin strategy decapitated Colombian cartels, atomized organizations took their place; as those fell, Mexican gangs stepped in. When coca sources all but dried up under tough militarization and aerial coca eradication in Colombia, the Mexican DTOs found easy substitutes in Bolivia and Peru. When interdiction efforts along the U.S.-Mexico border ramped up, distributors opened new routes through Central America and the Caribbean. When those were constricted under programs like Operation Martillo, Mexican smugglers dug tunnels and shifted to methamphetamines and synthetic opioids.[4]

An active-duty Colombian police officer gives Russell Crandall (then serving as the principal director for the Western Hemisphere at the Office of the Secretary of Defense) and aide Ashley Richardson an orientation on a mock clandestine cocaine laboratory used in training exercises at the Western Hemisphere Institute for Hemispheric Cooperation, Fort Benning, Georgia, circa 2009

The Bad and the Ugly

Beyond its internal failures, our punitive, militarized drug strategy has also yielded onerous negative externalities.[5]

THE MILITARY-INDUSTRIAL-NARCOTICS COMPLEX

First, and most perniciously, the drug war has given rise to a military-industrial-narcotics complex that is sustained wholly on its own internal logic, however flawed that logic might be. On departing the White House in January 1961, President Eisenhower famously admonished the nation about the military-industrial complex: a costly and ineradicable alliance between the country's military and defense-contractor industry at the expense of the public interest. (Some later said that it should really be the military-industrial-congressional complex to reflect the key role that Capitol Hill plays in keeping the machine going.) In the war on drugs, there is a parallel complex with its own momentum. It exists to ensure its own existence and remuneration.

When Congress gave anti-drug authorities the license to pursue supply-side strategies in the late 1980s and early 1990s, it essentially gave the executive branch carte blanche to fulfill its duties. (The federal budget allocation for the drug war was roughly $25 billion in 2015; 55 percent went to supply-side and domestic law enforcement and 45 percent to prevention, education, and treatment.) A colleague of mine at the Office of the Secretary of Defense often bragged that his office alone controlled anti-drug programs costing over $1 billion annually. A billion dollars is an awful lot of money, but over the many years we've been fighting the drug war, it is barely a drop in the ocean.

I never once got the sense that the anti-drug agencies and officials were carrying out their duties cynically. But the unreflective fulfillment of duty, year in and year out, created its own inertia. The words of one U.S. military veteran and self-described "ultra right-winger" interviewed in 2008 are illustrative: "If the drug war goes away, I might be unemployed." A State Department publication released the following year showed that one company, DynCorp International, had been paid $164 million to oversee coca eradication programs in Colombia in 2007. This sum was 25 percent of the aid intended for Colombia's security forces, and twice what the corporation had earned in 2002, when its annual report stated that its "primary responsibility" in Colombia was teaching Colombian counterparts how to do the work themselves.[6]

A ZERO-LEARNING ENVIRONMENT

Another hallmark of the drug war is that the strategy has had no rearview mirror. There was never, at any point, an effective mechanism to track or assess whether policies were meeting expressed goals. Whether the policy intervention was to regulate pharma companies to reduce prescription drug abuse in the 1910s or to spray Colombian coca fields from the 1980s through the 2010s, each one had its own motivation and logic. When confronted with a new set of challenges, policymakers far too often chose to extend a failing program or, worse, to reintroduce a program that had been tried and abandoned in the past, without ever attempting to determine why the previous policies had not succeeded.[7]

Thus it was no surprise that the Obama administration put out a "Goals to Be Attained by 2015" document that included decreasing the prevalence of drug use among teenagers by 15 percent and reducing the number of chronic abusers by 15 percent. Lamentably, if we had met an almost identical set of goals outlined by the Reagan administration three decades before, there might not have still been a major drug problem in the United States. Instead, drug abuse stubbornly persisted, even if the popularity of particular drugs, such as heroin and cocaine, ebbed and flowed.

At the same time, the war's longevity institutionalized a sense that "any motion is forward motion." This produced a self-referential justification: As long as we were spending money and matériel on interdiction or eradication, we were making progress, regardless of whether the policies were succeeding on any external measures. A Reuters headline in May 2018—"Colombia, U.S. Seek to Halve Cocaine Output in Five Years"—suggested that inertia was alive and well in this corner of the vast drug war playroom. Invariably, drug war hawks—or even those who just want to see better policy—will retort that trying and failing is better than not trying at all. And this is of course correct. But such a mind-set cannot allow us to tolerate the pitiful policy outcomes over the course of our drug war.[8]

A Foreign Policy Elephant

The militarized drug war has also defined our relationships with several other countries, particularly in Latin America, at the expense of other policy priorities. In September 2017, President Trump shocked drug warriors when he announced that his administration "seriously considered" decertifying Colombia for failing to meet its international counternarcotics obligations. The president cited the "extraordinary growth of coca cultivation over the past three years." Decertification would have placed one of the closest U.S. allies in South America in the same basket as drug war nemeses like Bolivia and Venezuela. Part of Trump's ire may have resulted from Colombia's president Juan Manuel Santos, a winner of the Nobel Peace Prize, saying that the war on drugs was "perhaps more harmful than all the wars in the world combined." Another part may have derived from the perception that Santos had neglected anti-cocaine goals to boost his peace negotiations with the FARC. Said the State Department's top anti-drug diplomat William Brownfield: "It is my personal belief that the government of Colombia and its president overwhelmingly focused on the peace negotiations and the peace accord. I believe that by so focusing their attention, they by definition focused less on the issue of drugs and drug trafficking. I believe in addition they concluded that in order to reach a successful peace accord, they had to cede to the FARC on issues related to drugs." The Santos administration responded forcefully by saying: "Colombia is without a doubt the country which has most fought drugs, and which has had the most success on that front. . . . No one has to threaten us to confront this challenge."9

Signals of Change

Given the discouraging realities, there was an increasing sense in American public opinion, as in Beltway circles, that drug policy was ripe for reform. In recent years there have been several developments that could prove to be early signals of change, although this of course does not automatically entail progress. The most prominent was widespread liberalization of cannabis, which left roughly two-thirds of American citizens living in states where the drug was legal in some form; in 2019, 67 percent of citizens supported legal medicinal *and* recreational use, double the rate from a decade earlier. On the issue of medicinal marijuana, the approval rate was over 90 percent. It's important to bear in mind, though, that the recent trend has an imperfect precedent: cannabis enjoyed a similar phase of popularity in the 1970s, and it, like all drugs, had been entirely unregulated in the United States before 1911.[10]

The opioid crisis of the 2010s was another shifting issue that touched the American mainstream as no other drug addiction epidemic had before. Almost one in two people in 2017 knew someone who was or had once been addicted to opioids. The problem affected all corners of American society, from underemployed assembly plant workers in the heartland to lawyers at the pinnacles of high-profile careers. In one especially tragic case, the former vice chair of Obama's Joint Chiefs of Staff, Admiral Sandy Winnefeld—a venerable public servant I admired tremendously from my time in the Pentagon when we collaborated on counternarcotics policy—lost his son, a college freshman, to an opioid overdose in the autumn of 2017. The key difference between this crisis and the crack crisis of the 1980s and the heroin crisis that preceded that one, is that in the recent wave, so many people had a story to share on social media.[11]

As Senator Joe Manchin of West Virginia described the situation in an interview in 2016, "It's an epidemic because we have a business model for it. Follow the money. Look at the amount of pills they shipped in to certain parts of our state. It was a business model." In this case, the driver of that business model was a licit, licensed industry. The reach of the crisis, the embeddedness of politicians and the pharmaceutical industry, and the extent to which the crisis eroded public trust in government changed the conversation. For the first time, politicians on both sides of the aisle began to talk publicly about addiction as an illness to be treated rather than as a vice to be eradicated. Some of the most vocal were longtime drug war hawks. We can also look to nascent medical research on hallucinogens as a signal of change. The implication of renewed medical interest in drugs like psilocybin and LSD is a more nuanced and perhaps more technocratic approach to the scheduling and regulation of drugs.[12]

It would be imprudent to draw sweeping conclusions about these modest shifts in public awareness and attitude as indicators of an impending radical end to the drug war. It is ambitious enough to suggest that they have the potential to contribute to future policy shifts. We may eventually look back on the last decade as an inflection point. However, I fear that the apt metaphor is actually of a sine wave, and we are at a peak right now.

Unacceptable Extremes

Whether or not change was under way, the question remained whether the drug war *ought* to change. The fact is, there is little chance that continuing to prosecute the drug war in its current form will further reduce drug consumption and abuse. Narratives like the Department of Defense's summary of Operation Martillo and the op-ed by Walters and Murray obscure this reality with one-off statistics suggesting that what we've done for the past thirty years on the supply side is a winning prescription. In fact, the drug war's weak record of lasting supply-side gains would be entirely laughable—if the costs in treasure and trauma were not so great, that is. If we accept this as we have done for at least the past half century, we will not succeed.

As for escalating the war, the only cases where aggressive supply-side and punitive domestic policies have substantially reduced drug use and abuse have entailed costs that would be unjustifiable under the rules of America's liberal democracy. Singapore's draconian drug laws make the possession, use, and sale of all drugs illegal and punishable by caning and prison sentences or a mandatory death penalty. Singapore long had one of the world's lowest rates of drug use—.005 per 100,000 people for cannabis, .003 for ecstasy, .002 for opioids. The policy was supported by social intolerance and stigmatization of drug users and drug addicts. But the iron fist of draconian punishments was an inescapable pillar of this controversial approach. In 2018 Singapore's ambassador to Washington, Ashok Kumar Mirpuri, explained the Asian city-state's reasoning for the hard line: "When expressing sympathy for drug traffickers, let us remember the immense harm drugs cause abusers and their families, especially children." Yet even Singapore was not immune from the forces of drugs and drug addiction.[13]

In the Philippines, Rodrigo Duterte won the 2016 presidential election on a hysterical anti-drug and anti-corruption line. One pro-Duterte senator explained his political mentor's thinking: "He was bullheaded in telling people our problem is drugs. We're nearly a narco-state, and our police are afraid. Our judges, fiscals [prosecutors] are either afraid or on the take. Congressmen are in it, mayors are in it." For Duterte, drugs were a "contamination" that would ruin the country unless something drastic was done. For methamphetamine addicts in particular, "They are of no use to society anymore." Soon after taking office, Duterte held a rally in a park attended by two hundred thousand of his supporters. He threatened drug crooks: "You sons of bitches. I really will kill." He received a raucous response. Duterte was also very clear about how he would go about it, explaining, "There are 3 million drug addicts [in the Philippines]. I'd be happy to slaughter them . . . [and] finish the problem of my country and save the next generation from perdition." Duterte's controversial anti-drug strategy sparked a surge in extrajudicial killings that allegedly topped over three thousand victims (most reported as drug dealers and addicts) in a four-month span.[14]

Duterte's iron-fist drug strategy was condemned internationally, but he and his strategy have remained popular in the Philippines, having met the expectations of those who voted for him. In one poll, almost 90 percent of Filipinos agreed that in the time since Duterte's inauguration, there had been a decrease in drug-related incidents in their neighborhoods. Even the English journalist and vocal Duterte critic James Fenton acknowledged, "There's less of a drug problem. You can walk the streets at night, one is told." And yet, Fenton cautions his readers, the "price paid is striking."[15]

Such draconian approaches to drug enforcement have popped up from time to time in White House rhetoric. We have already seen that, in 1989, Bush drug czar William J. Bennett declared, "Morally, I don't have any problem at all" with beheading as a means of deterring drug dealers (though he acknowledged that pursuing such a policy would be legally challenging in the United States). Bennett further clarified, "What we need to do is find some constitutional and legally permissible way to . . . make the punishment fit the crime—and the crime is horrible." In 2018, President Trump advocated capital

Men in handcuffs after the Philippine National Bureau of Investigation seized $67 million worth of methamphetamine, locally known as "shabu," in a raid in San Juan City, Metropolitan Manila, December 23, 2016 (Reuters, permission to author)

punishment for convicted dealers and indicated that his administration was investigating policy changes that could enable federal prosecutors to pursue the death penalty. Whether this was an example of Trump's typical bombast or a substantive policy plan remained unclear at the time of publication.[16]

On the other hand, sweeping legalization of drugs is also unlikely to achieve acceptable results and will almost certainly bring other pernicious side effects. The "legalize it" case is captured well in the following argument, from Nicholas Kristof of the *New York Times:* "For decades, America has waged an ineffective war on drug pushers and drug lords, from Bronx street corners to Medellín, Colombia, regarding them as among the most contemptible specimens of humanity." The way to win, Kristof and others counter, is simply to follow the commonsense reforms of progressive governments like those of Portugal and Canada. Daniel Denvir of *Slate* made a similar point by outlining a stark contrast. First, he highlighted how Trump's first attorney general, Jeff Sessions, instructed prosecutors in 2017 to pursue the most severe charges in federal drug cases, "presenting the conventional drug war wisdom as though its veracity required little explanation." Then he described how Lucie Charlebois, Québec's minister of public health, held back tears as she unveiled two new treatment centers in Montreal that would allow addicts to receive supervised methadone injections. For Denvir, a tour of one of these "remarkably banal" Montreal injection clinics proved a "striking repudiation of the drug war."[17]

The model favored by the legalization camp is generally known as "harm reduction." Proponents describe this as "a public health approach to drug use premised on the idea that the aim of policy should be to maximize health and minimize damage." For advocates, the Trump administration's doubling down on the drug war represented "a wholesale rejection of science." One U.S.-based activist expanded: "It's completely regressive. Utterly draconian policies, utter hysteria around the crack epidemic and the result then was to lock everyone up. The idea is if we put a dent in the supply then demand will go down accordingly. It's not what happens." Why was Washington so unwilling to genuinely entertain a seemingly logical alternative? Because, Denvir explained, "it would require legalization, and that would be the end of the drug war."[18]

Critics are correct to point out the drug war's failures, massive expense, and damage inflicted on marginal segments of American society, as well as on source and transit countries. Demilitarization and legalization might well be preferable to the status quo. But as people become more open-minded about drug legalization, it is worth remembering the climate of the "Just Say No" days of the late 1980s, when families, communities, and politicians were terrified of an apparent crack cocaine scourge. These sentiments might seem trivial now, but there were legitimate reasons that the United States (and often its Latin American allies) clamored to escalate the war on drugs: because drugs, on their own, do cause personal and social harm.[19]

In considering demilitarization and legalization, it is important to be clear about the full range of consequences. Alcohol-related deaths plummeted during the dry years of Prohibition. This is not to argue that repealing Prohibition was a bad move but to remind the reader that punitive approaches at the very core of the anti-drug strategy can have positive effects. Today, rates of use and addiction are higher for alcohol and tobacco than for other substances in part because they are legal. This caution stands in full view of the reality that most recreational use of drugs is not harmful abuse, and full permissiveness on more dangerous drugs, such as opiates and amphetamines, is likely to come with its own burdens in the form of higher addiction rates, social dysfunction, and costs of treatment. The notion that the drug war can simply be transformed through legalization writ large remains naive until more specific details are developed and successfully implemented. This is especially true now that state-level policies are moving in the direction of cannabis legalization. It is rarely mentioned that state marijuana legalizations violate more than one U.N. treaty on drug production, the very international statutes that Washington has spent the past several decades insisting that other countries obey.

Another Way Forward

The unsuitability of each of the three options above—continuation, escalation, and reversal—creates a conundrum. There is no magic pill to make the drug issue go away. Instead, what we have are suboptimal policy options for social problems that are tenacious. The question, then, is not, "How can we win the drug war?" but "What are the least bad ways to make incremental progress?"

Mark Kleiman, a recently deceased professor of public policy at New York University and one of America's wisest voices on drug policy, offered, to my mind, the most cogent and reasonable prescriptions for drug war reform. Kleiman's sage guidance was that we first acknowledge that there will never be a single "solution" to the drug problem. This is partly because the potential for drug use and drug abuse is wired into humans' brains. For Kleiman, "Left to their own devices, and subject to the sway of fashion and the blandishments of advertising, many people will wind up ruining their lives and the lives of those around them by falling under the spell of one drug or another." Any realistic alternate future requires accepting that substance abuse and the associated impacts on users, their families, their workplaces, and the general public will continue. It requires accepting "some level of damage" from the illegal markets and police enforcement. In his estimation, we aren't going to solve the problems of drugs by either "winning the drug war" or "ending prohibition." The only feasible, and therefore preferable option, involves trade-offs and tolerance levels that we must pursue with exceptionally sober deliberation.[20]

Kleiman's stuff is sharp indeed, but we should proceed with caution. One of his principles turns on the cost-benefit calculation idea. "We should act only when we can do more good than harm, not merely to express our righteousness. Since lawbreakers and their families are human beings, their suffering counts, too: Arrests and prison terms are costs, not benefits, of policy." This is admirably high-minded but, alas, also often unrealistic. There is usually no way to calculate the costs of any policy before it's implemented. This is one of the insights this book's historical analysis gives us, and one upshot of this insight is that it's not unreasonable to expect decision-makers to do better than simply estimating the (extremely hypothetical) potential costs and benefits of an idea. Instead, we expect them to make choices in the absence of perfect information, which means that we expect them to rely on first principles and a priori claims about the good and the less good and virtue. As Kleiman would most certainly have agreed, smart drug policymaking must embody values, rather than just cost-benefit analyses.[21]

A crucial point is that in order to make any change or progress on drugs or drug war, we need to change the terms of the debate. This is a concrete step that policymakers, scholars, and media can take. The debate is still stuck in this old and persistent discursive field that considers drug use a question of morality. From the right, if you use drugs, you're a condemnable person, and drug use in America is a signal of moral decline. From the left, prohibition is a restriction on civil liberties and a malign attempt by the privileged to terrorize classes and races that are already marginalized. There's not much middle ground available between those two poles.

My guess is that if we instead acknowledge the phenomena related to drug use as facts and quit thinking about them in terms of individual or national virtue, we will have a lot more flexibility in the policy options we have to address drugs' harms and avoid creating new ones. (Some of those phenomena, in my interpretation, are: people do use drugs and will continue to use them; the drug trade is a market like any other and is subject to forces of supply and demand; our assumptions about the permissibility of drug use are contingent and have ebbed and flowed substantially over the past two centuries; addiction is a low-instance illness with high treatment success rates; most drugs are physically benign; the substances with the highest health risks and social costs in the United States are alcohol and tobacco, which are already permitted; and there are indeed substances that damage people's physical and mental health, economic prospects, family lives.)

There are some areas where the United States should consider going more maximalist. One in particular is basically calling it quits in the global supply-side war where American taxpayer dollars are diverted to funding and training local security force operators—whether in Colombia, Mexico, Afghanistan, or elsewhere—to bust clandestine cocaine, opium, or meth labs. As we learned, egged on by Congress and an equally frantic American public, President Bush Sr. took the drug war "downtown" in Latin America. If you had asked any of these policymakers at the time, after seeing the results of the billions spent during this quarter century supply-side mini-era, only the most rigid observers could conclude it was anything other than myriad localized tactical successes and setbacks but an elusive strategic win. Part of the problem, though, is that the drug warriors, as our drug war veteran put it above, would be out of a job—or at least out of an argument or ideology.

Drug war proponents will certainly respond that, despite all its failures, you simply must prosecute both the supply and the demand sides, that giving up on the former will undermine the latter. Yet this is the logic that has justified our rigid supply-side policies that appear stuck as if it were still back in the global drug war's halcyon days in the late 1980s and 1990s. If Washington wants to continue the supply-side game, it should instead do the smaller-ticket, less sexy initiatives like bolstering key public institutions like the judiciary, prisons, and law enforcement. Ironically, this prescription is indeed still supply side in nature but represents a kinder, gentler, and more effective approach. And a qualitatively better supply-side outlook in the short and medium term is an improvement on the status quo until we can undertake massive reconsideration of our global anti-drug campaign.

The question remains whether our leaders have the courage to apply a new approach within the broader war on drugs and own the fact that the old way of addressing drugs and their harms doesn't work. Only courage can enable change. So far there has been little sign of it.

Postscript

One gorgeous crisp fall morning in 2018 as I was putting the final touches on this manuscript, I opened my email to find a message sharing the news that my friend and former Davidson College colleague Patrick Braxton-Andrew had passed away in Mexico. I first got to know Patrick back in 2012 when, in his late twenties, he served as my assistant in Davidson's study abroad program in Peru, which meant that he spent an intensive six months in the South American country with my entire family in tow. Patrick was a bright, adored local kid attending Davidson whose dad was a beloved cross country and track coach at the college. After three stints aiding the Peru program, he returned to the town of Davidson to teach high school Spanish.

An inveterate traveler, Patrick rarely missed an opportunity to grab his tattered backpack and travel abroad, usually in Latin America but also in Asia. On this last weeklong Mexico trip, Patrick's plan was to take the scenic train passage into the Copper Canyon between the northern provincial city of Chihuahua to the Pacific port city of Los Mochis before meeting up with his brother Kerry in Mexico City for a couple of days. So when Patrick did not

Patrick Braxton-Andrew (1983–2018) with friends in Guatemala in 2016

show up in the capital on the appointed day, it was clear that something was wrong.

It was on the next day that I got the news. We all thought (and hoped) that he must have gotten lost on a hike in this majestic but also inhospitable arid desert mountain landscape. In the back of everyone's mind, though, was that this remote region of southwestern Chihuahua state into Sinaloa had, like myriad other spots in the country, a well-earned reputation for drug gang activity and violence. After an incredible search and investigation conducted by the Mexican authorities—especially the governor and attorney general of Chihuahua—we learned that Patrick had taken a short hike on the outskirts of the isolated pueblo of Urique, about 450 miles southwest of El Paso, when he ran into a Sinaloa cartel cell run by José Noriel Portillo Gil, alias "El Chueco" (the crooked one), who summarily executed him.

One of the many mysteries involved the motive, given that Mexican narcos try to steer clear of killing gringos. Some villagers who witnessed the cold-blooded murder told the press or Chihuahua authorities that El Chueco might have killed Patrick because, due to his olive skin and fluent Spanish, he mistook him for a DEA agent.

In this deep tragedy of Patrick's all too young death, no matter how much I wanted to deny it, I was once again confronted with the war on drugs. Here we had the successes of courageous Mexican officials who did the right thing to rescue Patrick. El Chueco was, at least in my opinion, a heinous human being who I hope will meet justice, but I also couldn't help thinking that all of this violence, tragedy, and evil was part of a broader war whose central culpability rested with our personal and societal desires, hypocrisies, and policy failures. Long may you run, PBA. For your spirit and love of foreign cultures and people-to-people exchanges, I dedicate this book to you.[22]

NOTES

Only the key sources for each note are listed here. A full listing and other topical and source information can be viewed at: russellcrandall.com.

Introduction

1. Zachary Siegel, "How Joe Biden's Policies Made the Opioid Crisis Harder to Treat," *Politico*, May 23, 2019.

2. Annabelle Buggle, "After 40-Year Fight, Illicit Drug Use at All-Time High," *Huffington Post*, December 6, 2017; Seth Daggett, "Costs of Major U.S. Wars," Congressional Research Service, June 29, 2010; UNODCP, "The Global Cocaine Market," *World Drug Report,* 2010; E. Ann Carson, "Prisoners in 2014," Office of Justice Programs, U.S. Department of Justice, September 2015; Beau Kilmer and Greg Midgette, "Mixed Messages: Is Cocaine Consumption in the U.S. Going Up or Going Down?" Brookings Institution, April 28, 2017.

3. "Prescription Narcotics Are Potent Painkillers, but They Can Be Deadly," *Washington Post,* November 10, 2014; Jeanne Whalen, "The Children of the Opioid Crisis," WSJ.com; Jennifer Levitz and Scott Calvert, "Vermont's Radical Experiment to Break the Addiction Cycle," WSJ.com; Lauryn Higgins, "In North Carolina, Heroin Is More Accessible and Cheaper Than Alcohol," *Salon,* August 6, 2017.

4. Abby Phillip and Katie Zezima, "GOP Contenders Are Talking About Drug Abuse, but Racial and Partisan Rifts Persist," *Washington Post,* November 27, 2015.

5. Phillip and Zezima, "GOP Contenders Are Talking."

6. Jason Wahler, "The Grey Area with the New Green: Cannabis for Addicts in Recovery," *Huffington Post,* January 9, 2018.

7. Jason Gay, "When Boxing Goes Low, I Go High," *Wall Street Journal,* August 27, 2017.

8. Russell Crandall, "The Drug War Divide," *The American Interest,* October 3, 2014.

9. Dan Lamonthe, "The U.S. Begins Bombing Taliban Drug Labs as Trump's Afghanistan Strategy Takes Hold," *Washington Post*, November 20, 2017.

10. "Remarks by President Trump Before a Briefing on the Opioid Crisis," The White House, August 8, 2017.

11. Yves Lavigne, *Hell's Angels: "Three Can Keep a Secret if Two Are Dead"* (New York: Kensington, 1989), 94; Benjamin Breen, "From the Lab to the Street: How 3 Illegal Drugs Came to Be," *Atlantic*, August 25, 2013; Crandall, "Drug War Divide"; Betsy Pearl, "Ending the War on Drugs: By the Numbers," Center for American Progress, June 27, 2018.

Chapter 1. Drugs 101

1. Agata Blaszczak-Boxe, "Prehistoric High Times: Early Humans Used Magic Mushrooms, Opium," *LiveScience*, February 2, 2015; Ezekiel Gebissa, "Khat in the Horn of Africa: Historical Perspectives and Current Trends," *Journal of Ethnopharmacology* 132, no. 3 (December 1, 2010), 607–14; John Otis, "The Tradition of Chewing Coca," *The World*, PRI, April 1, 2011; Johann Hari, *Chasing the Scream: The First and Last Days of the War on Drugs* (London: Bloomsbury, 2015), 149; Anthony Lydgate, "Shakespeare's Lost Weed Sonnets," *New Yorker*, August 13, 2015; Rod Phillips, *Alcohol: A History* (Chapel Hill: University of North Carolina Press, 2014), 183.

2. Johann Hari, "Why Animals Eat Psychoactive Plants," *Boing Boing*, January 20, 2015; Steven Kotler, "Animals on Psychedelics: Survival of the Trippiest," *Psychology Today*, December 29, 2010; Ronald K. Siegel, *Intoxication: The Universal Drive for Mind-Altering Substances* (Rochester, Vt.: Park Street Press, 2005), 208; Hari, *Chasing the Scream*, 152.

3. Sam Harris, "Drugs and the Meaning of Life," *Huffington Post*, September 5, 2011.

4. Amresh Shrivastava et al., "Cannabis and Psychosis: Neurobiology," *Indian Journal of Psychiatry* 56, no. 1 (2014): 8–16.

5. Mark Kleiman, Jonathan Caulkins, and Angela Hawken, *Drugs and Drug Policy* (New York: Oxford University Press, 2011).

6. Ana Maria Rosso, "Poppy and Opium in Ancient Times: Remedy or Narcotic?" *Biomedicine International* 1 (2010): 81–87.

7. David T. Courtwright, *Forces of Habit: Drugs and the Making of the Modern World* (Cambridge: Harvard University Press, 2001), 1–2.

8. Massachusetts Cannabis Reform Coalition, "Social History of Marijuana," available at http://masscann.org/cannabis-the-plant/social-history-of-marijuana.

9. Substance Abuse and Mental Health Services Administration, "Key Substance Use and Mental Health Indicators in the United States: Results from the 2016 National Survey on Drug Use and Health," September 2017.

10. Stephanie Lanza, "Trends Among High School Seniors in Recent Marijuana Use and Associations with Other Substances, 1976–2013," *Journal of Adolescent Health* 57 (August 2015): 198–204.

11. Hari, *Chasing the Scream,* 148; Zachary Siegel, "Ending the Drug War: An Interview with Johann Hari," *The Fix,* February 12, 2015.

12. Bruce Barcott, *Weed the People: The Future of Legal Marijuana in America* (New York: Time Books, 2015), 165.

13. Ira Flatow, "A Tale of Two Addicts: Freud, Halsted, and Cocaine," interview with Howard Markel, *Talk of the Nation,* NPR, November 25, 2011. See also Howard Markel, *An Anatomy of Addiction: Sigmund Freud, William Halsted, and the Miracle Drug Cocaine* (New York: Vintage, 2012).

14. David T. Courtwright, "A Century of American Narcotic Policy," in *Treating Drug Problems: Volume 2: Commissioned Papers on Historical, Institutional, and Economic Contexts of Drug Treatment,* ed. Dean R. Gerstein and Henrick J. Harwood (Washington, D.C.: National Academies Press, 1992); Courtwright, *Forces of Habit,* 97.

15. Gabor Maté, *In the Realm of Hungry Ghosts: Close Encounters with Addiction* (Berkeley: North Atlantic, 2008), 14; Dan Levin, "Vancouver Prescriptions for Addicts Gain Attention as Heroin and Opioid Use Rises," *New York Times,* April 21, 2016.

16. Nils Bejerot, *Addiction: An Artificially Induced Drive* (Springfield, Ill.: Thomas, 1972); Courtwright, *Forces of Habit,* 95.

17. Maté, *In the Realm of Hungry Ghosts,* 38; Carolyn Gregoire, "Why This Doctor Believes Addictions Start in Childhood," *Huffington Post,* January 27, 2016.

18. Johann Hari, "Everything You Think You Know About Addiction Is Wrong," TED Talks, June 2015.

19. Andrew Dobbs, "4 Things Johann Hari Gets Wrong About Addiction—Updated with a Response from Hari," *The Fix,* July 29, 2015.

20. Mark Kleiman, "Dopey, Boozy, Smoky—and Stupid," *American Interest,* January 1, 2007; Bruce L. Benson and David W. Rasmussen, *The Economic Anatomy of a Drug War* (Lanham, Md.: Rowman & Littlefield, 1994).

21. Gene M. Heyman, *Addiction: A Disorder of Choice* (Cambridge: Harvard University Press, 2009), 112; Kleiman, "Dopey, Boozy, Smokey—and Stupid"; David Boyum and Mark A. R. Kleiman, "Breaking the Drug-Crime Link," *The Public Interest,* Summer 2003.

22. Hari, "Why Animals Eat Psychoactive Plants"; Hari, *Chasing the Scream,* 148.

23. Kleiman et al., *Drugs and Drug Policy,* 1–9.

24. Robert K. Massie, *Peter the Great: His Life and World* (New York: Random House, 2012), 212; Abigail Cutler, "The Ashtray of History," *Atlantic,* January 2007; Sean Gabb, *Smoking, Class, and the Legitimation of Power* (Lulu, 2011), 57.

25. Courtwright, *Forces of Habit,* 194.

26. "Noam Chomsky Dialogue with Trade Unionists, Cambridge, Massachusetts, February 2, 1999." Available at https://archive.org/details/NoamChomsky-1999-02-02-DialogueWithTradeUnionists-Cambridge.

27. Kleiman et al., *Drugs and Drug Policy,* 44–45.

28. Kleiman et al., *Drugs and Drug Policy,* 45–47.

29. Kleiman et al., *Drugs and Drug Policy,* 46–47; George F. Will, "Should the U.S. Legalize Hard Drugs?" *Washington Post,* April 11, 2012.

30. Kleiman et al., *Drugs and Drug Policy,* 45–47.

31. Kleiman et al., *Drugs and Drug Policy,* 44–45; "A Social History of America's Most Popular Drugs," *Frontline,* PBS, October 2000.

Chapter 2. Alcohol

1. Dylan Matthews, "Mark Kleiman on Why We Need to Solve Our Alcohol Problem to Solve Our Crime Problem," *Washington Post,* March 28, 2013.

2. "Alcohol Use and Your Health," factsheet, Centers for Disease Control and Prevention, available at www.cdc.gov/alcohol/fact-sheets/alcohol-use.htm; Matthews, "Mark Kleiman on Why We Need."

3. Iain Gately, *Drink: A Cultural History of Alcohol* (New York: Penguin, 2008), 1–2.

4. Gately, *Drink,* 1–12.

5. Peter C. Mancall, *Deadly Medicine: Indians and Alcohol in Early America* (Ithaca, N.Y.: Cornell University Press, 1997), 136; Tanya Basu, "Have We Found the Lost Colony of Roanoke Island?" *National Geographic,* December 8, 2013; Gately, *Drink,* 120.

6. Gately, *Drink,* 122–24.

7. Gately, *Drink,* 124–27; Susan Cheever, *Drinking in America: Our Secret History* (New York: Grand Central, 2016), 34.

8. Gately, *Drink,* 128; Cheever, *Drinking in America,* 34; W. J. Rorabaugh, *The Alcoholic Republic* (Oxford, U.K.: Oxford University Press, 1981), 5–21; W. J. Rorabaugh, "A Nation of Sots: When Drinking Was a Patriotic Duty," *New Republic,* September 29, 1979; Lisa McGirr, *The War on Alcohol: Prohibition and the Rise of the American State* (New York: Norton, 2016), Mark E. Lender and James K. Martin, *Drinking in America: A History* (New York: Free Press, 1987); Andrew Barr, *Drink: A Social History of America* (New York: Carroll and Graf, 1999).

9. Gately, *Drink,* 123–56; Mancall, *Deadly Medicine.*

10. Cheever, *Drinking in America,* 66; Timothy Egan, "The Wrath of Grapes," *New York Times,* April 21, 2012; Daniel Okrent, *Last Call: The Rise and Fall of Prohibition* (New York: Scribner, 2010), 47; Rorabaugh, *Alcoholic Republic,* 152; Robert J. Dinkin, *Campaigning in America: A History of Election Practices* (Westport, Conn.: Greenwood, 1989), 3.

11. Cheever, *Drinking in America,* 65.

12. Kelefa Sanneh, "Drunk with Power," *New Yorker,* December 21, 2015.

13. Egan, "Wrath of Grapes"; Cheever, *Drinking in America,* 66–67.

14. Cheever, *Drinking in America,* 67.

15. Cheever, *Drinking in America,* 67; Rorabaugh, *Alcoholic Republic,* 50–53; Thomas P. Slaughter, *The Whiskey Rebellion: Frontier Epilogue to the American Revolution* (Oxford, U.K.: Oxford University Press, 1988), 101.

16. Rorabaugh, *Alcoholic Republic,* 53–55; Egan, "Wrath of Grapes."

17. Egan, "Wrath of Grapes"; Cheever, *Drinking in America*, 77–78; Rorabaugh, "Nation of Sots"; Emma Green, "Colonial Americans Drank Roughly Three Times as Much as Americans Do Now," *Atlantic*, June 29, 2015.

18. "Benjamin Rush (1746–1813)," Penn Archives and Records Center, available at https://archives.upenn.edu/exhibits/penn-people/biography/benjamin-rush.

19. Edward Behr, *Prohibition: Thirteen Years That Changed America* (New York: Arcade, 1996), 15; Benjamin Rush, *An Inquiry into the Effect of Ardent Spirits Upon the Human Body and Mind, With an Account of the Means of Preventing and of the Remedies for Curing Them* (Boston: James Loring, 1823), 8; Rorabaugh, *Alcoholic Republic*, 41.

20. Rorabaugh, "Nation of Sots"; Rorabaugh, *Alcoholic Republic*, 6; Patrick Radden Keefe, "The Jefferson Bottles," *New Yorker*, September 3, 2007.

21. James Hamblin, "How Much Water Do People Drink?" *Atlantic*, March 12, 2013; Howard Means, *Johnny Appleseed: The Man, The Myth, and the American Story* (New York: Simon and Schuster, 2011), 97; Michael Pollan, *The Botany of Desire: A Plant's-Eye View of the World* (New York: Random House, 2002).

22. Rorabaugh, "Nation of Sots"; Eric Burns, *The Spirits of America: A Social History of Alcohol* (Philadelphia: Temple University Press, 2004), 11; Dawson Burns, *The Bases of the Temperance Reform: An Exposition and Appeal* (New York: National Temperance Society and Publication House, 1873); McGirr, *War on Alcohol*, 6; Sanneh, "Drunk with Power."

23. Sanneh, "Drunk with Power"; Norman H. Clark, *Deliver Us from Evil* (New York: Norton, 1976), 14–24.

24. Ronald K. Siegel, *Intoxication: The Universal Drive for Mind-Altering Substances* (Rochester, N.Y.: Park Street Press, 2005), 257.

25. McGirr, *War on Alcohol*, 6; James A. Morone, " 'The War on Alcohol,' by Lisa McGirr," *New York Times*, December 30, 2015; Julia M. Klein, " 'The War on Alcohol' by Lisa McGirr," *Boston Globe*, December 10, 2015.

26. Rorabaugh, *Alcoholic Republic*, 191–94; Jack S. Blocker, David M. Fahey, and Ian R. Tyrrell, *Alcohol and Temperance in Modern History: An International Encyclopedia* (Santa Barbara: ABC-CLIO, 2003), 215; Jack S. Blocker Jr., "Did Prohibition Really Work? Alcohol Prohibition as a Public Health Innovation," *American Journal of Public Health* 96, no. 2 (2006): 233–43.

27. Sarah W. Tracy and Caroline Jean Acker, "Psychoactive Drugs—An American Way of Life," in *Altering American Consciousness: The History of Alcohol and Drug Use in the United States, 1800–2000*, ed. Tracy and Acker (Amherst: University of Massachusetts Press, 2004), 1–32; Rorabaugh, *Alcoholic Republic*, 195; Blocker, "Did Prohibition Really Work?"

28. Sanneh, "Drunk with Power"; McGirr, *War on Alcohol*, 6–8.

29. Christopher Finan, *Drunks: An American History* (Boston: Beacon Press, 2017), 31; McGirr, *War on Alcohol*, 5.

30. Tracy and Acker, "Psychoactive Drugs," 4; Ian Tyrrel, *Sobering Up: From Temperance to Prohibition in Antebellum America, 1800–1860* (Westport, Conn.: Greenwood,

1979); Jonathan Zimmerman, "Dethroning King Alcohol: The Washingtonians in Baltimore, 1840–1854," *Maryland Historical Magazine* 87, no. 4 (1992): 374–98; McGirr, *War on Alcohol*, 6–8; Okrent, *Last Call*, 10; Rorabaugh, *Alcoholic Republic*, 200–214.

31. McGirr, *War on Alcohol*, 6–8; Okrent, *Last Call*, 10; Rorabaugh, *Alcoholic Republic*, 200–214.

32. Sanneh, "Drunk with Power"; Norman H. Clark, *Deliver Us from Evil: An Interpretation of American Prohibition* (New York: Norton, 1976), 8.

33. Egan, "Wrath of Grapes"; Siegel, *Intoxication*, 257; Lucas E. Morel, "Lincoln Among the Reformers: Tempering the Temperance Movement," *Journal of the Abraham Lincoln Association* 20, no. 1 (Winter 1999): 1–34.

34. Paul M. Angle and Earl Schenck Miers, *The Living Lincoln: The Man and His Times, in His Own Words* (New Brunswick, N.J.: Rutgers University Press, 1955), 49.

35. Siegel, *Intoxication*, 260.

36. Okrent, *Last Call*, 15.

37. Sanneh, "Drunk with Power"; Okrent, *Last Call*, 15; Carry Amelia Nation, *The Use and Need of the Life of Carry A. Nation* (Topeka, Kans.: F.M. Steves & Sons, 1908).

38. Sanneh, "Drunk with Power"; Okrent, *Last Call*, 15.

Chapter 3. Cocaine

1. National Institute on Drug Abuse, "Nationwide Trends," available at www.drugabuse.gov/publications/drugfacts/nationwide-trends; "International Statistics," The Truth About Cocaine, Foundation for a Drug Free World, available at www.drugfreeworld.org/drugfacts/cocaine/international-statistics.html.

2. Mattathias Schwartz, "A Mission Gone Wrong: Why Are We Still Fighting the Drug War?" *New Yorker*, January 6, 2014.

3. U.S. Congress, Office of Technology Assessment, *Alternative Coca Reduction Strategies in the Andean Region* (Washington D.C.: U.S. Government Printing Office, 1993), 189.

4. John Otis, "The Tradition of Chewing Coca," *The World*, PRI, April 1, 2011; Siegel, *Intoxication*, 1–2; Dominic Streatfeild, *Cocaine: An Unauthorized Biography* (New York: Picador, 2001); Paul Gootenberg, ed., *Cocaine: Global Histories* (London: Routledge, 1999); Tim Madge, *White Mischief: A Cultural History of Cocaine* (Edinburgh: Mainstream, 2001); Joseph F. Spillane, *Cocaine: From Medical Marvel to Modern Menace in the United States, 1884–1920* (Baltimore: Johns Hopkins University Press, 2000); Thomas Feiling, *The Candy Machine: How Cocaine Took Over the World* (New York: Penguin, 2009); Thomas Feiling, *Cocaine Nation: How the White Trade Took Over the World* (New York: Pegasus, 2010); Courtwright, *Forces of Habit*; Jill Jonnes, *Hep-Cats, Narcs, and Pipe Dreams: A History of America's Romance with Illegal Drugs* (New York: Scribner, 1996).

5. Paul M. Gahlinger, *Illegal Drugs: A Complete Guide to Their History, Chemistry, Use, and Abuse* (New York: Penguin, 2001), 38; Kenneth Duane Lehman, *Bolivia and the United States: A Limited Partnership* (Athens: University of Georgia Press, 1999), 190.

6. Feiling, *Cocaine Nation*, 1.

7. Bill Drake, ed., *The Coca Leaf Papers: Long-Lost Knowledge from 17th–19th Century Explorers, Madmen Visionaries, and Geniuses*, Amazon Kindle Services; William R. Long, "Peasants' Way of Life: Coca Leaf—Not Just for Getting High," *Los Angeles Times*, August 29, 1988; Feiling, *Cocaine Nation*; Otis, "Tradition of Chewing Coca"; Mike Jay, "Miracle or Menace? The Arrival of Cocaine, 1860–1900," *International Review of Neurobiology* 120 (2015): 27–39; Joseph A. Gagliano, "The Coca Debate in Colonial Peru," *The Americas* 20, no. 1 (1963): 43–63.

8. Andrew O'Hagan and Sophie McNicholl, "Treading the Fine White Line: Cocaine Trafficking," *Forensic Research and Criminology International Journal* 1, no. 2 (2015); Gootenberg, ed., *Cocaine*, 82–85.

9. Terry Gross, interview with Norman Ohler, "Author Says Hitler Was 'Blitzed' on Cocaine and Opiates During the War," *Fresh Air*, NPR, March 7, 2017.

10. Feiling, *Cocaine Nation*, 1–5; David Cohen, *Freud on Coke* (London: Cutting Edge Press, 2011).

11. Courtwright, *Forces of Habit*, 48; Markel, *Anatomy of Addiction*, 48.

12. Paul Gootenberg, *Andean Cocaine: The Making of a Global Drug* (Chapel Hill: University of North Carolina Press, 2008), 1.

13. Flatow, "Tale of Two Addicts"; Joseph A. Gagliano, *Coca Prohibition in Peru: The Historical Debates* (Tucson: University of Arizona Press, 1994), 111.

14. Brent Staples, "Coke Wars," *New York Times*, February 4, 1994; Louis Menand, "Why Freud Survives," *New Yorker*, August 28, 2017; Scott Oliver, "A Brief History of Freud's Love Affair with Cocaine: The Founder of Psychoanalysis Had a Serious Blow Habit," *Vice*, June 23, 2017; Flatow, "Tale of Two Addicts"; Sherwin Nuland, "Sigmund Freud's Cocaine Years," *New York Times*, July 21, 2011.

15. Flatow, "Tale of Two Addicts"; Markel, *Anatomy of Addiction*, 98–99, 269; Martin Torgoff, *Can't Find My Way Home in the Great Stoned Age, 1945–2000* (New York: Simon & Schuster, 2004), 316–18.

16. Mark Townsend, "Drugs in Literature: A Brief History," *Guardian*, November 15, 2008; Markel, *Anatomy of Addiction*, 98–99.

17. Flatow, "Tale of Two Addicts."

18. "Cocaine: How 'Miracle Drug' Nearly Destroyed Sigmund Freud, William Halsted," *PBS NewsHour*, October 27, 2011.

19. Maria Godoy, " 'Cocaine for Snowblindness': What Polar Explorers Packed for First Aid," NPR, September 28, 2012.

20. Howard Wayne Morgan, *Drugs in America: A Social History, 1800–1980* (Syracuse, N.Y.: Syracuse University Press, 1981), 17; Markel, *Anatomy of Addiction*,

54–59; James Hamblin, "Why We Took Cocaine Out of Soda," *Atlantic,* January 31, 2013.

21. Siegel, *Intoxication,* 260–61; Mark Perry, *Grant and Twain: The Story of a Friendship That Changed America* (New York: Random House, 2004), 220; John Waugh, *U.S. Grant: American Hero, American Myth* (Chapel Hill: University of North Carolina Press, 2009), 317; Ron Chernow, *Grant* (New York: Penguin, 2018), xvii.

22. Hamblin, "Why We Took"; Grace Elizabeth Hale, "When Jim Crow Drank Coke," *New York Times,* January 28, 2013.

23. Hamblin, "Why We Took"; Clifford D. May, "How Coca-Cola Obtains Its Coca," *New York Times,* July 1, 1988.

24. Karch, *A Brief History,* 41.

25. May, "How Coca-Cola Obtains."

26. May, "How Coca-Cola Obtains."

27. "A Social History," *Frontline,* PBS; Jonnes, *Hep-Cats,* 22–25; David F. Musto, "The History of Legislative Control Over Opium, Cocaine, and Their Derivatives," *Shaffer Library of Drug Policy;* Courtwright, "Century of American Narcotic Policy"; David Kestenbaum, *Why Coke Cost a Nickel for 70 Years,* NPR Morning Edition, podcast audio, November 15, 2012.

28. "Cocaine Debauchery in the South," *New York Medical Journal,* December 8, 1900; Jonnes, *Hep-Cats,* 32; Joseph Helfman, ed., *The Bulletin of Pharmacy* 15, no. 1 (January 1901).

29. David F. Musto, ed., *Drugs in America: A Documentary History* (New York: New York University Press, 2002), 363; Gahlinger, *Illegal Drugs,* 42; Edward Huntington Williams, "Negro Cocaine 'Fiends' Are a New Southern Menace," *New York Times,* February 8, 1914.

30. Jonnes, *Hep-Cats,* 32.

31. Jonnes, *Hep-Cats,* 32.

32. Jonnes, *Hep-Cats,* 32–33.

33. Jonnes, *Hep-Cats,* 25, 31, 35.

Chapter 4. Opium

1. Jonnes, *Hep-Cats,* 15.

2. Jonnes, *Hep-Cats,* 15; Jeremy Agnew, *Alcohol and Opium in the Old West: Use, Abuse, and Influence* (Jefferson, N.C.: McFarland, 2013), 63; Lorraine Berry, "Confessions of an American Opium Eater," *Brooklyn Magazine,* February 16, 2017.

3. Jonnes, *Hep-Cats,* 16; Richard Holmes, "De Quincey: So Original, So Truly Weird," *New York Review of Books,* November 24, 2016.

4. Jonnes, *Hep-Cats,* 16.

5. Sam Quinones, *Dreamland: The True Tale of America's Opiate Epidemic* (New York: Bloomsbury Press, 2015), 52; Lucy Inglis, *Milk of Paradise: A History of Opium* (New York: Pegasus, 2019), 3–70.

6. Musto, ed., *Drugs in America*, 184; David F. Musto, "Opium, Cocaine, and Marijuana in American History," *Scientific American* 265, no. 1 (July 1991): 40–47; Joshua Shenk, "Lincoln's Great Depression," *Atlantic*, October 2005.

7. Courtwright, *Forces of Habit*, 33.

8. Melissa Bull, *Governing the Heroin Trade: From Treaties to Treatment* (Abingdon, U.K.: Routledge, 2008), 55.

9. Courtwright, *Forces of Habit*, 35.

10. Courtwright, *Forces of Habit*, 35; Karl E. Meyer, "The Opium War's Secret History," *New York Times*, June 28, 1997.

11. Richard J. Grace, *Opium and Empire: The Lives and Careers of William Jardine and James Matheson* (Montreal: McGill-Queen's University Press, 2014), 87; Courtwright, *Forces of Habit*, 34–36.

12. Norman Ohler, *Blitzed: Drugs in the Third Reich* (Boston: Houghton Mifflin Harcourt, 2017); Antony Beevor, "The Very Drugged Nazis," *New York Review of Books*, March 9, 2017.

13. David Courtwright, *Dark Paradise: A History of Opiate Addiction in America* (Cambridge: Harvard University Press, 2001).

14. Courtwright, *Forces of Habit*, 37.

15. Courtwright, *Forces of Habit*, 37.

16. Courtwright, *Forces of Habit*, 37.

17. Jonnes, *Hep-Cats*, 30; "Opium Throughout History," *Frontline*, PBS, available at www.pbs.org/wgbh/pages/frontline/shows/heroin/etc/history.html.

18. Jonnes, *Hep-Cats*, 30–31; June Sawyers, "When Opium Was Really the Opiate of the Masses," *Chicago Tribune*, January 3, 1988.

19. Musto, "Opium, Cocaine, and Marijuana in American History"; Courtwright, *Forces of Habit*, 33–37.

20. Jonnes, *Hep-Cats*, 17.

21. Stephen R. Kandall, *Substance and Shadow: Women and Addiction in the United States* (Cambridge: Harvard University Press, 1999), 24.

22. David F. Musto, *The American Disease: Origins of Narcotic Controls* (New Haven, Conn.: Yale University Press, 1973); Quinones, *Dreamland*, 53; Jonnes, *Hep-Cats*, 17.

23. Denise Hofmann, "Nineteenth-Century Protestant Missionaries and British Merchants in China: Mutual Dependence in the Context of Opium Smuggling," Department of History, Middlebury College, January 2011, 58.

24. Meyer, "Opium War's Secret History."

25. Meyer, "Opium War's Secret History."

26. Meyer, "Opium War's Secret History," 93–96; Schwartz, "Mission Gone Wrong."

27. Musto, *American Disease*, 37–40; Jonnes, *Hep-Cats*, 40–41; Schwartz, "Mission Gone Wrong."

28. Courtwright, *Dark Paradise*, 79–82; Jonnes, *Hep-Cats*, 44; Morgan, *Drugs in America*, 98; Ernest Abel, *Marijuana: The First Twelve Thousand Years* (New York: Springer, 1980); Musto, *American Disease*, 38–39.

29. Courtwright, *Dark Paradise*, 81; Musto, *American Disease*, 37–40.

30. Jonnes, *Hep-Cats*, 36.

31. Jonnes, *Hep-Cats*, 36–37; Quinones, *Dreamland*, 53; Musto, "Opium, Cocaine, and Marijuana in American History"; Jim Edwards, "Yes, Bayer Promoted Heroin for Children—Here Are the Ads That Prove It," *Business Insider*, November 17, 2011.

32. Jill Jonnes, "Public Health Then and Now: The Rise of the Modern Addict," *American Journal of Public Health*, 85, no. 8 (August 1995): 1157–62.

33. Jonnes, *Hep-Cats*, 37.

Chapter 5. Cannabis

1. Martin A. Lee, *Smoke Signals: A Social History of Marijuana-Medical, Recreational, and Scientific* (New York: Scribner, 2013), 3.

2. Lee, *Smoke Signals*, 4.

3. Lee, *Smoke Signals*, 3–5.

4. Kristin Romey, "Ancient Cannabis 'Burial Shroud' Discovered in Desert Oasis," *National Geographic*, October 4, 2016.

5. Lee, *Smoke Signals*, 4; Courtwright, *Forces of Habit*, 40.

6. Lee, *Smoke Signals*, 4.

7. Fitz Hugh Ludlow and David M. Gross, *The Annotated Hasheesh Eater* (CreateSpace Independent Publishing Platform, 2007), 6.

8. Doug Fine, *Hemp Bound: Dispatches from the Front Lines of the Next Agricultural Revolution* (Hartford, Vt.: Chelsea Green, 2014), xxiii.

9. Lee, *Smoke Signals*, 16; James McClure, "The English Once Had to Grow Hemp, or Be Punished for Not Doing So," *Civilized*, September 7, 2016, available at www.civilized.life/articles/english-hemp-elizabeth-i.

10. Lee, *Smoke Signals*, 16; Siegel, *Intoxication*, 256.

11. Lee, *Smoke Signals*, 18–19.

12. Lee, *Smoke Signals*, 19.

13. Ludlow and Gross, *Hasheesh Eater*, 15; Lee, *Smoke Signals*, 31–33.

14. Lee, *Smoke Signals*, 31–33; Ludlow and Gross, *Hasheesh Eater*, xi; Martin Booth, *Cannabis: A History* (New York: Picador, 2005), 95.

15. Lee, *Smoke Signals*, 33.

16. Booth, *Cannabis*, 82; Lee, *Smoke Signals*, 36.

17. David W. Maurer, "The Argot of the Underworld Narcotic Addict," *American Speech* 11 (1936): 116–27.

18. Lee, *Smoke Signals*, 39; Lily Rothman, "Here's What People Called Marijuana in the 1940s," *Time*, April 20, 2015.

19. Courtwright, *Forces of Habit*, 43; "The Buyers: A Social History of America's Most Popular Drugs," *Frontline*, PBS; Matt Thompson, "The Mysterious History of 'Marijuana,'" *Code Switch*, NPR, July 22, 2013.

20. "A Hashish House in New York," *Harper's New Monthly Magazine*, 67, no. 402 (1883): 945.

21. Booth, *Cannabis*, 164; Hari, *Chasing the Scream*, 15.

22. David Bienenstock, "I Just Smoked Legal Weed," *Vice*, January 3, 2014.

23. Courtwright, *Forces of Habit*, 43; Wendy Chapkis and Richard Webb, *Dying to Get High: Marijuana as Medicine* (New York: New York University Press, 2008), 28.

24. Mezz Mezzrow, *Really the Blues* (New York: NYRB Classics, 2016), 66; Courtwright, *Forces of Habit*, 43–44; Lee, *Smoke Signals*, 44; Booth, *Cannabis*, 201; Larry Sloman, *Reefer Madness: A History of Marijuana* (New York: St. Martin's Griffin, 1998), 86.

25. Lee, *Smoke Signals*, 10–11; Sander Gilman and Xun Zhou, *Smoke: A Global History of Smoking* (London: Reaktion, 2004), 155.

26. Louis Armstrong, *Louis Armstrong, In His Own Words: Selected Writings* (Oxford, U.K.: Oxford University Press, 2001), 112; Lee, *Smoke Signals*, 11; Sanjay Gupta, "Why I Changed My Mind on Weed," CNN, August 9, 2013.

Chapter 6. Tobacco

1. Sandra Blakeslee, "Nicotine: Harder to Kick . . . Than Heroin," *New York Times*, March 29, 1987; U.S. Department of Health and Human Services, *Preventing Tobacco Use Among Youth and Young Adults: A Report of the Surgeon General*, Office on Smoking and Health, National Center for Chronic Disease Prevention and Health Promotion, Center for Disease Control and Prevention, 2012.

2. Blakeslee, "Nicotine Harder to Kick."

3. Blakeslee, "Nicotine Harder to Kick"; Michael C. Moynihan, "Cigarettes Are Still Sublime," *Wall Street Journal*, January 20, 2017; Gregor Hens, "The Last Last Cigarette," *New Yorker*, December 1, 2016.

4. Courtwright, *Forces of Habit*, 14.

5. Emily Jones Salmon and John Salmon, "Tobacco in Colonial Virginia," *Encyclopedia Virginia*, January 29, 2013.

6. Gately, *Drink*, 120–23.

7. Dr. Judith Mackar and Dr. Michael Erikson, *The Tobacco Atlas* (Geneva: World Health Organization, 2002).

8. Antonio Escohotado, *A Brief History of Drugs: From the Stone Age to the Stoned Age* (Rochester, N.Y.: Inner Traditions, 1999), 56–57; Courtwright, *Forces of Habit*, 100).

9. Courtwright, *Forces of Habit*, 16; Siegel, *Intoxication*, 253; Keith T. Krawczynski, *Daily Life in the Colonial City* (Westport, Conn.: Greenwood, 2012); Escohotado, *Brief History of Drugs*; Blakeslee, "Nicotine: Harder to Kick."

10. Raymond Goldberg, *Drugs Across the Spectrum* (Belmont, Calif.: Cengage Learning, 2009), 14.

11. Heidi Pierson, *Tobacco Pipes* (Vancouver: National Park Service, Fort Vancouver National Historic Site, 2010); Escohotado, *Brief History of Drugs*, 57.

12. Courtwright, *Forces of Habit*, 18.

13. William Kremer, "James Buchanan Duke: Father of the Modern Cigarette," BBC, November 3, 2012, available at www.bbc.com/news/magazine-20042217.

14. Courtwright, *Forces of Habit*, 114.

15. Courtwright, *Forces of Habit*, 114; Kremer, "James Buchanan Duke."

16. Daniel Miller, *Consumption: Critical Concepts in the Social Sciences* (Abingdon, U.K.: Routledge, 2001), 490; Courtwright, *Forces of Habit*, 114; Richard Kluger, *Ashes to Ashes: America's Hundred-Year Cigarette War, the Public Health, and the Unabashed Triumph of Philip Morris* (New York: Knopf Doubleday, 2010), 69.

17. *The Health Consequences of Smoking: 50 Years of Progress: A Report of the Surgeon General*, Office on Smoking and Health, National Center for Chronic Disease Prevention and Health Promotion, Centers for Disease Control and Prevention, 2014; K. Michael Cummings, "Programs and Policies to Discourage the Use of Tobacco Products," *Oncogene* 21, no. 48 (2002): 7349–64.

18. Courtwright, *Forces of Habit*, 122–24.

19. Courtwright, *Forces of Habit*, 18, 103–4, 124; Sarah W. Tracy, *Alcoholism in America: From Reconstruction to Prohibition* (Baltimore: Johns Hopkins University Press, 2009); Frank McCourt, *Angela's Ashes: A Memoir* (New York: Scribner, 1996), 344.

20. Courtwright, *Forces of Habit*, 192; *The Health Consequences of Smoking;* see also Kleiman, "Dopey, Boozy, Smokey—and Stupid."

Chapter 7. Crackdown

1. Lee, *Smoke Signals*, 41.

2. Hamblin, "Why We Took"; James Markham, "The American Disease," *New York Times*, April 29, 1973.

3. Jonnes, *Hep-Cats*, 35–36.

4. Nancy Tomes, *Remaking the American Patient: How Madison Avenue and Modern Medicine Turned Patients into Consumers* (Chapel Hill: University of North Carolina Press, 2016), 33; James Harvey Young, *The Medical Messiahs: A Social History of Medical Quackery in Twentieth Century America* (Princeton, N.J.: Princeton University Press, 1975), 30.

5. Lee, *Smoke Signals*, 41; Gahlinger, *Illegal Drugs*, 43; Musto, ed., *Drugs in America*, 185.

6. Courtwright, "Century of American Narcotic Policy"; James H. Mills, "Cocaine and the British Empire: The Drug and the Diplomats at the Hague Opium Conference, 1911–12," *Journal of Imperial and Commonwealth History* 42, no. 3 (2014): 400–419.

7. Nancy Marion and William Oliver, eds., *Drugs in American Society: An Encyclopedia of History, Politics, Culture, and the Law* (Santa Barbara, Calif.: ABC-CLIO, 2014), 995; Eric Schneider, "A Hundred Years' Failure," *Politico*, January 2, 2015; Jonnes, *Hep-Cats*, 47.

8. Bernard Segal, *Perspectives on Drug Use in the United States* (Philadelphia: Haworth Press, 1986), 6.

9. Feiling, *Cocaine Nation*, 24.

10. Robert Hardaway, *No Price Too High: Victimless Crimes and the Ninth Amendment* (Santa Barbara, Calif.: Praeger, 2003), 110; Tom de Castella, "100 Years of the War on Drugs," *BBC News Magazine*, January 24, 2012.

11. Musto, "Opium, Cocaine, and Marijuana in American History."

12. Jonnes, *Hep-Cats*, 114; Courtwright, *Dark Paradise*, 110; Quinones, *Dreamland*, 54.

13. Jonnes, *Hep-Cats*, 39, 48.

14. Jonnes, *Hep-Cats*, 39, 50; Jonnes, "Public Health Then and Now."

15. Musto, ed., *Drugs in America*, 187–89; Feiling, *Cocaine Nation*; Philip Bean, ed., *Cocaine and Crack: Supply and Use* (New York: St. Martin's, 1975), 21.

16. Jonnes, *Hep-Cats*, 66.

17. Jonnes, *Hep-Cats*, 115.

18. Feiling, *Cocaine Nation*, 19.

19. Joseph Tumulty, "Wilson's Part in the National Prohibition Fight," *New York Times*, December 1, 1921; Kathel Austin Kerr, *The Politics of Moral Behavior: Prohibition and Drug Abuse* (Reading, Mass.: Addison-Wesley, 1973), 97.

20. Tumulty, "Wilson's Part"; Kerr, *Politics of Moral Behavior*, 97.

21. Feiling, *Cocaine Nation*, 19–20.

22. Kerr, *Politics of Moral Behavior*, 97–102.

23. Okrent, *Last Call*, 1; Johann Hari, "The Parable of Prohibition," *Slate*, June 3, 2010; Cheever, *Drinking in America*, 135–46.

24. Sanneh, "Drunk with Power."

25. Okrent, *Last Call*, 1–3; "Prohibition: Speakeasies, Loopholes, and Politics," *Fresh Air*, NPR, June 10, 2011.

26. Okrent, *Last Call*, 118; Martin Gitlin, *The Prohibition Era* (Minneapolis: Essential Library of Social Change, 2010), 14.

27. Sanneh, "Drunk with Power."

28. Jeffrey Miron and Jeffrey Zwiebal, "Alcohol Consumption During Prohibition," *American Economic Review* 81, no. 2 (May 1991): 242–47.

29. H. L. Mencken, "Five Years of Prohibition," *American Mercury* 3 (December 1924): 420–22.

30. Cheever, *Drinking in America*, 156; Hardaway, *No Price Too High*, 65.

31. John Joseph Fenton, *Toxicology: A Case-Oriented Approach* (Boca Raton, Fla.: CRC Press, 2002), 141.

32. Sanneh, "Drunk with Power."

33. Cheever, *Drinking in America*, 142–43; Karen Abbott, "Prohibition's Premier Hooch Hounds," *Smithsonian Magazine*, January 10, 2012; Michael Lerner, *Dry Manhattan: Prohibition in New York City* (Cambridge: Harvard University Press, 2008), 1.

34. Ted Robert Gurr, *Violence in America: The History of Crime* (California: SAGE Publications, 1989), 220.

35. Okrent, *Last Call*, 373; Cheever, *Drinking in America*, 157; Hari, "Parable of Prohibition"; Daniel Okrent, "Wayne B. Wheeler: The Man Who Turned Off the Taps," *Smithsonian Magazine*, May 2010.

36. Okrent, *Last Call*, 373–74.

37. Cheever, *Drinking in America*, 157.

38. Sanneh, "Drunk with Power."

39. Blocker, "Did Prohibition Really Work?"

40. Okrent, *Last Call*, 374.

41. McGirr, *War on Alcohol*, 205–10; Sanneh, "Drunk with Power."

42. Lee, *Smoke Signals*, 54; David F. Musto, "The History of the Marihuana Tax Act of 1937," *Archives of General Psychiatry* 26 (February 1972).

43. Lee, *Smoke Signals*, 48–55.

44. Jonnes, *Hep-Cats*, 91; Sloman, *Reefer Madness*, 31.

45. Jonnes, *Hep-Cats*, 91–92.

46. Lee, *Smoke Signals*, 48.

47. Lee, *Smoke Signals*, 49; Barcott, *Weed the People*, 18–20.

48. Lee, *Smoke Signals*, 50–51.

49. Lee, *Smoke Signals*, 49–55.

50. Lee, *Smoke Signals*, 55; Eric Schlosser, "Reefer Madness," *The Atlantic*, August 1994.

51. Hari, *Chasing the Scream*, 7–11.

Chapter 8. Amphetamines

1. Nick Reding, *Methland: The Death and Life of an American Small Town* (New York: Bloomsbury USA, 2009), 24; Alan Jacobs, "The Lost World of Benzedrine," *Atlantic*, April 15, 2012; Lukasz Kamienski, "The Drugs That Built a Super Soldier," *Atlantic*, April 8, 2012.

2. Judith Warner, "Overselling Overmedication," *New York Times*, February 14, 2008.

3. Beevor, "Very Drugged Nazis."

4. Beevor, "Very Drugged Nazis."

5. Beevor, "Very Drugged Nazis"; Megan Garber, "Pilot's Salt: The Third Reich Kept Its Soldiers Alert with Meth," *The Atlantic*, May 31, 2013; Norman Ohler, *Blitzed: Drugs in the Third Reich* (Boston: Houghton Mifflin Harcourt, 2017), 52.

6. Beevor, "Very Drugged Nazis"; Rachel Cooke, "High Hitler: How Nazi Drug Abuse Steered the Course of History," *Guardian*, September 25, 2016; "Author Says Hitler Was 'Blitzed' on Cocaine and Opiates During the War," *Fresh Air*, NPR, March 7, 2017.

7. Reding, *Methland*, 45.

8. Beevor, "Very Drugged Nazis."

9. Reding, *Methland*, 24–25; Dennis Breo, "Hitler's Medical File: Drug and Pain Ruled His Last Days," *Chicago Tribune*, October 14, 1985.

10. Beevor, "Very Drugged Nazis."

11. Reding, *Methland*, 24.

12. Reding, *Methland*, 29; David Liss, "Book Review: 'Methland' By Nick Reding," *Washington Post*, June 14, 2009; Andrew Cohen, "How White Users Made Heroin a Public Health Problem," *Atlantic*, August 12, 2015.

13. Ruth Reichl, *For You Mom, Finally* (New York: Penguin, 2009); Frank Owen, *No Speed Limit: The Highs and Lows of Meth* (Basingstoke, U.K.: St. Martin's Griffin, 2008).

14. Courtwright, *Forces of Habit*, 78.

15. Peter Keating, "The Strange Saga of JFK and the Original 'Dr. Feelgood,' " *New York Magazine*, November 22, 2013.

16. Ryan Grim, *This Is Your Country on Drugs: The Secret History of Getting High in America* (Nashville, Tenn.: Turner, 2010), ch. 4.

Chapter 9. Alternative Consciousness

1. Jonnes, *Hep-Cats*, 113.

2. Barcott, *Weed the People*, 31.

3. Phil Baker, *William S. Burroughs* (London: Reaktion, 2010), 35; Jonnes, *Hep-Cats*, 208; Barcott, *Weed the People*, 31–34.

4. Jonnes, *Hep-Cats*, 208.

5. Barcott, *Weed the People*, 32–34; Bruce Barcott, *Marijuana Goes Main Street* (New York: Time, 2017).

6. Lee, *Smoke Signals*, 74; Barcott, *Weed the People*, 34; Sloman, *Reefer Madness*, 180.

7. Jonnes, *Hep-Cats*, 207–8; Norman Mailer, "The White Negro (Fall 1957)," *Dissent Magazine*, June 20, 2007.

8. Gary Lachman, "Holy Smoke: A Review of *Breaking Open the Head*," *Guardian*, February 8, 2003; Daniel Pinchbeck, *Breaking Open the Head: A Psychedelic Journey into the Heart of Contemporary Shamanism* (New York: Broadway, 2003).

9. Pinchbeck, *Breaking Open the Head*, 36.

10. Jay Stevens, *Storming Heaven: LSD and the American Dream* (New York: Grove, 1998), 44–46; Michael Pollan, *How to Change Your Mind: What the New Science of Psychedelics Teaches Us About Consciousness, Dying, Addiction, Depression, and Transcendence* (New York: Penguin, 2018); Rafael dos Santos et al., "Antidepressive, Anxiolytic, and Antiaddictive Effects of Ayahuasca, Psilocybin and Lysergic Acid Diethylamide (LSD): A Systematic Review of Clinical Trials Published in the Last Twenty-Five Years," *Therapeutic Advances in Psychopharmacology* 6, no. 3 (June 2016): 193–213; Daniel

Perrine, "Visions of the Night: Western Medicine Meets Peyote, 1887–1899," *Heffter Review of Psychedelic Research* 2 (2001): 6–52.

11. Dave Stewart, *Sweet Dreams Are Made of This: A Life in Music* (New York: Berkeley, 2016), 45.

12. Pinchbeck, *Breaking Open the Head*, 125; Stevens, *Storming Heaven*, 1–12, 49.

13. Stevens, *Storming Heaven*, 1–12.

14. Albert Hofmann, "Exploring an Alternate Universe: Albert Hofmann Discovers the Effects of LSD" (1943), reprinted in *Lapham's Quarterly*; Albert Hofmann, *LSD: My Problem Child*, reprint edition (United Kingdom: Oxford University Press, 2013); Bankole Johnson, ed., *Addiction Medicine: Science and Practice*, vol. 1, 2011 ed. (New York: Springer, 2012), 586.

15. Stevens, *Storming Heaven*, 1–22.

16. Stevens, *Storming Heaven*, 171–84; Tom Shroder, "Can Psychedelic Trips Cure PTSD and Other Maladies?" *Washington Post*, November 17, 2014.

17. Pinchbeck, *Breaking Open the Head*, 125, 179; Michael Pollan, "Trip Treatment," *New Yorker*, February 9, 2015.

18. Stevens, *Storming Heaven*, 77–87; W. Henry Wall Jr., "How the CIA's LSD Mind-Control Experiments Destroyed My Healthy, High Functioning Father's Brilliant Mind," *Alternet*, August 8, 2012.

19. Stevens, *Storming Heaven*, 74–84.

20. Frances E. Karttunen, *Between Worlds: Interpreters, Guides, and Survivors* (New Brunswick, N.J.: Rutgers University Press, 1994), 229; Martin A. Lee and Bruce Shlain, *Acid Dreams: The Complete Social History of LSD—The CIA, the Sixties, and Beyond* (New York: Grove, 1985), 72; R. Gordon Wasson, "Magic Mushroom," *Life*, May 13, 1957; Jeremy Narby and Francis Huxley, ed., *Shamans Through Time: 500 Years on the Path to Knowledge* (New York: Tarcher, 2001).

21. Stewart Tendler and David May, "Timothy Leary, LSD, and Harvard," in *Wildest Dreams: An Anthology of Drug-Related Literature*, ed. Richard Rudgley (United Kingdom: Arktos Media, 2014), 297; Robert Forte, ed., *Timothy Leary: Outside Looking In: Appreciations, Castigations, and Reminiscences* (Rochester, Vt.: Inner Traditions, 1999).

22. Gary Lachman, *Turn Off Your Mind: The Mystic Sixties and the Dark Side of the Age of Aquaris* (New York: Disinformation Company, 2001), 164; Pinchbeck, *Breaking Open the Head*, 181–82; Jim Keith, *Mind Control, World Control* (Kempton, Ill.: Adventure Unlimited Press, 1997); Louis Menand, "Acid Redux," *New Yorker*, June 26, 2006; Timothy Leary and Gunther Weil, "The Religious Experience: Its Production and Interpretation," *Journal of Psychedelic Drugs* 1, no. 2 (1968): 3–23.

23. Lee and Shlain, *Acid Dreams*, 78; Menand, "Acid Redux"; Matthew Collin, *Altered State: The Story of Ecstasy Culture and Acid House* (London: Serpent's Tail, 1997), 60.

24. Robert Cottrell, *Sex, Drugs, and Rock 'n' Roll: The Rise of America's 1960s Counterculture* (Lanham, Md.: Rowman & Littlefield, 2015), 71–80; Timothy Leary, *High Priest* (Berkeley, Calif.: Ronin, 1995), xix.

25. Lee and Shlain, *Acid Dreams*, 79.

26. "Ginsberg on Drugs," *Harvard Crimson*, December 12, 1962; Stevens, *Storming Heaven*, xv; Timothy Leary, *Turn On, Tune In, Drop Out* (Berkeley, Calif.: Ronin, 1999).

27. Stevens, *Storming Heaven*, 221–27; Mick Brown, "Tom Wolfe Interview: 'I Never Took LSD—It Was Far Too Dangerous,' " *The Telegraph*, November 4, 2016; Christopher Lehmann-Haupt, "Ken Kesey, Author of 'Cuckoo's Nest,' Who Defined the Psychedelic Era, Dies at 66," *New York Times*, November 11, 2001; Blair Jackson, *Garcia: An American Life* (New York: Penguin, 2000), 78.

28. Lee and Shlain, *Acid Dreams*, 119–20; Stevens, *Storming Heaven*, 226–27.

29. Michaela Elias, "Remembering Stanford's Bohemian Quarter," *Stanford Daily*, October 14, 2016; Lee and Shlain, *Acid Dreams*, 119; Sandy Brundage, "Fate of Merry Prankster Tree in Limbo as Neighbors Rally," *The Almanac*, July 9, 2013; Sam Whiting, "The Edge of Civilization/Perry Lane, Land of Ambiguity," *San Francisco Chronicle*, June 26, 2005.

30. Lee and Shlain, *Acid Dreams*, 120; Stevens, *Storming Heaven*, 226.

31. Lee and Shlain, *Acid Dreams*, 120–21; Peter Conners, *White Hand Society: The Psychedelic Partnership of Timothy Leary and Allen Ginsberg* (San Francisco: City Lights Book, 2010).

32. Lee and Shlain, *Acid Dreams*, 122.

33. Stevens, *Storming Heaven*, 221–35.

34. Stevens, *Storming Heaven*, xvi, 101–20, 291–309; "Psychiatry: An Epidemic of Acid Heads," *Time*, March 11, 1966.

35. Stevens, *Storming Heaven*, xvi.

36. Robert Greenfield, *Timothy Leary: A Biography* (Boston: Mariner, 2007), 271; Tom Shroder, "Apparently Useless: The Accidental Discovery of LSD," *Atlantic*, September 9, 2014; Jesse Jarnow, "LSD Now: How the Psychedelic Renaissance Changed Acid," *Rolling Stone*, October 6, 2016.

37. Pinchbeck, *Breaking Open the Head*, 1; Pollan, *How to Change Your Mind*, 185–218; " 'Reluctant Psychonaut' Michael Pollan Embraces the 'New Science' of Psychedelics," *Fresh Air*, NPR, May 15, 2018; Laura Miller, "The Trip of a Lifetime," *Slate*, May 14, 2018.

38. Laura Mansnerus, "Timothy Leary, Pied Piper of Psychedelic 60s, Dies at 75," *New York Times*, June 1, 1996; Will Giles, "Come Together: Timothy Leary's 'Bad Trip' for 'High' Office," *Duke Political Review*, January 30, 2014; Larry Welborn, "They Murdered to Avoid a Robbery Conviction," *Orange County Register*, November 13, 2009.

Chapter 10. Nixon's War

1. Jonnes, *Hep-Cats*, 254–57.

2. Jonnes, *Hep-Cats*, 262; Stephen R. Kandall, *Substance and Shadow: Women and Addiction in the United States* (Cambridge: Harvard University Press, 1999), 119; Harry S. Truman, "287. Statement by the President Upon Signing Bill Relating

to Narcotics Laws Violations," Truman Public Papers—Harry S. Truman Presidential Library, November 2, 1951.

3. Kathleen J. Frydl, *The Drug Wars in America, 1940–1973* (Cambridge: Cambridge University Press, 2013), 51; Nancy E. Marion and Willard M. Oliver, *Drugs in American Society: An Encyclopedia of History, Politics, Culture, and the Law* (Santa Barbara, Calif.: ABC-CLIO, 2014), 359.

4. Jonnes, *Hep-Cats*, 262; John F. Kennedy, "Remarks to White House Conference on Narcotics and Drug Abuse," Kennedy Presidential Papers—John F. Kennedy Presidential Library, September 27, 1962; Musto, ed., *Drugs in America*, 300; Beth Weinman, "A Historical Perspective on Offender Drug Abuse Treatment," *Handbook of Evidence-Based Substance Abuse Treatment in Criminal Justice Settings*, vol. II (2011), 1–12.

5. Jonnes, *Hep-Cats*, 279.

6. Quinones, *Dreamland*, 55.

7. Thom L. Jones, "The Man Who Stole the French Connection," *Gangsters Inc.*, May 2, 2011, available at http://gangstersinc.ning.com/profiles/blogs/the-man-who-stole-the-french.

8. Edna Buchanan, "Lucky Luciano: Criminal Mastermind," *Time*, December 7, 1998.

9. Timothy Newark, *The Mafia at War: Allied Collusion with the Mob* (Barnsley, U.K.: Frontline, 2012), 269; Jonnes, *Hep-Cats*, 145–46, 468; Salvatore Lupo, *History of the Mafia* (New York: Columbia University Press, 2011), 189; John Dickie, *Cosa Nostra: A History of the Sicilian Mafia* (New York: St. Martin's Griffin, 2005), 312–18.

10. Newark, *Mafia at War*, 269.

11. Quinones, *Dreamland*, 54–55; Dickie, *Cosa Nostra*, 312–18; Daniel Rosenblum et al., "Urban Segregation and the U.S. Heroin Market: A Quantitative Model of Anthropological Hypotheses from an Inner-City Drug Market," *International Journal of Drug Policy* 25, no. 3 (May 2014): 543–55; Feiling, *Cocaine Nation*, 30; Maia Szalavitz, "A Brief History of New York City's Heroin Scene," *Vice*, December 14, 2015.

12. Jonnes, *Hep-Cats*, 269; Ben Wallace-Wells, "How America Lost the War on Drugs," *Rolling Stone*, March 24, 2011.

13. Jonnes, *Hep-Cats*, 280.

14. Kate Doyle, "Operation Intercept: The Perils of Unilateralism," *National Security Archive*, April 13, 2003; Richard M. Nixon, "Special Message to the Congress on Control of Narcotics and Dangerous Drugs," The American Presidency Project, July 14, 1969.

15. Victoria Bruce and Karin Hayes with Jorge Enrique Botero, *Hostage Nation: Colombia's Guerilla Army and the Failed War on Drugs* (New York: Knopf, 2010), 74.

16. Doyle, "Operation Intercept"; Lawrence Gooberman, *Operation Intercept: The Multiple Consequences of Public Policy* (Oxford, U.K.: Pergamon, 1974), ch. 1.

17. Doyle, "Operation Intercept"; Gooberman, *Operation Intercept*, ch. 1; "Mexico: Operation Impossible," *Time*, October 17, 1969.

18. Peter Maguire, "Regulate It, Man," *New York Review of Books,* December 20, 2018.

19. Sanjay Gupta, "Why I Changed My Mind on Weed," CNN, August 8, 2013.

20. Siegel, *Intoxication,* 273.

21. Robert L. DuPont, "Where Does One Run When He's Already in the Promised Land?" paper presented at the Fifth National Conference on Methadone Treatment, March 1973, p. 1395; Jonnes, *Hep-Cats,* 272.

22. Jonnes, *Hep-Cats,* 272; Alfred W. McCoy, *The Politics of Heroin in Southeast Asia* (New York: Harper & Row, 1972).

23. Alvin Shuster, "G.I. Heroin Addiction Epidemic in Vietnam," *New York Times,* May 6, 1971.

24. Feiling, *Cocaine Nation,* 33; Jonnes, *Hep-Cats,* 272–73; Ed Vulliamy, "Nixon's 'War on Drugs' Began 40 Years Ago, and the Battle Is Still Raging," *Guardian,* July 24.

25. Jonnes, *Hep-Cats,* 274–76; William M. Leary, "CIA Air Operations in Laos, 1955–1974: Supporting the Secret War," *CSI Publications—Studies in Intelligence* (Winter 1999–2000).

26. Peter Carlson, "When Elvis Met Nixon," *Smithsonian Magazine,* December 2010; Jonnes, *Hep-Cats,* 271; "Presley's Doctor on Trial over Prescriptions," *New York Times,* September 30, 1981.

27. Jonnes, *Hep-Cats,* 269–70.

28. Jonnes, *Hep-Cats,* 269–70.

29. Jonnes, *Hep-Cats,* 270.

30. Richard Reeves, *President Nixon: Alone in the White House* (New York: Simon & Schuster, 2002), 641; "Summary, Narcotic Meeting, State Dining Room, June 3, 1971," U.S. Department of State Archive—Foreign Relations, 1969–1976, Volume E-1, Documents on Global Issues, 1969–1972, June 3, 1971; Vulliamy, "Nixon's 'War on Drugs,' "; Richard M. Nixon, "202—Remarks About an Intensified Program for Drug Abuse Prevention and Control," The American Presidency Project, June 17, 1971; Emily Dufton, "The War on Drugs: How President Nixon Tied Addiction to Crime," *Atlantic,* March 26, 2012.

31. Jonnes, *Hep-Cats,* 281.

32. David Downs, "The Science Behind the DEA's Long War on Marijuana," *Scientific American,* April 19, 2016.

33. Richard M. Nixon, "74—Radio Address About the State of the Union Message on Law Enforcement and Drug Abuse Prevention," American Presidency Project, March 10, 1973; Emily Dufton, *Grass Roots: The Rise and Fall and Rise of Marijuana in America* (New York: Basic, 2017), 57–72.

34. Lee, *Smoke Signals,* 128; Eva Bertram, Morris Blachman, Kenneth Sharpe, and Peter Andreas, *Drug War Politics: The Price of Denial* (Berkeley: University of California Press, 1996), 94; William F. Buckley Jr., "The War on Drugs Is Lost," *National Review,* February 12, 1996.

35. Lee, *Smoke Signals,* 128; Dufton, *Grass Roots,* 29–44, 221–22.

36. Bryan Burrough, "The Other Green Revolution," *Wall Street Journal*, January 10, 2018.

37. Albin Krebs, "Harry J. Anslinger Dies at 83; Hard-Hitting Foe of Narcotics," *New York Times*, November 18, 1975; Jonnes, *Hep-Cats*, 298.

38. Howard Padwa and Jacob Cunningham, eds., *Addiction: A Reference Encyclopedia* (New York: ABC-CLIO, 2010), 305.

39. Jonnes, *Hep-Cats*, 292–97.

40. Jonnes, *Hep-Cats*, 275–76.

41. Quinones, *Dreamland*, 65; Christopher Wren, "Holding an Uneasy Line in the Long War on Heroin; Methadone Emerged in City Now Debating Its Use," *New York Times*, October 3, 1998.

42. Quinones, *Dreamland*, 63–64.

43. Quinones, *Dreamland*, 64.

44. Quinones, *Dreamland*, 63–65.

Chapter 11. Reagan's War

1. Jonnes, *Hep-Cats*, 304.

2. Feiling, *Cocaine Nation*, 37.

3. Nathan Michael Corzine, *Team Chemistry: The History of Drugs and Alcohol in Major League Baseball* (Urbana: University of Illinois Press, 2016), 96; Streatfeild, *Cocaine*, 209; Jonnes, *Hep-Cats*, 310. Ann Crittenden and Michael Ruby, "Cocaine: The Champagne of Drugs," *New York Times*, September 1, 1974.

4. Torgoff, *Can't Find My Way Home*, 322–24, 332; Madge, *White Mischief*, 148.

5. Michael Demarest, "Cocaine: Middle Class High," *Time*, July 6, 1981; Feiling, *Cocaine Nation*, ch. 2; Madge, *White Mischief*, 148; Robert Reinhold, "Wide Marijuana and Cocaine Use Reported Among Professionals," *New York Times*, July 22, 1976; David Musto, "Illicit Price of Cocaine in Two Eras: 1908–14 and 1982–89," *Pharmacy in History* 33, no. 1 (1991): 3–10.

6. Carlos Suárez De Jesús, "Cocaine and Me: A Memoir," *Miami New Times*, October 13, 2005.

7. Guy Gugliotta and Jeff Leen, *Kings of Cocaine: Inside the Medellin Cartel—An Astonishing True Story of Murder, Money, and International Corruption* (New York: Simon and Schuster, 1989), ch. 6.

8. Gugliotta and Leen, *Kings of Cocaine*, ch. 1.

9. Jonnes, *Hep-Cats*, 333.

10. Jonnes, *Hep-Cats*, 347.

11. Ronald Reagan, "Radio Address to the Nation on Federal Drug Policy," October 2, 1982.

12. Reagan, "Radio Address," October 2, 1982.

13. Barcott, *Weed the People*, 53; Dufton, *Grass Roots*, 123–49, 160–63; Peter Maguire, "Regulate It, Man," *New York Review of Books*, December 20, 2018.

14. Michelle Alexander, *The New Jim Crow: Mass Incarceration in the Age of Color-blindness* (New York: New Press, 2012), 23, 71; David A. Harris, "Driving While Black: Racial Profiling on Our Nation's Highways," *ACLU Special Report*, June 1999.

15. Feiling, *Cocaine Nation*, 48–49.

16. David Franklin Allen and James Jekel, *Crack: The Broken Promise* (Basingstoke, U.K.: Palgrave Macmillan, 1991), 17–19, 199; "Price of Cocaine Has Risen," Associated Press, September 2, 1984.

17. Feiling, *Cocaine Nation*, 53; Erich Goode and Nachman Ben-Yehuda, *Moral Panics: The Social Construction of Deviance* (Hoboken, N.J.: Blackwell, 1994), ch. 12; Siegel, *Intoxication*, 287.

18. Riley, *Snow Job*, 21; Michael Massing, "Crack's Destructive Sprint Across America," *New York Times*, October 1, 1989.

19. Gene Johnson, "3 Decades Later, a Mixed Legacy for 'Just Say No,' " *U.S. News and World Report*, March 8, 2016; Vanessa Romo, "Will Melania Trump 'Just Say No' in Her Own Way?" NPR, August 10, 2017.

20. David Boaz, ed., *The Crisis in Drug Prohibition* (Washington, D.C.: Cato Institute, 1991), 119.

21. Feiling, *Cocaine Nation*, 65–66; Barcott, *Weed the People*, 52.

22. Dufton, *Grass Roots*, 101–5; Booth, *Cannabis*, 307.

23. Dufton, *Grass Roots*, 102–5; Tessa Stuart, "Pop-Culture Legacy of Nancy Reagan's 'Just Say No' Campaign," *Rolling Stone*, March 7, 2016.

24. Wallace-Wells, "How America Lost the War on Drugs."

25. "The 50 Best Commercials of All Time," *Entertainment Weekly*, March 28, 1997.

26. Jane Gross, "A New, Purified Form of Cocaine Causes Alarm as Abuse Increases," *New York Times*, November 29, 1985; John Corry, "TV Reviews: CBS on 'Crack Street,' " *New York Times*, September 4, 1986; William Grimes, ed., *The Times of the Eighties: The Culture, Politics, and Personalities That Shaped the Decade* (Philadelphia: Running Press, 2013).

27. Elise Viebeck, "How an Early Biden Crime Bill Created the Sentencing Disparity for Crack and Cocaine Trafficking," *Washington Post*, July 28, 2019; Beverly Watkins and Mindy Fullilove, "Crack Cocaine and Harlem's Health," *Souls*, vol. 1, June 5, 2009; Richard P. Conaboy, *Cocaine and Federal Sentencing Policy* (Collingdale, Penn.: Diane, 1995), 112; Maia Szalavitz, "Cracked Up," *Salon*, May 11, 1999.

28. Michelle Alexander, *New Jim Crow*, 52; Edith Fairman Cooper, *The Emergence of Crack Cocaine Abuse* (Hauppauge, N.Y.: Nova Science, 2002), 1, 21–23; Jane Gross, "A New, Purified Form of Cocaine Causes Alarm as Abuse Increases," *New York Times*, November 29, 1985; Gary Silverman, "Caring for Crack Babies Could Cost Billions," United Press International, March 8, 1990.

29. Silverman, "Caring for Crack Babies"; "The Cost of Not Preventing Crack Babies," editorial, *New York Times*, October 10, 1991; Vann R. Newkirk III, "What the

'Crack Baby' Panic Reveals About the Opioid Epidemic," *Atlantic,* July 16, 2017; Torgoff, *Can't Find My Way Home,* 352.

30. Torgoff, *Can't Find My Way Home,* 352–58; Ellen Hopkins, "Childhood's End: What Life Is Like for Crack Babies," *Rolling Stone,* October 18, 1990; Susan Okie, "The Epidemic That Wasn't," *New York Times,* January 26, 2009; "Slandering the Unborn," *New York Times,* January 3, 2019.

31. Torgoff, *Can't Find My Way Home,* 354; Gerald Boyd, "Reagans Advocate 'Crusade' on Drugs," *New York Times,* September 15, 1986.

32. Dana Priest, *The Mission: Waging War and Keeping Peace with America's Military* (New York: Norton, 2004), 204; Mattathias Schwartz, "Mission Gone Wrong," *New Yorker,* January 6, 2014.

33. William N. Elwood, *Rhetoric in the War on Drugs: The Triumphs and Tragedies of Public Relations* (Santa Barbara, Calif.: ABC-CLIO, 1994), 29.

34. Jonathan Easley, "The Day the Drug War Really Started," *Salon,* June 19, 2011.

35. Easley, "Day the Drug War Really Started."

36. Feiling, *Cocaine Nation,* 69–72; Schwartz, "Mission Gone Wrong."

37. Easley, "Day the Drug War Really Started"; Chris Thangham, "5 Grams of Crack Gets You 5 Years, 499 Grams of Cocaine Gets You Maximally 1 Year," *Digital Journal,* March 21, 2007; Randall Shelden et al., *Crime and Criminal Justice in American Society* (Long Grove, Ill.: Waveland Press, 2015), 212.

38. Peter Reuter, "Why Has U.S. Drug Policy Changed So Little Over 30 Years?" *University of Chicago,* May 21, 2013.

39. Deborah J. Vagins and Jesselyn McCurdy, "Cracks in the System: Twenty Years of the Unjust Federal Crack Cocaine Laws," American Civil Liberties Union, October 2006; "Written Submission of the ACLU on Racial Disparities in Sentencing, Hearing on Reports of Racism in the Justice System of the United States, Submitted to the Inter-American Commission on Human Rights, 153rd Session," American Civil Liberties Union, October 27, 2014.

40. "Written Submission."

41. Eva Bertram et al., *Drug War Politics,* 140.

42. Sewell Menzel, *Cocaine Quagmire: Implementing the U.S. Anti-Drug Policy in the North Andes-Colombia* (Lanham, Md.: UPA, 1997), 57.

43. J. P. Caulkins, "Is Crack Cheaper Than (Powder) Cocaine?" *Addiction Journal* 92, no. 11 (November 1997): 1437–43.

44. Eric Sterling, "Is Sentencing Reform Debate a Move Toward Drug Legalization?" *Huffington Post,* April 21, 2014; Ashley Nellis, "The Color of Justice: Racial and Ethnic Disparity in State Prisons," The Sentencing Project, June 14, 2016.

45. Vagins and McCurdy, "Cracks in the System."

46. Vagins and McCurdy, "Cracks in the System."

47. Pepe Lozano, "Thousands to Be Released Early in Crack Cocaine Sentences," *People's World,* November 1, 2011.

48. Richard Thompson Ford, "Locked In," *American Interest,* August 7, 2017; James Forman Jr., *Locking Up Our Own: Crime and Punishment in Black America* (New York: Farrar, Straus and Giroux, 2017), 136, 158, 195; Jennifer Senior, " 'Locking Up Our Own': What Led to Mass Incarceration of Black Men," *New York Times,* April 11, 2017.

49. Lee, *Smoke Signals,* 178–79.

50. Lee, *Smoke Signals,* 178–82.

51. Lee, *Smoke Signals,* 179–80.

52. Lee, *Smoke Signals,* 205–8; Jodi Cohen and David Mendell, "Something Wild in Field Gone to Pot: Low Grade of Marijuana Luring Teens to Summit," *Chicago Tribune,* August 6, 1998.

53. Lee, *Smoke Signals,* 180; Barcott, *Weed the People,* 120–21.

54. Torgoff, *Can't Find My Way Home,* 357–60.

55. Torgoff, *Can't Find My Way Home,* 358–59; Snoop Dogg and Davin Seay, *The Doggfather: The Times, Trials, and Hardcore Truths of Snoop Dogg* (New York: Harper Paperbacks, 2000); Christopher Partridge and Eric Christianson, *The Lure of the Dark Side: Satan and Western Demonology in Popular Culture* (Abingdon, U.K.: Routledge, 2014), 70.

56. Torgoff, *Can't Find My Way Home,* 358–60.

57. Torgoff, *Can't Find My Way Home,* 361–62.

Chapter 12. Supply Side

1. Bill Yousman, *Prime Time Prisons on U.S. TV: Representations of Incarceration and Culture* (New York: Peter Lang, 2009), 11; Beth Schwartzapfel and Bill Keller, "Willie Horton Revisited," *The Marshall Project,* May 13, 2015; M. J. Stephey, "Top 10 Memorable Debate Moments: Dukakis' Deadly Response," *Time,* September 26, 2008; "The Second Bush-Dukakis Presidential Debate, Debate Transcript," October 13, 1988.

2. Siegel, "How Joe Biden's Policies."

3. Richard Harwood, "Hyperbole Epidemic," *Washington Post,* October 1, 1989; Michael Isikoff, "Drug Buy Set Up for Bush Speech," *Washington Post,* September 22, 1989; United States Department of Health and Human Services, National Institutes of Health, National Institute on Drug Abuse, *National Household Survey on Drug Abuse, 1990* (Ann Arbor, Mich.: Inter-University Consortium for Political and Social Research, 2013).

4. James Swartz, *Substance Abuse in America: A Documentary and Reference Guide* (Santa Barbara, Calif.: Greenwood, 2012), 226; Jonnes, *Hep-Cats,* 400; Jerome Beck and Marsha Rosenbaum, *Pursuit of Ecstasy: The MDMA Experience* (Albany: State University of New York Press, 1994), 137.

5. Diane M. Canova, "The National Drug Control Strategy: A Synopsis," in *Handbook of Drug Control in the United States,* ed. James A. Inciardi (Westport, Conn.: Greenwood, 1990), 340; Clarence Lusane, *Pipe Dream Blues: Racism and the War on Drugs*

(Boston: South End Press, 1991), 74; Rudolph J. Gerber, *Legalizing Marijuana: Drug Policy Reform and Prohibition Politics* (Westport, Conn.: Praeger, 2004), 45.

6. Lee, *Smoke Signals*, 203–6.

7. Milton Friedman, "An Open Letter to Bill Bennett," in *Drug Legalization: For and Against*, ed. Rod L. Evans and Irwin M. Berent (Chicago: Open Court, 1992), 50.

8. Russell Crandall, *Driven by Drugs: U.S. Policy Toward Colombia* (Boulder, Colo.: Lynne Rienner, 2002); Mark Bowden, *Killing Pablo: The Hunt for the World's Greatest Outlaw* (New York: Atlantic Monthly Press, 2001), 65; Colman McCarthy, "Bennett's Addiction a Chance to Help Others," *Washington Post*, January 28, 1989; Michael Reed, *Forgotten Continent: The Battle for Latin America's Soul* (New Haven, Conn.: Yale University Press, 2007), 255; Scott Steward, "From Colombia to New York City: The Narconomics of Cocaine," *Business Insider*, June 27, 2016.

9. Mark Matthews, "Drug War Portrayed as a Failure: Andean Strategy Has Failed to Curb Cocaine Production," *Baltimore Sun*, February 20, 1992; Ronald Reagan, "National Security Decision, Directive Number 221, April 8, 1986," *The Public Papers of President Ronald W. Reagan*, April 8, 1986; Bruce et al., *Hostage Nation*, 48; Reid, *Forgotten Continent*, 255; Steward, "From Colombia to New York City."

10. Russell Crandall, *Gunboat Democracy: U.S. Interventions in the Dominican Republic, Grenada, and Panama* (Lanham, Md.: Rowman & Littlefield, 2006), 171–223.

11. Crandall, *Gunboat Democracy*.

12. Crandall, *Gunboat Democracy*.

13. Crandall, *Gunboat Democracy*.

14. Crandall, *Gunboat Democracy*.

15. Crandall, *Gunboat Democracy*.

16. Crandall, *Gunboat Democracy*.

17. Crandall, *Gunboat Democracy*.

18. Crandall, *Gunboat Democracy*.

19. Crandall, *Gunboat Democracy*.

20. Crandall, *Gunboat Democracy*.

21. Gugliotta and Leen, *Kings of Cocaine*, 34; Philip Shenon, "Noriega Indicted by U.S. for Links to Illegal Drugs," *New York Times*, February 6, 1988.

22. Frederick Kempe, *Divorcing the Dictator: America's Bungled Affair with Noriega* (New York: Putnam, 1990), 168.

23. Jonnes, *Hep-Cats*, 361–62.

24. Crandall, *Gunboat Democracy*, 171–223.

25. Crandall, *Gunboat Democracy*.

26. Crandall, *Gunboat Democracy*.

27. Crandall, *Gunboat Democracy*.

28. Crandall, *Gunboat Democracy*.

29. Crandall, *Gunboat Democracy*.

30. Crandall, *Gunboat Democracy*.

31. Crandall, *Gunboat Democracy*.

32. Crandall, *Gunboat Democracy*.

33. Crandall, *Gunboat Democracy*.

34. Crandall, *Gunboat Democracy*.

35. Crandall, *Gunboat Democracy*.

36. Crandall, *Gunboat Democracy*.

37. Crandall, *Gunboat Democracy*.

38. Crandall, *Gunboat Democracy*.

39. Kim MacQuarrie, *Life and Death in the Andes: On the Trail of Bandits, Heroes, and Revolutionaries* (New York: Simon & Schuster, 2015), 45; Wallace-Wells, "How America Lost the War on Drugs."

40. Robert D. McFadden, "U.S. Colonel's Wife Named in Bogota Drug Smuggling," *New York Times*, August 7, 1999.

41. Kim Housego, "How Greed and Opportunity Turned U.S. Soldiers into Drug Traffickers," Associated Press, September 3, 2005.

Chapter 13. Kingpin

1. Scott Stewart, "From Colombia to New York City: The Narconomics of Cocaine," *Business Insider*, June 27, 2016.

2. Robert Stone, "The Autumn of the Drug Lord," *New York Times*, June 15, 1997; Alan Riding, "Cocaine Billionaires: The Men Who Hold Colombia Hostage," *New York Times*, March 8, 1987.

3. William Yardley, "Juan David Ochoa Vasquez, Co-Founder of the Medellin Cartel, Dies at 65," *New York Times*, July 30, 2013; Stewart, "Narconomics of Cocaine"; Peter Green, "Cocainenomics: The Syndicate," *Wall Street Journal*, February 25, 2018; Patrick Radden Keefe, "Cocaine Incorporated," *New York Times*, June 15, 2012.

4. MacQuarrie, *Life and Death in the Andes*, 24; James Brooke, "A Drug Lord Is Buried as a Folk Hero," *New York Times*, December 4, 1993; Robert Kaplan, *Imperial Grunts: On the Ground with the American Military, from Mongolia to the Philippines to Iraq and Beyond* (New York: Vintage, 2006), 67; Mark Bowden, *Killing Pablo: The Hunt for the World's Greatest Outlaw* (New York: Grove, 2015), ch. 1.

5. Bowden, *Killing Pablo*, 17; Robert D. McFadden, "Head of Medellin Cocaine Cartel Is Killed by Troops in Colombia," *New York Times*, December 3, 1993.

6. Bowden, *Killing Pablo*, 24; McFadden, "Head of Medellin Cocaine Cartel."

7. MacQuarrie, *Life and Death in the Andes*, 26.

8. MacQuarrie, *Life and Death in the Andes*, 26; Bowden, *Killing Pablo*, 24.

9. MacQuarrie, *Life and Death in the Andes*, 27; Gugliotta and Lee, *Kings of Cocaine*, 28–52.

10. MacQuarrie, *Life and Death in the Andes*, 36; Bowden, *Killing Pablo*, 24, 40, 50–51, 95; Steven Dudley, *Walking Ghosts: Murder and Guerrilla Politics in Colombia* (Abing-

don, U.K.: Routledge, 2003), 72–73; Gary Marx, "Drug Lord, or Ghost, Stalks Colombian Town," *Chicago Tribune*, July 28, 1991; Patrick Micolta, "Illicit Interest Groups: The Political Impact of the Medellin Drug Trafficking Organizations in Colombia," *FIU Electronic Theses and Dissertations*, March 30, 2012; Elaine Shannon, "New Kings of Coke," *Time*, June 24, 2001; William Rempel, "The Man Who Took Down Cali," *Los Angeles Times*, February 24, 2007.

11. Gugliotta and Lee, *Kings of Cocaine*, 28–52; Bowden, *Killing Pablo*, 25–30; Alma Guillermoprieto, *The Heart That Bleeds: Latin American Now* (New York: Vintage, 1995), 320.

12. MacQuarrie, *Life and Death in the Andes*, 4; Steven Dudley et al., "Colombia Elites and Organized Crime," *InSight Crime*, August 9, 2016.

13. Michael Harris, "Book Review: Simple Tale of How U.S. Helped Bring Down a Drug King," *Los Angeles Times*, July 3, 2001.

14. Bowden, *Killing Pablo*, 24–34; Christopher Woody, "U.S. Agents Nearly Caught $194 Million Worth of Cocaine in a Narco Submarine," *Business Insider*, March 28, 2016.

15. Alma Guillermoprieto, "Our New War in Colombia," *New York Review of Books*, April 13, 2000.

16. "Revolutionary Armed Forces of Colombia—People's Army," *Stanford University Mapping Militant Organizations*, August 15, 2015.

17. Guillermoprieto, "Our New War in Colombia."

18. Dudley, *Walking Ghosts*, 40, 81–84.

19. Dudley, *Walking Ghosts*, 82; Bowden, *Killing Pablo*, 33.

20. Alma Guillermoprieto, *Looking for History: Dispatches from Latin America* (New York: Vintage, 2002), 31; Guillermoprieto, "Our New War in Colombia."

21. Gugliotta and Lee, *Kings of Cocaine*, 92–93; Bowden, *Killing Pablo*, 33; Alma Guillermoprieto, "Exit El Patrón," *New Yorker*, December 3, 1993; Jeremy McDermott, "Colombia Elites and Organized Crime: Don Berna," *InSight Crime*, August 9, 2016.

22. Dudley, *Walking Ghosts*, 73–74; Gugliotta and Lee, *Kings of Cocaine*, 91–98; Bowden, *Killing Pablo*, 33.

23. Guillermoprieto, *Looking for History*, 31; Guillermoprieto, "Our New War in Colombia"; Alma Guillermoprieto, "Colombia: Violence Without End," *New York Review of Books*, April 27, 2000; Jon Lee Anderson, "Colombia's Guerrillas Come Out of the Jungle," *New Yorker*, May 1, 2017.

24. Crandall, *Driven by Drugs*, ch. 1.

25. MacQuarrie, *Life and Death in the Andes*, 30–31; Gugliotta and Lee, *Kings of Cocaine*, 91–98; Bowden, *Killing Pablo*, 33–34.

26. Bowden, *Killing Pablo*, 32–35; Gugliotta and Lee, *Kings of Cocaine*, 97.

27. Bowden, *Killing Pablo*, 36–40; Hannah Parry, "Descendants of Escobar's Hippos Are Castrated in Colombia, Decades After Animals Escaped Drug Lord's Zoo and Thrived in the Wild," *Daily Mail*, May 29, 2016.

28. Bowden, *Killing Pablo*, 43–44; MacQuarrie, *Life and Death in the Andes*, 29; Riding, "Cocaine Billionaires."

29. John Otis, "Colombia's Drug Extraditions: Are They Worth It?" *Time*, February 24, 2009.

30. Bowden, *Killing Pablo*, 41; MacQuarrie, *Life and Death in the Andes*, 29–30.

31. Gabriel García Márquez, *News of a Kidnapping* (New York: Penguin, 1998), 22–24; Gugliotta and Lee, *Kings of Cocaine*, 99–101; Stone, "Autumn of the Drug Lord"; Aldo Civico, *The Para-State: An Ethnography of Colombia's Death Squads* (Berkeley: University of California Press, 2015), 219.

32. Bowden, *Killing Pablo*, 58; Gugliotta and Lee, *Kings of Cocaine*, 105–8; Guillermoprieto, "Exit El Patrón"; Juan Pablo Escobar, *Pablo Escobar: My Father* (New York: Thomas Dunne, 2016), 136.

33. Bowden, *Killing Pablo*, 53, 93, 131; Juan Francisco Lanao Anzola, "Palace of Justice Siege: Colombia Can't Be Built Without Justice," *Colombia Reports*, April 21, 2010.

34. García Márquez, *News of a Kidnapping*, 20–21, 128–32; Gugliotta and Lee, *Kings of Cocaine*, epilogue; Riding, "Cocaine Billionaires."

35. Bowden, *Killing Pablo*, 80–82.

36. Andrew Cockburn, *Kill Chain: The Rise of the High-Tech Assassins* (London: Picador, 2016), 98.

37. García Márquez, *News of a Kidnapping*, 180; Stone, "Autumn of the Drug Lord."

38. Douglas Martin, "Alberto Villamizar, 62, Foe of Colombian Drug Cartel, Dies," *New York Times*, July 28, 2007.

39. Bowden, *Killing Pablo*, 99; García Márquez, *News of a Kidnapping*, 273–86.

40. García Márquez, *News of a Kidnapping*, 255–56.

41. Joseph Treaster, "Drug Baron Gives Up in Colombia as End to Extradition Is Approved," *New York Times*, June 20, 1991.

42. Bowden, *Killing Pablo*, 144–47; Guillermoprieto, *The Heart That Bleeds*, 320.

43. Bowden, *Killing Pablo*, 143.

44. García Márquez, *News of a Kidnapping*, 288–89; Richard Boudreaux, "Colombia Drug Lord Surrenders," *Los Angeles Times*, June 20, 1991.

45. Bowden, *Killing Pablo*, 139–55; Sean Naylor, "Inside the Pentagon's Manhunting Machine: A Brief History of Special Operations, from Panama to the War on Terror," *Atlantic*, August 28, 2015.

46. MacQuarrie, *Life and Death in the Andes*, 34; García Márquez, *News of a Kidnapping*, 178, 198.

47. Bowden, *Killing Pablo*, 188–93; Guillermoprieto, *The Heart That Bleeds*, 324; Guillermoprieto, "Exit El Patrón"; William Rempel, *At the Devil's Table: The Untold Story of the Insider Who Brought Down the Cali Cartel* (New York: Random House, 2011), 103; Douglas Farah, "The Crackup," *Washington Post*, July 21, 1996.

48. Farah, "The Crackup."

49. García Márquez, *News of a Kidnapping*, 289.

50. MacQuarrie, *Life and Death in the Andes*, 44; García Márquez, *News of a Kidnapping*, 290; Bowden, *Killing Pablo*, 15.

51. Bowden, *Killing Pablo*, 15.

52. Wallace-Wells, "How America Lost the War on Drugs"; Bruce et al., *Hostage Nation*, 51.

Chapter 14. Plan Colombia

1. Russell Crandall, "City on a Hill: A Letter from Medellin," *American Interest*, May 1, 2011; Russell Crandall, "Colombia's Protean Drug Wars," *American Interest*, April 17, 2014; "Los capos del cartel de Cali," *El Espectador*, August 24, 2012.

2. Steven Cohen, "What *Narcos* Still Gets Wrong About the War on Drugs," *New Republic*, September 9, 2016; Robert Stone, "The Autumn of the Drug Lord," *New York Times*, June 15, 1997.

3. Joseph Treaster, "The World: Cocaine Manufacturing Is No Longer Just a Colombian Monopoly," *New York Times*, June 30, 1991; William Yardley, "Juan David Ochoa Vásquez, Co-Founder of Medellín Cartel, Dies at 65," *New York Times*, July 30, 2013.

4. "Los capos del cartel de Cali."

5. William Rempel, "Drug War: One Cartel Falls, Another Rises," *Los Angeles Times*, June 19, 2011.

6. Crandall, *Driven by Drugs*, 101–42; Farah, "The Crackup."

7. Ana María Saavedra, "Los herederos del último gran cartel colombiano," *El País*, April 23, 2009.

8. Bruce et al., *Hostage Nation*, 74–75.

9. Daniel Wilkinson, "Death and Drugs in Colombia," *New York Review of Books*, June 23, 2011.

10. Russell Crandall, "Requiem for the FARC?" *Survival* 53, no. 4 (August–September 2011): 233–40; Crandall, "Colombia's Protean Drug Wars."

11. Crandall, "Colombia's Protean Drug Wars."

12. Reid, *Forgotten Continent*, 255.

13. Guillermoprieto, "Colombia: Violence Without End."

14. Guillermoprieto, *Looking for History*, 42–48.

15. Peter DeShazo et al., "Colombia's Plan de Consolidación Integral de la Macarena," *Center for Strategic and International Studies*, June 2, 2009.

16. Civico, *Para-State*, 55.

17. Russell Crandall, "Colombia Needs a Stronger Military," *Wall Street Journal*, June 12, 1998.

18. Guillermoprieto, *Looking for History*, 36.

19. Civico, *Para-State*, 131–35.

20. Civico, *Para-State*.

21. Russell Crandall, "Clinton, Bush, and Plan Colombia," *Survival: Global Politics and Strategy*, Spring 2002.

22. Crandall, "Clinton, Bush, and Plan Colombia."

23. Crandall, "Clinton, Bush, and Plan Colombia."

24. Horacio Godoy, "Plan Colombia's Strategic Weaknesses," *Latin American Studies Association*, March 27, 2003.

25. Crandall, "Clinton, Bush, and Plan Colombia."

26. Crandall, "Clinton, Bush, and Plan Colombia."

27. Crandall, "Clinton, Bush, and Plan Colombia."

28. Crandall, "Clinton, Bush, and Plan Colombia."

29. Crandall, "Clinton, Bush, and Plan Colombia."

30. Crandall, "Clinton, Bush, and Plan Colombia."

31. Natalia Cosoy, "Has Plan Colombia Really Worked?" BBC, February 4, 2016.

32. Russell Crandall, "Colombia's Catastrophic Success," *American Interest*, December 19, 2013.

33. Crandall, "Colombia's Catastrophic Success."

34. "Colombia Restarts Controversial Glyphosate Fumigation of Coca," *Telesur*, January 11, 2017.

35. Crandall, "Colombia's Catastrophic Success."

36. Crandall, "Colombia's Catastrophic Success."

37. John Negroponte, "Latin America: Helping Colombia Is in Our National Interest," *Miami Herald*, May 22, 2007.

Chapter 15. Catastrophic Success

1. Bruce et al., *Hostage Nation*, 93–96; Ana Carrigan, "Looking for Allies in Colombia," *New York Times*, March 10, 2002.

2. Bruce et al., *Hostage Nation*, 95–96; Juan Forero, "Colombian Rebels Hijack a Plane and Kidnap a Senator," *New York Times*, February 21, 2002.

3. Bruce et al., *Hostage Nation*, 94–96.

4. Bruce et al., *Hostage Nation*, 97–99; Alvin Powell, "Six Years a Hostage," *Harvard Gazette*, December 9, 2010.

5. Bruce et al., *Hostage Nation*, 102–3.

6. Crandall, "Colombia's Catastrophic Success"; Claire Felter and Danielle Renwick, "Colombia's Civil Conflict," *Council on Foreign Relations*, January 11, 2017.

7. Bruce et al., *Hostage Nation*, 4; Juan Carlos Torres, *Operación Jaque: La verdadera historia* (Bogota: Planeta, 2008); Crandall, "Requiem for the FARC?"

8. Bruce et al., *Hostage Nation*, 5; Marc Gonsalves, Tom Howes, Keith Stansell, and Gary Brozek, *Out of Captivity: Surviving 1,967 Days in the Colombian Jungle* (New York: William Morrow, 2009).

9. Bruce et al., *Hostage Nation*, 9.

10. Bruce et al., *Hostage Nation*, 3–15; Gonsalves et al., *Out of Captivity*, 26.

11. "Hostages for Prisoners: A Way to Peace in Colombia?" International Crisis Group, March 8, 2004.

12. Bruce et al., *Hostage Nation*, 53; Gonsalves et al., *Out of Captivity*, xv, 15, 63.

13. Bruce et al., *Hostage Nation*, 141; Gonsalves et al., *Out of Captivity*, 188.

14. Tim Padgett, "Colombia's Stunning Hostage Rescue," *Time*, July 2, 2008; Dana Priest, "Covert Action in Colombia: U.S. Intelligence, GPS Bomb Kits Help Latin American Nation Cripple Rebel Forces," *Washington Post*, December 21, 2013.

15. Priest, "Covert Action in Colombia," *Washington Post*, December 21, 2013; Simon Romero, "U.S. Aid Was a Key to Hostage Rescue in Colombia," *New York Times*, July 13, 2008.

16. Bruce et al., *Hostage Nation*, 216–17.

17. Bruce et al., *Hostage Nation*, 20–21, 161–63; "FARC incluyen a 'Simón Trinidad' en la lista de canjeables," *El País*, January 14, 2004.

18. Bruce et al., *Hostage Nation*, 191.

19. Bruce et al., *Hostage Nation*, 194–95.

20. Bruce et al., *Hostage Nation*, 210–11.

21. "Colombia's Peace Process: The Moment of Truth," *Economist*, August 30, 2014.

22. Deborah Sontag, "The Secret History of Colombia's Paramilitaries and the U.S. War on Drugs," *New York Times*, September 10, 2016.

23. Sontag, "Secret History."

24. Sontag, "Secret History."

25. Sontag, "Secret History."

26. Sontag, "Secret History."

27. Caroline McDermott and Russell Crandall, "City on a Hill: A Letter from Medellin," *American Interest*, May 1, 2011.

28. Civico, *Para-State*, 51.

29. Adriaan Alsema, "Thanks to Medellin and Cali, Colombia Boasts Least Homicides in Decades," *Colombia Reports*, January 5, 2015.

30. Steven Dudley et al., "Colombia Elites and Organized Crime," *InSight Crime*, August 9, 2016.

31. Crandall, "Requiem for the FARC?"

32. Bruce et al., *Hostage Nation*, 240–42; Orth, "Inside Colombia's Hostage War."

33. Bruce et al., *Hostage Nation*, 245–47.

34. Bruce et al., *Hostage Nation*, 245–47.

35. Bruce et al., *Hostage Nation*, 251; Karl Penhaul, "Uribe: Betancourt Rescuers Used Red Cross," CNN, July 16, 2008.

36. Bruce et al., *Hostage Nation*, 252–53.

37. Bruce et al., *Hostage Nation*, 253.

38. Bruce et al., *Hostage Nation*, 253.

39. Bruce et al., *Hostage Nation*, 253.

40. Bradley Graham, "Public Honors for Secret Combat," *Washington Post*, May 6, 1996.

41. Simon Romero, "Manuel Marulanda, Top Commander of Colombia's Largest Guerrilla Group, Is Dead," *New York Times,* May 26, 2008.

42. Crandall, "Requiem for the FARC?"; Crandall, "Colombia's Catastrophic Success."

43. Crandall, "Requiem for the FARC?"; Crandall, *America's Dirty Wars: Irregular Warfare from 1776 to the War on Terror* (Cambridge: Cambridge University Press, 2014), 354.

44. Crandall, "Colombia's Catastrophic Success."

45. Virginia Bouvier, "Gender and the Role of Women in Colombia's Peace Process," UN Women, United Nations, March 4, 2016.

46. Jon Lee Anderson, "Out of the Jungle," *New Yorker,* May 1, 2017.

47. Crandall, "Colombia's Catastrophic Success."

48. Crandall, "Colombia's Catastrophic Success."

49. Crandall, "Colombia's Catastrophic Success."

50. Crandall, "Colombia's Catastrophic Success."

51. Christopher Woody, "Cocaine Prices in the U.S. Have Barely Moved in Decades—Here's How Cartels Distort the Market," *Business Insider,* October 13, 2016.

52. William Neuman, "Defying U.S., Colombia Halts Aerial Spraying of Crops Used to Make Cocaine," *New York Times,* May 14, 2015.

53. Adam Isacson, "As Its Coca Crop Increases, Colombia Doesn't Need to Fumigate. But It Needs to Do Something," Washington Office on Latin America, September 23, 2016.

Chapter 16. Our Man in Lima

1. William Rempel and Sebastian Rotella, "Arms Dealer Implicates Peru Spy Chief in Smuggling Ring," *Los Angeles Times,* November 1, 2000; Abraham Lama, "Drogas y Narcotrafico—Peru: Edecán y ex avión presidencial involucrados en narcotráfico," *Inter Press Service Agencia de Noticias,* May 19, 1996.

2. Lama, "Drogas y Narcotrafico—Peru."

3. Lama, "Drogas y Narcotrafico—Peru"; Marguerite Cawley, "Montesinos Is Gone, But Peru's Narco-Political Brokers Continue Tradition," *InSight Crime,* October 20, 2014; "El Coronel Absuelto," *Caretas,* June 23, 2005; "La Intervención de Alberto Fujimori Fujimori," Corte Suprema de Justicia de la República (2001), available at www.gacetajuridica.com.pe/noticias/sente-fujimori/P2C15_Intervencion.pdf.

4. Alfonso Quiroz, *Corrupt Circles: A History of Unbound Graft in Peru* (Baltimore: John Hopkins University Press, 2008), 361; Karen DeYoung, " 'The Doctor' Divided U.S. Officials," *Washington Post,* September 22, 2000; "Montesinos: The End of the Road," BBC, June 24, 2001.

5. Coletta Youngers and Eileen Rosin, eds., *Drugs and Democracy in Latin America: The Impact of U.S. Policy* (Boulder, Colo.: Lynne Rienner, 2004), 92–94; Cynthia

McClintock and Fabian Vallas, *The United States and Peru: Cooperation—At a Cost* (London: Routledge, 2002), 55–58; DeYoung, " 'The Doctor.' "

6. DeYoung, " 'The Doctor.' "

7. DeYoung, " 'The Doctor.' "

8. "CIA Gave at Least $10 Million to Peru's Ex-Spymaster Montesinos," Center for Public Integrity, July 28, 2001.

9. DeYoung, " 'The Doctor' "; "CIA Gave at Least"; Kevin Drum, "But He's Our Son of a Bitch," *Washington Monthly*, May 16, 2006.

10. Quiroz, *Corrupt Circles*, 412; DeYoung, " 'The Doctor' "; Dennis Jett, "Ending Peru's Masquerade," *Christian Science Monitor*, September 25, 2000; Tamara Feinstein, ed., "Montesinos: Blind Ambition—The Peruvian Townsend Commission Report and Declassified U.S. Documentation," *National Security Archive Electronic Briefing Book No. 72*, June 26, 2002; "Montesinos protegió el narcotráfico en Perú y Colombia," *El País*, November 12, 2002.

11. Feinstein, ed., "Montesinos"; Youngers and Cameron, "U.S. Drug Czar Backs 'Peruvian Rasputin' "; *Human Rights Watch World Report, 1999* (New York: Human Rights Watch, 1998), 144.

12. Rempel and Rotella, "Arms Dealer Implicates Peru Spy Chief"; Tim Golden, "CIA Links Cited on Peru Arms Deal That Backfired," *New York Times*, November 6, 2000.

13. Quiroz, *Corrupt Circles*, 416; Youngers and Rosin, eds., *Drugs and Democracy in Latin America*, 43; McClintock and Vallas, *United States and Peru*, 87; Juan Tamayo, "Peru's Link to Arms Deal Worried U.S.," *Miami Herald*, September 20, 2000.

14. Leslie Alan Horvitz and Christopher Catherwood, *Encyclopedia of War Crimes and Genocide* (New York: Infobase, 2014), 307; DeYoung, " 'The Doctor.' "

15. Rempel and Rotella, "Arms Dealer Implicates Peru Spy Chief"; T. Christian Miller, "Venezuela's Feud with Peru Flares," *Los Angeles Times*, June 30, 2001; Carla Salazar, "Peru Ex-Spymaster Sentenced to 20 Years," *Washington Post*, September 22, 2006.

16. Anthony Faiola, "Army Played a 'Key Role' in Departure of Fujimori; Intelligence Service Scandals Rankled Peruvian Military," *Washington Post*, September 18, 2000; DeYoung, " 'The Doctor.' "

17. Coletta Youngers, "Cocaine Madness: Counternarcotics and Militarization in the Andes," *North American Congress on Latin America*, September 25, 2007.

18. R. Evan Ellis, "Narcotrafficking, the Shining Path, and the Strategic Importance of Peru," *War on the Rocks*, March 31, 2015.

19. Romina Mella and Gustavo Gorriti, "Peruvian Authorities Switch Gears in Combating Cocaine Air Bridge," *InSight Crime*, September 17, 2015.

20. Keegan Hamilton, "The Golden Age of Drug Trafficking: How Meth, Cocaine, and Heroin Move Around the World," *Vice*, April 25, 2016.

21. Frank Bajak, "Narco Planes Ferry Cocaine Under Nose of Peru's Military," Associated Press, October 14, 2015.

22. "Peru Approves Shooting Down of Drug Smuggling Planes," BBC, August 21, 2015.

Chapter 17. Bolivian Backlash

1. Russell Crandall, "Blow Hard," *American Interest*, January 1, 2008; Russell Crandall, "Reports from the Revolution," *Survival: Global Politics and Strategy* 50, no. 6 (2008): 193–98.

2. Alma Guillermoprieto, "Bolivia's Parched Future," *New York Review of Books*, December 18, 2009.

3. Duncan Campbell, "Bolivia's Leftwing Upstart Alarms U.S.," *Guardian*, July 15, 2002.

4. Jean Friedman-Rudovsky, "Bolivia's Surprising Anti-Drug Success," *Time*, August 5, 2008; Juan Forero and Larry Rohter, "Bolivia's Leader Solidifies Region's Leftward Tilt," *New York Times*, January 22, 2006.

5. Jackie Briski, "Bolivia Says No to Cocaine, but Yes to Coca," *Christian Science Monitor*, March 20, 2012.

6. Crandall, "Blow Hard."

7. Crandall, "Blow Hard"; Abraham Kim, "The Plight of Bolivian Coca Leaves: Bolivia's Quest for Decriminalization in the Face of Inconsistent International Legislation," *Washington University Global Studies Law Review* 13, no. 3 (2014): 559–81.

8. Crandall, "Blow Hard."

9. Linda C. Farthing and Kathryn Ledebur, "Habeas Coca: Bolivia's Community Coca Control," Open Society Foundations, July 2015.

10. Peter Kerr, "Bolivia, with U.S. Aid, Battles Cocaine at the Root," *New York Times*, April 17, 1988.

11. "Con Nueva Ley Relanzarán Industrialización de la Coca," *Los Tiempos*, February 27, 2017.

12. Crandall, "Blow Hard."

13. Chrystelle Barbier, "Bolivia Resists Global Pressure to Do Away with Coca Crop," *Guardian*, April 24, 2015.

14. Crandall, "Blow Hard."

15. Crandall, "Blow Hard."

16. "Bolivian President Evo Morales Expels USAID," BBC, May 1, 2013.

17. Jamie Doward, "Bolivians Demand the Right to Chew Coca Leaves," *Guardian*, January 12, 2013.

18. Evo Morales Ayma, "Let Me Chew My Coca Leaves," *New York Times*, March 13, 2009.

19. Jamie Doward, "Leaked Paper Reveals UN Split over War on Drugs," *Guardian*, November 30, 2013.

20. Jon Lee Anderson, "The Pope of Latin America," *New Yorker*, July 17, 2015.

21. Simeon Tegel, "Bolivia Ended Its Drug War by Kicking Out the DEA and Legalizing Coca," *Vice*, September 21, 2016.

22. Max Radwin, "Is Bolivia's Coca Policy a Solution to Drug Trafficking—or Part of the Problem?" *World Politics Review*, June 5, 2018; "How Bolivia Fights the Drug Scourge," *New York Times*, September 14, 2016.

23. Juan Montes and José de Córdoba, "Evo Morales Offers to Sit Out Bolivia's Next Election If He Can Finish Term," *Wall Street Journal*, November 20, 2019.

Chapter 18. El Narco Mexicano

1. David Luhnow and José de Córdoba, "The Perilous State of Mexico," *Wall Street Journal*, February 21, 2009.

2. Ioan Grillo, *El Narco: Inside Mexico's Criminal Insurgency* (New York: Bloomsbury Press, 2012), 60; Anabel Hernández, *Narcoland: The Mexican Drug Lords and Their Godfathers* (London: Verso, 2013).

3. Russell Crandall, "Democracy and the Mexican Cartels," *Survival: Global Politics and Strategy* 56, no. 3 (2014): 233–44; Grillo, *El Narco*, 64; Keefe, "Cocaine Incorporated."

4. Keefe, "Cocaine Incorporated"; Grillo, *El Narco*, 64.

5. Christopher Looft and Steven Dudley, "Most Guns in Mexico Traced to U.S. Dealers: Gov't Data," *InSight Crime*, May 1, 2012.

6. Bruce M. Bagley and Jonathan D. Rosen, eds., *Drug Trafficking, Organized Crime, and Violence in the Americas Today* (Gainesville: University Press of Florida, 2015); Grillo, *El Narco*, 155–68.

7. Grillo, *El Narco*, 8, 171–90.

8. Dane Schiller, "DEA Agent Tells Details of Now-Infamous 1999 Confrontation with Mexican Drug Kingpin," *Dallas News*, March 2010.

9. "Mexico Drug War Fast Facts," CNN, February 20, 2018.

10. George W. Grayson, *Mexico: Narco-Violence and a Failed State?* (New Brunswick, N.J.: Transaction, 2010), 180.

11. Grayson, *Mexico*; Fred Burton, "Mexico's Cartel Wars: The Threat Beyond the U.S. Border," *Stratfor*, October 26, 2006; Patrick Radden Keefe, "The Hunt for El Chapo," *New Yorker*, May 5, 2014.

12. William Finnegan, "Silver or Lead," *New Yorker*, May 31, 2010; Edith Honan et al., "El Chapo Trial Provides a Deep Look Inside the Sinaloa Drug Empire," *Washington Post*, January 31, 2019.

13. Cimino, *Drug Wars*; Feiling, *Cocaine Nation*.

14. Ed Vulliamy, *Amexica: War Along the Borderline* (New York: Farrar, Straus and Giroux, 2011), 254; Nancy E. Marion and Willard M. Oliver, *Drugs in American Society: An Encyclopedia of History, Politics, Culture, and the Law* (Santa Barbara, Calif.: ABC-CLIO, 2014), 452.

15. John Gibler, *To Die in Mexico: Dispatches from Inside the Drug War* (San Francisco: City Lights, 2011).

16. Alexis Okeowo, "A Mexican Town Wages Its Own War on Drugs," *New Yorker*, November 27, 2017.

17. Grillo, *El Narco*, 102–4; Crandall, "Democracy and the Mexican Cartels"; Steven Dudley, "The Zetas and the Battle for Monterrey," *InSight Crime*, December 18, 2012; John Burnett, "Mexico's Ferocious Zetas Cartel Reigns Through Fear," NPR, October 2, 2009.

18. Ioan Grillo, *Gangster Warlords: Drug Dollars, Killing Fields, and the New Politics of Latin America* (New York: Bloomsbury, 2016), 297; José Luis Pardo Veiras, "A Decade of Failure in the War on Drugs," *New York Times*, October 9, 2016; Russell Crandall and Savannah Haeger, "Latin America's Invisible War," *Survival: Global Politics and Strategy* 58, no. 5 (2016): 159–66.

19. Paul Rexton Kan, *Cartels at War: Mexico's Drug-Fueled Violence and the Threat to U.S. National Security* (Washington, D.C.: Potomac, 2012).

20. R. Evan Ellis, "Strategic Insights: Mexico—New Directions, Continuity, and Obstacles in the Fight Against Transnational Organized Crime," U.S. Army War College, March 31, 2016.

21. Bruce et al., *Hostage Nation*, 209, 279–80; Michael Osborne, "More Than a Mexican Problem: How the U.S. Can Adapt Plan Colombia to Mexico," *Small Wars Journal;* Christopher Hobson, "Privatising the War on Drugs," *Third World Quarterly* 35 no. 8 (2014): 1441–56.

22. Luhnow and de Cordoba, "Perilous State of Mexico."

23. Crandall, "Democracy and the Mexican Cartels."

24. Bernd Debusmann, "Among Top U.S. Fears: A Failed Mexican State," *New York Times*, January 9, 2009.

25. Keefe, "Cocaine Incorporated."

26. Keefe, "Cocaine Incorporated"; Jeremy Raff, "The Border Patrol's Corruption Problem," *Atlantic*, May 5, 2017; Garrett M. Graff, "The Border Patrol Hits a Breaking Point," *Politico*, July 15, 2019.

27. Keefe, "Cocaine Incorporated"; Ron Nixon, "The Enemy Within: Bribes Bore a Hole in the U.S. Border," *New York Times*, December 28, 2016.

28. Raff, "Border Patrol's Corruption Problem"; Garrett M. Graff, "The Green Monster," *Politico*, November/December 2014.

29. Graff, "Green Monster"; Doris Meissner, "Border Budget Is Already Enormous," *New York Times*, January 31, 2013.

30. Christopher Woody, "Mexico's Ascendant Cartel Is Making a Deadly Addition to a Trafficking Hub on the U.S. Border," *Business Insider*, March 4, 2017.

31. Lawrence Downes, "Borderline Insanity at the Fence in Nogales," *New York Times*, December 7, 2013; Matt Flegenheimer, "Paul Ryan Tours Texas Border Area Where Trump Wants a Wall," *New York Times*, February 22, 2017.

32. Arthur H. Rotstein, "Napolitano: National Guard Being Considered for Border Duty," *Tucson Citizen*, April 16, 2009; Alma Guillermoprieto, "Mexico: The Murder of the Young," *New York Review of Books*, December 2014; Sarah Stillman, "Where Are the Children?" *New Yorker*, April 2, 2015.

33. Randal C. Archibold, "Obama to Send Up to 1,200 Troops to Border," *New York Times*, May 25, 2010.

34. George W. Grayson, "The Evolution of Los Zetas in Mexico and Central America: Sadism as an Instrument of Cartel Warfare," Army War College, April 2014.

35. Grayson, "Evolution of Los Zetas"; Douglas Lovelace, *Terrorism Commentary on Security Document*, volume 138: *The Resurgent Terrorist Threat* (Oxford: Oxford University Press, 2015), 376.

36. Lovelace, *Terrorism Commentary*; Randal C. Archibold, "Mexico Kills a Drug Kingpin, but the Body Gets Away," *New York Times*, October 9, 2012.

37. Alfredo Corchado, *Midnight in Mexico: A Reporter's Journey Through a Country's Descent into Darkness* (New York: Penguin, 2013); Grayson, "Evolution of Los Zetas."

38. Randal C. Archibold and Ginger Thompson, "Capture of Mexican Crime Boss Appears to End a Brutal Chapter," *New York Times*, July 16, 2013.

39. Russell Crandall, *America's Dirty Wars: Irregular Warfare from 1776 to the War on Terror* (New York: Cambridge University Press, 2014), 89–100; Joshua Partlow, "How Mexico Secretly Launched a Crackdown After Penn Met 'El Chapo,' " *Washington Post*, January 16, 2016.

40. William Neuman and Azam Ahmed, "Public Enemy? At Home in Mexico, 'El Chapo' Is Folk Hero No. 1," *New York Times*, July 17, 2015.

41. Crandall, "Democracy and the Mexican Cartels"; Pascal Tréguer, "The First 'Public Enemy Number One' Was Al Capone," *World Histories*, available at https://wordhistories.net/2017/08/03/public-enemy-number-one.

42. Keefe, "Cocaine Incorporated"; Keefe, "Hunt for El Chapo."

43. Malcolm Beith, "After Six Years of Bloodshed, Mexico's Drug War Shows Little Sign of Waning," *Atlantic*, June 4, 2013.

44. Keefe, "Hunt for El Chapo."

45. Keefe, "Hunt for El Chapo."

46. Alma Guillermoprieto, "Killing Arturo Beltrán," *New Yorker*, January 6, 2010.

47. Crandall, "Democracy and the Mexican Cartels."

48. Crandall, "Democracy and the Mexican Cartels."

49. Keefe, "Hunt for El Chapo."

50. Associated Press, "Mexico Rules Out 'El Chapo' Extradition," *Guardian*, January 28, 2015.

51. Sean Penn, "El Chapo Speaks," *Rolling Stone*, January 9, 2016; Ravi Somaiya, "Sean Penn Met with 'El Chapo' for Interview in His Hide-Out," *New York Times*, January 9, 2016.

52. Patrick Radden Keefe, "The Tragic Farce of El Chapo," *New Yorker*, January 11, 2016; Deanna Paul and Devlin Barrett, "Joaquín Guzmán Receives Life Sentence in U.S. Federal Court," *Washington Post*, July 17, 2019.

53. Vanda Felbab-Brown, "Peña Nieto's Piñata: The Promise and Pitfalls of Mexico's New Security Policy Against Organized Crime," *Brookings*, February 2013.

54. Max Fisher, "Losing Faith in the State," *New York Times*, January 7, 2018.

55. Joshua Partlow, "In Mexico, the Price of America's Hunger for Heroin," *Washington Post*, May 30, 2017; Crandall, "Democracy and the Mexican Cartels."

Chapter 19. Fear and Loathing in Central America

1. Nils Gilman, "The Twin Insurgency," *American Interest*, June 15, 2014; Russell Crandall and Savannah Haeger, "Something Wicked This Way Comes," *American Interest*, April 15, 2016.

2. Grillo, *Gangster Warlords*, 3–13.

3. Russell Crandall, "Syria in Our Backyard," *American Interest*, June 7, 2016; Russell Crandall and Paige Donnelly, "The Fragile Victory," *American Interest*, March 28, 2013; Russell Crandall and Paige Donnelly, "El Salvador's Delicate Balance," *American Interest*, March 28, 2013.

4. Alejandra Sanchez Inzunza and Jose Luis Pardo Veiras, "Life Where the Murder Rate Is Sky High," *New York Times*, July 15, 2017.

5. Douglas Farah, "Central America's Gangs Are All Grown Up," *Foreign Policy*, January 19, 2016.

6. Farah, "Central America's Gangs."

7. Jared Goyette, "Oscar Martinez on Why El Salvador Is a 'Good Place to Kill,' " PRI, April 20, 2016.

8. Carlos Chavez, "For El Salvador Funeral Homes, Business Is Booming," *InSight Crime*, October 15, 2015; Harris, "Murder Capital of the World"; "Barrio 18," *InSight Crime*, February 13, 2018.

9. Elisabeth Malkin and Alberto Arce, "Files Suggest Honduran Police Leaders Ordered Killing of Antidrug Officials," *New York Times*, April 15, 2016.

10. Malkin, "Files Suggest"; Malkin, "Two Dozen Police Commanders."

11. Sarah Stillman, "When Deportation Is a Death Sentence," *New Yorker*, January 15, 2018.

12. Michael Miller, "People Here Live in Fear," *Washington Post*, December 20, 2017.

13. Natalie Tomlin and Ana Mulero, "Langley Park Residents Say Brothels Operate Openly Yet Elude Police," *CNS Maryland*, May 27, 2015.

14. Farah, "Central America's Gangs"; Jonathan Blitzer, "The Teens Trapped Between a Gang and the Law," *New Yorker*, January 1, 2018; Schwartz, "Mission Gone Wrong"; Crandall, "Drug War Divide."

15. Russell Crandall, "Drug Wars," *Survival: Global Politics and Strategy* 55, no. 4 (2013): 229–40; Crandall, "Drug War Divide."

16. Schwartz, "Mission Gone Wrong."

17. Joseph R. Biden Jr., "Joe Biden: A Plan for Central America," *New York Times*, January 29, 2015; Jennifer Shutt, "Biden Urges Support for Central America Aid Package," *Politico*, January 29, 2015; Oscar Martinez, *A History of Violence: Living and Dying in Central America* (New York: Verso, 2016).

18. Alma Guillermoprieto, "In the New Gangland of El Salvador," *New York Review of Books*, November 10, 2011.

19. Peter Katel, "Central American Gangs: Can Violence in the Region Be Stopped?" *CQ Press*, January 30, 2015.

20. Walter Ewing, "New Report Evaluates Scale of the Central American Refugee Influx," *Immigration Impact*, September 4, 2015.

21. Kristof, "Obama's Death Sentence."

22. Elyssa Pachico, "El Salvador Gangs Accept Proposal to Create 'Peace Zones,'" *InSight Crime*, December 5, 2012.

23. "Rivers of Blood: A Crackdown on Gangs Has so Far Made Things Worse," *Economist*, October 10, 2015; Guillermoprieto, "In the New Gangland"; Daniel Alarcón, "The Executioners of El Salvador," *New Yorker*, August 4, 2015; Carlos Dada, "Corruption Charges Turn Guatemala Upside Down," *New Yorker*, September 4, 2015.

24. David Gagne, "El Salvador Moves Gang Leaders Back to Max-Security Prison," *InSight Crime*, January 19, 2015; Alberto Arce, "El Salvador Throws Out Gang Truce and Officials Who Put It in Place," *New York Times*, May 20, 2016; Eric L. Olson, "Four Questions and Observations About El Salvador's Deteriorating Security Situation," Wilson Center, December 15, 2015.

25. Evan Ellis, "The New Offensive Against Gangs in El Salvador," *Global Americans*, May 2, 2016.

Chapter 20. The Global War

1. Ginger Thompson, "Trafficking in Terror," *New Yorker*, December 14, 2015; Alex Chitty and Jana Kozlowski, "Lines in the Sand: Tracing Cocaine's Path Through Africa to Europe," *Vice*, March 27, 2015; William K. Rashbaum, "U.S. Charges 3 Malians in Drug Plot," *New York Times*, December 18, 2009.

2. Thompson, "Trafficking in Terror"; Chitty and Kozlowski, "Lines in the Sand"; Rashbaum, "U.S. Charges 3 Malians in Drug Plot"; Office of the Inspector General, "The Handling of Sexual Harassment and Misconduct Allegations by the Department's Law Enforcement Components," U.S. Department of Justice, March 2015.

3. Neil C. M. Carrier and Gernot Klantschnig, *Africa and the War on Drugs* (London: Zed, 2012); Max Hoffman and Conor Lane, "Guinea-Bissau and the South Atlantic Cocaine Trade," Center for American Progress, August 22, 2013.

4. "Guerrilla seguiría lucrándose de narcotráfico," *El Nuevo Siglo*, September 20, 2012.

5. David Brown, "The Looming Narco-State in Afghanistan," *Atlantic*, January 15, 2014; Gretchen Peters, *Seeds of Terror: How Drugs, Thugs, and Crime Are Reshaping the Afghan War* (New York: Picador, 2010).

6. Kim Sengupta, "U.S. Wants to Bring Colombia Tactics to Afghan Drugs War," *Independent*, October 3, 2007; Scott Wilson, "Which Way in Afghanistan? Ask Colombia for Directions," *Washington Post*, April 5, 2009.

7. Kirk Semple and Tim Golden, "Afghans Pressed by U.S. on Plan to Spray Poppies," *New York Times*, October 8, 2007; Carlotta Gall, "Record Opium Crop Possible in Afghanistan, U.N. Study Predicts," *New York Times*, March 6, 2007; Sengupta, "U.S. Wants to Bring"; Wilson, "Which Way in Afghanistan?"

8. Brown, "Looming Narco-State"; Rachel Donadio, "New Course for Antidrug Efforts in Afghanistan," *New York Times*, June 27, 2009.

9. Brown, "Looming Narco-State."

10. Azam Ahmed, "Tasked with Combating Opium, Afghan Officials Profit from It," *New York Times*, February 15, 2016.

11. Shah and Mashal, "Bountiful Afghan Opium Harvest."

12. Alissa J. Rubin, "Drug Use Has Increased in Afghanistan, U.N. Report Says," *New York Times*, June 21, 2010; Sengupta, "U.S. Wants to Bring"; Wilson, "Which Way in Afghanistan?"

13. Jonnes, *Hep-Cats*, 363–66.

14. Jonnes, *Hep-Cats*, 363–66; Dan Lamothe, "The U.S. Begins Bombing Taliban Drug Labs as Trump's Afghanistan Strategy Takes Hold," *Washington Post*, November 20, 2017.

Chapter 21. The War over the War on Drugs

1. Lee, *Smoke Signals*, 298; Sam Harris, "Drugs and the Meaning of Life," *Making Sense* podcast, episode 1, July 24, 2011; Eric Schneider, "A Hundred Years' Failure: How Did a Law to Regulate Heroin Traffic Turn into the Costly, Futile War on Drugs," *Politico*, January 2, 2015; José Luis Pardo Veiras, "A Decade of Failure in the War on Drugs," *New York Times*, October 9, 2016; Christopher J. Coyne and Abigail R. Hall, "Four Decades and Counting: The Continued Failure of the War on Drugs," Cato Institute, April 12, 2017; Eric Schneider, "A Hundred Years' Failure: How Did a Law to Regulate Heroin Traffic Turn into the Costly, Futile War on Drugs," *Politico*, January 2, 2015; Annabelle Buggle, "After 40-Year Fight, Illicit Drug Use at All-Time High," *Huffington Post*, July 23, 2013; José Luis Pardo Veiras, "A Decade of Failure in the War on Drugs," *New York Times*, October 9, 2016.

2. Shirley Warshaw, *Presidential Profiles: The Clinton Years* (New York: Facts on File, 2004), 217; Francis Wilkinson, "A Separate Peace: The Clinton Administration Has Abandoned the Rhetoric of the War on Drugs, but It Hasn't Stopped Fighting the War," *Rolling Stone*, May 5, 1994; " 'War' on Drugs Stumbles Along," *Los Angeles Times*, October 22, 2000; "General Barry R. McCaffrey Sworn In as New Drug Czar,"

National Drug Strategy Network, March 1996; James G. Stavridis, *Partnership for the Americas: Western Hemisphere Strategy and U.S. Southern Command* (Washington, D.C.: National Defense University Press, 2010), ch. 4; Holly Yeager, "New Drug Czar Prepares for Tough Campaign," *San Francisco Chronicle*, March 4, 1996.

3. Kate Linthicum, "Mexico's Bloody Drug War Is Killing More People Than Ever," *Los Angeles Times*, July 22, 2017.

4. Veiras, "A Decade of Failure."

5. Nicholas Kristof, "How to Win a War on Drugs: Portugal Treats Addiction as a Disease, Not a Crime," *New York Times*, September 22, 2017; Samuel Oakford, "Portugal's Example: What Happened After It Decriminalized All Drugs, from Weed to Heroin," *Vice*, April 19, 2016.

6. Maia Szalavitz, "Drugs in Portugal: Did Decriminalization Work?" *Time*, April 26, 2009; Artur Domoslawski, *Drug Policy in Portugal: The Benefits of Decriminalizing Drug Use* (Warsaw: Open Society Foundations, 2011).

7. Lauren Frayer, "In Portugal, Drug Use Is Treated as a Medical Issue, Not a Crime," *Morning Edition*, NPR, April 18, 2017; Brian Vastag, "5 Years After: Portugal's Drug Decriminalization Policy Shows Positive Results: Street Drug-Related Deaths from Overdoses Drop and the Rate of HIV Cases Crashes," *Scientific American*, April 7, 2009; Chris Ingraham, "Portugal Decriminalised Drugs 14 Years Ago—and Now Hardly Anyone Dies from Overdosing," *Independent*, June 6, 2015; Kristof, "How to Win a War on Drugs."

8. Danielle Allen, "The Trump Administration's Surreal Desire for 'More Law Enforcement,' " *Washington Post*, June 21, 2017.

9. Kristof, "How to Win a War on Drugs."

10. Crandall, "Drug War Divide"; Russell Crandall, "Is the U.S. the Last Country Still Fighting the Drug War?" *New Republic*, January 1, 2014; Crandall, "Drug Wars."

11. "The Global War on Drugs Has Failed: It Is Time for a New Approach," *Transforming Neighborhood's Initiative*, November 21, 2011.

12. Juan Forero, "Latin American Countries Pursue Alternatives to U.S. Drug War," *Washington Post*, April 10, 2012.

13. Nicholas Casey, "With Rebels Gone, Colombia Jumps into the Pot Industry," *New York Times*, March 9, 2017; Robin Yapp, "Colombian President Calls for Legislation of Marijuana," *Telegraph*, October 26, 2011; Jared Wade, "Colombia Approves First Medical Marijuana License," *City Paper Bogotá*, June 30, 2016; Sibylla Brodzinsky, "Colombia's Clandestine Cannabis Farmers Keen to Come Out of the Shadow," *Guardian*, September 16, 2016.

14. Crandall, "Is the U.S. the Last Country?"

15. Crandall, "Is the U.S. the Last Country?"

16. Crandall, "Is the U.S. the Last Country?"

17. "A Conversation with President José Mujica," *Economist*, August 21, 2014.

18. Crandall, "Is the U.S. the Last Country?"

19. Crandall, "Is the U.S. the Last Country?"

20. Crandall, "Is the U.S. the Last Country?"

21. Amanda Erickson, "Mexico Just Legalized Medical Marijuana," *Washington Post*, June 21, 2017.

22. Massimo F. T. Calabresi, "State Drug Laws and U.S. Foreign Policy—Event with Barry R. McCaffrey and Russell Crandall," Council on Foreign Relations, June 12, 2014.

23. Calabresi, "State Drug Laws and U.S. Foreign Policy"; Barcott, *Marijuana Goes Main Street;* Szasz, *Pharmacracy,* 136.

24. Stuart S. Taylor, "Marijuana Policy and Presidential Leadership: How to Avoid a Federal-State Train Wreck," Brookings Institution, April 11, 2013.

25. Gabor Maté, *In the Realm of Hungry Ghosts: Close Encounters with Addiction* (Las Vegas: Central Recovery Press, 2011), xv; Schwartz, "Mission Gone Wrong."

26. Schwartz, "Mission Gone Wrong"; Terry Gross, " 'Narconomics': How the Drug Cartels Operate Like Wal-Mart and McDonald's," *Fresh Air*, NPR, February 15, 2016.

Chapter 22. Law Enforcement and Incarceration

1. Joseph Goldstein, "Undercover Officers Ask Addicts to Buy Drugs, Snaring Them but Not Dealers," *New York Times*, April 4, 2016.

2. Goldstein, "Undercover Officers Ask."

3. Charles Lane, "The Age of Mass Incarceration May Actually Be Abating," *Washington Post*, April 19, 2017; Goldstein, "Undercover Officers Ask."

4. Ta-Nehisi Coates, "The Black Family in the Age of Mass Incarceration," *Atlantic*, October 2015; Matt Thompson, "Imagining the Presence of Justice," *Atlantic*, May 3, 2017; Goldstein, "Undercover Officers Ask."

5. Alexander, *New Jim Crow*, 56; Marc Mauer, "Bill Clinton, 'Black Lives,' and the Myths of the 1994 Crime Bill," The Marshall Project, April 11, 2016.

6. Bret Stephens, "Joe Biden: Be Proud of Your Crime Bill," *New York Times*, May 30, 2019.

7. Frank Schmalleger, *Criminology Today: An Integrative Introduction*, 4th ed. (California: Content Technologies, 2017); Mauer, "Bill Clinton, 'Black Lives' "; John DiIulio, "Criminals and Getting Truth-in-Sentencing Laws," Heritage Foundation, February 22, 1995.

8. Alexander, *New Jim Crow*, 55–58; Jamelle Bouie, "The Messy, Very Human Politics of Bill Clinton's Crime Bill," *Slate*, April 11, 2016; Erik Eckholm, "Prison Rate Was Rising Years Before 1994 Law," *New York Times*, April 10, 2016.

9. Jessica Lussenhop, "Clinton Crime Bill: Why Is It So Controversial," BBC, April 18, 2016.

10. Alexander, *New Jim Crow*, 57; "No Second Chance: People with Criminal Records Denied Access to Public Housing," *Human Rights Watch*, November 17, 2004.

11. U.S. Department of Justice, *Violent Crime Control and Law Enforcement Act of 1994*, National Criminal Justice Reference Service, 1995.

12. Holly Harris, "The Prisoner Dilemma: Ending America's Incarceration Epidemic," *Foreign Affairs*, March/April 2017, 118–29; Adam Gopnik, "How We Misunderstand Mass Incarceration," *New Yorker*, April 10, 2017.

13. Bret Stephens, "Joe Biden: Be Proud of Your Crime Bill," *New York Times*, May 30, 2019.

14. Dexter Filkins, " 'Do Not Resist' and the Crisis of Police Militarization," *New Yorker*, May 13, 2016; Anna North, "When a SWAT Team Comes to Your House," *New York Times*, July 6, 2017.

15. Alexander, *New Jim Crow*, 74–78.

16. Richard Fausset, Alan Blinder, and Yamiche Alcindor, "Yielding to Pressure, Charlotte Releases Videos of Keith Scott Shooting," *New York Times*, September 24, 2016.

17. Stuart Miller, "Do Not Resist: New Film Shows How U.S. Police Have Become an Occupying Army," *Guardian*, September 30, 2016.

18. Alexander, *New Jim Crow*, 60; Eric Markowitz, "Making Profits on the Captive Prison Market," *New Yorker*, September 4, 2016; James Surowiecki, "Trump Sets Private Prisons Free," *New Yorker*, December 5, 2016; Eric Schlosser, "The Prison-Industrial Complex," *Atlantic*, December 1998; Clint Smith, "Why the U.S. Is Right to Move Away from Private Prisons," *New Yorker*, August 24, 2016.

19. Heather Long, "Private Prison Stocks Up 100% Since Trump's Win," *CNN Money*, February 24, 2017; Surowiecki, "Trump Sets Private Prisons Free"; Smith, "Private Prisons"; Bozelko, "The GOP's War"; Shane Bauer, "Chapter 1: 'Inmates Run This Bitch,' " *Mother Jones*, July/August 2016; Adam Hochschild, "Our Awful Prisons: How They Can Be Changed," *New York Review of Books*, May 26, 2016; Jed S. Rakoff, "Why Innocent People Plead Guilty," *New York Review of Books*, November 20, 2014.

20. Hochschild, "Our Awful Prisons"; Jeff Smith, *Mr. Smith Goes to Prison: What My Year Behind Bars Taught Me About America's Prison Crisis* (New York: St. Martin's, 2015), 272; James Kilgore, *Understanding Mass Incarceration: A People's Guide to the Key Civil Rights Struggle of Our Time* (New York: New Press, 2015), 264; Naomi Murakawa, *The First Civil Right: How Liberals Built Prison America* (New York: Oxford University Press, 2015), 260; Elizabeth Hinton, *From the War on Poverty to the War on Crime: The Making of Mass Incarceration in America* (Cambridge: Harvard University Press, 2016), 449; Marie Gottschalk, *Caught: The Prison State and the Lockdown of American Politics* (Princeton, N.J.: Princeton University Press, 2016), 474.

21. Eckholm, "Prison Rate"; Gopnik, "How We Misunderstand."

22. Alexander, *New Jim Crow*, 59–61, 84–86; Tom Kertscher, "U.S. Incarcerates More People Than China or Russia, State Supreme Court Candidate Joe Donald Says," *Politifact*, December 9, 2015.

23. Alexander, *New Jim Crow*, 89–93; "Federal Judge Quits over Sentencing Rules," *Chicago Tribune*, October 1, 1990.

24. Alexander, *New Jim Crow*, 93; Ethan Brown, *Snitch: Informants, Cooperators, and the Corruption of Justice* (New York: Public Affairs, 2007), 16; Robert Perkinson, "The 'Jim Crow' Injustice of Crack Cocaine Continues," *Root*, May 13, 2010; "Legal Scholar: Jim Crow Still Exists in America," *Fresh Air*, NPR, January 16, 2012; "Interview Michael S. Gelacek," *Frontline*, PBS; Vagins and McCurdy, "Cracks in the System"; Caroline Fredrickson, Deborah J. Vagins, and Jesselyn McCurdy, "Dear Commissioners," American Civil Liberties Union, March 16, 2007.

25. Siegel, "How Joe Biden's Policies"; German Lopez, "Joe Biden's Long Record Supporting the War on Drugs and Mass Incarceration, Explained," *Vox*, April 25, 2019.

26. Sadie Gurman and Eric Tucker, "Justice Department Guidance Could Lead to Harsher Prison Sentences," *Chicago Tribune*, May 9, 2017.

27. Gottschalk, *Caught: The Prison State*, 170; Alex Altman, "Koch Brother Teams Up with Liberals on Criminal Justice Reform," *Time*, January 29, 2015.

28. John Gramlich and Kristen Bialik, "Obama Used Clemency Power More Often Than Any President Since Truman," Pew Research Center, January 20, 2017; Heather MacDonald, "Mandatory Minimums Don't Deserve Your Ire," *Wall Street Journal*, May 25, 2017.

29. "America's Prisons Are Failing. Here's How to Make Them Work," *Economist*, May 27, 2017.

30. Gopnik, "How We Misunderstand"; Lane, "Age of Mass Incarceration"; Matt Ford, "Rethinking Mass Incarceration in America," *Atlantic*, March 2, 2017.

31. Lane, "Age of Mass Incarceration"; Jelani Cobb, "A Drawdown in the War on Drugs," *New Yorker*, August 29, 2016; Forman, *Locking Up Our Own*; John Pfaff, *Locked In: The True Causes of Mass Incarceration and How to Achieve Real Reform* (New York: Basic, 2017); Ford, "Rethinking Mass Incarceration"; Gopnik, "How We Misunderstand"; Eli Hager and Bill Keller, "Everything You Think You Know About Mass Incarceration Is Wrong," The Marshall Project, February 9, 2017.

32. John J. DiIulio Jr., "Prisons Are a Bargain, by Any Measure," *Brookings Institution*, January 16, 1996.

33. Eckholm, "Prison Rate."

34. Eckholm, "Prison Rate"; David Cole, "The Truth About Our Prison Crisis," *New York Review of Books*, June 22, 2017; Gopnik, "How We Misunderstand"; Baz Dreisinger, "Prison: America's Most Vile Export?" *Atlantic*, September 30, 2015.

35. Lane, "Age of Mass Incarceration."

36. Josh Keller and Adam Pearce, "This Small Indiana County Sends More People to Prison Than San Francisco and Durham, N.C., Combined. Why?" *New York Times*, September 2, 2016; Sarah Stillman, "Get Out of Jail, Inc.," *New Yorker*, June 23, 2014.

37. Keller and Pearce, "This Small Indiana County."

38. Keller and Pearce, "This Small Indiana County."

39. Hochschild, "Our Awful Prisons."

40. Hochschild, "Our Awful Prisons"; John Wagner and Philip Rucker, "House Backs Bipartisan Criminal Justice Overhaul, Sends Bill to Trump," *Washington Post,* December 20, 2018; Elise Viebeck, "How an Early Biden Crime Bill Created the Sentencing Disparity for Crack and Cocaine Trafficking," *Washington Post,* July 28, 2019.

Chapter 23. Cannabis Revisited

1. "Operation Mountain Sweep," Military, *Global Security;* "Mexican Attitudes to Marijuana Mellow," *Economist,* December 24, 2016; Christian Hageseth and Joseph D'Agnese, *Big Weed: An Entrepreneur's High-Stakes Adventures in the Budding Legal Marijuana Business* (New York: St. Martin's, 2015); Torgoff, *Can't Find My Way Home;* Patrick Anderson, *High in America: The True Story Behind NORML and the Politics of Marijuana* (New York: Viking, 1981); Doug Fine, *Too High to Fail: Cannabis and the New Green Economic Revolution* (New York: Gotham, 2013); Doug Fine, *Hemp Bound: Dispatches from the Front Lines of the Next Agricultural Revolution* (White River Junction, Vt.: Chelsea Green, 2014); Crandall, "Drug War Divide."

2. Lee, *Smoke Signals,* 141–43.

3. Lee, *Smoke Signals;* Joe Nickell, "Cancer Patient's Message: Medical Marijuana Really Does Help," *Missoulian,* April 9, 2011; Dufton, *Grass Roots,* 208–13, 222, 224.

4. Margalit Fox, "Tod H. Mikuriya, 73, Dies; Backed Medical Marijuana," *New York Times,* May 29, 2007; Lee, *Smoke Signals,* 140–43; Tim Fernholz, "Puff Piece," *New Republic,* August 20, 2012.

5. Lee, *Smoke Signals,* 130; Jessica Roy, "California's Been Rejecting Legalized Marijuana for More Than a Century. Here's Why This Time Is Different," *Los Angeles Times,* September 13, 2016; Dufton, *Grass Roots,* 218.

6. Lee, *Smoke Signals,* 232; Nuala Sawyer, "The Legacy of Brownie Mary," *SF Weekly,* April 19, 2017; Michael Malott, *Medical Marijuana: The Story of Dennis Peron, the San Francisco Cannabis Buyers Club, and the Ensuing Road to Decriminalization* (Charleston, S.C.: CreateSpace, 2009).

7. Lee, *Smoke Signals,* 232–34; Dufton, *Grass Roots,* 213–24.

8. Andrew Gumbel, "Obituary: Brownie Mary," *Independent,* April 14, 1999.

9. Eric Bailey, "6 Wealthy Donors Aid Measure on Marijuana," *Los Angeles Times,* November 2, 1996.

10. Lee, *Smoke Signals,* 243.

11. Paul Chabot, "Marijuana Legalization Proposition Is a Train Wreck," Illinois Family Institute, March 9, 2011.

12. Sloman, *Reefer Madness,* 413.

13. Barcott, *Weed the People,* 301.

14. Lee, *Smoke Signals,* 264; Michael Pollan, "Living with Medical Marijuana," *New York Times,* July 20, 1997; Barcott, *Weed the People.*

15. Megan Rose, "What Does an Innocent Man Have to Do to Go Free? Plead Guilty," ProPublica, September 7.

16. Barcott, *Weed the People*, 97–98; Lee, *Smoke Signals*, 253–70; Lee V. Barton, ed., *Illegal Drugs and Governmental Policies* (New York: Nova Science, 2007), 87.

17. Lee, *Smoke Signals*, 295–97; Ethan A. Nadelmann, "Change of Tune in Drug Policy," *Los Angeles Times*, May 18, 2001.

18. David Firestone, "Let States Decide on Marijuana," *New York Times*, July 26, 2014.

19. Samuel P. Jacobs, "Marijuana Initiative Could Make or Break Obama in Colorado," Reuters, June 2, 2012.

20. Christopher Ingraham, "Scientists Have Found That Smoking Weed Does Not Make You Stupid After All," *Washington Post*, January 18, 2016.

21. Richard Fausset, "Following Its Country Music, Nashville May Loosen Up on Marijuana," *New York Times*, September 18, 2016.

22. Ingraham, "Scientists Have Found"; Christopher Ingraham, "Every Minute, Someone Gets Arrested for Marijuana Possession in the U.S.," *Washington Post*, September 28, 2015; Glenn Kessler, "Fact Checker: John Boehner's Claim That We 'Have Literally Filled Up Our Jails' with People for Minor Marijuana Possession," *Washington Post*, April 16, 2018.

23. "Clinton Tried Marijuana as a Student, He Says," *New York Times*, March 30, 1992; Jonathan Karl, "Barack Obama and His Pot-Smoking 'Choom Gang,' " ABC News, May 25, 2012; Frank James, "Inhale to the Chief: More Details of Obama's Pot Smoking Youth Revealed," NPR, May 25, 2012; Natalie Jennings, "The Choom Gang: President Obama's Pot-Smoking High School Days Detailed in Maraniss Book," *Washington Post*, May 25, 2012; Caitlin Dickson and Matthew Deluca, "David Maraniss's Biography Spills on Obama's Pot-Smoking & More," *Daily Beast*, May 25, 2012.

24. Abby Haglage, "The DEA Just Blew It on Pot," *Daily Beast*, August 11, 2016.

25. Matt Ferner, "Eric Holder Signals Support for Marijuana Reform Just as He's Heading Out the Door," *Huffington Post*, September 25, 2014; Alex Berenson, "What Advocates of Legalizing Pot Don't Want You to Know," *New York Times*, January 4, 2019; Alex Berenson, "Marijuana Is More Dangerous Than You Think," *Wall Street Journal*, January 4, 2019; Malcolm Gladwell, "Is Marijuana as Safe as We Think?" *New Yorker*, January 14, 2019; James Hamblin, "If Legal Marijuana Leads to Murder, What's Up in the Netherlands?" *Atlantic*, January 14, 2019; Kenneth L. Davis and Mary Jeanne Kreek, "Marijuana Damages Young Brains," *New York Times*, June 16, 2019.

26. Berenson, "What Advocates of Legalizing Pot"; Tony Mecia, "Reefer Madness," *Weekly Standard*, June 8, 2018.

27. Berenson, "What Advocates of Legalizing Pot"; Christopher Ingraham, "11 Charts That Show Marijuana Has Truly Gone Mainstream," *Washington Post*, April 19, 2017.

28. Richard A. Friedman, "Marijuana Can Save Lives," *New York Times*, February 8, 2018.

29. Elizabeth Bruenig, "The Wonder Drug: Inside the Medical Marijuana Industry's Wild New Frontier," *New Republic,* September 27, 2015; Laurie McGinley, "First Marijuana-Derived Drug Approved, Will Target Severe Epilepsy," *Washington Post,* June 25, 2018.

30. Bruenig, "Wonder Drug"; Sanjay Gupta, "It's Time for a Medical Marijuana Revolution," CNN, April 20, 2015.

31. Bruenig, "Wonder Drug."

32. "DEA Announces Actions Related to Marijuana and Industrial Hemp," U.S. Drug Enforcement Administration, August 11, 2016.

33. Ian Lovett, "In California, Marijuana Is Smelling More Like Big Business," *New York Times,* April 11, 2016; Harry Enten, "Everyone Agrees That Weed Is Great—Except Politicians," *FiveThirtyEight,* October 27, 2017; Katie Zezima, "Marijuana Is Legal in California Jan. 1. But You Won't Be Able to Buy It Everywhere," *Washington Post,* December 31, 2017; Thomas Fuller, "Marijuana Goes Industrial in California," *New York Times,* April 15, 2017; "State Marijuana Laws in 2018 Map," *Governing: The States and Localities.*

34. Thomas Fuller, "Californians Legalize Marijuana in Vote That Could Echo Nationally," *New York Times,* November 9, 2016; Zezima, "Marijuana Is Legal."

35. Fuller, "Californians Legalize Marijuana."

36. Fuller, "Californians Legalize Marijuana"; Timothy Egan, "Reefer Republic," *New York Times,* October 7, 2016.

37. Jeremy Berke, "Here's Where You Can Legally Consume Marijuana in the U.S. in 2018," *Business Insider,* November 7, 2018.

38. Hal Arkowitz and Scott O. Lilienfeld, "Experts Tell the Truth About Pot," *Scientific American,* March 1, 2012.

39. Mark A. R. Kleiman, "High Stakes: The Future of U.S. Drug Policy," *Majalla,* March 1, 2017; Brian Root, "A Return to the Failed 'War on Drugs' in the U.S.?" Human Rights Watch, March 16, 2017.

40. Hampton Sides, "Science Seeks to Unlock Marijuana Secrets," *National Geographic,* June 2015; Zusha Elinson, "California's Next Buzzy Varietal May Not Come from Grapes," *Wall Street Journal,* February 5, 2017; Melati Kaye, "Burgeoning Marijuana Market Prompts Concerns About Crop's Environmental Impact," *Scientific American,* February 2, 2017; Thomas Fuller, "California's 'Green Rush' Takes Hmong Back to Their Opium-Growing Roots," *New York Times,* June 3, 2017; Zezima, "Marijuana Is Legal."

41. Lovett, "In California"; Conor Dougherty, "Cannabis, Marijuana, Weed, Pot? Just Call It a Job Machine," *New York Times,* April 25, 2019.

42. Lovett, "In California"; "State Marijuana Laws in 2018 Map," *Governing: The States and Localities.*

43. Lovett, "In California"; Fuller, "Marijuana Goes Industrial."

44. Lovett, "In California"; Thomas Fuller, "Medical Marijuana Is Legal in California. Except When It's Not," *New York Times,* November 21, 2016; Lester Black, "Legal

Weed Isn't the Boon Small Businesses Thought It Would Be," *FiveThirtyEight*, December 29, 2017; Borchardt, "Marijuana Prices Fall"; David Gelles, "A Real Estate Boom, Powered by Pot," *New York Times*, April 1, 2017; Fuller, "Marijuana Goes Industrial"; Thomas Fuller, "Now for the Hard Part: Getting Californians to Buy Legal Weed," *New York Times*, January 2, 2019.

45. Kaye, "Burgeoning Marijuana Market."

46. Jefferson B. Sessions, III, attorney general, "Memorandum for All United States Attorneys: Marijuana Enforcement," January 4, 2018.

47. Kleiman, "High Stakes."

Chapter 24. Big Tobacco

1. Courtwright, *Forces of Habit*, 18, 125, 204.

2. James W. Brock, *The Structure of American Industry* (Long Grove, Ill.: Waveland, 2016), 93.

3. Brock, *Structure of American Industry*, 93.

4. D. Kirk Davidson, *Selling Sin: The Marketing of Socially Unacceptable Products* (Westport, Conn.: Praeger, 2003), 163; Courtwright, *Forces of Habit*, 128, 148.

5. William Wan, "America's New Tobacco Crisis: The Rich Stopped Smoking, the Poor Didn't," *Washington Post*, June 13, 2017.

6. Joseph A. Califano, *High Society: How Substance Abuse Ravages America and What to Do About It* (New York: Public Affairs, 2007), 14; Jacob Sullum, *For Your Own Good: The Anti-Smoking Crusade and the Tyranny of Public Health* (New York: Free Press, 1998), 57.

7. Martin Tolchin, "Surgeon General Asserts Smoking Is an Addiction," *New York Times*, May 17, 1988.

8. Pierre Thomas and John Schwartz, "Government Intensifies Tobacco Company Probe," *Washington Post*, May 3, 1997.

9. Philip J. Hilts, *Smoke Screen: The Truth Behind the Tobacco Industry Cover-Up* (Boston: Addison-Wesley, 1996).

10. David Heath, "Contesting the Science of Smoking," *Atlantic*, May 4, 2016; Jennifer Maloney and Saabira Chaudhuri, "Against All Odds, the U.S. Tobacco Industry Is Rolling in Money," *Wall Street Journal*, April 23, 2017.

11. Heath, "Contesting the Science of Smoking"; Maloney and Chaudhuri, "Against All Odds."

12. Courtwright, *Forces of Habit*, 129, 204; Maloney and Chaudhuri, "Against All Odds."

13. Barry Meier, "Court Rules F.D.A. Lacks Authority to Limit Tobacco," *New York Times*, August 1, 1998.

14. Courtwright, *Forces of Habit*, 19; Maloney and Chaudhuri, "Against All Odds."

15. Maloney and Chaudhuri, "Against All Odds."

16. Jennifer Kaplan, "Philip Morris: World's Second Largest Tobacco Company Tells People to Quit Smoking," *Independent*, October 24, 2016; Simon Chapman, "Big Tobacco's Smoke and Mirrors Won't Work This Time," ABC News, July 20, 2014; "A Common-Sense Approach for Public Health," Philip Morris International; Jia Tolentino, "The Vapors," *New Yorker*, May 14, 2018; Laurie McGinley and Lenny Bernstein, "FDA Unveils Sweeping Anti-Tobacco Effort to Reduce Underage Vaping and Smoking," *Washington Post*, November 16, 2018.

Chapter 25. Psychedelics 2.0

1. Rick J. Strassman, "Hallucinogenic Drugs in Psychiatric Research and Treatment: Perspectives and Prospects," *The Journal of Nervous and Mental Disease* 183, no. 3 (1995): 127–38.

2. Pinchbeck, *Breaking Open the Head*; Joan Didion, *Slouching Towards Bethlehem* (1968; repr. New York: Farrar, Straus and Giroux, 2008); Ryan Grim, *This Is Your Country on Drugs: The Secret History of Getting High in America* (Hoboken, N.J.: John Wiley & Sons, 2009); Jesse Jarnow, *Heads: A Biography of Psychedelic America* (Boston: Da Capo, 2016); Michael Pollan, "The Trip Treatment," *New Yorker*, February 9, 2015.

3. Pollan, "Trip Treatment"; Pollan, *How to Change Your Mind*; A. J. Lees, " 'Scuse Me While I Kiss the Sky," *New York Review of Books*, August 16, 2018.

4. Pollan, "Trip Treatment"; Mark A. R. Kleiman, "Psychedelic Experiences Might 'Cure' Smoking and OCD. Should We Allow Them?" *Vox*, December 26, 2016; "Mindfulness Performance Enhancing Drugs—Part 2," *Mindfulness Based Health*, September 4, 2015.

5. Pollan, "Trip Treatment"; Michael M. Hughes, "Sacred Intentions," *Baltimore City Paper*, October 16, 2008.

6. Hua Hsu, "The Lingering Legacy of Psychedelia," *New Yorker*, May 17, 2016; William Wan, "Ecstasy Could Be 'Breakthrough' Therapy for Soldiers, Others Suffering from PTSD," *Washington Post*, August 26, 2017.

7. Ariel Levy, "The Drug of Choice for the Age of Kale," *New Yorker*, September 12, 2016.

8. Levy, "Drug of Choice."

9. Levy, "Drug of Choice"; Wan, "Ecstasy Could Be 'Breakthrough.' "

10. Wan, "Ecstasy Could Be 'Breakthrough.' "

11. Susumu Tonegawa, Michele Pignatelli, Dheeraj S. Roy, and Tomás J. Ryan, "Memory Engram Storage and Retrieval," *Current Opinion in Neurobiology* 35 (2015): 101–9; Sara Chodosh, "The FDA Says Ecstasy Is a 'Breakthrough' Drug for PTSD," *Popular Science*, August 31, 2017.

12. Wan, "Ecstasy Could Be 'Breakthrough.' "

13. Wan, "Ecstasy Could Be 'Breakthrough.' "

14. Wan, "Ecstasy Could Be 'Breakthrough.' "

15. Amy Maxmen, "Psychedelic Compound in Ecstasy Moves Closer to Approval to Treat PTSD," *Nature,* April 28, 2017; Andrew Sullivan, "Why We Should Say Yes to Drugs," *New York Magazine,* May 25, 2018.

16. Kai Kupferschmidt, "All Clear for the Decisive Trial of Ecstasy in PTSD Patients," *Science,* August 26, 2017; "A Multi-Site Phase 3 Study of MDMA-Assisted Psychotherapy for PTSD," U.S. National Library of Medicine, National Institutes of Health, May 25, 2018.

17. Dorian Rolston, "A Trip That Doesn't End," *New Yorker,* May 17, 2013.

18. Jun Yan, "Percentage of Americans Taking Antidepressants Climbs," *Psychiatric News: American Psychiatric Association,* September 15, 2017.

19. "Active Ingredient in Magic Mushrooms Synthesized," *Biocompare,* August 28, 2017.

20. Sharon Begley, "Scientists Are Starting to Test Claims About 'Microdosing,' " *Scientific American,* August 24, 2018.

21. Tom Jackman, "Denver Voters Approve Decriminalization of 'Magic Mushrooms,' " *Washington Post,* May 8, 2019; Lilly Dancyger, "Psilocybin for the Masses: Oregon Considering Legalizing Mushrooms," *Rolling Stone,* December 4, 2018; Michael Pollan, "Not So Fast on Psychedelic Mushrooms," *New York Times,* May 10, 2019.

Chapter 26. The Most American Drug

1. Courtwright, *Forces of Habit,* 81; Brian C. Kelly, Amy LeClair, and Jeffrey T. Parsons, "Methamphetamine Use in Club Subcultures," *Substance Use and Misuse* 48, no. 14 (2013): 1541–52; Law Reform, Drugs and Crime Prevention Committee, "Inquiry into the Supply and Use of Methamphetamines, Particularly ICE, in Victoria, Volume 1 of 2," Parliament of Victoria, September 2, 2014; Alan Schwarz, "Drowned in a Stream of Prescriptions," *New York Times,* February 2, 2013; Ioan Grillo, "Mexican Meth Production Goes on Speed," Reuters, May 10, 2012; "The Meth Epidemic Timeline," *Frontline,* PBS, February 14, 2006; Jonah Engle, "Merchants of Meth: How Big Pharma Keeps the Cooks in Business," *Mother Jones,* July/August 2013.

2. Reding, *Methland,* 45–46; "Methamphetamine," Wikipedia entry; Joshua Foer, "The Adderall Me," *Slate,* May 10, 2005; "What Is Meth Cut With?" *American Addiction Centers,* available at https://americanaddictioncenters.org/meth-treatment/cut-with; Timothy Egan, "Methland vs. Mythland," *New York Times,* July 20, 2009.

3. Reding, *Methland,* 33–47, 54; Richard A. Friedman, "What Cookies and Meth Have in Common," *New York Times,* June 30, 2017; Sandra Blakeslee, "Brain Studies Tie Marijuana to Other Drugs," *New York Times,* June 27, 1997; Joe Martin, "Heartache in America's Heartland," *Real Change,* November 19, 2009.

4. Egan, "Methland vs. Mythland"; Patrick Sauer, "An Interview with Nick Reding, Author of Methland," *Huffington Post,* August 20, 2009; Robert Siegel and Melissa Block, "Author Paints Small Town's Struggle in 'Methland,' " NPR, July 8, 2009;

Reding, *Methland*, 46; Nicolas Rasmussen, "America's First Amphetamine Epidemic, 1929–1971," *American Journal of Public Health* 98, no. 6 (2008): 974–85; Walter Kirn, "Wasted Land," *New York Times*, July 1, 2009.

5. Travis Linneman, *Meth Wars: Police, Media, Power* (New York: New York University Press, 2016), 158; Reding, *Methland*, 32–34.

6. Reding, *Methland*, 33.

7. Stephanie Wilbur Ash, "Iowa Town Split over Portrayal in 'Methland,'." *Star Tribune*, July 17, 2009; Eric Andersen, "Iowa Meth Town No Myth," *Daily Iowan*, July 22, 2009; Kirn, "Wasted Land"; Scott Martelle, "Book Review: The Small-Town Nightmare of 'Methland,' " *Los Angeles Times*, June 8, 2009; Reding, *Methland*, 35; Linneman, *Meth Wars*, 159.

8. Pamela M. Prah, "Methamphetamine: Are Tougher Anti-Meth Laws Needed?" *CQ Press*, July 15, 2005.

9. Prah, "Methamphetamine."

10. Carmel Perez Snyder, "Officials Praise Anti-Meth Law," *News OK*, January 17, 2005; Julie Bisbee, "Oklahoma Meth Makers Flout Laws," *News OK*, April 5, 2010; Sean Murphy, "Police, Drug Lobby Clash over State's Meth Bill," *Claremore Daily Progress*, October 31, 2011; Prah, "Methamphetamine"; Euan McKirdy, "Philippines' War on Drugs," CNN, September 3, 2016; Clifton Adcock, "Ice Meth," *Tulsa World*, November 12, 2007.

11. Prah, "Methamphetamine."

12. Reding, *Methland*, 240–41.

13. Keegan Hamilton, "The Golden Age of Drug Trafficking: How Meth, Cocaine, and Heroin Move Around the World," *Vice*, April 25, 2016; "The Combat Methamphetamine Epidemic Act of 2005," *Frontline*, PBS, February 14, 2006; Reding, *Methland*, 175–77; "Mexican Meth," *Frontline*, PBS, February 14, 2006; "Combat Methamphetamine Epidemic Act of 2005," U.S. Drug Enforcement Administration; "2003–2008," History, U.S. Drug Enforcement Administration, July 23, 2007; The White House, "National Drug Control Strategy," *NCJRS*, February 2006; U.S. Department of Justice, "National Methamphetamine Threat Assessment," *National Drug Intelligence Center*, December 2007; "President Bush Signs Voting Rights Act Reauthorization and Amendments Act of 2006," *George W. Bush White House*, July 27, 2006; Executive Office of the President, "Synthetic Drug Control Strategy: A Focus on Methamphetamine and Prescription Drug Abuse," U.S. Drug Enforcement Administration, June 1, 2006; Office of National Drug Control Policy, "National Synthetic Drugs Action Plan," National Criminal Justice Reference Service, October 2004; "Interview Rep. Mark Souder (R-IN)," *Frontline*, PBS, February 14, 2006; Justin Glawe, "How Drug Trafficking Conspiracy Laws Put Regular People in Prison for Life," *Vice*, September 30, 2015; Julian Morgans, "A Brief History of Meth," *Vice*, October 22, 2015.

14. Prah, "Methamphetamine."

15. "DEA Eliminates Major Source of U.S. Meth," U.S. Drug Enforcement Administration, September 23, 2004; Reding, *Methland*, 175–77; "Legal Requirements for the

Sale and Purchase of Drug Products Containing Pseudoephedrine, Ephedrine, and Phenylpropanolamine," FDA; Hamilton, "Golden Age of Drug Trafficking."

16. Carl Byker, "Transcript: The Meth Epidemic," *Frontline*, PBS, February 14, 2006; Jane Carlisle Maxwell, "Methamphetamine: Here We Go Again?" *Addictive Behaviors* 36, no. 12 (2011): 1168–73.

17. "National Survey on Drug Use and Health (NSDUH), 2012," Substance Abuse and Mental Health Services Administration, 2012.

18. Kristina Davis, "Drugs Made in Mexican 'Superlabs' Are More Potent Than Ever, Fueling the Addiction Epidemic," *Los Angeles Times*, November 20, 2017; Phil Villarreal, "CBP: Teen Tried to Sneak Meth Hidden in Bra Across Border," *KGUN9*, August 17, 2016; Rachael Revesz, "Mexican Teenager Dies After Drinking Liquid Meth in Front of Smiling U.S. Border Officers," *Independent*, July 31, 2017.

19. Stuart Ramsay, "Inside Mexico's Infamous Meth 'Super Labs,' " *Sky News*, July 8, 2015.

20. Ramsay, "Inside Mexico's Infamous Meth 'Super Labs' "; "The Buyers: A Social History of America's Most Popular Drugs," *Frontline*; Chiara Menguzzato, "How Mexico Became the U.S.'s Main Meth Supplier," *Talking Drugs*, December 18, 2014; Elijah Stevens, "U.S. Meth Production Falls as Mexican Imports Increase," *InSight Crime*, September 16, 2015; Associated Press, "Spike in Meth Seen from Mexico as U.S. Production Low," *AZ Central*, June 17, 2015; Associated Press, "Arizona Meth Confiscations Skyrocket Due to Booming Drug Market in Mexico," *Guardian*, June 16, 2015.

21. Jamie Fellner, "Race, Drugs, and Law Enforcement in the United States," Human Rights Watch, June 19, 2009; Morgans, "Brief History of Meth."

22. Jon Schuppe, "Twin Plagues: Meth Rises in Shadow of Opioids," NBC News, July 5, 2017.

Chapter 27. Opioid Nation

1. Martin Booth, *Opium: A History* (New York: St. Martin's Griffin, 1996); Nancy D. Campbell, J. P. Olsen, and Luke Walden, *The Narcotic Farm: The Rise and Fall of America's First Prison for Drug Addicts* (New York: Abrams, 2008); Jim Hogshire, *Opium for the Masses: Harvesting Nature's Best Pain Medication* (Port Townsend, Wash.: Feral House, 2009); W. Travis Hanes III and Frank Sanello, *The Opium Wars: The Addiction of One Empire and the Corruption of Another* (Naperville, Ill.: Sourcebooks, 2002); Tracey Helton Mitchell, *The Big Fix: Hope After Heroin* (Berkeley, Calif.: Seal, 2016); William S. Burroughs, *Junky: The Definitive Text of Junk* (New York: Grove, 1953); Courtwright, *Dark Paradise*; Barry Meier, *Pain Killer: A "Wonder" Drug's Trail of Addiction and Death* (Emmaus, Penn.: Rodale, 2003).

2. Ian Frazier, "The Antidote," *New Yorker*, September 8, 2014; Quinones, *Dreamland*, 95; Olga Khazan, "The New Heroin Epidemic," *Atlantic*, October 30, 2014; Josh Katz, "Drug Deaths in America Are Rising Faster Than Ever," *New York Times*, June 5,

2017; Margaret Talbot, "The Addicts Next Door," *New Yorker*, June 5, 2017; Sheelah Kolhatkar, "The Cost of the Opioid Crisis," *New Yorker*, September 18, 2017.

3. Rod Dreher, "Tragedy of the American Dreamland," *American Conservative*, June 24, 2015; "How Heroin Made Its Way from Rural Mexico to Small-Town America," *Morning Edition*, NPR, May 19, 2015.

4. Quinones, *Dreamland*, 95–96; Celine Gounder, "Who Is Responsible for the Pain Pill Epidemic?" *New Yorker*, November 8, 2013.

5. Quinones, *Dreamland*, 95–96.

6. Khazan, "New Heroin Epidemic"; Carol Gentry, "Clinic's Painkiller Pith Sparks Ethics Debate," Yahoo! Groups, April 22, 2006.

7. Quinones, *Dreamland*, 124–28; Frazier, "Antidote"; Khazan, "New Heroin Epidemic."

8. Quinones, *Dreamland*, 134–37, 265–66; John Fauber, "Chronic Pain Fuels Boom in Opioids," *Medpage Today*, February 19, 2012; Susan Zalkind, "CDC Issues Guidelines Against Opiod Prescriptions to Treat Chronic Pain," *Guardian*, March 17, 2016; American-Statesman Investigative Team, "Critics Say Pharmaceutical Firms Spurred the Increase in Prescriptions for Narcotic Painkillers," *Statesman*, September 29, 2012; Karen Howlett, "Purdue Pharma Agrees to Settle Oxycontin Class-Action Suit," *Globe and Mail*, May 1, 2017; "Ohio Opioids Complaint—Final," Ohio Attorney General, May 31, 2017.

9. Quinones, *Dreamland*, 134.

10. Crandall, "Drug War Divide."

11. Nicholas Kristof, "Drugs Dealers in Lab Coats," *New York Times*, October 18, 2017; Patrick Radden Keefe, "The Family That Built an Empire of Pain," *New Yorker*, October 30, 2017.

12. Quinones, *Dreamland*, 138–39; Beth Macy, *Dopesick: Dealers, Doctors, and the Drug Company That Addicted America* (New York: Little, Brown, 2018); Marcia Angell, "Opioid Nation," *New York Review of Books*, December 6, 2018; Meier, *Pain Killer;* Chris McGreal, *American Overdose: The Opioid Tragedy in Three Acts* (New York: Public Affairs, 2018); Ryan Hampton with Claire Rudy Foster, *American Fix: Inside the Opioid Addiction Crisis—and How to End It* (New York: All Points, 2018).

13. Mark A. R. Kleiman, "Panel Paper: Strategic Options for Managing the U.S. Opioid Epidemic," *APPAM Conference*, November 2, 2017; "Sam Quinones: Dreamland—The True Tale of America's Opiate Epidemic (Bloomsbury)," *Herald Scotland*, June 27, 2015; Kleiman, "High Stakes."

14. Nancy Rommelmann, "The Great Opiate Boom," *Wall Street Journal*, June 5, 2015.

15. Frazier, "Antidote"; Alana Semuels, "Are Pharmaceutical Companies to Blame for the Opioid Epidemic?" *Atlantic*, June 2, 2017; Barry Meier, "In Guilty Plea, OxyContin Maker to Pay $600 Million," *New York Times*, May 10, 2007; Anna Lembke, *Drug Dealer, M.D.: How Doctors Were Duped, Patients Got Hooked, and Why It's So Hard to Stop* (Baltimore: Johns Hopkins University Press, 2016), 71; Barry Meier, "Origins of

an Epidemic: Purdue Pharms Knew Its Opioids Were Widely Abused," *New York Times,* May 29, 2018; Angell, "Opioid Nation;" Lenny Bernstein et al., "Purdue Pharma Reaches Tentative Deal in Federal, State, Opioid Lawsuits," *Washington Post,* September 11, 2019; Renae Merle and Lenny Bernstein, "Purdue Pharma's Bankruptcy Plan Includes Special Protection for the Sackler Family Fortune," *Washington Post,* September 18, 2019; Christopher Rowland, "Purdue Pharma, Drugmakers Accused of Fueling the Opioid Epidemic, Files for Bankruptcy," *Washington Post,* September 15, 2019.

16. Jon Kamp and Arian Campo-Flores, "Hooked: One Family's Ordeal with Fentanyl," *Wall Street Journal,* May 19, 2016.

17. Frazier, "Antidote."

18. "The Global Afghan Opium Trade: A Threat Assessment," United Nations Office on Drugs and Crime, July 2011; "The Numbers Behind America's Heroin Epidemic," *New York Times,* October 30, 2015.

19. Miriam Coleman, "Philip Seymour Hoffman Autopsy Reveals Actor Died of Toxic Drug Mix," *Rolling Stone,* March 1, 2014.

20. Angell, "Opioid Nation."

21. Khazan, "Heroin Epidemic"; Talbot, "Addicts Next Door"; Park, "Deaths Rippled Across America"; Olga Khazan, "Is Marijuana More Addictive Than Alcohol?" *Atlantic,* September 17, 2014.

22. Talbot, "Addicts Next Door"; Anne Case and Angus Deaton, "Mortality and Morbidity in the 21st Century," *Brookings Papers on Economic Activity,* Brookings, March 17, 2017.

23. Jonah Engel Bromwich, "Prince Overdoses on Fentanyl. What Is It?" *New York Times,* June 2, 2016; Benjamin Rachlin, "A Small-Town Police Officer's War on Drugs," *New York Times,* July 12, 2017; Scott Higham et al., "The Fentanyl Failure," *Washington Post,* March 13, 2019.

24. Katharine Q. Seelye, "Heroin Epidemic Is Yielding to a Deadlier Cousin: Fentanyl," *New York Times,* March 25, 2016; Nicole Lewis, Emma Ockerman, Joel Achenbach, and Wesley Lowery, "Fentanyl Linked to Thousands of Urban Overdose Deaths," *Washington Post,* August 15, 2017; Scott Higham et al., "The Fentanyl Failure," *Washington Post,* March 13, 2019.

25. Joel Achenbach, "Wave of Addiction Linked to Fentanyl Worsens as Drugs, Distribution, Evolve," *Washington Post,* October 24, 2017.

26. Seelye, "Deadlier Cousin"; Lewis et al., "Fentanyl Linked"; Jeanne Whalen, "For Small-Town Cops, Opioid Scourge Hits Close to Home," *Wall Street Journal,* September 28, 2016.

27. Katharine Q. Seelye, "Addicted Parents Get Their Fix, Even with Their Children Watching," *New York Times,* September 27, 2016.

28. Lewis et al., "Fentanyl Linked"; Alicia Victoria Lozano, "Philadelphia No Longer Leads State in Fatal Drug Overdose Rate, but Deaths Continue to Rise in Opioid Epidemic," *NBC Philadelphia,* July 27, 2017.

29. Lewis et al., "Fentanyl Linked"; Katz, "Drug Deaths in America"; Nicholas Kristof, "Opioids, a Mass Killer We're Meeting with a Shrug," *New York Times,* June 22, 2017.

30. Azam Ahmed, "Drug That Killed Prince Is Making Mexican Cartels Richer, U.S. Says," *New York Times,* June 9, 2016; Sheelah Kolhatkar, "The Cost of the Opioid Crisis," *New Yorker,* September 18, 2017.

31. Julie Lurie, "Drugs Kill More People Than Cars or Guns," *Mother Jones,* September 19, 2016.

32. Keegan Hamilton, "America's New Deadliest Drug Is Fentanyl," *Vice,* August 30, 2016; Nick Miroff, "U.S. Border Officers Make Largest-Ever Fentanyl Bust: 254 Pounds Hidden Under Cucumbers," *Washington Post,* January 31, 2019.

33. Frazier, "Antidote"; Lenny Bernstein, "Four in 10 Say They Know Someone Who Has Been Addicted to Prescription Painkillers," *Washington Post,* November 24, 2015.

34. Frazier, "Antidote"; German Lopez, "If We Want to Save People from Opioid Overdoses, a New Study Shows Naloxone Works," *Vox,* February 27, 2017; Siegel, "How Joe Biden's Policies."

35. Seelye, "Naloxone Saves Lives"; Chris McGreal, "Don't Blame Addicts for America's Opioid Crisis. Here Are the Real Culprits," *Guardian,* August 13, 2017.

36. Colin Campbell, "Chris Christie's Emotional Speech About Drug Addiction Is Going Viral," *Business Insider,* November 5, 2015; John Cassidy, "Carly Fiorina Tests Donald Trump's Indestructibility," *New Yorker,* September 17, 2015.

37. Abby Phillip and Katie Zezima, "GOP Contenders Are Talking About Drug Abuse, but Racial and Partisan Rifts Persist," *Washington Post,* November 27, 2015.

38. Joseph Walker, "Prosecutors Treat Opioid Overdoses as Homicides, Snagging Friends, Relatives," *Wall Street Journal,* December 17, 2017.

39. Dan Levin, "Vancouver Prescriptions for Addicts Gain Attention as Heroin and Opioid Use Rises," *New York Times,* April 21, 2016.

40. Levin, "Vancouver Prescriptions"; Denise Ryan, "Part 1: Heroin Addiction on the Rise Among Young Drug Users (with Video)," *Vancouver Sun,* June 3, 2014; Siegel, "How Joe Biden's Policies"; Manish Krishnan, "In Canada the Actual Dollar Cost of Addiction for an Individual Can Be Catastrophic," *Vice,* March 8, 2016.

41. David Lapp, "The War Zone in White America," *National Review,* January 14, 2016.

42. Steve Birr, "Ohio Lawsuit Likens Big Pharma to Tobacco over Their 'Scheme to Deceive Doctors,'" *Daily Caller,* June 1, 2017; Masha Gessen, "Nan Goldin Leads a Protest at the Guggenheim Against the Sackler Family," *New Yorker,* February 10, 2019; Purdue Pharma and the Sackler family agreed in late March 2019 to provide close to $275 million to resolve a lawsuit from the state of Oklahoma, of which about one-third would fund the establishment of an addiction response and research institute at Oklahoma State University. See Jan Hoffman, "Purdue Pharma and Sacklers

Reach $275 Million Settlement in Opioid Lawsuit," *New York Times*, March 26, 2019; Lenny Bernstein and Katie Zezima, "Big Pharma, State of Oklahoma Reach Settlement in Landmark Opioid Suit," *Washington Post*, March 26, 2019; Ken Miller and Geoff Mulvihill, "Oklahoma Opioid Case to Fund Addiction Center in Tulsa," *Tulsa World*, March 26, 2019.

43. Katie Zezima, "Counterfeit Opioid Pills Are Tricking Users—Sometimes with Lethal Results," *Washington Post*, November 19, 2017.

44. Margaret Talbot, "Trump Says His Wall Will Stop Opioids—Two High-Profile Legal Cases Suggest That He's Wrong," *New Yorker*, January 21, 2019.

Concluding Thoughts and a Tentative Way Forward

1. "Opioid Addiction 2016 Facts & Figures," *American Society of Addiction Medicine*, available at www.asam.org/docs/default-source/advocacy/opioid-addiction-disease-facts-figures.pdf; German Lopez, "Drug Overdose Deaths Skyrocketed in 2016—and Traditional Opioid Painkillers Weren't the Cause," *Vox*, September 5, 2017; "Prescription Nation 2016: Addressing America's Drug Epidemic," National Safety Council; Dina Gusovsky, "Americans Consume Vast Majority of the World's Opioids," CNBC, April 27, 2016; Erin Brodwin, "Death from Opioid Overdoses Have Jumped—and One Age Group Is Being Affected at Stark Rates," *Business Insider*, February 28, 2017; Lester Black, "Legal Weed Isn't the Boon Small Businesses Thought It Would Be," *FiveThirtyEight*, December 29, 2017; Debra Borchardt, "Marijuana Sales Totaled $6.7 Billion in 2016," *Forbes*, January 3, 2017; Debra Borchardt, "Marijuana Prices Fall in 2016 as Growers Flood the Market with Pot," *Forbes*, January 31, 2017; Josh Katz, "Drug Deaths in America Are Rising Faster Than Ever," *New York Times*, June 5, 2017; "National Survey of Drug Use and Health," National Institute of Drug Abuse, National Institutes of Health, available at www.drugabuse.gov/national-survey-drug-use-health; "Drug Abuse at Highest Level in Nearly a Decade," December 1, 2010, National Institute of Drug Abuse, National Institutes of Health, available at https://archives.drugabuse.gov/news-events/nida-notes/2010/12/drug-abuse-highest-level-in-nearly-decade.

2. David W. Murray, Brian Blake, and John P. Walters, "A Strategy to Counter the Opioid Epidemic: Contain, Reduce, Extinguish," Hudson Institute, April 21, 2017.

3. John P. Walters and David W. Murray, "Trump Can Save Lives by Stopping Illegal Opioids at Their Source," *Wall Street Journal*, August 14, 2017; "Overdose Death Rates," National Institute on Drug Abuse; Mark Kleiman, "Surgical Strikes in the Drug Wars," *Foreign Affairs*, September/October 2011; George P. Shultz and Pedro Aspe, "The Failed War on Drugs," *New York Times*, December 31, 2017; "Treatment Episode Data Set (TEDS), 2001–2011: State Admissions to Substance Abuse Treatment Services," Substance Abuse and Mental Health Services Administration; "Results from the 2015 National Survey on Drug Use and Health: Detailed Tables," Substance Abuse and Mental Health Services Administration, September 8, 2016; Jeffrey A. Miron and

Katherine Waldock, "The Budgetary Impact of Ending Drug Prohibition," CATO, 2010.

4. Ioan Grillo, "Mexican Drug Smugglers to Trump: Thanks!" *New York Times*, May 5, 2017; U.S. Department of Justice, "2016 National Drug Threat Assessment Summary," U.S. Drug Enforcement Administration, November 2016; U.S. Department of Justice, "Drug Movement Into and Within the United States," National Drug Intelligence Center, February 2010; U.S. Department of Justice, "National Drug Threat Assessment 2011," National Drug Intelligence Center, August 2011; June S. Beittel, "Mexico: Organized Crime and Drug Trafficking Organizations," Congressional Research Service, April 25, 2017; José Luis Pardo Veiras, "A Decade of Failure in the War on Drugs," *New York Times*, October 9, 2016; Karen Piero, "U.S. and Mexico to Set Up Joint Team to Fight Drug Cartels," Reuters, August 15, 2018.

5. Kleiman, "Dopey, Boozy, Smoky—and Stupid."

6. Liana W. Rosen, "International Drug Control Policy: Background and U.S. Responses," Congressional Research Service, March 16, 2015; Miron and Waldock, "Budgetary Impact"; "The Federal Drug Control Budget: New Rhetoric, Same Failed Drug War," *Drug Policy*, February 2015; Art Carden, "Let's Be Blunt: It's Time to End the Drug War," *Forbes*, April 19, 2012; Renee Montagne, "Ike's Warning of Military Expansion, 50 Years Later," *Morning Edition*, NPR, January 17, 2011; Christopher Hobson, "Privatising the War on Drugs," *Third World Quarterly* 35, no. 8 (2014): 1441–56; "Eisenhower Farewell Address (Full)," available at www.youtube.com/watch?v=CWiIYW_fBfY; Bruce et al., *Hostage Nation*, 278; Louis Uchitelle, "The U.S. Still Leans on the Military-Industrial Complex," *New York Times*, September 22, 2017; William J. Lynn III, "The End of the Military-Industrial Complex: How the Pentagon Is Adapting to Globalization," *Foreign Affairs*, November/December 2014; Barbara Maranzani, "Dwight Eisenhower's Shocking—and Prescient—Military Warning," *History*, March 22, 2017; Crandall, *Driven by Drugs*, 7.

7. Crandall, "Drug War Divide."

8. Josh Phillips, "Operation Martillo Drops the Hammer on Smugglers," USO, June 27, 2013; "Operation Martillo," *Global Security*, available at www.globalsecurity.org/military/ops/martillo.htm; Román D. Ortiz, "La cocaína regresa a Colombia," *El País*, May 12, 2018; "Colombia, U.S. Seek to Halve Cocaine Output in Five Years," Reuters, March 1, 2018.

9. "Presidential Memorandum for the Secretary of State," The White House, September 13, 2017; Adriaan Alsema, "Trump Threatens to Decertify Colombia as Partner in War on Drugs," *Colombia Reports*, September 14, 2017; Christopher Woody, "U.S. Officials Are Raising Alarm over Colombia's Cocaine Boom, but They May Be 'Missing Most of the Picture,' " *Business Insider*, September 16, 2017; José Luis Pardo Veiras, "A Decade of Failure in the War on Drugs," *New York Times*, October 9, 2016; Reuters, "Colombia Defends Anti-Drug Efforts After Trump Critique," *Business Insider*, September 14, 2017.

10. Chris Nichols, "Do a Majority of American Live in States with Legal Marijuana?" *Politifact*, April 19, 2018; Andrew Daniller, "Two-Thirds of Americans Support Marijuana Legalization," Pew Research Center, November 14, 2019.

11. German Lopez, "Survey: Nearly Half of Americans Have a Family Member or Close Friend Who's Been Addicted to Drugs," *Vox*, October 31, 2017; Josh Katz, "Short Answers to Hard Questions About the Opioid Crisis," *New York Times*, August 10, 2017; "44% of Americans Know Someone Who Has Been Addicted to Prescription Painkillers," National Council on Alcoholism and Drug Dependence, May 5, 2016; John Gramlich, "Nearly Half of Americans Have a Family Member or Close Friend Who's Been Addicted to Drugs," Pew Research Center, October 26, 2017; Amanda Holpuch, "Life After Opioid Addiction: Three Survivors Tell How They Got Clean," *Guardian*, June 25, 2017.

12. Chris McGreal, "Don't Blame Addicts for America's Opioid Crisis. Here Are the Real Culprits," *Guardian*, August 13, 2017; Brian Alexander, "When a Company Is Making Money from the Opioid Crisis," *Atlantic*, September 6, 2017; Bill Whitaker, "Ex-DEA Agent: Opioid Crisis Fueled by Drug Industry and Congress," CBS News, October 15, 2017; Nancy Smith, "Sorry, Big Pharma: Opioids Intoxicated Tiger Woods, Not Marijuana," *Sunshine State News*, August 17, 2017; Sarah Ferris, "Democrat Vows to Go After Opioid Makers—Including Daughter's Company," *The Hill*, September 22, 2016; Julie Bosman, "Inside a Killer Drug Epidemic: A Look at America's Opioid Crisis," *New York Times*, January 6, 2017; Sarah Childress, "Michelle Alexander: 'A System of Racial and Social Control,' " *Frontline*, PBS, April 29, 2014.

13. Michael Teo, "Singapore's Policy Keeps Drugs at Bay," *Guardian*, June 5, 2010; Ashok Kumar Mirpuri, "Singapore Is Winning the War on Drugs. Here's How," *Washington Post*, March 11, 2018; Simon Kent, "Draconian Singapore Has Low Rate of Drug Abuse," *Toronto Sun*, July 14, 2013.

14. James Fenton, "Murderous Manila: On the Night Shift," *New York Review of Books*, February 9, 2017; James Fenton, "Duterte's Last Hurrah: On the Road to Martial Law," *New York Review of Books*, February 23, 2017; Oliver Holmes, "Rodrigo Duterte Vows to Kill 3 Million Drug Addicts and Likens Himself to Hitler," *Guardian*, September 30, 2016; Felipe Villamor, "Duterte, Citing Hitler, Says He Wants to Kill 3 Million Addicts in Philippines," *New York Times*, September 30, 2016; Seung Min Kim, Jenna Johnson, and Philip Rucker, "At Pennsylvania Rally, Trump Again Calls for the Death Penalty for Drug Dealers," *Washington Post*, March 10, 2018; Miguel Syjuco, "The Wrong Way to Fight a Drug War," *New York Times*, August 8, 2018.

15. Fenton, "Murderous Manila"; Fenton, "Duterte's Last Hurrah"; Alexandra Sims, "Rodrigo Duterte Compares Himself to Hitler and Pledges to 'Slaughter Three Million Drug Addicts,' " *Independent*, September 30, 2016.

16. Reuters, "Beheading of Convicted Drug Dealers Discussed by Bennett," *Los Angeles Times*, June 16, 1989; Kim, Johnson, and Rucker, "At Pennsylvania Rally."

17. Nicholas Kristof, "Drugs Dealers in Lab Coats," *New York Times*, October 18, 2017; Daniel Denvir, "Canada Figured Out How to Win the Drug War," *Slate*, May 30,

2017; Kristof, "How to Win a War on Drugs"; Christopher Curtis, "Two Montreal Safe-Injection Sites to Open Within Weeks: Minister," *Montreal Gazette*, May 12, 2017.

18. Denvir, "Canada Figured Out"; Aubrey Whelan and Don Sapatkin, "DA Candidate Endorses Safe Injection Sites for Heroin," *Philadelphia Inquirer*, September 14, 2017; Maura Ewing, "Protecting Heroin Clinics from Prosecution," *Atlantic*, October 5, 2017; Bobby Allyn, "Desperate Cities Consider 'Safe Injection' Sites for Opioid Users, *Morning Edition*, NPR, January 10, 2018.

19. Russell Crandall, "Is the U.S. the Last Country Still Fighting the Drug War?" *New Republic*, January 1, 2014; Robb London, "Is the War on Drugs Succeeding?" *Harvard Law Today*, July 1, 2005; Andrew Cohen, "How White Users Made Heroin a Public-Health Problem," *Atlantic*, August 12, 2015; Michael Massing, "Crack's Destructive Sprint Across America," *New York Times*, Oct 1, 1989.

20. Kleiman, "Dopey, Boozy, Smoky—and Stupid"; Kleiman, "High Stakes"; Kleiman, "Surgical Strikes"; Graeme Wood, "The Life-Changing Magic of Tripping," *The Atlantic*, July 29, 2019.

21. Jason Schwartz, "Dopey, Boozy, Smoky—and Stupid," response to Mark Kleiman article, *Addiction and Recovery News*, January 30, 2007; Román D. Ortiz, "La cocaína regresa a Colombia," *El País*, May 12, 2018; Andrew Sullivan, "Why We Should Say Yes to Drugs," *New York Magazine*, May 25, 2018.

22. Daniel Borunda, "Officials: Sinaloa Drug Cartel Killed U.S. Tourist Patrick Braxton-Andrew in Chihuahua," *El Paso Times*, November 21, 2018.

GRATITUDE

A whole host of policymaking and academic colleagues, friends and family, and dozens of former and current Davidson College students helped make this book immeasurably better. I do, however, take full responsibility for any errors, omissions, or other lapses in scholarly judgment or temperament. The metaphor of a dwarf standing on the shoulders of giants is very much in play with my book. I have called out all of them throughout the tome, but these authors in particular offered ideas, insights, and evidence that challenged and expanded my own analysis: Bruce Barcott, Jill Jonnes, David Courtwright, Sam Quinones, Nick Reding, Daniel Okrent, Mark Kleiman, Ronald Siegel, Alma Guillermoprieto, Martin Lee, Mark Bowden, Gabriel García Márquez.

I had a veritable Dream Team of research assistants who were invaluable in all aspects of the book's research, writing, and publishing phases. All of these students first started working with me when they were undergraduates at Davidson. In some cases, this is the second (or, gasp, third) book project on which they have assisted me. I was especially fortunate to have Marshall Worsham to collaborate with me from the draft's earliest days. Now a Ph.D. student in environmental science at UC Berkeley, Marshall gamely wrestled what was my initial bloated draft into something infinitely more reader-friendly and logical; his intellectual and literary fingerprints are on every page of this work—as they were on my last book, *America's Dirty Wars: Irregular Warfare from 1776 to the War on Terror.*

The intrepid researcher assistants were Iain Addleton, Lauren Martinez, Savannah Haeger, Maria Antonia Bravo, Jack Richardson, David Samberg, Laura Dunnagan, and Jennie Goodell. My exceptional colleagues at Davidson's Little Library once again aided me in myriad ways: James Sponsel, Joe

Gutenkanst, Trish Johnson, Jeremy Martin, Jean Coates, Jason Radcliff, Lisa Forrest, Sharon Byrd, and Jill Gremmels. At Yale University Press, Jaya Aninda Chatterjee has been everything a writer could want in an editor: proactive, loyal, and deeply patient. Yale's Phillip King came into the manuscript production process late but was a real shot in the arm. Martin Schneider did an absolutely stellar job copyediting the draft backward and forward. The five anonymous reviewers solicited by the press provided pages of constructive feedback—and thankfully so much of this is now part of the final version. My dear friend and literary agent Gillian MacKenzie first proposed the idea for a general audience book on this subject. Once again, Tanya Buckingham at the University of Wisconsin–Madison's Cartography Lab was a reliable source for the maps (drawn by Wisconsin's Alex Nelson and Christopher Archuleta). Marshall Felix and Gwenn Miller opened up their secluded midcoast Maine cabin for a monastic week of furious lobster-fueled writing that got the 'script over the finish line.

Here is my decidedly incomplete honor role of additional folks who helped with the book: Britta Crandall, Chris Chivvis, Allen Wells, Amelia Anderson, Michael Mandelbaum, Eliot Cohen, Riordan Roett, Guadalupe Paz, Hal Brands, Mike Hammer, Philip Jefferson, Dane Erickson, Francisco Gonzalez, Dan Pearson, Mike Sullivan, Rebecca Bill-Chavez, Greg Buppert, Dan Black, Allie Francis, Haley Rhodes, Isabel Soto, Patrick Baetjer, Eduardo Estrada, Augusto Chian, Tom Rynne, Brian Nichols, Bill Brownfield, Ken Menkhaus, Jane Zimmerman, Wendy Raymond, Carol Quillen, Matt Samson, Ralph Levering, Andy Rhodes, Caroline McDermott, Frank Mora, Fuji Lozada, Amy Klett, Chris Klett, Greg Weeks, Clayton Rose, Mike McKinley, Michael Shifter, Marin Strmecki, Brian Winter, Chris Sabatini, Rob Bose, Mark Ferrari, Paul Ream, Sarah Sears, Heidi Bustos, Kim Breier, John Kuykendall, Paul DiFiore, Jonathan Stevenson, Carolyn West, Dana Allin, Matthew Harries, Richard Feinberg, Tom Shannon, Kevin Whitaker, Andrea Becerra, Warren Bass, Jeff Michael, Drew Tucker, Gustavo Orozco, Denis McDonough, Kari McDonough, Pam Dykstra, Brian Orland, Bill Crandall Jr., Lee Veltri, Rebecca Barrow, Ebony Stubbs, Nathan Higdon, Wilson Pava, Jamie Hess, Dan Kurtz-Phelan, Melati Kaye, and Daniel Lynds.

I had the grave misfortune of losing both of my parents, Janet and William, during the three years spent researching and writing this book. Their own love of travel and cultures instilled in me a passion for international politics and history from a young age. Their faith in education is what helped form my vocation as a teacher and scholar. It is through these books and students that I pay forward a bit of their enormous gift. I miss them dearly.

INDEX